COACH OF THE YEAR CLINIC NOTES

LECTURES BY
PREMIER HIGH SCHOOL COACHES

Edited by Earl Browning

www.coacheschoice.com

Printed in the United States.

ISBN: 978-1-60679-172-1

ISSN: 1945-1202

Telecoach, Inc. Transcription: Emmerson Browning, Kent Browning, and Tom Cheaney

Diagrams: Steve Haag and Travis Rose

Book layout and cover design: Bean Creek Studio

Cover photo (front): Angie Ledbetter, freelance photographer, Batesville, MS

Cover photos (back): Angie Ledbetter, freelance photographer, Batesville, MS (top)
©Sun-Sentinel/ZUMApress.com (bottom)

Special thanks to the Nike clinic managers for having the lectures taped.

Coaches Choice
P.O. Box 1828
Monterey, CA 93942
www.coacheschoice.com

Contents

Contents

Clint Alexander

DEFENSE: FROM PRACTICE TO GAMES

Woodberry Forest School, Virginia

This is my 16th year as a head coach, and it seems like I just started. I have been to many clinics and seen numerous amounts of X's and O's in that time. At one time, I felt I did not know enough about running a great practice. Each year, we go to colleges and watch what they do and ask the staffs for tips, hints, and clues about how to practice with a purpose and do a great job.

Woodberry Forest School is a private boarding school with about 400 boys in grades 9 through 12. It is an old and very traditional school. I started out coaching in a small country school and later went to a large public school with an enrollment of 2,200 students. From there, I came to Woodberry, which was an entirely new environment. It is more like a college rather than a high school as to the way they handle everything.

We had to make some changes on the things we did to be successful. Our practices ended at 5:40 on the dot and dinner was at 6:15 sharp. We had to be very efficient with everything we did.

I am a big military historian buff, and this statement by Napoleon is our foundation principle: "Morale is to material as three is to one." When Napoleon took over the army in Italy, the Italian army had not won a battle in two years. He defeated Austria with an army that did not have muskets, shoes, or any of the conventional tools for fighting. He made his troops believe they could win. We wanted to do the same thing with our players. We wanted them to believe they could be successful.

COACHING PHILOSOPHY

- Winning must be more than just winning games.
- Emphasize life lessons and character development.
- Study great leaders and military history. How did they overcome adversity?
- Empower your coaches.
- Do not be a micromanager.
- Listen to your players. Do not ask if you do not want their answers.

We all want to win games because we are competitive. Sometimes, it takes a loss to get your team to build success. The last three years, we have a record of 24-3. Two of the three losses were overtime losses. We have found studying how military leaders overcame adversity is a great way to get better as a coach.

You have to empower your coaches. Give people the plan, and turn them loose to execute the play. If you try to micromanage everything, you will slowly but surely destroy their enthusiasm for the job. They will not work as hard, and it becomes the "it is not my idea" syndrome. If it is not their idea, it will not be successful.

If your players are doing something you do not like, do not jump on them. Talk to their coach, and change it that way. The more I help the player, the less he listens to his position coach and the more he listens to me. I do not want that to happen. He has to listen to his position coach and do it his way.

Everybody says we listen to our players, but I am not sure we do. If you ask them, you have to respect what they say. When our defense comes off the field, the first thing I ask them is, "What are they doing? Is it what we thought they would do? What is not working?"

TEAM VALUES

You must have a core set of values that you build your program on. This is what you will rely on to solve the problems you will face as a program. You cannot be a rudderless ship.

Unselfish

If your players value the role they have instead of valuing the role other players have, you have a chance at a great team.

—Mike Krzyzewski

When we started here, we had to build on something. They had never won, so we could not build on that foundation. We went back to core values. When we turned this thing around three years ago, we decided we were going to do three things. We were going to be unselfish, disciplined, and leaders. We were not going to talk about anything else. We did not talk about winning, playoffs, ranking, or any of the unimportant things. We had many thoughts on unselfishness. Our players bought into what Coach Krzyzewski said about the players' role on a team. He said to embrace their role and not covet the next player's role.

In three years, I have not had a parent call me, complaining about anything going on in the program. It cost $42,000 dollars a year to send their sons to this school. There are no scholarships, but there is financial aid. It goes before a financial aid board, and the fee that comes out of that board is what you pay, or you do not come to Woodberry. The academic standards are astronomical.

Leadership

Leadership is leaders inducing followers to act for certain goals that represent the values and the motivations, the wants and the needs, the aspirations and expectations, of both leader and followers. The genius of leadership lies in the manner in which leaders see and act on their own and their follower's values and motivations.

—Abraham Lincoln

Leadership is a full-time job. At Woodberry, we have 400 hundred students, which amounts to about eight students to a class. My football players cannot hide in a class. The teachers and students know you play football and see everything you do. You have to be a leader and remember the little things.

Discipline

Nothing is more harmful to the service than the neglect of discipline; for the discipline, more than numbers gives one's army superiority over another.

—George Washington

You must have discipline and take pride in the little things. The one thing we were not taking advantage of at Woodberry was how smart our players were. This is the smartest group of players I have ever coached. If the players ask you something, do not tell them the wrong answer. If you do not know, find out, but do not be wrong.

BUILDING A PROGRAM

- Winning in a hurry forces you to make compromises on your values.
- Build a two-platoon program.
- Be patient; look for the little victories.
- Barometer—Landon School scores in seven years: 0-48, 21-42, 3-7, 14-17, 17-3, 21-28 (OT), 15-14

I started my head coaching career with the greatest job you could have. It was in a small town called Concord, Michigan. There were 329 students, and four seniors played football. I applied for the head job at that school.

I waited two months for the interview. I was so excited about getting my first head coaching job. I met the athletic director at one of the local restaurants. He said, "Congratulations, you got the job." I asked him why I did not have to answer any questions about my expectations or about what I believed. He told me I did not need to because I was the only one to apply for the job.

I took over that program in 1997. They last had a winning season in 1988. They went 5-4 that season. Since then, there was not a kid in the school who had ever won a game. Our numbers were so small I went to the superintendent and told him if someone were hurt in the first two weeks, we would have to cancel the football season. He told me I could not do that. I went to the band and recruited some bodies. I told them they could still play at halftime of the games.

We were close to turning the program in those early years. We won some games and lost many close ones. We were in the game and playing competitively. In the first meeting I had with the players, I told them in five years we would be playing for championships. In four years, we went 10-2, won our district, and one regional.

When I came to Woodberry, one of our goals was to be a two-platoon program. Today, we two-platoon at all three levels. We all have special players who play both sides of the ball.

That first year at Concord, we went to overtime and lost, but we celebrated. We celebrated because we were close, and that was a little victory for us. I told the players they were the foundation that would lead us to the Silverdome to play in the playoffs. We went 1-9 the first year.

When I went to Woodberry, we had 52 players in the varsity program. They had good numbers, but they only played 12 to 15 players. We had to develop the depth and improve the numbers.

The barometer for our program has been the Landon School. They are a great school in Bethesda, Maryland, and do a good job with their players.

WHY COMMIT TO A TWO-PLATOON PROGRAM?

- Do not let the size of your team dictate how many kids you play.
- Concord High School: 27 players/22 starters
- Can do it with limited coaches. Share positions. Use unit drills.
- Develops players. Make them great at something.
- Makes practice better.
- Prepares you for injuries.
- Expands your ability to make changes with your game plans. Creates role players.
- Makes more kids want to be part of the program.
- First season in 2005: 52 players on the varsity team.
- In 2011: 95 players on our varsity roster.
- 396 boys in the school.

This is what we have learned about two-platoon football. The second thing on this list sounds crazy, but we did it. Our thinking was, why take a B player and make him do two different things? Let him do one thing and make him a B+ player. We make our living by taking B players and making them do one thing really, really well. I did this with a small staff, and I am doing it with the staff I now have. I have a great staff of coaches.

When you play as many players as we do, it makes your practices better. When we practice, we go fast, and we compete. We can make changes and adjustments to the game plan because I have the defensive players 99 percent of the time.

We have 396 boys in our school, and 96 of them are on our varsity roster. I probably have 30 real "football players." We had two boys on our team this year who did not play a down. One of them told me the reason he played was because he did not want to go quietly into the night. He wanted to rage against the night. He had a great experience with us because he said he was a football player.

Defensive Philosophy

He who defends everything defends nothing.

—Fredrick the Great

- Create negative plays and turnovers.
- Tackle well.
- If you cannot tackle, you cannot play.
- Stop what our opponents do best.
- Take away the best plays.
- Do not let one player beat you.
- Pursuit is the key to our defense.

Every team has that one player who is capable of beating you. We work hard on stopping that from happening. We must pursue the ball. We have a statement about that: "A defensive player's commitment to his teammates can be measured by the distance from the ball at the end of each play."

Our Defensive System

Be extremely subtle, even to the point of formlessness. Be extremely mysterious, even to the point of soundlessness. Thereby you can be the director of the opponent's fate.

—Sun Tzu

That quote describes what we do defensively. The formlessness means like water. If you watch us play defense in five games, you may not see the same defense in any of those films. We do not really have a system. I tell our players we are a 3-4 defense, but we are a 50 front. We may never be in the 50 front based on what the offense does. If we have to be in a 42 defense that week, we play 42. If we have to be in a 33 defense, we will be in that front. We put the players on the field who can win that week.

DEFENSIVE SYSTEM

- Consistently have the bodies to run a 34 or 52.
- Do not have the 3- or 1-technique players to run a 4-3
- Embrace change.
- Use the logo concept.
- What do we need to do each week to win?
- Teach in parts, must be able to install during early ball/no summer contact.
- Create tags based on packages or players (Hopkins, 42 Wolf Pack, Bowie).

Sometimes, the system of defense does not work with the personnel you have. We have to be adaptable to play at a high level. I love change. If there is an idea, I think will work, we try it. If it does not work, it does not work. However, I do not eliminate things because we have never done it before. When I got to Woodberry, all the levels were doing different things and systems. I had to change that.

I told our players the way we were going to play, we would win many games. If we decided not to play with a strong safety this particular week, we have a chance to win the game. We will have a better chance of winning if your parents do not call me all week asking why you are not playing strong safety this week. If I have to spend the entire week defending what we are going to do on the phone, we are not going to win. The team bought into those ideas, and we have not had that problem.

Teaching in parts was the biggest change for me. I came from a big public school that worked all summer. We played in the 7-on-7 leagues, and we installed everything we needed for the season. When the season started, we installed everything we were going to use. At Woodberry, we say goodbye on June 21, and they show back up on August 21. Our players go all over the world during their summers. They are involved with exchange programs and all kinds of activities.

We have no contact with our players over the summer. When they come back to school, we have to do it all immediately. If we have to create a package or change something, we tag it with something the players know and can remember. We had a player received a scholarship to Johns Hopkins and had to miss a game. He had to accept the scholarship in person. Instead of making a big deal out of his missing the game, we made a celebration out of the award. The next week, we named a package in the defense, Hopkins, and everyone immediately knew what to do.

Defensive Musts

Maneuver according to circumstance.

—Napoleon

- Be flexible, do what it takes to win that week.
- Use halftime adjustments.
- Be wolves, not dogs.
- Do not make your players afraid to make mistakes.
- Support them; do not pull them.

Napoleon made that statement to one of his commanders. It simply means that he is not with him, and the commander has to make the best decision possible. That same thing happens in coaching. In the game, things happen quickly, and you must make decisions. Do the best you can.

Probably the most important thing I learned in coaching is about halftime adjustments. I used to go to Penn State to their camps and spring practice. I was a big Joe Paterno fan. I asked him one day what he did at halftime. He said, "Don't lose the game." I thought he was blowing me off. He said, "Do not let the coaches go into the locker and rip your team a new one. They will never recover." He told me, "Never go into the locker room without a plan. Get together with the coaches and discuss what is going to happen in the locker room."

There was a study done in Alabama by a sport psychologist, comparing the behavior of wolves and dogs to football players. Some coaches want dogs. They want obedient players that do exactly what the coach tells them. Wolves never became domesticated and were more independent than dogs. They make quick decisions, but at the same time are cautious. You have to make up your mind if you want your players to be wolves or dogs. If something happens in a game that we have not worked on, we want the player to make a decision instead of looking to the sidelines for help.

If you pull a player out of the game every time he makes a mistake, you do not help him. They are going to make mistakes and get beat. You have to work on his attitude and keep it positive. The first thing we told the defensive backs was if they did not get beat on occasion, they are not playing hard. We want them going after the ball and not afraid of giving up a score. If they are not aggressive, they are passive, and you cannot do that at the defensive back position.

Play Great Defense and Special Teams

Invincibility lies in defense; the possibility of victory in the attack.

—Sun Tzu

- We believe this philosophy will always give us a chance to win the game.
- Set up short field for our offense.

If you want to win, you must play great defense. Every defeat we suffered the last three years was the result of turning the ball over and giving the opponent the short field.

DOWNHILL PURSUIT DRILL

Keys to the Drill: Sprint! Start with a great huddle and break (Diagram #1).

- The coach calls the play, and the defense aligns correctly to the formation.
- The coach snaps the ball, and the defense reacts to their gap and pursues downhill to the direction the coach points to outside of the numbers five yards behind the line of scrimmage.
- Two other coaches push block the ball out in the way of the defense to force them to pursue over the top of the blocks. The defense breaks down as a unit and sprints back to the huddle.

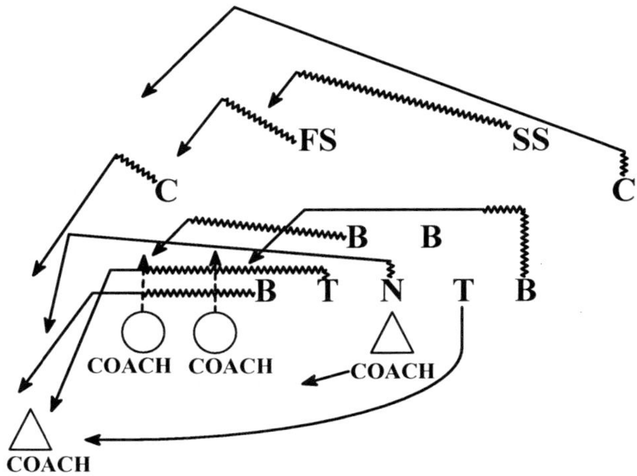

Diagram #1. Downhill Pursuit Drill

- The same group goes three times in a row.

Coaching Points: The backside safety has the cutback alley. The backside corner has deep pursuit. The backside outside linebacker plays reverse and counter. The inside linebacker slides and stays square until he gets outside the tackle or tight end. Have waiting players go work techniques on the sled until they go. There will be no rest for any players during this drill. Downhill pursuit is critical in creating negative plays and taking away cutback lanes.

Everyone does the pursuit drills the same way. I hate those drills because the defense pursues the ball as if it is a long run by the offense. The mentality is we are giving up a 15- to 30-yard run. We want to pursue downhill.

We teach a similar drill, but we added a large ball on the outside of the drill to make the defenders fight over that ball to get to the ballcarrier. We use this as a conditioning drill. The players not in the drill work on sleds, using the techniques we taught them. They are not standing around and watching. Everyone works on something. We play good defense and get downhill in our pursuit. We fight over blocks and get to the ball.

SIDELINE STRIP AND RETURN PURSUIT DRILL

Blocking after a turnover can result in a game winning play, and all players contribute (Diagram #2).

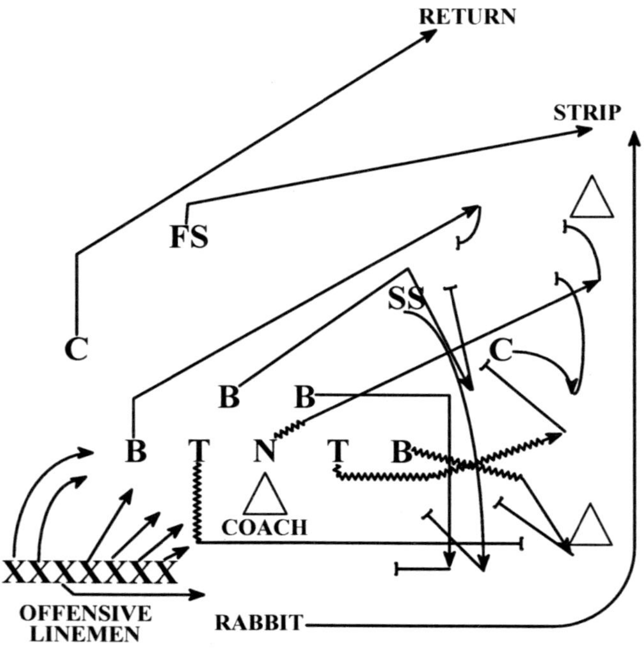

Diagram #2. Sideline Strip and Return Pursuit Drill

Keys to the Drill: Sprint! Sprint! "Let the rabbit run!"

- Starts with a great huddle and break.
- The coach calls the play, and the defense aligns correctly to formation.
- The coach snaps the ball, and the "rabbit" runs down one sideline.
- The defense reacts to their gap and pursues to the ball, taking a deep angle.
- The last two defenders strip, scoop, and score with the ball.
- Have seven offensive players with shields react to the strip and try to touch the returner. Defensive players must block.

We do the traditional sideline pursuit drill with the rabbit, except we use it as a strip and return drill. The last two defenders in the pursuit line make the play. The next-to-last defender strips the ball from the rabbit. The last defender scoops the ball and returns it. The rest of the defensive team becomes blocker for the return players. When we get the ball, we want to score. We have seven offensive linemen who run through a chute down the line of scrimmage and try to touch the fumble returner. They have shields, and the defenders try to block them.

These two drills account for about 60 percent of the success we have on defense. We do these drills almost every day. In pre-season camp, we do one in the morning and one in the afternoon. The second drill is hard to do right. Too many things can go wrong in running the drill.

DEFENSIVE GAME PLAN

- *Sunday:* Film and corrections—all coaches have a role in the game plan.
- *Monday:* Corrections install—what do you choose to stop first?
- *Tuesday:* Full pads—get physical.
- *Wednesday:* Pads or shells—last chance to make adjustments
- *Thursday:* Finalize the game plan.
- *Friday:* Pre-game practice

When we do our game plan, all the coaches get a say in what we do. We want our offensive coaches there because sometimes they see things we do not see. We also try to help them on the offensive side of the ball. On Monday, we do the correction from the game and install the adjustment to stop the opponent's favorite play. The two things we have to stop are the tunnel screen and the zone read. You can see the chart as to what we do the rest of the week.

When we get into defensive practice planning, we want to balance what we need to improve on with what we need to change to be successful this week. You want to create specific drills to work against your opponent's strengths. Make up your own drills to deal with what you have to do. Practice planning is the most important thing I do as a head coach.

The position coaches must carry out the defensive game planning. They have to go through their individual position techniques. We want to work special teams every day—at least some part of it. We have to install the game plan and make our formation adjustments to what we anticipate seeing. We work our pursuit drills and game plan at the same time. We work 1-on-1 with our offensive positions best against the best.

On Tuesday, we work specific team drills. We work on the tunnel and wall screen in our 7-on-7 drills. We work the inside drill, and we work a 5-on-11 drill. We take our five defensive linemen and work against our pass offense. The quarterback and receivers work on their passing game, and the offensive linemen work on their pass blocking against our defensive front. It is actually a better offensive drill than defensive drill. In the drill, the defensive line does all their line stunts against the offensive line.

We work off a practice schedule and timer. We do not deviate from the schedule, and we are on time with the horn. We have all the individual, group, and team periods for the day on a strict schedule. If we run the plays as part of our offense that the opponents run, we time and practice those plays against our defense. Both units get work at the same time.

An important point for the practice field is working from all parts of the field. Do not spend all your time working from the middle of the field. Move the ball so the linebackers know where their drops are in relationship to the field. If the middle linebacker tilts to run to his hook zone when all he has to do is back up, that needs to be covered. We cover that in a period on our practice schedule.

I do not ask the position coaches what they do during their individual periods. They know what they need to do, and they work on that. We work a similar practice schedule as far as time and drills for Monday, Tuesday, and Wednesday. Each day should bring improvement in doing the schedule for that week. Following are examples of what the defensive backs did in those three days:

- Ballistic stretch: 18 minutes
- Individual techniques: 44 minutes
- Formation adjustments: 24 minutes
- Tunnel and wall screens: 28 minutes
- 1-on-1: 8 minutes
- Dallas drill: 8 minutes
- 7-on-7: 38 minutes
- Defensive game plan/downhill pursuit: 28 minutes
- Team defense: 22 minutes
- Goal line defense: 20 minutes
- Scout defense: 38 minutes

That is an accumulative time for the defensive backs for Monday, Tuesday, and Wednesday. You can see where we spend the time. We work individual technique because it is fundamental to the game. The scout period is not a wasted period. When he plays on a scout team or position, he works his technique.

We break down each of our positions the same way. In addition to the defensive backs, we do the same breakdown for the inside and outside linebackers, defensive line, and special teams.

We work on special teams every day. Each week, we spend 34 minutes of practice kicking extra points and field goal. Those are team drills in practice; it is not the amount of time we spend on kicking. The punt and punt return teams are 34 minutes a week. We work the same with our kickoff and kickoff return for 34 minutes a week.

We have been tremendously successful with our special teams. In 2008 and 2009, we had an all-state kicker. In 2010, we had a second-team, all-state kicker and a first-team, all-state punter. The punter played inside linebacker for us. In the last two years, we have had long snappers go to the University of Richmond and Auburn University.

We do not have all the answers, and we work in a unique environment. However, I coached in the public schools, and I know what you coaches are going through. We try to do the best job, regardless of where we are. Thank you for your attention.

COACHING THE KICKING GAME

Memphis University School, Tennessee

When I was first asked to speak at this clinic, they asked me to speak on special teams. At that time, I started looking at other games, especially the bowl games. Two games jumped out at me after I agreed to talk on special teams. Knowing how important special teams play is, we can learn a great deal by watching other games.

First, we watched the Sugar Bowl. With most of our staff, we root for the teams from the South, and we do not cheer a great deal for the Big Ten teams. In the Sugar Bowl this past season, the University of Arkansas played The Ohio State University. I did not think Arkansas played very well in the bowl game. They got behind early in the game, but they were good enough to battle back into the game. They had a chance to win the game near the end of the game with a play from their special teams. They blocked a punt by Ohio State near the end of the game, deep in Ohio State's end of the field.

In my mind, there is never a reason when the team that blocks the punt should try to fall on the ball and not pick it up and run with the ball. Pick the thing up and run it into the end zone. Odds are, unless you fumble the ball after you pick it up, it is going to be your ball.

Arkansas blocked the punt, and the defender fell on the ball behind the line of scrimmage. Had he picked the ball up, he could have walked into the end zone. I expect, when the Arkansas staff got back home, they probably went through the film and pointed that issue out to the team.

My concern on that punt block goes back to a basic issue about coaching. What do we practice on blocking a punt? Do we practice blocking the punt and then falling on it? Do we practice blocking the punt and then trying to pick the blocked punt up and trying to score with the blocked punt? To me, you always try to score with a blocked kick.

The other game that hit me about the special teams was the game between the Colts and the Jets in the playoffs. Peyton Manning drove the Colts down to the end zone near the end of the game and the Colts scored the go-ahead touchdown. By all rights, they should have advanced into the next round of the NFL playoffs. However, they did not cover the kickoff to the Jets very well. The Jets ran the kickoff back to midfield. They made a couple of first downs, and then kicked a field goal and won the game. Those two incidents reminded me how important the whole concept of special teams is to the game of football.

Briefly, let me talk about the specialist. Just about every punter we have had at MUS has gone on to punt at the college level. In fact, my son got an Ivy League education. He went to Cornell University because he could punt. We have even had punters punt in the NFL. When we talk about the specialists, I have some general rules. Following are the specialist rules we have used over the years.

Specialist General Rules

- Trying harder does not make you better.
- Coach these guys more like golfers.
- Quality reps are more important than quantity.
- Don't mess with what is working (too many chefs in the kitchen).

Trying harder does not make you better, and you should coach these guys more like they are golfers. When I give instructions to my punters, I try to present it the same way a golf coach would coach his player when making adjustments. The punter requires a specific skill set to be effective. I believe the quality of repetitions is more important than the quantity of repetitions. I have found that if we just kick, kick, kick all the time in practice, then by the middle of the season, our legs are dead and sore. We lose about five yards on the distance of our kicks as well. I also believe that if a kicker is kicking well, then you do not want to keep messing with his style and technique. You can always nitpick and find something wrong to improve on, but you could do more damage than good. If they are in a groove and feel comfortable with what they are doing, I do not believe in messing with them.

Most of my good kicking specialists have, at one time or another, gone to a kicking camp. It does not hurt my feelings for someone to get coaching from another coach that knows much more about the kicking game than I do. I just do not like for them to go to a bunch of coaches and get different opinions on how they should be kicking the ball. I think they can get too much coaching and get confused.

I do not believe that the kicker and the punter have to be the same player. Sometimes, at the high school level, you may feel that you have one guy that has a really strong leg and you want to make him your specialist. I have found over the years that if I have one person doing both kicking and punting, they end up being mediocre at both of them. The skill set of punting and kicking is so similar to each other, but yet they are different. Punting is best done in a linear motion or down the line. Placekicking utilizes a rotary movement.

If you were never a punter, but you are in charge of coaching the punters, you might look at the chart I have called "Punting for Dummies."

Punting for Dummies

- Drop, drop, drop
- Steps short and straight (two steps and punt the line)
- See what you hit
- Film it (trust but verify)

I would stick to these points and I would not try to go any further than this. If this does not work, then your punter probably is not a very good punter. Drop, drop, drop. There are many different ideas on how to drop the ball for a punt. I do not know that there is any one that is better than the other. I believe it is what the punter feels comfortable with. All of our punters have held the ball a little bit different than each other. If they are not hitting the punt good, then I explained to them that they just have to drop it. Just drop it. Drop it straight every time and make it the same way every time.

The next thing I look for is how big their steps are that they are taking prior to their punt. Many times, they take too long of a step and get off balance, which throws their punt off. We are looking for short steps in a straight line. I am looking for the punter to kick the ball within two steps, and I would prefer a step and a half. You have to be able to catch, step, and kick it. I do not believe in three-step punting at all.

We want the punter to be able to see what he is kicking. I will stand in front of the kicker and watch his eyes to see if he is watching what he is kicking. It is like shooting free throws. You can tell a good free-throw shooter by what he does with his eyes after he shoots the ball. Is he focused on the basket or is he focused on the flight of the ball? The best shooters have their eyes focused on the rim. It is the same thing with kickers. We want them to see what they hit. We do not want them to track the flight of the ball.

We like to film our kicking game so we can go back and analyze it to make sure that we really saw what we saw. Sometimes on the sideline during a game, you think you see something, but when you get back to the film room, it really was something else. That is what we mean by trust but verify. This is a very simple punting philosophy, but if you are not a punting expert, you do not need to go any further than this. I have a "Kicking for Dummies" philosophy as well.

Kicking for Dummies

- Alignment
- Plant foot
- Kick them all the same
- Film it

The most common problem we have in the kicking game is that our kickers do not line up the same way every time. The reason is geometry. They have not advanced through geometry yet. In the NFL, you are kicking straight almost all of the time because the hash marks are so close together.

In high school, the hash marks are much farther apart, so we are rarely kicking straight down the field. Most of the time, we are kicking at an angle. Often, I will see a kicker put down his kicking tee the same way and take his alignment steps away from the tee the same way, no matter what angle he is kicking from. If he has lined up the same way every time, but he is kicking to a different angle every time, he is not setting up the same way every time. I will paint a straight line on the kicking tee and tell the kicker, "Point the line on the tee to the place he wants to kick the ball." I then have him take his alignment steps along that same line that represents the angle that he is kicking. This way, he is lined up toward the angle of the kick and the same way every time.

If we have problems, at this point, in getting the kick to where we want it to go, I will focus on the plant foot. I will coach the kicker to focus on where he wants his plant foot to land and not to focus on the ball. We want the plant foot to hit the same spot every time. If you have a good kicker and he is not kicking very well, then it is usually something to do with his plant foot. Again, we want to kick it the same way every time. I want the kicker to swing his leg on an extra point the same way he would on a 50-yard field goal. You have to be consistent when kicking and have a natural rhythm. Film it and verify it.

Snappers come in all shapes and sizes. If you do not have a natural snapper, look at your backup quarterback. The backup quarterback will usually make a pretty good snapper. We try to start finding our long snappers at the seventh and eighth grade level. We encourage those guys to practice it and to keep getting better at it. All the snapper has to do is snap the football. I never ask them to block anybody. Their job is to snap. If I have a snapper that is all over the place with his snaps, the first thing I check is where his hands are at the finish. If his snaps are getting high or wide, I will tell him to finish with his hands down low.

When we look for a holder, we are looking for someone that has quick hands. We also want him to have really good chemistry with the kicker. If I have three guys that are pretty good holders, I will ask the kicker who he feels most comfortable with. I want them to feel good about what they are doing together. It may not be the guy I think is the best holder, but it is the holder that the kicker feels the most comfortable with.

The number one key statistic that determines your success in a football game is where you start with the football. I believe the formula for scoring is an inverse of where you start with the ball. If you start 10 yards away from the goal, then you have a 90 percent chance of scoring. If you start from the 50, you have a 50 percent chance of scoring. If you start 80 yards away from your goal, you have a 20 percent chance of scoring. What determines where you start? Most of the time it is special teams. For this reason, I preach the importance of special teams to all of our coaches and all of our players.

If we are playing a game against an evenly matched opponent, or an opponent where we are a little bit of an underdog, I think it is important to have your best players on the field. Why would you not have your best players on the field as much as possible? You want your best players on the field all of the time so that you have the best opportunity to be successful. Sometimes we will find a kid that feels that he is a star and does not want to play on the special teams because he is too good or too tired. For this reason, we have changed the organization of our special teams.

Organization

Make it an offensive or defensive play.

Goal: Field position

Coaching and personnel:

- Offense
  - ✓ PAT-FG (offensive line)
  - ✓ KO return (backs and receivers)
- Defense
  - ✓ Punt (linebackers and defensive backs)
  - ✓ KO (linebackers and defensive backs)
  - ✓ Punt defense
  - ✓ PAT defense

We have gotten to the point where we have assigned the kicking game to the offense and the defense. My hope is that when we say it like that, we can get our best defenders to want to play on these teams because their success as a unit very much depends on where the offense starts. Our defensive coaches are responsible for staffing the punt and kickoff teams. Our offensive coaches take care of field goals, points after touchdown, and kickoff returns. Punt return stays with the defense.

We consider the point after touchdown, the field goal, and the kickoff return to be offensive plays. The kickoff return is considered an offensive play because it determines where we are starting with the ball in order to try to score. The punt, kickoff, punt return, and point after touchdown defense are considered defensive plays. A punt is a defensive play because it determines where an opponent is going to start with the ball. The defensive guys, both players and coaches, will be more concerned with how well we can cover a punt than the offensive guys who are mad because they did not get a first down. I try to make it to where special teams is just another play. The first play of defense is either a punt or a kickoff.

If my defensive coordinator likes to play a lot of young guys on the punt coverage team and we do not cover well, all I have to do is ask him on the headsets, "Why are we playing the junior varsity team on our first play of defense?" I think we should have our best players on the field for punt coverage. That is just my philosophy.

We keep a lot of statistics on the kicking game. It is not anything fancy. It is just a way for us to trust but verify. If you want to know if you are doing well in the kicking game, then keep statistics and find out. We keep them long-term to make sure that we stay on track with what we are doing. Our current chart goes from 2004-2010. This is just a sample using 2009-2010.

One of the things here I really like to look at is where the opponent started their drive. In 2007, our opponents started at the 26-yard line; in 2008, they started at the 26-yard line; in 2009, they started at the 19-yard line. That is pretty hard to do. This year, we were back up to the 27-yard line.

Our practice organization incorporates both the importance of special teams and also the importance of having all of our best players on special teams.

	2009	2010	Avg.
Punting—MUS			
Number	40	41	
Total yards	1430	1723	
Average	35.8	42.0	
Net punting	31.1	37.9	34.5
Punting—Opp.			
Number	59	47	
Total yards	2067	1657	
Average	35.0	35.3	
Net punting	30.0	30.1	30.1
Punt Returns—MUS			
Number	27	19	
Total yards	227	222	
Average	8.4	11.7	
Touchdowns	1	1	
Punt Returns—Opp.			
Number	13	16	
Total yards	127	129	
Average	9.8	8.1	
Touchdowns	0	0	
Field Goal			
Attempts	20	6	
Made	18	4	
Percentage	90%	67%	85%
Extra Point			
Attempts	60	44	
Made	59	44	
Percentage	98%	100%	99%
Blocked Kicks—MUS			
Punts	0	0	
Field goals & PATs	0	1	
Blocked Kicks—Opp.			
Punts	2	0	
Field goals & PATs	1	0	

	2009	2010	Avg.
Kick Returns—MUS			
Total	40	41	
Yards	1430	1723	
Average	35.8	42.0	
Touchdowns	31.1	37.9	34.5
Kick Returns—Opp.			
Number	59	47	
Total	2067	1657	
Yards	35.0	35.3	
Average	30.0	30.1	30.1
Kickoffs—MUS			
Total	94	60	
Yards	5128	2913	
Average	54.6	48.5	
Touchbacks	7	5	
Net	40.3	32.4	
Field position	19	27	23
Punt Returns—Opp.			
Total	38	42	
Yards	1782	2038	
Average	46.9	48.5	
Touchbacks	1	0	
Net	38.1	33.2	
Field position	21	36	29

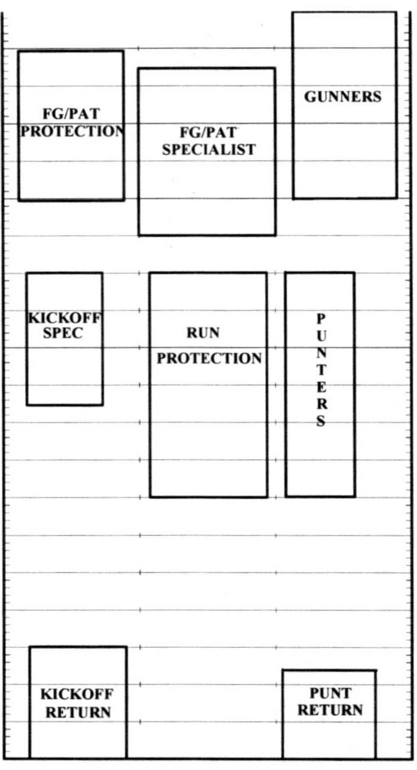

Diagram #1. First Period (5 to 10 Minutes)

Practice Organization

- Field setup
- Week 1—Early and often (specialist, punt, and PAT groups)
- Game week—Practice schedule
- Game winners

We set the field up in a certain way in order to have an organized approach to practicing special teams. I encourage the specialists to get on the field about five minutes early to warm up. When we go to the field, it is to practice. When practice starts, every player is on special teams because they are offensive and defensive players (Diagram #1). If you are an offensive lineman, then practice begins with PAT protection. The tight ends are there with them. Our backs and receivers are typically catching kickoffs and punts.

If you are a defensive lineman or a linebacker, then you know that you are going to be on the punt protection team. We can get five or six field goal or PAT attempts. We can get four or five punts and kickoffs. We can get some repetitions on punt protection. We are not sending down our guys to cover during this first five minutes, we are just practicing on repetitions.

In the second period, we may go to punt coverage and field goal or PAT. We are covering at this point (Diagram #2). The third period might be kickoff and kickoff return (Diagram #3).

We can get three or four good reps with ones against ones and twos against twos. We have special teams time allocated in our practice plan. Following is an example of what our practice plan might look like. We have this on a spreadsheet program. There would be a column for all positions and we group the X and Z players as a group and the guards and tackles as a group.

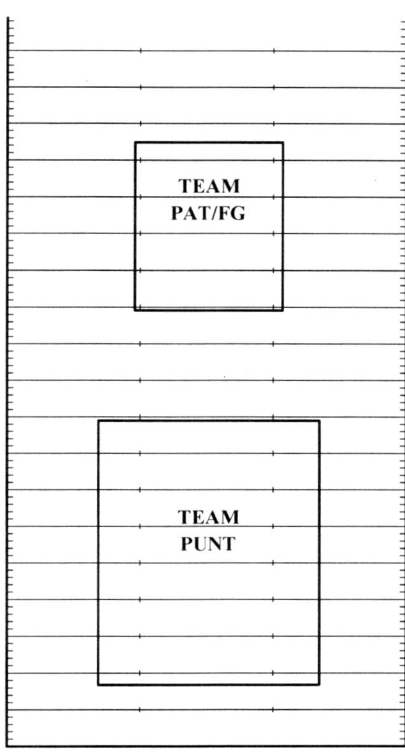

Diagram #2. Second Period (Five Minutes)

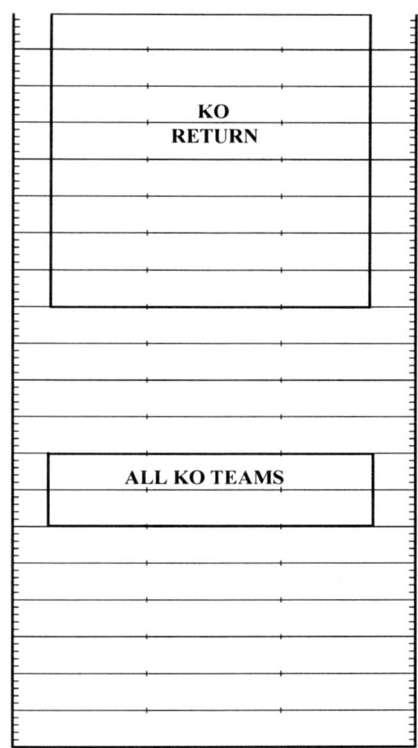

Diagram #3. Third Period Kickoff/Kickoff Return (Five Minutes)

OFFENSIVE PRACTICE PLAN

Pd	Start	Time	Skill	QB	Y
1	3:45	:05	S.T.	PAT	>
2	3:50	:05	S.T.	Punt & Ret	>
3	3:55	:05	S.T.	KO & Ret	>
4	4:00	:05	Indy	Noose	Sled

We get a lot of work done in the first 10 to 15 minutes of our special teams practice because of how things are setup from the beginning. We cover our bases in a pretty short period of time. Let's talk about our special teams playbook.

Kickoff

- Kick ball in target zone with as much height as possible
- Defenders sprint as a group
- Arrive at the ball as a unit
- Pursue to the ball until the whistle blows
- Safety needs to "fit"

Number one is the kickoff (Diagram #4). The first rule is the kicker has to kick the ball into the target zone. Whenever we have a bad kickoff return, it is almost always because the kicker kicked the ball to the middle of the field. The depth of the target zone will depend on your particular kicker. If he cannot kick it far, then he has to kick it high. We do not want him to kick a line drive short kick. We want to sprint down the field as a group and avoid blockers any way we can and then get back into our lane as fast as we can. We would like to arrive at the ball as a unit and pursue the ball until the whistle blows.

Once we get to the red zone, we have to play gap control defense. We want to take on the blockers in the red zone with our left shoulder. If they have two players to receive the kickoff, we will plan ahead of time as to whom we want to kick the ball to and where the target zone is.

It is my feeling that if we have a pretty good kickoff return man, we are going to have success with our kickoff return team. Obviously, we need to secure the ball first.

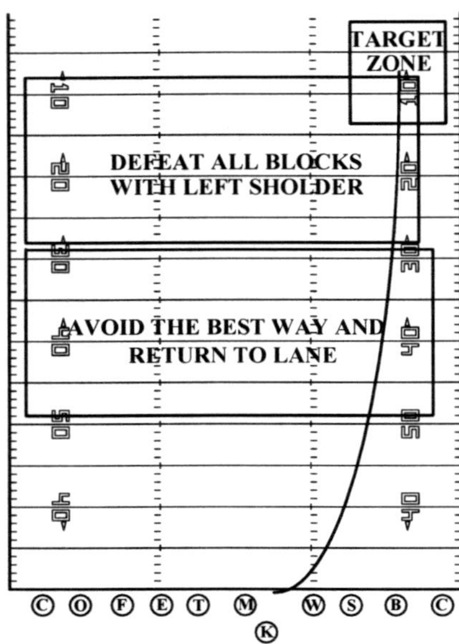

Diagram #4. Kickoff

Kickoff Return

- Secure the ball
- No penalties
- Return man runs north/south
- Timing of cross-block
- Ball security

I get very frustrated when we have a penalty on a kickoff return. At that point, it does not matter how good our kickoff return is, we are going to be pushed back into a hole to start our offensive series. I would rather miss a block than to have a penalty for blocking in the back.

We emphasize to our receiver that he is to run north and south. We like to run a cross-block scheme on our kickoff return. The timing of the cross-block needs to be when the receiver is ready to hit the gap behind the cross-block. What is hard about the kickoff return is that all of the kickers we face are different. I would rather go against a pretty good kicker that will kick it in the same area each time with a little height because I can plan my return and have a good feeling about what is going to happen. If we play against a poor kicker, he could kick it anywhere and we do not know where it is going. It takes a lot of time to practice all of the places the ball can go.

We try to take a backup offensive player and coach him up to be a badass type of player. We put him at one of the X positions and ask him to crack on somebody and make a big hit. We will take two players as a double-team and kick the next defender out. We want to hit it up between those two blocks.

If we call 2 Roger, we are going to crackback block on the second defender from the outside. We double-team and block out the first defender on the outside (Diagram #5). We want that crackback block to be a highlight film type of block. We may pick out one of the better players on the opponent's kickoff team to run that crackback on because we want him to know that we are here to play and we are going to be on him all night long. We like to get in his head and get his attention to slow him down a little bit.

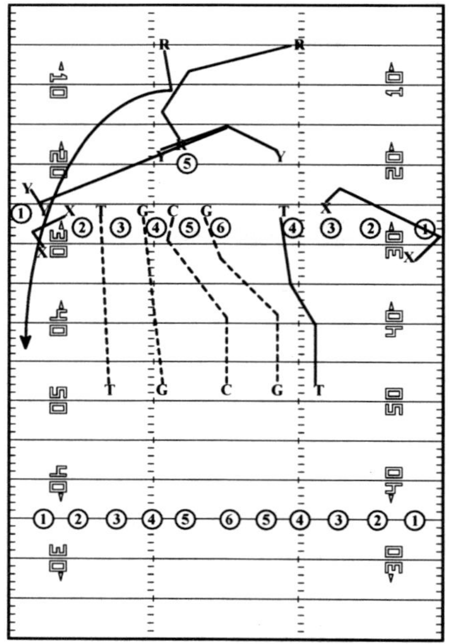

Diagram #5. Kickoff Return 2 Roger

We can do the same thing with a 3 Roger where we crack back on the third man from the outside and double-team the second man from the outside; and a 4 Roger where we will crack back on the fourth man from the outside and double-team the third man from the outside (Diagrams #6 and #7).

We can do the same thing on the other side. We will call 2 Lucy, 3 Lucy, or 4 Lucy. It looks the same; just flip it to the left side.

We try to take all of our receivers and put them on the front line, which is a little bit different than

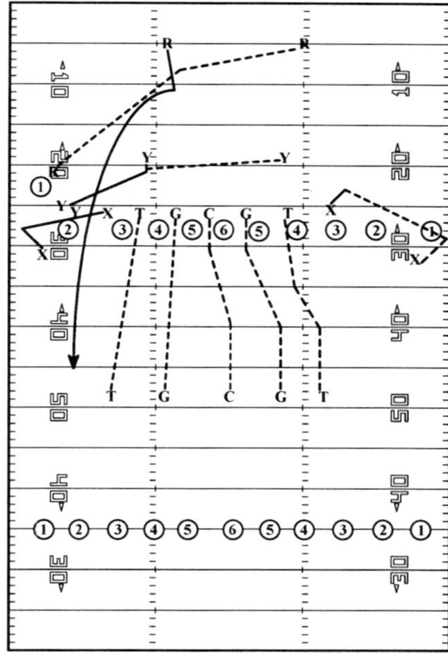

Diagram #6. Kickoff Return 3 Roger

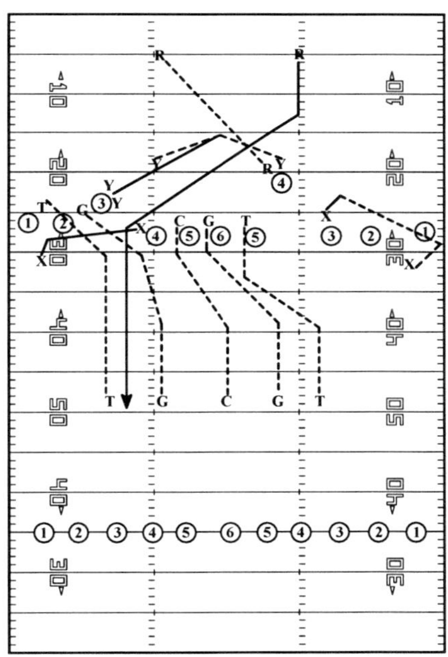

Diagram #7. Kickoff Return 4 Roger

most people think. We want our receivers to be good blockers and they get a lot of practice stock blocking in practice. This reinforces to them that they are not out there just to catch the ball, but they also have to block. Plus, if the kick is bad, we have guys out there that are supposed to be able to catch the ball. Our backup fullback or running back will be the X man, typically. If we have a backup linebacker that is a good athlete, we may put him in the X position. A lot of times, we end up with our tight ends being the double-team players.

For an obvious onside kick, we make sure we assign key roles to key players (Diagram #8).

Onside

- Assign key roles
- A shortstop and two rebounders
- Block their threats
- Fight to the finish

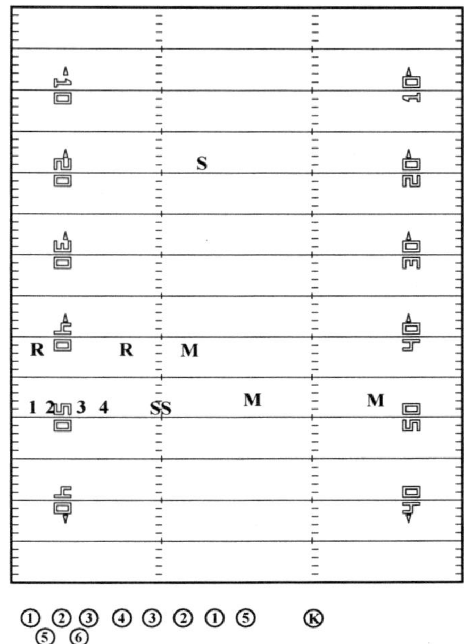

Diagram #8. Onside Kick

We take our best baseball player and put him at "shortstop." We take our two best basketball players and put them at the "rebounder" positions. We want our four front players to run up and knock the snot out of the kicking team players trying to rush down as fast as they can to cover the ball. We teach the "shortstop" that if he can catch it, then catch it and get over. If it is kicked too hard or he does not feel that he can catch it, then he lets it go. We then let our "rebounders" catch the ball. I think it is important to assign two or three players to be responsible for getting the ball. It is important to assign four or five players to go out there and knock the snot out of the defenders coming down against us.

Punt Protection

- Man—Zone principles
- Form the pocket
- Punter must know call
- A holding penalty is always better than a blocking penalty
- Have a trick if the rush team is unsound

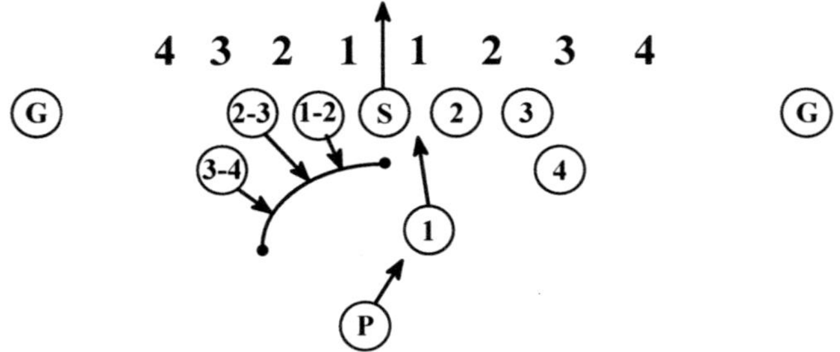

Diagram #9. Punt Protection—Even

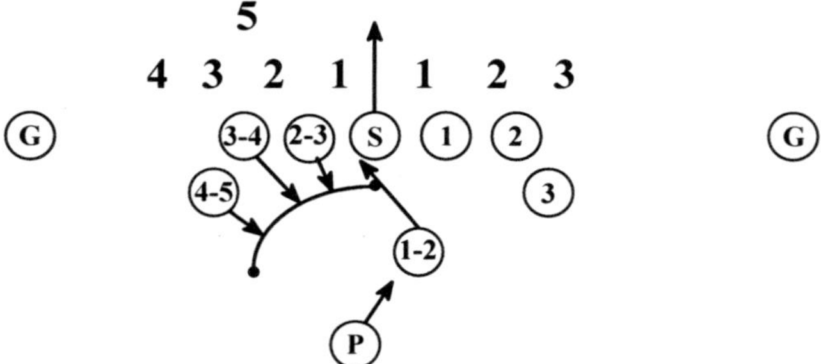

Diagram #10. Punt Protect—Left

We feel that you can only line up eight players to rush if you have players covering our two gunners and someone back to catch the punt. We are going to protect with seven players. We have a man and zone blocking scheme based on how you line up. We are going to form a pocket and block zone and we are going to be aggressive on the playside and block man-to-man.

The punter has to know where the playside is and where the zone side is so that he sets the pocket behind the guard or back to the side that we are man protecting. On the zone side, we are going to shuffle back, shuffle back, shuffle back and protect the pocket. On the playside, we are going to get up in their face, man-to-man, and we are going to stuff them. Whether we block even, left, or right is going to depend on how our opponent lines up. This is against a fairly typical lineup.

If we play against a team that has a funky punt alignment, this tells me that they have to practice it a lot. I have found that teams do not practice it enough to have sound protection. One of the worst plays in football is a blocked punt. We block more punts against a funky punt protection team than a traditional protection team. I want something in our punt protection that is sound all of the time—something that we can practice and be competent in. If you do not line up correctly, we will have a trick in our bag to take advantage of it.

We are going to send three players to cover the punt as soon as we make the snap. We do this with the snapper and the two gunners. They should make most of the tackles (Diagram #11).

Punt Coverage

- Most tackles made by gunners and center
- GTWs must always expect to have to make tackle
- Practice downing the ball

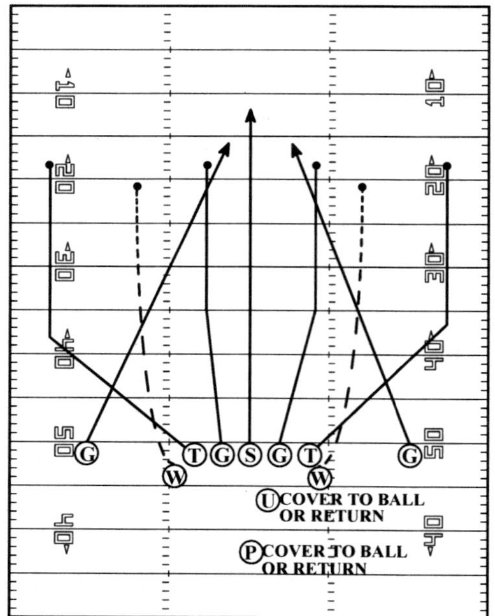

Diagram #11. Punt Coverage

Punt coverage is a defensive play because it establishes where the opponent is going to get the ball. The snapper and the two gunners have to be able to tackle. They cannot just be fast; they have to be able to tackle. When we practice our punts, we typically do that from the 40- or 50-yard line.

This enables us to practice downing the ball. This is important. You have to reinforce to the down linemen that they have to sprint downfield and be ready to make a tackle. The down linemen will get lazy and expect the gunners to make the tackle and they will not be in good position to make the tackle when they are needed.

In closing, I would want to say that we try to keep it simple, but keep it sound. We practice the special teams aspect of football very seriously and we prepare for our success. We always want to coach the specialists in a positive manner and keep their confidence up. We believe in field position. Everything that we do is to try to get the ball closer to the goal line in order to score, and have our opponent go as far as possible in order to score.

I would like to thank Nike® and Larry Blackmon for having me here this weekend. I have been fortunate to have some success because of a great group of players and a great group of coaches that coach along with me.

Tim Baechler

THE STRAIGHT T FORMATION OFFENSE

Canton High School, Michigan

Thank you. In the past several years, we have been successful in our football program. I want to start with some of the things we have achieved in the last 10 years.

2000-10 ACHIEVEMENTS

- 105-23 record
- 6 league championships
- 6 district championships
- 2 regional championships
- 1 Division I state finalist

The next area I want to discuss is the question coaches often ask me. Why the T? Let me give you a few reasons why we run the straight-T formation.

- Statistics
- Builds toughness, entire team
- A system; not a grab-bag approach
- We can practice it faster and better than our opponents.
- Continuity; It's how we play football.
- Quarterback does not have to win for us.
- It's what I know. We learn and get better every year as a staff.
- You can hide some linemen.
- You can hide some backs as well if you are not hiding any linemen.

Now that you know why we run the straight-T offense, let me talk about the philosophy behind our practices. If you don't do it in a game, you should not be doing it in practice.

PRACTICE PHILOSOPHY

- Practice should be harder than the games.
- Repetitions. No waiting in lines.
- Scripts are great and so is staying on schedule, but a piece of paper does not trump doing it until you do it right.
- What happens on the field is either coached, or it is allowed to happen. Film doesn't lie.

We do not have middle school football. There are about 2,000 students in our school. We share a campus with Plymouth and Salem High Schools. I know a lot of people believe that Canton High School gets all of the football players. That is not true, and that is not how it works. The middle school kids are sent home with a letter telling them which high school they have been assigned to for their ninth grade. They are not allowed to make that choice for themselves. We do not have open enrollment or selecting a school of their choice.

We typically get around 40 kids out for football. We do have a youth league in our district, but we usually get around 12 kids who have played organized football, and that is it. However, our system allows these kids to become good football players.

Our freshmen team does not do as much as we do at the varsity level, but they have been very successful with our base program. They win at the freshman level, and they win at the JV level. When they come up to the varsity, they expect to win.

Our quarterback does not have to have a hot night for us to win a game. We are not going to throw the ball 20 to 30 times a game. Typically, we will get two or three really good players. We get a lot of good players, but we have a lot of average joes that we hide out on the field. Nevertheless, they can play football. The reason for that is because our offense is based on double-teaming at the point of attack, and down blocking. We do base block, but not very much. It allows those 175 to 185 pound kids to play in the line and to play well.

As I entered the coaching profession, I studied the game to implement my ideas. I loved Lou Holtz, and I read everything I could that he said. I got all of his books and studied them.

I talk with my coaches about the things they do with their players. If I see a coach teaching a player to log roll, I ask him if the player will be doing the log roll in the games. My belief is this: if you don't do it in a game, you should not be doing it in practice.

Another thing I have a problem with is when we have two players doing a drill and 10 to 12 other players standing around watching the drill. That is just a waste of time. It may be a great rep, but we need to get everyone involved in the reps.

We say we are going to practice two hours, but we are going to practice a play until we get it right. We are going to practice two hours even if it takes us six hours to do it right. We may have to run the play repeatedly, but we are going to get it right. A couple of years ago I had an assistant coach who complained about running the plays repeatedly. He was concerned about breaking up continuity in the practice. I do not care about continuity if we can't run the plays correctly.

A few years ago, when I got the head job, I had a chance to interview the entire former staff. I asked them why they were so bad. That entire staff, except for two of the coaches, blamed how bad they were on the kids. "They are not competitive. They do not work hard. They are not very athletic." Only two of the coaches said it was because of the job the staff did as coaches.

We practice both offense and defense every day. That is my way of doing things. I know a lot of coaches have one day for offense and one day for defense, and then the other two days are for both offense and defense. I just do not feel comfortable doing that.

I believe steps and blocking techniques are more important than the plays. We really aren't tricking anybody. This is especially true in our league. We have been at Canton for 13 years. We have tried to hide the ball and run deceptive plays. We really are not fooling anyone who knows us well.

Effort and attitude are more important than the plays. Winning football is consistent domination. Win every down. Go for the jugular now.

We have seen a lot of teams that made a perfect huddle, and they come up to the line of scrimmage, line up, and look great. However, when the ball is snapped, they do not come off the ball with a real effort, and they exhibit an attitude that they are not concerned with blocking anyone. They are not competing. I do not care what offense you run; if you do not have good effort, you are not playing good football.

We tell the kids we are concrete breakers. We are going to go through it, around it, or over it, but be patient, and the system will break it.

Some teams take wide splits with their line when running this offense. At times, we take large splits as well. We want to teach our kids when we want them to split more, and when to tighten down on their splits. This is true on the backside, where we may only split one foot. We do not line up in a tight set a great deal of the time.

I have included a copy of our practice schedule. The reason I have included this schedule is because coaches come to watch us practice during the playoffs, so I thought it would assist them in knowing what we were working on that day. I am not going to go into details; you can see what we are doing.

MONDAY PRACTICE SCHEDULE—DEFENSE

2:55-3:05	Form run and flex
3:05-3:20	Repeats (conditioning)
3:20-3:25	Water
3:25-3:30	Punt
3:30-3:40	Offensive individuals
3:40-4:10	Offensive walk and talk (bird dog versus expected fronts, personnel, extras (if any new plays or schemes, put them in now)
4:10-4:30	Defensive individual: Any two-way players go with defense, offensive players only go to offensive coach.
4:30-5:00	Front seven/skelly (defense). Remaining offensive players scheme.
5:00-5:40	Team defense. Remaining starters on offense. Film, chalk talk, trap drill, guard steps, basically whatever needs fixing, offensive line coaches work on it.
5:40-5:55	Conditioning

We do some conditioning at the beginning of practice as well at the end of practice. I believe in working them hard when they are tired.

I am not sure if everyone knows what we mean by bird dog. I call out, "Down, set, hit," and the players take a step and then pause. They stand there as if they were statues. Then I will say, "Two." The players take a second step. Then I call out "Three," and they continue on that next step. They have to pause on each step. It is a great way for the coaches to watch the players step on every single play. It is a great way to practice the little things without beating the crap out of them.

On Monday, we will go over the scouting report on our opponent. The great thing about our offense is the fact that we do not have to game plan a great deal. We do practice against their defense, but we have seen almost every defense you could draw up against us.

We watch the film of the opponent's offense in our coaching meeting on Sunday night. The staff looks at the past year and the present year of the offense we will be playing. Mostly, they are looking at personnel.

TUESDAY PRACTICE SCHEDULE—OFFENSE

2:55-3:05	Form run and flex
3:05-3:20	Repeats (conditioning)
3:20-3:25	Water
3:25-3:30	Punt return team
3:30-3:50	Offensive individuals (two-way players go offense)

- Lineman—Backs
- Base—Stance and steps
  - ✓ Footwork: Base block—seven seconds
  - ✓ Ball protection: Down blocks
  - ✓ Blocks: Double-teams—technique depends on what we have
- Reach and overtakes: Rocker steps, pulling

3:50-4:25	Muscle/skelly (Muscle is our inside run game) ones on ones Muscle—twos on twos Skelly then outside run game; switch
4:25-4:55	Team offense: Huddle but with two plays
4:55-5:15	Front seven/skelly
5:15-5:45	Team defense
5:45-5:55	Conditioning

Before Plymouth High School opened, we were a total two-platoon team. We still had good numbers with 65 to 70 players on our team, but our depth was terrible. We only had 20 players with 50 others just out there. Now, we have players going both ways. This year, we have six players going both ways. We play teams now that have several players going both ways, and we do it as well, even though we do not like to do it.

We call two plays in the huddle in our two-minute drill. We are still in the full house set. That is how we practice the two-minute drill.

WEDNESDAY PRACTICE SCHEDULE

2:55-3:05	Form run and flex
3:05-3:15	Repeats (two sets)
3:15-3:20	Punt team
3:20-3:25	Kickoff team
3:25-3:55	Muscle/skelly (offense)
3:55-4:25	Team offense
4:25-4:55	Front seven/skelly
4:55-5:30	Team defense
5:30-5:40	Conditioning

THURSDAY PRACTICE SCHEDULE

2:45-2:55	Pre-game flex
2:55-3:05	Special teams punting contest
3:05-3:10	Punt
3:10-3:15	Punt return
3:15-3:20	Kickoff and onside
3:20-3:25	Kick return
3:25-3:30	Hands unit
3:30-3:35	PAT/field goal
3:35-3:40	PAT block
3:40-4:10	Team offense
4:10-4:40	Team defense
4:40-4:45	10x10s for the Falcons
4:45-5:05	Scouting report
5:05-6:00	Spaghetti dinner

I want to talk about our muscle drill. This is the best drill we do. This is a good drill early in the year. It helps with the players developing the tough mentality of three yards and a cloud of dust type plays. It is like the old Woody and Bo type plays. That is what I grew up with when I played football. That is winning football to me, and it is what we do.

We line up two cones four yards past the line of scrimmage. We space the cones where the area to run is not very wide. The goal is to gain the four yards for seven straight times. We can tackle the ballcarrier, we can thud the runner, or we can tag him. They have to gain the four yards on seven consecutive plays.

The drill can get brutal. We may have five or six plays where we are successful, and then someone misses a block or makes a mistake, and we do not gain the four yards. "We have to start over." We start back at zero. The kids get so frustrated and disgusted. We play into them with comments such as this: "You guys just can't get it right." "It is getting late, and we need to go to the next drill." "You guys are not good enough to run this drill, and we are going to move on." No! They will not let us move on because they want to complete the drill successfully.

That is what you want out of the drill. You want to build that tough mentality in the players that they can be successful even when they are tired and it is late in practice. We want them to develop the intestinal fortitude that we can gain four yards every time we run the ball.

We do not huddle on this drill. We run back to the line and get ready to run the next play. I signal in the play, and we execute the play. We are getting a lot of repetitions, and we are not wasting any time getting in and out of the huddle.

I want to go over our base package and the adjustment as well.

- Trap
- Off-tackle trap
- Quarterback keep
- Quarterback keep pass

The first play is the trap against an odd defense (Diagram #1). I am not going to bore with our blocking, as I am sure most of you know how to block the

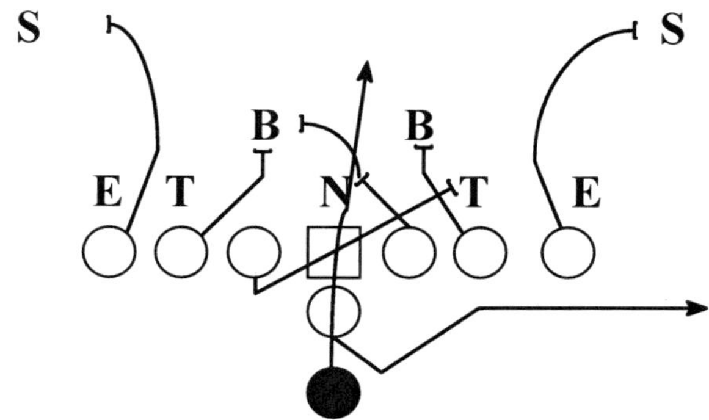

Diagram #1. Trap vs. Odd

plays. We face two safeties so our tight ends must get downfield to block those safeties.

We block the Eagle defense two different ways (Diagram #2). I like to double-team at the point of attack. My favorite way is to have our center and guard double-team block. We want to cut the offside defensive tackle. We want our left tackle to take a step with his right foot inside and then dive to get his outside arm on the defender on his thigh board. We are not trying to hurt the defensive man we are cutting. He wants to dive and roll into the defender.

Diagram #2. Trap vs. Eagle

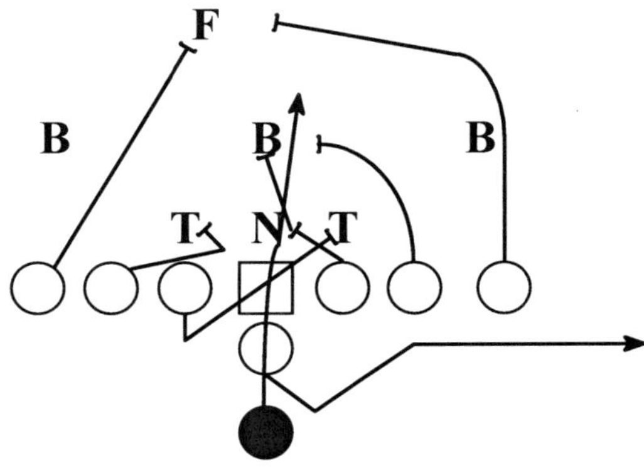

We consider the midline to be a part of our trap package, and we can talk about that in the adjustments.

Our off-tackle trap is the next part of our offense (Diagram #3). We run the play with the fullback faking the trap inside, and the frontside halfback blocking on the defensive end. This is the odd man defense.

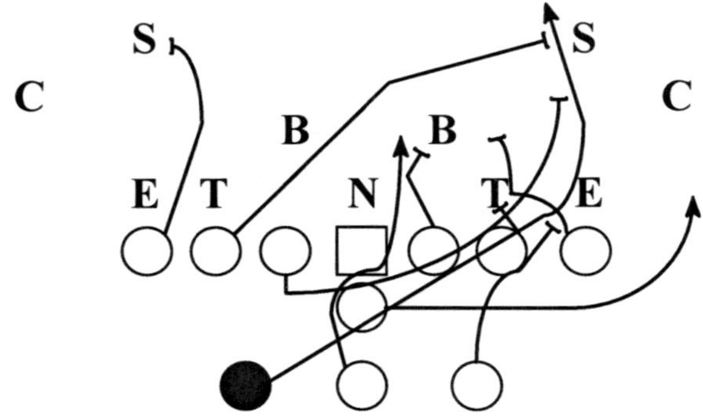

Diagram #3. Off-Tackle Trap

We want to get the double-team block with the right tackle and the tight end on the playside. We worry about the linebacker after we move the tackle back off the line of scrimmage. The backside guard pulls and is responsible to lead the play upfield. The big question is: can we handle the tackle long enough to run the play?

We want to prevent the defensive end from coming inside to make the play. We have the halfback take a right lead step and then an inside step with the back foot so he can gain an inside-out leverage position on the defensive end. We want to prevent him from coming down inside. If we get a stalemate, that is okay as long as he does not close down the running lane. We know the end is a better defensive player than our back is a blocker. We just need a stalemate to stop him. I hope that the running back can hit the hole and have enough speed to get inside the end and through the hole.

The fullback is stepping toward the halfback, who is getting the ball. He steps slightly to his left and then cuts toward the center. The ballcarrier wants to aim at the hands of the fullback on his first step. The second step should be planted and turned toward the off-tackle hole. It should be turned slightly upfield. He should get the ball by on his third step. By his fourth step, he is hitting the hole with his shoulders square to the line of scrimmage.

When some teams start installing this play, they get caught up in the minutiae of how to block the play against the Eagle look (Diagram #4). You could down block on the 2 technique inside. I want to double-team the 2 technique and then have him come off on the tackle coming down on the middle linebacker. I like the double-team block at the point

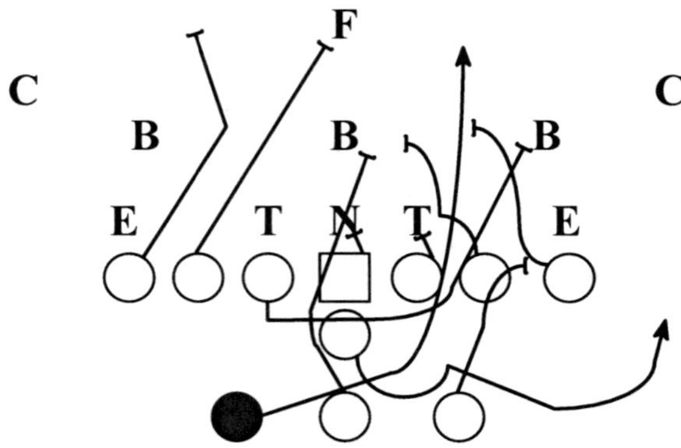

Diagram #4. Off-Tackle Trap vs. Eagle

of attack. The fullback is running the midline, and we hope he absorbs the linebacker. We must have a different scheme in case he can't do it.

We have a fan scheme in our package (Diagram #5). It is great if we can get the pulling guard on the outside linebacker. We have the fullback cut it over past the center on the fake. The onside tackle comes inside on the middle linebacker. The halfback gets inside the tackle, and the pulling guard leads the play, looking for that outside linebacker. We block the end out with our end.

Diagram #5. Fan Scheme

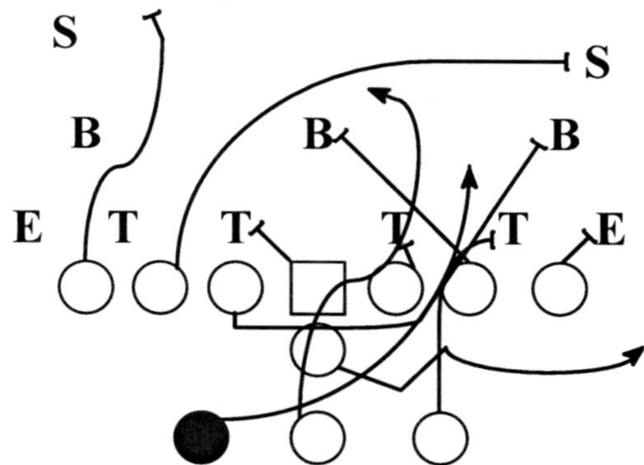

Another variation is our base scheme (Diagram #6). We still pull the backside guard, and he leads he play up inside to the linebacker on the playside. Our onside tackle has a tough block on the tackle. He wants to take him outside and have the back run the ball inside his hip.

Our quarterback keep play has been a good play for us. We never want to chase a defender outside in our offense. If we are attempting to block a man and he runs outside, it is not going to do us any good

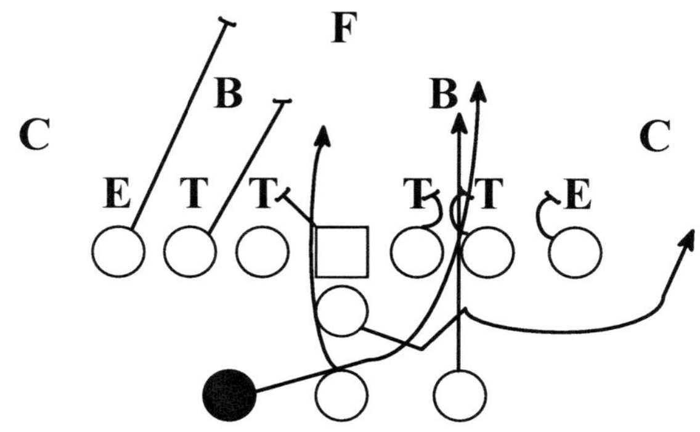

Diagram #6. Base Scheme

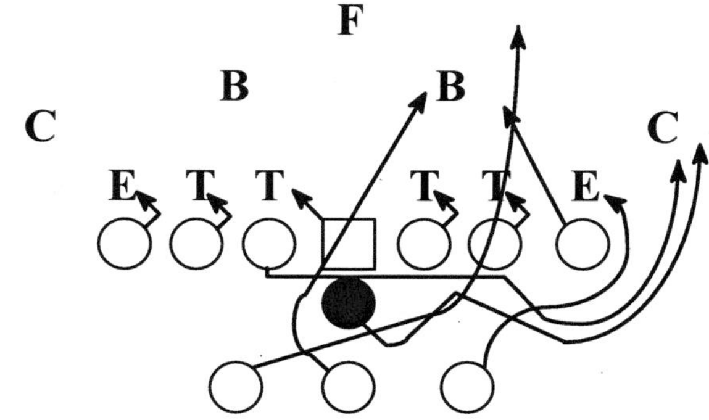

Diagram #8. Quarterback Keep vs. Even

to chase him. We want the offensive man to block the first man he sees inside in that case.

In the diagram here, we are double-teaming the tackle with the tight end. It is a quick double-team (Diagram #7). We co-opt on the tackle. However, our end is only tapping the tackle slightly. We do want to get the frontside linebacker sealed down inside. The way our tackle approaches the play is this, He is going to reach block the defensive tackle by himself.

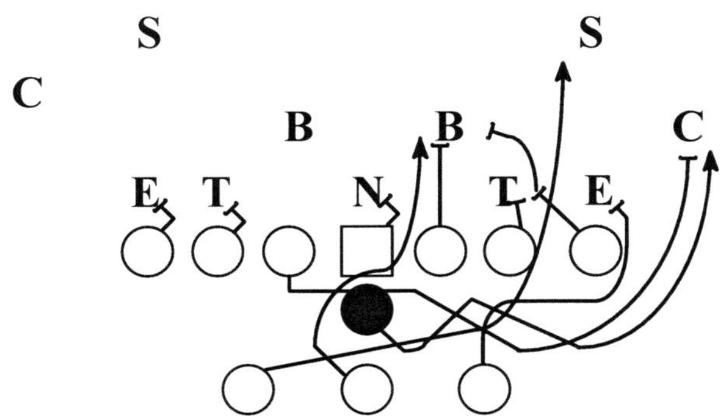

Diagram #7. Quarterback Keep vs. Odd

The quarterback is coming outside to get on the corner. The backside guard is pulling and going outside to lead the play. The quarterback must have energy on the play, and he has to make the play look the same all of the time. He may hide the ball on his back hip, or he may fake the handoff and then tuck the ball and run.

Against the even front, we still pull the backside guard on the quarterback keep (Diagram #8). He leads the quarterback outside the end. The center must block back on the 2 technique. We want the fullback to hit up in the off-tackle hole. This is a good play to run on the goal line. It is an easy play to run, and it simple to block. Our main offensive goal is to make the trap, off-tackle trap, quarterback keep, and keep pass all look identical. That is a big coaching point. We want to make all four plays look the same.

Quickly, I want to move on to our adjustments. If we call "wall," it is our off-tackle blocking, but we give the ball to the fullback. Our fullbacks have not been the big, heavy, bulldozer-type fullbacks. They have been halfback-type runners. We have had some good runners in that position, however. On the adjustment for the trap, we run a second man trap (Diagram #9). I want to show the play against the even front. The backside guard pulls and traps the second man past the center. The fullback bends the play around the guard's block on the 2 technique.

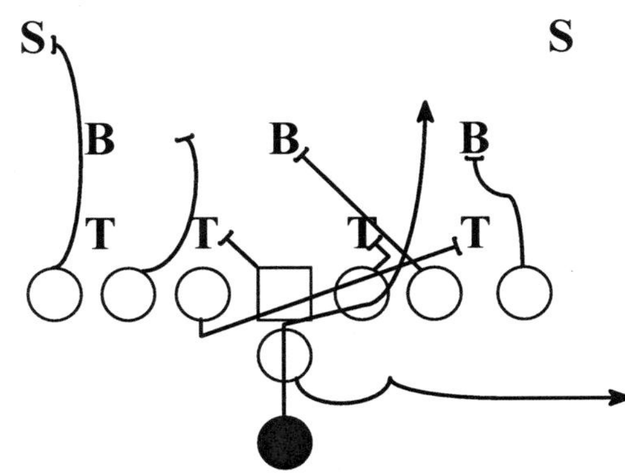

Diagram #9. Second Man Trap vs. Even Cover 2

We do not read the play. We want to eliminate any doubt on the part of the handoff. The big rule here is this: if the tackle is covered, he blocks the man, and he wants to block him outside. If the tight end is covered, he wants to try to block him man out. The fullback steps straight ahead and in front of the quarterback. The quarterback takes two steps back deep, and rides hip-to-hip. It is a double quarterback isolation play.

If you are a trap team, you should run the midline. If you are a midline team, you should run the trap. It would not make any sense not to run them both. This is especially true against the even fronts (Diagram #10).

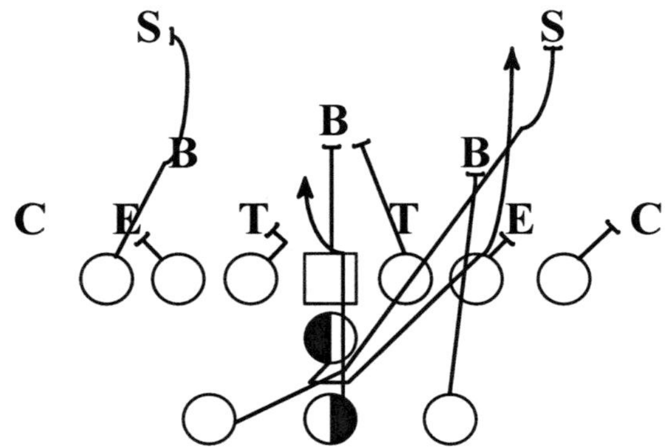

Diagram #10. Midline vs. Even Front

We can run the play on the goal line because it is a great quarterback isolation play. We do not have to work hard on this play because it is a simple play. I think this is what scares people away from running the play. The rules are so simple. If you are a lineman and you are covered, block him. If the defense goes inside, and the B gap is not there, the quarterback takes the ball outside.

We do have an off-tackle power play. When our offensive players hear the word power, they know the guard is not pulling. The fullback is going take the role of the pulling guard, and he will lead the play through the hole to the linebacker.

Counters are plays that I have considered getting rid of because since we have so much offense, it is hard to practice all of the plays. There are some games when you do decide to run the counter in a game. You run the counter, and the defense can't stop the play. Your comment is something like this: "I am sure glad we had that counter play in our offense."

When I was the coach at Hudson High School, I tried to run the reverse play. I was a young 23-year-old coach then. We were not too successful on the play. I had the fullback running into the tight end, and we were all confused. I have never used the reverse play since. If you are going to run this scheme and you face an Eagle defense, you are going to lose your double-team at the point of attack.

I want to talk about our sweep play (Diagram #11). It is our version of the outside zone play. It has been good for us. I am going to try to talk you through the play. We start with the tight end to the playside. He wants to reach block on one half of the defender lined up on his outside shoulder or head-up. If the defender strings the tight end to the sideline, he wants to run him to the sideline.

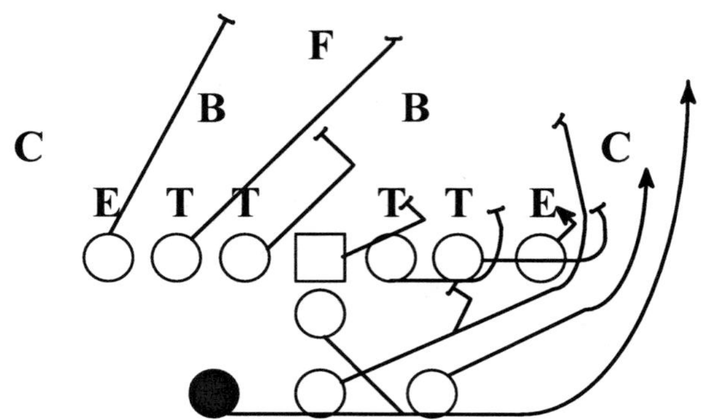

Diagram #11. Power Sweep

If the end does get the seal, our tackle overtakes that defender, and the end comes off to the next linebacker. If the tackle sees the defensive end going to the outside, he has to come upfield and block the nearest linebacker. Those are the most important blocks on the play. It is not hard to make these blocks for those two linemen. You have to work on the blocks, but the players can get it done even against zone teams. The onside guard and tackle pull and overtake. They are looking upfield for the linebackers.

The halfback on the playside sprints five yards outside the end. He wants to get to that spot as fast as he can. If the corner is not there, he turns inside and hooks the corner. If the corner is there when the halfback reaches that spot, block him to the sideline.

The rule for the fullback is this: he takes two steps and aims for two yards outside of our tight end, keeping his eyes on the frontside linebacker. If that linebacker blitzes, he has to stop and pick him up because he is the only player who can block him. We teach the fullback this technique the first week of practice, and we do not have a problem with that block the rest of the year. In that first week, we run the play, and I will send the linebacker a few times, and the fullback learns to pick him up. It is not a problem for us after that first week of practice.

If the linebacker does not blitz, the fullback stays one yard outside our tight end and cleans up any defender in the path. If there is no one to clean up, he looks up inside for the next ugly jersey. Everyone else is releasing and trying to get in front of the football.

The halfback carrying the football gets on his train track. He is reading the block of the tight end. If the end is hooked, he goes outside. If the end is stringing the play out, the ballcarrier turns up inside.

The quarterback opens straight out to the playside and hands the ball to the back coming across the ball. It is similar to the handoff made on the stretch play.

Next is our keep pass (Diagram #12). It is a run-pass option for us. We tell our quarterback he is running keep out. We want him to come out as soon as he gets the snap. We do not want him getting too deep on the play.

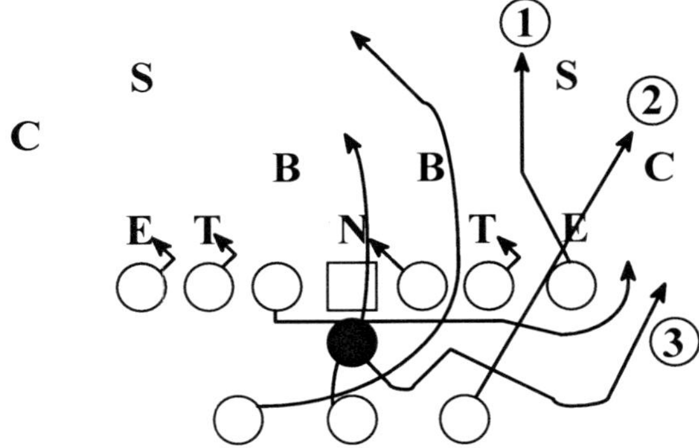

Diagram #12. Keep Pass Option

The key on the play is the block on the tackle. The guard is pulling behind the tackle. The fullback runs inside the B gap. We do not want the defensive linemen to beat us to the outside. If they are going to beat us, we want them to beat us to the inside. We are going to get the ball outside.

We sent the tight end on a deep flag. The onside halfback runs at the corner. If the corner comes up, we want to throw the ball to the halfback as soon as possible because the corner can sack the quarterback on a blitz. If the corner stays back, we want the halfback to run him deep and outside. If the quarterback has to run the ball, that is fine as we feel we can gain four to five yards on the play. The options for the quarterback are first the tight end, second the halfback, and third the run on the keeper. It is deep, shallow, and then it is a run. It is a big play for us.

The keep stay pass has been a good companion play for us. This is good against teams that have the defensive backs keying our tight end down blocks. We have the tight end stay in and block. The halfback runs the same route. Next, we read the corner. If the corner comes up, we throw the ball. If the corner stays back, we run the ball.

Coaches ask me if it is confusing pulling the guards on play-action passes. It is, but if we run a bootleg pass, we are only running it to one side. When we run our vertical pass, it is only to one side. We do run the keep passes to both sides. We do not want the guards confused, and we do not want both guards pulling and running into each other.

It is important for the linemen blocking to know where the mesh point is on plays. We do not work a great deal on pass blocking. We block for two counts, and they come outside.

On the bootleg pass, the fullback does not rush his moves to start out. He wants to allow the guard enough room to pull. Then, the fullback slips out into the pattern last (Diagram #13).

The tight end is the #1 target. The fullback fakes and goes through the line. He chop-steps to allow the guard to pull. After the fake, he comes outside on the playside and is the #2 receiver. The backside tight end drags across the formation and he is the #3 target. The quarterback is the #4 option as he comes outside looking for the open receivers. If he can't find an open receiver, he runs the football. For the offside halfback, we can tag the call for him and have him run a peek at the post, or flag. If the backside corner is cheating over to help on the playside, we can run the peek with the halfback.

The question is: could we pass more? We could, but it does not fit our philosophy. We want to play defense with our offense. We want to work the clock and keep our defense off the field.

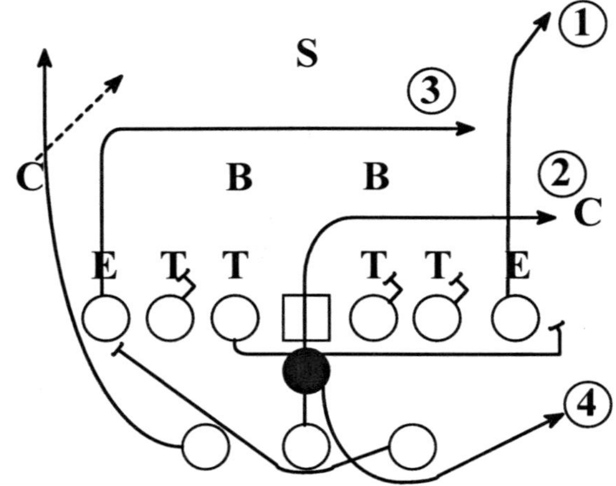

Diagram #13. Bootleg Pass vs. Even

I want to get to the vertical pass (Diagram #14). It is great against the two-deep look. The ends run eight-yard flag routes. The halfback goes down the seam. We are sending three receivers into the three-deep zones. The quarterback makes a three-step drop on the play. He reads the receivers across the secondary.

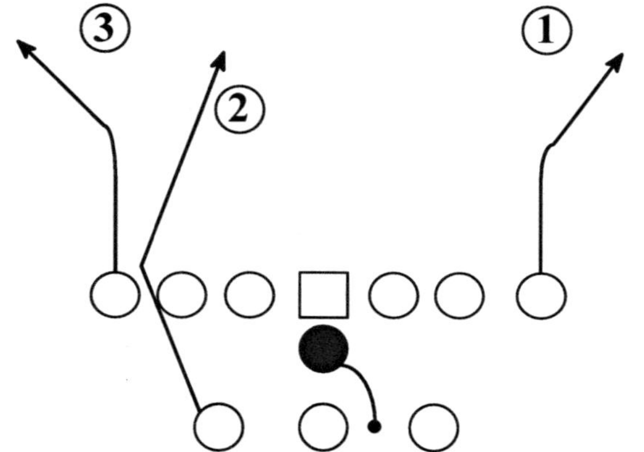

Diagram #14. Vertical Route—Three Receivers Deep, Halfback Post

We can change the patterns for the halfback and end. The left end changes his route and runs the post, and the halfback runs the flag or seam route on the left side (Diagram #15).

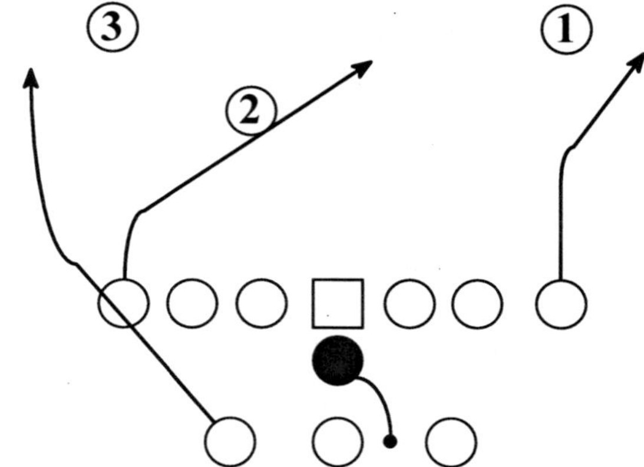

Diagram #15. Vertical Route—Three Receivers Deep, Halfback Flag/Seam

We want the quarterback to read the receivers. He cannot make up his mind that he is going to throw before the ball is snapped. He has to read the play. This is a great play against two-deep coverage.

In this offense, I have beaten every defense on earth, and I have been beaten by every defense on earth. It is not the defense or the scheme. It is the Johnnys and Joes that make the difference. I feel the technique is more important than the scheme.

Thank you very much. We will be around.

Adam Barth

FUNDAMENTALS OF THE 3-3 STACK DEFENSE

Cathedral High School, Indiana

It is a pleasure to be here today. I want to talk about our 3-3 stack defense. I will be going into my sixth year at Cathedral High School. The first two years, we ran a 4-3 defense. Why did we change to the 3-3 stack from the 4-3? Three years ago, we got to the point where we did not feel we had two safeties that were good downhill cover 4 and cover 2 safeties.

We also felt we did not have enough depth at the defensive line position. Our kids are typically smaller athletic kids. We do not get a lot of Division I kids. We have a lot of good Division II and III kids, which is why we have been successful. This defense gives us a chance to get those kids on the field and get different pressures from a lot of different areas on the field. When we changed to the 3-3 stack, I got my information from Gordon Elliott in Seattle, Washington.

WHY 3-3 STACK?

- Lack of defensive linemen and lack of efficient safeties
- Allows us to get more athletes on the field and utilize the speed we have
- Allows us to pressure from multiple places versus multiple formations
- We can involve more players more often, which equals more enthusiasm for the defense.

With the 3-3 defense, we use three down linemen and they can be moving all the time. At least 50 percent of the time, we are bringing one linebacker, if not two. That also means 50 percent of the time we are not blitzing. We want the offense to read and think we are blitzing on every down. The defense is high impact, high energy, and our players get into it. Kids like to blitz.

Players today want to see an immediate impact of what they are accomplishing and to see results. We give them goals so they have something to look at and to measure their performance against.

MAJOR TEAM DEFENSIVE GOALS

- Create one or more turnovers than touchdowns against in each game.
- Cause and recover two fumbles each game.
- No runs over 15 yards
- Stop 75 percent of all third and fourth downs.
- Score or set up a score.
- Five minus-yards plays per game (three sacks)
- No passes over 20 yards

These goals are self-explanatory. You have probably seen something similar at other clinics. Following are what we use as position names. You may have seen other position names for the same defense. We tried to use old terminology from our previous 4-3 defense.

- Nose
- Anchor end (strongside)
- Blood end (weakside)
- Mike (middle inside linebacker)
- Sam (strongside inside linebacker)
- Will (weakside inside linebacker)
- Snake (strongside outside linebacker)
- Bear (weakside outside linebacker)
- Corners
- Free safety

The following diagram shows how we number our defensive techniques (Diagram #1). We teach them to all of our defensive players.

Diagram #1. Defensive Technique

This is how we break down our alignments, keys, and responsibilities for our base defense. I will start with the nose and work my way down the list.

Nose

Our nose man is in a 0 technique. We are head-up on the center all the time. We have used two types of noseguards. We have had big players that could not be moved on defense. We have had smaller, quicker guys that we could use to slant. Both types of players have been effective for us. You can fit this position to the type of players you have.

Alignment: 0 technique, and a yard to a yard and a half off of the ball.

Key: Ball

Technique: Predetermined slant to A gap given by the Mike or attack the center, read his block, and keep him off the Mike backer.

Ends

Alignment: 5 technique or outside shade of the tackle. We never call for the tackle to line up head-up on the offensive tackle, so we do not have a technique number for that situation. This helps keep the defensive end from being hooked by the offensive tackle.

- Anchor goes to callside, tight or wide.
- Blood goes *away* from callside, open or short.

Key: Ball

Technique (base): He will attack the outside shoulder of the tackle, and then he will read. What the offensive tackle does will determine the gap responsibility of the defensive end. The defensive end and the stack linebacker have gap exchange responsibility for the B and C gaps when we are in base. If we get a down read, the defensive end will close hard and be the B-gap player. We are not running upfield. For any trap or counter, we are wrong-arming everything.

Mike

Alignment: Four and a half yards deep and stacked behind the nose.

Key: Varies based on formation and game plan. It could be the tailback or the fullback. If the offense is in the gun with one tailback, he will key the tailback. If it is a gun formation with two backs, he will key the quarterback to the first back he goes to.

Technique:

- Run—A gap to C gap. Mike has the A gap opposite the A gap of the nose slant. If the ball goes to the nose slant side, he will come over the top from A gap to C gap. If his key goes to that side, he will fill the A gap hard and bend pursuit to the ball. He will check for crossers. If Mike's key goes away from the assigned A gap, he will fill the C gap to flow. Check for crossers. Crossers are guards or tackles coming on traps or counters. We work crosser drills every single day of practice. He has to have a point two yards behind the line of scrimmage to where he looks for any crossers coming. He will then redirect, dip, and rip to come through.
- Pass—His pass drop is to the #3 receiver. If we are blitzing, he will take over for the blitzing linebacker.

Sam/Will

Alignment: 50 Technique on the heels of the defensive end. We want them right on top of the defensive end. This gets them closer to the line of scrimmage, and when they get their read, it looks like a blitz.

Key: Varies based on formation and game plan. If the offense is in an I formation backfield, he will read the tailback most of the time. We read backs most of the time. If it is a shotgun formation, we will cross read.

Technique:

- Run to—Fill assigned gap, B or C, depending on where the defensive end goes. Fill like a blitz. Use clear/cloudy fit off the defensive end. For an iso technique, he will take on blocks with his outside arm and keep his inside arm free. He will spill all plays outside to fit to the free safety or Mike.

- Run away—Shuffle in and check for crossers, pulling offensive linemen, or backs coming back across from the opposite direction.
- Pass—Drop off to the #2 receiver. We will make an outlaw call if the #2 receiver is too wide and detached, or if there is a trips formation. Sam or Will makes an outlaw call that sends the defensive end to Sam or Will's side into the B gap and widens Sam and Will's alignment outside of the stack. He will bump out and split the difference, or at least a third of the way toward the #2 receiver. He will now have C-gap responsibility. This will make it easier for him to get onto the #2 receiver. All gaps are still covered. An outlaw call overrules any call from the sideline.

We do not have a lot of coverages. We use cover 2, cover 4, and Bronco, which is our blitz coverage. These are our three main coverages. We will throw in a man-to-man coverage on occasion if we are blitzing. Our philosophy is the less we have, the better our players can know it.

Bear/Snake

Alignment:

- Cover 4—Creep inside before the snap using the prowl technique to a 4x5 alignment off the offensive tackle. We give this as a landmark, but they should never be standing in one spot at the snap of the ball. We want them moving back and forth to give the quarterback a possible blitz look. We do not want the quarterback to read the outside linebacker and determine what type of coverage we are playing. Once the outside linebacker gets to his alignment, he must get his shoulders square and buzz his feet.
- Cover 2—Align one to two yards outside the #1 wide receiver at a depth of five yards. At the snap, he should not backpedal. He should sit at five yards and wait for the #1 receiver to come to him. He should make sure he gets contact. If the football is not in the air, we are going to hit receivers.

Key: Guard or tackle based on the game plan. The outside linebackers will read linemen every single play.

Technique:

- Run to—If they get a run read and flow is coming toward them, they are the contain player. They are a controlled contain player. Take on kick-out blockers, but never get deeper than two yards past the line of scrimmage. It will create a seam for the running back, if they are too far upfield. They want to force the ball back inside and let our flow come from over the top to make the tackle.

On the option, they have the pitchman, and they slow play it. They bait the quarterback, so he does not know what we are going to do. He is not just going to attack; he is going to sit at the line of scrimmage. Most high school quarterbacks do not know what to do if a defender is just sitting there. We have 10 other guys that are running over to make the tackle. They cannot come up the field too far. We teach our kids to build a fence. If they come upfield too far, they open the gate.

- Run away—CRCB means the counter/reverse/cutback/boot. That is their main responsibility. They stay home. Take the back out of the backfield in the flat or any shallow receiver in the flat.
- Pass, cover 4—Open to the #1 receiver and get under the #1 receiver. His aiming point is six yards. That usually ends up at four yards when you are talking about a high school player coming at his angle. Our outside linebacker should be able to stop any hitch the quarterback will throw. Continue to sink or trail the #1 receiver until the flat is pressured by the #2 or #3 receiver. He will not come off of the #1 receiver; he will split the difference until the quarterback totally commits to the out. We want to keep everything in front until we have to rally to get to anything in front of us.
- Pass, cover 2—Typical cover 2 corner technique, which means they will outside trail the #1 receiver with their butts to the sideline as long as the #2 receiver is going vertical or inside. If the #2 or #3 receiver comes outside, the outside linebacker will squat and reroute the #1 inside and level out over the #2 or #3 receiver at 10 to 12 yards. They stay on top of the flat route and break on the ball.

Corners

Alignment: Split the #1 and #2 receivers at a depth of seven yards. It does not matter what coverage we are in, the corners are half-field players. They have to range as deep as the deepest receiver does. To do that from seven yards is tough. If it is a long distance situation, we may let them drop back a little farther.

Key: Quarterback to backfield action.

Technique:

- Run—Initial backpedal and check the #1 receiver for play-action or crackback. His eyes are on the quarterback. If he gets run action his way, he checks #1 to see if a crack is coming. If there is, he will come up and replace right now. On any other play, he is a half-field player.
- Pass, three-step drop—Be ready to break on the ball at the interception point, where the ball will be, not where the man is when the football is thrown.
- Pass, five-step drop—Backpedal until his cushion is threatened, then open and play as deep as the deepest, while ranging.

Free Safety

Our free safety is our best player on the field. He is our Stud. Everything has to go through him. If he cannot make plays, he is a wasted player on the field. Any offense has to change their blocking scheme to account for our free safety. If the offense does not account for him, he will be unblocked and he is our best tackler. Our free safety has been our leading tackler for the past three years. When you line up and pick out the best football player on your team, you want to put him at free safety.

Alignment: He will line up 10 yards deep over the center and guard gap to the #2 or #3 receiver side. His alignment is based on formation. It is not based on the call. Calls do not matter to him.

Key: He will always read linemen. He will read the guard to the #2 or #3 receiver side for run or pass. The guard is uncovered, so it is an easy read for him. He will look for a low hat or high hat from the guard. He does not have a specific gap responsibility.

Technique:

- Run—He goes to the ball. The free safety takes on the block with his outside arm and bounces the play to our Bear or Snake. On the option, the free safety has the quarterback. He does not worry about the handoff, he only worries about the quarterback.
- Pass—Coverage is based on the offensive formation, not on our defensive call.
- Pass, 2 back—He will be in a robber technique off the #2 receiver. If #2 goes six or seven yards vertical behind our linebackers, he locks on man-to-man. If #2 goes out to the flat, the free safety is going to drop and rob underneath #1. If #2 drags across the field, he will stay on top of the drag and look for something to come back at him. He will drop off the drag to take the dig if it shows.
- Pass, trips with 1 back—Robber technique off the #3 receiver.
- Pass, any other 1 back—High hole player under their #2 receivers.
- Pass, empty—High hole player under the #2 and #3 receivers. The corners have over-the-top; the free safety has underneath those receivers. He will play robber off of the #3 receiver. We can change this in our game planning, but he will be ranging on the #3 to the #2 receiver.

We have little variation to different formations we see. Adjustments are minimal. Our players do not have to do a lot of thinking. You will see them aggressively running to the football.

When we look at the overall gap responsibility, the nose and the Mike linebacker are responsible for the two A gaps. The ends and the Sam and Will linebackers are responsible for the B and C gaps.

We are a two-platoon team. Our defensive linemen get a lot of practice versus different types of blocks they will see on any given week. We will work specifically on each type of block based on our scouting report. We have 20 minutes of individual time to work on fundamentals and 20 minutes of group time to work on any specific scheme blocking our opponent will throw at us. Even if they get double-teamed, they have to stay at the line of scrimmage, they cannot get pushed back.

I will close with something we go by at Cathedral High School. We put a lot of emphasis and importance into this.

CATHEDRAL FOOTBALL PLAYERS: POINTS TO LIVE BY

- We will never compromise our standards. It takes 100 years to grow an oak tree. It takes 10 minutes to chop it down. There are many young men who have worn the gold helmet before you, which is why we are representing the school with the most wins in the state of Indiana.
- Play with tremendous enthusiasm 100 percent of the time. Remember, 100 percent of the body and 100 percent of the mind!
- Remember, character is the ability to stand up for the things that are right and say no to the things that are wrong, even when no one is watching.
- Live in the *past*, you die in the *present*. You have to be able to move on to the next play in practice or in the game.
- Academic integrity, athletic integrity, and character are the key ingredients of a Cathedral football player.

We play good, hard football at Cathedral. We have good kids, we have good parents, we have a good coaching staff, and we have a tremendous tradition at Cathedral High School. We love our football. It has been a pleasure to be invited to speak to you this weekend.

John Bartolovic

THE JET AND ROCKET SWEEP SERIES

Ford City High School, Pennsylvania

Thank you. First, I want to explain a few points about our system. We have everyone in our program running the same offense. In addition, our youth league teams run our system. Another factor that has helped us with this system is the fact that we have not had a lot of turnover in our coaching staff. The coaches have been with our program for several years and they know our system. That makes it so that we are teaching the players the plays they have been using for several years in our program.

Our players know what is coming when we add our plays to the system. We do not come out to practice on Monday and start adding plays that we plan on running that Friday.

When we teach new plays, the line coaches have their players for one hour. They teach all of the aspects of the plays. They may go over as many as three plays on that first day of practice, depending on the plays we are adding. It may be the sweep, trap, or another play.

We may only add one and perhaps two plays a day if we have an advanced group of players. It is not as if we are going fast on adding the plays to our offense. By the end of the summer, we have a lot of our offense included in our package.

During the time the line is working on the plays, I work with the individual running backs instructing them on the plays. We spend a lot of time putting the plays together so our players know what to do on the plays by the time we finish that one-hour session.

Following are some reasons why we use the jet and rocket sweep series:

- Small linemen are very effective.
- Fastest players are sprinting when the ball is snapped.
- Blocks do not have to be devastating.
- Run from various formations (Check the defensive alignment.)
- We can run to the weakside or the strongside.
- We run all of our basic wing-T plays with the jet and the rocket.
- All backs can run the ball.
- Great misdirection plays
- Very good play-action passing game
- We can throw to multiple receivers.
- The key: Run your plays over and over against every defensive front you see, including against the blitzes.

When we run our drills for the jet sweep, I work with the running backs. I make sure they know their assignment on who to block on the play. If we are running the jet sweep to the right side, I am going to teach them to left shoulder block the outside defenders. We have some teams that want to run upfield against our jet sweep. Against those teams, we are going to turn and right shoulder block them and go around them, as we do on our Buck sweep play.

I am going to go slow so you can see some of the different plays we run with our jet sweep and rocket series. I have a playbook with close to 125 plays in it. We have dealt with Carnegie Mellon University so long as we have been going to visit with them for 23 years. I take all of their plays, run them off, and add them to our playbook. It saves me a lot of work. I do not want to show all of their plays here today. I will tell you I worked with Chuck Klausing for several years and we ran these plays then.

Many of the plays we run we have taken from someone else. I will go over some of the things we do that you may be interested in that may be different from what you use now. When the quarterback wants the ball snapped, we do it on time. Sometimes, we may do it with a nod of the head or with a foot motion.

We try to snap the ball when the motion back, which is our wingback, is somewhere close to the B gap on the backside. He takes the handoff near the A gap on the playside. When we do this, the motion back is running between 85 and 90 percent (Diagram #1). I am not sure he can run 100 percent and still get the handoff from the quarterback. That is our 448 jet sweep. I will show the play against the 4-4 defense. Our rules hold up 99 percent of the time against most defenses.

Diagram #1. 448 Jet Sweep

Assignments for the 448 Jet Sweep	
Position	**Assignment**
QB	Snap the ball when the wingback is in the B gap. Open to the back receiving the ball.
RH	Block #2 from the B gap.
LH	Rip motion—Receive the ball in playside A gap.
FB	Step right foot, then left foot. Make a good fake running the trap right.
TE	Shut off.
BT	Shut off.
BG	Shut off.
C	Reach on area to the 3 technique.
PG	Pull step—Wall inside and grab grass.
PT	Block #1 from B gap.
SE	Block man on you. Can call with a crackback block.

We run our trap series off this series. The fullback starts out on his left foot as he does on the Buck series. It is left foot, right foot, and then he comes back and runs the trap route over the center.

Our tight end on the backside shuts off to the inside. A lot of our tight ends play both ways and I am not sure they are going to make much of an effort to go downfield on the play every time. If we have one-way players, we send them downfield on the play. The backside defensive end is not going to make the play. You can send him downfield if you want.

Our center reads to the 3 technique. We have to block the play that way. We have never had the play stopped by the 3 technique. Our center uses a reach block on him and tries to take a piece of him. That gives us enough room to move up front.

Our guard pulls and leads upfield. The playside tackle is going to block the first man on the line of scrimmage from the B gap.

I have two specific plays I want to cover. First is our 448 jet sweep pass (Diagram #2). We are going to fake the jet and run everything the same as we do on the running play. Our timing is all the same. We work on the timing of this play repeatedly. By the time the end of the season comes around, we may have run the jet sweep play 200 times or even more. The jet sweep is not a play we install in only one day. We do not just say, "Let's run the jet sweep." We work hard on our base plays.

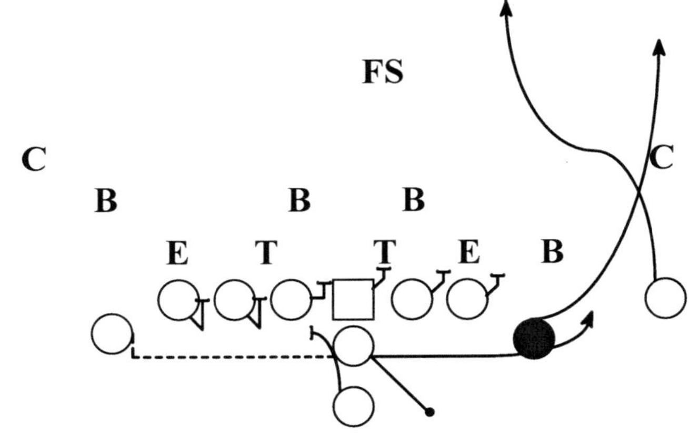

Diagram #2. 448 Jet Sweep Pass

Position	Assignment
QB	Snap the ball when the wingback is in the B gap. Open to the back fake. Fake the jet sweep. Three steps 45-degree angle. Look post to wheel routes.
RH	Look like you are blocking the jet sweep, run a wheel route.
LH	Drop-step, make a good hard fake on the jet sweep. Block the first man past the tackle.
FB	Fake jet and block the first man outside the BST.
TE	Zone block or run drag route depending what is called.
BT	Gap on area
BG	Gap on area
C	Reach on area
PG	Reach on area
PT	Reach on area
SE	Post route

On the backside, we are blocking back on the area. The quarterback fakes the jet sweep. After the fake, he takes a three-step drop and reads the safety. I looked at the stats recently and I noticed our split end had 10 touchdowns off this play. The reason for this is because the safety comes up to support on the jet sweep play.

You can run different routes with the split end on the play. We have had the split end fake the post and then cut back to the flag. If the defense is playing the pass, you can mix it up on them and run different routes with the split end.

I think everyone that runs this offense runs the trap play. I want to cover the 431 jet trap and then I will show you some plays that go along with this play (Diagram #3). We can trap both sides of the formation.

We are running the play to the wingback side. The quarterback signals for the snap when the motion man gets to the B gap. I tell the quarterback to open to the back that is coming in motion. It makes it easier for him to remember the steps on the jet and the waggle series. After the quarterback has run the plays a ton of times, it becomes second nature. In the beginning, they may have a problem with the steps.

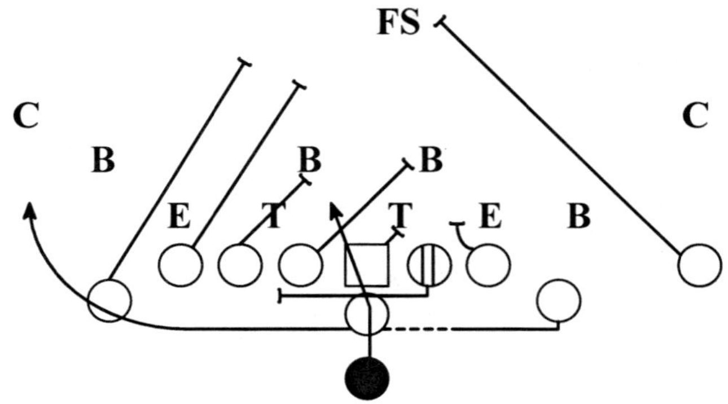

Diagram #3. 431 Jet Trap

Position	Assignment
QB	Snap the ball when the wingback is in the B gap. Open to the back receiving the ball. Fake the handoff to the man in motion.
RH	Liz motion. Aim two feet behind the quarterback. Make a good, hard fake of the sweep.
LH	Block at the point of attack.
FB	Step left foot then right foot. Angle back to the left foot of the center.
TE	Block at the point of attack.
BT	Inside release to playside LB
BG	Pull steps—Trap first man past the center, left shoulder (listen for call)
C	On away
PG	Double to opposite ILB.
PT	Inside release to playside ILB
SE	Block at POA.

What we generally see is a 3 technique on the left tackle. We have the left guard inside release and we trap at the 1 hole. We have the line make a call if a defender is playing in the A gap or in a 2 technique. We can make a call and have the guard block down inside and we would trap the 2-technique defender. If we get a 1 technique or a gap defensive player, our guard is going to make a call. That means we are going to trap the next man outside of the gap or 1 technique. We do give them some leeway to do this.

Our aiming point is two feet behind the quarterback. We want a good fake by the motion man on the jet sweep action. I think it is important to have a lot of good eyes watching the different positions on their fakes on this offense. One coach cannot watch all of the positions. I have been lucky to have the same coaches working with me and they all have positions they watch when we run our offense. We tell all our backs, including the quarterback, to make a good fake. If we do not get a good fake on the jet sweep, the trap play is no good to us.

We run several plays off this play. We run influence plays to keep the defense honest on the trap series. Most of the trap plays go to the side of the sweep plays. You trap most of the time to that side. When teams start stunting to motion and they get a feel for the trap to the side of the sweep, we need to run some other plays. We can fake the jet sweep left and run the trap back to the right side.

We are going to look at some of the plays I selected that may be something you may want to consider. I am not a big AV technician so I may need help with this fancy AV setup.

I want to show you the rip 448 jet waggle play. We run this similar to the other teams that run the jet and rocket series. I have three examples to show you. I want to make sure you see the way we run our right halfback on his passing route (Diagram #4). He is not going deep down the field. We want him to drag across the formation just behind the linebackers. We fake the jet sweep to the right and run the waggle back to the left side. There are times when we run the waggle when we do not pull our guards. If we are having trouble with quick people inside, we can keep them at home to pick up the blitz.

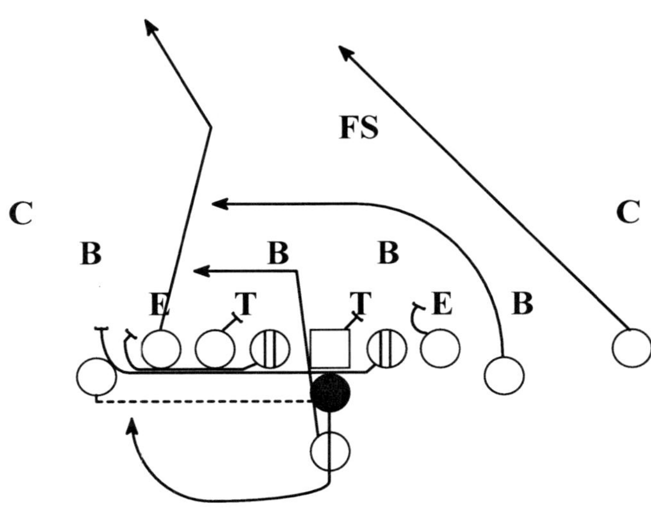

Diagram #4. Rip 448 Jet Waggle

Position	Assignment
QB	Snap the ball when the wingback is in the B gap. Open to the back receiving the ball fake. Fake the handoff to the fullback, and waggle outside.
RH	Run 10- to 12-yard drag route just behind the linebackers but across the field.
LH	Rip motion—Aim two feet behind the quarterback. Make a good hard fake of the jet sweep.
FB	Step left foot then right foot. Blitz control first. Run a two- to five-yard pattern into the flat.
TE	Inside release and run a flag route.
BT	Gap down-on rule
BG	Pull steps—Let the fullback clear and then lead the quarterback outside.
C	On away
PG	Pull outside—Block first man past the offensive tackle.
PT	Gap down-on rule
SE	Run through center field deep.

We want to be careful when we start adding a lot of plays for our guys. Most of our guys play both sides of the ball. We make our quarterback learn the plays for the halfbacks, or the split ends plays. At times, when we move the quarterback to another position on a pass play, he will ask one of the coaches what pattern he should run. Of course, the coach replies, “You are the quarterback. You should know what the pattern is.” The quarterback may not know all of these things. We try to give him a cross section of what is going on so he has a grasp of what we are trying to do on a play.

We can have as many as 10 different ways to run the waggle play. You can come up with your own ideas on the play. We tell the quarterback to read from long to short on the pattern. It is difficult to teach them to read the other way of short and then long.

People ask me why we run the jet and rocket series. I am an old wing-T coach and we can still run some of those plays with the jet plays. We like to run our belly plays from these formations. We try to tie some of the same actions together in the two

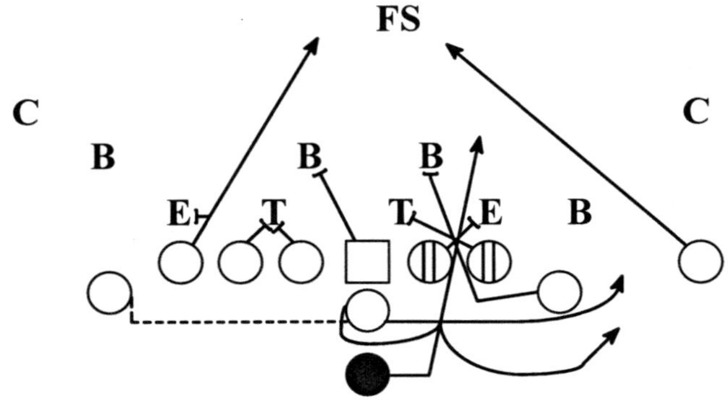

Diagram #5. 434 Jet Belly

Position	Assignment
QB	Fake jet sweep. Step on at a 45-degree angle for three steps and hand the ball to the fullback, then fake the pass.
RH	Drop the left foot inside him; block the ILB.
LH	Rip motion—Fake jet right and go behind the right halfback.
FB	Ballcarrier (steps—crossover step) and follow the right halfback.
TE	Zone to POA
BT	Zone
BG	Pull around the center and wall off.
C	On area
PG	Pull steps—Kick out first man on or past the PT.
PT	Go down. (Listen for call.)
SE	Block at POA.

concepts. I will show you our 434 jet belly play. We work hard on the timing on the play (Diagram #5).

We run every wing-T play you could think of, plus some other things on offense. I will not add any more plays if it does not fit our blocking schemes. I do not think our players can handle any more plays.

I do want to mention one thing we see from the defense that is different from game to game. They put a defender on our center, and they put defensive linemen on our two guards. They do this because they think we cannot pull our guards and still run the jet sweep. The way we handle that defense is by having the center make a special call for our blocking. We reach block with both guards and the center. The center reach blocks the defender to the playside. The backside guard reaches the noseguard, and the frontside guard reaches outside to the tackle or the man on his outside. We work against this alignment enough where we know we can handle the blocks.

We run the jet Sally play with an inside handoff to the halfback (Diagram #6). This is what we see most of the time on our 423 jet Sally play.

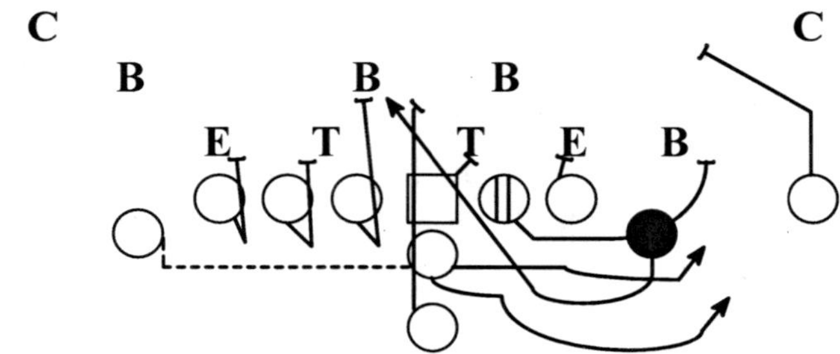

Diagram #6. 423 Jet Sally

Position	Assignment
QB	Fake jet sweep. Steps at a 45-degree angle; inside handoff to right halfback behind the BST.
RH	Ballcarrier-Drop-step, inside handoff at 1 hole.
LH	Rip motion—Fake jet right. Go behind the right halfback.
FB	Fake jet sweep. Block first ILB at 1 hole.
TE	Cup block to linebacker.
BT	On area
BG	Pull just like the jet sweep.
C	On reach block
PG	Cup block to linebacker.
PT	Cup block to linebacker.
SE	Block at POA

In our playoff game we ran this play but we had some problems with the defensive tackle on the playside. He lined up in the 3 gap and when the guard pulled to the outside, that tackle came across the line and made a play at the point of the exchange.

We are going to look at the play and see if we need to change the blocking on the play.

We can run pass plays from this Sally action. On the backside when we cup block, we make sure we can use that block. If a defender is in the gaps and giving us a hard time, we will aggressively block him. If the lineman does not think he can cup block the defender, they will go after him in an aggressive type block.

We are not a huge rocket team. However, we do run it. We are giving the fast players the ball on the play. If you have skilled athletes, you can run the rocket series and get some good yardage with the action. We have a lot of different plays that complement each play.

First, I want to cover the 448 rocket pitch (Diagram #7). Our quarterback reverse pivots and fakes the midline play. He pitches the ball to the wingback coming behind the fullback in motion. We want to snap the ball so the timing allows the quarterback to make the pitch to the wingback in rocket motion between the C and D gaps.

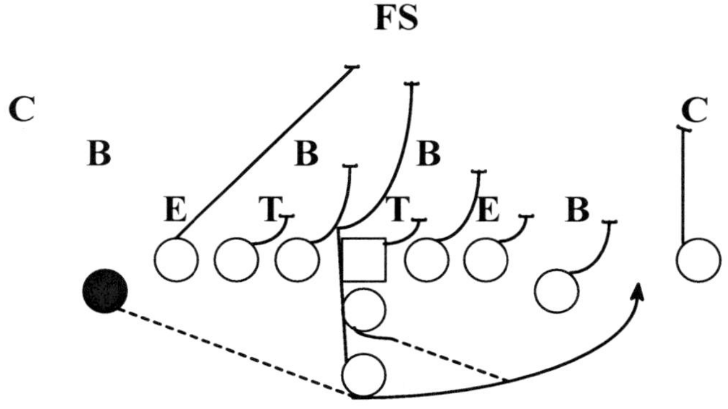

Diagram #7. 448 Rocket Pitch

We are not going to block the 5-technique tackle. If we can get our playside tackle across the face of that defensive tackle, we do not block him. We want the onside lineman to take a flat step and turn and get across the face of the defensive man in front of him and get upfield to block on the play. We do not believe those defenders are going to make the play.

We can fake the rocket pitch and run our power counter spy play (Diagram #8). We fake the rocket to the left side here. We pull the left guard on the play and he comes over and picks up the linebacker. The right guard double-teams with the center on the 1 technique. The fullback kicks out the defensive end or the first man outside of the offensive tackle. The end on the playside does not want the defensive end crossing his face. The left halfback takes the pitch from the quarterback. The right halfback is faking the rocket pitch on the play.

If you are not running the rocket pitch, this is not a good play. However, if the rocket pitch is doing well, it helps to have this play in your offense. We run all of the counters out of the rocket, and we run all the plays to the other side as well. We are not one-dimensional in that we are going to run only one type of play from the rocket action.

Position	Assignment
QB	Reverse pivot over the midline, pitch to the wingback, and waggle away from the play.
RH	Left shoulder block the #1 outside C gap.
LH	Motion—Receive pitch from the quarterback in the C or D gap.
FB	Lateral step; run trap right. Don't get too close to QB on the reverse pivot.
TE	Zone
BT	Zone
BG	Zone
C	Reach on area
PG	Zone—Pull and wall off.
PT	If uncovered, pull. Must block the 5 technique if he crosses in front of you.
SE	Block at POA.

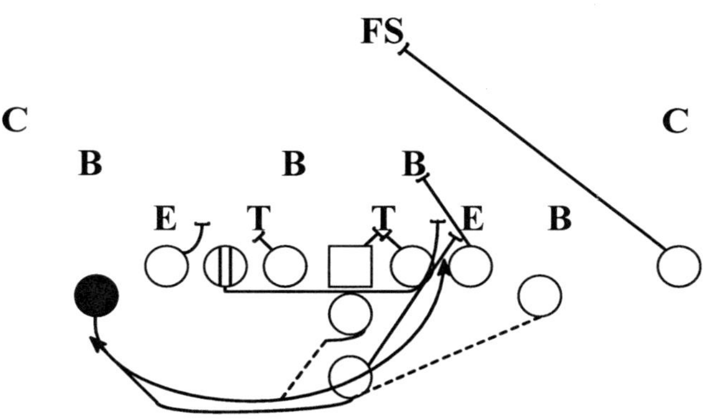

Diagram #8. 444 Power Counter Spy

The toss to the halfback is only a two- to three-yard toss. It is not as if the quarterback is throwing the ball hard on the toss. We pull the backside guard and we are looking for the double-team. We like to get the double-team block first, and then we slide off the double-team block to the linebacker.

When we add plays, we add key words that are within our own language. Here the "spy" means we fake the rocket action. If we call 444, it means the formation is the 4 with the 4-back going through the 4-hole. The word "power" tells the fullback to kick out, and it tells the backside guard to lead through the hole. We do not add a lot of new terms. We let the kids come up with key words that help them with the different plays. We asked them what name we could use when we wanted to fake the rocket action. They came up with the term "spy."

A companion play of the power counter is our joker spy series (Diagram #9). Joker to us means we are going to pull both the guard and tackle on the play. It looks like the power counter, but we bring the ball back inside with our right halfback over the center. He must take a counter step to give the play a slight counter move to set up the blocking. Again, the left halfback is faking the rocket counter play.

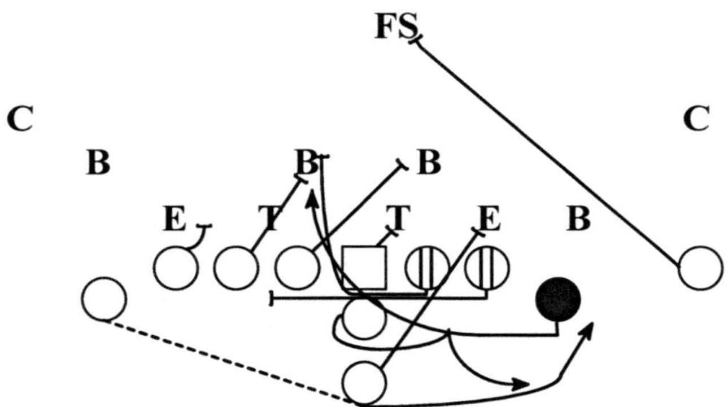

Diagram #9. 423 Joker Spy

We want the quarterback to reverse pivot over the midline. He fakes the pitch to the left halfback. He gives the ball to the right halfback on an inside handoff. We pull both the backside guard and tackle on the play. The pulling guard pulls and traps the first man on the line of scrimmage past our onside guard. The tackle fold blocks up in the 1 gap. Our center blocks onside or away. Again, I talked about this before. If we get a defender in the 1 gap or in a 2 technique on the callside, we are not going to trap that man. He is too tight for us to trap block him.

We do run a pass play off the same action. It is our joker keep pass (Diagram #10). Everything is the same with the backfield action. We run the split end on a skinny post route. We drag the tight end across the center of the field. The fullback runs an out route after he clears the line. We still run the right halfback inside to fake the joker spy play. The quarterback fakes the handoff to the halfback and comes outside on the waggle action. The left halfback comes outside on the rocket action and can block for the quarterback.

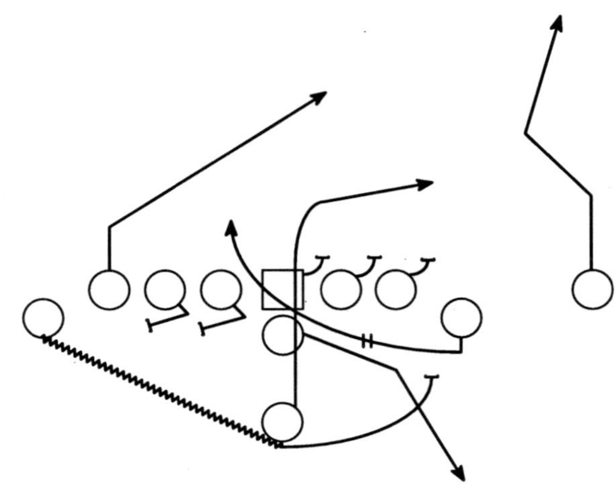

Diagram #10. Joker Keep Pass

I want to cover one play that I wanted to cover when we were talking about the jet sweep. We fake the jet and run a toss to our fullback. We can give this play different names, but we call it 38 because the ball is going to the fullback on the outside to the right (Diagram #11). Here, we are calling the play "38 toss."

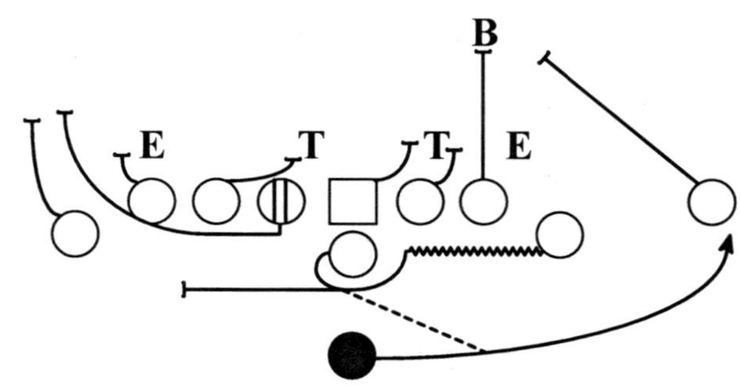

Diagram #11. 38 Toss

We want the play to look like the jet sweep as much as possible. The right halfback comes in motion as he does on the sweep. We pull the backside guard to sell the sweep play. The tight end blocks the end by reaching his outside shoulder. The backside tackle checks the down lineman on the pulling guard. Our center reaches onside on the 2 technique. We want our onside tackle to make sure he blocks the inside linebacker.

We do not want to block any player in the back to the point the defensive man is injured. Our split end has an open shot on the first man inside on the second level. We do get some great blocks on this play. We do not block the corner because not many defenders want to take on our fullback in the openfield.

The fullback takes an open step and slides to the outside trying to make sure he keeps his depth. He does not want to get low toward the line of scrimmage where the defensive end can cover him on the toss. The quarterback fakes the jet sweep and then tosses the ball to the fullback on the outside play.

I have enjoyed this experience. This is the first time I have done a lecture of this type. This is what we do on offense. I hope I have given you something that can help you in your program. Over 20 years ago, I attended a clinic and someone said that if you could only get one or two points out of a clinic, it would be beneficial to your coaching career. That is what I do when I go to a clinic. I am not going to change much of what we do. We may change a formation and look at a play or two.

I want to thank you for your time.

Mark Batton

DRAWS, SCREENS, AND THE SPRINT-OUT PASS

Magnolia High School, West Virginia

I want to start out with something a little different from what you may have seen before. I will get to draws and screens in just a minute. I found this at a clinic that I went to a few years ago. I had never seen this at a clinic before, and I have not seen it at any clinic since then. I have been going to clinics for a long, long time. I wanted to give you something that you could take back with you that might be of benefit, even if it is not on sprint-outs, draws, or screens. This really helped me out a lot, especially in my relationship with our parents and my players.

I meet with my parents in the first week of August. This is what I go by. This is what I use to build the relationship with my parents. For our purposes, I will list the items that I cover on our agenda and make a few comments about some of them.

- Weight room: We discuss the importance of the weight room, and we make attendance as mandatory as possible. I include a calendar that shows the days and times the weight room is open. I include information on the proper ways to hydrate and prevent heat illness. This information comes from the *Journal of Athletic Training*. I also include what not to drink and why.
- Attendance at practice: Attendance is mandatory. Move your haircuts and dental appointments around so that you can be a practice.
- Practice clothes and personal hygiene: I usually have a lot of mothers look at me and laugh when I bring this up. I do discuss it, and stress it with our parents. I include documents from the West Virginia Department of Health and Human Resources, Bureau for Public Health that covers staph infections and ways to prevent skin infections.
- Magnolia football concussion management program
  - ✓ WVSSAC return to play (RTP) protocol: We implemented the concussion management program this year at Magnolia. Focus on concussions started with the NFL and then moved to the college level, and now it is at the high school level. We include a letter that that describes the impact test that we give.
  - ✓ Impact testing: We bought the software program this year, and we give every player the impact test at the beginning of the season. If there is a problem later on, we have a baseline to go off from the beginning of the year. I include the National Federation of State High School Associations publication, entitled "A Parent's Guide to Concussion in Sports" and a copy of the West Virginia State Return to Play Protocol.
- Zero tolerance: This covers being good citizens, whether it is in or out of school. The Magnolia High School Athletic Department puts together an athletic participation packet that includes information from physicals to insurance. We also include information from the state of West Virginia and Magnolia High School, concerning athletes, policies, and agreements. We cover personal conduct, use of tobacco, alcohol, or drugs, reasons for suspension or removal from the team. There is a piece in there about the role of parents in interscholastic athletics, as well as guidelines for parents' behavior.
- Uniforms and equipment
- What I expect from players
  - ✓ At practice
  - ✓ At school (attendance)
  - ✓ In public

- Field house and facilities
- Laundry service: The laundry service fee is a school fee that must be paid before report cards are issued or records released.

I include the varsity and junior varsity football schedule in our packet and information about the tradition of the football program at Magnolia High School. I include the history so the parents can see the tradition that we have had at Magnolia. We started football in 1902, and we are one of the few teams in the state of West Virginia that has over 600 wins. We have two state championships, with the last being this past season.

I finish off the packet with forms that must be completed and signed by the parents, indicating that they have attended our meeting and understand the contents and requirements of our program, including the concussion management program.

I hope this is something that you can use; again, it has helped me a lot. When I first started meeting with the parents prior to the season, my assistants thought I was nuts. I have received a great reception from our parents with this, and everybody knows the rules from the beginning.

We are an AA school in the state of West Virginia. We average about 40 to 45 players each year. We are the second-smallest AA school in West Virginia. I generally only have one quarterback, so I cannot afford to lose my quarterback. We pass a lot out of the sprint-out. We use these two base formations. We can run this from under center, or out of the shotgun, it does not matter. Generally, we operate out of the gun.

When we call this formation to the right, we call it River (Diagram #1). When we run this formation to the left, we call it Lake. It is R for right (and for River), and L for left (and Lake).

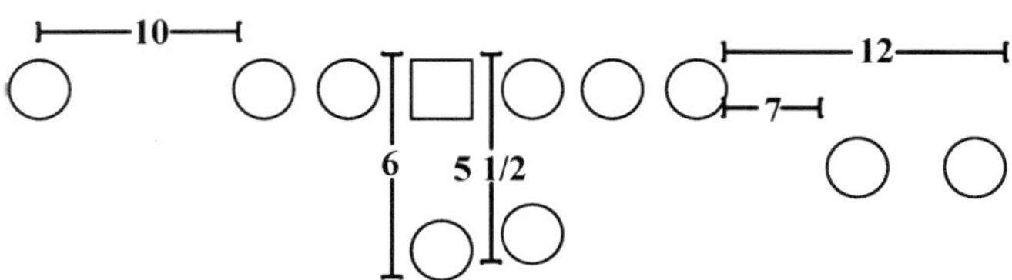

Diagram #1. River Formation

We call Rip to the right, and we call Lip to the left (Diagram #2). We tell our receivers to have their inside foot up.

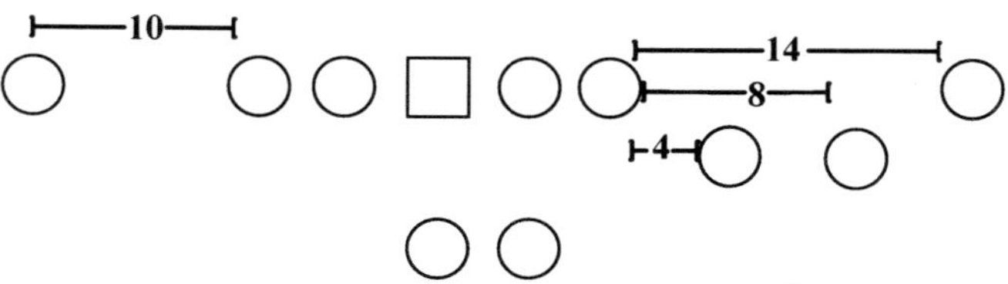

Diagram #2. Rip Formation

Our sprint-out is a run/pass option. A couple of years ago, we had a quarterback who liked to run the ball. He was a tailback playing quarterback. He liked the idea of getting on the edge. If he did not like what he saw when he got on the edge, he would tuck the ball and run. He ran for 1,700 yards and passed for 1,300 yards out of this offense.

Let me draw up our top play out of this formation (Diagram #3). If we have the ball in the middle of the field, the outside receiver is located just outside of the numbers. The inside receiver is located on the hash marks. It is crucial that the outside receiver runs to 12 yards, and then back to 10. He comes back at an angle to put the defender on his inside shoulder, so he has his outside shoulder and hand free. We will sprint to him.

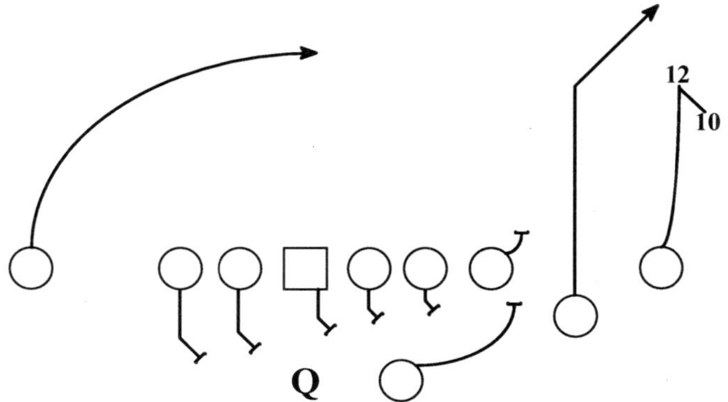

Diagram #3. Top Play

We hinge block on the line of scrimmage. The focus of the tight end is to get to the outside shoulder of the defensive end and keep him pinned inside. The running back will come up to the outside shoulder of our tight end. Our interior linemen will hinge-block. When we hinge-block here, we retreat.

All we are doing is forming a wall. We do not attack it, we do not slide; we hinge block, and the pivot point is the tight end.

We tell the quarterback the ball must be delivered before the receiver makes his cut. If the receiver sticks it at 12 and pivots out, the ball is going to be on its way. Not every quarterback can throw the ball on the run. We have drills that we use to make him better at it. The quarterback is opening up, and he gets depth. He has to get depth because the deeper the quarterback, the better off he is. The quarterback will sprint out with the ball, armpit-to-armpit, and then get his shoulders square to the receiver. He will throw it and follow through.

Another play we like to use in the sprint-out is this (Diagram #4). There is no tight end now, so we hinge off of the right tackle. The right tackle must get his head to the outside of the defensive end. The outside or #1 receiver will run everybody off. The #2 receiver gets into the flat right away. Our #3 receiver runs an 8- to 10-yard banana route. We tell our quarterback to deliver the ball to the #2 receiver, if he is open, right away. What this amounts to is a long handoff. The quarterback is reading the strong safety. If the strong safety covers the flat, the window is open behind him. We will now throw the ball to the #3 receiver in that window.

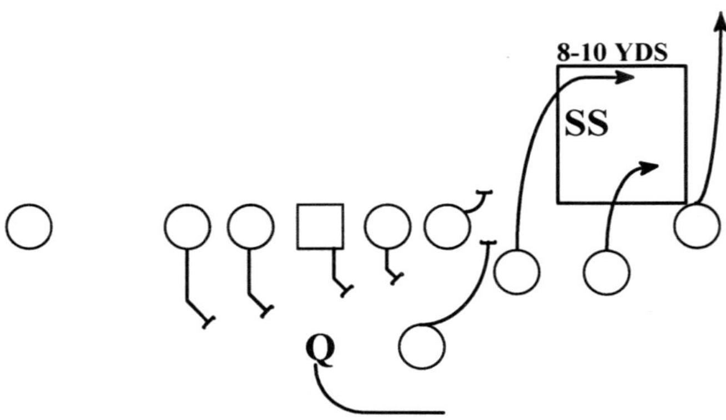

Diagram #4. Another Play

We can move our receivers in closer together into a bunch formation (Diagram #5). We have the same thing.

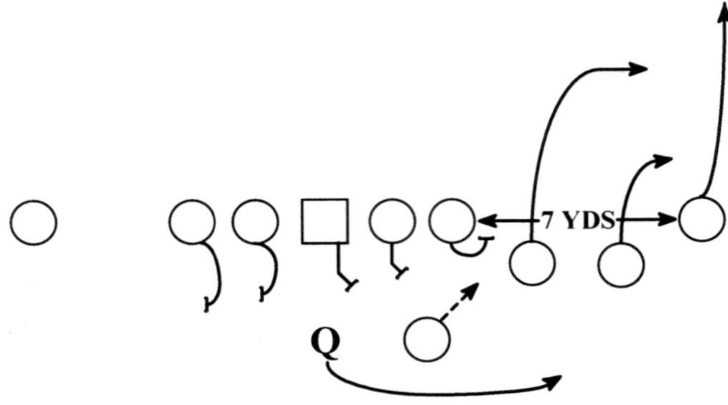

Diagram #5. Bunch Formation

We like to run these plays with motion (Diagram #6). Some time around game five, our opponent has identified our go-to guy. Now, all of a sudden, that go-to guy is double covered. It is hard to double-cover a receiver who is in motion.

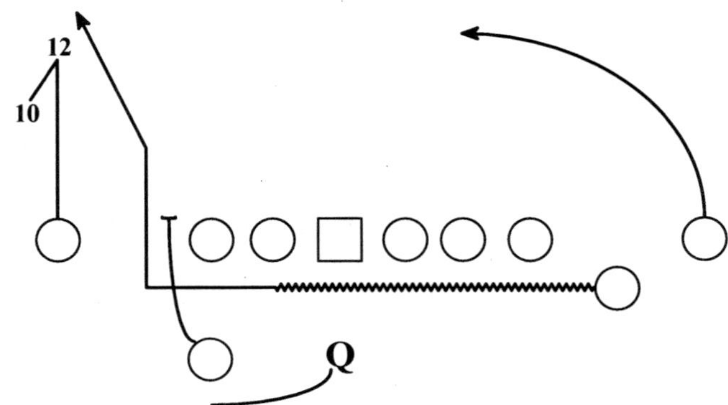

Diagram #6. With Motion

We can line up in our River formation and throw to the left, to our motion receiver. It is the same read, just to the left side. We are sprinting back toward the weakside of the defense. We have found that, in this formation, the defense will line up with their strongside to our right side. This can give us an advantage. When we throw this to the left, the quarterback has to get his shoulders turned around and square to the receiver.

Let me show you a couple of drills that we use for the sprint-out pass (Diagram #7).

In this first drill, the quarterback is going to jog for five yards, keep his shoulders square to the receiver, and throw the ball for 10 yards. We will get 8 to 10 reps in each direction.

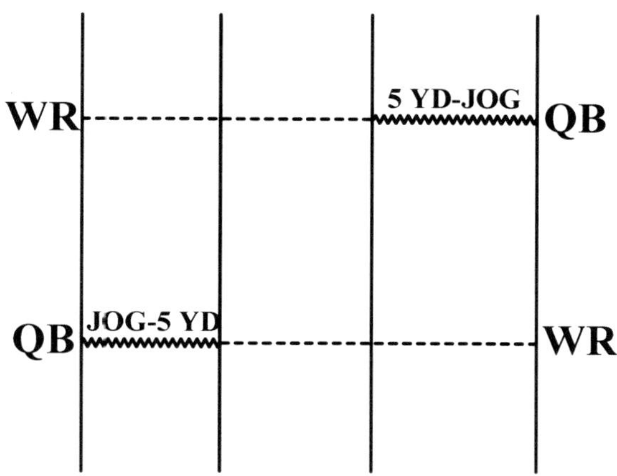

Diagram #7. Sprint-Out Drill #1

In the second drill, we set out three cones that the quarterback has to go around in order to get depth (Diagram #8). If he can get depth, then he can get his shoulders square. If you want to find out whether or not your quarterback can throw the ball on the run, put him through this drill a few times. We can run this drill from the shotgun or from under center.

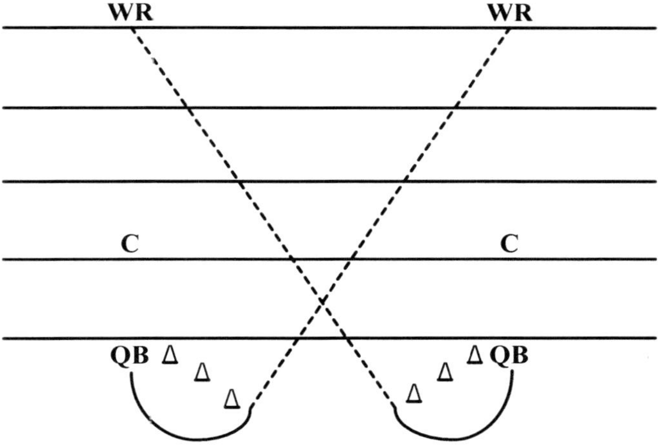

Diagram #8. Sprint-Out Drill #2

Our philosophy on screens is you can run them out of any formation. If you are not running screens in high school football, you are missing out. We will run a screen three or four times during a game. We will do most of the screen practicing during team time because of the coordination and relationship the back has with the offensive linemen.

We do have to put some time in on it. We have found that most defensive coaches do not put a lot of time in defending the screen. I know our defensive coordinator puts in a lot of time to stop the screen, and we still get screened on. This is why we put so much time in, offensively, on the screen pass. The screen play will get into the defensive players' heads. If they are looking for the screen, they cannot be as aggressive as they normally would be. This is to our advantage.

If we are going to screen to the left, we will set our running back to the right (Diagram #9). At the snap, the back will sprint directly toward the left guard. We want him to stay low and hide behind the left guard.

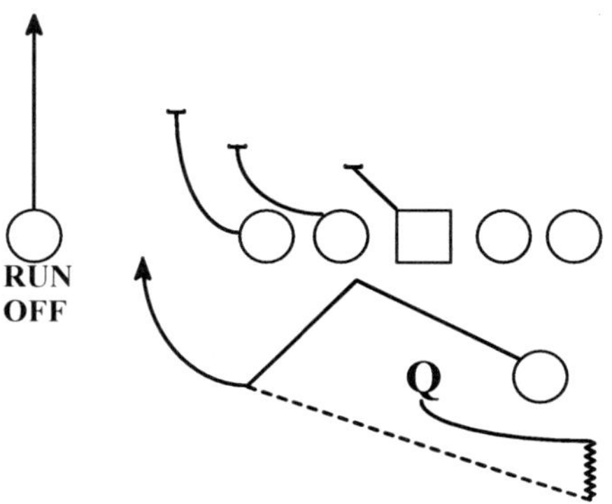

Diagram #9. Screen From the Shotgun

On our screens, we will send the tackle, guard, and center out to block. They will set for a count of 1001, and then go. If someone is bleeding through, our center is usually the mop-up guy. Once the left guard has left, the back must come back at an angle. We emphasize he is coming back at an angle, not going down the line of scrimmage. We do not want our running back to drift across the line of scrimmage, where we get a penalty. We tell the running back not to cross anybody's face as he approaches the left guard. The minute he crosses the defender's face, the defender will go with him. The running back will just let him go.

We tell the quarterback to sprint until he gets to a position behind the right tackle, he stops, and then we have him backpedal to get depth. Let those 6'4" and 6'5" defensive lineman who weigh 240 and 250 come.

When we run this out of the two-back set, we always screen to the fullback (Diagram #10). The fullback will hide behind the guard. The quarterback will reverse out. We will fake the power, isolation,

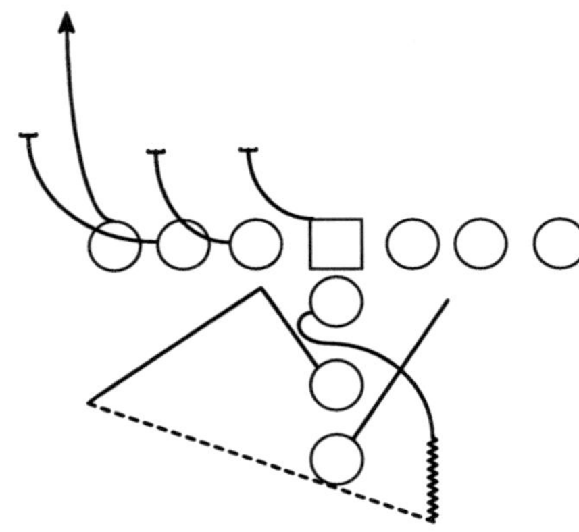

Diagram #10. Screen Two-Back Set

or slam. The quarterback will set behind the right tackle and backpedal once again. The quarterback has to work on this. It can be difficult to backpedal and throw the football. The tight end on the left must release and clear downfield. If he does not release downfield, the corner will stay. Any screen to the tight end side, the tight end must release. The back must come back away from the line of scrimmage.

The last thing I want to cover is the draw play (Diagram #11). Our draw is based on the sprint-out series. We use the same type of formations. The running back is going to set back just a little bit on the draw. We are still going to hinge-block it, we are just not going to retreat quite so quickly. We are going to take a few retreat steps, and then we are going to get into them.

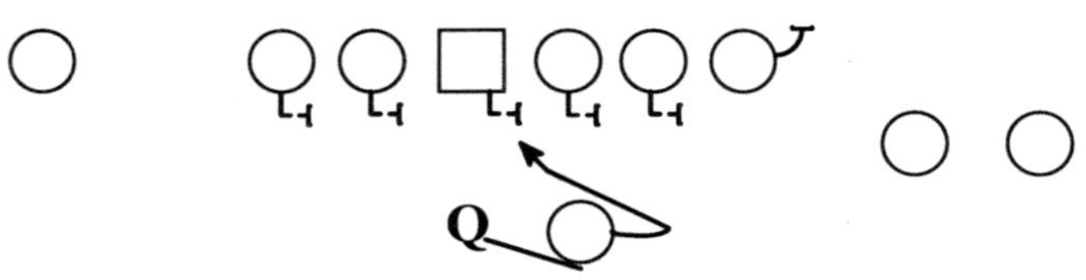

Diagram #11. Draw Right

Our linemen cannot get beat to the inside. We want to force the defender to the outside, and we will take him wherever he wants to go. The quarterback will take the ball like a sprint-out, and then he will hand it to the running back as he is coming back upstream. The running back will act as if he is going to attack to the right, and then we are going to give the ball to him with an inside handoff.

We can also run the draw right with a lead concept (Diagram #12). The quarterback will reverse out. Both the tailback and the fullback will step together. On all of our draws, the wide receivers will run off their defenders.

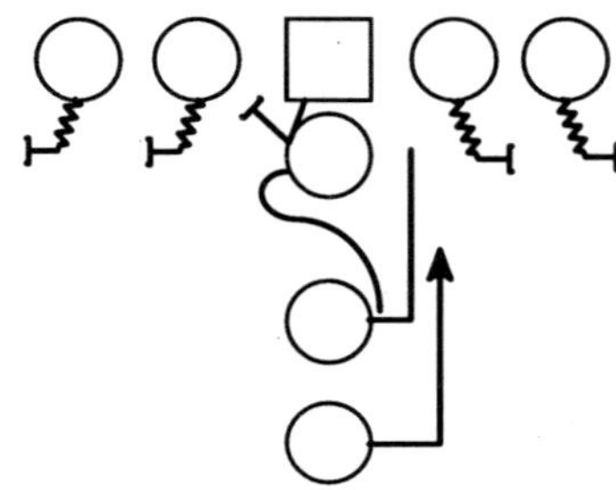

Diagram #12. Draw Right Lead Concept

I have used up my time. I appreciate your attention. Thank you very much.

Thurman Bell

DEFENDING THE SPREAD OFFENSE

Roseburg High School, Oregon

Thank you. I am going to do something a little different today. I want you to know I tried to get out of doing this lecture. You would think, at my age, I would learn how to say no. The last clinic I spoke at, I used chalk and a chalkboard. I remember one of the first clinics I spoke at was in a basement, and we were using 16 mm film. We had to use a splicer to put together those highlight tapes. Now, they have all these unbelievable machines. I bet 80 percent of the coaches who know me are here to see if I can figure out how to run this fancy A-V equipment.

One of my assistant coaches, Beau Canfield, talked me into doing a PowerPoint® presentation. I did not know what a PowerPoint was when he told me that. He put the lecture together and handed me a disc. I said, "What is this?" He told me it was my lecture. I had to go take some in-service hours on how to use this thing. Using this presentation may be more stressful than doing the lecture.

Dave Johnson, who is the director of the Portland clinic, was my student teacher. I had been teaching one year and he was supposed to follow me to learn how to teach. Between the two of us, we got into a lot of trouble. We go back a long way. Dave is a great person.

I feel I am a better technician than anything else I do. However, you have to put the bodies in the right position and know something about X's and O's. You have to find a system that works for you. I have tried a little of everything. My topic today is: "Defending the Spread Offense." I do not think you can stop the spread offense. I have a secret way I used in our first two football games, which worked well. I will show you the one we used for two games. When you see these offenses today, it makes you think hard about how to slow them down. Either you think of something, or you get out of the business of coaching.

It has been a good run, and I have had many good players. The best thing I can tell you about all those players is that I have had 28 players or coaches who have gone on to be head coaches in high school or college. I know we are all about the kids who play the game, but I am proud of that fact as well. Players who come into our program learn something and take it somewhere else. Many extremely successful coaches have come through our program.

I do appreciate you coaches showing up to listen to an old coach. I do not have all the answers, and I am not sure anyone does. All you have to do is believe in what you are doing. We have had some great players. You can enjoy watching them go on and play in college. When I get in the stands and watch them, I get somewhat emotional. Troy Calhoun, the coach at the U.S. Air Force Academy was our quarterback in 1984. He is doing a wonderful job at the Air Force Academy.

I am going to follow this outline because, if I do not, I will start rambling and talking about nothing, which I am doing right now.

We played this defense for two games. We played Oregon City on the road and Sprague High School at home. It just goes to show you that the officials are fair at home and on the road. If you want to slow down the spread teams, play this defense. I did not realize it until one day we were in our film room, watching the game film. One of my players asks me if it was illegal to play 12 players on defense (Diagram #1). The bottom line was: I was not cheating; I was not smart enough to see it, but neither were the officials. I hope you do not believe that.

If you look at this alignment and think about some adjustment you would make, it can be an effective defense. Of course, you must take one

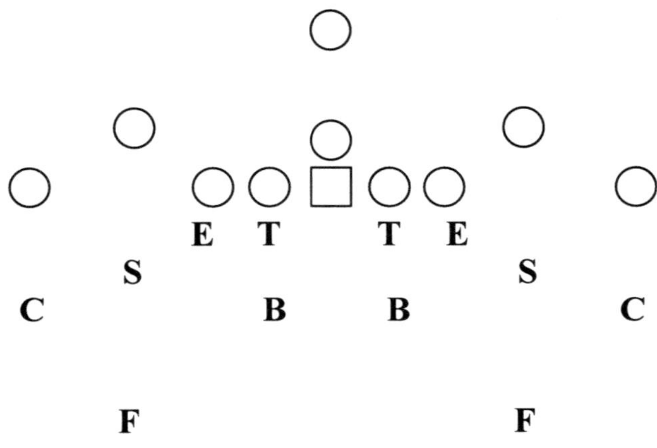

Diagram #1. The Perfect Defense—12 Men

defender out of the secondary or one out of the front. That is essentially what I want to show you. I do not think you can stop the spread offense with X's and O's. I think you stop the spread offense with personnel.

It is not only who you put on the field; it is where you put them. If you watch spread teams, about 80 percent of the offense goes to the wideside of the field. The wideside of the field gives the offense more to work with, and they can put more receivers into that area. It makes sense to me to put my best defensive players into the wideside of the field.

We put our personnel to the side of the field that is not necessarily into the formation. Many coaches always declare their defense to the tight end or some other condition. I have gotten away from that. Not all the players we put on the field are superstars. Within your personnel, there are players you have to hide. They can still help you, but we do not want the offense to find them and take advantage of them. When you get in trouble is when you try to hide eight defenders.

I have been at Roseburg High School for a long time. Two years ago, we played a spread team. However, they only threw the ball three or four times a game. I had a corner who could not tackle my mother. He was a good cover corner, but could not tackle. Naturally, his father was on the school board. This is a true story. The opponent wanted to spread us out and run the ball right at him.

We decided to replace the corner with a safety who could tackle. Some parents know a lot more about coaching than you do. We told the player what we were going to do. I got the phone call that night from the parent. The first thing he wanted me to know was that he was on the school board. He could not understand how I could replace his son. He has started for a year-and-a-half. I told him why we were doing what we did.

On Thursday, the rumors began to circulate that Coach Bell was senile and it was time to get him out of the profession. Rumors had this going before the school board. Nothing came of it, and the player played the next week and did a better job. That is one thing about being around for a long time. You make a tremendous amount of friends, but you make some enemies, too.

The point is to do what you believe is right for the team. Put your best players in positions so they can help the team.

When you start to defense the spread offense, there are some things you must consider. What type of spread offense is it? People think because you have the quarterback in the shotgun or a pistol, you are a spread offense. We play teams that align in the pistol offense and run the same things they did from a regular two-back offense. You have to find out what the purpose of their spread is. Do they want to spread you out and run the ball? You have to decide whether they are in the spread formation to run the ball or throw it. After you find out their primary objective, you need to know if they are a balanced offense.

If the quarterback is under the center and has a single running back behind him, I classify that as a one-back set. This set may have the quarterback in the pistol or shotgun, but it is a one-back set.

The two-back set has an I formation in the backfield. The offset I is the formation we see today from the two-back set. The Wildcat formation is a form of the two-back set. The I formation, offset I, and split backs, are examples of a two-back offense.

The three-back look is the wishbone, double wing, and two-back formations that use motion to put three in the backfield. I do not count jet motion as a back in the backfield. When I refer to one-back, two-back, and three-back sets, I am talking about players with the potential to attack the line of scrimmage. We have to decide what type of offense they run, and then decide what we have to do to defend the offense.

The first thing we do is to meet as a coaching staff. I let our coaches have Saturday off so they can go to a college game or do whatever they want. We come in early on Sunday, have an all-day meeting, and plan what we are going to do. The players come in on Sunday night around 6:00 p.m.

We send out staff members in person to scout the other team. I think too many coaches rely too much on game tape. I think it is important for someone to see the game live. I always have one or two coaches watch the game live. They could be off the freshman staff, but someone needs to see the game. I know you can watch the games online, but it is a lot different to see the game in person.

The scouts come to the meeting and give the staff a scouting report on the team we will play next. The first thing we do is record all the formations they use. It is very difficult to prepare for teams today because of the multiple formations they use.

The next thing we do is view the tapes we have on the opponent. In our league, we are supposed to exchange two tapes with the opponents. You are supposed to send the tapes of the two previous games. For all I know, the opponent is going into the game with 18 tapes on us. They may be from the previous year. The rules say we exchange two tapes.

We put the tapes on and watch them. I have each coach charting individual things about the team. If you do not go back and watch the previous year's game tape, you are making a big mistake. You may formulate a plan and find out it is exactly what you did the previous year. I do not like to duplicate the same plan. I want to do something different. You need to see what you did against them and what they did against you from the previous year's tape.

You need to evaluate all their formations and personnel. When we look at personnel, we want to find out where they align and what they do. You will find some teams flip-flop linemen and run over the same players each time. You need to detail what they do with the personnel, not just look at his athletic ability. You need to look at the personnel in detail and find out what they do with them.

The most important player to evaluate is the quarterback. You need to know if he runs the ball or simply throws it. Can he throw it? How does he handle pressure?

After we collect all the information about the team, we start putting together a plan. Back when I was younger, I coached everything. Most coaches of that era did. We did not specialize in just football. The head football coach was the assistant basketball coach. He was the head track coach or baseball coach. That is all we did.

Today, you coach football for 9 to 12 hours a day and 365 days a year. Some of you do it that way. I think that is a mistake. I think the thing that kept me going and fresh was when football season was over, I did something else for a while. Some coaches spend 12 months a year coaching football and face the possibility of burnout. That is another lecture.

The fact that I coached basketball helps me with my preparation for playing a spread team. When I start putting the plan together, I think about putting match-ups together like a basketball game plan. Matching up in football is the same thing you do in basketball, except football requires more match-ups. We do not play a base defense against all sets. We play base alignments, but the personnel in those alignments are not the same. We do not want the offense to use formations to match their best personnel on our weakest players.

What you plan to do in the box dictates what you do in the secondary. We go through all their tendencies and evaluate what they want to do. The first thing we have to do is stop the run. If a team can run the ball on you, it makes their passing game almost impossible to stop. When a team can run the ball, the play-action pass becomes a tremendously big weapon.

We need to decide how many people we need to put in the box to stop the run. I am not talking about blitzing people from outside the box. I am talking about the number of bodies we need in the base defense to stop the run.

If we play five defenders in the box, with a 3-4 look, we flip/flop the ends (Diagram #2). We

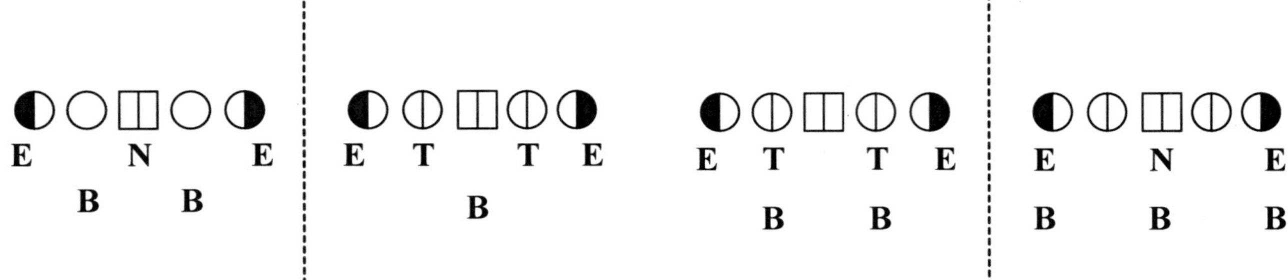

Diagram #2. Five-Defender Box

Diagram #3. Six-Defender Box

want to put our best personnel into the field. We also play five in the box, using a 5-1 look. Among the advantages of playing with five defenders in the box is the defense has more people to play the pass. When we put five defenders in the box, we tell the offense we can stop the running game with five defenders. That lets us play the pass with six defenders.

The reason we like to play an odd front against spread teams is the center. With so many teams in the shotgun set, the center has to snap a blind snap and be accurate with it. You make it harder when you put someone on his nose. When you put a defender over the center, it is worth three to four bad snaps a game. He has to snap the ball and block someone immediately. We evaluate the center. If he is not strong enough, we cover him and put the pressure on him. If you have a good noseguard, the pressure increases on the center.

Three or four bad plays a game make the game turn in your favor. That is particularly true if they lead to turnovers instead of just bad plays. There are disadvantages with playing five defenders in the box. You get less pass rush from five defenders.

You can play with a six-man box (Diagram #3). The advantages of putting six bodies in the box are obvious. We can play the 3-3 stack and get the nose over the center. We can also play a 4-2 look. We get more pass rush with six defenders. We can stop the run better, and we can add more confusion to the offensive line blocking. If a team does not block well, you want more defenders in the box.

Among the disadvantages with six in the box is fewer in the secondary. With fewer defenders in the secondary, it limits the number of things you can do with a pass defense scheme. This is a good change-up for the defense, but I do not think you can play defense doing one thing. You have to play the defense you know how to play and adjust to what the offense does. That means the base will allow the defense to get into multiple looks verses the spread teams.

Your scheme must be able to handle a five-wide set. To make that determination, you need to evaluate the empty set as you did the spread. What do they do from the empty set? Do they want to put a great running quarterback against a thin box, or is it a passing set meant to overload the secondary?

You have to decide what they want to do from the empty. The empty set all starts with the player taking the snap. There are two different kinds of quarterbacks in the spread formation. There is the running back who can throw, or the quarterback who can run. You have to decide which one they are playing.

The thing you must remember is you cannot do the same thing every time. People ask the same question all the time. They want to know how we play a certain situation. We do not play a certain situation the same way every time. If you do that, you form strong tendencies. Give offenses the same adjustment every time, and they will figure out how to beat it. If the offense calls a man-beater pattern and you play a zone, the advantage is yours.

When I draw up the spread formation to talk about the secondary, it will be a double slot set. That is not the only spread formation. There are triple sets and tight end sets in the spread offense. You must decide how to adjust to all the formations by using the same evaluations I talked about earlier. All our adjustments come off what the offense does from each formation.

One of the problems we have with alignment to the spread formation is the position of the offensive line. The rules say when the offensive lineman gets in a stance, his helmet is supposed to be on the beltline of the center. The problem is they never get in a stance. I cannot tell the running back from the offensive linemen because they have so many in the backfield. I believe that is the most abused rule in football.

I am not going into the adjustment with the different formations. I will give you our base alignments and calls. We have a checklist of things we can do. We go over it with our coaches so we can work on all adjustments against the spread formation.

I am going to cover the formations out of the six-man box. When you run cover 3, you must disguise what it is. You cannot align in a cover 3 and wave a flag telling the offense we are in cover 3.

In our base cover 3, we disguise the coverage and roll the strong safety down into the strong flat zone (Diagram #4). The strong safety and weakside linebacker play the flat/curl zones. The Mike and Sam linebackers inside play the hook/curl zone, and we play a three-deep zone behind them.

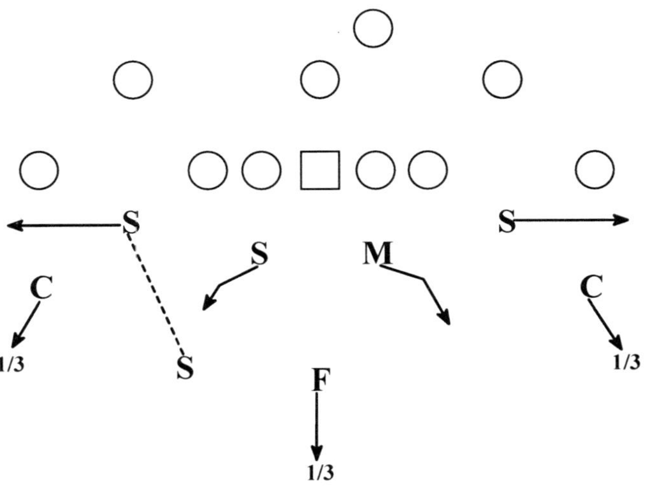

Diagram #4. Base Cover 3

The next coverage we can play is a base cover 1 (Diagram #5). One thing I do not like to do in cover 1 is run defenders across our formations. If motion goes from one side of the formation to the other, I like to invert through the secondary instead of running

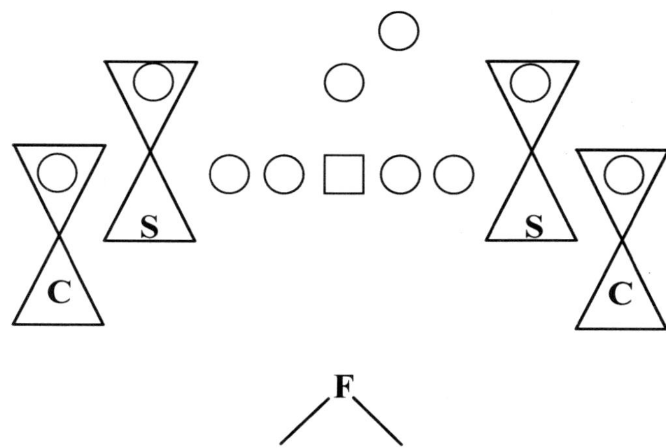

Diagram #5. Cover-1 Man-Free

a corner across the formation with the motion. That is not our only option, but I will do something not to run defenders from one side of the defense to the other. Many coaches like to do that with their defenders. They want their best defenders covering a certain receiver and they follow him across.

We run a cover zero, which is cover 1 with no free safety and generally run it with a blitzing game of some kind. In the diagram, we run a dog-stunt off the edge. When we run the dog stunt, we send the outside linebacker off the weakside and drop the free safety down to cover the slot receiver (Diagram #6). It is an elementary stunt and not difficult to run. The disguise is what makes the stunt go. If you move too early, the offense knows what you are doing.

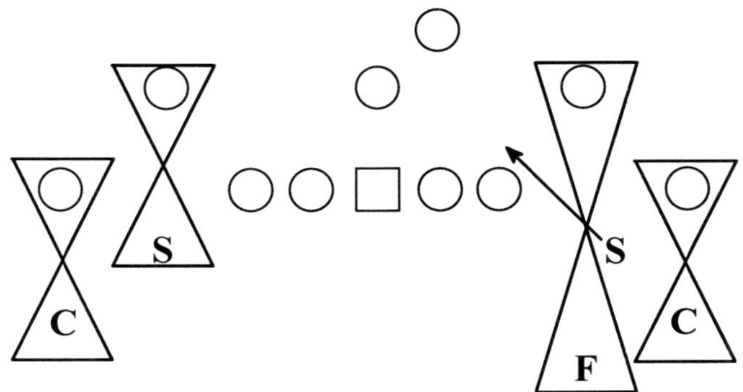

Diagram #6. Cover-Zero Dog

The next one is what I call "cover-1 combo" (Diagram #7). If the offense has a great receiver, it is hard for a defender to take him 1-on-1 and cover

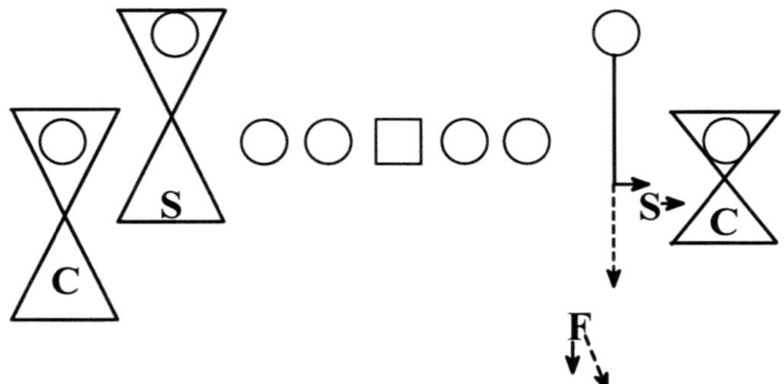

Diagram #7. Cover-1 Combo

him. In this case, we use the free safety and the outside linebacker in combination coverage on the slot receiver.

In combination coverage on a single receiver to the wideside, the linebacker aligns to the slots outside and takes him on all outside breaking patterns. If the receiver runs an outside pattern, the linebacker takes him, and the free safety is free. If the receiver goes vertical, the free safety is slightly deeper to the inside and picks him up. The outside defender releases the slot to the free safety, and he becomes free. He can help the corner on the #1 receiver to the outside or zone across for any crossing pattern.

We can play a combo mix coverage to a trips set (Diagram #8). We mix two coverages on the three receivers. The corner locks up on the outside receiver in a man-to-man coverage. In this coverage, the three defenders take the two receivers in an inside-out combo. It is linebacker, strong safety, and free safety in the combo coverage on the #2 and #3 receivers. The linebacker and strong safety play inside-out coverage on the receivers, and the free safety is over the top of both of them. We work with five defensive backs in the secondary.

Late in the game or in a special situation when we want to cover a primary receiver, we call "cover-1 star" (Diagram #9). That simply is a double-team call on a particular receiver. I am the one who makes that determination. We take two defenders and bracket the star receiver. We take him out of the equation. He is not going to catch the ball. If you know who the offense is going to throw the ball to and you do not cover him, that is a big mistake. Do not let one player beat you. There are ways to take anyone away in a critical situation. If you are wrong in the call, you force them to throw the ball to someone else.

Diagram #9. Cover-1 Star

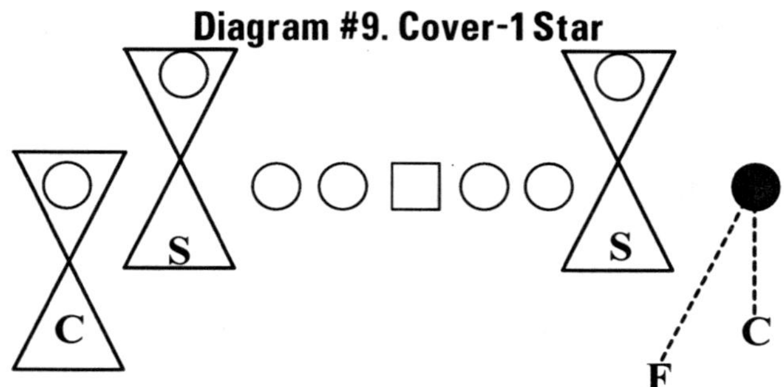

This next coverage comes from a basketball defense. We call it cover 30 (Diagram #10). It is a triangle-and-two basketball defense. The coverage is cover 3 with a double coverage on the primary wide receivers. That comes from the scouting report. If they like to throw the ball to the slot

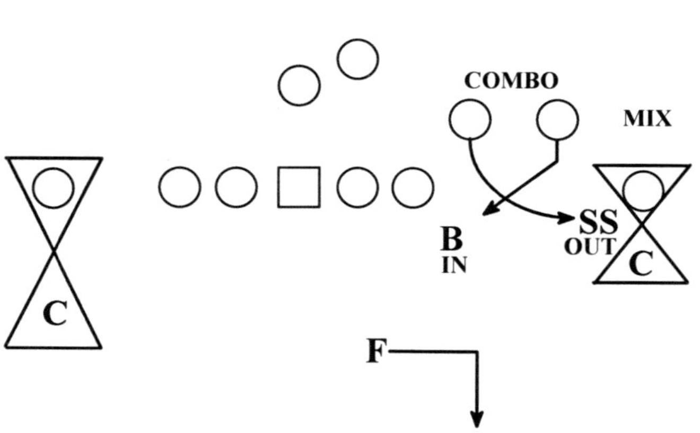

Diagram #8. Combo—Mix Vs. Trips

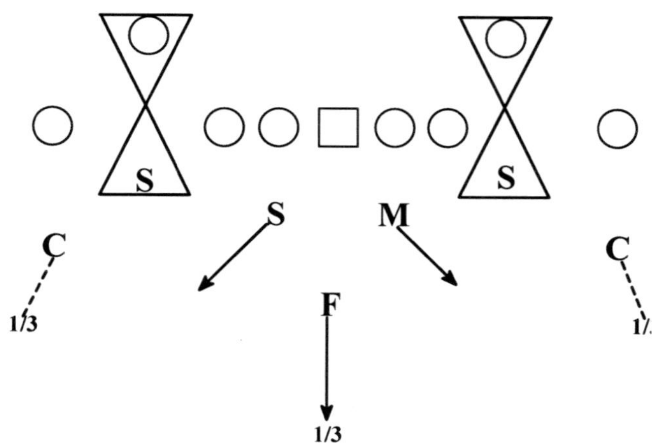

Diagram #10. Cover 30 (Triangle-and-Two)

receivers, we double those receivers. We use those coverages with a six-man box.

If we have a five-man box, that gives us more options in the secondary. I have six defenders in the secondary. I want to put my best defenders into the field. The safeties, corners, and outside linebackers flip-flop. If you have a real difference between two players in the same position, you want to flip-flop those players. If one plays the run better and the other is faster and plays the pass, use what they do best to align them.

We play cover 4 and cover 2 with this alignment. In Diagram #11, we align in a cover-2 scheme. We disguise what we do and get into a corner roll to both sides with the safeties playing the half fields. In this coverage, we can drop eight into the coverage or use combinations of blitzes to pressure the quarterback. The corners roll down into the flat zones. The outside linebackers play the seam/curl zone, and the safeties play the hash marks.

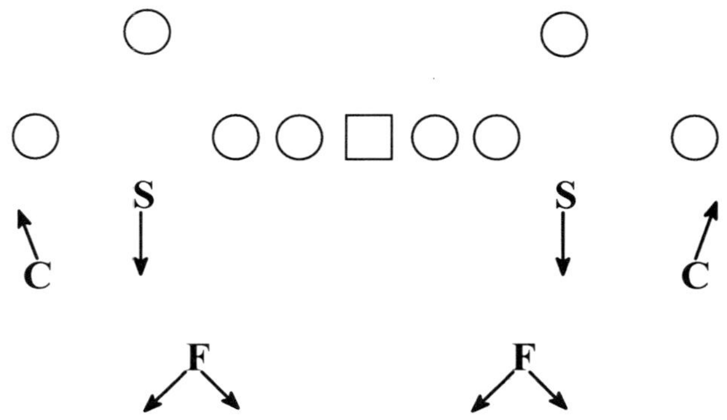

Diagram #11. Cover 2

From the same alignment, we can play a cover 4 or quarter coverage (Diagram #12). We base the coverage off the read on the #2 receiver. If he goes out, the outside linebacker has the flat zone in that area. If he releases vertical, the safety picks him up. The corner aligns on the wide receiver but reads the #2 receiver and reacts off what he does. If he releases outside, he takes the wide receiver and gets help from the safety on the inside.

As part of our game plan, we have a rule that determines what we do in the secondary. The rule for this game is man coverage, and will stay man coverage. If we are in zone coverage, we stay in zone coverage. It does not matter what the offense

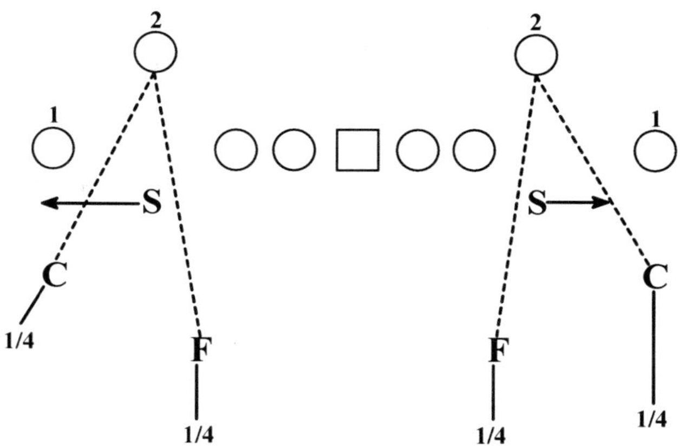

Diagram #12. Cover 4

does or what type of movement they give us; we do not change the secondary scheme. However, in the next game, we may want to change the rule. If they give us a certain formation, we play zone. If they shift to another formation, we can go to a man coverage. It does not matter what the rule is, but you must have a plan to handle the adjustments.

We can run dog or double-dog and play man in the secondary (Diagram #13). If we bring a dog stunt from the weakside, we can play cover 1 and bring the strong safety to the middle. We drop the free safety down on the slot receiver to play man coverage when the outside linebacker blitzes. If we want to double-dog, we play cover 2 and bring both outside linebackers on the blitz.

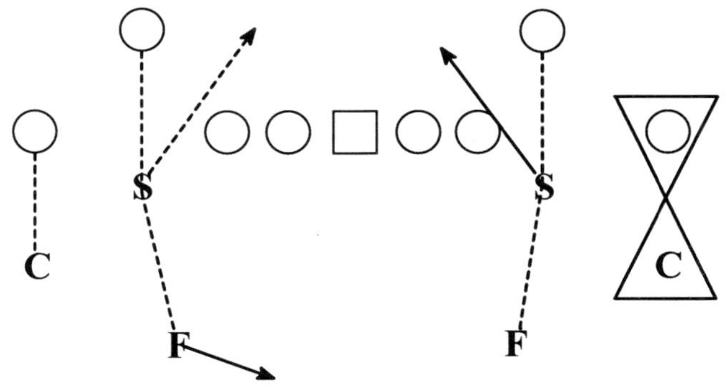

Diagram #13. Cover-1 Dog/Double Dog

We have an adjustment from this coverage. We call "cover-1 snug." That is man-under, two-deep zone coverage. We take the outside linebackers and corners and play press coverage on the wide and slot receivers. They play man-to-man in a trail position with safety help over the top on both sides.

The adapted coverage from the cover-1 snug is cover-1 combo. The coverage is the same in-and-out adjustment I talked about earlier. It is the same combo coverage to both sides with safeties deep over the top. It is man coverage with a combo on the route of the slot and wide receivers.

We can adjust to the trips set and integrate the calls to match the receiver. We can call the star coverage with this formation.

We can play a cover 40, which is the basketball defense, out of the cover-2 alignment. We double the primary receivers and play zone on everyone else. This defensive coverage has holes in it, but it is an option to cover what the offense likes to do. Do not let the offense dictate how you play. Make them adjust to what you do.

We make our plan according to what the offense does. We want them to do something else to beat us. We do not want them to beat us doing what they like to do. We want to make them play left-handed and adjust to the way we play.

We do all the planning on Sunday and give the players the game plan as soon as we can. I am retired, and on Monday, I do not have a damn thing to do. I spend more time working on football now than I did when I worked full-time. I work on the game plan, study, and watch film until the assistant coaches come in after school. We meet, and I give them the game plan we worked out on Sunday with the adjustment I put into it.

On Monday, when we go to practice, we introduce the base game plan for the upcoming week. We talk about the game plan and start our adjustments to the sets we will see. We walk through all the adjustments to the sets we see. We use two defenses in the walk through and a scout offense.

After the walk-through, we take half the linebackers and perimeter personnel and work on pass coverage, and the other half and the linebacker and defensive line work on run fits. Halfway through the drills, we switch linebackers.

We work on the base defense on Monday and Tuesday. On Tuesday, we introduce the back-up plan. You need an ace in the hole when things start to fall apart. On Wednesday, we work on the base, additional fronts, and adjustments to both plans. On Thursday, we repeat and review everything, and we play on Friday.

This is all simple, and it is not complicated. It is what I picked up over the years. I appreciate your attention. I gave you want we do, and I hope you can use some of it. Thank you very much.

Steve Belles

PLAY-ACTION PASSES FROM OUR BEST PLAYS

Hamilton High School, Arizona

How many head coaches do we have here today? Our record since I have been at Hamilton High School is 67-3. We have a phenomenal coaching staff, we have great players, and we have a great administration. Trust me, it is not me, it is the program itself. I took over for John Wrenn who is at Arizona State University now working in athletic administration.

In my first year, we were 13-1 and defeated Mt. View High School in the finals. In my second year, we ended up getting beat by Brophy College Preparatory in a monsoon that night. That was not the reason we lost, however. We ended up with a 12-1 record. The next morning I woke up, looked into the mirror, and asked myself this question: What am I not doing right? I was about as miserable as I could be. We were 12-1 for the year and I was miserable. Something is wrong with that.

I knew it is not about winning. I was not happy with the direction of our program in terms of how our kids were reacting and overall how we were perceived in the state. I just did not like the status of our football team. I decided we needed to make some changes.

I told my wife I was going to go talk with our principal, Dr. Fred DePrez. I was prepared to let him know there had to be some changes made in our program philosophywise or I would not mind resigning as head coach. I had no problem with that move. Dr. DePrez told me to make the changes I needed to make in the program. At that point, I knew this was the place I wanted to be.

I came into a great program and I did not want to rock the boat, but it did not feel as if it was my program. So after that second year, we made some changes. For time's sake I will not get into all of the changes. As a head coach, it has to be your program. You have to feel comfortable with the program.

I heard Bret Bielema of the University of Wisconsin-Madison lecture at the AFCA Convention this year. What he said holds truth for what we are doing at Hamilton High School. This is what I took from that lecture.

First, you must have a loyal coaching staff. You must have assistants that believe in what you believe in. If you do not have coaches that believe in what you believe in, they need to go somewhere else to coach. I am sorry; but, if they do not believe in what you believe in, you are going to have coaches stabbing you in the back left and right.

We have 35 guys in our program from the freshman level to the varsity. They are either volunteers or paid coaches. We have 24 varsity coaches and we are all on the same page. Our kids get coaching. All of these 35 guys are former players or state championship coaches, but they all check their egos at the door, including myself. I am no better than the other coaches, except I have to lay down the law and define the expectations that I have.

Everyone is on the same page. I am not saying that we all agree on everything. We made an agreement a few years ago that if we have a problem with one another, we would not discuss the problem on the field. We agreed to come in after practice and talk about it. When we leave the locker room it is over and done.

What we have now is a situation where we can work together to better our program. When we come into our Sunday meeting, we break down the game films and we make our plans for the week. After that, we are done. There is no griping, moaning, and complaining. When you can reach that level as a head coach or as an assistant coach, you are going to be so much happier as a coach. You can have your say on what we decide to do for each game.

We platoon our players. We do not have anyone going both ways. We did have one kid that played both ways. He got an offer to go to Boise State University today. The point I am making is the fact that everyone has a chance to have input in our program. If you feel you do not have an opportunity for input, you need to go somewhere else to coach.

Everyone has to accept our rules on this. It may be a scout team coach. We have two young coaches that do our scouting. They put their heart and soul into scouting the opponents. We review where we are as a staff each year. Four weeks ago, we had a four-hour meeting discussing where we are and where we can get better.

Anytime you do a lecture it makes you look at what you do well and what you do not do well. Where can you get some ideas that can make your program better? I put together some materials on our play-action passing game. I was at another clinic and I heard a coach talking about their play-action passes. I picked up one point from that lecture that I liked. "Make sure your players are accountable for doing the play-action passes great."

I want to get into the philosophy we base our offense on. First, we want to attack the defense.

PHILOSOPHY

- Attack the defense.
- Control the situation.
- Know the situation.
- Play with a plan.
- Coach your quarterback, running back, and linemen.
- Look for big play opportunities.

We feel play-action passing is a worthy attack phase of the game. We want you to think it is a running play, but we are going to throw the ball. When we throw the ball, we are going for the home run. We are not going for five yards; we are going for broke. We do have outlet passes depending on what the defense does, but, realistically, we want to go deep against you six or seven times a game. If we can complete three of those deep passes, they can make a difference in the outcome of a game. They could result in three touchdowns in a game and help us win the game.

We want to control the situation on offense. We do not want the defense to dictate to us what we can and cannot do on offense. You run what you want to run. If the defense puts nine men in the box, you have to throw the ball to keep them honest.

If you have a coach in the press box, make sure that coach knows what is going on in the game. He must know the situation. "What did you see on that play, Coach?" "Well, I saw 11 players on the field." That is not what we want from the coach in the press box. We have special situations we want to know about. If they have an alley player, we want to know that.

We believe you must play with a plan. I have a playsheet that I carry with me on the sideline. The coach that calls the plays does not use a playsheet, but he knows the game plan.

Each week we want to come up with a plan and coach our quarterback up. All of our position coaches make sure they coach their players up on what is expected and what we must do. The big thing we must improve on is the fake on the play-action pass. We must work on making the play look like a run.

We look for big-play opportunities. No question about this. This is a real key. You want to make sure the right personnel is on the field for these big plays. Make sure the players know who should be in the game in the big-play situations. You do not want a third-team player in the game that has to make a big play for you.

Coaches must know the situation and they must know what we are trying to accomplish. It is important to use the coach that is in the press box. Use him effectively. Our coaches in the press box give us great information on what is going on in the game. For example, they can let us know what coverage we are seeing and if the safeties are coming up strong to fill for the run.

What we look for is if the defense has one safety or two safeties. If the deep safety is cheating over on plays, we are going to try to take away the middle of the field with certain plays. The coaches in the box can be a big help if you use them right.

We must coach the play-action passing game. That is what we are doing now. Following are a few points we stress with the players regarding the play-action passing game:

- We let the players know how important faking is in the play-action game.
- Film after the game shows how well your play-action pass game worked.
- Demand greatness out of this and you will be surprised how many big plays you will have next year.
- Must give feedback—good or bad.

One of our sponsors provides us with Gatorade®. We tell our players if they can fake the cameraman out on a play-action pass, they are rewarded with a Gatorade. This is a big deal for our players on film day.

We want our backs running the fake to make it look as if they have the football. They do not need a herky-jerky motion on the fake. Have them run the same way as they do when they run the ball on the regular play.

When we tell a player he did a good job, we need to tell him why it was a good job. The player may not know why he did a good job. "The coach told me I did a good job."

It is the same thing when you tell a player he made a bad play. Tell him why he is sitting on the bench. Let him know what he did wrong.

When a player scores a touchdown on a play-action pass, we tell him he is only one of the 11 players that scored the touchdown. We have every player do what we call "touch it up." That means everyone is a part of that play-action touchdown. The other 10 players go to the end zone and "touch them up" because they are a part of that score. When everyone feels a part of the touchdown, I think you get better results. You may want to think about doing that.

You must demand the backs and quarterback make a good fake on all of their plays. Don't let them off the hook. You can work on that during the 7-on-7 summer games. Demand good fakes by everyone involved.

At this time of the year we have what we call "advisory time" for all of our students. The students get 25 minutes to meet with teachers, to make up tests, etc. I have the quarterbacks come in with me and we have sessions for the quarterbacks. They get on a whiteboard and work on the things related to their position. I do not coach them. I tell them what I want them to do, and they have to describe it on the whiteboard. We make them write the things on the board and we make sure they understand what they are talking about on the situation. We want to make them accountable on game night.

We have three days a week where we go on the field. On Monday, we go over everything in the classroom. On Tuesday, we go over what we covered on Monday on the board. We go on the field and run through everything. We get loosened up and then do 7-on-7.

On Friday, we are on the field for about one hour and fifteen minutes with the kids. We have two hours a week built into our school day. We lift three times a week. We get enough out of those three days. We do not feel it is how big our players get. If we get a player that is too big, he is not going to be able to move for us in a game. We do a lot of agility drills. We want to make sure we are flexible. If you do not have good hips, you cannot move.

THREE TYPES OF PLAY-ACTION FAKES

- Quarterback must make it look like the run play.
- Quarterback must show the defense the football for a short period of time, then pull it back in, and set up to pass.
- The third fake is a fake that quickly shows the football but does not affect the rhythm of a timing pattern.

We have run this offense out of the wing-T formation, but we have also run it from the shotgun formation. We have done boot pass out of the shotgun. You can incorporate all of this into your offense. We are under the center 90 percent of the time.

LINEMAN KEYS

Linemen must know at the point of attack, they must make contact at the line of scrimmage. Do not retreat into a normal pass protection.

This, however, means that the protection is not as sound as normal protection and can break down at times.

I want to put on the film to show you our play-action passes in game situations. I will go fast, but if you want a copy of this disk, drop me a note and I will be glad to send you a copy. If you have questions, I will sit down with you after the film and talk as long as you want.

I will tell you, our offensive line was good this year and did a great job of protecting our quarterback. We had one player sign with Auburn University, one with the University of Oregon, one with Fresno State, and two with San Diego State University. They were five good football players.

I talked about the veer being one of our best plays. This is the play-action pass against the 4-3 defense (Diagram #1).

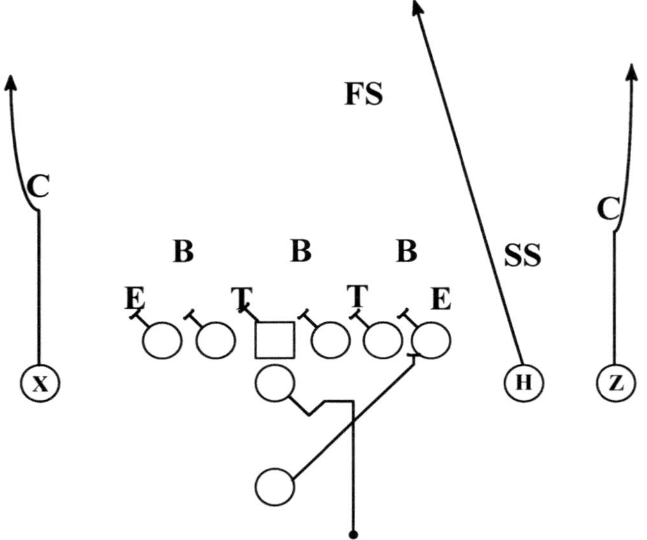

Diagram #1. Trey Right Veer Right Pass H-Seam

We can run a variation off the play by changing the route of the fullback. Now the fullback runs the outlet route to the trips side (Diagram #2). We keep the tight end in to block on the end man. Our H-back is still running the seam route. We are keying the free safety on the play.

We have two X-receivers on the next play. We want to go deep on this play so we slip in a second X-receiver that has some speed. We pull both guards on the play (Diagram #3). The Z back goes in deep motion faking the sweep play. Our fullback is in the flat.

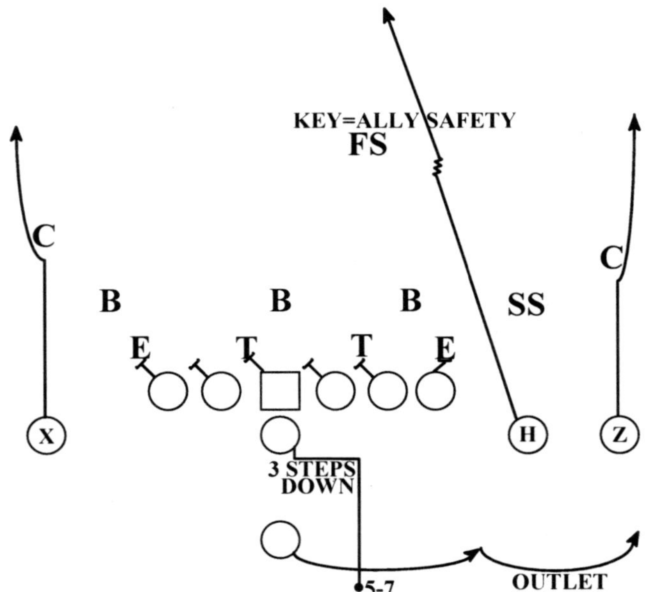

Diagram #2. Trey Right 44 pass H-Seam

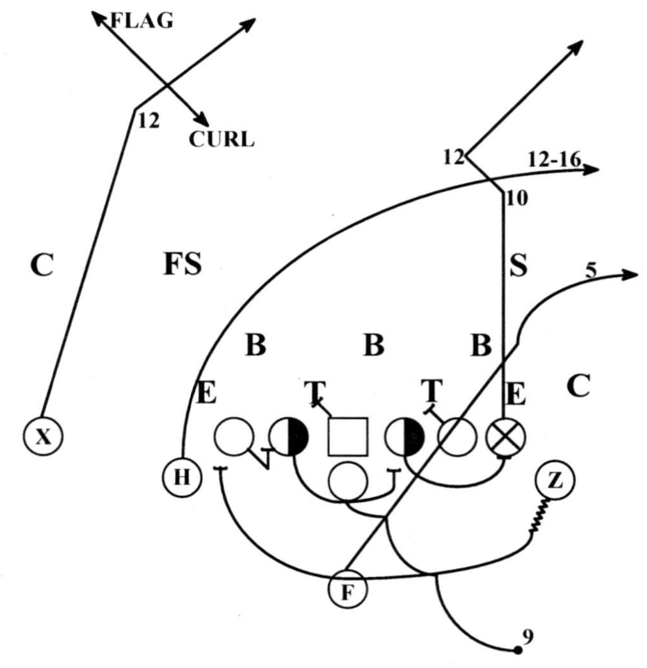

Diagram #3. Right Boot Right Pass

Another play where we use the two X-receivers is in an X cross route. We call it "left boot right pass X cross" (Diagram #4). We have the same action by the backs and both guards are pulling. The X-receiver that is running the crossing route splits seven yards from his tackle. He wants to find the hole behind the safety on the play.

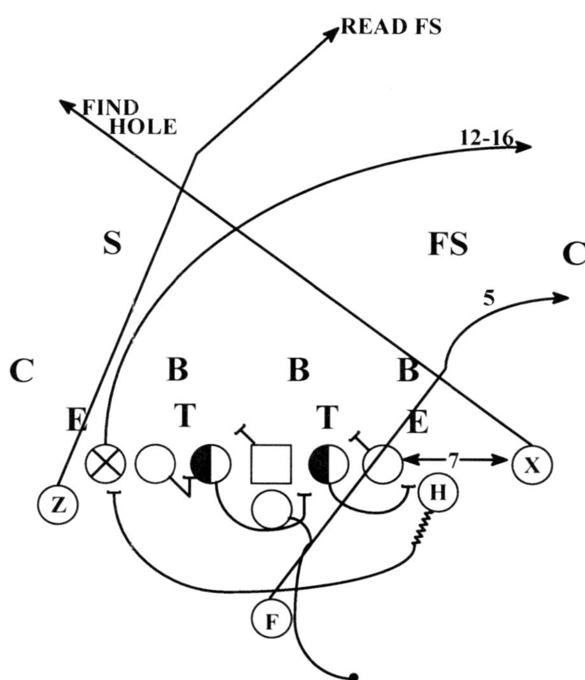

Diagram #4. Left Boot Right Pass X Cross

We ran a naked boot play and threw a delayed route to the tight end that was very successful (Diagram #5). The tight end holds for two counts and then runs an arrow route outside two to four yards deep. If the defense goes with the outside Z receiver, the tight end has a lot of room to run once he catches the ball.

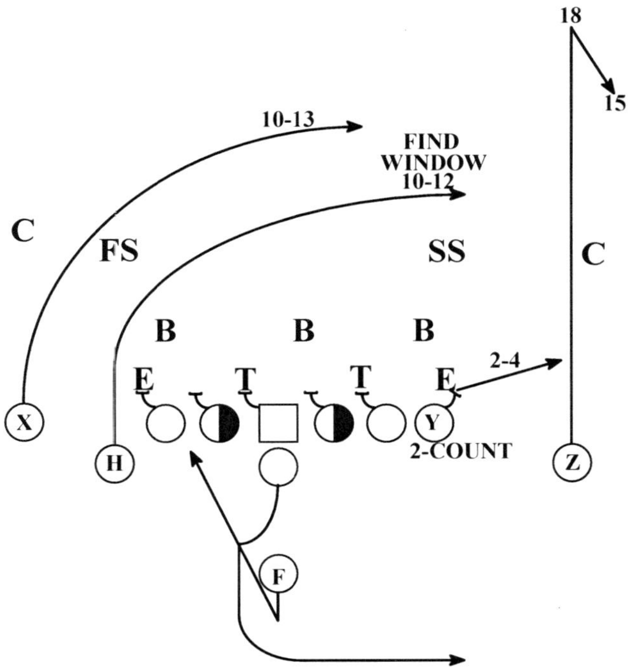

Diagram #5. Split Right Iowa Left Pass Naked

In a 2x2 look, we can run our fullback to the flat after his fake. The H-back runs a deep route clearing the free safety so the X-receiver can run a dig route underneath the free safety (Diagram #6). The fullback is the first man the quarterback reads, and the X is the second choice route. We call the pass "digger" for the dig route. The Z receiver runs a clearing route on the tight end side. The tight end stays and blocks.

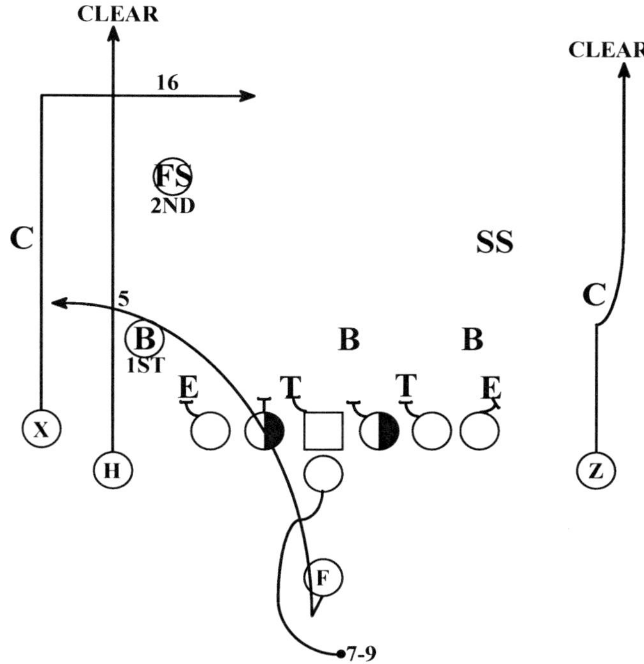

Diagram #6. Rex Zone Left Pass Digger

If we see a team that wants to play us with press coverage on the tight end side of the formation, we can run the play-action pass a lot of different ways. We use a second X-end and send him wide to the slot side. He runs a buttonhook route (Diagram #7). The quarterback is reading the Will linebacker. If Will has the X-receiver covered, he can run a deeper route.

The quarterback reads the Mike linebacker. If the Mike backer does not go with the other X-receiver, he throws him the ball across the middle. If he does not get the ball, he continues to run a crossing route 12 to 15 yards deep.

The action of the backs is the same. The fullback runs his flat route. The quarterback should be able to find the split end open on the buttonhook or the fullback open in the flat. Here, it was second down

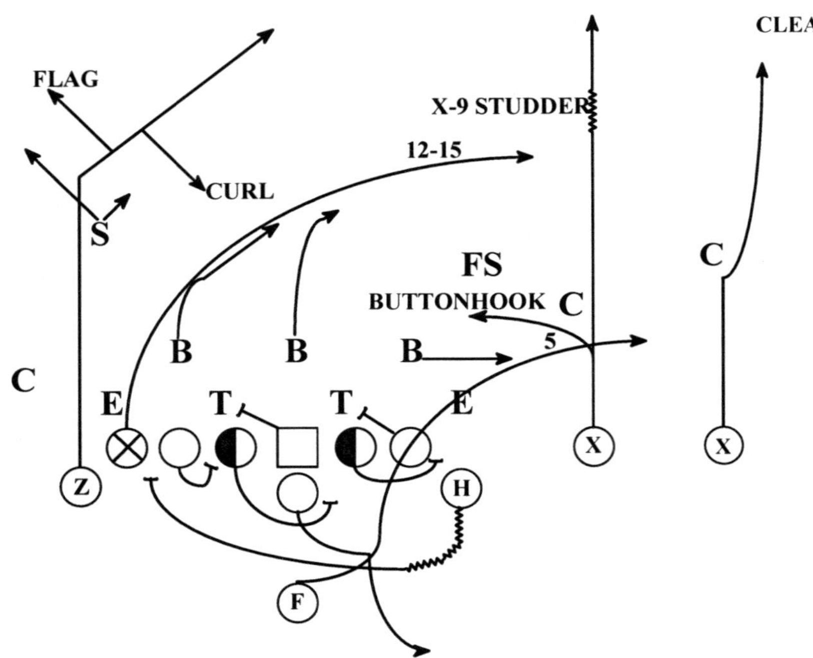

Diagram #7. Left Boot Right Pass

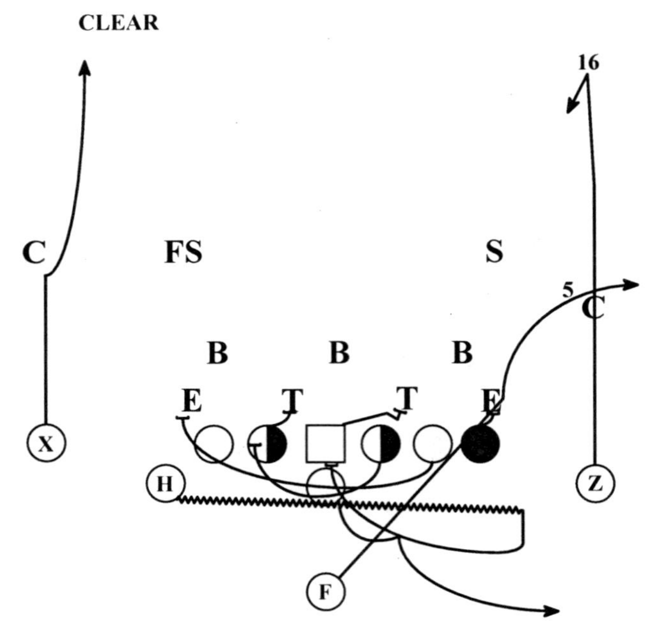

Diagram #8. Split Right Counter Left Pass Naked

and eight to go for the first down, and we were just looking to move the chains. If that backer goes with the fullback, the end sits in the window inside on the buttonhook.

We can run a similar play by splitting the X-end and have the H-back go in motion from his wing position. He crosses the center and comes back on a fake over the center. The fullback runs the same route as before (Diagram #8). The guards pull toward the split end. We keep the tight end in to block on the play. The quarterback is looking for the fullback in the flat.

When is the best time to throw the play-action pass? It is on first down or on second-and-short. Those are the best downs to hit the long pass. The thing you must be aware of is the fact that in the 7-on-7 games, the time factor is a problem in running play-action passes.

If you just want to talk football, you can email me anytime you want. I will be glad to talk with you.

Fred Brown

KICKING GAME COVER STRATEGIES

Spartanburg High School, South Carolina

Thank you very much. I am from Charlotte, North Carolina, but I coach in South Carolina. I went to Wofford College and played in the wishbone there. I got into coaching to give back to the game what it has given to me.

In football today, the one thing that many coaches overlook is field position. That has to do with kicking the ball. If you look at the game of football, how many games come down to field position? Our goal is to win the field position battle in every game.

When we punt the ball, we want to kick it 40 yards and have no return yardage from that kick. We want them to drop the ball and give us a 40-yard gain on one play. We want to kick the ball 40 plus yards and not give up any return yardage on the play. We want the opponent's offense to go as far as we can make them go to score.

Let's look at the kickoff. If you have a goal to limit the return team to a 20-yard return, that is a good goal as long as you kick it deep. If you kick the ball to the 20-yard line and they return it 20 yards, you have met your goal. However, you are in trouble because you gave up 20 yards of field position. If you cannot kick the ball into the end zone, you must come up with another strategy. With the kickoff and in the punting game, we want to limit the amount of yardage we give up in a return.

When you play special teams, you cannot afford to fill the team with second-line players who do not have talent. Special teams play is so important. The kickoff team used to be the place you gave players a chance to get into the game. However, today the kickoff is a momentum-swinger in the game. If you want to get the stadium crowd into the game quickly, get a long return on the opening kickoff.

If you want to win the game, block a punt. Blocked kicks are the biggest momentum-changers in the game of football today. A blocked punt usually means a quick touchdown or a score of some kind. I want to expand on that topic in the remaining time for this lecture.

I want to get into the topic right away. My topic is three bear protection. When we talk about three bears, we refer to the three big players in the punt protection scheme. We affectionately call them shields.

Many coaches at the Division I level have gone to this type of protection scheme. They recognize the advantage of using this type of protection. If you use a kick-slide, area-blocking scheme as they use in the NFL, the coverage suffers. The blockers are going backward instead of forward. The rules in the NFL that prohibit the majority of the coverage team from leaving the line of scrimmage before they kick the ball does not fit well with this scheme. We use the three bears scheme for a number of reasons.

WHY THE THREE BEAR PUNT?

- Inexperience of the punter and snapper
- Can utilize bigger athletes in protection, moving block spot
- Directional kicking to limit coverage area
- Protection solid

Long snapping in the punting situation is a hard job. We all have had the center that tells you he can get it back to the punter, but it may not be where he wants it. This punt protection gives you maximum protection when you get the bad snap. It builds confidence in the snapper that his mistakes do not become critical.

We want to snap the ball to the punter in .8 of a second. That is with a good zip on the ball. The total operation time for punting the ball is 2.0 seconds. If we are slow, we need to speed up the operation time. However, if we are too quick, the punter is rushing his technique, which can produce bad punts. We do not want the punter taking his time, but we want him to use good mechanics and hit the punt with consistency.

The situation always dictates how much time your punter takes to punt the ball. A backed up situation requires a quicker time because the distance from the center to the punter is less. Late in a game, if you have to punt the ball to preserve the victory, the only important thing is to catch and kick. It does not matter if the ball spirals or goes end over end. You must get it out.

The big offensive linemen types do not play special teams except on the extra point and field goal teams. This gives you an opportunity to use the personnel you have available to you. The big boys want to cover the punts. They relish the thought of going down and hitting someone.

We have two types of shields. We have a speed shield, and we have a bad shield. Players who are more athletic make up the speed shield. They are not as big, but they are faster in their coverage. We also play the bad shield made up of big players. When we absolutely have to get the punt off, we play the big shield. The coverage is not essential. Getting the punt off is the important thing. We work both groups.

This adds prestige to your group and fires them up. We call the group the "Renegades." It is the rallying call for the team. It jacks up a team and gets them into an attack frame of mind. When you hear the yells and screams of "Renegades" going up and down the sidelines, you know your players are ready to get on the field. It is time to get crazy on the field.

When you directional kick the ball, you give up statistics in some situations. The punters must be willing to kick the ball into areas of the field that may mean less yardage and better coverage. To cover any kick, you must be motivated and ready to turn it loose. We want to have fun and get the job done. People who love contact are great special team players.

We directional kick with our punters. When they catch the ball, they quarter turn to the side they are kicking. The shield blockers form a moving block spot for the punter. If we kick the ball to the right, that is a red punt situation, and the shield is stepping in that direction. The shields take three short steps to the right side. They must maintain their positions and keep their shoulders tight as not to create any seams in the shield wall. When he kicks the ball, the punter must stay in the framework of the shields.

It is difficult to block a kick when you do not know where the punt is coming from. This allows your kicker to punt the ball into a particular area of the field. If we can kick the ball to a certain area and have three converge people in that area, I feel good about our chances. If we punt the ball and the coverage team does not know where it is going, the kick return team has the advantage. If we have a players stuck out on an island, one running where he should not be, and they catch the ball between them, we have a problem situation developing.

This type of punt formation gives us solid protection, and we do not worry about getting the kick off. When the punt coverage team spreads out along the line of scrimmage, it makes the defense do something. If the defense does not cover down on all coverage personnel, they open themselves up for a fake or a pass play. They have to honor the coverage team and match up with the blockers. That means they cannot rush the punt with a mass of people.

When we punt the ball, we want a positive field position mistake. At the least, we want a positive change of field position. Our objective is to punt the ball and hope someone makes a mistake with fielding the punt. We want to punt the ball 40 yards, let it hit the ground, and roll another 10 yards. Alternatively, we want to punt the ball and get a muffed punt or fumble.

We do not want to punt the ball and let the return team make a return of any substantial distance. You are trying to maximize the field position in the exchange of the ball.

When we kick the ball, the punter takes a quarter turn to his left or right to angle kick the ball. We seldom kick the ball down the middle of the field. Directional kicking makes this punting game successful.

Why do we use the spread punt? You can use this punt formation anywhere on the field. If they back you up, you can secure the punt with this protection scheme.

Our linemen in the punt formation are in a good fundamental football position. They are in a two-point stance along the line of scrimmage. On the snap of the ball, they want to step and stop the defenders' momentum at the line of scrimmage. We want to punch the rusher and stymie his charge at the line of scrimmage.

They do not have to drive the defenders off the line of scrimmage, but they must have a physical presence on the rusher. If we can stop or cause the rusher to hesitate, they cannot block the punt. We will punt the ball in 2.0 seconds—that is providing all the elements of the punt go as planned. The snap must be good and delivered with speed.

WHAT PERSONNEL TO RECRUIT?

- Lineman should be athletic people who can tackle, but have a physical presence.
- Ends will need to be the best tacklers.
- The shield will need athletic players who are disciplined enough to protect.
- Punter needs to directional kick.

When you pick your personnel for the guards and tackles, you want players who can step in front of a rusher and stop him before they release. The gunners and people to the outside of the formations can be corners or receiver-type players. Generally, in the punt-blocking scheme, one or both of the outside rushers are turned loose on the play.

The shield blocker must be a good athlete, but he must be disciplined enough to protect. The shield blockers are eight yards from the ball. The right and left shield blockers are post players. They align in the A gaps of the center. They set in position and do not move. The middle shield is the movement player. He has to fill the gap between the outside shields. The shield can take on four blockers. When they move, they step in unison, taking three steps to the right or left, depending on the direction call of the punt. As long as the punter stays inside the width of the shield, no one will block the punt.

The block point for the punt is two-and-a-half yards behind the shield. The angle coming from the outside to the block point cannot get past the shield to the ball. They may be able to hit the punter, but they cannot get to the ball. If they hit the punter and do not hit the ball, that is roughing the punter.

How—Technique

- Linemen alignment: Heels of snapper, minimum of two yards apart
- Shield: Eight yards from ball, gate open, align based on the kicker leg
- Punter depth 15 yards, adjust alignment based on the snapper and shield

We align the toes of the linemen even with the heels of the snapper (Diagram #1). That put the line off the line of scrimmage slightly. The splits between the linemen are a minimum of two yards. That forces the rushers to let you know what their intentions are. They are going to rush the kick or try to block you at the line of scrimmage. In order to block you, they have to align on you.

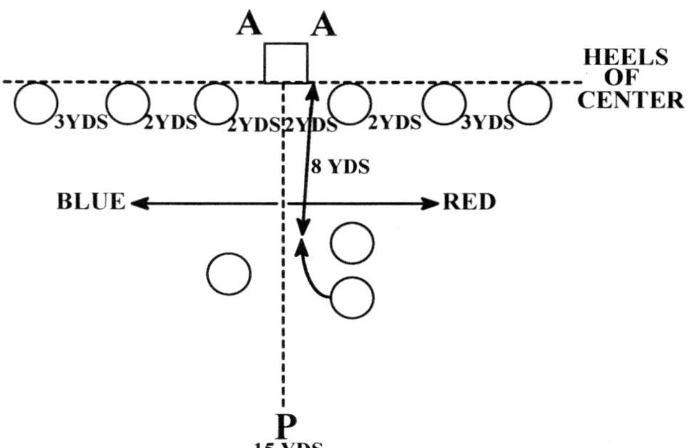

Diagram #1. Three Bear Formation

Our punter needs to directional kick the football. We happen to have a left-footed punter. When he catches the ball, he takes a quarter turn and kicks the ball. We have a red and a blue punt. The red punt is the directional kick to the right. The blue punt is the directional kick to the left.

His depth is 15 yards if I have a snapper who can snap it that distance. If I do not, his depth is 12 yards. If you move the punter up, make sure you adjust the depth of the shield to protect the block spot. The block spot is two-and-a-half yards behind the shield, whether they align at eight yards or seven yards.

- Read demeanor how to block front (man versus zone)
- Kick to the least amount of down linemen.
- Protection versus 55

The blocker reads the rushers at the line of scrimmage. To block a kick, the defender has to have a certain demeanor. If he is coming after the ball, he is in a gap and in a sprinter stance or down low ready to explode off the ball when it moves. He is tight and anxious for the ball to move. The blocker must disrupt the path of a defender with that demeanor. However, if the rusher is standing up and looking at the blocker, he is not coming. He is going to block for the return.

We block the rusher whether we think he is coming or not. When we step and shoot the hands, we read the defender. If he is trying to shoot his hand and make contact, we shed the blocker and get down the field to cover the punt.

Some coaches in their blocking scheme call for a zone block. They take the guard, tackle, and end and zone to the outside. They step to their outside and block the man in their outside gap. I believe that allows too much leakage on the shields. Also, if everyone zone-blocks to the side of the kick, that is not a good idea. When you do that, it catches the backside blockers in the wash of rush players, and the coverage is not as good. That is particularly true if you miskick the ball. Everyone is running to the right and the ball is down the middle.

When we block, we use the count system. We want to try to kick the ball to the least amount of down linemen. If the return team has a 6-4 overload, we want to kick the ball to the side where there are four rushers. With six defenders to one side of the punt formation, they will double-team the gunner to that side and try to hold him up. We want to kick the ball away from that side, where we have more coverage people than they have blockers.

When we count for our blocking assignments, we only count defenders on the line of scrimmage. We do not count linebackers or anyone off the line of scrimmage. They cannot block the punt from that position. If the linebacker walks up within the heels of the defensive line, we count him. If the linebacker can run from his position and through the shields in less than two seconds, we need to find another shield player, or the linebacker does not need to be playing high school football.

One of the reasons we take large splits is a rule of geometry. It takes the defender further from the ball and makes the angle he must run sharper. If the defender comes off the outside of our punt formation, he is eight yards wide and 13 yards from where the ball comes out. For him to cover that distance in 2.0 seconds, he has to be flying.

When you use this kind of punt protection scheme, it is not the best for coverage. It is the best scheme for protection. It makes up for the slow snapper or slow punter. If your punter takes too long kicking the ball, this is more secure. If the snapper cannot get zip on the ball you want, you should use this in your protection scheme.

I want to talk about 55 protection (Diagram #2). The most frequent rush pattern we see is 55 protection. That has five rushers on each side of the center. The center has to snap the ball and not worry about blocking anyone. With the huge splits we take, we see the defensive coaches put the fastest players that they have in the A gaps. That puts two rushers in the A gaps on either side of the center. They put one defender outside each end to make sure we do not fake the punt and that we kick the ball. That leaves two defenders between the guards and the end on each side.

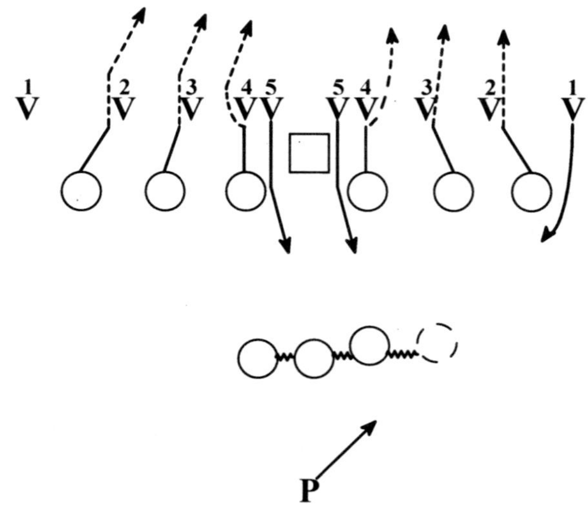

Diagram #2. 55 Protection

The shield can block the four rushers coming through the A gap. It does not matter if they stunt or rush straight, the shield will take them on. If one of the rushers gets too anxious or stumbles, none of them has a chance of getting to the punt. He will interfere with the rush of the others. We count the defenders from the outside to the inside. The widest defender to the outside is #1 and each defender going to the inside gets a number. The blocking assignment for the end, tackle, and guard is the #2, #3, and #4 rushers, respectively.

We do not block the #1 defender outside the end. We do not feel he can get to the ball. If he does try to block the kick, there is no one to cover the end on that play. If the guard gets a good punch on the #4 rusher, that may be enough to stop the #5 rusher inside of him. All we have to do is knock them off their initial charge. That leaves the #5 defenders unblocked coming up the middle. We have three shield blocks in a wall. The outside shield to the side of the kick is aware of the rusher coming off the edge. He does not step out or aggressively go to him. He stays in the formation of the shield. For that rusher to block the ball, he has to come through the outside shield to get to the block spot.

That is generally a mismatch, physically. The shield player is a big, bad offensive lineman or a bull of a defensive lineman. If the speed rusher tries to come through the lineman, he destroys him. If he tries to go to the outside, the shield lineman punches him and diverts his charge to the ball. If he goes outside and is untouched, he may hit the punter but cannot get to the ball.

Last year, our quarterback was the punter. He had good hands, was very athletic, and had a good leg. He was confident and could field any snap that came close to him. I did not worry about him. We have always had a snapper who could zip the ball and get it to the punter. The question you have to answer is: what do you do if you do not have a good snapper? You cannot put the punter in a formation with a bad snapper unless you can protect him. I know the snaps are going to be on the ground or high sometimes. Those things take the punter out of his rhythm and steps. I would rather have a solid secure punt protection for situations like that.

If we face a team that has that type of punting game, it discourages me from rushing the kick. If they have an excellent punter and snapper, and the punts come out in 2.0, it is a waste of time for me to rush the punter. The only thing I will work on is to make sure he punts the ball. I want to cover from the outsides in case there is a passed ball or high snap. I want someone to force the punter to punt the ball in a timely manner. I can spend the practice time working on something that will help me in a game. Practice time is tight, and we do not need to spend time working on something we will not do.

The shield blocker to the short side of the field does not step out at any rusher coming from that side. However, if the rusher is trying to close the angle to get to the block point, the shield wants to punch him off his track. He cannot open a gap between the middle shield and himself, but he can extend his arm and punch the rusher off his track. It is like the wingback on an extra point. He has to block inside, but he must get a hand on the outside rusher, if there is no threat to the inside. It is the same technique the directional shield has on the outside rusher.

If you are effective in the punt protection scheme, the defense will stop rushing and try to return the ball. If we can keep the returns to a minimum, we get a positive field change. The problem with high school punters is their eyes. They have to catch the ball and kick it. They cannot look up to see what is coming. They have to trust the shields to hold up and punt the ball. I try to get the punter to take a rocker step, one step, and punt. However, I do not change their style unless it becomes a timing issue.

If the punter is a two-step punter, we try to work on his mechanics to improve his time in getting the ball off. If he is a three-step punter, we have to change that. A key to a good punter is to catch the ball clean. He must have good hands and use them. He cannot catch the ball into his body and get it off with any consistency.

Another thing you have to consider is the number of times the rusher will attack the shields. Some defenders like to try to punish the blocker with their running start. However, more times than not, they are the ones who takes the hit and punishment. It does not take too many times attacking the shield blockers for defenders to stop running into them. When that happens, you get what you want. You get the punter punting the ball with no rush.

It is almost like a kamikaze attack. They may try to penetrate it once or maybe twice, but most of them stop short of the shields and get into the return.

If the defense backs us up and we think we will get a rush, we can give a max call. That means we are going to take as many rushers off the shield as we can. It may require the blockers cutting down their splits to make the blocks. We are in a two-point stance and can adjust in and out with our alignment. The middle shield player makes the adjustments. The shields are generally offensive linemen and used to communicating calls to one another. They understand overloads and point them out.

In our blocking scheme, we release the coverage team based on the demeanor of the rushers. If the defender is rushing, we hold for a count of two seconds. If he is trying to hold up the coverage player, we shed and get into our coverage lanes. If he has no blocking assignment or the defender retreats off the line, he releases and covers downfield. We tell the blocker, when in doubt, block. If he turns the rusher loose and he rushes, he may not get to the punter, but we do not want to take that chance.

Blocked kicks are one of the biggest momentum-changers in the game of football. If you get a punt blocked, it generally leads to a score immediately, or it sets up one. That is another reason to secure the punt.

When we start to teach the blocking assignments with the punt protection team, we do not talk about time. We do not teach two seconds before the release. We teach them to stop the forward progress of the rusher. That means to stop him from coming forward. After we understand what that means, we can start talking about a timed release by the blockers.

I hope I gave you something to think about in your blocking scheme. Remember your role as coaches. That is why I am in coaching today. I wanted to give back to the people who gave so much to me. We are the only role models some of our players have. Make sure their experiences with you are positive. Wins and losses do not make a difference in this sport. Development of young men and the impact you have on their lives is what is important in this sport. Thank you for your attention.

Chris Chambless

THE 5-2 BASE DEFENSE AND STUNTS

West Point High School, Mississippi

I want to keep this very informal, so if you have any questions, please feel free to ask them. I am going to do the best I can to tell you what we do. We line up and play a base defense. We give our players a job to do and they go do it. We are a read team. We try to teach our players to come off the ball and do those types of things.

We have been successful and have won the state championship the last two years, but our players are humble. We know you must have good players to win ball games. I joke around all the time and say, "If we can get our players on the bus, we have a chance." We have good players and we are fortunate enough to have fast players. That is how you win games.

When I talk to our players, I do not talk for any length of time. I tell them if I talk for more than 20 seconds, they need to tell me to shut up. We try to keep things in perspective.

In the Bible Belt, if you can show it written in the Bible, it is true.

All hard work brings a profit, but mere talk leads only to poverty.

—Proverbs 14:23

- Hard work beats talent when talent doesn't work hard.
- Blue-collar, lunch-bucket, and hard-hat mentality
- Outwork opponents in the off-season.

We have had success because our players work hard. We won many football games because we outworked the other team. We want the mentality of our football team to be blue-collar, and we point that out to them. When we prepare for some teams, we refer to them as a bunch of pretty boys that do not know how to work. In our football program, we train 11 months out of the year. We give them two weeks off at Christmas, one week at spring break, and one week in the summer. The rest of the time, we work on football. I will talk about that later on. I want to share with you our defensive philosophy.

DEFENSIVE PHILOSOPHY

- Play fast and aggressive.
- Put pressure on the opponent from multiple places.
- Be unpredictable.
- Win the turnover battle.
- Film study/scout emphasized
- Be coachable.

We tell them to play fast but be patient. We want them to play fast, but we do not want them to overrun the football. We want to pressure the opponent from multiple places. If we play a team that throws the ball, we will pressure them through the weaknesses they have in their protection schemes. When we put the blitz package together, we will come from places where they have a weakness. When we do that, we want to be unpredictable.

We do a lot of film study. Our defensive players come in on Sunday to watch the film. They are not required to do this, but they do it every Sunday. On any given Sunday, we will have 10 to 15 players there. If they are not there, they let us know they are not coming. The defensive staff watches the film with them and we show it to the whole team on Mondays before we go out to practice.

The last point is tremendously important. We are always on our players about being coachable. We, as coaches, do not know everything, but we want the players to let us help them to be successful.

BASIC PRINCIPLES

- Fast flow, read hats, run to the ball
- Sound, technique football
- Man-to-man in the secondary
- Constant pressure from the defensive line
- Downhill linebackers

Every successful team does these things well. I am a big man-to-man coach. I have always been a man secondary, and we have had the speed to play that type of defense. I hope I will always have enough talent to do that. We will emphasize that principle every day. We play a lot of press coverage.

We want constant pressure from the defensive line. In every drill we do, from the simplest run read stance drill to the most aggressive drills we have, we want the players to think about moves to defeat a pass block. We want to swim, rip, spin, or some pass rush to get to the quarterback. We want our linebackers playing aggressively and heading downhill on every step. I do not want them to back up or move sideways. We want to attack the line of scrimmage. We are man-to-man so their coverage comes off the flow of the back.

Aggressive play is the style of linebacker play we want. On occasion, the linebackers make mistakes, but that is the way we teach them to play.

DEFENSIVE LINE STANCE

- Flat back
- Ball hand down
- Run stance = more square
- Pass stance = jet

These are basic principles. In our stance, we want a flat back with the hand nearest the ball on the ground. The players to the left of the ball align in a right-handed stance, and the players to the right align in a left-handed stance.

When we are expecting a run from the offense, we are squarer in our stance with a good base. As the offensive lineman comes off the ball, we read his hat and shoot the hands with the palms out and the thumbs up. We run a drill that emphasizes this point. We shoot the hands and get perfect placement. We lock out and lift. I blow the whistle and they escape into the hole. We want to play up and down the line of scrimmage.

The pass rush stance has more stagger in the feet and is narrower in the width of the stance. We want the tail slightly higher and we want to rush with speed. It is the classic sprinter stance. If the offensive linemen show the high hat, we go into our pass rush mode. They have in their minds the pass rush move they use before they come off the ball. I told you earlier, we develop that mind-set in all our drills. We want to have a move in mind so we can react and get pressure on the quarterback.

PRE-SNAP READS

- Listen for adjustments from Mike linebacker.
- Know the down-and-distance.
- Anticipate based on film/scout what your opponent is going to do.
- Read offensive line tip-offs (weight on/off hand, pass stance, etc.

We have been fortunate to have some very smart interior defensive linemen. Our three down linemen know how to execute because they are very smart. They are very good players. They make good decisions based on what the offense does. They use the scouting report and pre-snap reads. We have one signed at Mississippi State University, one signed with Louisiana Tech University, and one walking on at The University of Alabama.

Our Mike linebacker is our salutatorian. We are fortunate to have a very smart Mike linebacker. He gets our down three defensive linemen in the right place and relays tips and hints as to what the offense will run. He is very vocal and they will know what is going to happen.

They know the down-and-distance and can anticipate what is going to happen. This allows them to get in the proper stance and react. We want to take something away from the offense on our pre-snap reads. It may only be one play but that allows us to make big plays. The offense burns us on anticipation at times, but it also allows us to make big plays. We anticipate based on what we see on film and the scouting report.

We allow them to take a chance on occasion. Athletic ability allows you to get away with it sometimes. We had a noseguard run around the center and went the wrong way. However, he was fast enough to reverse his direction and make the tackle before the back got to the line of scrimmage. Of course, he ran 4.4 in the 40-yard dash. We allowed him to do that because he was fast enough to make the play.

At times you have players who can make plays for you. You do not want to mess them up by overcoaching what they can do. We put them in a scheme and let them make plays. We are no different from any other team; we look for offensive linemen tipping off what the play will be.

The first year I was at West Point High School, I wanted to leave because we got our butt whipped. My assistant coaches got me to stay. They told me to hang on and be patient. We knew we were going to be good. Some of our best battles are in practice. I think our defense is good but our offense kicks our butt in practice. They knock us off the ball and run the ball at us. I like that because it makes our defense better. It is a challenge in practice. We go full gear every day. We never practice in shorts, and we do not practice on Thursday. Our practices on Monday, Tuesday, and Wednesday are so physical that we need the downtime.

HAND PLACEMENT

- Hands inside
- Thumbs up, palms out
- Extend and win the hand battle.
- Reset the line of scrimmage.
- Pop eyes to the ball.

We want to read the offensive lineman's hat. We get off and shoot the hands. We want to get the hands inside the hands of the offensive lineman and strike with the palms out and thumbs up. We want to extend the arms and win the hand battle for inside position. However, you cannot let your feet go dead. You have to continue to work the feet to reset the line of scrimmage. We want to maintain leverage with our hands and pad level and pop our eyes to the football.

We drill the hand placement in a get-off drill. We come off the ball, place the hands, and keep the feet moving. On the whistle, we disengage and get to the ball. We do this drill in segments. We come off the ball and shoot the hands as the first part. We progress adding each segment of the movement. We work on these skills repeatedly. They make mistakes, but we do not spend too much time verbally chewing them out. We work on the skills until it becomes second nature to them. We work repetitions until we know the skill.

READ/REACT

- Flat and square
- Read hats.
- Outside arm free
- Never let your man off free.
- Always work your "half a man."
- No numbers on film

We want to read and react and play up and down the line of scrimmage. To do that, the defensive linemen must stay flat and square to the line. We tell them it is okay for the running back to get to the line of scrimmage. We do not make many plays behind the line of scrimmage. What we do not want to happen is the ball getting beyond the line of scrimmage. We do the best we can to get down the line of scrimmage and close all the cutback lanes. The linebackers fill where they are supposed to fill and we tackle from the inside out. We run the ball into the sideline. If the ball tries to cut back, we will be there.

We want no vertical seams in the defense. The defender makes the tackle or the ball has to break back inside. We want nothing outside and everything run to the sideline. When we watch the film, we do not want to see the numbers of the defenders. If we see the numbers of the defenders on film, that means his shoulders are turned and he is not square to the line of scrimmage. We do not want the players to turn and run to the sideline. That allows players to cut back on a tackler.

READ/REACT

- Use hands to shed cut blocks.
- Always engage to win inside.
- Shrug release the most used move we teach
- Play your area, don't leak upfield.

The rules of high school football in Mississippi do not allow cut blocking in the open field. However, the defensive linemen play in the cut zone. Defensive linemen have to use their hands to shed off cut blocks. We work hard on pushing down with the hands and moving away from cut blocks. We want to play with our outside arm free, but, at the same time, we want to engage to win the battles to the inside.

We do not want to leak too far upfield. We want to play our own area and track the ball. We pursue the ball all over the field and swarm to the ball. We want to let the play develop and close on the ball.

PASS RUSH

- Jet stance
- Foot back, dig your toe in, and tickle the ground.
- Have your move in your mind pre-snap.
- Stay in your rush lane.

This is our jet stance. We want to come off the ball and attack the quarterback when we read a high-hat move of the linemen. We want them to narrow their feet and increase the stagger in their stance. As they come off the ball, they have a move in their minds they will use. If the move does not work, the defender cannot stop working. He needs one counter move to use if the primary move does not work. However, they must be aware of the screen and draw as they attack the quarterback.

We work pass rush almost every day. We concentrate on staying in our rush lanes. We must have containment of the ball, but we cannot allow seams up the middle because someone is out of their lane. If they get out of the rush lane, they strive to get back into them.

LINEBACKERS' PRE-SNAP READS

- Read offensive line and running backs as they get set to snap.
- Listen for tip-offs from defensive line on pulls.
- Look for bird-dogging or eye gazing.

Our linebackers align five yards off the football. They adjust their depth relative to down-and-distance. We want them three yards from the heels of the noseguard and the defensive line. They align head-up the offensive guards and key through the guards to the backs. They key the triangle of the ball, backs, and offensive guards. Our offense, in practice, gives our linebackers good work with their reads. We pull our guard many times.

In their stance, we want them relaxed in a squat-like position. We want their hands in a ready position at all times. When they focus on the triangle key, they see the guard first. The linebacker bases his reaction off the action of the guard. If the guard comes out on the linebacker, we power step, gather, and head downhill. If we read high hat by the guard, the linebacker opens to a 45-degree angle and works to the wide receiver coming inside unless the running back to his side goes out. He has to listen for calls on crossing routes coming across the field. We want him to knock those receivers off their routes.

The linebacker cannot have concrete feet. He has to read, react, and run. He must take the correct first step because it is too hard to recover from a missed step. We tell them to be patient and make sure they know what is happening. When he fills, he has to understand what we call "clear and cloudy." A gap that has no opposite colored shirt in it is clear and he fills. If he reads cloudy, there is action in the gap and his fill is a scrape fill.

We do not always do the things I am talking about. We work hard at it in practice, but if you watch the film, you will always see plenty of mistakes. When everyone does what he is supposed to do, the defense looks great.

If the offense flares a back outside, the defensive ends pick up the flare back and the linebackers scrape for containment. We try to remain sound on the perimeter, but sometimes we lose containment on the quarterback. If we do, we run, react, and rally to the ball.

Our players are like every other teenager in America. They play football on the Xbox®. In that game, the player you control has a circle around him. We use the analogy to relate to our players. We tell our players not to play out of the circle. We tell the linebackers not to step out of the circle. We want them to be in control. We tell the defensive backs the same thing. Players stop, skip, and waste time.

We work on staying inside the circle and always being in control without false steps.

Every day at practice, the entire defense runs through bag drills and tackles. We do not miss a day of some kind of bag drill and some kind of tackling drill. We are a good tackling team because we work on it every day. We take the time to do it. We teach the defense to tackle the correct way, but the bottom line is to get the ballcarrier on the ground. We will finish the tackle some way. We want to get a hold of something and get them on the ground.

STUNT TECHNIQUES

- Skinny up.
- Attack half a man.
- Win the hand battle.
- If you are sent, you better get there.

The term "skinny up" is hard for linebackers to do because they want to look big. That is how you get home most of the time. If someone tries to pick up the linebacker, he wants to attack only half of the blocker instead of taking him down the middle. When we blitz, we do not want to expose the chest. We do that by winning the hand battle and keeping the blocker's hands off us. If we send the linebackers, they have to get home. We are a man-to-man team. If the pressure does not get to the quarterback, it puts the defensive backs on an island.

DEFENSIVE BACK ALIGNMENT

- Six yards
- Split the inside leg of the wide receiver.
- Eyes focused on the player you are defending (not in backfield)

We say six yards, but in most cases, we are about three yards off the receivers. If it gets into a long-yardage situation, that adjusts. We teach a lot of press coverage. We split the inside leg of the receiver and force them outside. We do not want them coming to the middle of the field.

We want to recognize the routes of the receivers as early as possible. We want to break on the pattern when we see the hands go up. When we break on the ball, we teach angles to the receivers. We want to break and make the tackle first. We want the outside hand in a position to make a tackle and the inside hand trying to knock the ball down.

When we backpedal, we want the feet under the defensive back. We want to keep the feet in the "circle." That is the Xbox term for control. When the ball is in the air, we want to beat the receiver to the ball. To beat him to the ball, we have to obtain a favorable body position. When reacting to a short route, plant with the feet in the "circle" and attack downhill. Route recognition is critical for switch calls between two defenders.

In our off-man coverage, if the corner's receiver makes an inside breaking pattern, the corner looks for a receiver coming to the outside. If he sees a receiver coming to him, he makes the switch call. We try to zone off two receivers that cross their patterns. The defenders have an in call and an out call. The corner makes the switch call to the inside defender. They zone off the play with the corner taking the receiver that breaks outside, and the inside defender takes the receiver that breaks to the inside. We never have a switch call when we are in press coverage on the receivers.

In man-to-man coverage, the defensive back must be "in phase" to make a play on the deep ball. A defense back that is in phase on a receiver is one that can get his elbow on the receiver's inside forearm. If he is in phase, he can look back for the ball and try to intercept it. If the defensive back is not in phase, he cannot look for the ball. He has to catch up before he can look for the ball. If the receiver puts his hands up and the defensive back is not in phase, the defensive back has to play through the hands of the receiver. He tries to separate the hands so the receiver cannot catch the ball.

In the secondary, we play primarily four coverages. We play cover 1, cover zero, cover 2, and cover 2 man under. Cover 1, for us, is man coverage with a free safety in the middle of the field. Cover zero is man-to-man coverage with no free safety. We use this coverage in a blitzing situation. We have schemes to bring all secondary defenders and linebackers on blitz stunts. We play some cover 2, when the situation dictates we do so. However, we are more likely to play cover 2 with a man-under concept. We do play zone on all triple sets or three-receiver sets.

PRE-SNAP RESPONSIBILITIES

- Everyone looks for the signals.
- Mike linebacker makes strength call and defensive adjustments based on formation/scout.
- Willie linebacker makes back call (one back, two backs, three backs).
- Strong safety makes down-and-distance calls.
- Free safety makes coverage calls based on stunt/call/formation/scout.
- All of this information is vital to ensure proper alignment to the offensive formation and a correct reaction to the call.

We are a no-huddle defense. Everyone looks to the sideline to get his defensive signals. The Mike linebacker makes the strength call based on the formation or our scouting report. He is responsible for the defensive adjustments. The Willie linebacker makes the back calls for the defense. He is responsible for making the call for the number of backs in the backfield.

The strong safety makes the down-and-distance calls for the defense. The free safety's responsibility is to make the coverage calls based on the situation. We base our coverage off the situation, stunt call, defensive call, or scouting report. Communication is important to any defense. We do not put all the calls on one player but all players must hear what calls we make.

Our base defense is a 50 defense (Diagram #1). In our base alignment, we play with two 9-technique ends. Since we flip-flop our personnel, we play with a strongside defensive end we call "ace" and a weakside defensive end called "Rover." The strongside end is more of a rush end, while the weakside end is a drop player. The ace is more of a run stopper, and the Rover is a strong safety type of hybrid player.

The defensive tackles are in 4 techniques aligned head-up on the offensive tackles. We play our bigger, more physical tackle to the strongside and the more agile tackle to the weakside of the defense. The weakside defensive tackle will have some pass containment as part of his responsibility on occasion. The noseguard aligns head-up the center in a 0 technique.

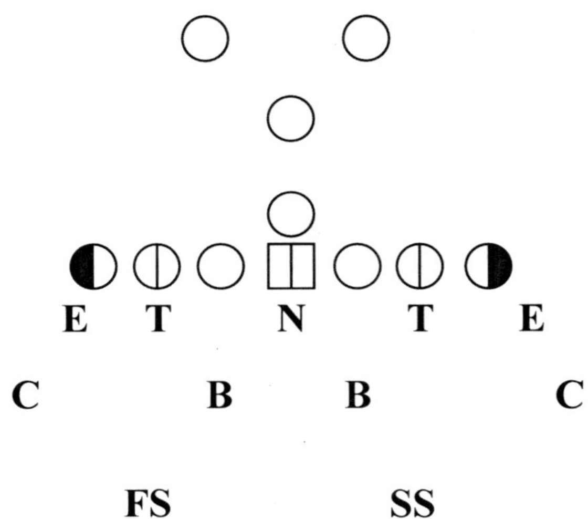

Diagram #1. Base Defense

The Mike linebacker aligns to the strongside of the defense, and the Willie linebacker aligns opposite him. The Mike linebacker is a run stopper and a more physical player. The Willie linebacker plays better in the passing game. We use him in our man-under scheme in pass coverage.

With no split receiver, the corners align at one yard deep and one yard outside the tight end or wing in the formation. The base alignment for the safeties is 10 yards. Situation and formation will affect the alignment of the defensive back. With detached receivers, the split rules vary according to the coverage we play.

We have an adjustment we use with one tight end (Diagram #2). If the offense aligns with a single tight end, we can use a 50 gap strong adjustment.

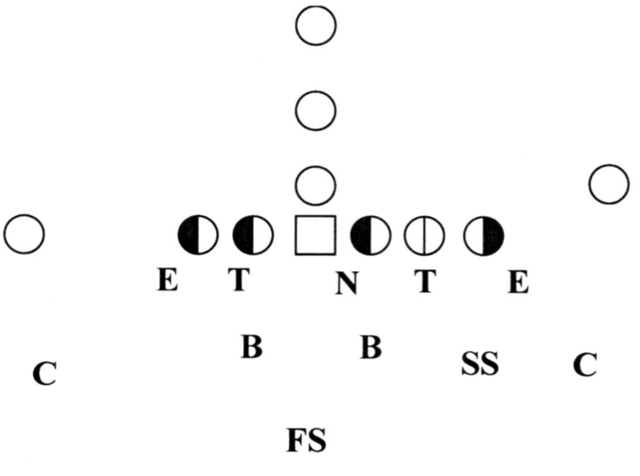

Diagram #2. 50 Gap Strong

In this alignment, the strongside defensive end and tackle to the tight end remain in a 9- and 4-technique alignment. We slide the noseguard from a 0 technique into a 1 technique (center/guard gap) to the tight end side. We reduce the backside, which has no tight end. The weakside defensive tackle moves from a 4 technique into a 3 technique on the outside shoulder of the guard. The backside Rover slides from a 9 technique into a 5 technique on the outside shoulder of the offensive tackle.

In the diagram, the secondary coverage is cover 1. The corners move out to cover the split and flanker. The strong safety moves down and plays man-to-man on the tight end. He has the tight end in pass coverage and the free safety is free in the middle of the field. The linebacker's alignment remains the same and they match up in coverage on the backs in the backfield.

The front we like to use against a 2x2 formation is 50 gap weak (Diagram #3). In this formation, we have no tight ends in the formation. We slide the noseguard to a 1 technique away from the strength call. If the ball is in the middle of the field, we go to a scouting report call or a left strength call. The strongside tackle and end reduce their techniques to inside techniques. They align in a 3 technique and a 5 technique on the offensive guard and tackle. The backside defensive tackle aligns in 5 technique on the outside shoulder of the offensive tackle.

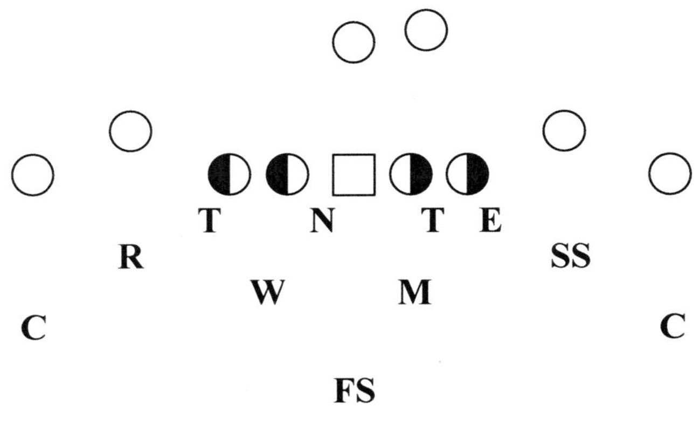

Diagram #3. 50 Gap Weak

The Rover drops off and aligns on the slot receiver to his side. If we play a heavy passing team, the 5-technique defender to the weakside is the agile tackle. The 5-technique defender has to contain in a passing situation. The walk-off Rover plays man-to-man on the slot receiver.

If we play a one-back team in a shotgun set, we can adjust the front to a 3-3 look (Diagram #4). Against the 2x2 shotgun set, we drop the ace end into a stack position behind the strongside defensive tackle. The tackles play 4 techniques head-up the offensive tackles. The Mike linebacker moves to a stack position behind the noseguard, and the Willie linebacker moves to the stack position behind the weakside defensive tackle.

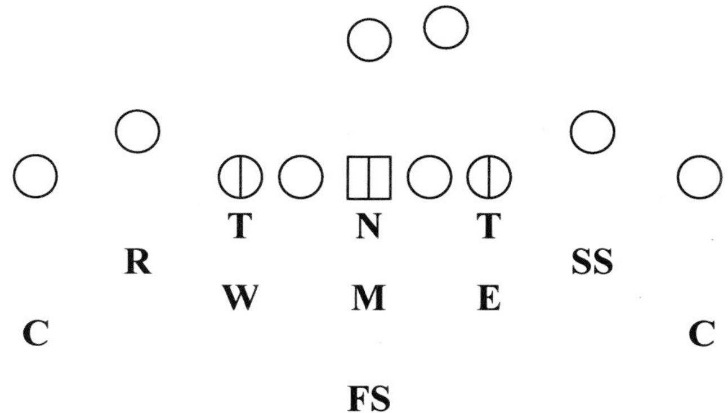

Diagram #4. 3-3 Alignment

The secondary aligns in a cover 3 look, but we will be in cover 1. This is a situation where the corners may have to use the switch with the strong safety or Rover.

An adjustment we use against this type of formation in a passing situation is cover 2 man under (Diagram #5). In this situation, we look like a 3-2 alignment to the inside. We move the Willie linebacker into the position played by the strong safety. He plays man-to-man coverage on the slot receiver to the strongside. The ace end moves into the Willie linebacker position to the weakside of

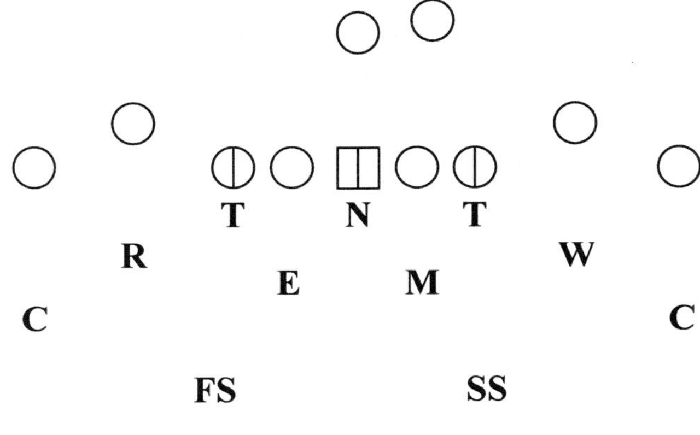

Diagram #5. Cover 2 Man Under

the formation. The Mike and ace play 20-technique alignment on the offensive guards. The strong and free safeties drop into a two-deep zone coverage over the five-under man coverage.

If we play a heavy running team or get into a short-yardage situation, we use a front called "50 solid" (Diagram #6). We slide our front to the weakside and drop the strong safety into a 6-technique alignment on the strongside tight end. The ace end moves to a 4 technique on the offensive tackle and the strong defensive tackle moves to a 2 technique head-up the guard. The noseguard moves to a head-up position on the weakside offensive guard. The weakside defensive tackle and Rover move to head-up the offensive tackle and the second tight end.

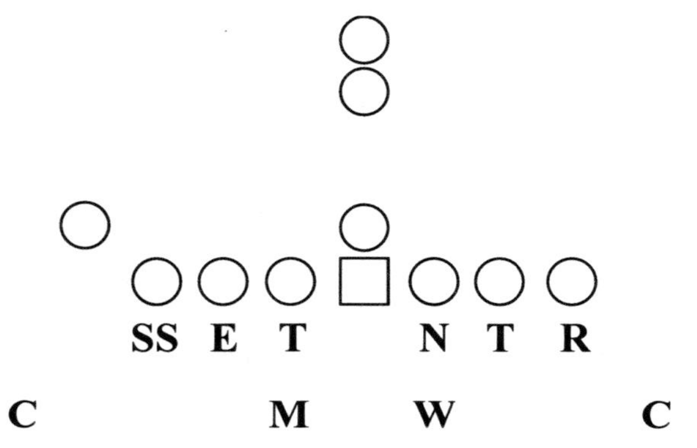

Diagram #6. 50 Solid

The Mike and Willie linebacker align in a stack position behind the strong tackle and noseguards. This is a 6-2 look for the defense. The secondary applies their rules for receivers and plays the coverage called. The weakside corner is one yard outside and one yard deep on the second tight end. The strongside corner aligns on the wing or flanker and covers him man-to-man.

I am running out of time. Before I stop, I want to show you two charts we use. The first one is a two-point chart. I need a chart for these situations. The HC in the chart stands for head coach. If we are one point behind, I make the decision on that call. This chart points out some situations and gives you some insight and thought of when to go for two points in a game.

Two-Point Chart			
Ahead By			
1 point—2 PT	6 points—Kick	11 points—Kick	16 points—Kick
2 points—Kick	7 points—Kick	12 points—2 PT	17 points—Kick
3 points—Kick	8 points—Kick	13 points—Kick	18 points—Kick
4 points—2 PT	9 points—Kick	14 points—Kick	19 points—2 PT
5 points—2 PT	10 points—Kick	15 points—2 PT	20 points—Kick
Behind By			
1 point—HC	6 points—Kick	11 points—2 PT	16 points—2 PT
2 points—2 PT	7 points—Kick	12 points—2 PT	17 points—Kick
3 points—Kick	8 points—Kick	13 points—Kick	
4 points—HC	9 points—2 PT	14 points—Kick	
5 points—2 PT	10 points—Kick	15 points—2 PT	

The second chart is a time management chart. It shows what to do with time running out in a game. It helps you decide when to take a knee and when to run a play. The chart shows the down in the downs column and the number of time outs the opponent has in the horizontal row.

Clock Management				
Down				
(Knee)	0	1	2	3
1	1:35	1:06	0:37	0:08
2	1:04	0:35	0:06	0:06
3	0:33	0:04	0:04	0:04
4	0:02	0:02	0:02	0:02
(Sweep)	0	1	2	3
1	2:10	1:39	1:08	0:37
2	1:29	0:58	0:27	0:27
3	0:04	0:17	0:17	0:17
4	0:07	0:07	0:07	0:07

Randy Coddington

THE 3-3-5 STACK DEFENSIVE SYSTEM

Concord High School, California

Before I get started, I want to give you an overview of Concord football. In 2004, when we arrived at Concord, it was a tough situation. What made it tougher was two-and-a-half miles down the road was De La Salle High School, which is the most prominent program in the state. We looked at that as a negative because they were a national power and were recruiting our players. In 2006, we turned the program around by sheer will. The campus turned into a positive environment. Also in 2006 as a staff, we made a philosophy change.

We made a decision to become a spread no-huddle offense. On defense, we went to a 3-3-5 so we could get more speed on the field. We decide not to punt the ball as much and go for two on extra points every time. It was fun to go and win it all this year with that crazy mentality because we did it our way.

We simply thought since we were right down the street from De La Salle, if we win or lose by 70 points, who would care. They will get all the headlines in the local papers anyway. We were willing to lose by 70 to win by one. Making aggressive decisions during the games have paid off as well. The players bought into it. During the game, we began to impose our will on the opponent and their coaching staff. I could see it happening from the booth. In 2006, that is the reason we went to the 3-3 stack. Since then, we have had nothing but success.

WHY RUN IT?

- Fewer defensive linemen
- More linebacker and safety-type players
- Speed on the field
- Attacking style
- Easy linebacker reads
- Create turnovers

I want to talk a little about our position groups. The defensive line is an important grouping in this defense. We refer to the nose tackle as the Stud. We named him that because he has to play that way. He is important because he must demand a double-team from the offense. If they do not double-team him, he will wreak havoc in their backfield. We call the defensive ends Eagle and Rover. The Eagle aligns to the left, and the Rover to the right.

The Rover end had 130 tackles this year. He is small, but extremely quick. He gets off the ball as fast as anyone I have seen. It is funny because my Stud and Rover were my two best linemen, and the Eagle ended up with a scholarship from San Diego State University. The three down linemen slant to the right, left, in, out, and pinch. It is very simple.

When we run an in or out movement by the defensive ends, the nose tackle goes into the left A gap (Diagram #1). On the in movement, the defensive end is a B-gap player, and on the out movement, he is a C-gap player. On the pinch call, they both are B-gap players. On the pinch movement, the Stud goes to the right A gap.

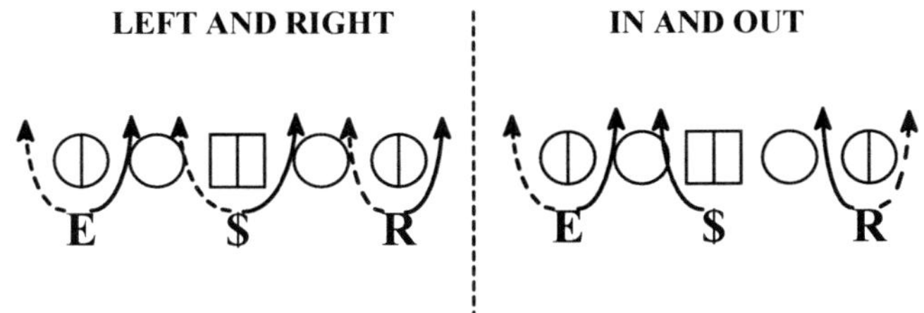

Diagram #1. Defensive Line Movement

It is very simple for the linemen. All they have to do is focus on their slant technique. We align all the linemen in a head-up position on the offensive center and tackles. Initially, when we teach their stance, we teach them with their right hand down and left foot back. The offensive lineman began to read the stances of the defensive ends. We now put them in both right- and left-handed stances to confuse the reads of the offensive linemen.

We use a sprinter stance with the feet beneath the hips with the butt high. We want them to get off the line and create havoc in the backfield. The defensive ends are spill players. If the offensive scheme does not block them at the line of scrimmage, they look inside and wrong-arm all blocks.

The linebackers are the next grouping of players. We give catchy names to all our players. We gave them patriotic names, and since they play like missiles, we named them Tomahawk and Patriot. The field linebacker is the Tomahawk, and the boundary linebacker is the Patriot. On the inside, we call them the conventional names of Sam, Mike, and Whip.

The inside linebackers align in a stack position behind the nose and defensive ends (Diagram #2). They align at a depth of three to four yards from the line of scrimmage. The Mike linebacker stacks behind the Stud. The Sam linebacker stacks behind the Eagle end, and the Whip linebacker stacks behind the Rover end. We align the Tomahawk and Patriot four yards wide by four yards deep off the end man on the line of scrimmage. At times, we have the linebackers moving, and sometimes they are stationary.

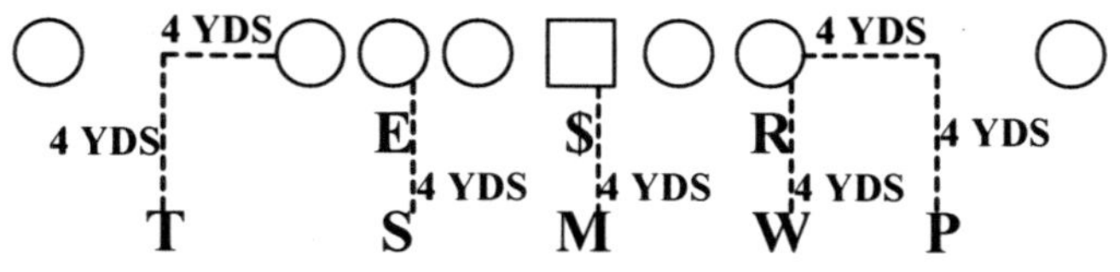

4 YDS 4 YDS
4 YDS E $ R 4 YDS
4 YDS 4 YDS 4 YDS
T S M W P

Diagram #2. Linebacker Alignment

The Tomahawk and Patriot have freedom to move in, out, up, and back from the line of scrimmage. They may align on the line of scrimmage, on a receiver slot receiver, or in the base alignment, depending on game planning. We use their alignment positions as disguise for their actual assignments.

The Sam and Whip linebackers are outside linebacker types. They can play the run effectively, but can also cover in tight areas. The Mike linebacker is a plugger type of linebacker and suited to stopping the run.

We are not concerned with the size of the defensive players we put on the field. We want speed instead of size. When we play bigger offensive linemen, we are very effective in our movement at getting by their blocks. The Rover end this year weighed 185 pounds and made a tremendous amount of tackles.

The big asset to our team was the ability to tackle in space. We work tackling in practice every day. We tackle on Thursday before we play on Friday. If you cannot tackle, you cannot play defense. Our personnel assignment puts wide receiver types at the Tomahawk and Patriot positions. The slower people on our defense are actually our corners.

The thing I like about this scheme is the advantage we gain on the outside. Sixteen-year-olds playing on offense have trouble deciphering the end defender on the line of scrimmage. We constantly change the defender as the end man on the line of scrimmage.

The first year we installed the defense, the offensive line coach talked about how he blocked the front. He said the offensive guard and tackle were responsible for the stack over the tackle. He did not mention the outside linebacker because they are coverage players. It made sense to me to send the outside linebacker to rush the quarterback instead of a bigger slower lineman. I love blitzing the outside linebacker because the offenses turn that responsibility over to a running back or a quarterback's hot read.

I generally send the outside linebacker early in the game to see how the offense is trying to account for them. Most of the players we have in these positions are 4.6 or better. They can get to the quarterback in a hurry.

Our blitz system is simple. When I began to learn this defense from research and other coaches, I had to learn the terminology that went with the blitz schemes. They all had names, and I knew the players would have trouble with remembering the different stunts. We play with many resource players in our defense. They are special-needs students in school. They need special attention in the classroom.

I knew I had to come up with a simple way to call our blitzing game to keep the players from getting confused. In this defense, you must bring pressure from a blitzing scheme. It is not a straight-up defense. You must move and confuse blocking assignments, or you will not survive in this front. I wanted to run many blitzes and keep it simple for them.

The way I did it was to number the linebackers (Diagram #3). We numbered the linebackers from left to right. The only people who had to think at all were the outside linebackers because they flipped from side to side. If the Tomahawk was on the left side of the defense, he was #1. If he was on the right side of the defense, he was #5.

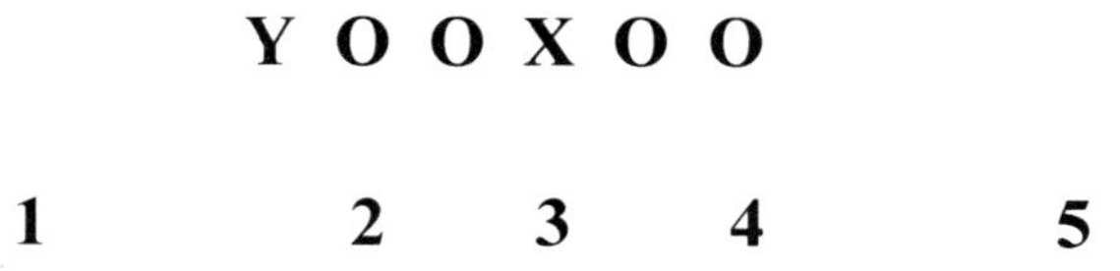

Diagram #3. Linebacker Numbering

The inside linebacker are #2, #3, and #4. If we call "24," the Sam and Whip linebacker blitz straight ahead. They blitz the opposite gap of the down linemen movement. If the blitz call is "left 24," the defensive line slants to the left, and the Sam linebacker blitzes his B gap (Diagram #4). The Whip linebacker knows the Rover goes inside and he blitzes the C gap.

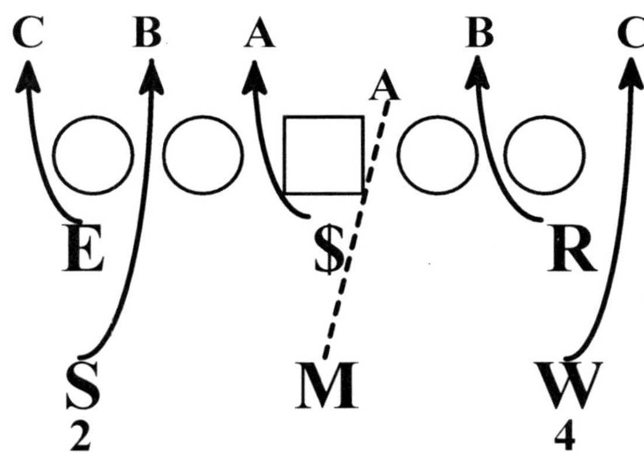

Diagram #4. Left 24

This allows us to call a limitless amount of stunts and not confuse our linebackers. We can call double numbers or triple numbers. We can call hundreds of blitz and stunt combinations. If we call "pinch 15," the defensive ends slant to the inside gaps, and the Stud slants into the right A gap. The "15" call gives us a double outside linebacker blitz off the edge. The defensive ends play the B gaps, and the outside linebackers are C-gap players.

An example of a three-digit call is "out 234" (Diagram #5). On this blitz, the defensive ends slant outside, and the Stud slants to the left A gap. The "234" call sends all three inside linebackers. The Sam and Whip linebacker blitz the B gap to their side and the Mike linebacker blitzes the right A gap.

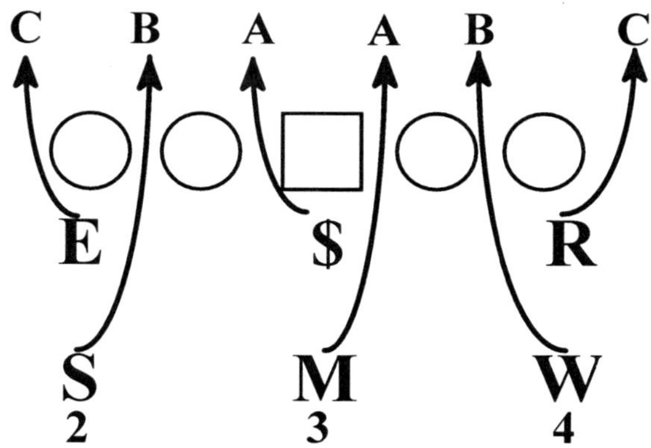

Diagram #5. Out 234

The players are playing at full speed and not trying to think where they are supposed to go. In the defense, you either blitz or drop into your coverage responsibility. We created many turnovers with the pressure we bring.

In our game planning each week, we may assign a mark to an offensive player. If the offense has a running back that we mark, that means to hit him on every blitz involving him. We run past all other defenders. We do not want to contact a blocker unless absolutely necessary.

We had two teams on our schedule that ran a double wing formation with two tight ends. In the last three years, I have not substituted linemen for my players. I want the speed on the field. If you do not see double wing in this area, you will soon. It is like a disease. It travels.

When we play these teams, we keep all the base players in the game. We have a smallish lineup, but we depend on speed to be the equalizer. The Tomahawk and Patriot linebackers walk up tight to the line of scrimmage on the outsides of the wing players (Diagram #6). They come off the edge, looking for the fullback on the power play. They want to wrong-arm him. If they cannot wrong-arm,

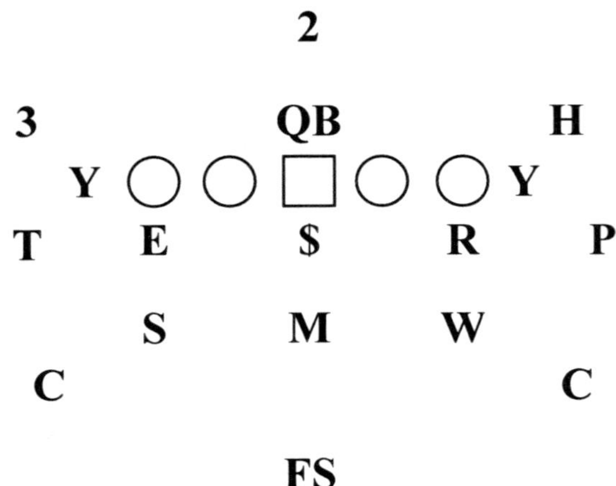

Diagram #6. Double-Wing Adjustment

they fall down and create a pile. If they want to play in a Neanderthal style of play, we do it.

Everyone else aligns in their normal position and runs the stunts and blitzes as normal. We run our stunts and blitzes off the alignment on the field or by their motion scheme. That is a game planning decision that we can automatic. The Mike linebacker makes the call, when he sees the motion.

When we played Northgate High School, they were 8-0 at the time. They ran the double wing formation. Our offense did not touch the ball until two minutes to go in the first quarter. We kicked off, and they hit us with a big play-action pass on the first play of the game. They onside kicked the kickoff and recovered. They hit a long play-action pass, but only got a field goal out of that possession. They onside kicked and recovered again. They got another field goal, and we were down 12-0 and had not run an offensive play. We made some adjustments on defense and won the game 78-12.

Since we play with smaller players, our tackles are gang tackles. We get people to the football. We pursue and swarm the ball. If the wing goes in motion, our corners are cross-keying the other side of the formation.

In practice, we coach the Tomahawk and Patriot on two different kinds of blocks. If they run the sweep, the guard pulls and tries to loop around the linebacker. On the power, the fullback comes at the linebacker and tries to kick him to the outside. The angle on the two blocks is different. With the looping guard, the linebacker attacks his outside shoulder. The fullback tries to kick him out, and he attacks the inside shoulder of the fullback. If the wing goes in motion, he looks for the counter coming away from the motion.

If the formation is a triple set, we like to run cover 3 or cover 1 (Diagram #7). The Tomahawk walks out and aligns on the #2 receiver. If we play cover 3, the Tomahawk is a flat/curl dropper. He drops to the short zone to that side. If we play cover 1, he has the #2 receiver in man coverage. To the inside, we want to keep the integrity of the box.

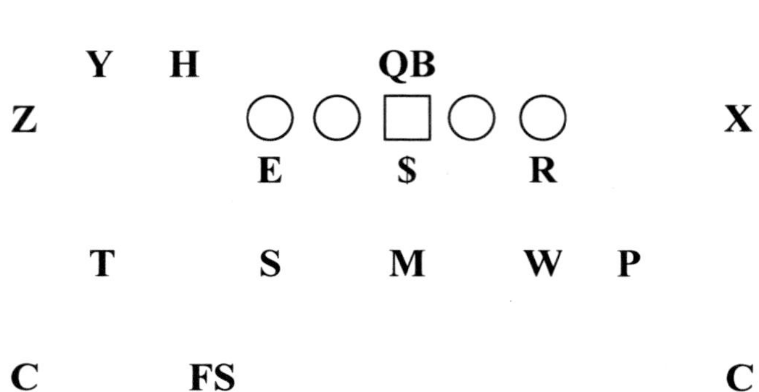

Diagram #7. Trips Formation

If we played a 4-2 defense, the linebacker would be over the guards. This alignment is like the 4-2, even though we stay in the stack position. We rush the three down linemen, and one of the linebackers will come on the blitz to give us four-man pressure. We end up in a 4-2 after they snap the ball.

If the offense empties the backfield, we like to keep two linebackers in the box (Diagram #8). We want to have five defenders in the box. That

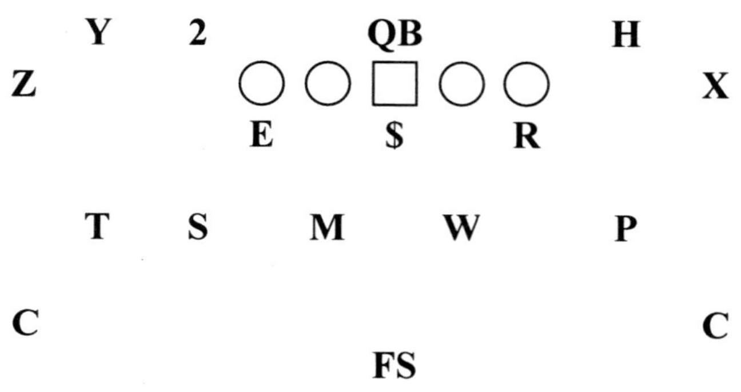

Y 2 QB H
Z X
E $ R
T S M W P
C C
FS

Diagram #8. Empty

keeps two linebackers in the box to defend the quarterback run. With the 3x2 formation, we adjust to the three-receiver side, as we did in the trips set. To the two-receiver side, we walk the Patriot out to cover the second receiver to the weakside. We can play cover-3 zone or go to a cover-1 man-free scheme.

The other alternative we had to the weakside was to expand the Patriot over the slot receiver to that side and play cover 4 or quarter coverage. The Patriot and corner play a cover-4 zone on the slot and wide receivers. They key the slot receiver and play according to what he does.

This year, our Sam linebacker was capable of moving back to the hash. He could play that seam better than the Patriot could. If we pulled the Sam linebacker back to the hash, the free safety moved over into the other half field and the Patriot moved into the Sam position. Next year, we may have to do something different, but we will figure it out.

If we get hurt with the running quarterback in the empty set, we bring the third linebacker back into the box and play the quarterback for the run. When we do that, we give up the bubble screen and the hitch patterns, but we will run those plays down with our speed.

The offense will try to overload the three-man front and outflank the linebacker (Diagram #9). The offense can put an offensive lineman over in the formation or move a tight end or blocking back into a wing set outside the tight end. If the offense unbalances the blocking side, we can do two different things. The first thing we can do is overshift the front, and everyone moves over one man in his defensive alignment.

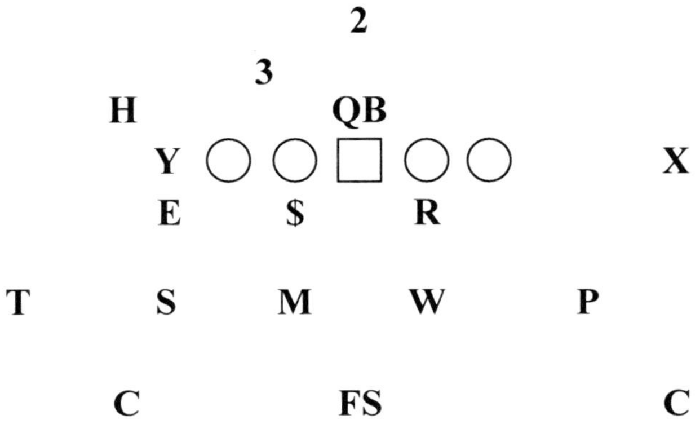

Diagram #9. Overload Shift (Base)

If we overshift the defensive line, we play our base defense, and nothing changes with the stunts, line movements, or blitzes. We do the same thing, except we do it from one gap beyond the center.

The second way we play the overload is to blitz into the overload. We call the blitz "thunder and lightning." Lightning is a left direction for the blitzing linebackers (Diagram #10). Thunder is a right blitz. However, we did not run the gap exchange blitz. The linebackers blitzed over one gap. The Sam linebacker and the Eagle end in a gap exchange blitz, switch gaps. On an out movement by the end and a blitz by the Sam linebacker, the Sam linebacker blitzed B gap and the end slants into the C gap.

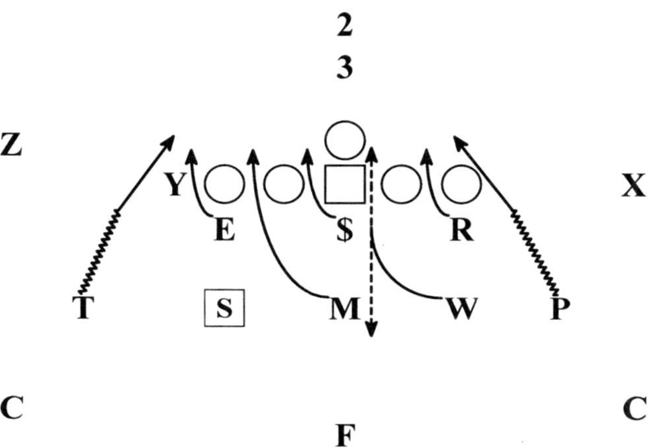

Diagram #10. Lightning

In a lightning blitz, the Eagle slants into the C gap, but the Mike linebacker blitzing over one gap fills the B gap. The Stud nose slants into the left A gap. The Whip linebacker blitzes into the backside A gap, and the Rover end slants into the backside B gap. The Tomahawk on flow to him is the D-gap player. The Sam linebacker has no gap and is a free-hitter.

The Sam linebacker is a freelance defender. If the ball runs in his direction, he can fill inside or outside, depending on how the Tomahawk plays. If the Tomahawk were to spill the play to the outside, the Sam linebacker is in position to make that play. If the play is a play-action pass, he locks on the tight end or #2 receiver to that side. The thunder stunt is the same thing going to the right. In that case, the Whip linebacker is the free-hitter.

The Sam and Whip linebackers know when they are free. On the snap of the ball, they may want to shuffle back to stay out of the traffic. It also gives him a good look at the #2 receiver.

This stunt brings the down linemen and the linebacker in the same direction. We like to run the thunder and lightning against a bunched set or a tight wing set. If the offense aligns with 21 personnel, we can run the lightning stunt to the tight end. If that is the tendency of the offense, we can run the thunder and lightning as a regular stunt. It does not have to be an overload.

This year, I did less coaching than I ever have. In 2004, when we took over here, I coached my butt off, and we went 1-9. This year, I coached considerably less than I did in 2004, and we went 13-1 and won the state championship. When you have better players who have experience, you do not need to work as hard. At least you can put your efforts into improving other parts of the scheme.

When you have better players, you coach them less so you do not mess them up. I let them play and make plays. The group we had this year were instinctive players.

We have teams that use a super-overload. They have a tight end set with two wings outside the tight end. We call the "Lion" stunt (Diagram #11). The adjustment to this set is a combination of the overshift and lightning stunt. We move the down linemen over one full man and run a lightning stunt into the overload. The offense has created so many gaps to one side that we have to overshift the front and slant into the overload.

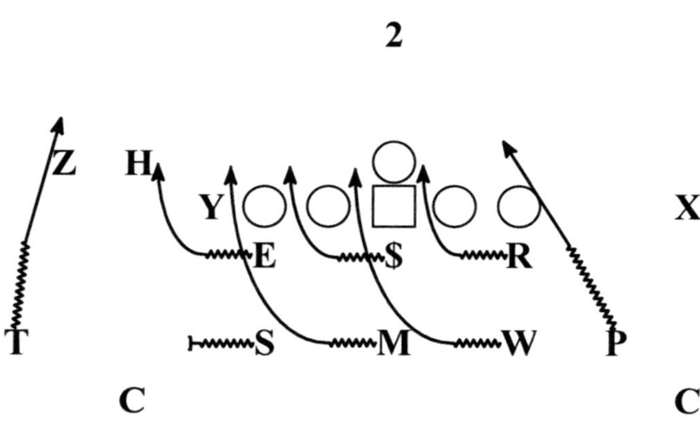

Diagram #11. Lion

If we need to call the front to the other side, we call "Tiger." We have a tight end and two leverage blockers to the outside. We have to get the bodies in that direction. I start teaching my Mike linebackers at the beginning of the year to recognize this set. If they do not adjust to it the first time the offense runs it, we may have to call a time-out to get them on the right page.

When you play thunder and lightning, you have to be sound to the backside if the offense runs the counter play (Diagram #12). When we run thunder or lightning, the linebackers involved with the stunt have a key as they start the stunt. Whatever the opponent does in their counter play, we give our linebackers a blocker to key. It could be the frontside tackle or guard. If we run the lightning stunt, the Whip and Mike linebackers are running the over blitzes. They read the frontside guard and tackle as they start the blitz path. On the third step, they will know where to go.

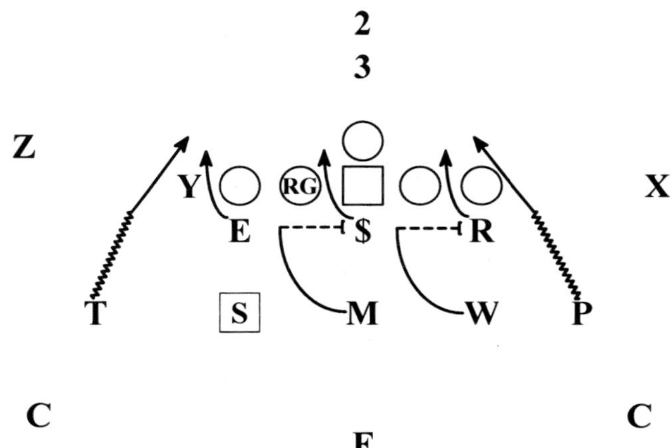

Diagram #12. Lightning Counter

If the guard or tackle pulls toward them, they redirect their charges on the third step. The Whip linebacker redirects back into the C gap to his side, and the Mike linebacker redirects into the backside A gap. The Rover end slants into the B gap and plays football. We have the Mike in the A gap, Rover in the B gap, Whip linebacker in the C gap, and the Patriot comes up on the outside in the D gap. The Sam linebacker is to the side of the stunt. When the action counters to the backside, he plays the frontside B gap for the cutback and pursues.

We drill this redirection every day in practice, and they have gotten good at the technique. We can be ultra-aggressive to the frontside and prepared to play the counter if it occurs. We were not very good at the redirect when we started doing it. When we worked on it and were persistent in the training, we became very good at that action. Some of our linebackers are so good at reading the counter, they see it on the first step of the guard. It does not look like a lightning stunt because they read it so quickly.

We see the triple option from the opponents we play (Diagram #13). I like to bring the Tomahawk up on the line of scrimmage and let him take the dive back in the outside veer. The Sam linebacker to that side has the quarterback, which is hard for him. The dive back comes right up in his face. If he takes the dive, the quarterback pulls the ball, and we are in trouble.

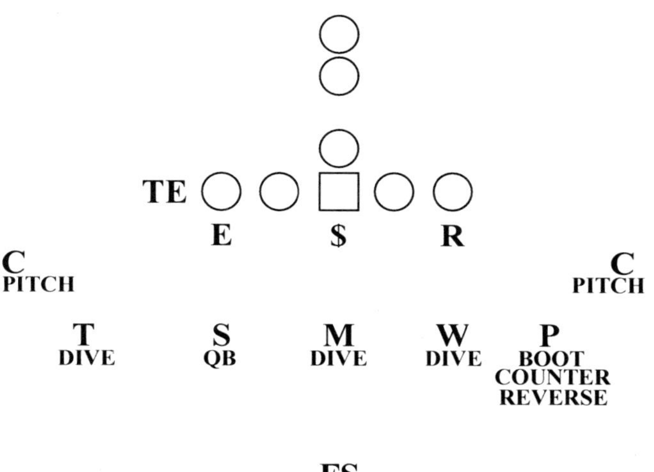

Diagram #13. Triple Option

You have to drill that into the Sam and Whip linebackers. The corner to that side has the pitchback. If they run the ball on an inside veer play, the Mike linebacker and backside linebacker play the dive. The Patriot to the backside plays the bootleg, counter, and reverse.

The secret to playing a triple option team is not to wait to the week you play them to work on the triple option. You must prepare all during the season if you have an option team on your schedule. We run triple option drill weekly. Preparation is the key for playing an option team. The defense must play assignment football.

In the championship game, I coached against a coach who has run the triple option longer than I have been alive. Someone told me he would figure out what we do by game time. He was right. He scored on his first two drives. In the game, there were seven lead changes. We ended up winning the game in a two-minute drill at the end of the game. We won 40-37.

We have a hammer call we use in a passing situation or if we want to lock up a star receiver. The hammer call is a man-under press technique by the Tomahawk and Sam linebacker. We press the wide receiver and slot with the Tomahawk and Sam linebacker and play a cover-3 corner behind them. We can play double hammer or use the hammer call for one receiver. If we call "hammer 85," we play press-man coverage on #85 and play a deep zone behind it.

The hammer call makes the quarterback hold the ball. When he holds the ball, our rush can get to him. We ran it twice in the championship and got two sacks. If I want to pressure on third down or double-team a receiver, I call the defense.

When we blitz, there are holes all over the coverage. However, we blitz fast people, and the quarterback does not have time to find those holes. They get into the quarterback's face quickly.

In practice, when our players get lazy and show their blitzes, I stop that immediately. If they show their blitzes, the offense blocks them. Blitzing from depth is good, but may not be good enough to get home. We bluff the blitz. When we show blitz, we always want to fake where we are not going. If they come up to the right side of a blocker, they will blitz to the left side. We must practice all those bluffs. When they tip or start early, I stop them and tell them, "Show me later." They understand what I want.

If we play cover 3, the corners come up into a press alignment. When the quarterback gets under the center or starts to call for the ball in the shotgun, the corners bail out into their third. We try to keep the offense honest with our disguises. Disguise is like a skill, and you must work on it in practice.

We are like any other high school program. If we have athletes who can play man coverage, we play it. This year, we played about 80 percent zone coverage. We had good corners, but they doubled at wide receiver and were more interested in catching the ball than playing defense.

Shawn Cutright

THE 50 ANGLE/SLANT DEFENSE

Colerain High School, Ohio

We call our defense the "angle 50," which we use to stop the run. When we try to get pressure on the passer, we call it our "six-pack." I am an old defensive coach who loves to sack the quarterback. When we go to the six-pack, my main objective is to defend the pass for about two seconds. After that time, four or five defenders had better get to the quarterback. If they do not, they will be watching the game from the sideline.

Colerain High School is in Cincinnati, Ohio and we have about 1000 boys in the school. I will go over the angle versus the six-pack. I want to talk about our defensive needs, calls, and techniques. If you have questions, shout them out and I will answer any I can.

WHY WE PLAY THE 50 DEFENSE

- Advantageous to our players—speed
- Difficult to get a pre-snap read
- Easy to adjust to power and spread
- Flexibility to change players
- Ability to run multiple coverages
- Keeps offense off balance with ability to angle

I came to Colerain several years ago when Kerry Coombs was there. We have players that love to play the game. We have to keep it as simple as possible. I want them to run fast and knock the crap out of somebody in the process. The scheme is flexible and we can adjust and run a few different coverages. Our alignment varies with our defensive line and the outside linebackers. In my opinion, the most important part of our defense is our outside linebacker. We want players on the field that make plays.

Our alignment for the defensive line is the old 50 defensive front (Diagram #1). The nose is head-

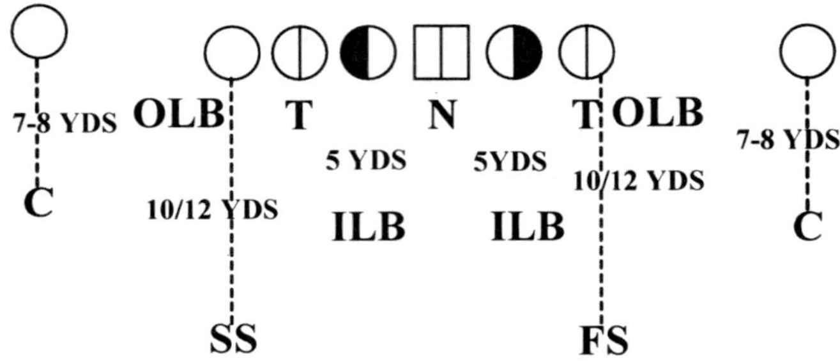

Diagram #1. 50 Angle Defense

up the center, and the defensive tackles align on the tackles. The tackles will angle almost every time. We very seldom play them straight. We want to move and use our speed. The linemen we play against are 280 to 290 pounds. We will not be as powerful or as physical as they are, but we will be faster. We move and cover gaps. We do not want them to know where we are going.

DEFENSIVE LINE—ANGLE DEFENSE

- Pass/run, reads guards to tackle
- Angles fast
- Ability to redirect quickly
- Plays flat on the line of scrimmage
- Takes up blockers so linebackers can run free
- Straight tackle sets the edge
- Angle tackle is a B-gap defender
- Tackles line up head-up on tackles
- Nose lines up head-up on center

We play with an *angle tackle* and a *straight tackle*. The angle tackle is a B-gap defender. The nose is an A-gap defender. The straight tackle sets the edge, depending on the way we angle. Through game planning, we decide what we are going to do.

DEFENSIVE LINE—ANGLE DEFENSE STANCE

- Modified linebacker stance (four-point)
- Hands barely touching the ground
- Heels in the dirt
- Feet
  - ✓ Parallel
  - ✓ Under arms
  - ✓ Weight on balls of feet

The stance is a modified linebacker stance. It is a four-point, but it has very little weight on their hands. We want them to get their feet about shoulder width. We want their hands down and the back flat. We want them to be able to move when they take off. If the tackle slants inside, he takes a 45-degree angle step through the *V* of the guard's neck. He aims for the onside foot of the center. The noseguard slants with an aiming point at the inside foot of the offensive tackle to the side he slants.

DEFENSIVE LINE—ANGLE DEFENSE TECHNIQUE

- Angle tackle
  - ✓ First step should be a 45-degree angle step with the inside foot through guard's neck to center's shoulder
  - ✓ Rips through the offensive person with opposite arm
- Nose
  - ✓ First step should be a 45-degree angle step with the inside foot through guard's neck to inside knee of tackle
  - ✓ Rips through the offensive person with opposite arm
- Straight tackle
  - ✓ First step is a six-inch movement straight ahead with outside foot
  - ✓ He sets the edge as a contain type player

We want the movement of the defensive line to take care of the front five blockers. We do not want any of the offensive linemen to get to the inside or outside linebackers. We want the TNT to control the offensive line from getting off the line of scrimmage. The thing we preach to the defensive line is to play flat-and-angle defense. We do not want them to penetrate and get upfield even if they can.

We want them to stay flat to the line of scrimmage. If they run the zone play away from the defender, he stays flat and runs it down. If the zone play comes to the defender, he redirects and plays crossface of the blocker. We do not teach running around the blocker. In our alignment, we are off the ball. We are from three-quarters to a yard off the ball. We very seldom jump offside. We may flinch, but we do not jump into the neutral zone.

We were fortunate enough to have a big noseguard this year. He was 6'6" and 330 pounds. He played great run defense but he was not very good at rushing the passer. When he rushes the passer, he has one move. He bull rushed the quarterback. When we run the six-pack scheme, we substitute for him. We put in a smaller player that could pass rush.

DEFENSIVE LINE—SIX-PACK

- Frequently utilize this into a package
- Reduce angles and press upfield more
- Move to three-point stance
- Nose alignment is still over center
- Tackles
  - ✓ Move to outside shade or completely outside the offensive tackle
  - ✓ Outside foot up, so power step is inside to reduce space
- If guard gives you his face, cross it; if he gives you his hip, you push upfield

In the six-pack package, we reduce the angles of the defensive line. We push up the field and do not stay as flat to the line of scrimmage. As soon as the defender gets to his gap, he penetrates and gets up the field. We align them in a three-point stance and we allow them to align wider. They align on the outside shoulder of the offensive tackle and in a wide split; they are one yard outside the offensive tackle.

The inside linebackers have the quarterback on the option. They make all the calls for the front seven. We have an automatic check to adjust to the look the offense shows. If the offense aligns in a pro formation with two backs, we check and go to the angle defense. If they come to the line and align in a double slot formation, we check, drop the ends off, and go straight to the six-pack look. We feel like from that set, they pass the ball 95 percent of the time.

The inside linebackers have to get us in the right call. They come in every week and watch extra film. They spend more time with me and must know all the checks we plan to use. If we play a zone team and the outside linebacker has the angle tackle, he may have to fill inside the tight end if they wash the tackle to the inside. If that happens, the outside linebacker fills inside and the inside linebacker plays over the top of him. They have to know they can mesh like that in that situation.

INSIDE LINEBACKERS—ANGLE DEFENSE TECHNIQUE

- Bench linebacker
  - ✓ Better at blitzing and filling isolation
  - ✓ Must be aware of the tight end and possible route combinations
  - ✓ Align outside shade of guards
  - ✓ Eyes on keys
  - ✓ Feet
    - ⇨ Parallel
    - ⇨ Under arms
    - ⇨ Weight on balls of feet
    - ⇨ Hands off knees
- Field linebacker
  - ✓ Better at coverage and running down outside zone/sweeps
  - ✓ Same as bench linebacker

The inside linebackers align at a depth of five yards. It does not matter whether we are in the six-pack or angle defense. They play an outside shade on the offensive guards. The *bench linebacker* is more physical and the better on the run. The *field linebacker* is more of a pass coverage defender. He runs well and can run down sweeps and zone plays.

The linebackers read the guards. If the guard pulls, they flow and fill over the top. If the guard blocks down, the linebacker fills and spills everything to the outside. We do not want anyone cutting up against us. We spill everything to the outside and run it down. We want everyone running to the sideline, and we feel our outside linebackers and safeties are good enough to make plays.

We are predominately a cover 3 team with the strong safety rolling down. He makes a ton of tackles. The inside linebacker reads run to pass. They play run first. One of those linebackers is the fourth rusher on the zone pressure package. If we can get pressure with four rushers, that is what we send. If it takes five to get pressure, I send five defenders. Fortunately, this year, four or five worked well in getting pressure. However, two years ago I had to send six to get pressure.

Two years ago, Princeton High School had a quarterback named Spencer Ware. He played running back for Louisiana State University this year as a true freshman. There was no way I wanted him to have any running lanes whatsoever. I brought pressure with six rushers about 85 percent of the time. They ran the midline and he liked to scramble to the weakside. That is how we dealt with him and his scrambling ability.

The outside linebackers on the angle defense are the most versatile and athletic players you have. They make most of the plays in this defense. We had a middle linebacker last year that was good. His name is Joe Bolden and happens to be the nephew of our head coach, Tom Bolden. I am moving him to outside linebacker next year and am going to take advantage of his playmaking ability. I want him coming off the edge and making plays in space.

OUTSIDE LINEBACKER—ANGLE DEFENSE

- Run/pass reads through tackle to quarterback
- Most athletic and versatile athlete
- Lines up on line of scrimmage
- Lines up on tight end almost all the time
- Tough enough to take on power runs
- Knowledgeable about alignment and formations

The outside linebacker lines up on the line of scrimmage against every set. It does not matter if it is trips or double slot. If there is a tight end, he aligns on the tight end. We have a bench and field outside linebacker.

- Strongside linebacker
  - ✓ Lines up over tight end
  - ✓ Eyes on keys
  - ✓ Plays better to powerside

- ✓ Alignment (feet)
  - ⇨ Splits crotch with inside foot
  - ⇨ Inside foot forward
  - ⇨ Weight on balls of feet
  - ⇨ Hands in a good defensive position
- ✓ Steps
  - ⇨ Inside foot jab-step into tight end
  - ⇨ Do not stand up, stay low
  - ⇨ Engage tight end shoving him inside to close gap and keep outside leverage

The fieldside linebacker was not as physical and had trouble playing over the tight end. He is more suited to playing in space and coverage. Teams last year aligned and traded the tight end. We ran with them and realigned on him. If they went to two tight ends, we walked the safety to that side down and helped the field linebacker with run coverage.

- Weakside linebacker
  - ✓ Lines up in space usually apex of #1 and #2 receiver
  - ✓ Eyes on keys
  - ✓ Plays better in space
  - ✓ Alignment (feet)
    - ⇨ Parallel stance on line of scrimmage
    - ⇨ Weight on balls of feet
    - ⇨ Hands in a good defensive position
  - ✓ Chase/tuck
    - ⇨ Rush linebacker chases down plays away when he has an angle tackle
    - ⇨ Off linebacker tucks when he has straight tackle on plays away

In his technique, the chase/tuck is the most important thing he does. If he is on the left and the angle of the line is right, he becomes a chase player off the backside because he is coming off the edge. If he has a straight tackle to his side and the flow goes away from him, he is a tuck-and-cutback player. He plays the cutback or reverse or any play coming back. He slow plays off the backside and does not chase the ball. It is easier to play chase and run after the ball than it is to tuck behind a tackle and slow play.

When the outside linebackers play in the six-pack, they are five yards off the ball at the inside linebacker depth. I want the outside linebackers to hit the line of scrimmage running as fast as they can. We want a linebacker running by a tackle trying to kick-slide outside to block him. They are curl/flat defenders. We know we are weak in the flat area. We will let the offense throw quick outs for a while. If they start to hurt, we roll the coverage and shut it off. We know the weakness is the three-step pass, but we have an answer to stop it.

We play with strong and weak safeties and corners. It should not matter because they do the same things. However, if the personnel fits, flip-flop them. Last year, we could go either way, but we were better when our strong safety rolled down and the free safety was in the middle. We have one player in the secondary to make all the calls. If he is wrong, who cares? The free safety makes all the calls and checks. He is the only one allowed to make the calls. That keeps everyone on the same page. The alignment of the free safety is between 10 to 12 yards.

The strong safety creeps down to seven to eight yards, plays hot on the #2 receiver, and is a curl/flat defender. He is the force play on a run to him and a cutback play on flow away from him. He is also involved with a big part of the blitz game.

The corners align at seven to eight yards and have a primary responsibility. They cannot get beat deep. They do not get involved with run support much, but they can with a defensive call.

To set the angle of the nose and angle tackle we use tight, split, field, or bench. The tight call goes to the tight end. That is the direction of the angle. If the call is tight right, the angle of the line is right (Diagram #2). The right tackle plays a straight technique. He takes a six-inch step into the tackle and reads the guard to his side. If the guard pulls,

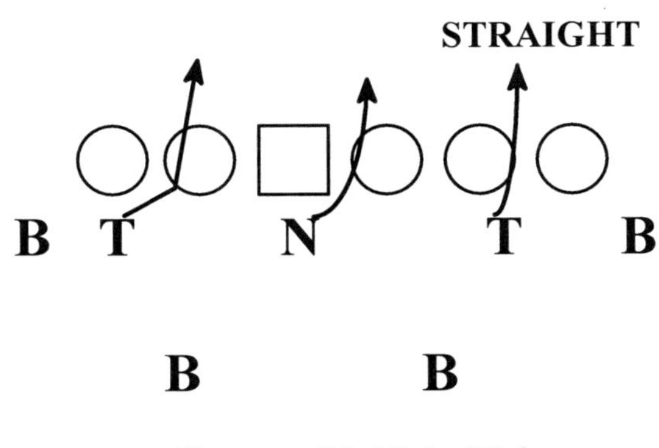

Diagram #2. Tight Right

he gets in the hip pocket and chases down the line of scrimmage. If he feels the tackle giving ground in a pass set, he jumps to the outside and has a contained rush.

The split call goes away from the tight end. We make the call in the huddle. When the offense comes to the line, the linebackers make both calls as a dummy call. If we call field or bench, it does not matter where the tight end aligns. We do not check out of a field or bench call. We can check out of tight or split calls if the offense is a trips set or unbalanced line. We only call the field and bench call from the hash mark.

If we call "crash," that is an aggressive stunt for the slanting linemen; they go two gaps instead of one (Diagram #3). If the angle tackle crashes, he goes all the way to the A gap. The tackle takes the guard into the A gap if he tries to get off the line. He uses the guard's body or his body to close the A gap. The outside linebacker slants into the B gap. The inside linebacker becomes the contain player on this movement. The nose goes from head-up the center to the B gap.

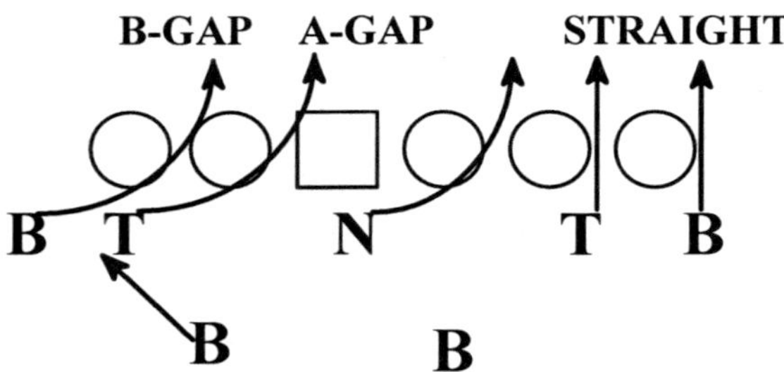

Diagram #3. Crash

The coaching point is for the inside linebacker. He has to fill the C gap and cannot bubble off the ball. He has to come straight into the C gap and not create a bubble. We never run the split crash. That slants the line away from the tight end and creates a problem in the C gap. If the outside linebacker has a tight end in front of him, we do not bring him on an inside blitz.

MOVEMENT CALLS—ANGLE DEFENSE

- Bird
  - ✓ Stunt where angle tackle and outside linebacker switch responsibility
- Double crash
  - ✓ Short-yardage call
  - ✓ Nose plays straight
- Double bird
  - ✓ Nose plays straight
- Pinch
  - ✓ Angle both sides
  - ✓ Nose plays straight

The bird movement involves the angle tackle and outside linebacker (Diagram #4). The tackle instead of slanting comes up the field and the linebacker blitzes the B gap.

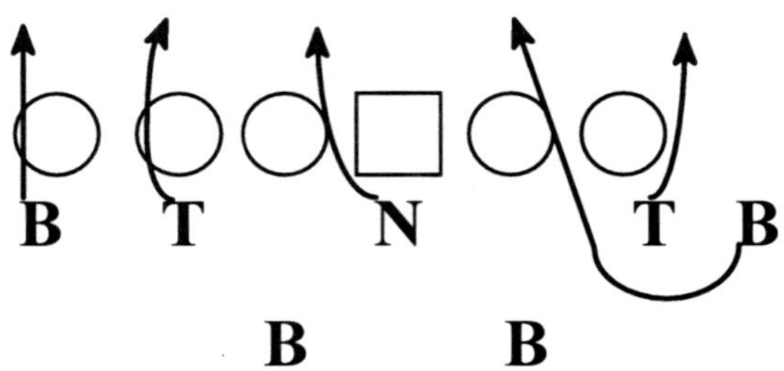

Diagram #4. Bird

In the double crash, both sides run the crash movement. If we get into a short-yardage situation with a double tight end formation, we check out of that and pinch (Diagram #5). On the pinch call, both sides pinch and the inside linebacker works outside. The nose, on the double call, plays straight up the center. The tackles come into the B gaps and the outside linebacker slants into the C gap. On the stunt, the inside linebacker flows with the action of the backs to the outside and makes the tackle. In short-yardage, we run more double crash than pinch.

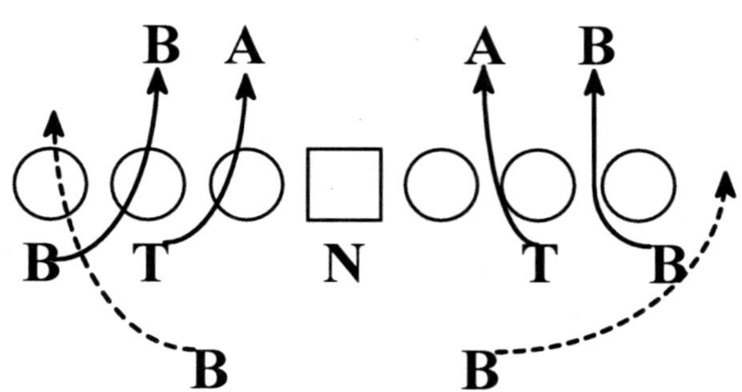

Diagram #5. Pinch

We have blitz calls we use. Some examples are "tight lighting" (Diagram #6). The angle of the line is to the tight end. The openside tackle and linebacker run a crash stunt. The safety cheats down and comes from the outside on this call.

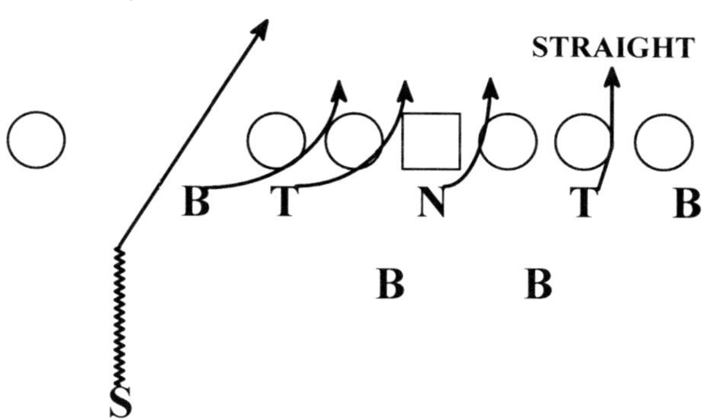

Diagram #6. Tight Lightning

In our base defense, if we angle to the right, the left outside linebacker comes off the edge for contain away from the angle. The straight tackle is the containment to the right. The field smoke is like a double end call (Diagram #7). The slant goes to the field. We bring the strong safety off the edge from the field. The straight tackle angles into the B gap. The boundary outside linebacker comes for containment away from the call, and the field safety comes off the edge. It is five-man pressure.

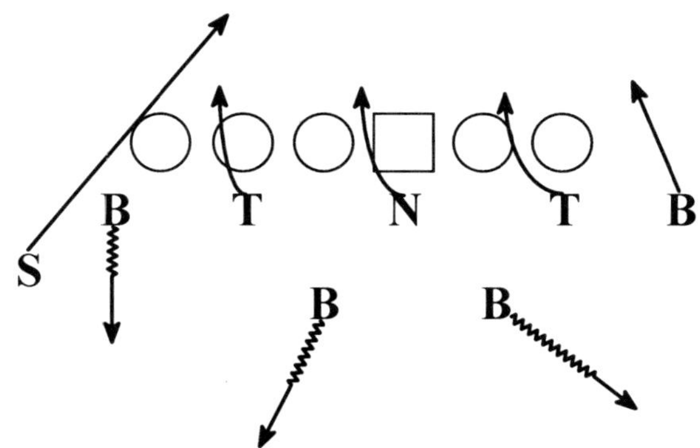

Diagram #7. Field Smoke

The "go" and "shoot" are blitz calls for our inside linebackers (Diagram #8). The go blitz sends the linebacker to the side of the call through the B gap.

The shoot call sends the inside linebacker through the A gap (Diagram #9). If the direction call is left. The right linebacker blitzes the A gap to his side.

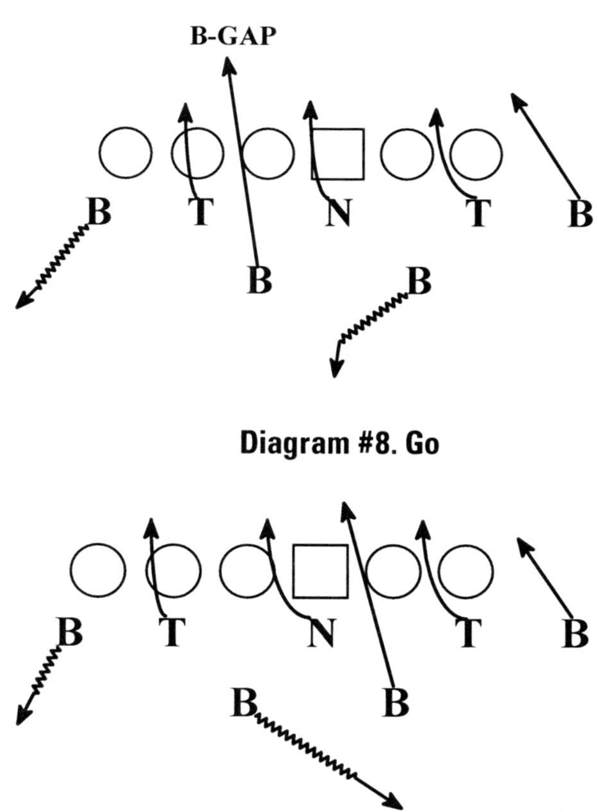

Diagram #8. Go

Diagram #9. Shoot

The go is in front of the angle and the shoot is behind the angle of the line. On the go call, the nose has to cut his angle so he does not collide with the linebacker going into the B gap. On the shoot call, the angle tackle has to do the same thing. He cannot run into the linebacker going through the A gap.

The four-man pressure game gets in to the six-pack scheme. The difference between the angle and the six-pack is the alignment of the outside linebacker and the tackles. The outside linebacker is five yards off the line of scrimmage and slightly wider. The tackles are wider in their alignments. The tackles in the six-pack scheme are primary contain defenders.

OUTSIDE LINEBACKER—SIX-PACK

- Pass/run reads through tackle to quarterback
- Must cover well in space
- Alignment varies for most formations—five yards of ball
- Coverage curl/flat
- Hold curl until inside linebacker gives go call

- Lines up on tight end in single width and sometimes when tight end is #2 receiver
- Is in motion and timing up blitzes to hit line of scrimmage full speed

When we use four-man pressure from the six-pack scheme, it is similar to the angle package. In the shoot, the linebackers run the stunt in A gap, but the angle tackle does not angle. If we call "end" with four-man pressure, the angle tackle and nose run their angle scheme and the outside linebacker away from the angle direction comes up the field for containment. He comes from five yards off the line of scrimmage. The bird stunt is the same as from the angle defense.

We run a four-man pressure called "fire" (Diagram #10). The noseguard and backside linebacker run through the A gaps. If the direction call is to the left, the nose goes to the left A gap, and the left inside linebacker runs through the right A gap.

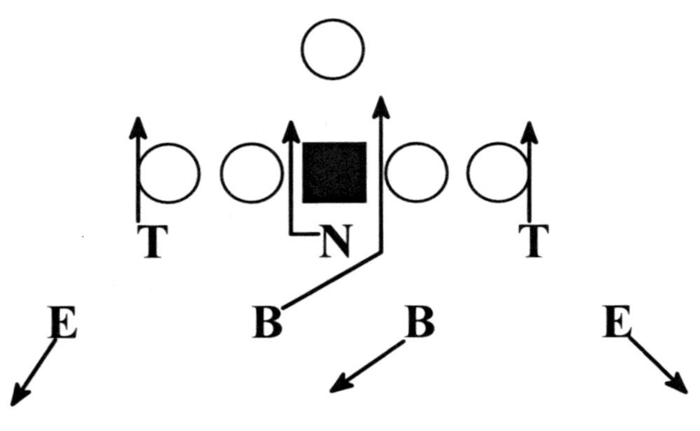

Diagram #10. Fire

In the six-pack scheme, we have a five-man scheme. We call this one "fire bird" (Diagram #11). This is a combination stunt. We run the "bird" call away from the direction call and the "fire" to the side of the call. The tackles are upfield for containment. The nose goes in the direction of the call and the linebacker from that side blitzes the backside A gap. Away from the call, the outside linebacker blitzes the B gap.

The coverage is cover 3 with the strong safety coming down into the strong flat/curl area. The free safety rotates into the middle of the field and the corners play the outside thirds. The bench outside

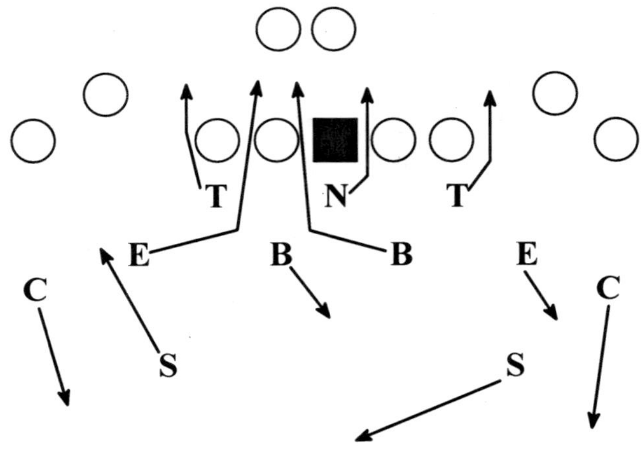

Diagram #11. Fire Bird

linebacker plays the boundary curl/flat area and the inside linebacker drops to the middle hook.

Another combination blitz we like is the shoot/end (Diagram #12). In the diagram, the angle charge is to the right. We run the shoot blitz with the inside linebacker in the A gap. The left outside linebacker blitzes off the edge from depth. The strong safety comes down and covers for the outside linebacker and we roll the secondary into cover 3.

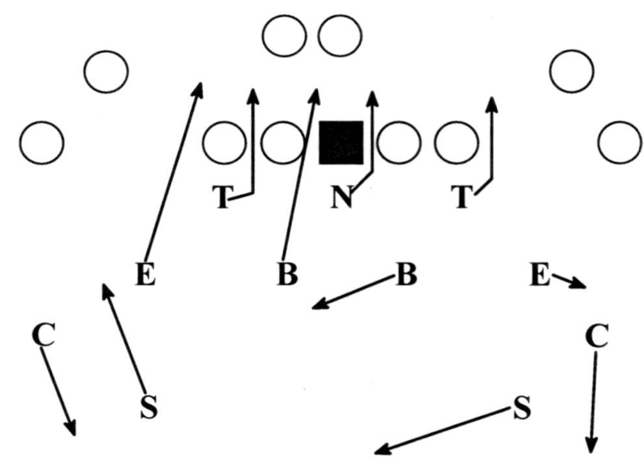

Diagram #12. Shoot/End

One of our best blitzes is "bolt" (Diagram #13). The direction of the angle is right. The left tackle goes two gaps into the A gap. The left inside linebacker comes off his butt into the B gap. The outside linebacker comes screaming off the edge. The nose slants in to the direction side A gap and the straight tackle moves up the field for containment. We can run a switch with this blitz. If we call the

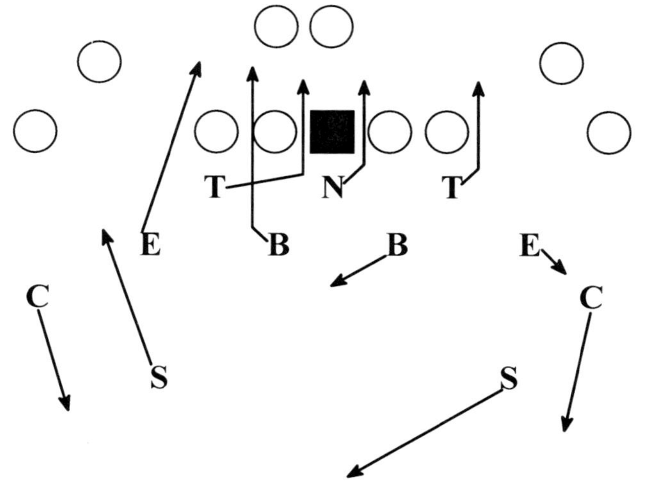

Diagram #13. Bolt

switch, the outside linebacker blitzes the B gap and the inside linebacker comes behind him off the edge.

When we roll the strong safety down to replace the outside linebacker, he comes down on the #2 receiver. We do not collision anything inside five yards from the line of scrimmage. If the receiver is over five yards, we want the strong safety to apply heavy pressure on the receiver. If #2 goes vertical, the strong safety runs with him. If #2 does not go vertical, the strong safety hangs in the curl area until the inside linebacker releases him to go to the flat.

We like to run the "Eagle pick" from the weakside (Diagram #14). The inside linebacker walks up into the line of scrimmage on the outside shoulder of the guard and he blitzes. The tackle takes a good outside charge to the outside of the offensive tackle. The nose goes into the opposite

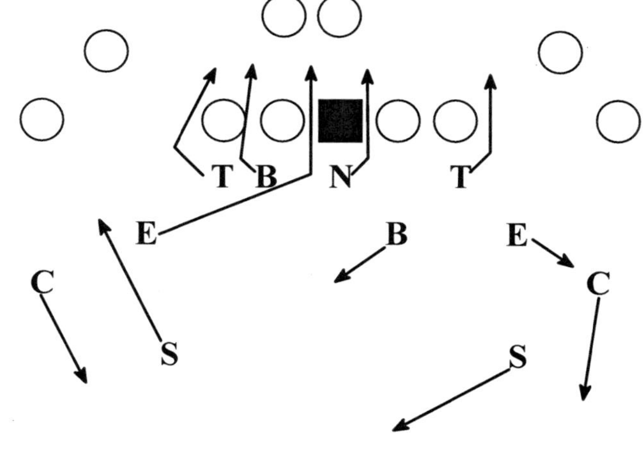

Diagram #14. Eagle Pick

A gap. The outside linebacker aligns on the #2 receiver, cheats back inside, and runs through the A gap. The blocking scheme has trouble finding the A-gap blitz runner. The center usually takes the noseguard pressing to his outside shoulder.

Anytime we hear a max call, the outside linebacker knows he is in coverage. If we hear a safety call, the linebacker knows the safety will replace a linebacker involved in a blitz. If we call a safety bolt, the outside linebacker stays in coverage and the safety blitzes off the edge instead of the outside linebacker. If the quarterback breaks contain, the inside linebackers are the secondary contain players. The outside linebackers and safeties stay in coverage and the inside linebacker goes to get the quarterback.

I appreciate the time. I enjoyed talking to you. If I can help you, send me an email.

David Ettinger

PLACEKICKING AND PUNTING MECHANICS

Garden City High School, New York

Thank you. I have been an assistant coach at Garden City High School since 1999. My credentials are from Hofstra University, where I was the kicker for four years and I was the punter for two years. I am the all-time scorer in a school that does not have a football team any longer. I was hoping someday I could walk out on the field and congratulate someone for breaking my record, but that is not going to happen now that Hofstra does not play football.

I am going to spend the first part of this lecture on placekicking and the second part on punting. I have broken down the kicking and punting into techniques. Is my way the only way? Of course not. I want to cover each phase as general as possible. Every kicker is a little different. When you leave here today, I hope you will have some basics for what you can look for with your kickers and punters that will help them. There are things you can look for when working with the kickers.

I like to compare the kicks to a golf swing. The key to the golf swing is consistency. As many of us know, if you swing one way the first time, and you swing another way the second time, the ball is going to go all over the place. It is the same with kicking. Every kick should look the same. It does not matter if it is a 20-yard extra point or a 50-yard field goal; the technique should be the same. If you had a video of the two kicks, you should not be able to tell if he kicked the first ball on the PAT or the second ball on the field goal. You should not be able to say the kicker put more into the second kick, so that must have been a field goal. On video, the kicks should look the same.

PLACEKICKING

Steps

- Will vary; start with three back, two side
- Make sure side steps are 90 degrees. (We will get back to why later.)
- Stance
- Toe of kicking foot even with heel of plant foot
- Weight forward (fall into kick).
- Kicking foot facing the ball; plant foot placing the plant
- Eyes on block or holder's hand.

The steps will vary, but the three back and two to the side is a good place to start. I tell my players they should start where they are going to plant the foot. If they take the first step with their right foot, it needs to be that same way every single time. If they take the first step with the left foot, that is fine, but it needs to be the same foot every single time. By doing this, you can develop a routine with the kicker. Everything he does on the kick should be the same every time. The more they practice the routine, the better they become. It all comes down to where that plant foot is going to take the kicker. If that spot changes, it makes a difference.

The easy way to make sure the kicker takes the side steps at 90 degrees is to have him put the arm out to the side and to follow his arm. You can make adjustments on the three and two steps, but that is a good place to start the steps.

That takes us to the next area and that is the stance. I am a right-footed kicker. The toe of my kicking foot is my right foot. It is even with the heel of my plant foot, which is my left foot. My right foot is always at the plant, and my kicking foot is always where the ball is going to be. For high school kickers, it is easy to see because they have a block on the mark where the ball goes down. For the college kickers, their toe should be where the holder's hand is on the ground.

The kicker should have his weight on the balls of his feet. He should be ready to go. He does not want to be leaning back. He wants his shoulders leaning forward. His hands should be relaxed and he should be ready to go. He should be able to fall into that first step.

Coaches ask me what the kicker should have his eyes on when he is ready to kick. After the play is set to go, I like to look up at the line again, and then I look at the holder's hands. In college, I would focus on the holder's back hand coming off the ground. It depends a lot on how quick the center is getting the ball back to the holder, and how good he is in getting the ball set for the kick.

I know a lot of high school kickers focus on when the ball is in the hands of the holder. It is a timing factor. A good snap and kick in high school should be successful in 1.5 seconds. Most high school plays on the placekick should be between 1.5 and 1.8; however, the longer it takes, the more the chances are that it will be blocked.

You need to figure out how good your snapper is and how good your holder is in getting the ball down. How good is he from the time he catches it to the time he gets it down to kick? How fast is your kicker? If you have a question on any of these elements, you may have to delay the kick time. You want to have a trigger point.

Approach

- First step is at the ball; stay on toes, not overextended, fall into first step.
- Second step (glide step) to plant, little air time as possible
- Keep hips and shoulders square (railroad tracks).
- Plant.
- One shoe size away from ball
- Two-inch block; toes even with back of block
- Off the ground; ball in middle of foot
- Plant foot must face target.
- Slight lateral lean, head and shoulders over the ball

The first step is toward the ball. This all has to do with hips and shoulders. We want to keep the hips and shoulders square and closed. Once we open them, it is hard to close the hip at contact of the ball. If the kicker takes a step off the track, his hips open too soon. On the second step, not only does he have to plant, but also he has to get the hip closed on contact or the ball is not going to go straight. If we keep everything square and stay on the railroad tracks, the ball should go straight. I want them to glide into the kick.

I tell my players if they follow the routine we establish in practice, even a bad kick is still going to go through the uprights. It is not going to look as pretty as a good kick. If the hips are all over the place, it is hard to get it closed at contact.

The plant foot is important. The plant foot should be one shoe size of the kicker's foot away from the ball (Diagram #1). This is going to matter on the kicks. If the plant is too close to the ball, the kicker will not be able to get through the ball. The right-footed kicker will leave it out to the right. If the plant is too far away from the ball, the kicker will not be able to get through the ball and it is going to the right as well. If the plant is too far back, the kicker brings his hips through the ball and it is going to miss to the left. With a two-inch kicking block used in high school, you want the toes of the kicking foot at the back of the block.

Diagram #1. Foot Position—Placekicks

If your kicker uses a one-inch kicking block, he should bring his toes a tad more. If you have a kicker that kicks the ball without a block, you want his foot in the middle of the spot where the ball is going to be placed.

If the kicker misses his plant foot on the two-inch block, he is going to have a low trajectory. Teams have a lot of soccer players converted to placekickers. I was one of those converted soccer players. They think they have to lean back to get the ball up. This is not what we want. We want the head and shoulders over the ball. You may have a little lean to the side, but you do not want to be leaning to the side to the point you are off balance.

Leg Swing

- Watch foot hit the ball (longer head down the better).
- Toe pointed down, kick with instep of foot.
- Opposite arm coming across the body.
- Skip straight through.
- Target.
- Three to six feet inside right pole for righties.
- First target check should be when block is placed.
- Second target check after steps back.
- Third target check after 90-degree steps to side.
- Hash mark kicks are the same once you get the target.
- Longer distance kick, the more you have to play angle.

The longer the kicker keeps his head down the better. The higher the ball will go if the head stays down. We try to get our kickers to keep their heads down all the way through the kick. Naturally, they want to see where it goes. When I was kicking in college, I could see when I missed a kick I was raising my head too soon. The left shoulder wants to come outside. When coaches yell at kickers to "Keep your head down!" that is the best advice you can give the kickers. It is one of the most important things you could say to the placekickers.

When the kick does not rotate end over end on the kick, it has to do with the flex of the toe. The kicking toe should point down on the kick. If the ball is not going end over end, it is because of the direction the toe is pointing. The problem you may have is the fact that the kicker may also be the quarterback and he does not have the flexibility in the kicking foot that he needs to kick. It may be harder for those types of players to develop that flexibility in the toe.

The opposite arm is important. It locks the shoulder in. If the swing is correct, it will keep the left shoulder down. The kicker cannot pull the shoulder out if he is swinging it across his body.

We want the follow-through to be a smooth skip through on the kick. The kicker needs to develop a consistency in his steps and in the follow-through. Kickers can work on this without kicking a football. They need to be sure they are taking the proper steps and that they follow through on the kicks against air. The more consistent the kickers can be, the more they are going to be successful.

Picking the target is important in kicking the ball through the uprights. There is an actual science to picking a target. For right-footed kickers, you want to aim three to six feet inside the right upright. The ball is naturally going to go from the right to the left. For a PAT, I did not have to aim three to six feet inside the upright. The short kicks are not as hard to aim the kick. Generally speaking, the longer the kick, the more you have to play that right to left movement.

A kick from the hash mark is the same as a kick from the middle of the field, except now you have to change targets. If I am kicking from the right hash mark, the only thing different is the target. I take the three steps back from the block. This is where the 90-degree steps to the side are important. It is one, two, and those are my 90-degree steps. It is not straight across the field. Now, my left foot is at the block; my right foot is at the ball. It is the same kick as the kick from the middle of the field. If we take a video of kicks from the left hash, middle of the field, and right hash, they should all look the same. The only thing different is going to be the angle of the block and it is turning. It is important to teach the kickers how to be successful from the hash marks.

The thing you must do with kickers is to figure out what targets are best for you. The factor to consider is the weather. You use the pre-game warm-up to figure out the weather factors. Each kicker must figure it out so they are comfortable to where their target is from each area of the field.

Another factor to consider in the pre-game is who your kicker is. If he is the best running back you have, you may not want him to kick as much during pre-game. Some kickers do not kick much the day before the games. I did not kick the day before a game. I felt fresher if I took the day off before a game.

We want to make contact with the ball just below the midpoint of the ball. This should happen through the swing. The kicker wants his head to be down and to watch the foot hit the ball. Keep the head down as long as you can after the foot hits the ball. The longer the head is down, and the higher the leg drive, the higher the ball is going to fly. If the kicker picks his head up, the foot hits higher on the ball. As long as the head is down, it should hit on the correct spot.

Most Common Placekicking Mistakes

- Picking the head up
- Opening opposite shoulder
- 90-degree side steps are off
- (follow the arm)
- Plant foot not in the right spot

Drills

- No step, one step
- Extreme angle
- Quick rise
- Rectangle

The first drill is what we call "no step." The ball is on the block, the holder is set up, and the kicker puts his plant foot in the correct spot. The left arm is up, and the kicker kicks the ball. He does not take a step when he kicks the ball. No steps! The ball will not go very far. What we are looking for is for the head to stay down. You are working on the muscle memory to get the motion on the lock on the ball. You close the left arm, and get the tip of the kicking foot through the ball. It is the skip-through.

What you are looking for on the ball is good end-over-end rotation and straight kicks. You do not need to put the kicker in front of the uprights on this drill. Put him on the side or on the endline. See if he can hit the upright from the sideline where he is kicking. Don't put him in front of the goalpost kicking PATs because all he is going to do is try to muscle the ball up over the crossbar. That is not the purpose of the drill.

The one step drill is just one more step. The kicker takes one step back and one step to the side. Everything else is the same. The kicking foot is forward and the plant foot is back. The ball will travel a greater distance now.

This drill is also good for all levels of kickers. If it is a bad snap, or if the holder muffs the ball and has a hard time getting the ball on the block, and the kicker starts his kicking motion, the one step can be effective. If the kicker has been in this spot before, hopefully, he reacts, gets the foot down, and still kicks the ball.

On the extreme angles drill, a good example is for the high school kicker to play on a college field where the goalposts are narrow. It can be intimidating for the kicker in this situation. The width is about six feet different between the high school and college goalpost. It is the same for a college kicker to go to an NFL field to kick. Then, we have the NFL kickers going to arena football, but we will not talk about that.

We work on the extreme kicks by placing the ball on the sideline for the kicks in practice. It is a lot tougher to kick the ball through the goal from the extreme angles. This drill can build the confidence of the kickers if they can practice those kicks before they get into those situations where the goalposts are different. You can challenge them to kick from the five-yard line through the uprights in practice. Then, you can have them kick from the four-, the three-, the two-, and the one-yard line from the side.

On the quick rise drill, we start on the goal line. We use a normal kick and time how quickly they can get the ball up over the line. We practice to see how far they can get the ball up and over the uprights.

Once our kickers are loose, I do not like them to kick from the same spot all of the time. We place a ball on the PAT line, then a ball on the right hash, and five back on each five-yard marker on that hash. We need to know their range of kicking. Some kids can kick form 40 yards, so we place the ball at different spots on the field as far back as the 45-yard line to challenge them on their kicks. Then, we take the ball to the other hash mark and work on bringing the ball back to the 45-yard line. Then, we go back down the middle of the field with the kicks. We do this so they do not end up just kicking PATs in the drills. In high school football, 95 percent of the placekicks are PATs, but you want the kids to have the experience of kicking the field goals, especially from the hash mark as well as the middle of the field. We try to make a rectangle with the drill by moving the ball around on the field.

I am trying to get my kicker stronger by having him come to the weight room. If a kicker can only kick 30 yards, if we can make him stronger, he may be able to kick 40 yards. If a kicker can blast the ball naturally, that is the kid we want kicking.

We consider a kickoff the same kick as a field goal, except it is farther back. The kickoff should not look much different. What I tell my kickers to do is to get a little more aggressive because it does not have to go through the uprights. They may need to develop a little more speed.

We want our kickoff kicker to put the ball on the 40-yard line and take his normal steps to kick the ball deep. Have the individual kicker figure out how many steps he needs to take until he finds the right spot. I may put my hat down on the field when a kid tells me he is comfortable kicking the ball from a certain spot. Have him put a marker of some type to check the steps for his kicks. We may tell the kicker he took nine steps back and three steps to the side on his last kickoff. I may tell the kicker to go eight steps back and three to the side. If he booms it into the end zone, that may just be his spot. In high school, the kickoff tee is two inches high. You want to have the kicker kicking from the kicking tee each time.

If you want to directional kick or kickoff left or right, it is the same as kicking the field goal. It is a matter of changing their target. I personally prefer to kick the ball to the right because the kickers are more accurate. If they miss the kick to the left, they have a tendency to kick the ball out of bounds.

PUNTING

Looking at punting, everyone who punts is unique in that they are all different. All of the NFL punters are a little different. I am going to give a basic description of the punting techniques.

Punting is similar to kicking field goals in that you want consistency. You want to be able to video your punter and see the same mechanics every single time. If you can develop the same mechanics, the punters will be consistent.

Pre-Snap

- Kicking foot back, toes even with heel of nonkicking foot
- Weight on balls of feet
- Feet shoulder width apart
- Upper body relaxed
- Eyes on ball

If I am a right-footed punter, my right foot, which is my kicking foot, is back and the toes are even with the left foot. I am on the balls of my feet, my hands are ready, and I am looking at the football. My feet are shoulder width apart. I want to be as relaxed as possible. I am looking at the snapper. I look for the signal that he is ready to go. It may be a nod of the head or it could be a verbal signal; you can make it whatever you choose. I want to keep my focus on the football. The center snaps the ball to the punter. That leads to the postsnap.

Postsnap

- Catch the ball, turn the ball, put the ball on the table.
- Kicking hand to back of ball, other hand on side (guide hand)
- Some air between ball and hand
- Elbow over kicking thigh

Steps

- First step with kicking foot at center's butt (ball fully extended)
- Second step with plant foot (feet should never cross over)
- Directional punting, change steps

After the snap, the punter must catch the ball, turn the ball, and put the ball on the table. Imagine a table about chest high in front of the punter. The punter catches the ball and places it on the table in the manner he wants to hold the ball immediately after the snap. After the catch of the snap, the punter wants to turn the ball so he will not have to kick the laces of the ball (Diagram #2).

As he turns the ball to the position he wants it, he extends the arms and puts the ball on the table. The kicking hand holds the ball at the back tip. The

Diagram #2. Placement of Hands

opposite hand is a guide hand and is on the front of the ball.

The one big problem high school kids have is that they do not have their arm extended far enough. On the position of the hands, it feels awkward to them. They have to put the ball to the foot. If my elbows are bent, I am going to kick the ball with a bent leg and it is going to go short. I want the elbow of the kicking-side arm fully extended over the kicking thigh.

There are many variations on how to hold the ball when punting. Some punters like it up at the chest and some on the kicking leg. I liked the snap to be on the side. You want a little air between the ball and your hands.

You want to develop the punters into two-step punters. You can get the ball off quicker using that style. The main thing is getting the consistent punt. The snap comes, the punter catches the ball, and he puts it out on the table on the first step. His kicking foot and leg are right at the center's butt. The second step is the plant foot. He never wants to cross the right track over the left track. He wants to keep the legs straight. He keeps his hips closed. The steps are controlled steps and are not going to get the hips out of whack.

If I keep my steps straight and I drop the ball properly, the ball is going to go somewhere good. It may not be a perfect spiral, but it should be a good kick.

On directional punting, the only thing that changes is the steps. If I want to go to the right, I catch the ball, put it out on the table, and now the steps are in the direction I want the ball to go. My body is telling the ball where to go. The key to directional punting comes down to the steps. The tendency is to bring the ball back into our body on the second step. That is the number one problem I have with the kids I coach. It is difficult to get them to keep the ball out in front of their bodies, especially on the second step. The kicking leg starts the swing toward the ball as the second step on the plant step.

The drop of the ball is the most important thing. The drop must be flat to kick a spiral. If the nose of the ball is down, you are not going to kick a spiral. A flat ball punted off a flat foot ends up as a spiral. This is all in the drop of the ball. If I do not get the flat drop, the punt is not going to be a good one. We are looking for consistency with a flat ball on a flat foot.

Leg Swing

- On the plant of the second step will start the leg swing
- With toe pointed down, make contact on leg lock.
- Drive up with the lower body and down with the upper body (do a crunch on the ball).
- Follow-through should be up and off the ground.
- Kick to your shoulder.
- Drop.
- Must be flat
- Little air time as possible
- On the table, pooch kick equals high ball and bad weather equals low ball
- Flat ball plus flat foot equals a spiral.

If do not extend my leg, I cannot lock my leg out. Get the ball out in front so you can extend the leg on the kick. You want the drop in as little time as possible. You want to get off the ground on the follow-through. We drop the front hand first and then come up and through the ball. We want to get the upper body to come down, and the lower body to come up as we kick. We do a crunch on the football.

If you want to pooch kick the punt, all you have to do is raise the ball and kick it from a higher point. The same idea in bad weather is to lower the ball on the punt to keep it from getting too high in the air. You want to bring the ball down and kick it right out of your hands.

Most Common Punting Mistakes

- Ball not extended from the body (bent leg)
- Drop not flat
- Toe not pointed down
- Leaning too far back

Drills

- Drop
- One step
- Tap
- Angle

The most common mistake I see relates to getting the arms extended. If the arms are not extended, the ball is going to go short. You want to be able to drop the ball on a hard surface and have it come back up to you. That is hard to do, and that is why spirals are hard to kick.

The other mistake I see is when the punters rear back. They need to have that lean to put the ball on the table. They can learn the drills in the gym in the off-season or in the summer camps. Another mistake is when the punters have the elbows bent too much. They need to keep the arms extended on the drop of the ball.

A good drill that I like is the tap drill. Two punters are 20 yards apart and they tap the punt back and forth to each other working on their technique. They go with a little more force on a regular punt, so this is a good drill.

Angle punting is a great drill. Get a sack of footballs and have a punter and a snapper working on the snap, with the punter kicking the ball out-of-bounds on the angle punts.

How to Choose a Kicker

- Leg strength
- Ex-soccer player, current soccer player
- Semi-normal in the head
- Someone who can practice

Eddie Eviston

SHOTGUN RUN-AND-SHOOT OFFENSE

Newport Central Catholic High School, Kentucky

I am very humbled and honored to be here today. There have been a lot of firsts for me this year, and this is one of them. It is my first year as a head coach, and I was fortunate enough to win the state championship this year. I know there are coaches out there thinking they can coach circles around me. So again, I am very humbled to be here.

We had a very successful year. I do not know if it was because of luck, or because our kids really bought into what we changed offensively. That is what I want to talk about today.

First, I want to talk about our season. We averaged over 42 points per game. People talk about the run-and-shoot and passing the ball all over the place, but that can be a misconception. We definitely put the run in the run-and-shoot this year. Our total offense was over 6,000 yards, 4,312 of those yards were rushing. It is a little unorthodox for this offense, but we had the kids who could do it.

Our passing game was still good. We passed for over 1,700 yards. What was good for me to see was that we had a 71 percent pass completion percentage. We only threw four interceptions through our 15 games. Our kids did a great job of picking up this offense and executing it.

When Earl Browning called me and asked me to be on the clinic this year, I was not sure what to call our offense. This was just an offense I learned while at Georgetown College. The principles are the run-and-shoot offense, but I really did not know what it was. I just ran it. I have done some research since that phone call, and I can now call it the run-and-shoot.

From my research, I found out the present principles of this offense started with Coach Glenn "Tiger" Ellison in Middletown, Ohio. Coach Ellison had a team that was struggling, and he wanted to put some fun back into football. From what I read, he wanted to keep it like backyard football. Those are some principles I will talk about.

Coach Darrel "Mouse" Davis picked up on the offense. From there, he brought in some innovative stuff and mastered the offense. It was from Coach Davis that this offense started to spread because of the great success he had.

It starts to get personal for me through Coach Stewart "Red" Faught. Coach Faught was a small-school, run-and-shoot guru. In his 30-plus years of coaching, I believe his quarterbacks were some of the leading quarterbacks in the country every year. Indirectly, he might be the reason I am standing here today. I went to Georgetown College as a defensive back. One day, one of our senior receivers needed somebody to throw him the football. I was a redshirt freshman, and I just started throwing the ball to him. Coach Faught was my coach during my first year. When Coach Bill Cronin took over at Georgetown College, Coach Faught mentioned that he might want to give me a look at quarterback. I moved to quarterback, and studied and ran his offense. Coach Cronin and Coach Craig Mullins taught me the ins and outs of this offense and gave me their tweaks on this offense. They are the real reason I am standing here today. They taught me everything I know about this offense and how to be a winner and a champion.

GOALS OF THE RUN-AND-SHOOT OFFENSE

- "Go where they ain't," Take what the defense gives you.
- Play fast.
- Employ controlled chaos (motions).
- Be up-tempo.
- Score now.

If you have been to a clinic and heard someone speak about the run-and-shoot, then I am sure you have heard this same lecture before. The first thing is to "go where they ain't." In other words, take what the defense gives you. It is vital for the quarterback to understand this concept. What we teach at the high school level is this: we are reading the defender. We are going to go opposite of where the defender is.

We want all of our players to play fast. We tell our players even if they are running the wrong direction or running the wrong play, we want them to play fast and go hard. When players hesitate, the defense has the advantage.

A big part of this offense is motion. We have long motion, short motion, and we have orbit motion. One of the big reasons we have players in motion is to get a read on the defense. We can figure out what type of coverage they are in from our motion. It has really helped us in the running game because of the angles and leverage that it gives us, especially on the outside when their linebackers adjust to our motion. We had players in motion about 80 percent of the time during the season. It really worked well for us.

We want to be up-tempo. What I mean by that is we want to get in and out of the huddle so we do not allow the defense to rest and regroup. Our play calling system is simplified. However, it was one thing we changed before this season. In the past, it took us a paragraph to call a play. We simplified it so that we could get in and out of the huddle and get flying around. If you are in a fistfight and you are throwing punches, you do not want to stop to let the guy in front of you catch his breath.

We want to score now. The concept is: no matter where you are on the field, you want to score on the very next play. I was taught there are no bad plays. Some plays are better than others. That is the kind of mind-set you want to take when running this type of offense.

KEYS TO OFFENSIVE SUCCESS

- Have confidence and belief in what you are doing.
- Players need to buy into the program.
- Get in the end zone during practice.
- Always have something to counter with; it must build off the foundation of your offense.
- Plan for all situations, and practice your plan as much as possible.

You have to have confidence and belief in what you are doing. When I got the job at Newport Central Catholic, I met with my defensive coach. We were talking about our opponents for the upcoming season. One of our opponents runs a variation of the run-and-shoot offense with an over or unbalanced look. It is very similar to something we also run. As we were talking about that team, my defensive coach says, "Yeah, they run that nonsense stuff." About the fifth game of our season, my defensive coach comes up to me and tells me to, "Run that unbalanced nonsense stuff because the defense cannot stop it." The point is that he started believing it what we were running on offense. That is the goal. You have to have your staff and your players to believe in it.

At this time last year, I met with my team, and we had a good group of seniors. There had not been any change in the head coach at Newport Central Catholic in 40 years. The biggest hurdle we had to overcome was having a new coach come in and change the entire offense. I told them they had to buy into the program. They had to believe in what we were teaching them, and they had to do it right off the bat.

We want to get the ball into the end zone during practice. You have to do it during practice. In practice, every team period we have, we move the ball down the field. If we start out on the 40-yard line, we will not stay on the 40-yard line. We will move the ball down the field. We will end that team period in the end zone as a team. Mentally, I believe that is the approach you need to take with your players. They need to know that the end zone is where we need to be.

We always have to have something to counter with. It must be built off the foundation of our offense. What I mean by that is you cannot change what you do. You cannot create a whole new offense. If the defense is doing something to disrupt what we are doing, we have to have something in our bag that will counter that.

We are a small program, and the majority of our players play both ways. That makes it hard, with the amount of time that we have, to practice our offense and defense as much as we would like. We plan for all situations and practice that plan as much as possible. When we had to run a two-point play during one of our games, my quarterback came over and asked me, "Do we want to run play A, B, or C?" Our players know what our options are, because we have worked on them in practice.

If we have a two-minute drill, we do not use our entire playbook. We reduce it down to a manageable amount of plays, and our players know what we are going to run in the two-minute drill. When we need to run out the clock, and we need a first down, we scale our playbook down and focus on just that situation, and we work on it. Our players know what we are going to do in that situation. We plan for those situations, and we practice them at least once a week. I think it is a mental thing, especially with high school kids. They feel confident in things because they have practiced them, and they know what is going on.

When we look at personnel and who we need in order to run this offense, I look at these tools from the players' standpoint:

- A mobile quarterback: Not necessarily fast, but can move
- Wingbacks: Kids who can do it all—run, catch, block, read a defense
- Super back: North-south type of runner
- Wide receivers: Run good routes, clutch hands
- Linemen: Must understand the concept of the play

Because I ran this offense myself, I know the importance of having a mobile quarterback. The quarterback does not necessarily have to be fast, but he has to be able to move a little bit. You are really able to open up the offense more when you have a quarterback who can run. The offense that we run sets up a lot of natural quarterback scramble opportunities.

We have two wingbacks. We put them one yard deep and two to three yards outside of the tackles. That will vary, depending on the play. These need to be players who can do it all. They have to be able to run, catch, and definitely block. What helped us this year is that we had two kids who were physical. They have to be able to read a defense so they can "go where they aren't." We tell them to go to the point where they are open.

We call our one back the super back. This player needs to be a north-south type of runner. You need a player who can hit the hole fast and slash the defense as quickly as possible. He has to pick up the dirty yards and get the job done. Obviously, he needs to be able to block, especially when it comes to the passing game.

Our wide receivers need to be able to run good routes. The run-and-shoot passing game is based on precision and timing, and receivers have to run good routes. You also need a player who has clutch hands.

As far as linemen are concerned, they must understand the concept of the play. Everybody wants that big, fast lineman that can knock people off the ball and pound the crap out of the defense. We all do not have those types of players. Every player must understand the concept of the play. We want the lineman to understand where the receivers are going and where the running backs are going. A lot of times, coaches teach their lineman just to pass-block during a passing play. In the run-and-shoot, they need to understand the entire concept.

NEWPORT CENTRAL CATHOLIC OFFENSIVE STRATEGY

- Ability to run the majority of all our plays from different looks—coach concepts, not just individual responsibilities
- Ability to have quarterback both under center and in the shotgun
- Ability to keep the same personnel in the game using various formations and looks

Having the ability to run our offense from different looks, no matter what, was very important to us. This goes back to teaching concepts and not just individual responsibilities. We want to be able to run any of our plays from any formation that we are in. Obviously, things may change, depending on the position we are in, but they are able to pick it up. It may take a little extra classroom time, but that is what you have to do.

Having the quarterback both under center and in the shotgun was key for us. We had a mobile quarterback this past season. It totally opened up our playbook. We were probably 50-50 this year, as far as being in the shotgun or having the quarterback under the center. This also keeps the defense guessing.

Unfortunately, we do not have a lot of athletes to pick from. It does make it easier for us to keep the same personnel in the game. The defense cannot key on certain personnel groups when you use the same players for every formation. There were times when we were in a different formation for every play of a drive. It makes it hard on a defense to deal with that. What made it easy for us is that we did not have to substitute anybody.

APPROACH TO THE 2010 SEASON

- Put the "run" in the run-and-shoot offense.
- Spread the ball out as much as possible.
- Attack an area of the defense.
- Utilize play-action pass efficiently.
- Use the quick passing game to put guys in space.

There is a misconception about the run-and-shoot offense. Most coaches believe you just throw the football in this offense. When I look back at college, we were very balanced, but I never really thought of it that way. Due to our personnel, the run was definitely a big thing for us.

We want to be a balanced offense as much as possible. We do not want to give the defense just one person they can stop and that stops our entire offense. Our approach is that you are going to have to stop everybody on our team. We want to get the ball in as many players' hands as possible.

We were fortunate this year in that we had a very good running back, who got the majority of our scores. However, he did not get all of them in a row. We spread it around pretty well. All of our kids know that if they can block and they can catch, they will get a time to shine, and they will get the ball. Our kids get excited about that.

We want to attack a special area of the defense. We read the defense and we try to pick out a weak defender. We approach the running game in a very similar manner. We look at what a particular linebacker might be doing. An example would be how he is adjusting to our motion. We decide if he does one thing, we are going to do something against that. That is how we approach the offense, both in the passing and running game.

In order to be successful, we have to utilize our play-action pass efficiently. This contributed to our 71 percent pass completion efficiency. We had some key plays come out of our play-action game. When you run as many plays as we do, the play-action play gets a lot of attention and is vital to us.

We like to use the quick passing game to put receivers in space. This is the whole run-and-shoot concept. The simple running game, coupled with the short passing game, is the approach that we wanted to take. We wanted to spread out the defense and put our guys in space. What I learned in college was 1-on-1 is one-on-none.

This is what our basic formation looked like (Diagram #1). We saw a lot of 4-4 defenses. I was talking to a friend of mine, who happens to be a defensive coordinator, and he told me the thing that gives him the most fits is the ace offense, where you have two tight ends, one on each side. That is what this is, except our tight ends are back one yard. Personnel-wise, the wingbacks have to be physical. They have to be able to attack linebackers and be able to block them.

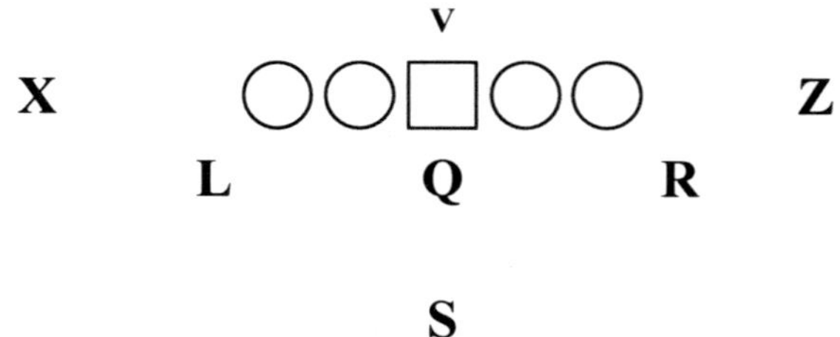

Diagram #1. Basic Formation

We build our run game offense off of the toss sweep play (Diagram #2). We send our wingback in motion. When we hand off the ball, we want him on the edge. Something we work on every day is to make sure that we are not fumbling the pitch. We want to put that linebacker in a bind. "This is coming at me, what am I going to do?" He has to make a decision.

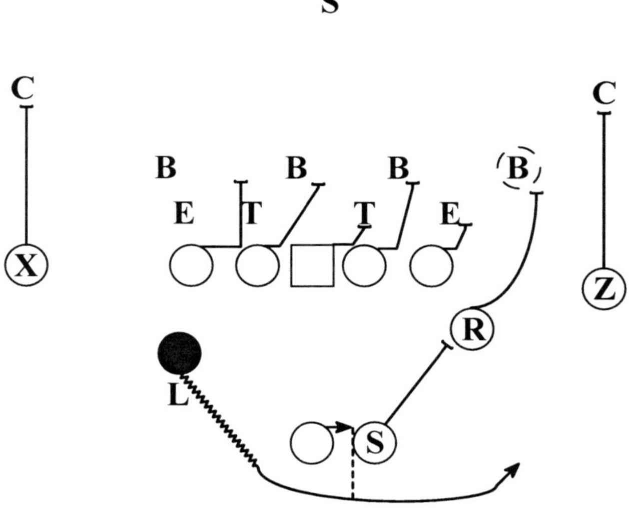

Diagram #2. Toss Sweep

If the linebacker tries to get a head start to try to disrupt the sweep, we will kick him outside. We will have our super back kick out the end and let our tackle block the linebacker. We will have the quarterback just run up between the guard and the tackle (Diagram #3). If the linebacker is going to fly, we are going to run it up inside of him.

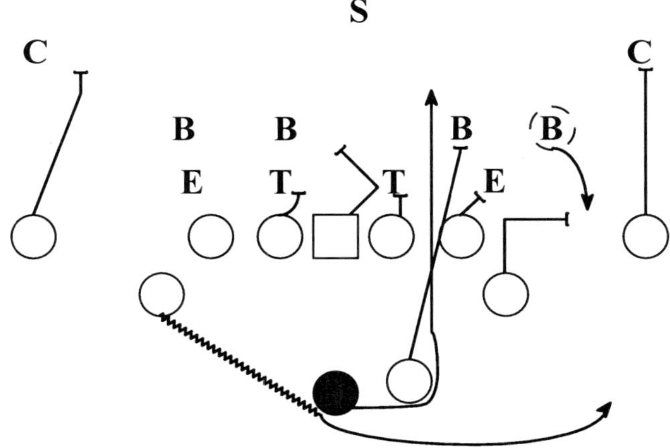

Diagram #3. Fake Sweep

If the defensive coordinator decides to bump all of the linebackers over when we show the motion, we will run an option to the weakside (Diagram #4). The whole goal of this offense is to have something to counter what you are trying to do.

All of these things are based off the power sweep. With this offense, you want everything to look the same. You do not want the defense to

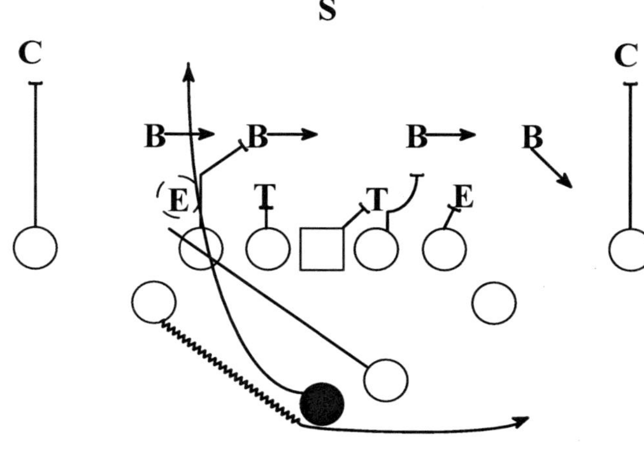

Diagram #4. Weakside Option

be able to tell if it is a run play or a pass play. You do have to get away from that just a little bit, but we try to get the same type of look as much as possible.

The way we set up our pass plays off of this looks something like this (Diagram #5). Our blocking up front is big-on-big. We have our wingback go in motion. A lot of our passing concepts come out of the trips formation. This is one way we can get into a trips look. We will have the super back block to the backside, 1 to 2. The center helps on the tackle, waiting for the linebacker that is coming. Our quarterback is going to read his hot read, a linebacker. He is looking right at him. We do not see many corner blitzes, I think probably because we keep the defense honest with our passing game.

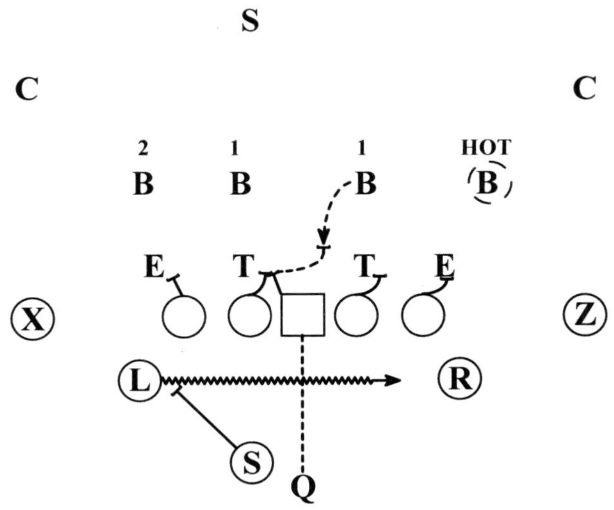

Diagram #5. Base Pass Concept

Let me show you one of my favorite passing plays. We ram our super back into a trips look. We have him run an in-and-out route, trying to step on both of the linebackers' toes. Our left wingback will do the same thing on the left side. We have our right wingback sneak in behind the linebackers, in the middle. We call that our triangle route (Diagram #6). We run a post over the top and a runoff on the backside. Obviously, the quarterback is reading the linebackers. This is the passing route we ran the most, out of an empty set.

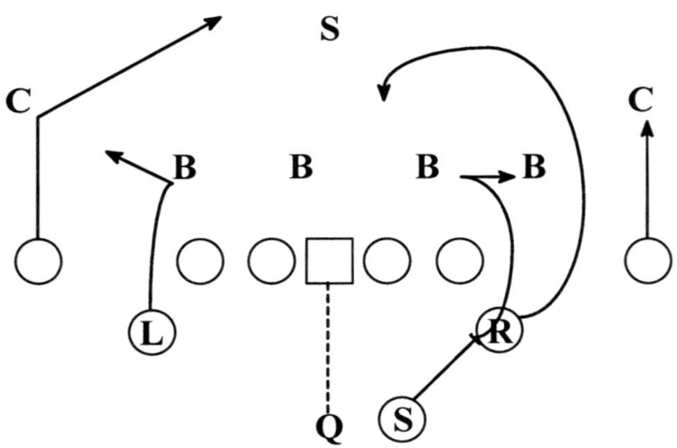

Diagram #6. Triangle Route

Another play we like to run out of a trips formation is an out route to the wingback on a short out pattern (Diagram #7). We motion into our trips. We are going to pick on that linebacker again. We pick on him a lot. This is a simple play, and a simple read.

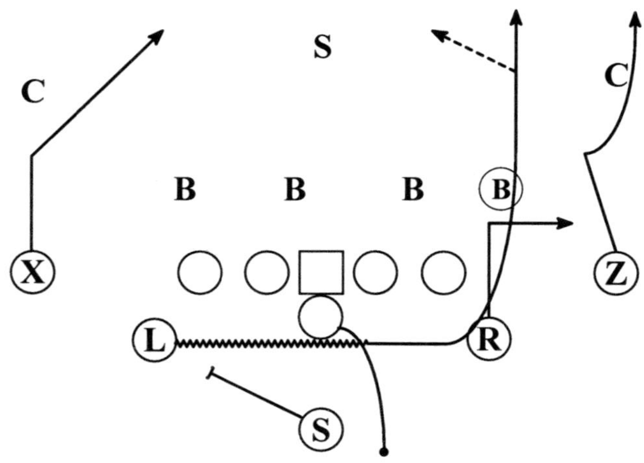

Diagram #7. Out Route to Right Wing

In going back to the run-and-shoot offensive principle of "go where they aren't," every pass play we have has at least one guy who will have an option route. On this play, it is our left wingback. After he goes in motion, he will go about 10 yards and then he will choose where he is going. Our right wingback will run about two yards and then turn out to the sideline. As soon as our left wingback goes in motion and is outside our right wingback, that linebacker is thinking that he has to get some leverage. If the linebacker starts to run with him, it becomes a natural pick. We want to get the ball to the right wingback in open space.

We were big on the speed option this past year. This is how we ran the speed option (Diagram #8). We are going to read the end. That is our rule. It is very simple. It is interesting to see what the end does when you motion toward him. Sometimes, they are quick to go, and our quarterback will sneak right inside of him. If the defensive end plays his rules and takes the quarterback, we are pitching, and it is just a matter of getting blocks.

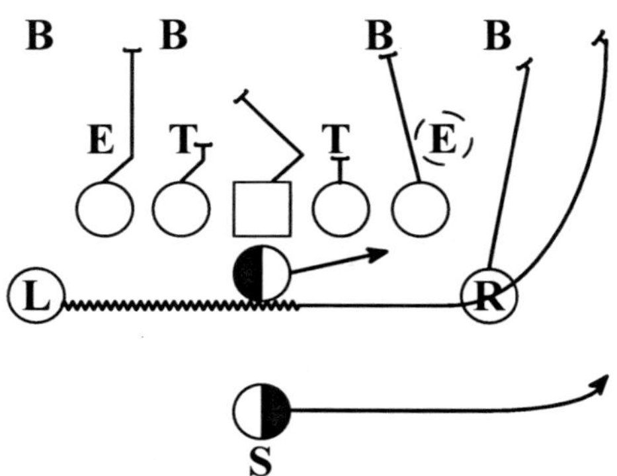

Diagram #8. Speed Option

We run unbalanced from time to time, and here is a play we run off of that (Diagram #9). We will bring our tackle over next to our other tackle. The X will move over to the tight end position. We will bring the left wing and put him behind our tight end. The super stays where he is. The right wing now moves two yards outside of the last guy on the end of the line of scrimmage. We will keep the Z where he is.

That is the basic look. The defense will adjust to this as much as they can. If we have a weak corner, we can motion the left wingback, or we can let him lead block on the end. We can bring our super back

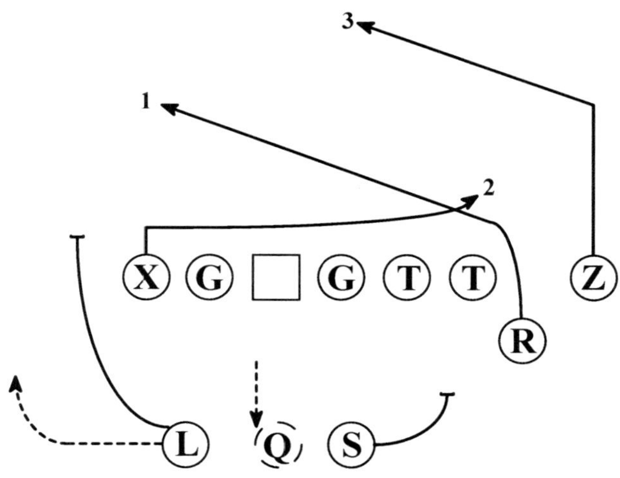

Diagram #9. Unbalanced

to lead block on the defensive end. Our X will have to go block the linebacker. As I told you before, our X has to be able to block.

All of our running plays are numbered. We will number our wingbacks as 4s, our super back is a 3, and our quarterback is a 1. If we run 38, it is our toss sweep to our fullback. We simplified it with our numbering system. All of our numbered plays are runs. All of our pass plays are names. We will let our players help in giving our pass plays a name. We will run an up-tempo huddle from time to time, or we can run a no-huddle.

My time is up. Again, I appreciate your time, and I am honored to be here today. I hope you will be able to take something useful back to your program. Thank you.

Rick Finotti

THE 4-3 DEFENSE SECONDARY COVERAGES

St. Edward High School, Ohio

I want to thank Nike and Earl Browning for giving me the opportunity to talk football and primarily about our defense. I want to say something about St. Edward's football. I have been a head coach for two years. I am 38 years old and was always an offensive line coach or a defensive linebackers coach. I have coached all levels of football. I have coached freshman and junior varsity; I have been an assistant coach, a defensive coordinator, and finally a head coach. St. Edward is notorious for championships. Currently, we are in a battle with St. Xavier High School for the most state championships in the state of Ohio.

Of all the state championships we have won at St. Edward, we did not have a football championship. That stuck in the throats of our alumni and the people of St. Edward. I got the job and we went 4-6 the first year. They almost ran me out of town.

St. Edward is located in Lakewood Ohio, which is on the west side of Cleveland. In our area, it is Saint Ignatius and us. We are the only schools to win the Division I championship from the northeastern section of Ohio. We are an all-male Catholic high school with 800 boys in grades 9 through 12. Our football squad has about 125 players on the team. We have been in existence for 61 years and have over 40 state championships in all sports. We were able to give them the first football championship this year.

We felt like we played the toughest schedule in the state of Ohio. Our defense gave up eight points a game during the regular season. We had a high-powered offense that averaged 38 points a game. We played many games that season with our substitutes in the game and still played great defense. Our players stuck to a very conservative game plan and did a good job.

You win championships with great players. The thing that set us apart was that four of the five Ivy League commitments played defense. Three of them played in the secondary.

My background was a 3-3 front. That is what we played when I was a coordinator. When we came to St. Edward, that was the defense they ran. We adapted that scheme and changed to a 4-4 base front. However, we realized we did not have the linebackers to play that defense. The teams we played were 12 and 11 personnel groups with good quarterbacks. We had a hard time with the fits and playing defense with the personnel we had on the field. We knew we needed to change the defense to take advantage of what we had in our school.

St. Edward is a renowned wrestling power in the state. The wrestling team had all-state wrestlers in the 160-pounds and up height-weight classes that did not play football. They focused so much on wrestling that they did not play both sports. This year, most of the second-team wrestlers played football and we got an all-state 160 pounder and a heavyweight to play for us. The discipline they got in wrestling carried over to football. We took advantage of that.

We changed our offensive scheme to more 21 personnel groups and ran power football. We ran the zone and isolation play and got physical in all our schemes. We did it in all phases of our game. We recognized we had to be successful in two ways. We had to play with the type of players we had in our school and the schemes had to fit the schedule. We had to win our schedule. We are not in a conference. We are independent and qualify for the playoffs by the wins on the schedule. We did not care about the record as long as we qualified for the playoffs.

We had to look in the mirror and figure out how to make our defense and program be successful and withstand the 10-week schedule. We went to a 4-3 defense and instilled some principles for it.

The number one thing we work on every day in practice, in double sessions, and in summer workouts is alignment. The state gives us 10 days in the summer for football practice. We do not have spring football. The time we get with our players, we work on alignment. We do not start until we work on alignment. We show them quad sets, all kinds of motion, and every bastard formation we can. We want to adjust and keep it within our base scheme.

We worked hard in the weight room and that is where we won most of our games. We became a strong and physical football team. We committed to the Olympic lifts. We used the power clean, clean and jerk, and hang snatch. What we did in the weight room helped us prepare for the style of football we played. We worked on five things that geared our defense:

- Work every day on *alignment* (cannot align, cannot compete).
- Run fits; stop the run first
- Tackle every day; circuits/ Indy/team/weight room
- Focus on fundamentals over scheme.
- Physical in everything we do

We did not talk about scheme because we wanted to look at the big picture of how we wanted our football team to look. When we work on alignment, we have an easy call system so we can communicate with one another. After we go over the alignments, we work in our individual drills on run fits. We feel you must stop the run first. We are a 4-3, cover 4 team and we spill everything to the outside. We use a wrong arm technique in our fits. The defensive ends are very aggressive.

We turn the young player loose to create havoc. We attack the pulling guard and fullback aggressively and spill the ball. We overlap with the linebackers in a gap exchange philosophy. We tackle every day in practice. We have to share a field with a local public school. After we stretch and before we go to our individual drills, we have a six-station tackling circuit. In that circuit, we work on different types of tackles. Every week after the game film, we evaluate our tackling. The assistant coaches evaluate their positions. We meet as a staff and figure what we need to concentrate on in the circuit to be better tacklers.

The good thing about stations is every coach gets to coach every player on the defense for two to three minutes every day. A defensive line coach gets to coach the corners, safeties, inside linebackers, and outside linebackers. That allows our players to get used to some other position coach working with them. In the game, their position coach may be in the box and not on the sideline. That leads to interaction of the players with another position coach. We work tackling in individual sessions, in team drills, and in the weight room. We give them exercise in the weight room that assimilates tackling. We do anything we can in the weight room to take our hips below parallel and drive them upward. We do something in the weight room year round to help us be better tacklers. You cannot wait for them to show up in fall practice to teach tackling.

Coach Matt Minnillo coaches our secondary. He is going to come up and talk about what we do. He can tell you about the specifics of the scheme. I think he does a great job of getting his corners and safeties ready to play. Our interceptions and tackling have improved by his coaching. Our defensive backs are very physical with receivers. As long as the quarterback has the ball, we have our hands all over the receivers.

ELEMENTS OF THE EAGLE DEFENSE

- All 11 players have a responsibility to stop the play.
- If you cannot align, you cannot play.
- As coaches, what we demand is what we will get.
- In every individual session of practice, coaches practice core technique and not a minute of time is wasted.
- Honest evaluation of players; we have a common standard of what a loaf is.
- We pride ourselves on a workman-type attitude.
- Ensure each player improves, especially our best players. This is essential. Demand more from best players; the average player usually gives more.
- Crossface to the football; never go backdoor.

I want to cover these elements quickly. On offense, you may have a specialist that does something individually for the offense. That does not happen on defense. When you put a player on the field, he is responsible to stop the play. All 11 players are responsible for stopping the play.

Coaches have to demand that their players execute what he teaches. You get what you emphasize and demand. We have a workman-type of attitude in our work ethics. We love to work. We evaluate our players with great intensity. We did it more as a staff this year than at any other time. The staff gets close to the players and is involved with all facets of the program. I am in charge of the weight program. I get used to the players and see the ones that work hard. I get to bond with the underachievers and want them to play just as much as their parents do.

During the summer, our staff works on a formula for evaluation. The one thing that is important for the coaches to understand is the definition of a "loaf." We punish players for loafing. We want every player in the screen when the ball goes down. Your value to your defensive teammate is your distance from the ball.

We want to make sure each player improves. When we got to St. Edward, there were many Division I players, but they were not worth a cent. They were major players. They did not have good attitudes and thought they were entitled to positions. They did not earn their playing time. We had to sit people down.

This year before the season started, we kicked five players off the team that were starters the previous year. They did not put the time in, had bad attitudes, did not work with their teammates, and did not follow the philosophy we believed in. We did without them. That gave some sophomores and juniors an opportunity, and they took advantage of it. That could have backfired on us. If we had an injury or two, I would not be standing up here talking to you. You take that risk.

The players today are different than they used to be. At a school like ours, everyone coming into the program thinks they will be the next greatest player and get a college scholarship. You have to be as honest and positive as you can, but you must make sure the best, most deserving players play.

A big part of our philosophy is playing crossface to the ball. A player pursuing the ball cannot use the back door. That cuts off the next defender trying to fit off your play. They may lose a little ground but will make it up in the pursuit of the ball.

The following goals and problems should guide instruction, drill work, and off-season work:

- Goals:
  - ✓ Stop run
  - ✓ Limit points
- Problems that deter these goals:
  - ✓ Alignment did not recognize unbalanced situations
  - ✓ Poor tackling
  - ✓ Poor eyes: misreading keys
  - ✓ Slow/improper footwork
  - ✓ Improper defensive technique
  - ✓ Improper run fits—stop the run

At the end of the season, we evaluate our defense. I do not want a long list of what we did well or what we did not do. It is simple. You won or lost; you could not stop the run or gave up too many points. We look at the two elements: stopping the run and giving up points. Cover 4 in our 4-3 scheme fit into that aspect. Two high safeties gave us a chance to eliminate the big play.

Improper fits is what led us to the spill technique. One of our linebackers coaches played in the NFL. He was big into bouncing the play. Our evaluation is what guides our planning and instruction in our drill work and off-season program. I wanted to share these things with you in limiting what you do in the off-season and your scheme. You should not use a scheme because you like it. I have done that, but it is part of the evolution of learning. When you coach, you try to look at things in a simplistic way.

MATT MINNILLO, SECONDARY/CO-DEFENSIVE COORDINATOR

When we get into the scheme, the first thing you have to do is count the receivers (Diagram #1). We use a half-field principle and count receivers from the outside moving to the inside. In the diagram, the formation is a 2x2 tight end set. The split end to the right is #1 and the slot receiver is #2. The #3 receiver is the single back behind the quarterback. On the left, the flanker is #1 and the tight end is #2.

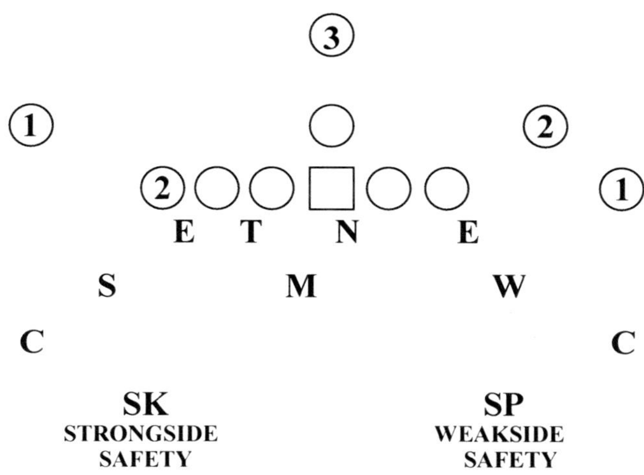

Diagram #1. Receiver Numbering

We stress landmarks to our defensive back (Diagram #2). We tell them that things on the field will help them with their coverage. That is particularly true with a four-vertical scheme. We used to play cover 3 and still have many elements of that coverage. The big point in stopping four-vertical routes is the defenders knowing where the landmarks are on the field. It starts with the numbers for the corner and hash marks for the safeties. In a four-vertical pattern, the corner splits the #1 and #2 receivers at the top of the numbers. The safeties either hold on the hash marks or push toward the numbers.

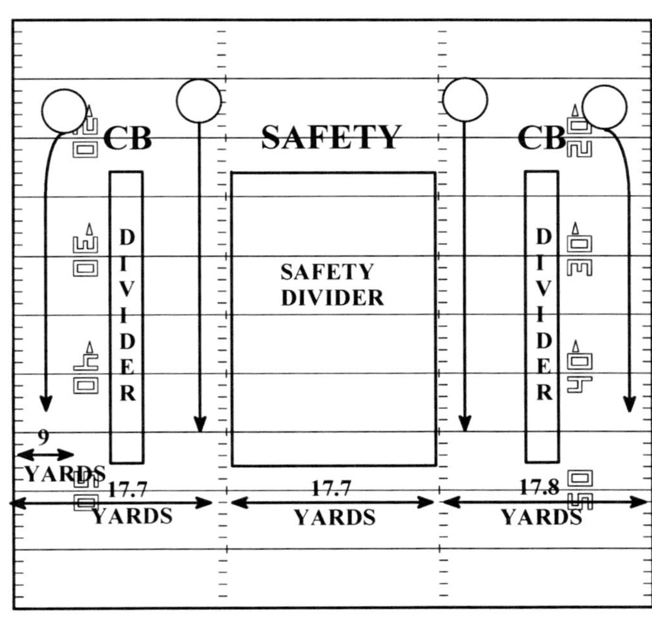

Diagram #2. Dividers

The defenders must know the size of the field. We know the hash marks split the width of the field into thirds. The numbers are nine yards off the sideline. When the wide receiver pushes vertical, it is a trouble zone for the corner. The corner has to push the vertical into the sideline while holding the numbers. When we play man coverage, we push the vertical pattern into the bench. When we play zone, we hug the numbers. We key the quarterback, zone turn to face him, and react to the ball in the air.

In practice, we do an insane amount of vertical releases with receivers and the ball in the air. That is the only way to effectively teach reaction to the deep ball. If they do not run deep, they cannot judge the ball in the air. They need to run. You can do it in a reduced space in the later part of the week. However, early in the week, we want them running deep and reacting to the deep ball.

On alignment, the corner's base rule is one yard outside and nine yards deep on the wide receiver (Diagram #3). The safety aligns two yards outside the tight end and 10 to 12 yards deep. If the #1 receiver aligns outside the numbers, the corner does not go with him. The corner hugs the numbers and deepens his alignment. Sometimes the corner is 10 to 12 yards deep because the wide receiver split to the sideline.

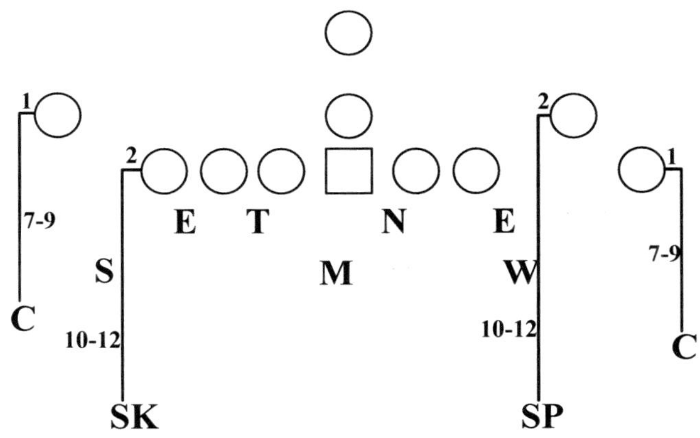

Diagram #3. Alignment

If the #2 receiver is a tight end, the safety has outside leverage on him. However, if the #2 receiver is a slot receiver, the safety has inside leverage on him. The weak linebacker or Will is the aspect player. On a rundown, he is a step closer to the box. In a pass situation, he is closer to the #2 receiver.

If the offense aligns in a pro with a twins set, we give our strength call to the tight end side of the set. We want the Sam linebacker to the tight end.

He knows how to handle all the tight end blocking schemes and his delay routes. The Will linebacker plays better to the openside of a formation and is better in pass coverage.

Our corners shuffle back into their coverage. They align with their inside foot back and tilted to the quarterback. They shuffle back into their coverage. If you see a corner that has his shoulders square to the line of scrimmage, the #1 receiver is outside the numbers. With the shoulders square to the line of scrimmage, the corner backpedals instead of shuffling.

COVER 4 NOTES

- All players in coverage, but Mike will read the release of the same receiver: #2 (Mike drops off #3)
- Route read #2 to #1
- There are only three things #2 receiver can do: in, out, vertical.
- Attack routes and combinations.
- *Cannot* cover grass
- Underneath player (Sam, Will, Mike) must reroute.

In the cover 4 scheme, everyone in the pass coverage scheme reads the #2 receivers except the Mike linebacker. The Mike linebacker reads the #3 receiver. He drops to the position of the #3 receiver. If the #3 receiver blocks, he becomes a spy. His assignment goes to where you want him during that week. He may spy a running quarterback or help with a popular receiver.

The Will and Sam linebackers read the #2 receiver to the #1 receiver. We pattern read and attack combination pass routes. The receiver can do three things when he runs a route. He can run a deep pattern, use an inside move, or use an outside move. The thing you need to teach your defensive backs is a stem is different from a release. That is the trickiest thing about teaching releases.

The defender cannot cover grass. That means he has to cover a receiver. He has to match the route the receiver runs. The Sam linebacker reads the #2 receiver. If the #2 receiver runs an out breaking pattern, the Sam linebacker's eyes go to the #1 receiver. The underneath players have to be physical with any receiver trying to get deep. They must reroute all vertical routes. The vulnerable play in this scheme is the inside vertical release by the #2 receiver. The Sam and Will linebackers cannot allow the #2 receivers to get an inside release on them. They must force them outside and reroute their routes. When they get a free release on the safeties is when we have problems in the secondary. It is their job to reroute the pattern and pound the crap out of the slot receiver.

We have a standard no-cover zone (Diagram #4). From the line of scrimmage to five yards downfield is the no-cover zone. Our linebackers cannot drive into those areas. If they cover someone in a no-cover zone, it opens up huge windows in the coverage. The linebacker must understand getting into windows in the coverage and attacking combinations. Passes thrown in those areas are given. We react back up and make the tackle. We mirror the depth and direction of pattern downfield. If the #2 receiver goes out, the #1 receiver is coming in.

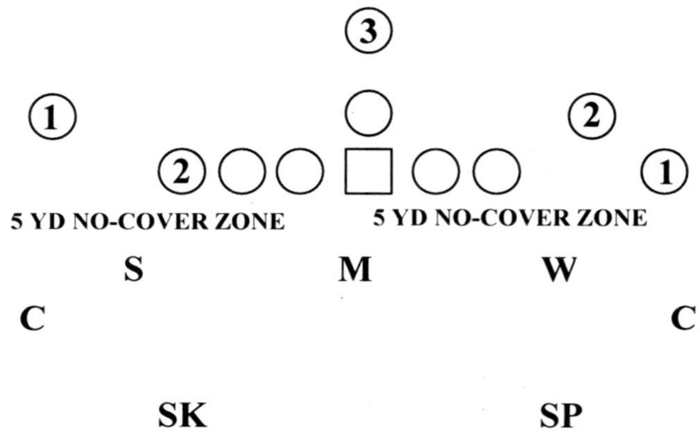

Diagram #4. No-Cover Zone

The weakside safety fills off the Will linebacker in his run support (Diagram #5). The Will and free safety read the #2 receiver. On running downs, the Will linebacker is closer to the box. If he reads run, he is inside the slot receiver with his fill. The free safety fits outside of the Will linebacker and outside the slot receiver.

We cannot have both defenders filling inside the slot receiver. In a pass situation, the Will linebacker is nearer the slot receiver. If a run develops, the Will linebacker fills up from the outside (Diagram #6). If the Will fits outside the slot receiver, the free safety fits inside the Will linebacker. The free

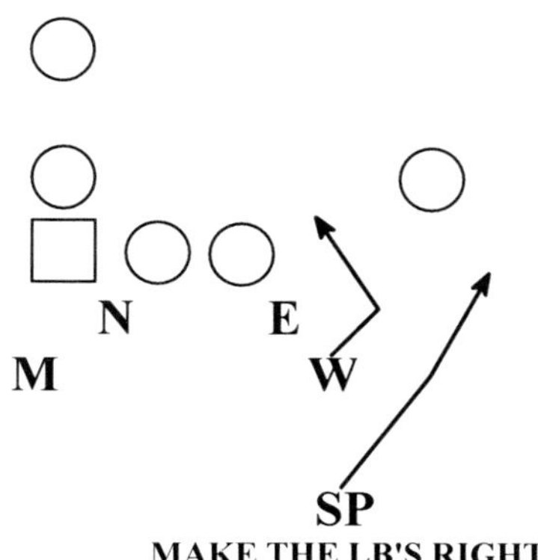

Diagram #5. Free Safety Inside

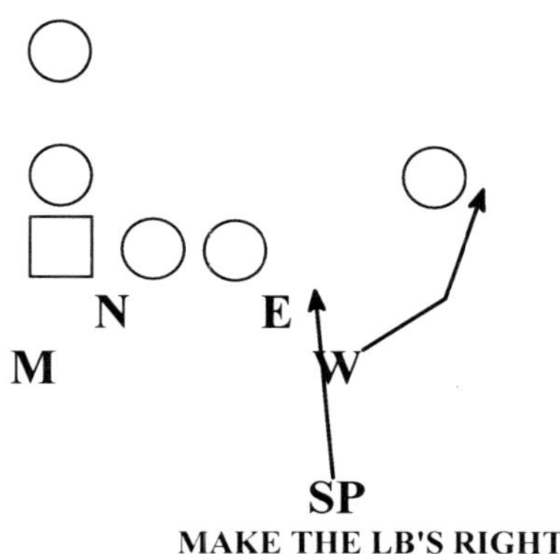

Diagram #6. Run Support Weak

safety overlaps the Will linebacker and always makes him right.

To the strongside, the strong safety's read is clear or cloudy (Diagram #7). If the situation is cloudy, he stays away. On a play-action pass, there is nowhere for the strong safety to fit. If he tries to fit into pursuit, there is no place for him to fit. We tell him to squat and watch for play-action. It also gives him time to overlap the Sam linebacker if he loses containment.

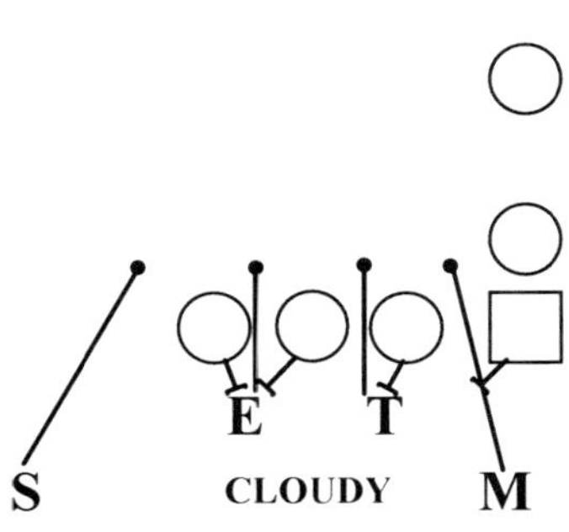

Diagram #7. Run Support Cloudy

If the strong safety has a clear window, he fits off the Sam linebacker. In this situation, the Sam linebacker takes on a block with the end attacking and the Mike linebacker scraping (Diagram #8). That is a clear window for the safety and he fills.

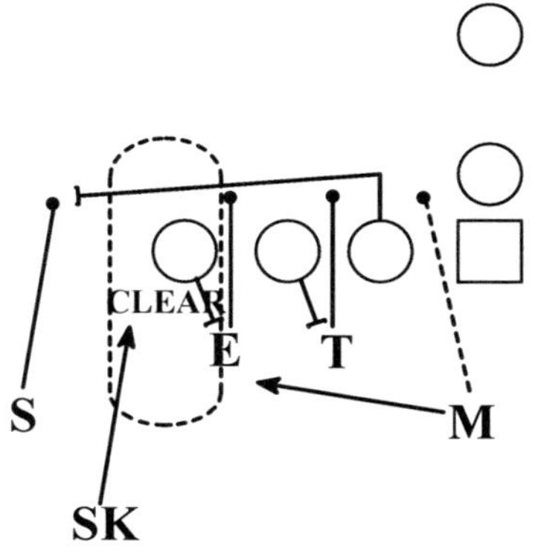

Diagram #8. Run Support Clear

The corner can have run support in certain situations (Diagram #9). If the corner gets a crackback block on the Sam linebacker, he has to replace the force. The important thing is to coach the corner not to read run until the receiver makes contact on the linebacker. The corner has to hold the vertical seam for the crack-and-go pattern from the receiver. If the corner drives too early, there is a big hole behind him.

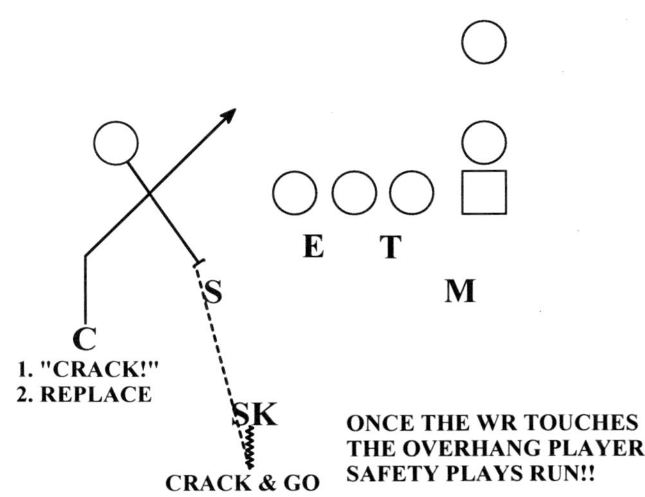

Diagram #9. Corner Run Support

We give the corner the analogy that the receiver has a match in his butt and the corner lights it. That is how tight we want the receiver coming off the receiver's block. We blitz the corner on occasion. When they blitz, they think too much about sacking the quarterback instead of what could happen. If it is not a pass, they have to play run. We have a crack alert call to the linebackers. The tighter the alignment of the receiver, the more vocal we are. The safety has the same type of read. He plays the vertical route until the receiver makes contact with the linebacker. At that point, he attacks the line of scrimmage using his running fit.

When the safety route reads, he needs to know the nearest inside vertical release (Diagram #10). In practice, they have to tell me where he is and point him out. Too many times, coaches assign yardage to routes. We have a "buy line." We tell the safety that if the #2 receiver pushes vertical and clears the linebacker, that is his route. We do not connect it to the depth of the pattern. When a defender buys a route, he matches the pattern. As long as the linebacker beats on the receiver, the safety stays out of the way. There is nowhere to throw the football. If they throw it, they hit the linebacker in the head.

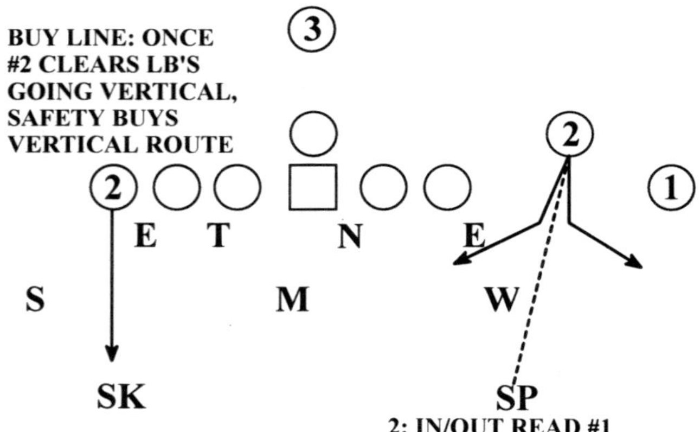

Diagram #10. Safety Route Read

We have a four-yard rule for engagement with a receiver. We do not allow the defenders to be within four yards of a receiver unless it is man coverage. We need to have space to drive on the football. The year before we came, they coached the defender to get right on top of the receivers. You cannot understand an interception point on a receiver if you are on top of him.

If the #2 receiver runs inside or outside, the safety immediately focuses on the #1 receiver. We do not play a robber technique with the safety on the #1 receiver. His technique is a vertical to protected post quarter coverage.

Our first year at St. Edward, we played against seven players that went to Division I programs. They went to places like Penn State and the University of Notre Dame. The curl pattern they threw was 20 to 25 yards down the field. They threw the post cut down the field. If you are thinking about going to quarter coverage, ask yourself what you want to do. If quarterbacks throw the curl with no depth, the robber coverage is what you need. However, if the vertical seam is what you see, you need to protect the post seam.

If the #2 receiver breaks to the outside and runs the wheel pattern up the sideline, the corner picks up that route (Diagram #11). We train the safety to look for the post. If the pattern is a dig, that is even better for the safety because he reads high to low and can drive on the dig route. He holds the hash and the inside move comes to him.

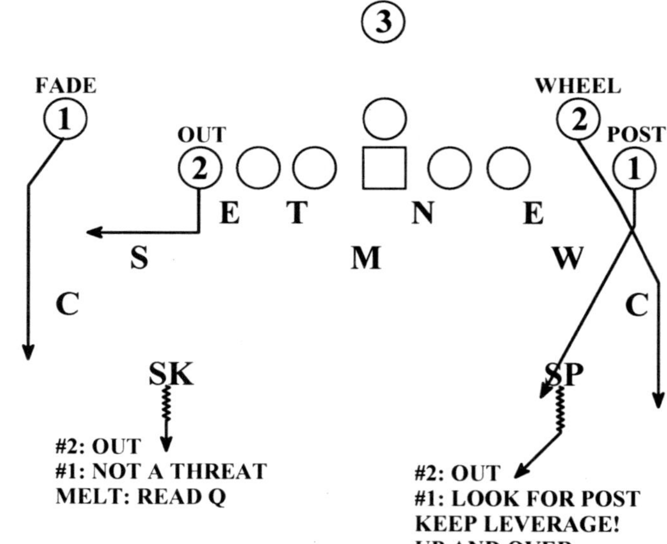

Diagram #11. #2 In and Out

The combination team's run to beat cover 2 is the flat/fade combination. If the #2 receiver goes out and the #1 receiver goes vertical, the corner stays on his divider and carries the #1 receiver deep.

The Sam linebacker reads the #2 receiver going out and #1 going vertical; he becomes the curl/flat dropper. When the safety reads those things, he becomes a free safety. He has no threat in his area. Even if the quarterback looks at the backside post, he has a play on the ball.

If the safety does not have work, we make them find work. They melt into the field and their reads. If the quarterback looks toward the fade, the safety leans toward the fade.

Our Mike linebacker drops on the #3 receiver. We build our screen game into this coverage. If the #3 receiver is involved in a screen, the Mike linebacker reads it immediately. The back steps up that and that becomes a screen alert for the Mike linebacker.

Our Mike linebacker and the outside linebackers will banjo their receivers. The Mike linebacker keys #3 to #2. If the #3 receiver runs to the flat, he looks for the #2 receiver coming inside. If #3 goes outside, the Sam linebacker or Will linebacker switch the #2 for the #3 receiver. The Mike linebacker picks up the #2 receiver coming inside and the outside linebacker matches the #3 receiver going outside. They exchange receivers crossing in and out patterns.

Cornerback Technique and Reads

- Shuffle technique
- Open and see the football.
- Do not break divider.
- Step, replace footwork
- Feet wider than framework of the body
- Break up on field foot, drive on downfield foot.

Quarterback Reads

- Reading the quarterback tells the corner if it is a three-step or a five-step drop.
  - ✓ Three-step: Stay in shuffle because the ball will come out quickly.
  - ✓ Five-step: Shuffle turns into crossover run; zone turn because of vertical route.

The corner aligns with outside leverage on the #1 receiver. He has his outside foot up in his stance and tilts inside to the quarterback. We use a shuffle step until the cushion breaks. In the shuffle, he steps with his inside foot, replaces it with the outside foot, and repeats the process until he has to zone turn and run. He reads the quarterback. That gives him the jump on the three-step drop. If he reads a five-step drop and the receiver vertical, he zone turns and matches the vertical route. When we read the quarterback, we know if the ball is coming out quickly or late.

We tell our secondary backs that quarterbacks will complete the pass. The important thing is what we do after they catch the football. We have to make the tackle and make them pay for catching the ball. We changed our production in pass defense by not allowing yardage after the catch. We became sure tacklers after the catch.

The last thing I want to show you is our adjustment to the triple set (Diagram #12). The safety's nearest vertical threat is the #3 receiver at tight end. It is hard to get a reroute on a third receiver going deep. We still read the #2 receiver to determine our coverage. To get four verticals from a trips set, the #3 receiver has to come to the backside safety. We are sound on the coverage. We play quarter coverage on the #1 and #2 receivers with the Mike linebacker under the #3 receiver short and the boundary safety taking him on the vertical.

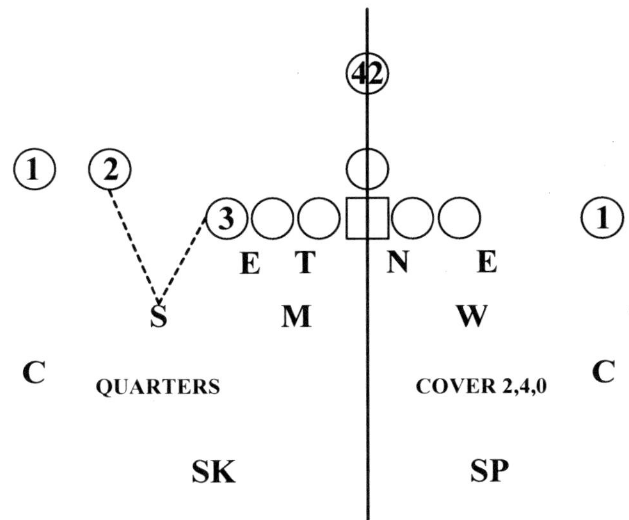

Diagram #12. Trips Alignment

I hope you enjoy the clinic. We will be around all weekend. If you want to talk football, we will be here. Thank you very much.

Bill Gierke

DEFENDING SPECIFIC WING-T-STYLE OFFENSES

Edgewater High School, Florida

Thank you. If I say something today that will help you in your program, it will be worth my time as well as yours. If you want to call me, feel free to do so. I cannot begin to tell you how many people helped me over the years. This includes college, high school, and youth coaches. It has been incredible the number of people that have helped me in my coaching career. I am a humble guy. The game has been good for me.

I am going to show you a film clip of a few plays of a team that has been on our schedule for several years. This offense hurt our defense when we first saw it. Our kids were confused on defense. As a staff, we spend a lot of time trying to defend this offense. It did not come overnight. The first two times we faced that offense we did not play very well.

No coach likes to lose. It does not matter the level you are coaching, you do not like to lose. You will see the coach on the other team did a great job with his offense. I want to point out a few things in the film that I hope will help you become a better defensive coach.

When we first faced this offense, we had a lot of long plays against us and a lot of long touchdowns. The offense is similar to the teams that used to run the double wing offense 10 or 12 years ago. They ran a lot of misdirection plays against us. This was confusing for our high school football players. I want you to count how many plays they ran that looked like wing-T plays. Count how many plays were successful because of missed tackles.

Twenty-five years ago, I had an All-American player that Coach Jimmy Johnson was recruiting at the University of Miami. I went down to watch them practice. I came back convinced we were going to run the 4-3 defense. That was a long time ago. I saw things they did that I could not believe. If you can't tackle, you are not going to win many games. If the players do not play technique, you are not going to win. Winning and losing still comes down to the team that plays the best techniques. Some coaches get carried away with X's and O's. That is not the answer.

Let me get back to the film. How many of these plays looked like the wing-T plays? We got tired of getting beat by those plays. Most of the pass plays they ran were play-action passes. They tried to beat us deep. We got together as a staff and decided we were going to come up with a defense to stop this offense.

Here is what we did on defense. There is so much technology available today you can learn from others. We went to a lot of clinics and got a lot of videos on this offense. We compiled everything we could find on the offense. We visited other high schools in Florida and studied what they did on the wing-T. You cannot stop an offense if you do not know how to run the offense. If you know how the offense works, you have a better chance of stopping it.

After going to the high schools, I went to visit college coaches. I showed them some of the film and asked how they would defend this offense. I went to several colleges and not one of them turned me down as far as spending time talking about this offense. That is one of the most wonderful things about being a coach. No one turned me down and I talked with a ton of coaches. What I am trying to tell you is this. We took all of those ideas and formulated our own ideas on how to stop that offense.

The first school I coached at, we were a big school with 3,300 students. The economy of Florida was falling apart. This last year we only had 1,700 students. Our enrollment in Orlando schools is decreasing every year. I was a head coach at Dr. Phillips High School for 11 years and I had six All-American players. I had three All-American offensive linemen. One of them is an All-American at The Ohio State University now. All of those linemen were 6'5" and over 300 pounds. They were great football players. We do not have that type of player today. This year we played with a noseguard that was 5'10" and 175 pounds. We are playing with players that are smaller, but we are playing with kids that can run. We do have some speed.

I visited with Dave Wannstedt and Butch Davis when they coached at Miami. I asked Dave to tell me about the 4-3 defense. This is what he told me. He said this is what defense is all about:

- Total determination
- Solid technique
- Consistent tackling

You practice defense differently than you do offense. The players have to be determined all of the time. If they do not want to be determined and focused, they can get off the field. In college, that is easier said than done. At times in high school, you have to get the players to meet you halfway. At least I do.

We talk all of the time about techniques. In Florida, it is against the rules to have footballs on the fields in the off-season. You can do almost anything else, but if you throw out a football, someone is going to turn you in to the state. However, you can teach technique in the off-season.

The most important thing Dave Wannstedt told me was to teach the players to be good tacklers. When it is said and done, running backs are going to break the line of scrimmage. Teams are going to drive the ball down the field if you do not tackle them. Can you tackle? Are you going to take the right pursuit angle to tackle the runner?

The advice Dave and Butch gave me 25 years ago is still true. If you can't tackle, you are going to get beat. They told me you must build mental toughness through your defensive players. They talked about four things to teach on defense in order to build mental toughness:

- Aggression
- Determination
- Technique
- Tackling

We do a tackling drill in the off-season. We do not use a football in the drill. We do not have football equipment on. Have you ever seen the big plastic Hula Hoops®? Some of the pro teams use them to work with their linemen. Warren Sapp played high school football for me. I was visiting him when he was playing with the Tampa Bay Buccaneers. They had these big Hula Hoops lying on the ground. The defensive linemen would do the figure eight through the Hula Hoops.

We use ropes instead of the Hula Hoops because the ropes are cheaper. I can make the circle as big as I want or as small as I want it. We put flags on the players. We put two players inside the circle. We have an offensive player and a defensive player. You blow the whistle and the drill starts. The offensive man cannot leave the circle until the defensive man has pulled all of the flags from the offensive man.

You may ask what this teaches. How many times have you see a tackler go for the ball and miss the tackle because he overextended his body on the attempt to make contact. What does this drill teach the kid? It teaches him to stay on his feet and not to overextend. He wants to get next to the offensive man and grab his flag. The drill takes 30 seconds. We do it twice a day and twice a week in the off-season. Kids love the drills. We have not had a player hurt in this drill since we put it into our program. I do not allow the players to wear the gloves that linemen wear.

The offensive man has to stay inside the circle. The defensive player cannot quit until he gets all of the flags. We may use three flags on the offensive man. We can put two on the sides and one in the back of the offensive man. The offensive man is trying to run away from the defensive man. This teaches the defensive man to stay on his feet. He does not want to overextend on the drill.

We do not allow the offensive player to use his hands in the drill. All he can do is run around inside the circle. If you run this drill in the off-season, it will help them become better tacklers in the fall.

I picked this drill up at a clinic in Atlanta. I was speaking at a clinic and this youth league coach was giving an on-the-field type lecture. I saw him do the drill and decided to put the drill into our program. We prefer to do this drill at the end of practice.

I went to coach at Edgewater High School 11 years ago. We only had two varsity players returning from the previous team. In our first meeting, this is what I told them. In the off-season workouts, the players are going to hold the other players accountable. Over the years, I have never had a problem doing that.

- Players hold players accountable.
- Unit goals are more important than individual awards.
- Both players and coaches pay the price to be part of a defense.
- Size is really not a major factor.

We hold our players accountable for their teammates. We tell them all of the time to check their egos at the door. The only thing that is important is how successful your unit is going to be. How many defensive linemen are going to come to the workout? You nominate players to be in charge of the groups. You can go around and ask the leaders of the groups, "How many players are missing from practice today?"

If the player tells me he does not know, I let him know that it is his fault and it is my fault, as well. It is my fault because I did not check on him at lunchtime. "It is also your fault for not having him here. I guess you do not want to have a good team." This is the difference in football and any other sport. I am not against other sports. I want my players to be around other players. I want them to play other sports. I want them with the other coaches because I believe coaches are good people. They have to be accountable if they are going to be there.

At our school, you cannot play on defense if you are not willing to commit to our program. I do not care how big you are; if you are not committed, you can't play defense if you are not committed to our program. If they play defense for us we may buy them a special T-shirt, award them with a decal on their helmet, or something to reward the defensive players that are committed.

Former Auburn University Coach Pat Dye told me to reward the different units. He said, "Offensive linemen must be first." They need to be first in the cafeteria line and first in all of the lines where football players are involved. The offensive linemen do not get the recognition they are due. The coaching staff must reward them as much as possible.

The last point we stress on defense is the fact that size is not a factor. It is a matter of commitment and determination. How well can you tackle? How well can you play your technique? Those are the only things we ask of our kids.

FOCUS ON TECHNIQUE

- Board drill
- Pass rush
- 7-on-7 drill
- Press coverage drill
- Pursuit drill
- Blind tackling drills

We focus on these six drills we got from Jimmy Johnson. We do these drills in our practice three days a week. We dress out in pads every day. Some coaches tell me they do not hit during the season. We are going to do those six drills three days a week.

Everyone knows what the board drill is. This drill is aggression and determination. We do that drill three days a week.

The reason we do the pass rush drill is because everyone in Florida is running a spread offense. Teams are throwing the ball 30 to 35 times a game. If you go to the playoffs, it gets worse. I think the players of south Florida are faster than kids are in central Florida. What is the best way to defend the pass? Sack the quarterback! Therefore, we work on the pass rush three days a week.

The 7-on-7 drill is the best drill Jimmy Johnson and Butch Davis taught me 25 years ago. I coached an offensive lineman at Evans High School in Orlando that was a first-round NFL draft choice. Leon Searcy was the eleventh pick in the NFL draft in 1992 out of the University of Miami. Leon Searcy and Russell Maryland would go against each other two or three times a week at the University of Miami. Russell Maryland was the number one NFL pick in the 1991 draft.

These players were all NFL players. All of the Miami players took part in this drill. Here was the key to the drill. No one took a man to the ground. No one could block or tackle below the waist. We all know if your best players get hurt, you are not going to be very good, especially in high school.

The thing I remember about that drill at Miami is that Jimmy Johnson had two whistles on plays. They lined up in the 4-3 defense and they worked against the I formation plays against the defense. One whistle was for everyone to stop, and the second whistle was for the ballcarrier to stop. It did not matter if the back was still running, he had to continue until the second whistle blew.

I am sure a lot of you use the press coverage drill. We use it because we play press coverages. We play man coverage. I picked this up from Howard Schnellenberger when he was the head coach at Miami. He only played his corners on press coverage.

We play press coverage where we play cover zero. We practice cover zero half line. We put two receivers to one side and cover them with press coverage. As soon as the play is over for that first group, the other side of the line comes up and gets ready to go and we work on press coverage on that side of the ball. We did this as a live drill. The only thing that was not live was that we did not allow tackling to the ground. You can't teach press coverage unless you do it live.

During the off-season, we do the pursuit drills. We do not run sprints in our program. I never have used wind sprints in my program. The offensive and defensive linemen push my truck around the track at school. I cannot bring a sled on our game field because that is where we practice. We do our sled work on the track with my truck and we do it at the end of practice. I hate that we can't put a sled on our field. We have to improvise.

The defensive backs and receivers and all other players are in pursuit drills. We set the cones up on the sideline and the defensive players must take the proper angle to run the ballcarrier down. I am sure all of you know the drill.

The blind tackling drill I picked up from a youth football coach. There are a ton of tackling drills, but we try to do this drill three days a week. We hang three canvas type tarps over the goalpost. Each tarp has a hook that we secure at the top of the crossbar.

We divide the linebackers on each side of the goalpost. One line is going to be the ballcarrier, and the other side is going to tackle the man with the ball. We have the three tarps, with a little room between each tarp. We give a snap count and the ballcarrier tries to score. The defense does not know where the ball is coming from. It teaches the defenders not to overextend on tackling. They have to be in a good football position and find the ball. The man with the ball can go through any of the holes or outside of the holes under the goalpost. I believe this drill helps us in tackling in a game.

I want to show you four formations. You do not have to call the formations the way we call them. We lined up the defense and we gave all of the backs and receivers a name. We call a formation with two tight ends and a wing and two backs in the backfield a tight formation (Diagram #1). We started researching this offense and we found the tight end was usually on the left side of the formation. In the tight formation, the line is unbalanced. They had a wingback one yard outside the end and one yard off the line. We called the second back inside between the two tackles the "sniffer back." All he is from that position is another guard. They had a quarterback and a tailback in the traditional spots in the backfield.

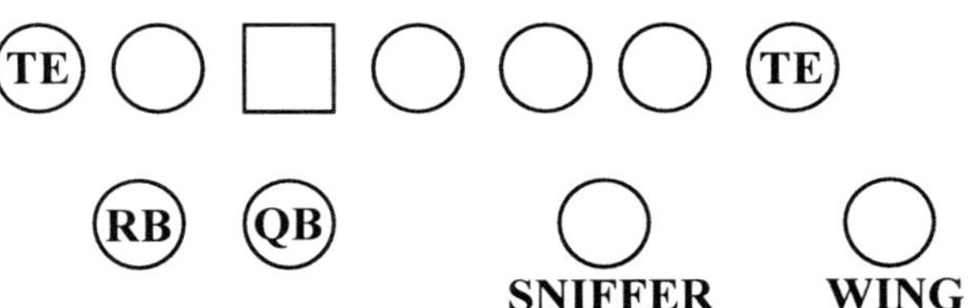

Diagram #1. Tight Formation

We studied the formation and tried to figure out what they could run from this formation. To me, this looks like a wing-T formation. They just have the sniffer sitting in the up position between the tackles.

The next formation we call a "pro look." They have split one end and moved the wingback to the other side of the formation (Diagram #2). It is unbalanced, but it resembles what we call a "pro set." As we studied the formation, we found they

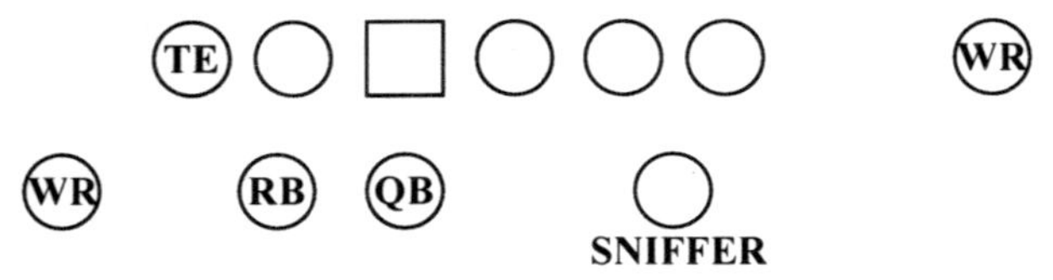

Diagram #2. Pro Formation

took the tight end from the weakside 90 percent of the time. At times, the tight end was ineligible. He would not have a jersey number where he was eligible to receive a pass most of the time.

We called the next formation "wide" (Diagram #3). It was the same situation with the tight end. The second man on the line from the inside was not a tight end. The first year we played them, I had a good strong safety. He covered that inside man on the line on passing situations. He spent the entire first quarter covering a player that was ineligible. I know players make mistakes, and I can assure you coaches make mistakes. We called that formation wide.

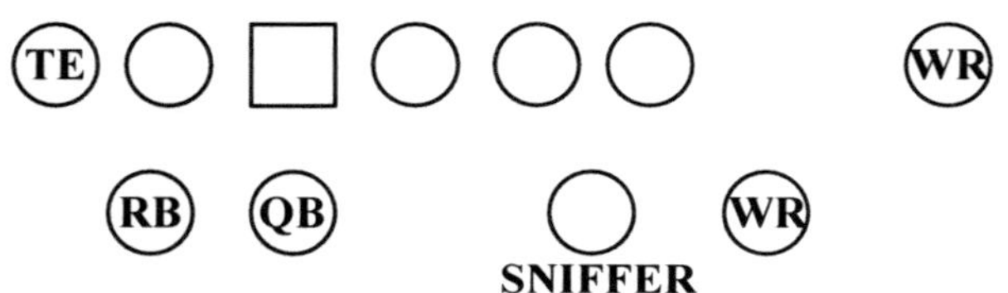

Diagram #3. Wide Formation

We called the next formation "weak" because the backs lined up on the weakside of the formation (Diagram #4). Again, the second man on the inside on the right side was ineligible. I can't begin to tell you how many films I saw where teams were covering that man. In a one-hour lecture, we do not have time to talk about the adjustments they make, or they can use motion and shifts. Do they line up in those formations and just stay there? No! Do you have to make adjustments in the secondary? Absolutely!

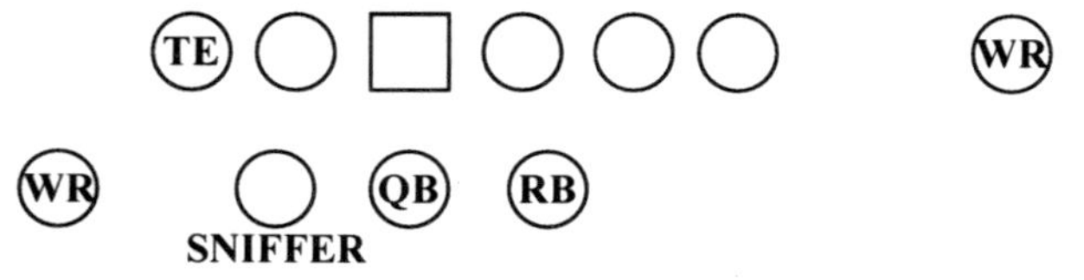

Diagram #4. Wide Formation Weak

We collected all of the information on the offense we wanted to learn how to defend. We gathered the data and put it into a computer program we purchased. This is what we found:

- Pass plays are deep routes, crossing patterns, play-action.
- Pullers are looking for easy kick-outs.
- Calculate the sniffer.

We wanted to prevent the offense from completing the long passes on us. We found that most of the deep routes were on first down. This was especially true if there was a turnover. We found out from the computer program if we turned the ball over, they were coming with a trick play or a deep passing route. We had to make sure our players were aware of this before they got on the field.

The pulling players, guards, ends, or the sniffer back were looking for the easy kick-outs. What did this offense remind you of? The wing-T offense. It is the old Buck sweep play where they are looking for the easy kick-out block.

The third point we researched was the number of times the sniffer back was involved in the blocking scheme. How many times did the sniffer back take you to the point of attack? Against this team, it was almost all of the time. He was leading us to where the ball was going.

FOUR BASIC ADJUSTMENTS

- Play man coverage.
- Don't be caught peeking in the backfield.
- Make running plays bounce.
- Make opponent go against tendencies.

We decided we would play man coverage against this team. That is our cover zero. When we play this team, we tell our players not to get caught peeking into the backfield. We were playing against a good football team and we were against a good coach. He knows what he is doing. We tell the secondary they do not have the ball. They have a man on defense and they must stay with their man.

We tell the defenders to make the ball bounce and not to give up the vertical creases. We do not want the runners busting through a seam and getting into the secondary. We want to make the play bounce.

The last point the computer told us was what we could expect the offense to do against us. We checked their tendencies and learned a great deal about what they were trying to accomplish against us.

Here is one of the best plays they ran against us. At times, they would down block, kick out with the sniffer, and pull the frontside guard up in the hole. That looked like the Buck sweep to me. That is the wing-T Buck sweep play (Diagram #5). They also zone blocked the play where everyone on the line used a reach block, and they tried to outrun us to the corner.

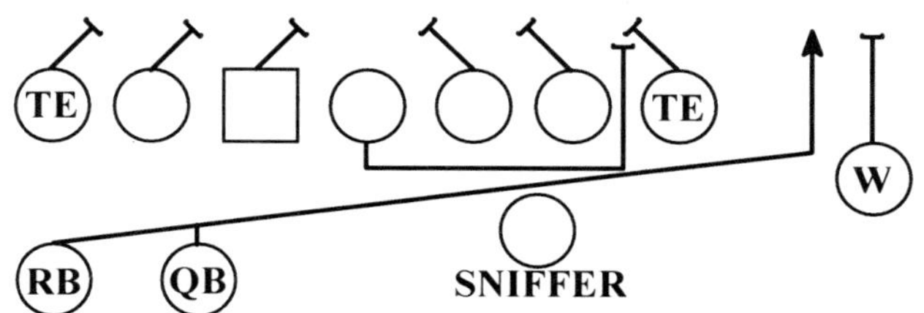

Diagram #5. Running Back Sweep

Sometimes, they would use the direct snap on the play. They move the backs over one-half a man and snap the ball to the running back. My guys could not see that on the field. They come to the line and... Boom! They snap the ball with no cadence. You may still be lining up on defense. They call that a "running back sweep."

The next play was their best play. It is the wingback counter play out of the same alignment (Diagram #6). They used a handoff to the wingback, and they handed the ball to him coming behind the running back. Those were complementary plays. They had a play-action pass off this play as well. They faked the sweep and threw the deep ball. They faked the counter and threw the deep ball.

At one of the clinics I attended when I was young, I heard a coach lecture on when to throw the football. Most of the pass plays are going to be deep off play-action passes. The defense needs to get the offense into a situation where the down-and-distance does not matter on a play-action pass—third-and-long. Now, the offense has to do

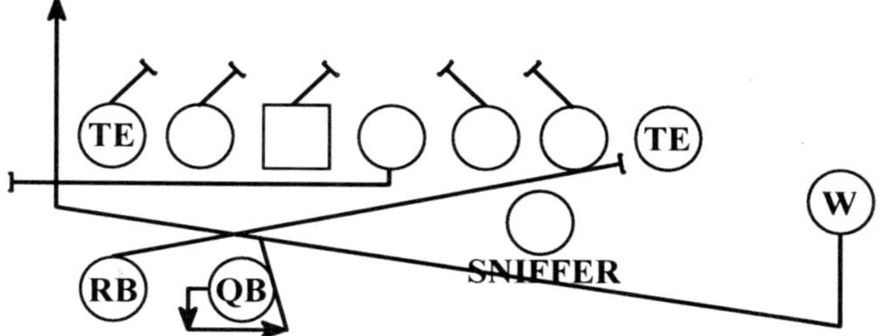

Diagram #6. Wingback Counter

something they do not want to do. This makes it easier to cover the play-action pass.

Another thing the offense did was to pull the tight end on the counter play. They pulled the guard, the sniffer, and the tight end on the wingback counter. They pull all three of them because that is their best play. The wing-T ran the same type play; when they ran the Buck sweep they ran the counter with the inside handoff to the wingback. This is the same play.

They ran a quarterback counter play as well (Diagram #7). The quarterback can run the play inside the end, or he can run the play outside. The quarterback does a complete spin on the play. He spins, and turns, and finds his hole.

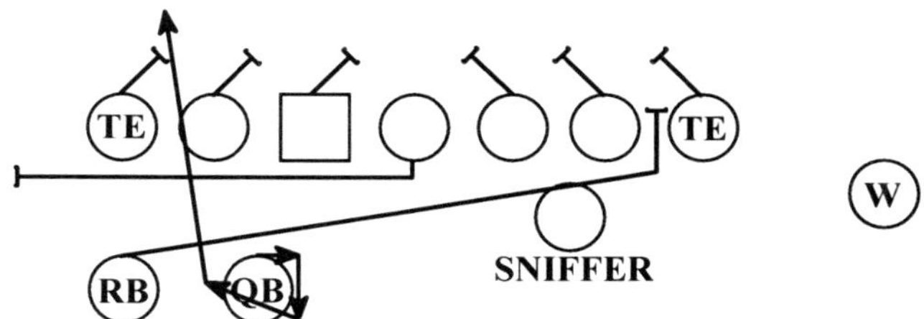

Diagram #7. Quarterback Counter

On the quarterback sweep, they try to outrun the defense (Diagram #8). They come to the line quick and snap the ball. The backs shift to the strongside and they try to get outside. They pull the onside guard and zone block the play.

Those are the four main plays and the play-action passes that we decided to concentrate on stopping. We wanted to take those four plays away from them and force them to run something else. At times, that can be easier said than done, but that was our game plan.

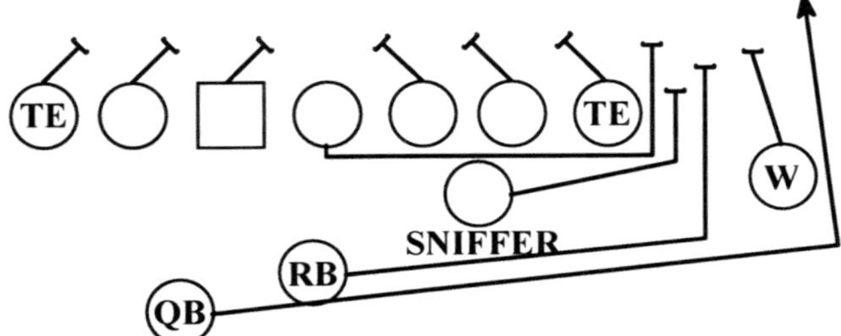

Diagram #8. Quarterback Sweep

I want to show you how we defended those formations. We do not have the big defensive linemen. We have players that can run, but they are not very big. We changed from our 3-5 defense and played with four down linemen. This is how we lined up against the tight set (Diagram #9). We played four down linemen. This is what we told those four down players. Remember, we have a 175-pound noseguard. We had the nose angle into the A gap. We told him to take as many blockers with him as he could. We did not expect him to make a single tackle. He is in a 0 technique.

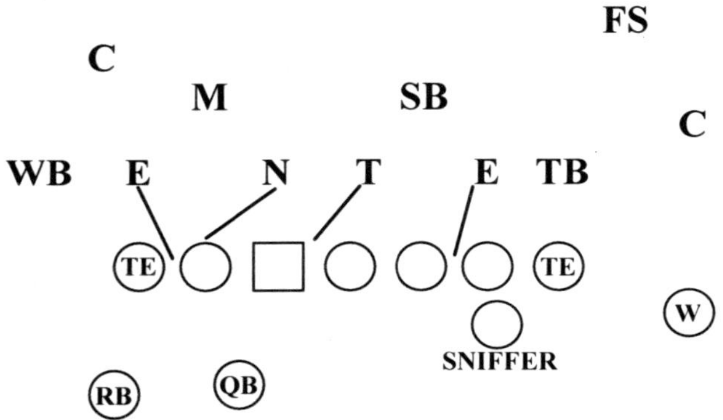

Diagram #9. Alignment vs. Tight

We played a 3 technique and he played with long sticks. This is where you are almost coming from two gaps over. We told him the same thing we told the noseguard: Take as many blockers with you as you can when you penetrate the A gap. We did not want to move out of the A gap. The ends played the C gaps. They used the same technique as the nose and tackle. We told them to stay down low and to protect the gaps.

We call our two ends the Will backer and the tight backer. We flip-flop the linebackers. The reason is because the techniques are easier to teach. The tight backer lines up on top of the tight end. He is not going to let that tight end release down inside. He must fight the tight end and keep him from using the reach block. On the weakside, the end was uncovered. We did play the Will backer on the line most of the time. That is how we lined up to defend the tight formation.

We told the weak backer if the ball goes away from him, he wants to stay on the line. If the ball comes to him, he wants to fight the tight end. We attack the pulling guards. Do not run up the field. Do not get kicked out of the hole. We want him to force everything inside to the Mike backer, who is our best player. We named one linebacker the sniffer backer. He had to cover the sniffer back. If the sniffer ran a pass route, the sniffer backer took him man-to-man. He covered the sniffer back on all plays.

The Mike backer has the running back. He is our best football player. He plays more like a safety man. He is athletic and he can run. He is fast and he loves to hit. If we could keep him unblocked, he would make the play for us.

If the sniffer backer keys through the guard to the sniffer back and sees the guard pulling, he calls out, "Pull, pull, pull" to the Mike linebacker. That means they are running the counter play. That is the reason we called the linebacker the sniffer backer.

It was easy for the secondary because they were playing man coverage. They did not want to get caught peeking in the backfield. We are playing cover zero. Against the pro set, the corner had the #1 receiver from the outside to the inside (Diagram #10). The free safety has the #2 receiver to the inside. If the #2 man inside is not eligible, he could be a free safety.

If the free safety lined up on the #2 man inside on the line of scrimmage, he was covering the wrong man. That man was not eligible. We want to help the free safety to cover the correct receiver. If we saw he was keying the wrong man, we called out from the sideline, "Tiger, tiger, tiger." He would have to go over on the other side and find the #2 receiver.

We mix the calls up on defense. Sometimes we angle weak, sometimes strong, and sometimes we

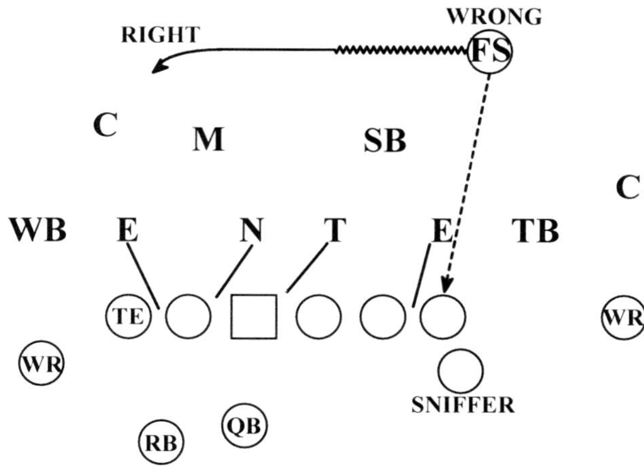

Diagram #10. Pro Set Adjustments

play our base defense. This is from the unbalanced set. This was a hard formation to defend. We never played the same coverage technique. The corners mixed up their techniques on the receivers.

Against the wide formation, we played the corner on the strongside deeper than the shortside of the formation (Diagram #11). The split end on that side was their best athlete. We played press coverage on the backside.

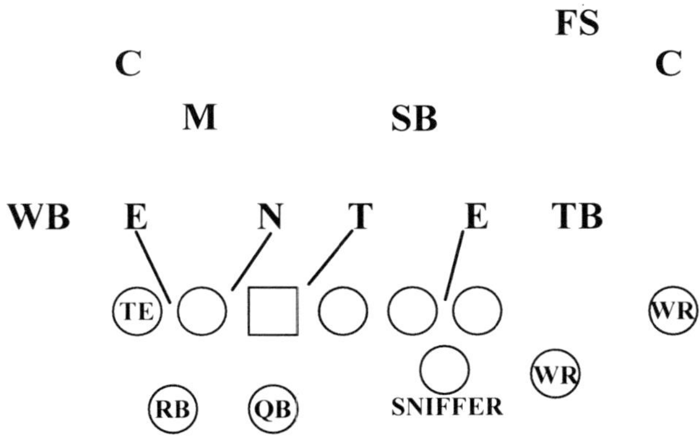

Diagram #11. Wide Set Adjustments

On the weak formation, we still have the front four and they can mix up their techniques (Diagram #12). We have our corner on the strongside off the line again. The backs on offense have lined up on the shortside of the formation.

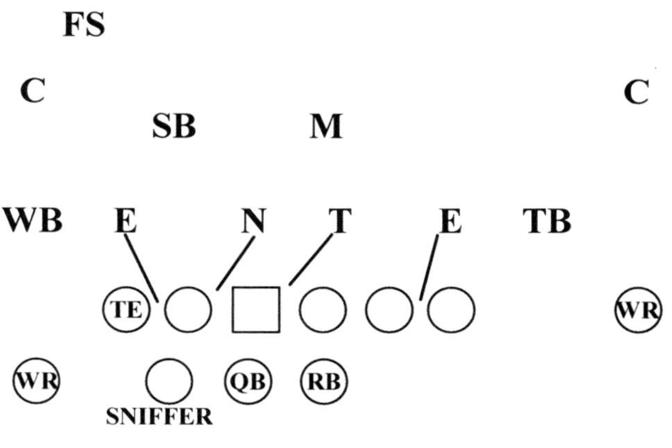

Diagram #12. Weak Set Adjustments

Tony Dungy spoke at our school recently. I asked him what separated the great players from the average players. He told me the players that could make decisions on the move made the great players. They have a knack for finding the football. That is what separates them from the average players.

If I touched on something you are interested in knowing more about, feel free to contact me. Thank you.

Andy Guyon

BALL DISRUPTION AND TACKLING DRILLS

Xavier High School, Connecticut

Thank you very much. I appreciate the opportunity to speak with you today. My topic is on team defense.

One of the things we emphasize is playing hard, physical defense. We call it playing "nasty." I am not talking about cheap shots. We emphasize playing within the rules. If we are taking cheap shots after the whistle, we are costing ourselves 15 yards. That might keep us from forcing a punt and getting the football. We tell our players that if they get a 15-yard penalty, they are out for the remainder of that game, and for the next game. We do not have a problem in that area.

Let me go over some statistics for this year. We had 12 forced fumbles, of which we recovered 10 of them. For as much time that we spend on trying to get the ball stripped, this is not something I am proud of. On the other hand, 26 interceptions is something that I get excited about. We also had 56 pass break-ups. These stats come from a number of things. We like to blitz, and we like to apply pressure. The ball comes out quick. We have done a good job of scheming when we drop eight. We are going to give you a pressure focus, and then we are going to drop eight. The quarterback thinks he sees pressure, and then he throws it to one of our outside linebackers. That happens more often than not.

We also had 62 tackles for a loss this year. On rundowns, we are coming with five- or six-man pressure. We move our defensive line, and we bring a ton of extra pressure.

In eight of our 13 games this year, we allowed one score or less. This comes from having great players. Also, I think it was important that our staff got together on Sunday nights to make sure that everyone was on the same page in what we were doing. Then, we would go out and practice during the week, in an organized manner, when implementing the game plan.

DEFENSIVE GAME GOALS

- Win
- 14 points or less
- Four takeaways
- 50 percent three-and-out
- Score or set up a score

The main part of my discussion today will revolve around ball disruptions. This is something that I took from Coach Bill Belichick. Following are five things you can do and teach to your kids as attempts by the defense to adversely affect the flow of the offense by applying direct pressure to the football on every play:

- Altered pass: Not necessarily a knockdown, but the pass was altered in some way
- Batted ball
- Forced fumble that you recover
- Pass break-ups
- Interceptions

BALL AWARENESS

Ball awareness requires a defensive player trained to locate the person handling the ball, and the position of the football at all times during the play. Most likely, we are going to attack the quarterback because he handles the football on every play. Next, we look at the running backs. How are they giving the running back the ball? Is it in the running game, or in the passing game? How is the running back carrying the ball? When they do throw, which one of their receivers is not good at putting the ball away?

- *The most important element is creating ball disruption:* We want to find out just how good their quarterback is when handling the ball.

- *For every play, know who has the ball or where it is going:* This goes back to the coach doing his work in finding the opponent's schemes and tendencies, whether it is down-and-distance or areas of the field.

This is what we use as the ball disruption formula:

- Add up ball disruptions/total plays = magic number.
- Magic number = 19 percent.
- You do that, and you win 70 percent of your games.

In our state championship game, we had disruptions on 21 of the 45 defensive plays. We were able to do one of those five things in 47 percent of our defensive plays. We had three interceptions in that game.

In our semifinal game, we had disruptions in 19 of our 54 defensive plays. That is a 35 percent ratio. We had one defensive touchdown, one fumble recovery, and seven sacks. We did a good job of changing personnel and defensive schemes to adjust to our opponent and to create these disruptions. Let's talk more specifically about our definitions.

Altered Pass

- *Prevent the quarterback from stepping up in the pocket:* When you get pressure on the quarterback, he wants to step up. If you can give the quarterback pressure in his face, he does not have anywhere to go. We want to make him sit there and throw the ball with a short arm throw.
- *Force the quarterback to release the ball before he wants to:* Most of today's passing game is a rhythm and timing throw. If we can disrupt his timing, our defense will benefit.
- *Prevent quarterback follow through:* We want to make the quarterback have to throw the ball up, or alter what he would like to do.
- *Make the quarterback progress to his second or third read:* At our level of football, we can usually tell which side or which receiver the quarterback or offensive coordinator will go to. We want to know, by down-and-distance, who he is getting the ball to, and we want to take that guy away. We want to make the quarterback do something he is not used to doing, like going to the second and third read. By the time the quarterback is into his second or third read, we have gotten to him with our pressure.
- *Force the quarterback to pull down and change the timing of pattern:* By forcing the quarterback to scramble, you have changed the timing of his pass. Once you force the quarterback to scramble, though, you have to do a good job of covering.
- *Change the quarterback's throwing motion.*
- *Sack.*

Our coaching points for altering throws include the following. If the quarterback is right-handed, and we are running at the quarterback, instead of running with both hands up, we are only going to put our left hand up. This will keep us on balance, so if the quarterback decides to tuck the ball and run, we can change direction and run after him. We want to get one arm up to disrupt the vision of the quarterback. This will give us an extra second for someone to get to the quarterback and get the sack.

We want to prevent the pump fake. If we have both hands up and have three guys running after the quarterback, he can pump fake us, get us off the ground, and duck under us. He will then have clear vision to his receivers. It is easier to jump up into the air with both hands up. If you only have one hand up, it is a lot harder to jump than it is for you to come forward.

We want to have more altered throws than we do sacks. By disrupting the rhythm of the quarterback and getting our hands in his face, he is not going to be as comfortable in the pocket and more apt to throw it to the defense.

An unbelievable statistic we have found to be true is, if you get a sack in a series, 75 percent of the time that series will result in a punt. That is just one sack in a series.

Batted Balls

- *Raising an arm into the throwing lane to deflect the pass:* This does not mean only the defensive line. Linebackers need to get their hands up to bat the ball down. Even if the defensive back knocks the ball down, that counts as a batted ball.

- *Defender can jump if there is a blocker between the quarterback and the rusher:* If the back steps up to block me, now I can jump. If I am getting blocked and can no longer come forward, we tell our guys to go ahead and jump. We want him to knock the ball down like it is a volleyball.
- *Hand up to the quarterback's throwing arm.*
- *Extend one arm to disrupt the throwing lane:* Even if you do not knock the ball down, just getting the hand up will disrupt the quarterback. It also will be harder for the receiver to see where the ball is coming from.
- *Free runner to the quarterback should run directly at the quarterback and extend your arm as the quarterback brings his arm back:* We teach this. We want the quarterback to fear getting hit, more than the hit itself.
- *Stay on your feet; use the opposite arm principle.*

Coaching points for batted balls are as follows. The motion of the ball is changed because of a deflection on the line of scrimmage. This will give our defense a chance to pick it off. Batted balls result in takeaways and disrupt the timing of pass patterns.

Forced Fumbles: When a Defender Dislodges the Ball From an Offensive Player

- *When sacking the quarterback be aware if you are on the ballside:* This goes back to what we tell the guys during the week. Is the quarterback left-handed, or is he right-handed? Does he carry the ball high and near his chest? Are his elbows out, or are his elbows in? Are both hands on the ball? If we think we can dislodge the ball, we will go after the ball first.
- *When sacking the quarterback from behind, have the awareness to put your hand on the ball.* If you are coming from behind the quarterback, we would rather strip the ball first and then go after the quarterback, rather than just trying to hit the quarterback.
- *Securing the tackle and allowing the pursuit to get hands on the ball:* We teach the first tackler to wrap the ballcarrier up. We teach the second, third, and fourth guys to find the ball and strip it out.
- *Attack the ball before the receiver can totally secure it:* When a receiver catches the football, the first thing he has to do is bring the ball into his body to secure it. We teach the defensive back if he cannot go around the receiver, to go up and under as the receiver brings the ball into his body, and try to pop the ball out.

For our coaching points, we want to spend more time on forcing fumbles. We will work on this in particular for next season. We will pay particular attention to where and how guys are carrying the ball.

We are going to talk about, "Where is the air?" Is the ballcarrier's elbow out, or is it in tight? Am I going to punch the ball, or am I going to try to strip his fingers off the ball? Am I going to try to chop his arm to try to get the ball out? How are we going to do it?

We want to red-dot the player who has the poorest ball security. The quarterback is the number-one focus in taking care of the ball. How good is your quarterback at protecting and sharing the football?

We want to locate the offensive player who puts the ball on the ground most frequently. We want to identify how that person specifically carries the ball, and what the best method is to get him to give up the football.

On Tuesdays, we run our tackling circuit, and we emphasize open-field tackles, sideline tackles, angle tackles, and tackling in space. On Wednesdays, we run our ball disruption stations.

The coaching points with this are: do we secure the fumble versus scoop and score? We try not to give them too many rules. If the ball is loose deep in the offensive backfield, we want the first guy on the scene to be a shortstop and scoop the ball and score. All of the other guys should be turning around and peeling back to hit the quarterback or anyone else who is trying to chase our guy. If the ball is fumbled on or somewhere around the line of scrimmage, we will just secure the football and let our offense score.

Pass Break-Ups

- *How to break on the route:* Every route, offensively, has a breaking point where the ball is going to be delivered. We teach the defensive back, based on the pattern, where the interception point is going to be. We want the defensive back to beat the receiver to the interception point.

- *Hand placement, secure the tackle:* If the receiver does catch the ball, where is the hand placement going to be in regards to how he is going to bring the receiver down, and am I going to be able to find a way to poke at the ball to get it out? I also need to know where my help is coming from.
- *Put your hand in the pocket:* This has to do with where the receiver catches the ball and what we need to do in order to get a hand on it before he puts it away.
- *In-phase with receiver versus out-of-phase:* If you can reach out and slap the receiver's thigh pads, you are in-phase with that receiver. If you are more than an arm's length away, you are not. We are always coaching to stay in-phase. If you are able to undercut a route and get two hands on it, we want you to pick it off. If you can only get one hand on it, we want to secure the tackle.
- *Out-of-phase—Play hands:* When the receiver's hands go up, that is when our hands should go up. We want to teach it so that we match the receiver's hands.
- *Defensive backs—Where is the sideline?* We want our players to be aware of their surroundings. If they are near a sideline, we want them to use the sideline as their friend.
- *Working with the sideline or not.*
- *How do you turn?* We want to teach our defensive backs how to turn with a receiver—how to turn if we are in zone coverage, and how to turn if we are in man-to-man coverage. We will teach our defensive backs how to turn into their receiver on different types of pass routes.
- *Red zone—Play through quarterback on defensive backs:* Play through the quarterback. Have vision to the quarterback to be able to play through the receiver back to the quarterback.
- *Box out for defensive backs:* We want to use our butt and use the sideline on the fade and the corner route in the back of the end zone. We want to be sure we are looking back so the referee cannot call interference on us. We teach our players to become the receiver and to go get it.

Interceptions

- *Shotgun—quarterback one-step—defensive backs:* If the quarterback is in the gun, it is a one-step catch and throw; it is a three-step drive. The ball is coming out quick, and we want to coach our kids to drive on the ball.
- *Quarterback under center—see quarterback:* If I am the defensive back, I am looking at the quarterback first. I am looking at the quarterback to see what he is doing as I am making my read cut.
- *Transition after interception—score:* We are looking to score.
- *Blockers get to numbers:* After we intercept the ball, we want our blockers to get to the numbers to make a lane so we can score.
- *Match—Jump on quarterback's eyes to the ball:* Some quarterbacks are good and will look to their left, middle, and right on their pre-snap read. Some quarterbacks will stare at where they are going with the football. Cheat by using the quarterback's eyes as a help.

Defensive Axioms

This is how we teach what we want our kids to do on every play:

- *Pursuit:* The first thing we teach is to pursue the ball. When you get to the ball, get there in a bad mood.
- *Tackling:* Make sure you are using the proper tackling fundamentals.
- *Takeaways:* We emphasize takeaways.
- *We teach defense in this order.*
- *Players know it takes zero talent to pursue:* Do you love your teammate enough to be there when you are supposed to be there? What happens if your teammate strips the ball and you are dogging it, and you are not there to get it? You have to have enough pride to get there and get the ball.
- *Coach effort on every play:* It is a lot, but it will get you to where you want to be.

PURSUIT DRILLS

Play Fast (Diagram #1)

Start out this drill in four lines. It does not matter who lines up where. Our defensive line coach stands in front of them and has them chop their feet. He tells them to hit it, and they do an up-down. He will point in a direction, and we have a coach positioned on each sideline. Once the players pop up, we are screaming at the players to haul ass toward the designated sideline. The biggest thing we want them to understand is that if they are running directly behind somebody, they are wrong. We will make them run it again. We want to find the open window and create a fence along the sideline.

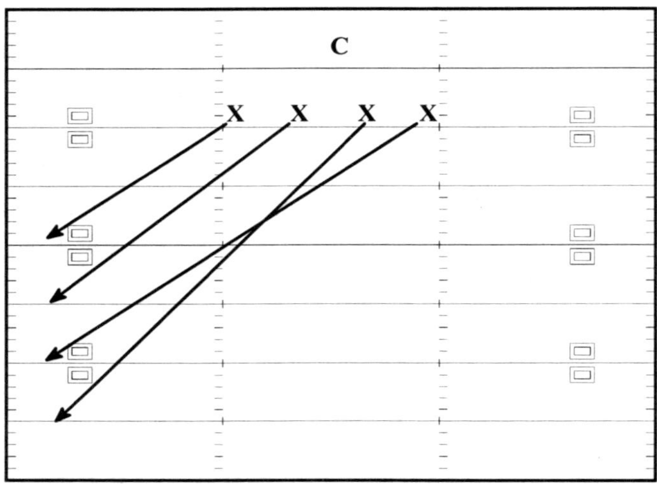

Diagram #1. Play Fast Drill

Assignment (Diagram #2)

Once we get the play fast drill in them and we see a lot of hustle, we want them to start to think as they are running toward the ball. We will put cones out to force leverage. The coach will get behind the garbage cans and throw the ball to one side or the other. We have the frontside force guys running toward their cone, which is lateral to the coach. The rest of the guys are running toward their cones located on the numbers.

The backside outside linebacker yells, "BCR." That stands for bootleg, counter, and reverse. He is going to balance his feet and make sure nothing is coming back at him, and then he takes off and sprints to the last cone. The backside corner is the

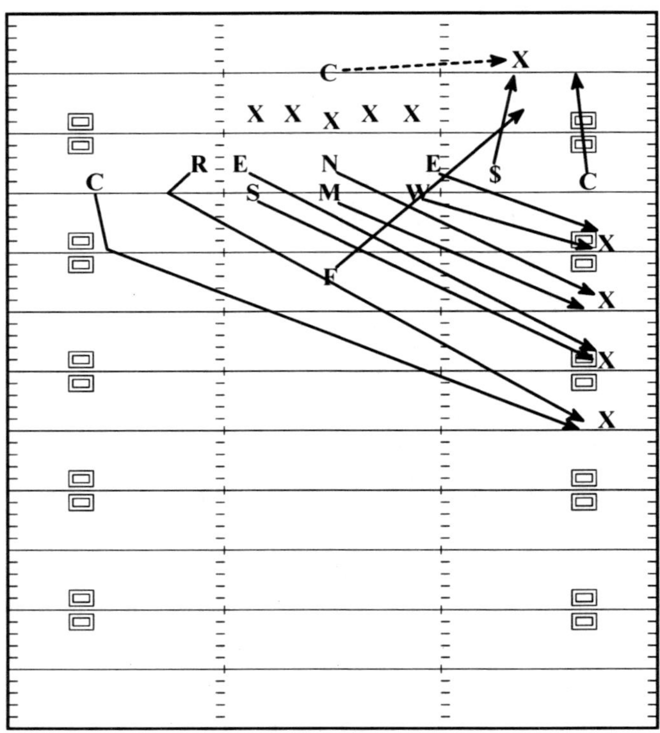

Diagram #2. Team Pursuit Drill

homerun player. He is going to take his two resets, help on bootleg, counter, and reverse, and then haul ass down the field. He is our last line of defense if it breaks.

Interception (Diagram #3)

The interception drill is a blast. This is a conditioning drill, without them knowing it is conditioning, because it is so much fun. We set the garbage cans

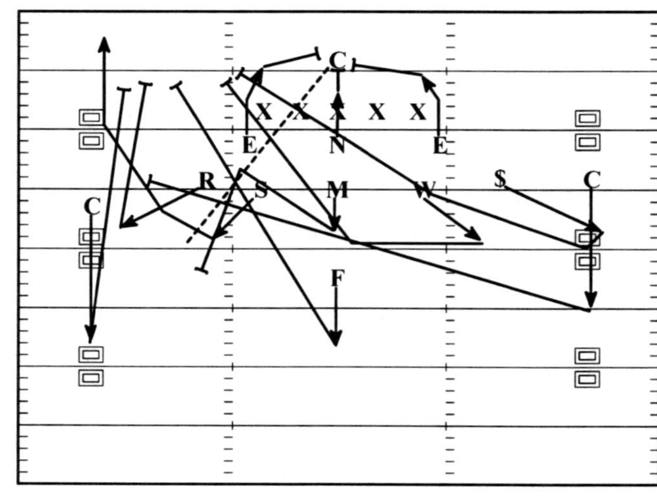

Diagram #3. Interception Drill

up front. We make our defensive calls, whether it is a blitz or base defense, whatever. We can get them working on their pass rush. If it is a base call, we want to get up the field.

I will play quarterback and take my drop and just lob it up there. Someone has to come up and high point the ball. If they do not high-point the ball, we do it over again. The closest defender to the defensive back making the interception will simulate throwing a block, and then will turn and run up the sideline. Everyone else is leading the ballcarrier up the sideline. The drill does not end until all 11 guys are in the end zone, celebrating. We emphasize to celebrate as a team.

If we want to make it a little more interesting, we can add three receivers into the drill. We make sure the receivers get blocked. If they do not get the receivers blocked, we do it over again. The receivers do not have to make the tackle. If we block somebody in the back, we do it over again.

Shimmy (Diagram #4)

Our kids hate this drill. However, it is a great drill. We have the full team up. We line up four guys on each side and outside of the hash marks. I stand in the middle at 20 yards down the field. I have one of my other coaches 20 yards behind me. At the start of the drill, they sprint for 15 yards straight down the field. They have to come out flying. When they get to me, I give them shimmy. They will start shimmying their feet with their inside foot forward. They sink their butt down, bend their knees, and bend their ankles. They shimmy and sit, sit, sit for five yards. They come to a complete stop when they get to me. When they do, we rip them again.

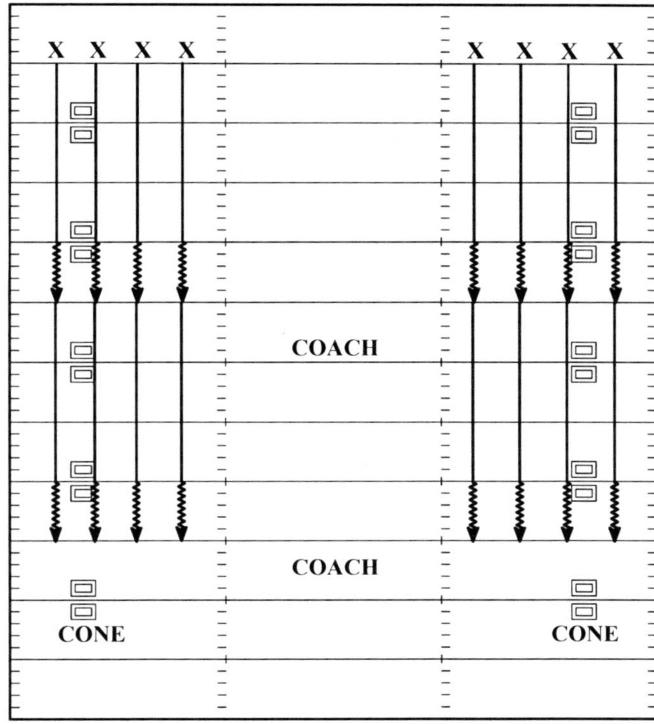

Diagram #4. Shimmy Drill

Once they get to the second coach, they have to shimmy for five yards again, come to a complete stop, and that coach will have them sprint off to the sideline and breakdown. They will jog back around and get in line again. This drill will gas them.

TACKLING

We teach two types of tackling. The first one is a profile tackle. I use the term profile because you can see the ballcarrier's profile from the side. This is an angle tackle, where you do not need to break down. You just roll your shoulder over and drive him into the bench.

The other type of tackle we call a shimmy tackle. This is when you are face-to-face and you have to shimmy and breakdown before you make the tackle.

The first drill we have for profile tackling is the one-step profile drill (Diagram #5). We place our running back and linebacker about five yards apart with a bag in the middle. We tell the running back to take one step to one side, and the linebacker will tackle him at an angle. We want him to wrap and run. We want to chest him up, throw our uppercuts, and run him back for five steps.

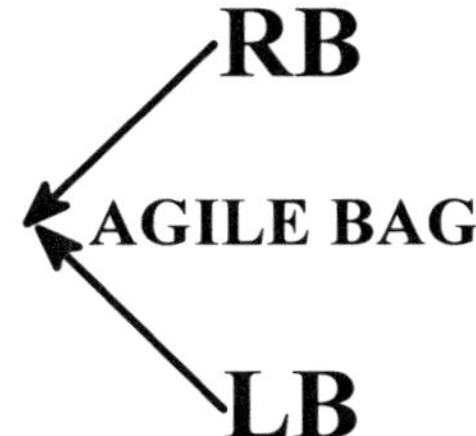

Diagram #5. One-Step Profile Drill

The 2-on-1 leverage drill is awesome for us (Diagram #6). We put two cones out for the running

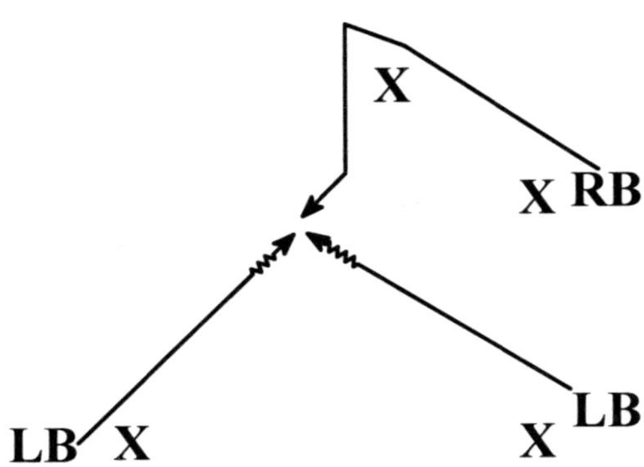

Diagram #6. 2-on-1 Leverage Drill

back to circle. Once the running back circles his cones, he will square up to the two defenders. The linebacker on the right will have his left foot up front. The linebacker on the left will have his right foot up front. This goes back to the shimmy drill we did earlier.

Now, we are attacking with leverage. I want to squeeze the running back back to my partner. Eventually, the running back should not have anywhere to go. We should be shoulder-to-shoulder and blasting the running back. We tell the ballcarrier to make as many moves as he needs to. This is where you get to coach them. This is where we also preach going after the ball.

In the two-step tackle drill, we put them on a line, facing each other (Diagram #7). In this drill, we take one step, wrap them up, and run our feet. We tell our guys to squeeze their butt cheeks together, bring their hips, and keep their elbows tight to their body. As they throw their uppercuts, keep their eyes to the sky, and drive the guy back. To keep it safe, we tell the running backs to let themselves be driven back. We will go with both left and right shoulders.

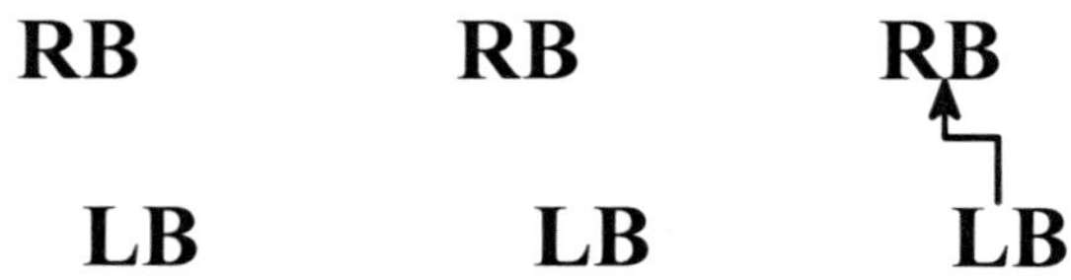

Diagram #7. Two-Step Tackle Drill

The last profile drill I have is the uppercuts drill (Diagram #8). The linebacker in this drill starts on one knee. The ballcarrier is lined up 10 yards away. The running back will jog downfield toward the linebacker. As soon as the running back is close enough to the linebacker, he will fire his uppercuts, stand up, and run. This drill really helps with the timing of the uppercuts. It helps with bringing the hips, too.

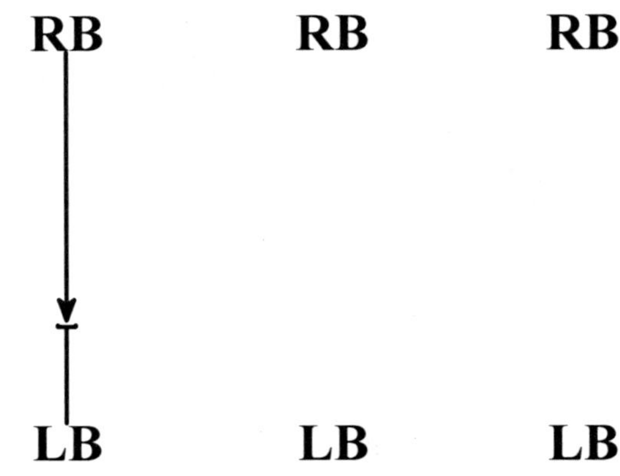

Diagram #8. Uppercuts Drill

Next, I want to go over some shimmy tackling drills. The first drill is the 2-on-1 big shimmy drill (Diagram #9). We use the sideline on this drill and make a big box with our cones. The ballcarrier is facing the coach, and he has the ball. The ballcarrier can choose to run at either linebacker. The linebacker that the running back is running away from better run at a full sprint. His job is to go for the strip. The linebacker that the ballcarrier

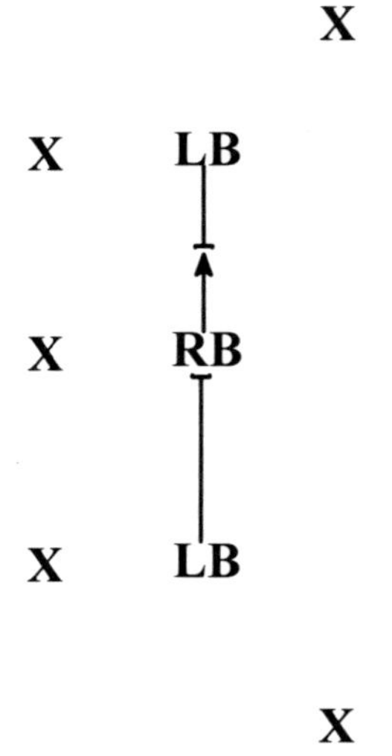

Diagram #9. 2-on-1 Big Shimmy Drill

is running toward will close the distance and make an open field shimmy tackle. The ballcarrier knows that he cannot make 27 moves, because a defender is coming at him from behind.

The shimmy wide drill utilizes a box on the sideline (Diagram #10). The running back and the linebacker are facing each other. I am in the middle of the field, and I just turn and throw. As soon as I turn, the linebacker can come out of his corner of the box and press. The linebacker is to track the running back's near hip to make sure that the running back does not cut back on him. We focus on either forcing the running back to the sideline and out-of-bounds, or to just get him down.

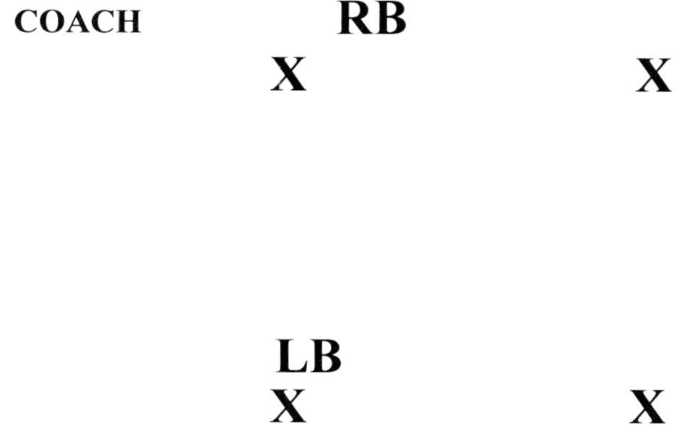

Diagram #10. Shimmy Wide Drill

In our shimmy screen drill, we are again on the sideline in a box (Diagram #11). This time, the wide receiver is on the sideline. The linebacker is watching me. I will turn and throw the ball to the receiver, and he will stay in the box. The linebacker is going to press the receiver, working inside-out, and make the tackle in space.

In the shimmy break drill, the running back and the defensive back or linebacker is lined up on the hash marks (Diagram #12). The defender will sprint downhill as fast as he can for 10 yards. We will put a cone out at five yards from the running back. As

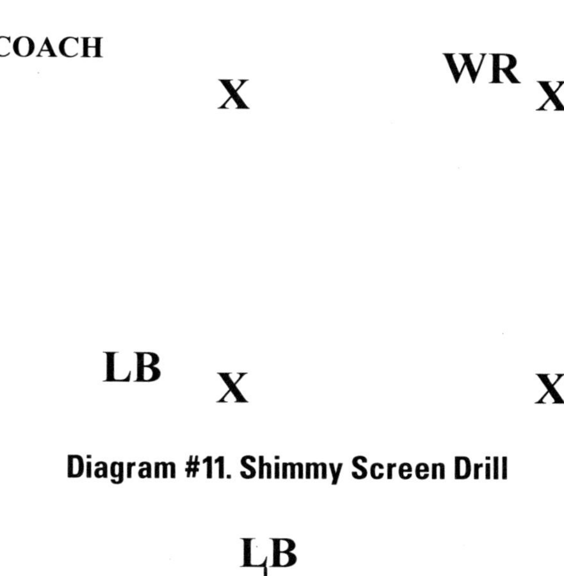

Diagram #11. Shimmy Screen Drill

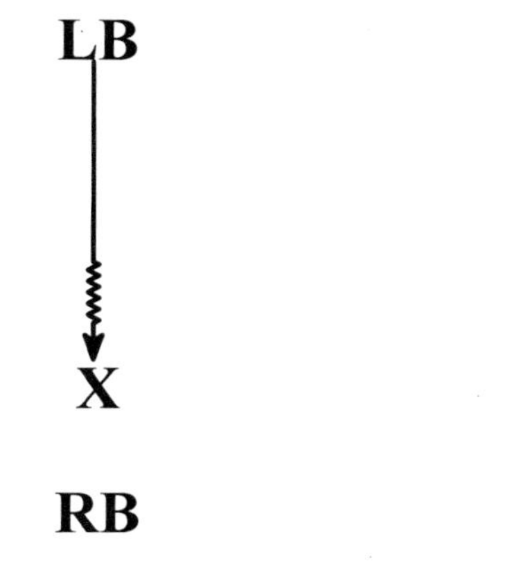

Diagram #12. Shimmy Break Drill

soon as the defensive player gets to that five-yard cone, the running back will try to make his move. This is where you get the title of the shimmy. We will complete the drill with a profile tackle.

In our team period, I stress to our defensive players that we need to get four takeaways. If we do not get four takeaways, we are going to run extra. In our games, we got 47 takeaways the first year we implemented this idea. In any of our 1-on-1 profile or shimmy tackling drills, we can add a second defender to practice stripping the ball.

I want to thank everyone for your attention. Good luck in your coaching career.

Bryon Hamilton

NO-HUDDLE SPREAD OFFENSE: FLY SWEEP

Foothill High School, California

Thank you. It is good to be with you today. I am going to talk to you about one play in our offense. I will show you how we install it, practice it, and execute it. We installed this offense in 2005. We have run it for five years with a great deal of success. In 2006, we decided to run this offense and nothing else.

WHAT IS THE SZF?

- Developed in 2005, the shotgun zone fly is a run-oriented offense that combines the traditional fly sweep, inside zone, and spread passing concepts.
- Since installing the SZF, Foothill High School has won three EAL championships, played in three NSCIF championships, and have a 46-13 record.
- The SZF utilizes the quarterback, the wide receivers, and a running back in order to produce a triple threat in the run game. By utilizing the quarterback and wide receivers in the run game, the SZF offense maintains a three-back threat on almost every play while at the same time spreading the field to create stress on the defense.

The system is the shotgun zone fly series. The SZF focuses on the run as a power running game. This offense uses the quarterback as a primary runner, which forces the defense to cover the field like a spread team. At the same time, the offense has the ability to run the ball inside the tackles as well as on the perimeter. It is versatile in its application.

We run the inside zone, quarterback zone, fly sweep, power, trap, and throw the ball. We throw, and we run. The entire idea behind this offense is it forces the defense to play sideline to sideline while we play goal line to goal line. We want to give the impression that we are a finesse football team and kick butt. We want to go at the defense. The reality of this offense is to get defenders out of the box. I do not want the linebackers coming downhill.

Penetration is the thing that stops the running game. We want to spread the field and get defenders out of the box, but we are going to kick some butt.

POINTS OF EMPHASIS

- Force the defense to defend the entire field on every play.
- Force the defense to commit defenders to the sweep on every play.
- Maintain a power run game while spreading the field.
- Create confusion and hesitation in the defensive linebackers and secondary.
- Use motion and formations to create a numerical and physical advantage over the defense.
- Cause defensive pass coverage to be predictable.

If I can keep the defense in their areas, I can usually find one area of the defense we can dominate. My goal is to keep your defense playing option-sound football in a contained area. I do not want a linebacker making plays hash mark to hash mark. If I can do that, we can find one area of field, and we can take an advantage.

SZF SWEEP

- Average 8 to 10 sweep calls per game
- 80 percent of all offense play calls include some motion. The most common motion is fly or pop motion.
- The fly sweep has averaged over nine yards per carry since 2006.
- Defense has to commit practice time to defend it and prepare for it.

If we can get the defense to show us in pre-snap what they are doing in coverage, it makes it easier for us. That is why we use so much motion. We use fly and pop motion. When we use the fly motion, people on the defense start to move, which give us tips and clues of what they are going to do.

I want to talk about the sweep play. We run the sweep play 8 to 10 times a game. We run the sweep motion considerably more than the sweep. We use motion from our wide receiver or slot. We use some kind of motion on 80 percent of the plays we call. The fly motion comes from the wide receiver, and the pop or short motion comes from the slot players. The defense can stop the sweep. The question is what they give up to stop the sweep. We do not run the sweep but 8 to 10 times a game, but the defense has to spend a lot of practice time preparing for it.

When we run the fly sweep, the first key element of the play is the mesh between the quarterback and sweeper. The heels of the quarterback are at four-and-a-half yards from the line of scrimmage with the weight on the inside of his feet. We spend many hours working on the snap and catching the snap. We want his knees slightly bent with the hands ready to receive the ball. We want the hands covering his numbers. His number-one priority is to get the snap.

The halfback aligns at six-and-a-half yards to the right or left of the quarterback in the shotgun. His depth is approximately two steps behind the quarterback. That depth can change with the timing of the play. If he is a faster running back, his depth could be seven-and-a-half yards. He aligns behind the guard and opposite the Z-receiver, which we call the Zebra. From that position, he can run the frontside and backside zone or the frontside power.

The spacing between the Zebra, halfback, and the guard pull is two steps. Two steps are the timing element we use on this play. The formation determines split of the Zebra. If it is a normal formation, his split is around the numbers.

When the Zebra starts in motion to the quarterback, he is running fast, but in a controlled manner. He uses a slide step (gets depth) at the outside leg of the tackle to move toward the quarterback's playside hip. That puts him on the sweep track. He rotates his shoulders slightly toward the quarterback. That puts his belly button to the ball and his back numbers to the linebackers. This is a tremendously important part of this play. This hides the ball and causes hesitation by the linebackers. This means the sweeper is responsible for hiding the ball.

As he takes the handoff, he immediately locates the block on the force defender and attacks according to his read. If he is executing a fake, he does exactly the same thing, except he keeps his hands in a fist position and does not clamp down on the ball. If he is supposed to get the ball and it is not on the track when he gets there, *do not slow down!* He is now the lead blocker for the quarterback, who runs the ball on the track.

The quarterback wants to snap the ball so that it arrives in his hands when the sweeper is two steps away. The landmark for the quarterback is the outside leg of the backside offensive tackle. He places the ball on the sweep track and hands the ball to the Zebra. He extends the ball forward into the path of the Zebra. That is the sweep track. The Zebra takes the ball from the quarterback.

After he hands the ball off, he rotates on the leg that is on the halfback's aligned side, and fakes a handoff to the halfback. If the halfback is on a blocking track, the quarterback fakes an inside run after the exchange. If the quarterback does not feel comfortable about the exchange, due to a bad snap, he does not attempt to hand the ball off. He must secure the ball and then become the runner on the called track.

If the quarterback is executing a handoff to the halfback, he brings the ball to his belt buckle, pivots/rotates on the leg toward the halfback, and places the ball on the inside run track. After the halfback takes the ball, the quarterback continues a run fake to the opposite side. He only rides a sweep fake with the ball when the halfback is on a blocking track or not aligned in the backfield. If the quarterback carries the ball, he executes the proper fake and attacks the called run lane.

When we run this play, we are not looking to get to the sidelines. If you do not have the speed to get to the sidelines, you simply run out-of-bounds with a five-yard loss. We cut the ball back, depending on the block on the force player. We practice that daily in our sweep drill. If you want this play to be effective, you must do something to slow down the linebackers and make them hesitate. You do that with ball handling and faking. You must pay attention to details and demand they do it correctly.

When we run the fly sweep drill, we run two groups at the same time (Diagram #1). We align two centers, facing one another 10 to 15 yards apart. The wide receivers align on the cones that mark their split to the outside of the centers. The quarterbacks align in their position with a halfback behind them. The sweeper comes in motion to the quarterback. The quarterback give the ball to the sweep, fakes to the halfback, and carries out his fake on the opposite side of the running back for one step past the line of scrimmage.

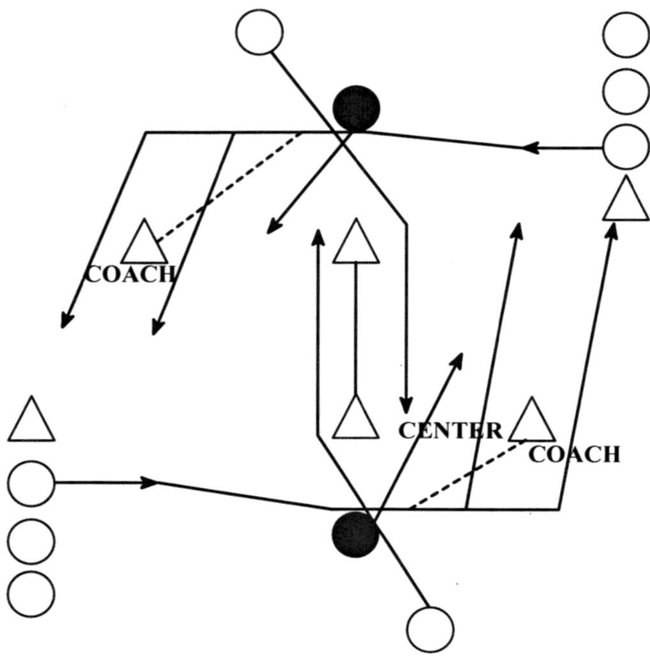

Diagram #1. Fly Sweep Drill

There are two coaches involved in the drill. They stand where the tight end's block would be and watch the mesh. He gives the sweeper a hook, a kick-out, or a head-up drive block read. The sweeper reacts to the block by cutting up (kick-out), running outside (hook), or dipping inside and accelerating outside (head-up block). The sweeper keeps the ball and runs for 10 yards off his read. He gives the ball to the other quarterback and returns to the sweep line on that side. We do this drill every day for five minutes. We try to get 25 reps during that time.

When we expand the drill, we take the coach out of the drill and replace him with a tight end or H-back, who actually performs the block for the key read. We can time and run all three plays in this drill. We can run the sweep, the zone to the running back, and the quarterback zone play.

We can block the sweep with three different methods. If we run the base sweep, we align and block the force from an alignment standpoint with no pull. We can run the G sweep and pull the playside guard. When we pull the frontside guard, the running back fills for the guard. We can run the lead sweep, where we lead with a back and a pulling guard.

SZF: FLY SWEEP

- Ballcarriers: Zebra (4), H-back (2), quarterback (1)
- Offensive line: Scoop/reach (outside zone) techniques.
- Center: Work hard to cut the 3 technique on the sweep side versus even, or call step it and back block on the noseguard, and the backside guard will pull around that back block.
- Pulling guard: Drop-step to a 45-degree angle, immediately read block on force, and track his leverage track downhill on the run lane, working inside to out on the first threat, never slow down, and stay square on the block.

We can run the play with the Zebra, H-back, and the quarterback. If we run 49, that is the Zebra sweep. If we run 29, that is the H-back sweep, or 19 is the quarterback play. If we run the play to the slot, we use pop motion instead of fly motion.

The offensive line uses a scoop technique. It is the same type of blocking used on an outside zone play. We talk to our offensive lineman in terms of covered or uncovered. If the defense covers the offensive lineman, his job is to get his inside hand on the upfield shoulder of the defender. He wants to work his butt to get into a square position and turn the defender. The depth of the offensive lineman's step depends on the width of the defender.

If the defender is head-up, the step is straight at the defender, working to get the inside hand on the upfield shoulder. We more than likely will be in a combination block of some sort on a head-up alignment. If the defender is inside, the blocking on the inside will take the defender, and the blocker punches him and works up to the second level. If the defender is outside the blocker, he has to lose ground to gain ground on the defender. He has to get depth off the line of scrimmage to get up to the outside of the defender.

To drill this type of blocking, we use the hoop drill (Diagram #2). We align two offensive blockers on one side of the hoop. It could be a tight end and tackle or a tackle and guard. We put the defensive lineman inside the hoop and the linebacker on the top of the hoop. On the snap, the two offensive linemen block the defensive lineman and the linebacker. We work the punch and go. On that block, the defender slants inside. The outside blocker punches him and goes to the second level. We use all our combination techniques in this drill. The hoop teaches proper angle to get to the linebacker. This is a good drill for scoop blocking.

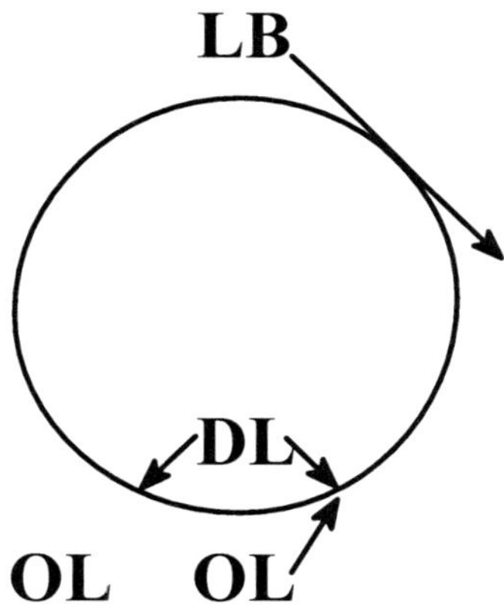

Diagram #2. Hoop Drill

The guard on the G sweep uses a square pull. We never want his shoulders or eyes to the sidelines. He pulls, keeps his shoulders square, and his eyes go to the force block immediately. Everything we do on the perimeter depends on what happens with the force block.

When we run this play, we do not talk about fronts. It does not matter whether it is a 4-3 or a 3-4. We talk in terms of covered or uncovered, the edge, and blocking the force. The offensive blocker on end the line of scrimmage blocks the force.

FORCE BLOCKING

- Tight end/wing playside force block: Fight for reach. Drive to the sideline when reach is not possible. When aligned away from sweep, inside release, and cut off the first fast-flow defender.
- Halfback: Carry inside zone fake 10 yards. Lead sweep; step to force block get downhill to first bad guy in alley working outside to inside.
- Quarterback: Place the ball on sweep track, complete an inside zone fake to the halfback, and carry out a boot or inside zone fake opposite of the halfback fake.
- Wide receiver: Drive hard to the inside number of the corner, squat with the butt to the sweep track, fighting for upfield shoulder leverage. When the game plan calls for first high defender responsibility, drive on slant route to safety, squat on numbers, fight to stay square on the block.

We call our sweep play "green." We can run it with a G, lead, or base scheme.

FORMATION RULES

- Always formation to have a minimum of three perimeter blockers (wide receiver, tight end/ wing/halfback, pulling guard).
- Never be in an alignment/formation that allows immediate inside penetration by force defender.
- Stress the defense with overloads, quick motion formations, and "nasty" splits.

When we align in a formation, we must have a minimum of three perimeter blockers on the play. We want a wide receiver, tight end, and pulling guard on the perimeter. We could have a wing, halfback, and pulling guard. We want to get a hat on a hat and turn the ball up if necessary.

When we align in our formation, we never want to take a split that allows the defender to jump inside and blow up the play. That is particularly true for the force defender. We take the defender as wide in our splits as he will go. However, we never want to get into a position where if the defender jumps inside, we cannot block him.

We want to stress the defense by using unbalanced sets and overloads. We want to use quick motion formations and "nasty" splits on the force defenders. If the tight end takes a three split, it puts the defender covering him in a dilemma.

The first play I want to show you comes from a tight trips formation. The play is a 49 green lead (Diagram #3). The force blocker is the tight end. He takes a nasty split on the outside linebacker. On this play, the playside guard is uncovered and pulls around the reach block of the tackle. The center scoops through the playside A gap and angles for the playside linebacker. If the linebacker blitzes that gap, the center blocks him.

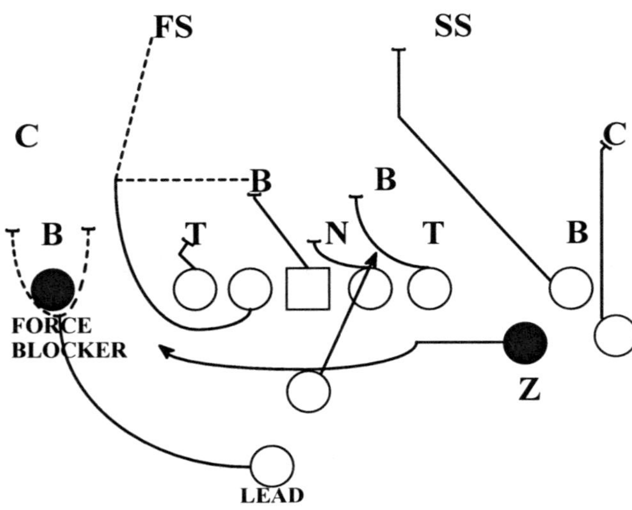

Diagram #3. 49 Green Lead

The backside guard scoops for the shade noseguard. The backside tackle scoops through the B gap, trying to get to the second level.

The play is a lead play. The running back becomes the lead blocker on this play. The quarterback has no fake with the running back. The quarterback can get a long ride with the Zebra since there is not a fake to the running back. After he rides the Zebra, he fakes the quarterback zone play to the backside.

The pulling guard uses a square pull and sees the playside linebacker. If the playside linebacker blitzes into the B gap, the guard attacks him at that point. He is square and in position to make that block. However, his primary path comes from the block on the force. If the tight end washes the force inside, he goes around the outside and looks back inside. If there is no linebacker, he goes up to the safety running in the alley.

The running back is the lead blocker on the play. He reads the force blocker and goes inside or outside his block, depending on his read. If the force blocker reaches the defender, he takes his block to the outside and blocks the corner. If the defender is working outside, the force blocker drives him outside, and the running back turns inside and blocks the first defender.

The Zebra runs the ball and reads the same thing the lead blocker reads. If the blocker and force defender lock up in a stalemate, the Zebra dips inside and back to the outside.

This set is an unbalanced formation with the tight end in a closed position to the right tackle (Diagram #4). The wingback in this set is the H-back set outside the tight end. The wide receiver and Zebra are off the line of scrimmage. The backside guard and tackle scoop through the backside A and B gaps and up to the second level. The center has to work hard and reach the 3-technique defender to the overload side. The best chance he has is to try to cut him.

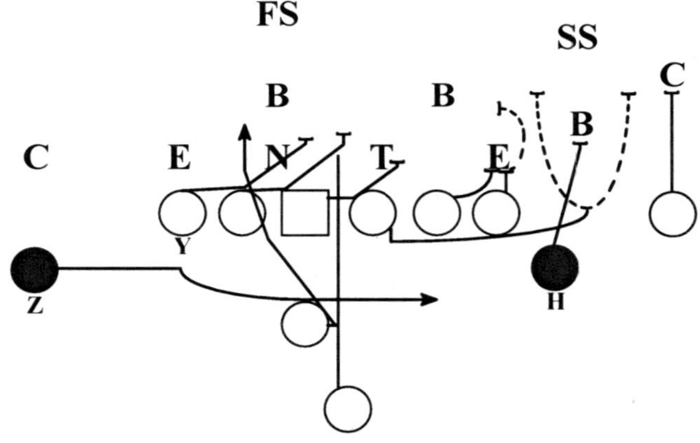

Diagram #4. G 48 Green Overload

The tackle and tight end run a combination block on the 6-technique defender. This is a zone blocking combination block, working for the 6 technique and the inside linebacker.

The H-back has the force block on the outside linebacker. He tries to reach-block him, but blocks him any way he can. If the defender goes inside, he seals him inside. If the defender runs outside, he drive-blocks him and kicks him out. If it is a stalemate situation, the back wants to dip to the inside and take the play to the outside.

The pulling guard uses the square pull and gets his eyes on the force blocker. He reads the direction of the block. If the H-back drives the force outside, the guard turns inside and up on the safety. He looks inside before he goes up to the safety and blocks the first defender who could make the play. The wide receiver stalk-blocks the corner.

The quarterback hands to the Zebra. He rotates and fakes to the running back on the inside zone play. The running back has to fill on anything coming into the A gap. The quarterback fakes the quarterback zone or the bootleg off the fake.

If, for some reason, the force blocker splits too wide and the force defender penetrates to his inside, the guard kicks him out, and we turn the ball inside immediately.

We use another overload formation called a closed-flex right tackle (Diagram #5). We run the G 49 green. The tight end uses a nasty split from the right tackle, and the H-back sits in the tight slot alignment outside the right tackle. The backside guard and tackle scoop through the A and B gaps and up to the second level. The defense uncovers the center, and he blocks the 3-technique defender. He tries to cut him down or entangle his feet so he cannot pursue down the line.

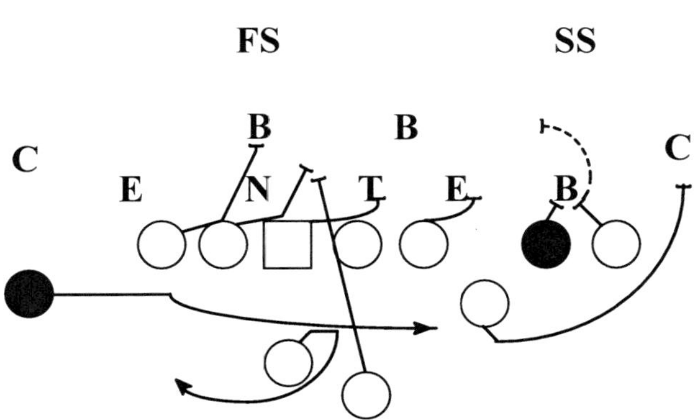

Diagram #5. Closed-Flex Right Tackle

The right tackle reaches the 5-technique defender on his outside shoulder. The tight end and wide receiver use a combination block on the outside linebacker with the wide receiver working off the block for the inside linebacker. We read this combination block as the force block. With a combination block, we should block the defender to the inside. However, the inside pulls have to read the block on the force.

The H-back has no defender aligned over him and pulls to the outside around the combination block of the tight end and wide receiver. The pulling guard square-pulls and reads the combination block. He goes inside or outside the block. The quarterback gives the ball to the Zebra, fakes the running back, and runs a bootleg fake to the backside.

This play is a 28 green G (Diagram #6). We run this to the H-back using pop motion. That is the short motion coming from the slot. The blocking is the same from the offensive line. If the defense is a 34 front, the tackle may have trouble with his reach block on a 5-technique defensive end, and he can call on the tight end to give him some help. The tight end reduces his split and helps the tackle. He punches the defender onto the block of the offensive tackle and gets off to the second level.

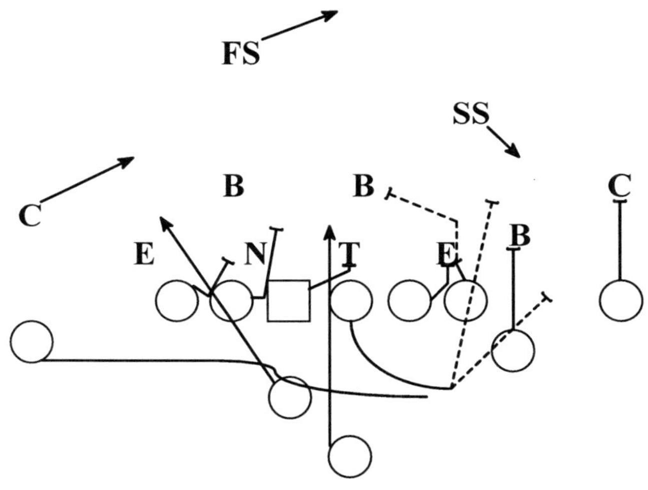

Diagram #6. 28 Green G

We can run the play from under the center. The quarterback wants to snap the ball at the same place and present the ball in the same fashion. The quarterback reverses to the motion and gets off the line of scrimmage. The running back runs the same fake, and the quarterback fakes the bootleg. The timing is the same from the quarterback and Zebra. The line blocking is the same, and the reads on the force block are the same. We run 5 to 10 percent of our snaps from under the center.

I appreciate you being here.

Joe Hemphill

BASIC 3-4 DEFENSE WITH MULTIPLE STUNTS

St. Elizabeth High School, Delaware

Thank you very much. It is a pleasure to be here today. I am going to talk about the 3-4 defense we use at St. Elizabeth High School. I got started with this defense from becoming frustrated with what we used in the past. I came across some new information on the 3-4 defense and I decided to look into it. As I looked into it further, it seemed very similar to what we had been doing previously, with just a few tweaks and changes. I wanted to see if I could take our old defense and old terminology and fit it into what people were calling the 3-4 defense.

We took what people normally call defensive tackles, and we called them "defensive ends." We kept hearing that we needed to get more speed on the field and to get away from those big, slower linemen. We started looking for guys that were faster and more athletic. We found two taller lanky kids, one was 6'2" and weighed 220 pounds, and the other was 6'3" and weighed 225 pounds. The reason we call them defensive ends is because our players do not want to be called defensive tackles. I made an agreement with them. I told them I would play them as defensive ends in a 4 technique in our new defensive package. They think to this day that they are defensive ends.

Our outside linebackers are kids that would have normally played linebacker in our old defense. Our noseguard is a noseguard. Our middle linebackers play at four yards off of the football.

We made some changes from a technique standpoint. We had used two defensive tackles in a 4 technique, and they were gap control type of guys. We asked them to step inside, keep the tackle off of them, and play football from the B gap. We were not an attack type of defense. We had our defensive ends reading helmets and sealing down.

With our new "defensive ends" in our base defense, we are aggressive and we come after you. We get into the B gap, get after the football, and make something happen (Diagram #1). I spend a lot of time with our two defensive ends. I teach the defensive ends once they get into the B gap, they have to read the guard out of the corner of their eye. If the offensive guard pulls away from us, we get in his hip pocket. If the offensive guard pulls to our side, we do the same thing.

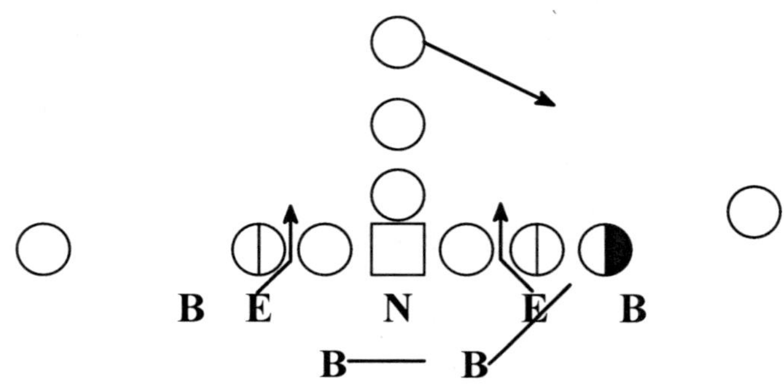

Diagram #1. Base

We fight through the tackle to get to the guard because he will take us to where the ball is going. If the offensive guard blocks down on the noseguard, the defensive end is going to get trapped by a pulling lineman. We practice hard on this. I stand behind our offensive linemen and tell them what I want. I tell the guards to pull, block down, and scoop.

We tell the nose and the defensive ends to be aggressive. When we get penetration, and we do not know where the ball is, we tell them to stop and find the ball before they go any farther.

The inside linebackers are responsible for the C gaps. The inside linebackers have a key, and if their key comes their way, they have the C gap. We coach them to come off of the tail of the defensive end when they go to the C gap. We do not want them to get too wide. If action goes away, we tell them to stop behind the noseguard and find out what is going on. He is responsible for the isolation play. The frontside linebacker is responsible for power; the backside linebacker is responsible for the isolation.

We tell the noseguard to make contact with the center and drive the center as far back as he can. I noticed a lot of offenses will take their weakest offensive lineman and make him their center. Do not get me wrong, I know there are some good centers out there, but the majority of them are the weakest link on the offensive line. We want our noseguard to control the center of the line of scrimmage.

The two outside linebackers cannot let the tight end get inside and on up to our inside linebacker, keeping him from getting to the C gap. We put the outside linebacker on the outside shoulder of the tight end. We still want him to read the hat of the tight end. If that hat goes outside, we want to get outside. If the hat goes inside, either the guard is coming down to trap him or the fullback is going to kick him out. He has to find out, right off the bat, which it is and he needs to attack the block.

The outside linebacker on the other side has one foot on the line of scrimmage, provided we have three or fewer threats to the openside. He is our contain guy on that side. We tell him if action goes away, check for faces coming his way. He cannot let anyone cross his face. If someone crosses his face, he either has to stop them or run with them. The guard cannot cross his face. The back cannot cross his face, and the quarterback cannot cross his face. His job is to take away the throwback. That is our base defense.

We have a few called moves we use. I will start with our defensive end calls. When we call a "step out," our end has the C gap, and the middle linebacker knows he has the B gap. They are just switching assignments. We run this if the offense is able to run power or the backside veer and we cannot get our linebacker to the C gap.

Another call we use is our "lock up." If we are having trouble defending the iso play and power plays, we call lock up. Our defensive end attacks the offensive tackle and drives him straight back. He is responsible for both the B and C gaps. The noseguard also uses this technique. This is not my favorite call and we will do other things before we make this call, but we do work on it. If we need to use it, we will.

Ends	Description
Step out	Opposite of base technique. Step to outside gap.
Lock up	Explode and lock out. Responsible for B and C gaps.
Shade	Shade to called shoulder and penetrate the gap.
Gap	One yard penetration. Find football. No redirect. No wash. Fight pressure.
Slant	Slant with directional call, drive to assigned gap.

It is really important, on our base call and on our gap call, that we do not get washed down to the inside. We want to get penetration and fight pressure. If the offense is trying to move us out of that gap, they are doing it for a reason. Our gap players have to fight pressure and find the football.

A simple rule for the nose man and defensive end is this: No matter where they are lined up, if they have no call, they are responsible for their inside gap. If they lined up in a gap, they are responsible for that gap.

We have a few calls for our outside linebackers. The "hard" call is used against an option team. We use this call if we want to get the linebacker on the quarterback right now. The linebacker comes off the tail of the offensive lineman on the end of the line. It might be the tight end, or it might be the offensive tackle.

Outside Linebackers	Description
Hard	Loosen and drive to quarterback (used on option)
Fire	Drive for outside shoulder of nearest back (pass rush)
Hug	Lock up tight end (no easy release off of line of scrimmage)
Plus	Drive through inside gap (usually called to tight end side)

The "fire" call is a pass rush call. We are not worried about the run; we want pressure and we want a quick pass rush. The aiming point is the outside shoulder of the near back. We want to come hard off the edge and we do not want to get caught inside.

We can make a "plus" call if we do not want the tight end to get off the line of scrimmage. We want to drive the tight end through the C gap.

The calls for the nose are simple. They are similar to the calls for the defensive ends.

Nose	Description
Slant	Slant with directional call. Drive to assigned A gap.
Gap	One yard penetration. Find football. No redirect. No wash. Fight pressure.
Shade	Shade to called shoulder and penetrate the gap.

Let me show you some fronts we use to change it up from our base. If we are having trouble getting our inside linebackers into the C gaps, we can call "Eagle" (Diagram #2) or "tite" (Diagram #3). Our linebackers line up over the C gaps. All they do is to come straight up and fill into the C gaps. They know, no matter where they line up, they are responsible for the inside gap.

I want to show you the other fronts on the overhead. I want you to see the different alignments we use. We do not use all of these alignments in a game (Diagrams #4 through #8). The fronts we use depend on two things. First, is the opponent's tendencies. Second, is how well we are performing against them.

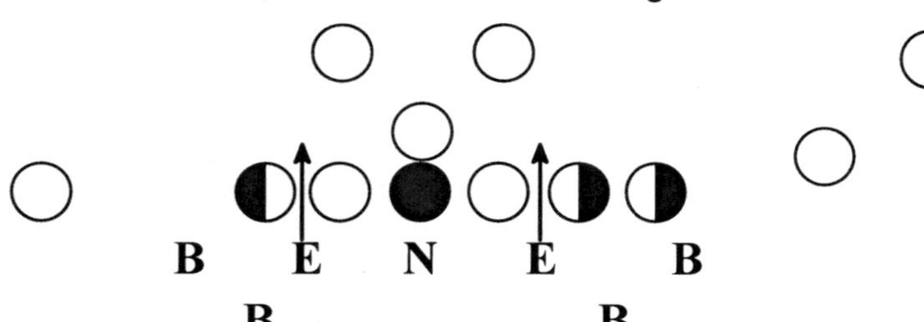

Diagram #2. Eagle

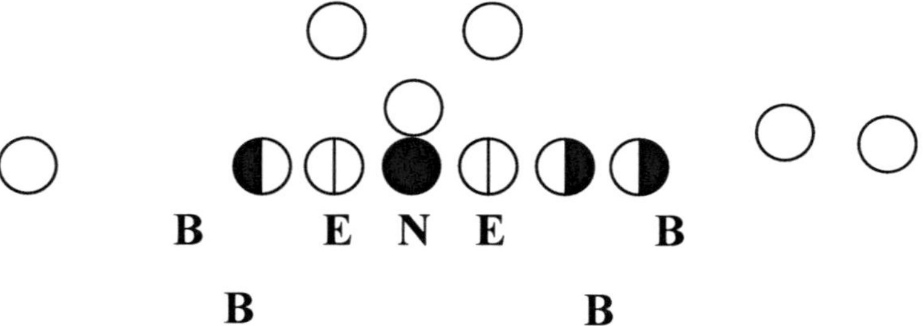

Diagram #3. Tite

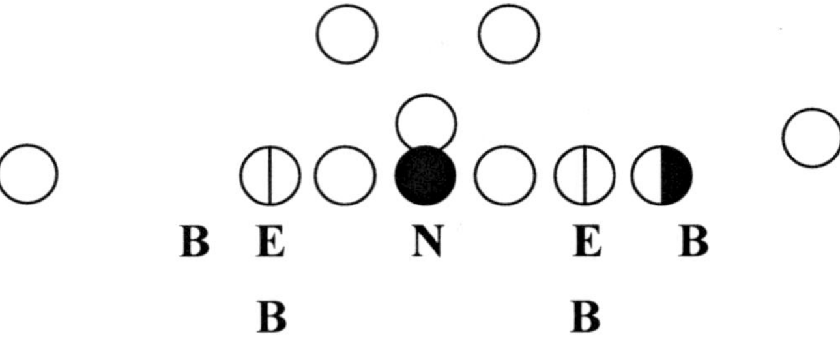

Diagram #4. Stack

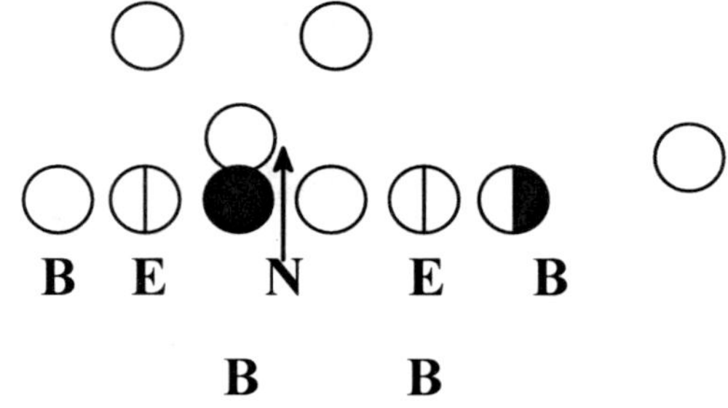

Diagram #5. Over

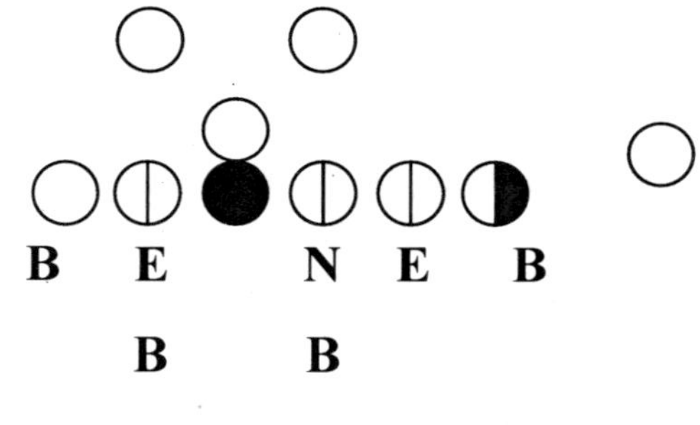

Diagram #6. Sink

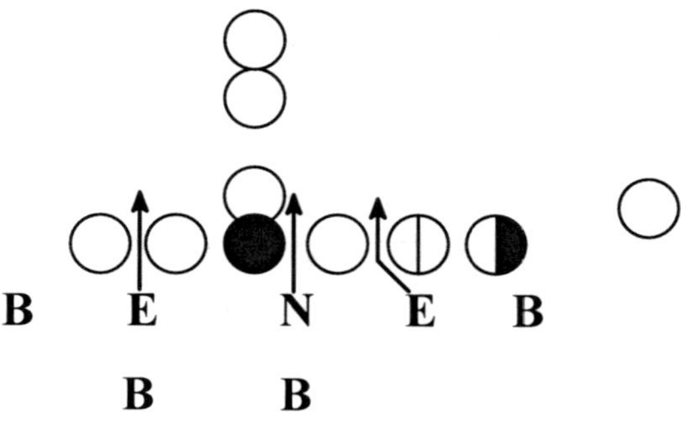

Diagram #7. Gap Stack Right

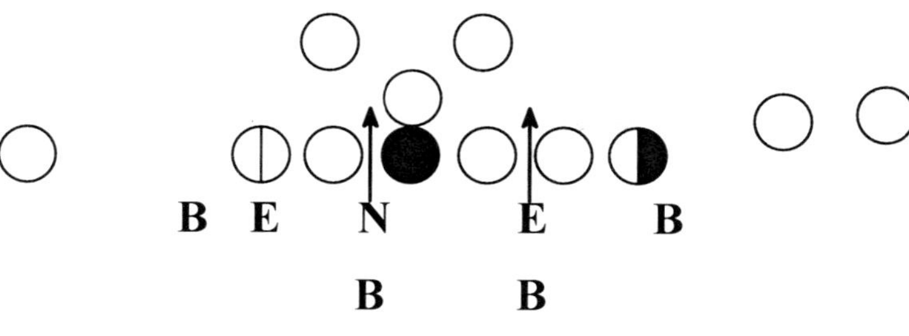

Diagram #8. Gap Stack Left

We are a pressure defense. We like to blitz in this defensive package. Our stunts are the same ones used by most 3-4 defensive teams. Let me show you the different blitzes we like to use (Diagrams #9 through #13).

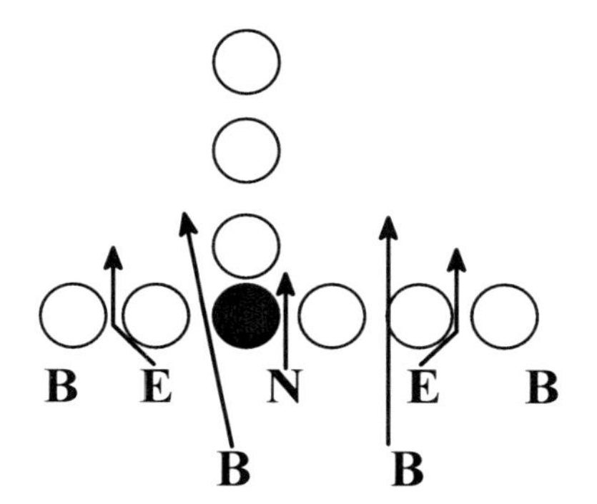

Diagram #9. Over Blitz

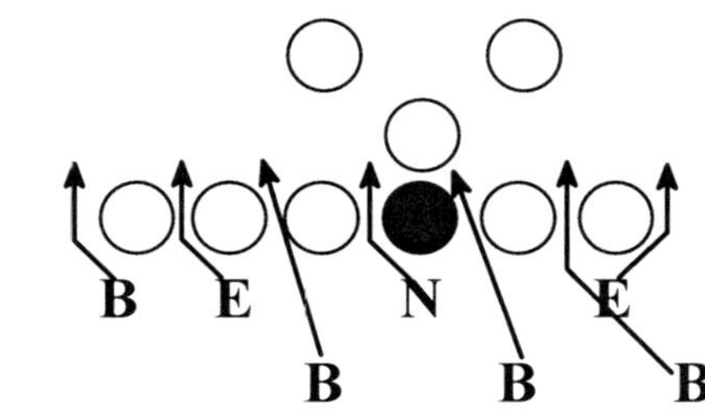

Diagram #10. Bingo

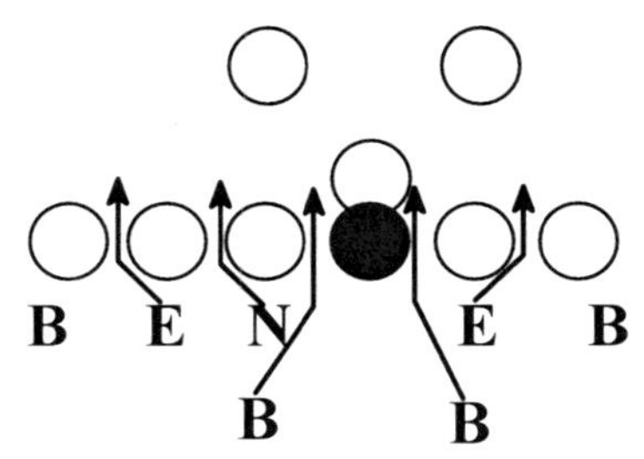

Diagram #11. Sink at A

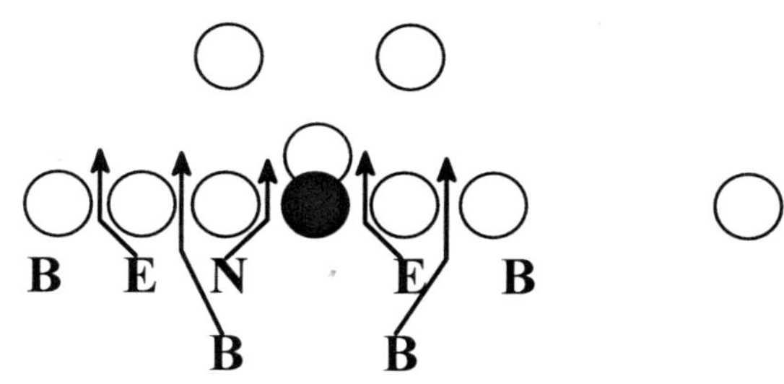

Diagram #12. Sink at B

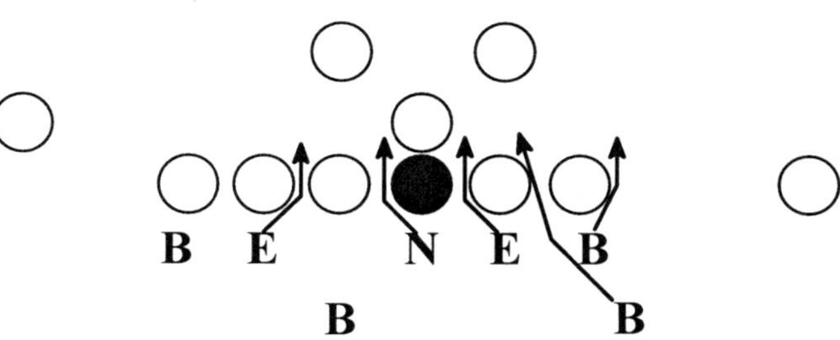

Diagram #13. Eagle Fire at B

Next, we need to spend some time with the secondary and their alignment. I do not have time to cover all of the calls we use but I will cover some of them. The first look is our "flex" call (Diagram #14). I want to cover a few points on each of our secondary calls.

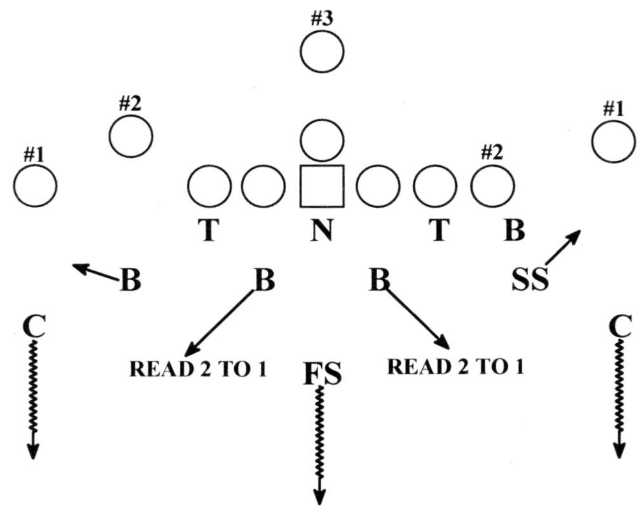

Diagram #14. Flex Call

The corners have the deep outside third. Our free safety has the middle third. Our strong safety has the flat responsibility as does the weakside linebacker. The middle linebackers first read the receiver nearest to them. They are looking for an inside route.

If we run a flex man free, we are going to be counting receivers (Diagram #15). We count from the outside to the inside. The corners have the first outside receivers to their side. Our outside linebackers have the #2 receivers to their side. Our inside backers have #3. The free safety is free.

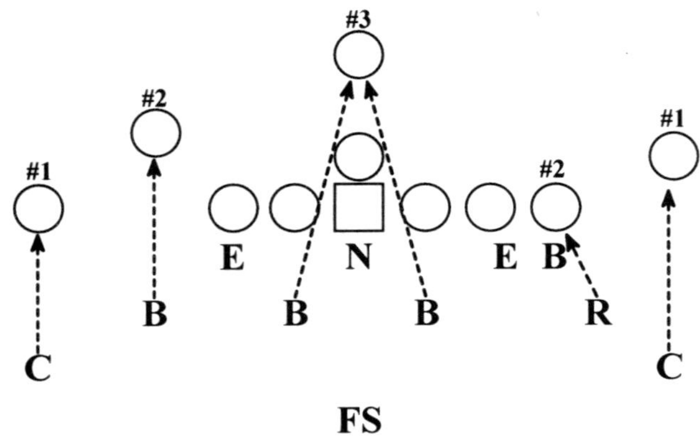

Diagram #15. Flex Man Free

Our flex fire call gives us a pass rush off the edge from both our outside linebacker and our Rover. The Rover is in a fire call where he times his rush on the cadence of the quarterback. He drives for the outside shoulder of the nearest back, the tailback in Diagram #16. The outside linebacker is in a plus call and he drives through the inside gap of the tight end.

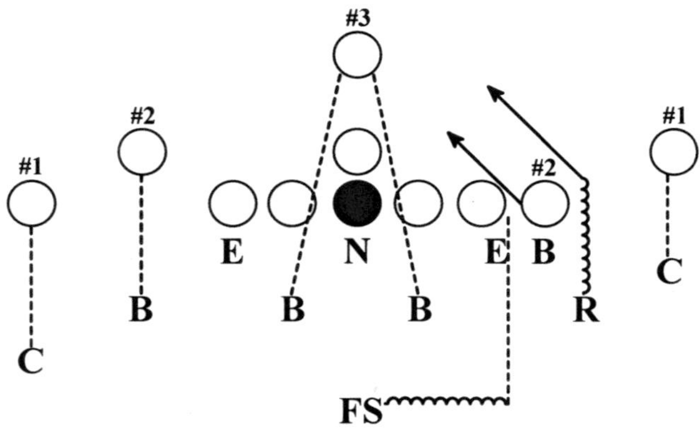

Diagram #16. Flex Fire

Both corners have man coverage on the #1 receivers. The weakside outside backer has the #2 receiver to his side. The free safety has the #2 receiver to the blitz side, in this case the tight end. The middle linebacker has the #3 receiver.

If the offense shows motion, we will make some adjustments (Diagram #17). The Rover takes the motion receiver and the free safety has the #3 receiver to the strongside, again the tight end. We rush our backside end and outside linebacker to get pressure on the quarterback.

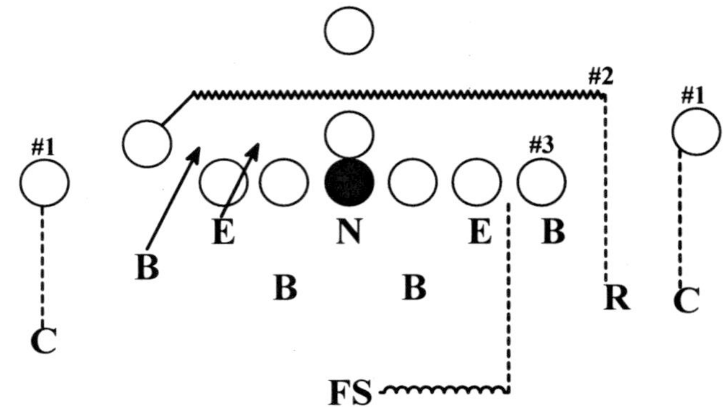

Diagram #17. Vs. Motion

Editor's Note: Due to technical difficulties, the remainder of the lecture was not recorded.

Ryan Hines

MULTIPLE COVERAGES VS. MULTIPLE OFFENSES

Urbana High School, Maryland

Thank you. Our strength is our defense. That is what I am going to talk about tonight. I am going to focus on what makes us unique and sets us apart.

WHY COVERAGES?

- New off-season rules make teaching opportunity more available.
- The two most important things to know are the offensive line and the secondary.
- Techniques overlap through different coverages.
- Easy to tag on the end of a defensive call.
- Easy to adjust to a no-huddle team.
- Ease to hide.
- Multiple coverages allow you to play multiple fronts.
- Gives the quarterback multiple reads.
- Have a plan B.
- It is what we do best.

People may ask, "Why talk about coverages?" The reason we did not have multiple coverages in our scheme was we did not have the time to work with the players to teach the technique and fine points of too many coverages. The rules changed and allowed us to play in 7-on-7 leagues in the summer. That provided us with an avenue to teach our players. By playing in the summer leagues, we had all the coverages we wanted to use in the defense before practice began.

The corner may have to learn 20 different coverages, but you only have to teach him four or five techniques. He can apply those four or five techniques in all the schemes you play. You need to teach him what he does with his feet, hands, and eyes when he plays pass defense.

You do not need to huddle to change the secondary coverage. That makes it adaptable to all no-huddle offenses. The defense can align, communicate the change, and never be threatened by time. We can call coverage and adjustment very easily. We can play at a high tempo or slow it down as low as it will go.

When you play multiple coverages, it allows your defense to play multiple fronts. If you are a 4-3 cover-2 team, it is easy to go to a 3-4 front. You must be able to adjust your front and coverage to the different types of offenses you play. However, when you adjust your front, the list of techniques your linemen must use it gets long quickly. The secondary is not that drastic. The techniques played in zone remain the same in all zones. The techniques in man-press coverage remain the same in all man coverages. The schemes are different, but the techniques are the same. A trail technique is a trail technique in cover 1 as it is in cover-2 man-under.

When the offensive coordinator starts to put together the game plan, he starts with his formations and puts down the defenses he expects to see. When I do my defensive game plan, I script my first eight plays on my call sheet. I use eight different plays from eight different formations or motion schemes to see what the defense needs to do.

On the defensive side, you must have a plan B to those formations. You cannot align the same way against the trips formation or the slot formation. If you play the same adjustment to a particular set, the offense will find a solution and use it every time. If you play the same coverage to a formation every game, the opponent will scheme to beat that coverage.

COACHING POINTS FOR THE SECONDARY

- Know your run support.
- Know your pursuit angle.

- Know your drop.
- Know your read.
- Know your technique.
- Read the drop of the quarterback.
- Recognize route combinations.
- Get to the top of your drop and break on the ball.
- Drop through your zone.
- Do not chase.
- Communicate.
- Run to the ball.
- Do not give up the big play.

The most important point for your secondary is run support. Most people think it is pass coverage. However, the number-one goal for any defense is to stop the run. When you play cover 2, it is difficult for the corner to understand his role in run support. He knows when he rolls down into flat coverage, he has run support on the edge. He has to understand that the edge of the defense is not outside the numbers. He has to squeeze to the inside. You have to teach them to knife to the ball and set the hard edge.

Everyone runs pursuit drills in practice. The thing you must engrain in your players is they are not running to the ball. They are running to the sideline at an angle to intercept the ball. They have to understand the angle at which they must pursue the ball to make a tackle.

In secondary coverage, the defender has to know his drop. He has to know the field and landmarks on it. They must understand dividers. They need to know their drops from the coverage we are playing.

Everything in defensive back play starts with the eyes and his visual key. That controls every movement he makes. The coach wants to be in a position to see the eyes of the players. He has to know where they are looking. If he is supposed to look at the #2 receiver, he cannot be looking at the ball. He has to see other things with his peripheral vision, but he has to look at his key.

The defensive back has to read the drop of the quarterback. In addition, he must read the shoulders of the quarterback. We teach our players to see the patterns of the receiver but react off the shoulders of the quarterback. If the inside receiver in a trips formation runs a bubble path, the linebacker cannot vacate his drop and react to that pattern until the quarterback's shoulders turn to throw that pattern. If the quarterback's shoulder turns in the downfield direction, that pattern could be the wheel and not the bubble.

We want to read the three- and five-step drop, but we have to read the shoulders to react to the receiver. Quarterbacks cannot turn the shoulders in one direction and throw the ball in any other direction. He can pump the ball in one direction, but to throw the ball the other way, he has to turn his shoulders in the direction he throws.

Another thing we read with the quarterback is the off hand on the ball. For the quarterback to throw the ball, he has to take the off hand off the ball. When we see the hand come off, we know the throw is coming. We react to the direction the quarterback's shoulders point us.

We spend a lot of time in 7-on-7. In that drill, we get to see route combinations and recognize them. We see the smash route and curl/flat route combinations. Walk the players through those combinations so they know what is happening.

We want the defender to get to the top of their drop and break back to the ball. If the defender is the curl/flat defender, we want him to get to the curl area. We want to stop the curl pattern first. The curl general gets to the depth of at least 10 yards. The flat receiver runs his route from one to four yards down the field. We do not want to give up a 10-yard pass to prevent a three-yard completion. We drop to the curl area and react back to the flat route.

We want to drop through the zone. If I am a seam/flat player, I want to drop to the seam first before I react to the flat. If the seam/flat player drops to the seam first, he passes through the curl area on the way to the flat. That allows him to help on the inside curl route run by the outside receiver.

Unless we play man coverage, the zone defender does not chase a receiver leaving his zone. In zone coverage, the receiver leaving an outside zone becomes an "in, in, in," receiver. That is what he yells to the defender in the next zone. He probably will get an "out, out, out" call coming from the inside zone player. Crossing two receivers is a technique to get the defenders to run into one another or lose coverage of their receiver. We want to banjo (switch) the receiver leaving a zone and pick up the receiver entering the zone.

Talking in the secondary is an essential skill. You have to teach your defenders to listen and talk. Communication is the hardest and most important thing to learn in secondary coverage. Calling the ins and outs is necessary in playing zone coverage. Communicating in the deep zone is essential because a mistake in that area leads to scores.

We talked about giving up the five-yard route to prevent the completion at 10 yards. However, do not give up the five-yard route and let the receiver run an additional five yards. When the ball is in the air, the defender breaks on the ball and runs to it. If they throw the five-yard hitch pattern, react and break up on the ball, and hold it to a five-yard gain. Everyone on the defense has to run to the ball.

We do a drill called "roll call." It can be a live team drill or dummy team drill. We run a pass or run play. When we make the tackle or stop the ball in a dummy drill, we blow the whistle and count "Three, two, and one." When we reach one, everyone on the defense should be at the ball except the backside corner. You must get the mind-set of running to the ball. Too many times, the ball pops out just before the whistle blows. If we do not run to the ball, we do not a have a shot of getting that ball.

It is important not to give up the big play. It is hard for a high school offense to run a 12-play drive for a score. Most of the time, the 15- to 18-year-old player cannot run 12 plays without making a mistake. They miss a block or jump offside. It is hard to drive the ball for 80 yards without making some type of mental or physical error. That is why it is so important not to give up the 30-yard run or the 20-yard pass play.

We play the following coverages: zero, 1, 2, 3, 4, 5, 6, 7, 8, 9, half coverage, quarter coverage, and corner coverage. That may look like too much coverage, but some of them are combination coverages, and we do not play them all within a season. They are in the playbook, and we play what best fits our personnel.

We are a 4-3 defense, and our base secondary shell is a cover-2 look (Diagram #1). When I show

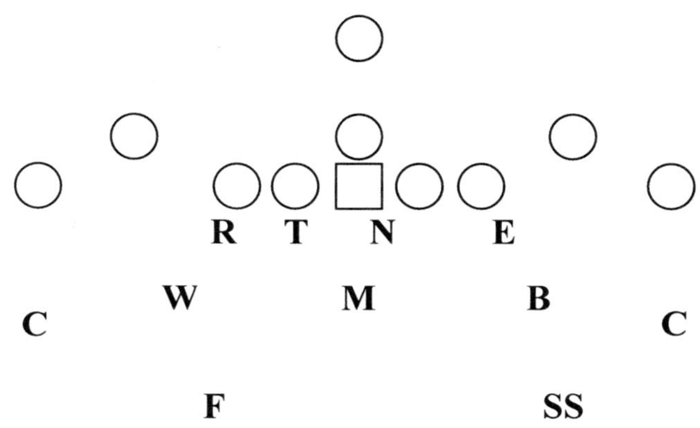

Diagram #1. Base Shell

you the coverages, I will try to show you different formations so you can see the alignments of the defensive backs.

I want to talk about our converge zones (Diagram #2). I am not trying to insult anyone's intelligence, but I want to make sure we are all on the same page. The area five yards deep to us is a no-cover zone. If the wide receiver moves outside to the sideline, the corner will not go with him. We never cover a receiver into the wide field that is within five yards of the out-of-bounds line. He widens to the numbers and gets depth off the ball but he does not go outside to the receiver. As that zone moves downfield, we expand it farther away from the sidelines.

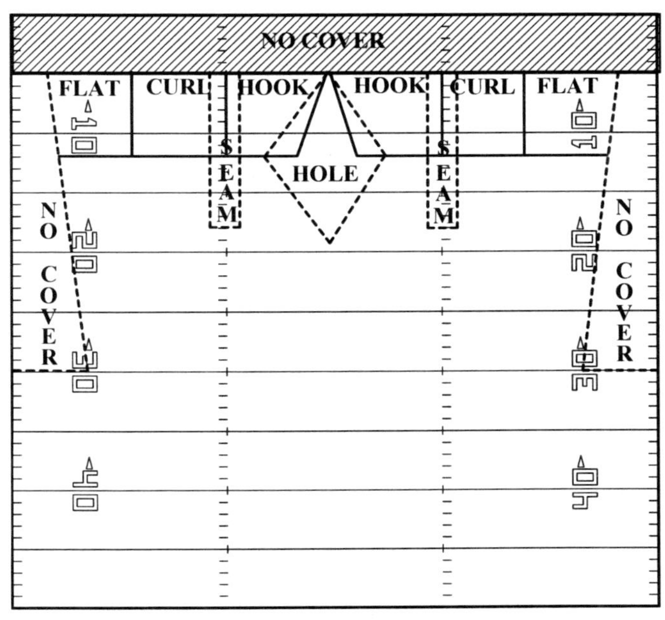

Diagram #2. Coverage Zones

The farther the ball travels into the sidelines on a downfield throw, the farther we can play off the receiver and react back to it. Unless we are in man coverage, we do not want a defender in the no-cover zones. If you put a receiver on the sideline at 22 yards and the quarterback in a five-step drop, the ball must travel 35 to 40 yards in the air to reach the receiver. If we break the safety off the hash mark, nine times out of 10, he can reach the receiver and knock the ball down. That is why we expand the no-cover zone as the area gets deeper.

The flat zone is up to 12 yards off the line of scrimmage. Too many times, the defender drops four steps, squares up, and covers grass. If there is no one in the zone, he continues to get depth and finds someone to cover. We define the curl area from the hash marks to two yards inside the numbers. The hook areas are inside the curl to the middle of the field.

The seam area of the field is down the hash marks up to 18 yards deep. The seam is the area in which teams want to attack the cover-3 safety with a four-vertical pattern. The deep thirds are from sideline to hash marks on either side and hash mark to hash mark in the middle of the field.

If we play quarter coverage, we divide the deep field into fourths instead of thirds. The hole is the middle linebacker area for a Tampa 2 or vertical route by a #3 receiver releasing up the middle of the field. We teach the Mike linebacker, if he has a receiver running down the middle of the field, Mike goes with him.

COVER ZERO

- Allows you to bring six or more on the rush.
- Cut the coverage time.
- Pressure the quarterback.

The first coverage we teach is cover zero. That is a dead locked up man-to-man coverage with no free safety. In this coverage, we want to stay on top of the receiver and are not as aggressive as we would be with a safety over the top. The corners lock up on the wide receivers, and the safeties take the #2 receivers to their side or the #3 receiver to the trips side. That leaves the Mike, Sam, and Will linebacker to cover the remaining back in the backfield. If we play a zero coverage, we bring the kitchen sink after the quarterback. This will be a six-man blitz or a seven-man add-on blitz.

We hope we never give the quarterback a chance to set his feet or get comfortable in the pocket. We want him to throw the ball before he wants to throw it.

COVER 1

- Allows you to bring five (or more) rushers.
- Cuts coverage time.
- Pressures the quarterback.
- Extra deep defender allows you to bring more pressure and not give up the big play.

Cover 1 is a man-free coverage. The corners play the wide receivers man-to-man. The strong safety and Will linebacker take the #2 receivers to their side or the #3 receiver in the trips set. The free safety roams the middle of the field, playing the quarterback. He keys the shoulders of the quarterback and plays over the top of the man defenders underneath.

The man technique in this cover can be more aggressive because of the free safety over the coverage. We can also game plan how to play the second slot receiver. We may insert a nickel back or use some other game plan situation. The Mike and Buck linebacker have a read coverage on the remaining receiver. If he releases the linebacker to the side, he releases him man-to-man. The other linebacker, according to the game plan, blitzes the quarterback or drops into the hole in the middle. We can bring both linebacker and turn the back over to the defensive end to the side he releases.

Playing cover zero and cover 1 depends on the capabilities of your personnel. If you do not have four defensive backs who can play man coverage, you do not need to run a cover zero. These coverages depend more on personnel than your zone coverages or combination zone and man coverages. The receiver who puts you in a bind is the slot receiver on your linebacker. In our alignments, we can play cover 31. We align in a cover 3 and play cover 1. We can align in a cover 32, where we align in a cover 3 and jump to a cover 2.

COVER 2

- Good edge support.
- Keep seven in the box.
- Easy adjustments for the outside linebackers.
- Five underneath defenders.
- Two deep defenders.
- Easy to convert to cover 4.

With the cover-2 alignment, the offensive set is a twin to the field and a wing set outside the tight end to the boundary (Diagram #3). To the twin set, the corner aligns on the wide receiver but keys the slot receiver. He cannot think he is going to play the flat and nothing else. The corner has outside leverage on the wide receiver and must funnel him to the inside. He cannot allow him to release outside of him and put pressure on the free safety over the top.

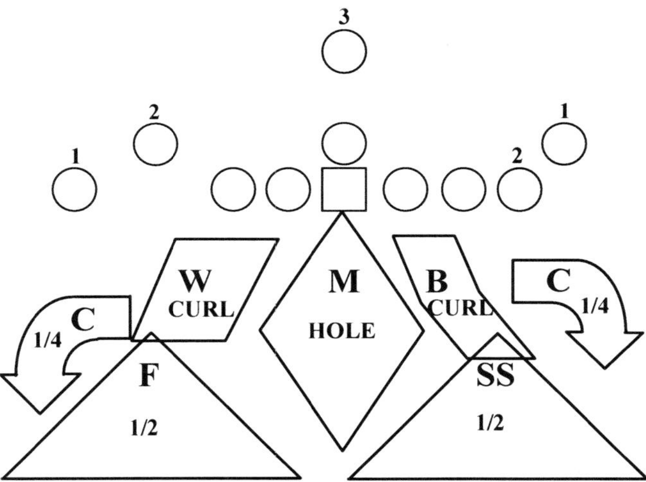

Diagram #3. Cover 2

If the corner allows the wide receiver to get to the sideline area at 15 to 18 yards deep, the safety cannot cover that throw. The corner becomes a quarter player unless there is a pattern threatening the flat area.

The safety aligns on the slot receiver to his side at a depth of 10 yards. On the snap of the ball, he retreats, stemming to widen his alignment to the middle of the slot and wide receivers. The backside on a 2x2 set plays the same way. However, with a winged tight end, their drops are tighter to the field. Their responsibility is the same as the split side.

The Will and Buck linebacker are curl droppers. The Will linebacker, playing under the slot, helps the safety play the smash route to his side. On the smash, the wide receiver hitches, and the slot runs a corner route. The Will linebacker drops to 12 yards under the slot receiver. His positioning makes the quarterback throw over him using an arced ball and giving the safety more time to get to the corner.

The Mike linebacker is responsibility for the running back to the #2 receiver. The coverage passes receivers from one underneath coverage linebacker to the other. They do not chase receivers out of their zone. They use in and out calls to pass off the receivers.

If the slot receiver breaks outside, the wide receiver is coming in. The Will linebacker's eyes go from the slot going out and find the wideout coming inside. If the running back goes out, the Mike linebacker looks for the slot receiver coming inside. The Will linebacker passes the slot receiver going inside to the Mike linebacker and looks for a receiver coming to him. Do not chase receivers out of the zone; communicate and exchange receivers.

The pattern people like to run is the double slant. The corner rides the wide receiver on all inside releases and sees the slot receiver. If the slot is releasing inside, he stays with the slant of the wide receiver. The Will linebacker sees the same thing.

To the wing side of the formation, the corner has to set the edge on run his way (Diagram #4).

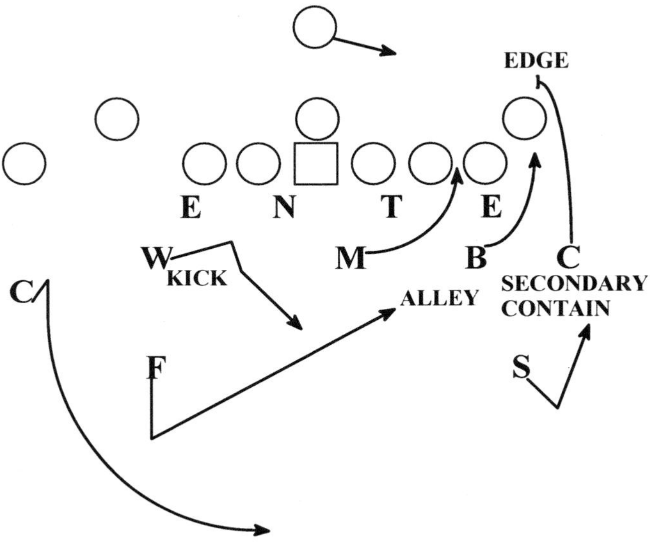

Diagram #4. Run Flow to Wing

That means we are at a physical mismatch most of the time. The tighter he can set the edge, the better off we will be. The Buck linebacker scrapes to the outside and plays through the window under the corner. The Mike linebacker is a shadow player on the running back. He plays one gap behind the running back, looking for the cutback. The Will linebacker takes a read step toward the B gap. He is what we call a kick defender.

He looks for the cutback run. As he kicks for depth, he has to read for the reverse, counter, or cutback. He is playing slow through the middle.

COVER 3

- Two linebackers in the box
- Three defenders deep
- Quick edge support

In cover 3, we want the corners seven yards off the wide receivers (Diagram #5). They align with inside leverage on the wide receiver. They want to force the ball to the outside in this coverage. The strong safety rolls down to linebacker depth outside the tight end and is a curl/flat player. The Will linebacker to the twin receiver side is the curl/flat player to that side. The Mike and Buck linebackers are the hook players, and the free safety plays the middle third.

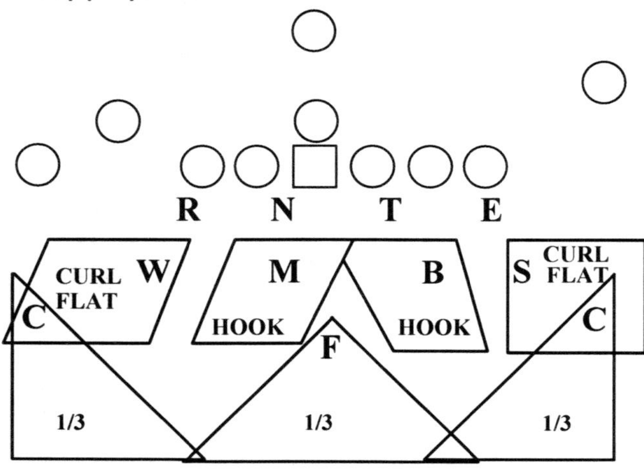

Diagram #5. Cover 3

If we have run flow to the twin receiver side, the Will linebacker is the edge player. He has to fight through the block of the slot receiver and set a tight edge. The Mike linebacker mirrors the back and reads the B gap first. If the back continues outside, he scrapes the C gap. The free safety rocks to his third, reads run, and fills the alley.

The Buck linebacker is the shadow player; he flows one gap behind the running back. The free safety plays the kick technique as the Will linebacker did on the cover-2 set. The playside corner is the secondary run support player.

COVER 4

- Nine in the box.
- Two deep defenders who can convert to four deep.
- Quick edge defender usually not accounted for in the blocking scheme.

Cover 4 is like an inverted cover 2 (Diagram #6). The corner aligns as he did on cover 3, but on the snap of the ball, he wants to stem inside to get between the #1 and #2 receivers. We do not like to run this to the two-receiver side. The free and strong safeties align on the #2 receivers and key them. The #2 receiver can do four things. He can release inside, outside, or vertical up the field. The fourth thing is he can block. The good thing about cover 4 is you can get nine in the box.

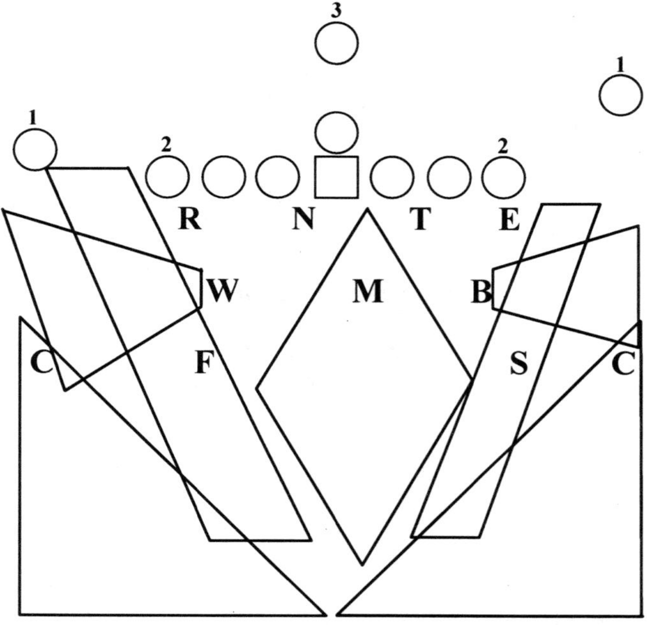

Diagram #6. Cover 4

If the #2 receivers block, the safeties come screaming for the run. If he releases vertical, the safety plays him. If the #2 receiver runs to the flat, the Will linebacker plays him, and the safety looks to help on the #1 receiver coming to the post, curl, or dig.

If we get run flow to the right, the strong safety comes screaming up from to set the edge (Diagram #7). He keys the tight end. The defensive end plays the C gap, and the Buck linebacker scrapes outside inside the strong safety. The Mike fills over the top as the shadow player on the running back. The Will linebacker becomes the kick players in the middle. The playside corner is the secondary contain player to that side.

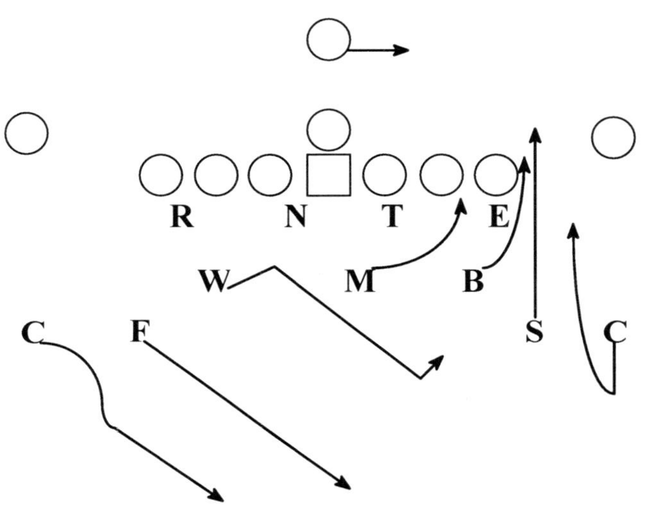

Diagram #7. Run Flow Right

Run support comes from the corner in cover 2, from the safety in cover 4, and the linebacker in cover 3.

Our two-deep man coverage is cover 5. We play man under with two deep safeties. When we play this defense, we teach the man defenders to play a trail position on the receivers. The defender is under the receiver but can touch his hip. He has help over the top and plays under him for all patterns. If he wants to run deep, we have a two-deep shell over the top. On occasion, we substitute to improve our coverage. We can take out a defensive lineman and play with two linebackers in the box or put in an extra defensive back for a linebacker.

We match the corners on the wide receiver and the linebackers on the slot receivers. The strong and free safeties are the deep defenders.

The next coverage is combination coverage. This is cover 6 (Diagram #8). To the two-receiver side of the formation, we play cover 2. To the tight side of the formation, we play a cover-4 scheme. Cover 6 is a combo coverage that gives us an extra defender in the box against an uneven run formation. It takes away the quick flat toward the flanker and gives you help over the top on play-action passes.

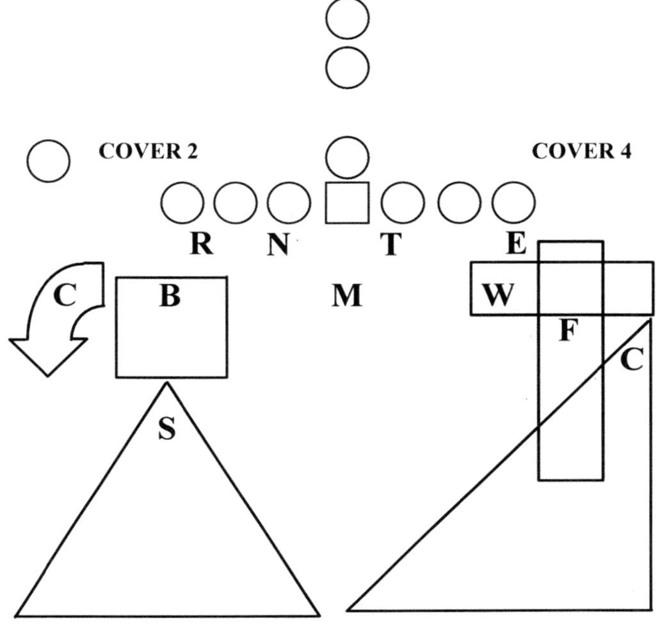

Diagram #8. Cover 6

If we have a team using jet motion, we run cover 7. This is nothing more than the corner roll to the jet motion. We want the corner to knife the jet sweep and shut the play down before it gets started. It is cover 3 with a cloud roll instead of a strong safety inverting down to the flat. If it is a pass, the rolled corner plays the flat, and the strong safety rolls to the outside third behind the corner. The free safety rolls to the middle, and the backside corner plays the opposite third.

Cover 7 forces the jet sweep inside. It prevents the stalk block because the corner is on the move to the line of scrimmage. It also provides a strong coverage against a trips formation. It allows you to keep your linebackers in the box so they can play the trap and dive plays run by the wing-T. This coverage allows you to play cover 2 into the motion.

We can run another cover-3 scheme. We call it cover 8. We use this to change the strength of the support to take care of short motion. If we get a short motion into the backfield, we invert our safeties. The strong safety rolls to the middle, and the free safety rolls down to the other side for support. This gives you an answer for the jet and rocket motions in the wing-T offense. We can use this coverage instead of cover 7 against the jet motion. The pass coverage is a cover-3 drop by everyone. We are three deep with four underneath in this scheme.

Cover 9 is specialty coverage (Diagram #9). We dropped the Mike linebacker into the line of scrimmage in a shade technique on the center to the tight end side. The noseguard moved to a 3 technique to the split end side. The Buck linebacker moves over to a stacked position behind the Mike linebacker, and the strong safety drops down into a linebacker position head-up the tight end.

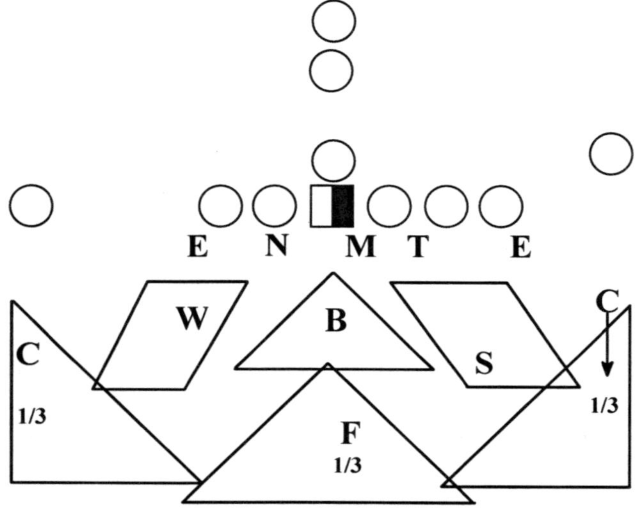

Diagram #9. Cover 9

The coverage is a three-deep secondary with three underneath defenders.

We designed half coverage to play a balanced running attack (Diagram #10). We play it against a two tight end double wing formation. This alignment has a 4-4 look. The corners are half-field players on the pass. The Will linebacker and strong safety are curl/flat defenders and can give you a quick outside edge on the power runs to the outside. The free safety in the middle has no pass coverage. He is like a Rover. All he has to do is get to the ball. He reads the center. The center blocks back on most of the plays coming from this set. He keys the center and fills opposite his movement.

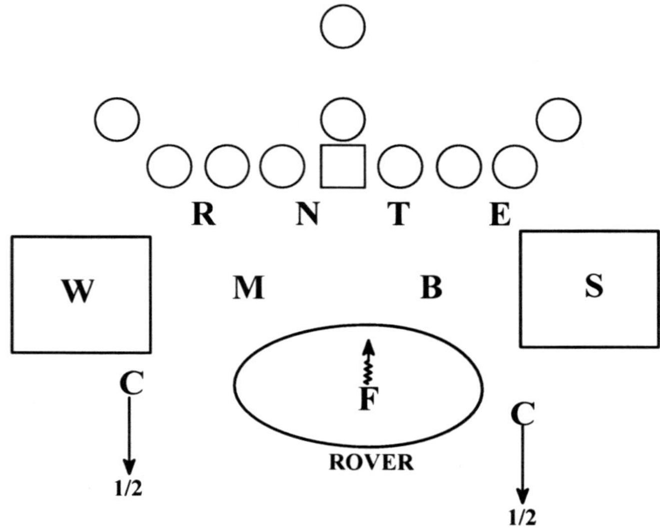

Diagram #10. Half Coverage

We oftentimes put a linebacker in the free safety position when we play this coverage.

I want to finish with what we call quarter coverage. We run this at the end of a half or a third-and-long situation. If it is third-and-18 for the first down, we will give up the hitches and short route patterns. We play this coverage to get a four-deep zone. It covers the seams and deep out routes. However, this coverage will give up the underneath routes. We want to keep people inbounds and prevent the deep ball. We allow the five-yard patterns, but prevent receivers from running the 12-yard out routes.

In this coverage, we have width and depth, and we have two defenders coming to any seam route. It eliminates the thought process for the secondary. They do not worry about anything except to keep the ball in front and inside.

Thank you.

Carl Johnson

SPREAD PUNT SCHEMES AND DRILLS

Jenks High School, Oklahoma

Thank you. I appreciate that fine introduction. I know when I go to a clinic, I want to pick up one or two nuggets to take back and incorporate. If I can do that, the clinic has been worthwhile. I hope that you will find something in this presentation you can use.

I have been at Jenks High School for seven years. When Coach Allan Trimble hired me seven years ago, he gave me an opportunity to coach the special teams. I had never been a special teams coach. I had always coached on the defensive side of the ball; I coached the defensive line. When I was a graduate assistant at the University of Houston, I worked for Coach Joe Robinson. He just recently took a job with The University of North Carolina at Chapel Hill. I learned a great deal from him. I learned not only about schemes, but also a great deal about organization. One thing that impressed me was his passion for special teams. He enjoyed that aspect of the game.

It rubbed off on me and I am into special teams and have great passion for it. I try to coach the special teams with the same passion that the offensive and defensive coordinators coach their areas. I think it has had an effect on our program at Jenks. We spend a lot of time working on special teams and it led to nine special teams scores this season.

We try to emphasize special teams scoring and I think it has helped us to be successful. I am going to talk about our spread punt team, including the personnel we like to use on the punt team. I will cover the fundamentals, identifying fronts, operation time, protections, drills, and coverage responsibilities.

We are a spread punt team. We have two gunners, two ends, two tackles, two guards, a center, a personal protector, and a punter. We have not had a punt blocked since I have been at Jenks.

Jenks Punt Basics

- We are a spread punt team.
  - ✓ Best way to protect the punter
  - ✓ Ability to cover and stop the returner
  - ✓ Allows us to run fakes
- We will gather on sideline on third down and go directly to the line of scrimmage.
- We are a man/zone protection team.

We want to stop the return. We punted 25 times this past season and gave up zero return yardages. We generally get a 4.5 hang time with our punter, but the coverage team works their butts off to get downfield. We had six punts inside the 10-yard line and five inside the five-yard line.

Our punter this year was also a quarterback. That is always a good situation to have in the punt game. That means the fake was always part of the punting scheme. The defense knew he was a quarterback and had to spend time defending the fake as well as the punt.

In a game situation, we have a five-yard-square box that extends from the 47-yard line to the 47-yard line on our sideline. On third down, we have a *punt team alert*. All the punt players huddle in that box. If we have to punt the ball, we go from that box directly to the field.

SPREAD PUNT PERSONNEL

In the *center*, you need a perfectionist. He has to be able to snap the ball to the punter in 0.8 seconds or less with accuracy. He has to have physical size so he can occupy space on the line. He is part of the protection scheme and must block an A gap. He has to be able to run and cover downfield and be a good tackler. The center this year was an offensive tackle. He snapped the ball in 0.72. The return team turns the center loose most of the time. He will be the first defender down and has to make an impact.

In the *guards*, we look for physical size because we do not want them overpowered or pulled out to one side or the other. They help the center with his spacing and splits. They have to hold the A-gap defender off on occasion. In this position, we want linebacker and fullback body types. They must be good tacklers.

The *tackles* must be physical but also have long reach. They have to protect as well as cover. When they cover, they must keep leverage on the returner. We want to use tight ends, linebackers, strong safeties, or fullbacks in this position.

The *wings* sit outside the tackles off the line of scrimmage. They must have athletic ability. They have to force the wide rushers around the punter. They have to stop a power rusher and they are contain coverage players. They cannot let the returner get outside of their coverage. We look for strong safeties, quick linebackers, big receivers, or fullbacks to play this position. They are responsible for echoing the calls from the personal protector to the rest of the coverage team.

The *bullets* are receivers or defensive backs that can get off jams at the line of scrimmage. Receivers get off jams all the time in their position play and defensive backs tackle well. They must have speed so they can get downfield and make plays. They must be great tacklers because they are the primary tacklers on the coverage team. They have to locate the ball quickly and know where it is.

The *personal protector* has to be a very smart player. He is the one who identifies the front and makes sure we have 11 players on the field. He makes all the protection calls and has to do it within the 25-second clock. He has to make good decisions and be willing to study the opponent. He must be able to block two rushers if necessary.

He is the pride leader of the punt team. He takes ownership of the unit and provides the leadership for the team. He is the player I hold accountable for what goes on with the punt team. I coach him individually so he can do what we ask. The quickest way to block a punt is up the middle. He is the player that does not let that happen.

The *punter* is an important member of the coverage team. He has to be athletic because he must have the capability to run fakes, handle bad snaps, and throw the ball. We have bad snap drills for the punter. We snap the ball low, high, right, left, and bounce them to him. He has to catch the ball cleanly. Catching the ball cleanly dictates his ability to establish a rhythm with good footwork. We want him to be able to use the traditional punt and to rugby punt the ball. He must have a strong leg with good hang time and distance on his kicks.

We have one stance when we align on the line of scrimmage. We are in a two-point stance for all players, with the hands on the knees and elbows bent slightly. The inside foot is up in the stance and the outside foot is back. We want a heel-to-toe stagger in the feet.

The offensive guards take a one-foot split from the center (Diagram #1). The depth of the guards off the ball should be the toes on the heels of the center. The outside foot in his stance should drop six inches. The tackles split two feet from the guard. They align their inside foot on the guard's inside foot. We want to make sure the tackle is even with the guard's alignment. We do not want the flying V formation. We want him legally on the line of scrimmage. His outside foot drops six inches.

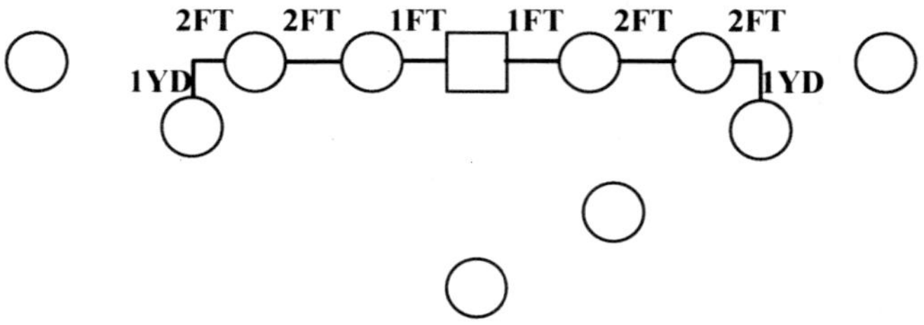

2FT 2FT 1FT 1FT 2FT 2FT
1YD 1YD

Diagram #1. Punt Team Line Splits

The wings take a two-foot split from the tackles and are one yard off the line of scrimmage. With the ball in the middle of the field, we want the bullets aligned on the inside edge of the numbers. If the ball is on the hash mark, the boundary bullet aligns on the outside edge of the numbers. The bullet to the field aligns halfway between the hash mark and numbers. If the ball is on the right hash mark, we kick the ball into the shortside of the field. The field bullet can cut his split down to about the hash mark so he has a chance to be in on the play.

The personal protector aligns five yards off the line of scrimmage and on the same side as the punter's kicking foot. His inside foot is directly behind the guard's outside leg. The punter aligns at 15 yards deep. If we have a slow snapper who has trouble getting the ball back 15 yards with zip, we cheat the punter forward.

We huddle on the sideline before we come on the field. When we get to the field and align, the personal protector looks at the front. He makes a series of calls depending on what he sees. The first thing he does is make a color call. The color is for our automatic changes. Here, for lecture's sake, green could mean we are going to kick the ball. If he calls red, that could be a call for a fake of some kind.

The next thing he calls is the alignment of the defensive front. If he calls 43, the front has four defenders to the left and three defenders to the right. The first number is left and the second number is right.

OPPONENT ALIGNMENT

- Six-man front = 3-3
- Seven-man front = 3-4 or 4-3
- Eight-man front = 4-4
- Nine-man (or more) front
  - ✓ Will look for either an open bullet or shift to tight punt, depending on situation
  - ✓ Various alerts: Stack, switch, or creeper

If the defense aligns in a nine-man (or more) front, we look for an uncovered bullet. If they do not cover one of the bullets, we can throw the ball to him. However, that depends on the situation of the game. We have the option of calling a tight punt. The personal protector points out and alerts everyone to stacks, switches, or creepers. A creeper is a defender that is moving somewhere other than where he originally aligned. He is an overload defender or a speed rusher from the outside.

The next thing the personal protector calls is a change in protection:

- Protection call
  - ✓ Solid (man)
  - ✓ Hinge (zone)
  - ✓ Zebra (zone)
  - ✓ Overload (man/zone)
- Ready call
  - ✓ After allowing everyone to point to their man, cut their splits, etc., the personal protector will make a ready call after everyone is set for one second.
  - ✓ No one is to move after this call.
  - ✓ The snapper can snap the ball at any time after the ready call.
  - ✓ If any bullet is uncovered, we have an alert call for that as well.

If the personal protector calls solid, we are in man protection. The hinge is a zone protection, but it could be only one side in a zone. The zebra call is zone all the way across the line. The overload is a combination call with man and zone blocking in the scheme.

The last call in the series of calls is the ready call. The personal protector gives the linemen a chance to adjust their splits and get set. Once he calls ready, the center is ready to snap the ball. When we call "ready," everyone has to freeze and not move. The snapper has to wait at least one second after the ready call before he can snap the ball. The center has to make sure we do not get into a rhythm in the interval between the ready call and the snap of the ball.

The line has to stand after the ready call and wait for the snap. We want them to see the ball with their peripheral vision. The defenders will react on the movement and we have to be ready. Everyone should see the flinch of the ball. We want to be the aggressor and get off first. Our goal is to get the punt off in 2.0 seconds. That is our operation time for getting the punt off:

- Snap time (15 yards) = 0.8 seconds
- Punter's time = 1.2 seconds
- Total punt time = 2.0 seconds

We have a coach in the press box with a stopwatch. He times every punt and tells me if he is fast or slow. If he is less than 2.0, he needs to slow down and concentrate on his mechanics. If he is too slow, we let him know he has to speed up a bit. Our goal for hang time is 4.2 seconds on a 40-yard punt.

I want to get into our protection schemes. We start with solid protection (Diagram #2). We start everything as man protection, so it is important to learn the calls and counting system. Any noseguard

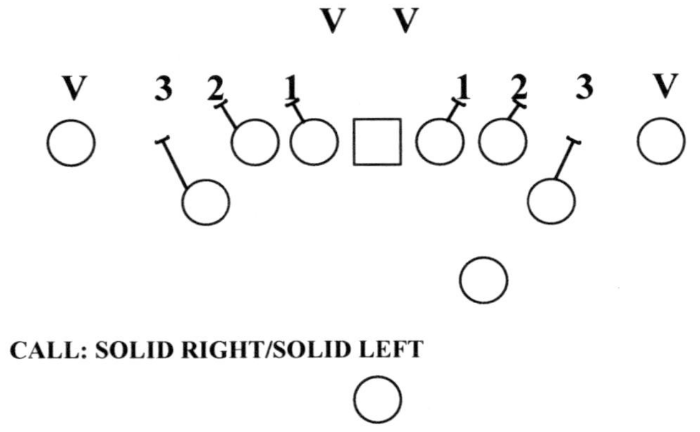

V V

V 3 2 1 1 2 3 V

CALL: SOLID RIGHT/SOLID LEFT

Diagram #2. Solid Protection

will be counted as "zero." We only count men at four yards depth or less. If someone is deeper, they cannot block the punt. If there is a stack, the man closest to the line of scrimmage gets the lower number and the man behind the higher number.

Any time there is a "zero," the personal protector adjusts his alignment to three yards behind the guard. Each side works independently after getting the call from the personal protector. We communicate all calls from the inside out (guards, tackles, and wings, in that order). We do not see many zero fronts in the punt protection schemes.

SOLID PROTECTION

- Guards are responsible for #1, tackles for #2, and wings for #3; the personal protector is responsible for a 0 technique.
- Communication is vital. Point to man and call out his jersey number (start with guards first). Example: "I've got 44!"
- See the ball and go on the center's flinch.
- Stay square to the defender and use a "step and jolt" technique as he commits to his rush lane.
- We do not want to wait on the rusher; be the aggressor; 1-on-1 protection.

When the players call out the communication of who they have, it stops the duplication of two blockers having the same man. We work from the guards out as we point to the defenders and call their numbers. It is critical and vital to do this. There should be no doubt in their minds.

When the blocker steps to the defender, he steps with the foot closest to the defender. If the defender is outside, he steps with his outside foot and gets square on the rusher. As we step, we want to jolt the man to a stop by staying low. We want pads under pads, while hitting with our hat and hands.

The goal is to bring their man to a stop and then get into coverage as quick as possible. If rusher drops off the line of scrimmage, we get into coverage immediately. The center immediately releases to the left and covers. When the coverage team gets off the line of scrimmage, they always escape to the coverage lane from the inside to the outside.

We can run a hinge protection from a seven- or eight-man front. We want to use this protection when we have four or more defenders to one side of the line.

HINGE PROTECTION

- Hinge protection is a zone concept that we will use anytime there is a threat of four or more rushers to one side.
  - ✓ This will bring the center into the protection scheme (goes to hinge callside).
  - ✓ Personal protector is responsible for a 0 technique.
- There are two parts of hinge protection.
  - ✓ The punch to help and buy time for our teammate inside
  - ✓ The block, pivot off our inside foot, exploding with our outside foot and attack the outside rusher.
- Cut split to one foot to get inside rusher as close as head-up as possible. Everyone must do this.

The hinge protection in the diagram is left (Diagram #3). The center hinges to the left A gap. The left guard punches the #1 defender to his inside but blocks the #2 defender on his outside. The tackle and wing have the same technique.

Each side works independently after getting the call from the personal protector. All communication is from the inside out. Communication is vital. Identify the number of the player on the punch and the block (punching #35; blocking #24). If there are

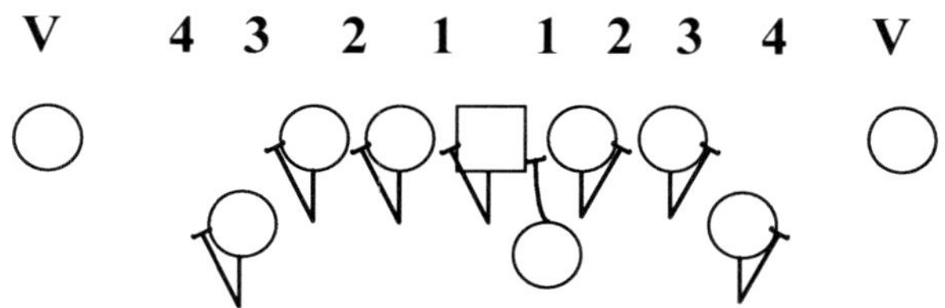

CALL: HINGE RIGHT/HINGE LEFT

Diagram #3. Hinge Protection

two rushers outside, block the widest rusher. That simply means that to get to the widest rusher, you have to go through the rusher closest to you. In essence, you block two men. Be explosive, but stay under control. On the snap of the ball, blockers get their depth. We take an inside-outside-inside (IOI) step, which will allow us to get depth and be able to see twists and games.

When we use the hinge protection, we use a kick-slide technique to get the depth off the line of scrimmage. We punch with the inside hand and kick-slide with the outside foot. It is the IOI step. We step on the inside foot, kick-slide with the outside foot, and drive outside with the inside foot. We want to attack the rusher on the outside number, wash him to the outside, and release on the coverage. If not everyone is on the same page, there will be seams in the protection. See the ball and go on the center's flinch.

The next protection is a combination of the solid and hinge protection (Diagram #4). In the diagram, we hinge to the left and are solid to the right. It is a seven-man front. We block man to the right and zone to the left.

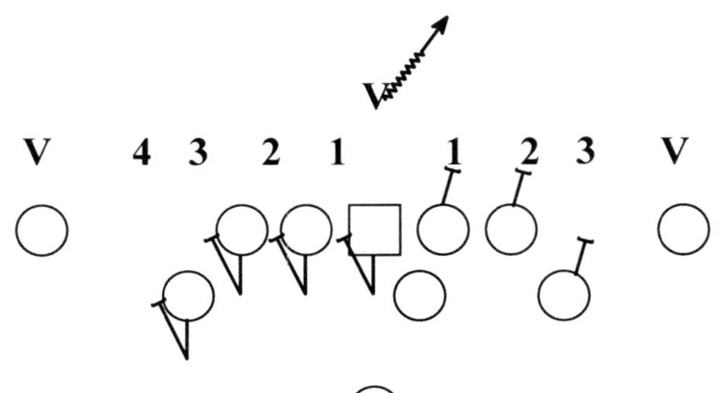

CALL: SOLID RIGHT/HINGE LEFT

Diagram #4. Hinge/Solid

This is a hinge left protection and the center blocks in the direction of the hinge. He blocks left. The personal protector blocks the opposite A gap. To the right side, we block the #1, #2, and #3 defenders on the line of scrimmage. We hinge to the left and zone defenders #1, #2, #3, and #4.

HINGE/SOLID PROTECTION

- If we get a seven-man front, we use a combo call that utilizes both man/zone rules
- We make a hinge call to the four-man rush side and a solid call to the three-man rush side.
- The snapper goes to the direction of the hinge call and the personal protector is then responsible for anyone else.

The personal protector has no one in the A gap, oversees the protection, and cleans up any seepage.

We make a zebra call when there is doubt by the personal protector (Diagram #5). The defense has lots of movement or a stack alignment in their front. If there is any question on protection by the personal protector, we call zebra. This is our safest protection scheme. Zebra is a *double hinge* scheme with the center blocking to the left and the personal protector to the right. We cut the splits down to one foot and the wings close down one half yard to the tackle's hip. The personal protector moves up to two feet from the line of scrimmage on the near foot of the center.

Diagram #5. Zebra

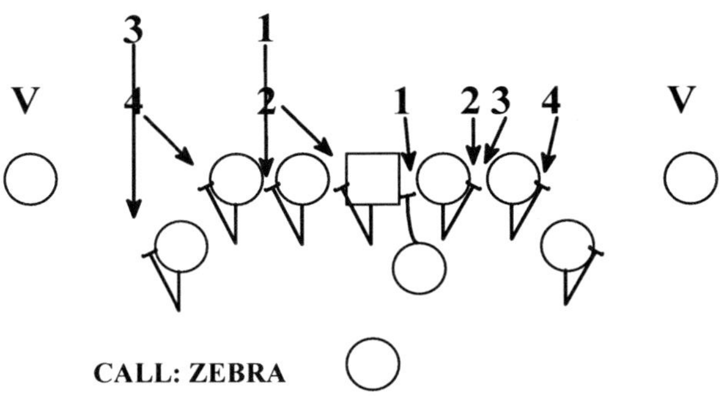

- Center is responsible for getting off a quick, accurate snap and then is responsible for our left A gap.

- Guards and tackles are responsible for holding off the inside rusher and then protecting their outside gap.
- Personal protector is to make zebra call, move up to a depth of two yards, and is then responsible for our right A gap.
- Punter moves his alignment up to 13 yards.

We use an overload protection if the punt block unit has at least six men to one side (Diagram #6). An overload right or overload left call tells the guard away from the overload side that he will need to block to his inside. We follow the call with a hinge call to the shiftside and a solid call away. We have automatics built in that we can check to if we see opportunities for a fake. We hinge to the left and the tackle and wing block solid to the right. The right guard blocks the inside A gap.

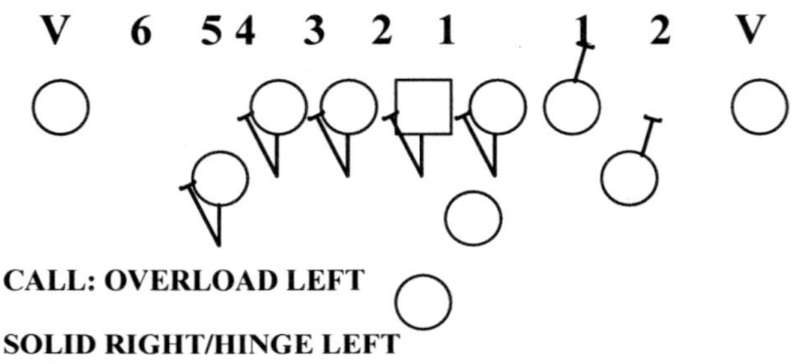

Diagram #6. Overload vs. Eight-Man Front

We will be in Trojan protection if we are inside our own five-yard line (Diagram #7). This protection is our maximum protection. Our bullets align two feet outside our wings and they block the inside number of the widest rusher before releasing to cover the punt. We use zebra protection whenever we are in this call. We can also call this out in the middle of the field in critical situations. If it is late in the game and we have to get the punt off, we use this formation regardless of where we are on the field.

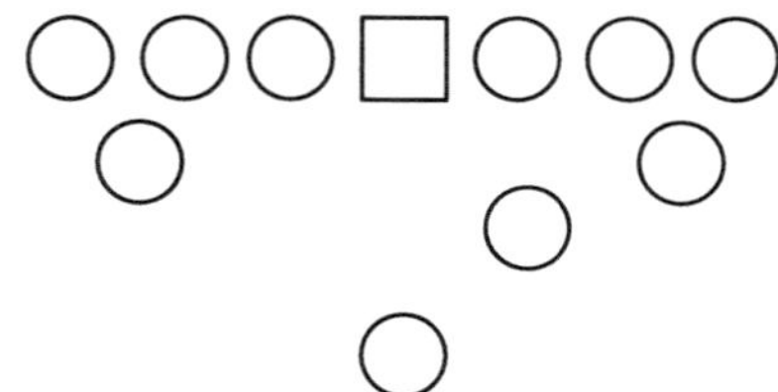

Diagram #7. Trojan Protection

We use a variety of formations, motions, and fakes in order to confuse our opponents. The more formations we can show them, the more work the special teams coordinator has. We want to make our opponent prepare for us on a weekly basis. The variety makes it fun for our team and breaks the monotony of doing the same thing all the time. We work on these situations every day so we can execute when we need to run something different.

Besides our automatics, we have at least one fake each week that we put in the game plan. A "Texas" call by the personal protector means that the opponent has not covered one of our receivers. It also tells everyone not to release into coverage until we punt the ball. There are two options by the punter. He can throw to the uncovered receiver who releases straight downfield under control, or he can punt the ball if the defense runs a defender out to the receiver late.

We can also make a "swat" call, which will allow us to switch out our first offensive unit with our second offensive unit. The goal is to make our opponent think that we are bringing the punt team onto the field, therefore bringing their punt return unit out as well. Timing is critical and we want to do it with as much deception as possible. The play we run in this situation will be a game planning decision.

We call a "swat alert" and align the second offense in the sideline box instead of the punt team. Everything looks the same except we run out an offense to run a play instead of the punt team. You must practice the situation because it cannot be done on a whim.

The different alignments we use in our punt formation are all simple to get into. They are all forms of the original formation. We use a 2x2 formation if we try to pooch kick the ball and pin an opponent deep. We call that formation "shoot." We widen the wings to get more coverage down the field.

We can get into a trips formation in the middle of the field or with the ball on the hash mark (Diagram #8). In the trips formation, we put both wings on the same side and reduce the bullets down inside away from the trips call. When we get into these special alignments, we can rugby punt the ball or use the traditional punt.

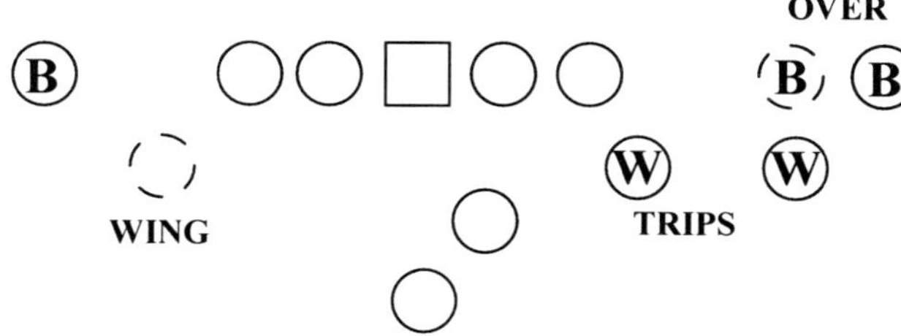

Diagram #8. Trips Formation

The "over" formation is a similar formation. We bring both bullets to the same side. The alignment of the over depends on the position of the ball. With the ball in the middle of the field, we go over right. If the ball is on the hash mark, we go over to the shortside of the field. The only time we did not do that was with a team that used a creeper off in inside bullet. We went to the wideside with the bullets and spread wide. The creeper had too far to go and had to uncover one of the bullets. The outside bullet is eligible for the pass and the inside bullet blocks the other defender.

The "poke" formation is a combination formation (Diagram #9). We bring both bullets and wings to the same side of the formation. With two blockers to the backside of the formation, we must rugby punt from this set.

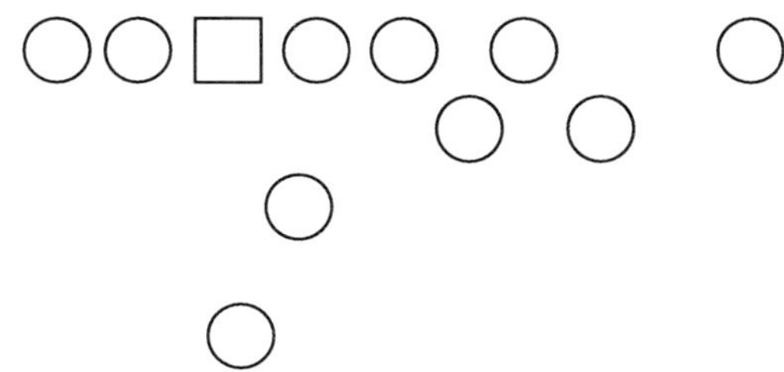

Diagram #9. Poke

When you punt the ball, you must cover it. That is essential to change the field position.

- Take great pride in covering punts. Win the field position battle.
- Be disciplined in hitting our landmarks and staying in our lanes.
- Squeeze the ball. Keep it inside and in front.
- We will try and hit our landmarks at 15 yards downfield.
- Key point: Hit landmarks *first* and then converge on the ball.

The coaching points and emphasis has to be on hitting the landmarks before doing anything else. Hit the landmarks, find the ball, and squeeze it.

The *bullets* are the "hit men" in your coverage scheme. They attack the ballcarrier on his right or left jugular vein. Getting off the line is essential to our success in this phase. They must defeat the press of the defensive backs off the line of scrimmage the way a receiver does on a pass release. The wide receiver coaches the bullets.

The *wings* have containment responsibility. At 15 yards downfield, they must be eight yards from the sideline and squeezing the football. We adjust distance if they are to the wideside of the field. They come down four yards outside the hash marks. They keep the outside shoulder free and keep the ball inside and in front of them. The *tackles*, at 15 yards downfield, must be four yards outside the hash marks and squeezing the football. He wants to keep the outside shoulder free and the ball inside and in front of him.

The *guards*, at 15 yards downfield, must be hitting their respective upright of the goalpost and squeezing the football. They keep the outside shoulder free and the ball inside and in front of them.

The *center* is a delayed hit man. He attacks the ballcarrier in a nose-up leverage position. The *personal protector* is a secondary hit man and attacks the ballcarrier nose-up. The *punter* is the safety on the coverage team. He keeps the ball nose-up and in front. He knows where the ball goes and stays even with it.

The coaching points that go with the coverage are important. The last four steps are critical. It does us no good to cover the punt but miss the tackle. They want to come to balance. They cannot break down too quick and they must keep the feet active. The feet should never stop moving. If the feet stop moving, it is hard to start them again.

Drills

- Kick-slides
- Kick-slides with bodies
- Half-line vs. scouts
- Full-line vs. scouts
- Gunner releases
- Leverage drill with gunners
- Team cover

When we start, we work the kick-slide on air. We want to be sure everyone has the technique before we start to work against people. When we add bodies to the drill, we use two rushers. We want the blocker to punch the inside rusher and block the outside rusher.

After work in individual drills we work in a half-line situation and finally in the full-line against the scout team. The gunners work with the wide receivers coach on their releases off the line of scrimmage. They also work on a leverage drill so they attack the ballcarrier on getting the right angle and getting the head in the appropriate place on the tackle. We want the head coming on the upfield side of the receiver.

When we work on team coverage, we go through the entire package of blocks and coverage. It is important to work from all positions on the field. We work down the middle and from each hash mark, which is important to understanding landmarks.

If there is ever anything we can do for you, do not hesitate to call on us. Our door is always open. I appreciate your attention and hope I gave you something you can use. Thank you very much for your time.

Bob Milloy

OFFENSIVE PRACTICE AND TWO-MINUTE OFFENSE

Our Lady of Good Counsel High School, Maryland

Thank you for that fine introduction. It sure does not feel like I have been coaching for 42 years. It feels like I have been coaching for 62 years. As I sat here watching some of the other coaches lecture, with all of the X's and O's, I realized how much the game of football has changed.

My first coaching job was back in 1961 coaching the eighth grade CYO youth football. I did that for six years. Then, I became the junior varsity coach at DeMatha Catholic High School for three years. I have coached at Whitman, Sherwood, and Springbrook High Schools in Maryland. I have learned X's and O's and a lot of other things about the game. I hope what I say will benefit you in your program.

This past fall, the newspaper did a story about all of the modern technology in football. They covered some of the area coaches about the way they scout the opponents with all of the modern equipment. I was in awe as I read that interesting article.

We do not use a computer to scout or do anything else related to football. I would not know how to turn on a PowerPoint. I can do a little with email, but I am not good with PowerPoint.

We still shoulder block teams. We still pull the guards to trap the defense. That is still a good play against teams that like to swim to get upfield rushing the quarterback. The guard trap is one of the best things we do on offense.

We have six basic core plays. The guard trap is at the top of our list. Our offense is a run first team. We are an off-tackle, belly type wing-T team. We can run the shotgun and the one-back offense and try to look current on offense. We still run our basic plays, which include: belly, trap, counter, toss sweep, midline, and option. We have the three- and five-step drop passing game. We run the sprint out passing game, and we have our screens and draw plays. We do fundos (fundamentals) two or three times each week.

The original title of my lecture, "Lessons Learned After 41 Years of Mistakes" would take too long to tell. I know you would prefer that I talk about our offense, so that is what I will do. However, I have learned a lot and I think some of those things I have learned are worth sharing. Last year, we lost to DeMatha in the regular season. However, in the playoffs we eked out a win over DeMatha. Our Lady of Good Counsel High School won its first championship of the WCAC. After going 51 years as "O-for...," we finally won a championship.

Last year it was a trying year for me because I received a lot of phone calls from parents. It was all about playing time. Parents were out of control on this subject.

One important lesson I have learned is this: Never call a parent back on game night. Let the situation settle. If you call the parent back on game night, you may be upset about the game, and chances are they are going to be upset. Don't call them back that night. Sleep on it, and think it over, and then call them the next morning.

It amazes me at the time and planning coaches put into a game. We work hard on Sunday getting a scouting report together. We work on a game plan on Monday. We practice a ton of plays we think we must have to be successful on Friday night. By Wednesday after practice, we try to assess what we really need to do to win the game Friday night. We get into the game and we only run 40 percent of the things we worked on all week. We think we need to be ready for all phases of the game.

We start looking at plays we can throw out of our offense and we find it hard to do. I may be one of the worst when it comes to having too much offense or defense. As coaches, we must realize the players can only comprehend so much. If we give them too much, we are not going to be as effective. It took me a long time to realize this, and I still have a hard time limiting the offense.

Let me talk about making mistakes. A few years back I was sitting in my office at Sherwood High School. I was at Sherwood High School nine years. One day this kid came to my office to see me. I knew who he was so I told him to come in. He sat down and he had a bag in his hand. He opened the bag and he had these small, skintight T-shirts. He wanted me to buy them to wear at practice. I could not imagine our players wearing skintight T-shirts. I said, "Kevin, I do not think this is a good idea. I just do not think our players will wear them."

You got it! Kevin Plank walked out of my office. Now, we all know who Kevin Plank is and the success he has had in the athletic world with Under Armour®. I could have been wearing Under Armour the rest of my life, but I did not buy into it. I did not see it at the time, but that was one of the biggest mistakes in my life.

One of the best things I ever did was in 1970 when I was coaching at Whitman High School. Our county schools did not have night football. On Friday night, we used to go down to Virginia and watch Ed Henry's team at George C. Marshall High School play. One game we saw was Marshall High play against T.C. Williams High School.

The next week, I called Coach Herman Boone up to set up a scrimmage with T.C. Williams High School. I told him we wanted to scrimmage his team the next year. He wanted to know who I was and what type of team we had. In the movie, *Remember the Titans* that game we watched was included in that film. They still had some of those Titans around on the team the next fall.

We had never had a winning season at Whitman High School in the history of the school. This was the football season of 1971. We practiced a couple of weeks in the early fall camps getting ready to scrimmage another high school. Scrimmage day came and we were the home team. These two buses pulled up at our stadium and the players started unloading.

On the first bus, 40 players came off the bus. The players on the first bus had red on red uniforms. On the second bus, they had 45 players. They had white on white uniforms. I started thinking, "What the hell have I gotten myself into?"

Actually, it was a great scrimmage. They beat us three to one in touchdowns. It worked out well for us. Coach Boone was impressed that a young high school coach would call him to scrimmage. It has worked out well for me. Coach Boone came over and talked to our team. He talked at my camps later. He was a great guy and became a loyal friend. Last week, I was in San Antonio, Texas at the U.S. Army All-American Bowl. The trophy they give out after the game each year is in honor of Coach Herman Boone.

The night before that game, I was sitting in the hotel lobby. I saw a crowd of people coming in the hotel. I looked up and Coach Herman Boone was in the center of the crowd. He had a big, black cowboy hat on. I stood up as they approached and said to him, "Coach Boone, I guess you are going to walk by me without speaking?" He looked under the big hat and said, "Bob Milloy, how in the world are you?" He sat down and we talked for 30 minutes.

I had six players with me in San Antonio. I had one player in the game and the other five players were taking part in the U.S. Army National Combine they have in conjunction with the all-star game. The parents of those players all knew who Coach Boone was. The players did not know the story, but those parents were busy getting Coach Boone to sign programs and other items for them.

If you want to hear me talk on X's and O's, you probably should leave. I can show you the right guard trap play if you want. I will talk about the two-minute offense at the end of the lecture. I will talk about practice organization first.

On offense, you are a running team, a passing team, or a combination of those two systems. The most important thing in setting up your offense is to decide what your quarterback can do. Can he run the ball; can he pass the ball; and can he think on his feet? Usually, you get one or two of those traits, and you may get three things he can do. You have to build your offense around him.

I have learned three things in the last several years. One of them was from Mike Dailey from McDaniel College. He is a great coach. One thing I learned from Mike Dailey relates to the stunts team's run. They have the wide receivers call out the possible stunts they see that the defense might run against them. For example, if the split end sees the corner cheating inside and up close to the line, he calls out, "Cowboy, cowboy." The corner may not come, but it alerts the offense that there is a possibility the corner may blitz. It is a call for cloud and sky coverage.

If the safety comes on a blitz, the receiver may call out, "Slew, slew." If the linebacker comes, they call out, "Badger, badger." These calls put the offense on alert. We started doing this on offense this year. After we got used to it, it helped.

The second thing I learned was how to use the scramble drill. Every day we do one scramble drill. We want to teach our receivers where to be if our quarterback has to scramble. If the quarterback scrambles to the right, the short receiver goes long, and the long receiver comes up on the play and goes to the sideline. The first-up man wants to get into the vision of the quarterback. The deep man tries to get to the post on that side of the field. We work on the play every day.

With all of the blitzing we are seeing, we started using what we call "repeat." We added it to our cadence. "Green 18, green 18, set, go." This helped us with the receivers calling the stunts out. It gives us more time to see the blitz developing. We repeat the first call.

We use this on pass and run plays to see what the defense is doing. It slows the defense down because they do not know if we are going to go on the first cadence or the repeat cadence. We work on this in practice and when we come into a game, it is second nature. This is a lot easier than going on a count of two.

EVERY GREAT IDEA WAS STOLEN FROM A THIEF

I did not invent anything. I am just like most coaches that go to clinics and write everything down. Three years ago, we completely redid our practice organization. This has helped us immensely. Before we revised our practice organization, I never used to script the plays in practice. I will never go back to the old ways of not having the plays written down. Never!

Once practice starts, we follow the script. As we run the plays, I make notes. When we meet after practice, the first thing we talk about is what we did with the plays on the script.

It takes more time in the beginning to do the script. It makes you be more selective in the plays you are going to run. We make sure we run the plays that we are planning to use in the game that week.

At our school, the team selects three captains and the coaches appoint one captain each week. The kids like this arrangement.

In our Wednesday practice schedule, the first thing we do is to stretch. Then, we go into our inside runs in the first part of practice. We have 12 running plays that day. The second team runs the last three plays on the script.

While we are running the plays, the receivers are working on their blocking. They work on stalk and crack blocks.

The next 20 minutes, the offense goes pass skelly. The offensive line is working on their blocks. We do not tell the players to do it again. We tell them to "fix it." Therefore, our line works on the plays we need to correct from the last week.

Next, we go for 20 minutes of team offense. We are still doing our fundo drills. Even at the end of the year, we are working on our fundamentals.

We work on the kicking game for 20 minutes every day. I think most football games are lost on misfielding punts. We use what we call the "punt hassle drill" once a week (Diagram #1). We line up two linemen as defenders, one on each side of the long snapper on punts. We use both offensive and defensive linemen in this drill.

We have the punt cover team go down on punts, one on the left side and one on the right side. We have one defender rush the punter and go in front of the punter. We have one defender rush the punter and go behind him. We do this drill for 10 minutes, but you would be amazed how much you can get done in those 10 minutes.

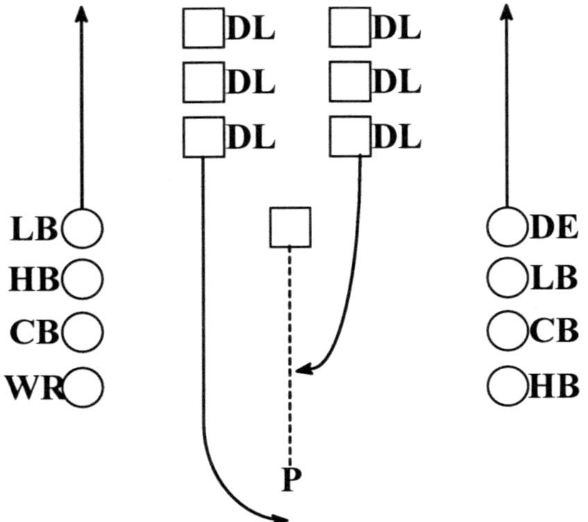

Diagram #1. Punt Hassle Drill

We are working on punting, and we are working on fielding punts. You can have two groups run the punt hassle drill. You can have the first defense and punt team on one end of the field and the second-team players at the other end of the field running the same drill. You get a lot done in those 10 minutes.

When our punt return players are back to receive a punt, there are three options on receiving the punt. The first option is this: If you are back to our 10-yard line, let the punt go. The second point is to fair catch the punt. The third option is if he is in the middle of the field, he can catch the ball and run. We make them practice all of these options. Those are little things, but they all count.

We have 10 minutes of the hassle drill. Then, we go to our punt team. We do this every day. We punt four of five times in that session. On Tuesday, we punt from the right hash, Wednesday from the left hash, and Thursday from the middle of the field. We work on protect and cover. Then, we run one of our four fake punts. We always have a fake punt ready.

We work on a second special teams period in the next drill. We work on a fake punt and a punt return. We do this drill for 20 minutes. The next day, we work on another phase of the special teams. We do not wait until the end of practice to work on our special teams. I can't remember when we last had a punt blocked. We use the traditional 7-2-1-1 alignment from the line back to the punter.

After this, we work on defense. I just ask my defensive coordinator, Billy Goodman, what he wants to work on and he sets it up. They have one hour to work in everything in that part of practice.

After our hassle drill, the defense gets 10 minutes of defensive fundos. It may be tackling. After that, they go to what we call "install." We have a front seven and a back seven. The linebackers have to switch during the drill because they are part of both groups. The install means the steps we take on the blitzes and any other movement we use on defense. We include the coverages, how we are going to handle motion, and shifts.

Next, the defense works on the front seven inside run drill and back seven pass skelly drill. Again, we switch the linebackers in the drill.

We do not run a lot of team defense. However, it changes daily. I am sure you do the same with your practice schedule. This is a typical practice for us. I am old-fashioned and we do sprints at the end of practice. We do not do them every day, but we do sprints and conditioning at the end of practice.

Thursday is the day we get on the game field. The practice I covered was our last game of the year. This is what we do in practice. It took a lot of years to evolve to this schedule. We are happy with this type of schedule, and I don't see it changing much in the future.

GAME PLANNING

I want to talk about game planning. We write down the defenses we expect to see in the upcoming games. Two years ago, we were set to play DeMatha High School on ESPN TV. We were 11-0 going into the championship game against them. DeMatha had been an even front defense from the time the game of football started. When you play good teams, they know what they are doing, and they were a good team. They are so good at what they do, we knew it would be difficult to fool them.

In our Tuesday night staff meeting before the game, we talked about the defense we expected to face for the upcoming game. I asked my staff if they thought DeMatha would ever run an odd defense against us. There was a dead silence for about a minute. Finally, they all said, "Nah, not a chance." The even front alignment was etched into their system over the years. As a result, we did not work against an odd defensive front that week.

Normally, we would work on both the odd and even fronts each week.

We started the game and I could not believe what DeMatha was doing on defense. They lined up in a 3-3-5 defense. They played that defense the entire game and we were not ready for the odd defense. They kicked our butt 35-7. It was embarrassing.

After that game, I made a promise to everyone. We would never go into a game where we did not work against both the odd and even front defenses. Never! We were going to work against both fronts every single day in practice. I give DeMatha credit for doing a good job against us. They put it on us and we were caught off guard. It was not as if we had not played against teams that ran an odd front defense, but we did not practice against it during the week of the DeMatha game.

In making our game plan and practice schedule for the week, we list the number one defense we expect to see that week. We list two or three stunts we may see from that number one defense. We look at a second defense and the stunts they run from each alignment. We look at a third defense and review what to expect from that alignment. We use these defenses to script the offensive plays we want to use against each of the three defenses. We select the plays we want to review and make them part of the script for the practice week. We do this for every game.

From there, we get into the inside runs. We list the plays we are going to run against all defenses. This is where we run the belly repeat. We are running the same play twice. We write down all plays we are going to use that week. Once you have it written down, it makes practice go a lot smoother. We run all of the plays on the script if possible. If not, we complete them the next day. That is how we run the inside drill.

We give the defensive coaches a copy of the script and they get the bird dog team, or scout team, ready to run the defenses we want to see for each play on the script. We do the same with the passing game. We script the pass plays we want to run against the defense we have written down. All of the coaches get a copy of the script and they all know what to expect.

When we are running the plays on the script, we list 12 plays. For the last three plays, we have our second unit run the plays. They run the plays that are the most difficult to run against the defenses. By the end of the week, they have run 12 plays against the defenses we expect to see for that week. We try to build depth by using those second-team players in the script.

We are off the practice field in two and a half hours. Once the season starts, we do not have a lot of contact. We go "thud" and we tag the ballcarriers, but we do not take them down to the ground. You can't play the game on the practice field on Wednesday. You play the game on Friday or Saturday.

When we go to the team script, we do not run the ball that much. We run enough running plays to keep the defense honest.

Our last phase of the game plan in practice is to work on our two-minute offense. The first thing your team must understand is what stops the clock. You would be amazed at how many players do not know this.

WHAT STOPS THE CLOCK?

- Incomplete pass
- Out-of-bounds
- Time-out

They must know a penalty may not stop the clock. It only stops the clock long enough for the official to enforce the penalty. As soon as the official marks the ball ready for play, the clock starts.

When the clock is running and we want to go to our two-minute offense, we call out, "Red ball, red ball," as soon as the official marks the ball for play. "Red ball" means we are going to line up in doubles, or the 2x2 alignment. We always keep the same personnel in the game. If we can huddle, we can go to trips, or we can use motion in our play selection. However, in red ball, it is all "read" for our receivers and backs. If we huddle, we still want to include our draws, screens, trips set, and the trap play. The trap is still a good play on third-and-long.

We must work on killing the clock. We call out, "Kill, kill" if we want to stop the clock. The quarterback must be under center when he takes the snap and spikes it to the ground. He can't kill the clock by spiking the ball if he is in the shotgun.

When you are in a one-back set, the back has to be at certain positions on certain plays. In our passing game, we have the three-, the five-, and the nine-step drop, which is the sprint-out pass. The wide receivers know what they are going to do on each play of the two-minute drill. The running back has to know to go right or left on the plays. We have to come up with a way to let the running back know where to go on plays.

The easiest way is to put the quarterback under center. Then, the running back can go right or left as the play develops. The second way is to *jump* the back to the area he needs to be. The third way is to *flash* him. To flash the running back, the quarterback gives a flash of the ball as he would if he were running the belly play. The fourth way to communicate with the running back to let him know where to line up is by putting him in the pistol offense. We do not run the pistol offense.

I said we have the three types of pass drops based on the steps by the quarterback. Our basic passing game is our three-step drop. We have five passes on the three-step drop. On the five-step drop, we have six passes. The deep is four-vertical routes. I plan to talk about the other routes later. The nine-step drop is our sprint-out series; we run those plays on the sprint-out action.

Three-Step Drop

- Smash
- Choice
- Crack flare
- Slant
- Double slant

Five-Step Drop

- Curl
- Deep
- Comeback
- Kirk
- Rudy
- Falcon crush

Nine-Step Drop

- Comeback
- Follow
- Flat
- Curl

Here is what we do on the two-minute offense. If we call doubles right, this is how we line up. Our X- and Y-receiver are to our right, and the T- and B-receiver are to our left (Diagram #2). The X and Y are our best receivers. The T is our third receiver and the B is our fullback. We have a wideout in for the fullback in this formation. If we are running a 30 set pass pattern, the X and Y are running the three-beater routes, and the T and B are running the two-beater routes. This never changes. However, the plays do change. We select the patterns we want to run on each play for that week. The 30 indicates three-step drop.

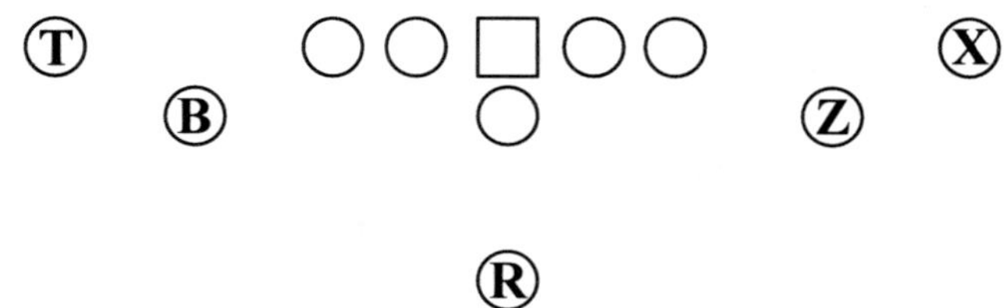

Diagram #2. 2x2 Alignment

When the quarterback comes to the line of scrimmage, he is reading he defense. If he reads the defense in cover 3, he knows the T and B are covered and he is going to the right side of the formation. We are going to run our crack flare pattern (Diagram #3). The outside receiver cracks back inside on the first man on the line, and we throw the bubble screen to our X-receiver in the slot.

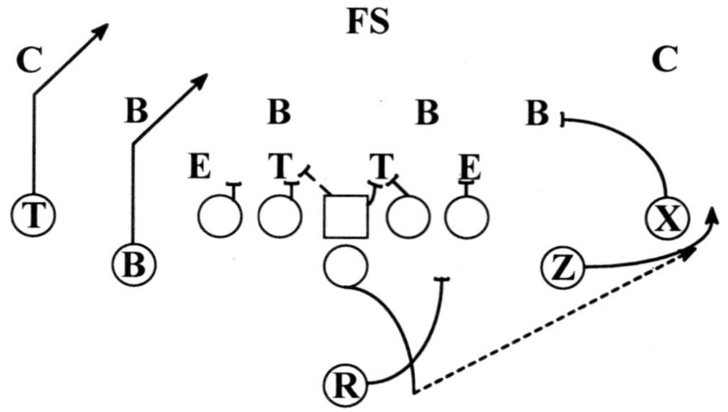

Diagram #3. Crack Flare Right Side

If the defense is in cover 2, the quarterback goes to the receivers on the left side, which is to our two-man beaters (Diagram #4). That is to our T- and B-receiver. The T runs a slant and the B-receiver runs the slant. The outside man should be open, but if the linebacker sits and reads the T-receiver, the B-receiver should be open on the slant.

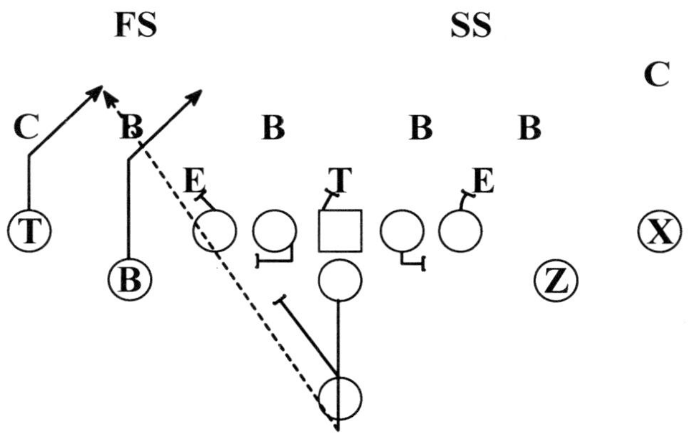

Diagram #4. Double Slant Left Side

The line knows they are blocking #1 and #2 on the line. The fullback knows his assignment. If we call 30 read, the line knows it is a three-step drop.

When we are in red ball, we do not huddle. If we throw an incomplete pass, we may call for a huddle. If we are in red ball, we line up in the 2x2 formation every time.

The next week we may be working with the five-step drop. We tell our two wide receivers on the right to run the curl route (Diagram #5). The inside man runs the flare, and the outside man runs the curl route.

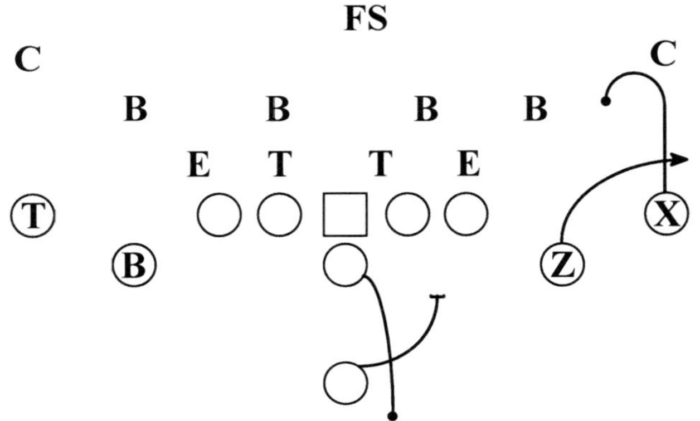

Diagram #5. Curl Routes Right Side

The receivers on the left are running the Kirk routes (Diagram #6). The Kirk is for our offensive coordinator, Kirk Davis, and he is the coach that wanted to use the pattern. The wide receiver runs the post, and the inside receiver runs a deep route toward the flag. The quarterback reads the free safety and throws to the open receiver.

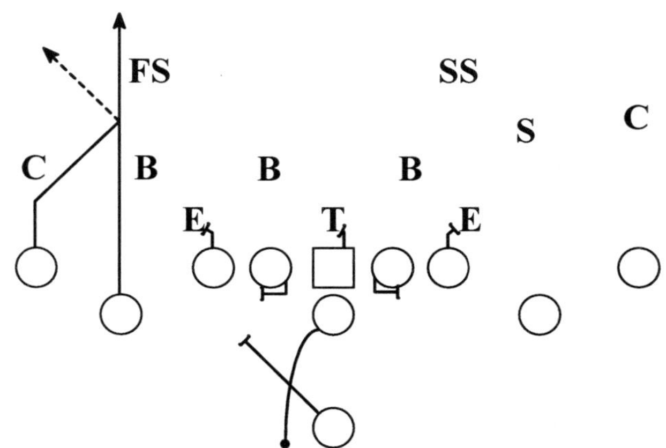

Diagram #6. Kirk Routes Left Side

If we come up to the line and see the cover 2 alignment, we are going to throw the curl route to the right side. The inside man runs the flare, and the outside man runs the curl route (Diagram #7). The fullback has the outside back and he cannot let the linebacker come outside and drop into a position to stop the curl route. The quarterback has to read the linebacker and make sure he is not on a drop to the curl receiver.

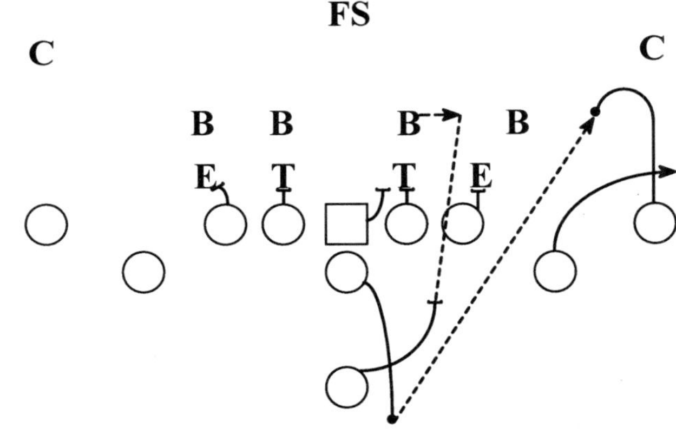

Diagram #7. Read Linebacker On Curl

On the left side, we are running the Rudy route (Diagram #8). The wide receiver runs a 10-yard post route, and the inside man runs a deep vertical route

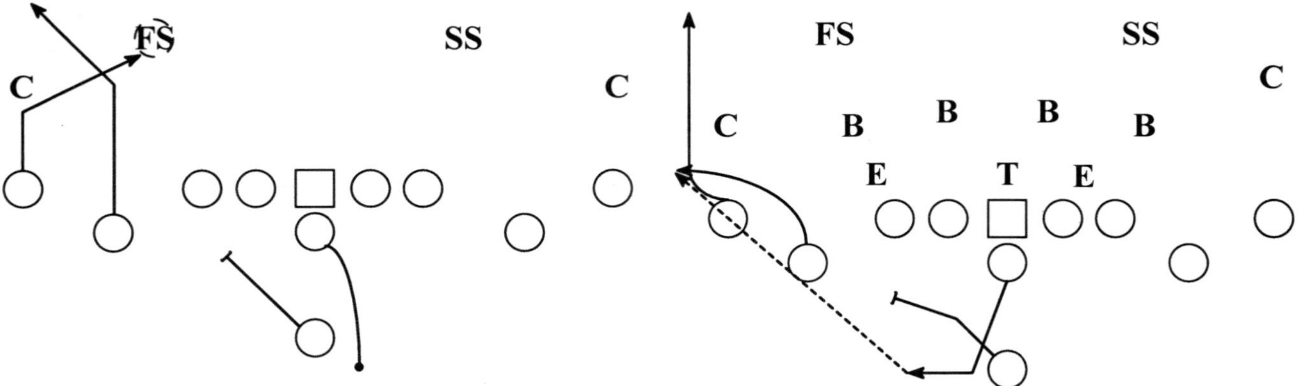

Diagram #8. Rudy Route Left Side

just outside of the spot where the safety is lined up. The quarterback reads the safety. If he takes the wide receiver on the post, he throws to the inside man. If he takes the inside receiver, the quarterback throws to the post route. It is a high-low read for the quarterback.

On the nine-step drop, we pick the comeback route for the three-man side (Diagram #9). The inside receiver runs the post and the outside man runs the comeback route at 10 yards. The fullback must know he has to protect the quarterback.

Diagram #9. Comeback Route Right Side

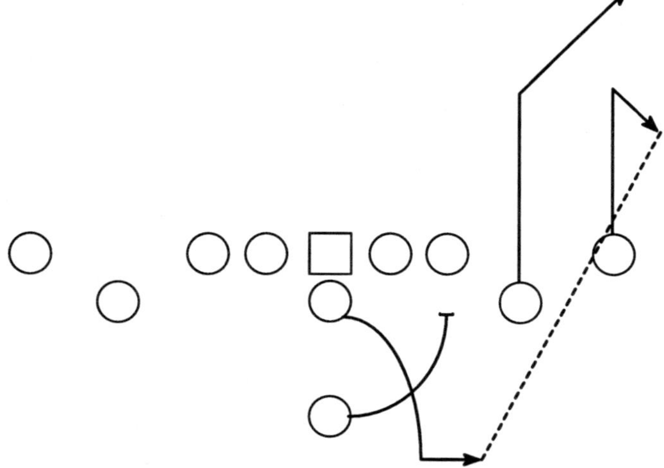

If we see a cover 2 on the two-man side, we are going to use the flat route (Diagram #10). The inside receiver runs the flat, and the outside man runs the fade down the sideline.

If the defense plays man-to-man, we throw the ball to our best player, Stefon Diggs, and let him run. Look out! He just may be the best player I have ever coached.

Diagram #10. Flat Route Left Side

The play we got from Stanford University is a five-step drop. We call it "Falcon crush." The two receivers on the left side run a smash route (Diagram #11). The outside receiver runs a hitch route at seven yards. The inside man runs the flag route. The fullback flares away from the route. The slot on the right side runs a six-yard dig route. The outside man on the right runs an 11-yard dig route, but he settles in the middle of the field. You have to cut the split down on the right side. If the safety overreacts on the flag route on the left side, the dig route comes open in the middle of the field. However, we will take the seven-yard hitch completion all day.

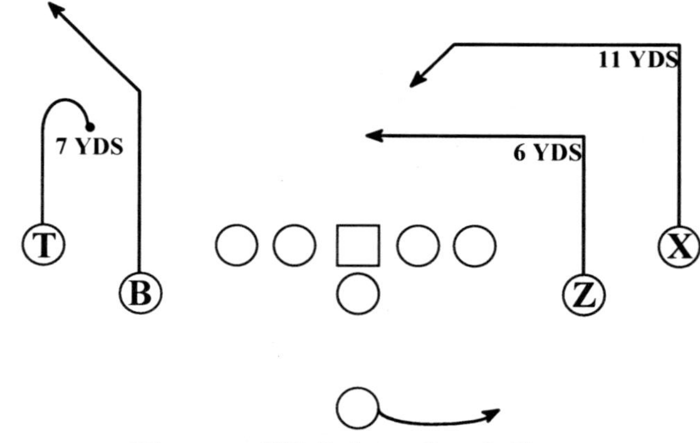

Diagram #11. Falcon Crush Pass

Early in my coaching career, I learned something that has stayed with me over the years. It goes something like this: If you don't talk too good, don't talk too long.

It is a privilege and an honor to be called, Coach. I have been doing it a long time and I would not trade it for the world. Thank you for having me at the clinic. I have enjoyed it.

Billy Mills

MIXING SCREEN PASSES WITH THE RUNNING GAME

Dinwiddie High School, Virginia

I appreciate that kind introduction. I am here today because we had a good season, and we have a pretty good football program. I have really good players and coaches. It is a big honor for me to be here because I cut my teeth on the Nike clinics. When I first got out of college, I had the opportunity, or misfortune depending on how you want to put it, of becoming a defensive coordinator. Like most guys out of college, I thought I had all the answers and knew what I was doing. That was one of the worst seasons of my life. It helped me understand that I had to learn a lot about football.

I went to my head coach and told him I needed some help and to get me to some clinics. He gave me three *Coach of the Year Clinics Football Manuals* and told me to go read them. If you are a young coach, I encourage you to pick up some of the Nike clinic manuals. They will help you learn about the game of football. When I was in Kentucky as a young coach, I would go down to the Galt House hotel for the Coach of the Year Clinic every year. I learned a lot of football that way.

When you go to a coaching clinic, you are always going to pick up something new. I sat in on a lecture yesterday with a coach talking about the counter trey. The counter trey is one of our base plays. I sat there for an hour and saw the same stuff that we do. I picked up a rule for the fullback read on play-action. That rule will help us become a better football team next year.

I guarantee you what I am going to show you today will make you a better football coach. I do not care what level you are coaching at, you are going to pick up something that you did not know before. I do not care what kind of athletes you have; I have run it with great athletes and without great athletes. My team chaplain also coaches eight and nine year olds. He won the championship using the same type of offense. I do not care what level your quarterback is on, you can have success with this offense.

I have been part of two turnaround programs. I went to Rockbridge County, where they had one winning season in the history of the school. Over time, we were able to win there. We moved up to Dinwiddie County, where they had won five games in five years. Since then, we have gone to the state championship game and just missed a chance to go again this year. I think it has a lot to do with our blueprint.

The first step in our blueprint is *commitment.* We base everything off of commitment and character. You have to have the commitment of everyone involved. You have to have commitment from your administration. The woman that hired me at Dinwiddie High School was fully committed to our program. I would not have been able to do what I have done there without her. I have been in situations where the administration was not committed. If you are in a situation like that, move on. You are not going to win there. If they are not behind you and do not back you, you will not be able to get it done.

The community has to be committed. They love football in Dinwiddie County. They empty the hollers out and get everybody to come watch our team play. That has lot to do with our success.

Your players have to be committed. They have to be committed to do what it takes in the off-season. They have to be committed to want to learn and get better, both on and off the football field.

Do not be afraid to go out and find help when you need it. Shane Sykes is one of the best strength and conditioning people in the Richmond area. He came to me in 2006 after working with several other teams in my district. Those teams did not need him anymore because they were comfortable with the program they had. I told him to give me all the help he could. He helped develop our off-season program and helped us with our speed, and he still works with our kids.

In 2005, when I went to Dinwiddie County from Rockbridge County, my offensive coordinator moved back to Kentucky. I could not find an offensive coordinator to come to Dinwiddie County that believed in what we were trying to do. I had to become the offensive coordinator after being a defensive coordinator for the previous 15 years. I took my own money and paid the $2,000 for the Tony Franklin system so I could learn the offense. It was the best thing I ever did as a coach.

You must have commitment from your staff. I have the best staff in the state of Virginia. If I can take credit for anything, it would be for hiring the staff I have. I have the luxury of telling my offensive line coaches that I want to do something and they will figure out how to do it. They get it done. It is important that we have been able to keep our coaches in our program for quite some time.

You need to be able to identify young talent. One of the best ideas I ever had came to me by accident. I was asked to go to a field day with elementary kids. They get outside and run relay races and have different sports related activities. We picked up one of the best running backs we have ever had in our program from that activities day. I asked him if he was playing football yet. We got him started in our program right away.

Competition is important. We compete with everything. We have an area just outside our weight room we call the "loser pit." If you lose at anything, whether it is hanging on a pole, doing power cleans, tire flips, it does not matter what it is, if you lose, you are going to do 50 up-downs in the pit. Our kids do not want any part of that. They do not care about the up-downs anymore; they just do not want to go into the pit. They come out and they compete every day. If you have ever watched us play, you know we scrap and we fight. That has a lot to do with it.

You have to be committed to defense and to special teams. I am an old defensive coach. I spend as much time focusing on our linebackers as I do with our offense. We are going to play good defense. Special teams is also important, and you have to put emphasis and time in on them.

Our coaches and our players have to be committed to the spread offense. Both programs that I came into had not won very many games. They were weak, they were small, and they were slow. That is not a good combination to start out with. We had to do something that would help us become successful. We are not going to be able to line up and run off-tackle and be successful. One of the teams in our conference is very good at doing that. They make fun of us and call us a gimmick team, but you know what, we beat them. I do not care what they do as long as we win the football game. They are starting to run some of our gimmick plays, too.

Just prior to going to Rockbridge, I had coached against a team that ran the spread offense. I knew I wanted to learn more about it. The coach at the University of Kentucky at the time was Hal Mumme and he was having a clinic for coaches. Coach Mumme was one of the best at running the spread offense. I went up there and picked up some concepts of it and decided that was what I was going to do. We were doing pieces of the spread concept, but we were not doing the whole program.

When I took it to Dinwiddie, I needed more structure, so I looked into the Tony Franklin system. One of the things he says is you have to be perfect at screens. I took everything he said to heart. I did not know anything about offense because I had been coaching defense for 15 years. I think being a defensive coordinator has helped me become a better offensive coach because I know where the holes are. I knew where I could attack the defense. The screens I will talk about have helped make us successful.

We started with this program in 2006. As you can see from my chart, we threw for 2,700 yards and almost half were from screens. Our offensive line was not very good. We were still able to have some success without being able to push people around. You can see we did not run the ball very much at all. We only had 853 yards rushing. We have done this every year since then and have averaged over 30 points a game.

Year	Tot. Off.	Rush Yds.	Pass Yds./ Screen	Yds./ Gm	Pts./ Gm
2005	1,549	622	927	155	10.8
2006	3,584	853	2,731 (1,256)	358	33.2
2007	4,018	1,710	2,308 (1,312)	365	36.5
2008	5,269	1,668	3,601 (918)	376	40.4
2009	4,133	1,455	2,678 (991)	376	32.0
2010	4,745	2,604	2,150 (722)	365	33.4

Why do I think it is important to run screens? First of all, it makes the defense cover the entire field and play assignment defense.

The first game of the first year we started doing this, we played Halifax County High School. For two quarters, we did nothing but move the ball backward. We ran a little screen play and our linemen waddled out and did not hit a single soul, but our running back was very good and busted it for an 80-yard touchdown. I believe I have heard the defense say, "Watch for the screen!" on every single play since. We have had people worried about our screens, and what we do with them, since 2006.

The screen helps us keep balanced on offense and keeps the defense from being able to lock down on one player. I have a man on the sideline that keeps a chart with all of our receivers on it. He lets me know if we have not distributed the ball evenly and to whom we need to get the ball to. We make sure we keep it balanced. If you are a defensive coordinator preparing to play us, you have to worry about everybody.

We consider screens to be an extension of our running game. Last year, we were a 45-percent pass and 55-percent run team. If you include screens in the run portion, we were 71-percent run and 29-percent pass.

Screens create dual responsibilities for the defense. What I mean by that is you will hear a defensive coach coaching his players that if the offense does this, you do this. Then, if the offense does that, then you do something else. They have about half a second to figure out what to do. Most of the time, they do not know what to do.

In 282 passing attempts, we had 12 sacks against us in 13 games. A lot of it had to do with the defensive ends that were afraid to come upfield because they had screen responsibility. That helps us throw the ball downfield because we have all day to throw it. Secondly, our base running play is a stretch play. The defensive ends were getting reached all day long because they were worried about the screen.

Running screens prevents blitzes and puts the defense in their base defense. Screens help us open up the running game if the defense overcompensates to stop our screens. We did not have as many yards running the screen this year, but we did have two 1,000-yard rushers, partly because the threat of the screen opened up our running game.

Screens will wear out the defensive line. When we play some of the bigger teams, we cannot line up and play toe to toe with them. We run them from sideline to sideline. We are going to cut them, and we are going to get in their head. We script our first 15 plays. I will have at least eight screens in those 15 plays. They know that before they play us, but they still have to defend it.

Teams do not practice defending the screen because they do not see it every Friday. We practice our screens, good versus good. I do not think our defense has given up a long play on a screen play in the past five years. The best screen defense we go against all year is our own defense. They see it so often they have become very good at defending the screen.

Screens help us take advantage of mismatches. We can get the ball in the hands of our playmakers. Through our film study, we pick on the weaker defenders you line up against us. We sell our kids on the idea that a five-yard screen is a good play. If I can get five yards, I have accomplished what I wanted to do. If we run the football for five yards, we are happy with that. When we catch a screen, we want to get vertical for five yards before we make any moves. Sometimes, kids think we are going to score a touchdown every time we run a screen. All I want is five yards, and then let the athletes do what they do.

If you are going to run the screen successfully, I believe these are things you must do in order to be successful. We designed our off-season program to develop all of the skills we use offensively and defensively, but especially for the skills required to run the screen game. We focus on reactive agility. That is just a fancy name for the wave drill. The wave drill is huge because it tests the ability to react to someone else. The mirror drill is similar.

We practice the ability to come to balance. If you are playing basketball, you sprint down the court to get into a defensive position; you come to a sudden stop and get into a balanced stance with your feet up underneath you. In football, we do the same thing when we stalk block.

You have to throw your fast screens in passing leagues so you can practice on timing and repetition. My guys want to win the passing league, but I tell them going into it that we are not trying to be the 7-on-7 champion of Virginia. We are going to practice what helps us in the regular football season. Even though we cannot block, these are things that are going to help us in the fall.

We devote a lot of time in our practice schedule to our screens. In the pre-season, we give it 15 minutes every practice, just as fast as we can go. We put in our fast screens on the first day. In day two, we put in our jailbreak screens. As we get into the season, we may cut it down to about 10 minutes. By that time, we have a better feel for what we are doing. I tell my coaches when we get to the screen drills, I want them to coach as if it is the most important thing they will do. I want them to amp up their coaching when we are practicing our screens. It is at a rapid-fire pace.

We film every practice and we coach off the film. I give each coach a DVD of practice and ask him to find one thing to coach to make a kid better. I do not want them to come up with 17 things. That kid is not going to fix any of those things. If we teach a player to do one thing better each day, we will be playing our best football at the end of the season.

TECHNIQUE AND DRILLS

Quarterback

Get big drill: I tell the quarterback to take the snap, and depending on what we are faking, he will take three big steps and get up on his toes. It is almost like a fadeaway jump shot. He is going to have a high release and drop the ball into the alley. They have to get good at doing it.

Grip and rip drill: This is practice for the fast screens. I coach quarterbacks with a linebacker mentality. I tell them to get it, grip it, and rip it. I do not care if it goes end over end. They get better at it as we go. The receiver is not looking for a pretty spiral when the corner is screaming down to hit him in his ear. He wants the ball right now—anyway he can get it. The quarterback adapts and learns how to do it, but you need to get him in the mentality of rapid-fire. I take 10 footballs and put them in the quarterback's hands and make him get them out as fast as he can. He throws five to the right and five to the left.

Screen of the day (PAT-and-GO): In the PAT-and-GO part of practice, we have the screen of the day. We are either going to do jailbreaks or fast screens that day. We practice on air every day.

Wide Receivers

Screen steps, releases, noose, and pat and go (wide base, fast feet, hands inside): I make our receivers block. They spend 30 minutes a day practicing their blocking. If my receivers mess up on their blocking, I send them down with the offensive line coaches to work with them. They do not want any part of that. If they do not block, I will not give them any touches.

On Thursday, we run through our 15 scripted plays. I will not give a receiver many touches if he has not been practicing or blocking to my liking. That gets his attention and gets in his head. Those guys will practice their fannies off the entire next week. They want that ball on Friday night.

Offensive Line

Cage drill: If you are going to run screens, you have to do this drill. It is an easy drill.

- Purpose
  - ✓ To perfect screen footwork and openfield blocking
- Tempo
  - ✓ Full
- Organization/Setup
  - ✓ Make a "cage" with four cones (five yards by

five yards) and place a defender inside the cage. Make one cage on the left and one on the right five to six yards away from the linemen.

- Coaching points
  - ✓ Practice each type of screen.
  - ✓ Release; get flat down the line and enter the cage.
  - ✓ Upon entering the cage, get a wide base and fast feet and work up to the defender. Wide base, fast feet. Hands and elbows inside.
  - ✓ The defender may move and "juke" anywhere within the cage.

You want somebody fast in the cage to practice against. We are not looking for a kill shot; we are looking to body up and occupy the defender.

If you are going to run screens, you have to have the attitude that this is what we do. We will be perfect at screens. If you ask any kid on our team what we are known for, they will say screens. I want it to be that way. Even though we only had 700 yards on it last year, it opens up everything else. In practice, our screens have to have a sense of urgency associated with them. We have to do our best coaching on screens. You will hear me amp it up when we start coaching screens in practice.

You must throw screens, even when they do not work. I had a really hard time with that one, because I want stuff to work. After I started doing it, I saw the benefits of it. It opens up so much more of our offense later in the game. I am not saying to throw a fast screen when you have a guy playing press coverage. We have another type of screen that can deal with that.

The first screen that we install is our fast screen (Diagram #1). Our 40 series goes to the right and our 50 series goes to the left. We number our receivers from the outside in. Our 41 fast screen goes to the right and to the outside receiver.

Everyone has the same technique across the offensive line. It is the same steps we use for our stretch play. We run a step over the bag, crossover step through the crotch, and get our screws in the armpit. We want to fight across. The right guard and tackle are going to try to get to the hole. We have to tell them what the hole is. The hole is any defender in the area that can blow up the play.

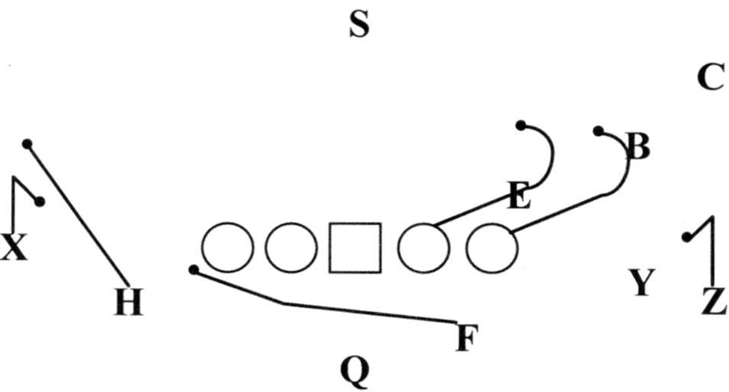

Diagram #1. 41 Fast Screen

Position	Rule
LT	Over bag—Through crotch right, uncovered work to LB
LG	Over bag—Through crotch right, uncovered work to LB
C	Over bag—Through crotch right, uncovered work to LB
RG	Over bag—Through crotch right, uncovered work to hole
RT	Over bag—Through crotch right, uncovered work to hole
X	Fast screen—Fast hands, fast feet
Y	Block #1 or MDM. (Be under control.)
Z	Fast screen—Fast hands, fast feet; get vertical for five yards before any moves
H	Block #1 or MDM. (Be under control.)
F	Flash across; create the fake (you will not mesh with the QB); block backside edge
QB Reads	Grip and rip—Catch and throw as fast as possible to upfield shoulder of Z

The fullback flashes across, but we are not going to stick the ball in his gut. The quarterback catches the ball and he is gripping and ripping, getting the ball out as fast as he can. We want to hit the Z on his upfield shoulder. The Z has to push hard for a couple of steps to get the corner to hold, and to allow the lineman to get in front of him.

The Y is the most important player on this play. We tell him we want him to come into balance and to take the most dangerous man. We do not say to take the number one defender anymore because coaches started playing games and moving defenders around. If the corner is bailing, we do not want to chase him down the field and have the safety rotate up and knock the crap out of our receiver.

The next screen we have is the bubble screen (Diagram #2). If we get a defense where they are splitting the difference on our Y, we like to run the bubble. The Z and H block for the Y.

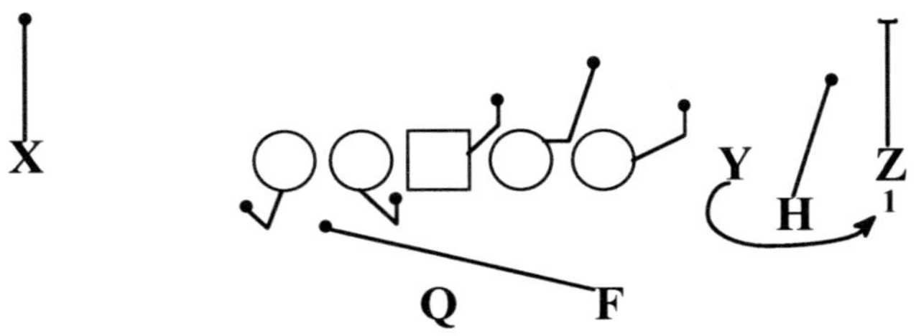

Diagram #2. Early 43 Bubble

Position	Rule
LT	Over bag—Through crotch right, uncovered work to LB
LG	Over bag—Through crotch right, uncovered work to LB
C	Over bag—Through crotch right, uncovered work to LB
RG	Over bag—Through crotch right, uncovered work to hole
RT	Over bag—Through crotch right, uncovered work to hole
X	Cutoff block FS
Y	Bubble—Arc at three-quarters speed and catch on run/attack and score
Z	Block #1 or MDM—Wide base, fast feet. (Be under control.)
H	Block #2 or MDM—Wide base, fast feet. (Be under control.)
F	Flash fake and protect edge
QB Reads	Grip and rip to Y

I want to show you 44 next (Diagram #3). You have to tell the Y, H, and C that they have to buy time. They can buy time by giving a false step or they can buy time by walking out. If they block the defender too early, the defender can recover and make the tackle. You just want your receivers and offensive line to cover somebody up. When they are blocking, they do not have to get the defender to the ground. They just have to occupy him and give the ballcarrier an opportunity to get down the field.

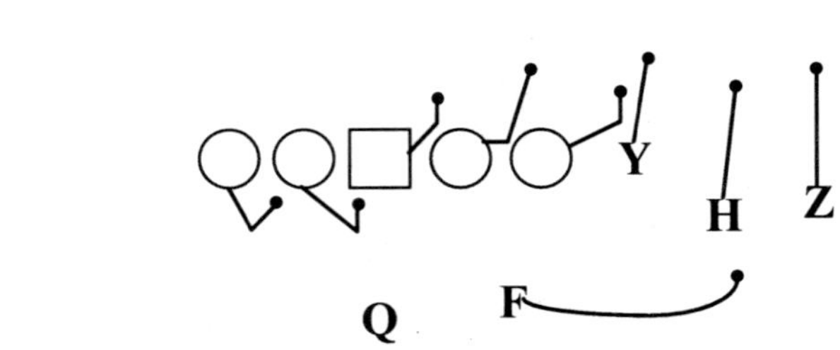

Diagram #3. Early 44

Position	Rule
LT	Over bag—Through crotch right, uncovered work to LB
LG	Over bag—Through crotch right, uncovered work to LB
C	Over bag—Through crotch right, uncovered work to LB
RG	Over bag—Through crotch right, uncovered work to hole
RT	Over bag—Through crotch right, uncovered work to hole
X	Cutoff block FS
Y	Block #3 or MDM. (Be under control; buy time.)
Z	Block #1. (Be under control; buy time.)
H	Block #2 or MDM. (Be under control; buy time.)
F	Free release swing-Cheat out to tackle's outside leg; look, immediately catch and score
QB Reads	Catch and throw as fast as possible to upfield shoulder of F

Let's look at early 41 Fox (Diagram #4). If the defense wants to walk up and press our receivers man-to-man, we can hit the Fox or the fade. There is always an answer. That is what you have to sell your kids on. If the corner totally bails out, we can go to the Z or the X as our backup.

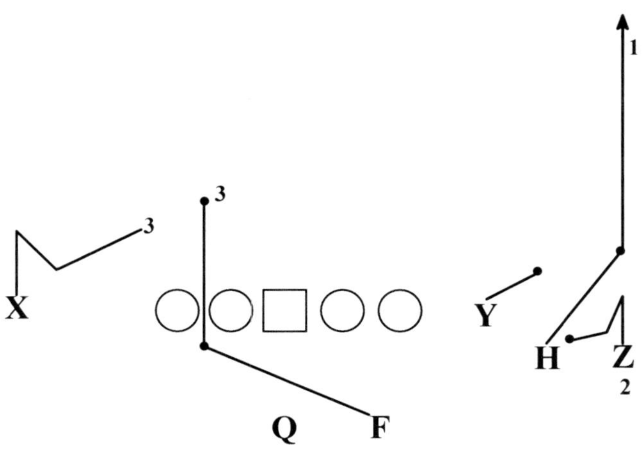

Diagram #4. Early 41 Fox

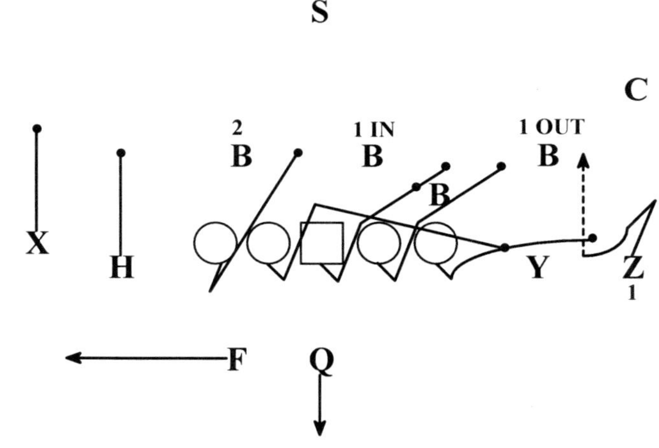

Diagram #5. 41 Jailbreak Screen

Position	Rule
LT	60s (slide protection)
LG	60s (slide protection)
C	60s (slide protection)
RG	60s (slide protection)
RT	60s (slide protection)
X	Fake fast screen—Convert to check down
Y	Block #2 or MDM. (Be flat on release and adjust up if necessary.)
Z	Fake fast screen, then convert check down
H	Flat, sell stalk on #1, rip through and get up numbers, stay away from safety
F	Fake zone left, check down
QB Reads	Catch and pump to Z, read H, F, and X on checkdowns

I am running out of time, but I would like to show you one of the jailbreak screens (Diagram #5).

Position	Rule
LT	90 set and show hands flat release block BSLB to safety
LG	90 set and show hands, flat release; peel block most dangerous defensive lineman chasing receiver
C	90 set and show hands, flat release; block #2 inside of box
RG	90 set and show hands, flat release; block #1 inside of box
RT	90 set and show hands, flat release; block #1 outside of box
X	Jailbreak—Three steps upfield, return at angle toward QB; do not go deeper than LOS
Y	Two steps upfield—Block #1 or MDM
Z	Jailbreak—Drive upfield three hard steps, come back at an angle toward the QB; attack the ball, catch, and score
H	Two steps upfield—Block #1 or MDM
F	Swing numbers
QB Reads	Five-step drop or pump fake opposite, retreat, get Big-Be Athletic, throw to Z as he comes down the line early

Joe Morris

THREE EFFECTIVE TYPES OF SCREEN PASSES

Mayfield High School, Kentucky

I appreciate the Nike Clinic having me speak here. We have had some success at Mayfield High School. I can attribute my success to the coaches that I have had the fortune to coach with. I brought five assistant coaches with me today to make sure somebody would show up to hear me speak. We definitely would not have won a state championship without the fine coaches I have with me at Mayfield. I will be the first one to tell you that you better have some players. My guys do a great job of coaching, but you have to have some players to start out with in order to be successful.

When I first started coaching at Mayfield, we were a wishbone team. We ran power off-tackle, counter trey, and the bootleg. Do not get me wrong; I still love that stuff. The makeup of our kids made us change to a spread offense and a no-huddle team. We do a lot of screens and a lot of quick passes in order to get the ball to our best athletes. It has been a great change for us. Our kids love playing in it. We took a couple of kids who weighed about 140 pounds off the basketball court, and they became very successful in our spread offense.

I am going to talk to you today about our screen passing game. I will cover our fast screen, solid screen, and jailbreak screen. They have been very successful for us over the past years.

WHY THROW SCREENS?

- Easy completion for quarterback (confidence)
- Gets the football in fast guys (best athletes) hands
- Offensive line gets to run and hit little guys (defensive backs)
- Makes defensive lineman run sideline to sideline, even if they don't work
- Can throw them in almost any situation
- Great against the blitz
- Practice them every day: team (6 to 10), warm-up drills (15 to 20), team screens (12 to 20), and quarterback individual.

Our screen plays are easy to complete, and that gives our quarterback confidence. Two years ago, we got a great receiver and a great quarterback. I think our quarterback was smarter than all of our coaches put together. In one of our games, we threw two screens on our first two passing plays of the game. My quarterback was two for two, and even though he only threw the ball about 20 yards, he had 158 yards passing and two touchdowns. That helps give our quarterback confidence and is one reason why we like to throw the screen. We do it early in order to get the quarterback in a rhythm and have some early success.

Screens allow us to get the ball into our best athletes' hands and do it very quickly. We have a couple of receivers; one weighs about 140 pounds, and another about 150 pounds, and he can run. They are very good athletes. If we put them in a two-tight-end wishbone formation, those guys could not make plays for us. We throw the ball out there to them and let them do their thing. They got better and tougher as the year went along.

Our offensive linemen get tired of taking on 250-pound defensive linemen or butting heads with 190-pound linebackers. My offensive linemen get to run around and hit little defensive backs. Every day in practice, we have a time period called "team screens," and they get to run around and hit little defensive backs. They love it. Those guys run out there, and they may not even make a block, but they may get in their way. Sometimes, they do not make a good block, and it still will work. For some reason, it makes our guys work harder, knowing that they get to go out and block little guys.

Even if the screen only goes for two yards and does not work, it makes the defensive line run from sideline to sideline. I know we put our best lineman on the defensive line, and some of them go both ways. The very first play we ran in the state championship was a fast screen. Our opponent had done a great job of scouting us and their defensive tackle got out there real quick and forced us to cut back.

I think we gained about 10 yards on the play. In the fourth quarter, that 260-pound defensive tackle was not getting out there as fast. He was tired. We were in the shotgun or no-huddle most of the game. Screens may not work early, but they will work late. If you try to run the ball early and are unsuccessful, I believe that if you run a bunch of screens, you can be successful running the ball later in the game.

We believe we can throw the screen in just about any situation. In a scrimmage this year against a very good team from Tennessee, we threw the jailbreak screen on third-and-three, down on the three-yard line. We had tried to run the ball on the first two plays and got nothing. I knew we were going to throw the ball, but my offensive coordinator called the jailbreak screen. I thought, "What is he doing?" We ran the play, our offensive linemen did not have to block anybody, and we walked into the end zone. You can throw the screen in just about every situation, except for forth-and-one. I will not let Coach Hatchell call a screen in that situation.

We found our screens work very well against the blitz. I believe some of the teams we faced would not blitz us because of our screens. If we would see a team getting ready to blitz us or in press coverage, we would run a solid screen or jailbreak screen, and we would make people pay. It also makes everything easier for our pass protection.

We practice our screens every day. When we are in our team period, at the end of practice, Coach Hatcher is going to script 6 to 10 screens for us to practice, every day. In our warm-up drills, we are going to throw 15 to 20 screens. Every day, our quarterback is going to practice the fast screen, the solid screen, and the jailbreak screen.

We practice team screens together as a group. This is where we get our offensive linemen all jacked up because they get to go and hit the little guys. We do put a defense over there to run against. We do it no-huddle, and our coach is yelling out the plays, so we can get as many repetitions as possible. We will put the ball on the 15-yard line going in, and we will score. We throw about 40 to 50 screens per day. It does not take us very long at all to do that. I feel this is why we have become good at throwing screens.

Let me go over our fast screens. As I said before, we are a no-huddle football team. When we throw a fast screen, 95 percent of the time it is going to be off of a freeze play. Either that, or the defense is leaving somebody uncovered, or they are in soft coverage. We have found that if the defense is up in our face and we try to run a fast screen, it does not work.

When we call a pass play, all of the 40s are to the right and 50s are to the left. Our guys have to be able to count. We can call 41, 42, 43, and 44, depending on the formation. If we call a 41, and I am the first receiver out there, I know I am getting the ball. 41 is to the right (Diagram #1).

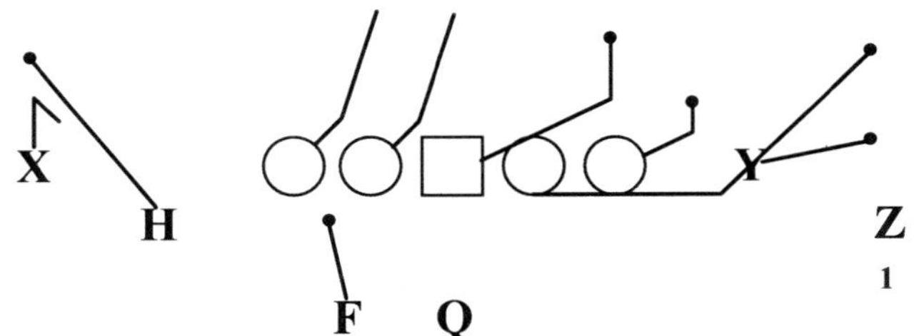

Diagram #1. Ace 41

On the 41, we are throwing the ball out to our Z. It is very important that our Y goes flat. We do not want him to go to where the defender is; we want him to go to where the defender is going to be. Again, we will not run this if they are in press coverage. The Y's job is to block the most dangerous defender that could tackle the Z. If the Y-back goes to where the cornerback is lined up, the corner is going to beat him and make the tackle. The more we practice it, the better we get at it.

We tell the Z-receiver, who is catching the ball, to put his near foot up. He is going to take one step, get his hands up, and then he is going to get the ball. I do a great job of coaching the receivers. When they catch the ball, I tell them to, "Get five yards, and then let the good Lord take over." I tell them to, "Go be an athlete, and go beat somebody, but give me five yards." I will take five yards every time.

We have tried blocking this several ways. These are our general rules for our Ace 41 screen.

ACE 41 RULES	
Position	**Rule**
Left tackle	Zone right, and work to the linebacker and then the safety.
Left guard	Zone right, and work to the linebacker and then the safety.
Center	Zone right; if uncovered, work to the linebacker.
Right guard	Pull to the alley player.
Right tackle	Zone right, hook end.
X	Fast screen, fast hands, fast feet
Y	Block #1 or most dangerous man (Be flat on release, and adjust up if necessary.)
Z	Fast screen, fast hands, fast feet (Run, attack, and score.)
H	Block #1 or most dangerous man (Be flat on release, and adjust up if necessary.)
F	Protect quick threat to the backside.
Quarterback reads	Catch and throw as fast as possible to the upfield shoulder of Z.

The right tackle's job is to block the outside edge zone player. We like to have the right guard pulling just as he is trapping to the outside. His job is to block the defender that the Y does not block, the second most dangerous man. Sometimes, he will not get there, but it does not matter because we are still going out there. The center is going to zone-step, and then get to the next level.

Our left and right guards will take their zone step and get to the next level. They do not have to worry about blocking the down lineman. The F-back will take a step up and protect the backside so the quarterback does not have to take a hit.

The quarterback, on the fast screen, is going to catch the ball and get it out as fast as he can. We work on it a lot. He does not grip the laces; he gets it in the receiver's hands, as fast as possible.

We can run the same thing out of a trips set (Diagram #2). The only difference is the H-back becomes the blocker on the most dangerous defender. Most of the time, we put the F-back away from the screen. We can change that, depending on how the defense lines up.

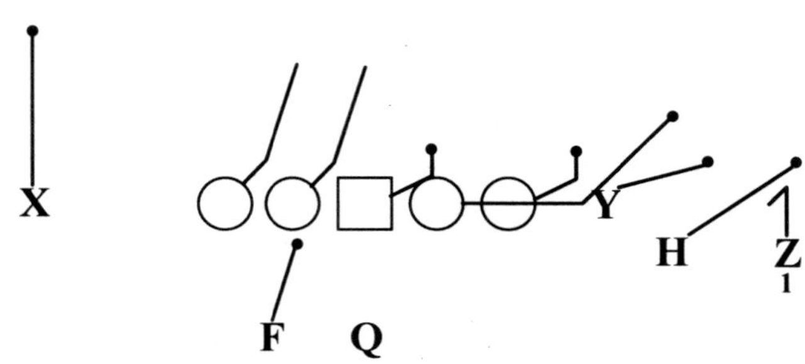

Diagram #2. Early 41

We can run the quick screen to our second receiver. All we need is to be able to count (Diagram #3).

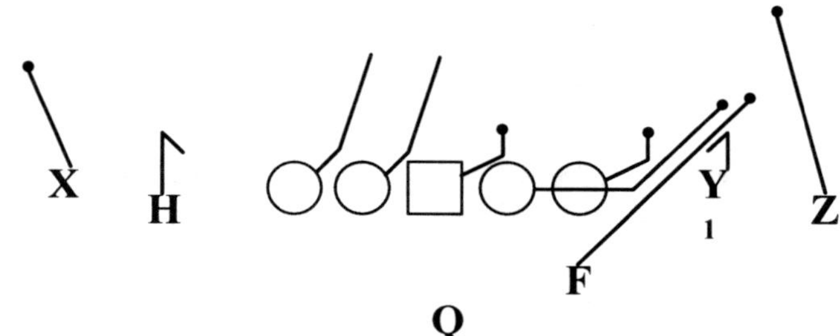

Diagram #3. Ace 42

If we run 43, we are going to go to our third receiver (Diagram #4). The Y back is going to block the most dangerous man, just like before.

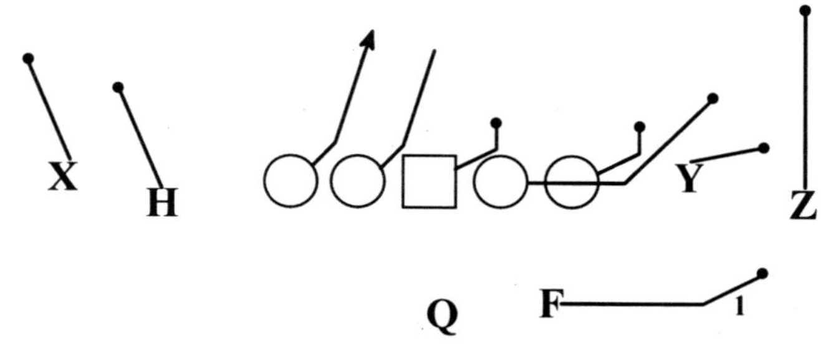

Diagram #4. Ace 43

Our quick screens are not very good when the defense plays press coverage. The exception is when we throw it to our back. We can run it in our trips set (Diagram #5). If the defense does not adjust to the trips formation, we can outnumber them. We run off all the defenders on our trips receivers, and throw it to the back. Any 40 play is blocked the same for our offensive lineman. This time, we put the F-back to the trips side. We just throw an easy completion for the quarterback, and get the ball in the fast guy's hands.

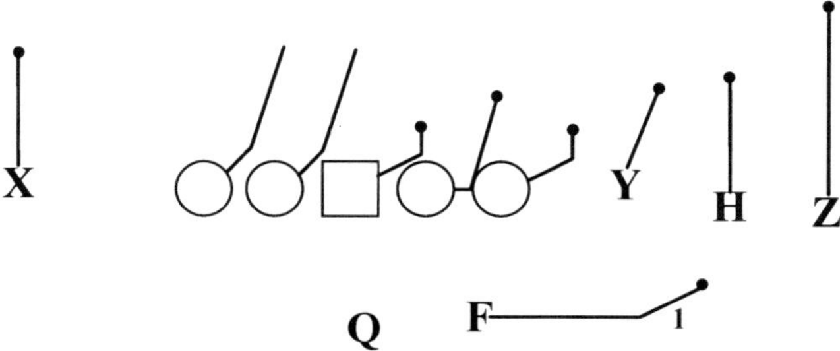

Diagram #5. Early 44

We can run the same plays to the left side. The only difference is we call it 50 (Diagram #6). The H-back is not told he has to kick out the corner. He just has to square up and occupy him. Most of the time, it does end up being a kick-out, but it does not have to be. We tell the receiver that it is his job to break off of that block. Everything else is just the same.

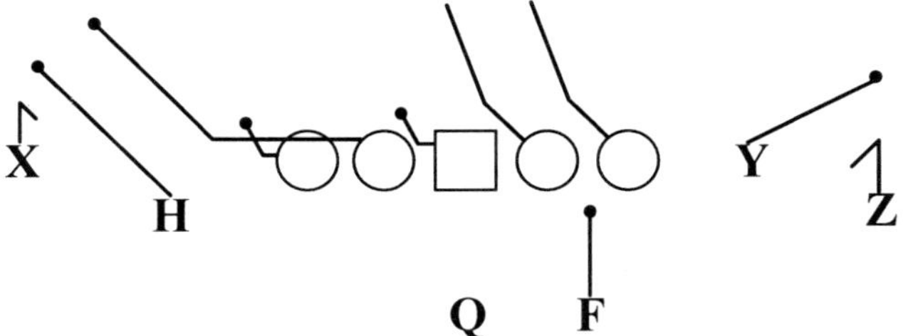

Diagram #6. Ace 51

We can run the quick screen to the left, away from the trips side. We like to do this against man coverage (Diagram #7).

The linemen need to know two plays. They need to know 41 and 51. The blocking for all the other 40 and 50 plays is the same. The receivers need to know how to count. The key is to get the ball to our athletes in space.

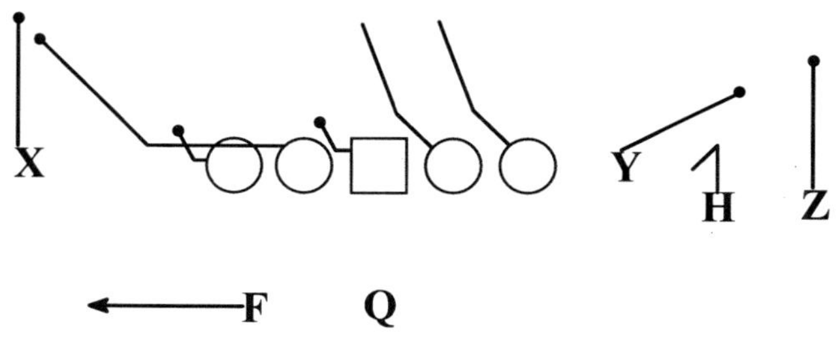

Diagram #7. Early 52

Let me get into our solid screen series (Diagram #8). This is probably the best screen that we run.

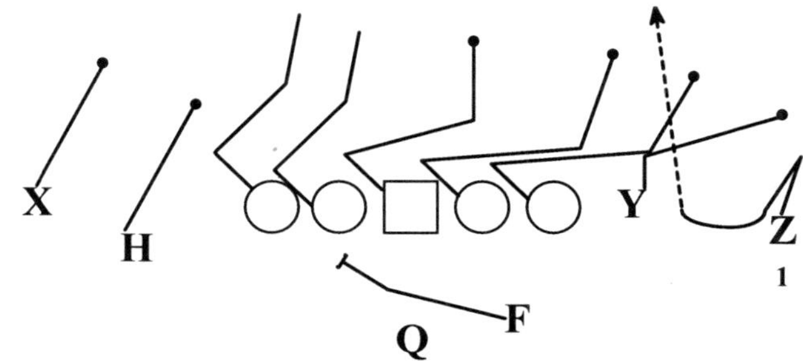

Diagram #8. Ace 41 Solid

We run a lot of zones. The biggest difference between a solid screen and the quick screen is our receiver will drive up three steps and then retrace his steps.

We tell him to come back about half to three-quarter speed, and to get behind the line of scrimmage. The other difference is our Y-receiver now drives up two steps and kicks out #1, or the most dangerous man. Before, he was going flat.

As I said, we run a lot of zone. Our best running play is a 33 zone play. It is just a regular inside zone play. Every one of our linemen is going to zone-step. Our quarterback is going to fake the zone play. Our tackle, after he takes his zone step, is going to come out and get the second-most dangerous man. All the other linemen take a zone step and then get to the next level. We like this type of play against the blitz and against press coverage. Most of the time, we will run this to our outside receivers, a 41 or a 51. It has been most successful to our outside receivers. We can run this out of our early (trips) set (Diagram #9).

The biggest thing we need to do is sell out on our zone step. Our offensive line was not very big, but we were athletic. They like running this type of offense.

ACE 41 SOLID RULES	
Position	**Rule**
Left tackle	Sell zone three steps to left, then release, work to the safety.
Left guard	Sell zone three steps to left, then release, third linebacker or the safety.
Center	Sell zone three steps to left, then release, second linebacker in box.
Right guard	Sell zone three steps to left, then release, first linebacker in box.
Right tackle	Sell zone three steps to left, then release, alley defender.
X	Cut off backside most dangerous man.
Y	Two steps upfield, block #1 or most dangerous man.
Z	Solid screen, three steps upfield, retrace, work toward quarterback, attack the ball, catch, and score.
H	Cut off backside most dangerous man.
F	Fake zone left and protect edge.
Quarterback reads	Flash fake zone left, get feet fast, and throw solid screen to Z as soon as he begins down the line of scrimmage.

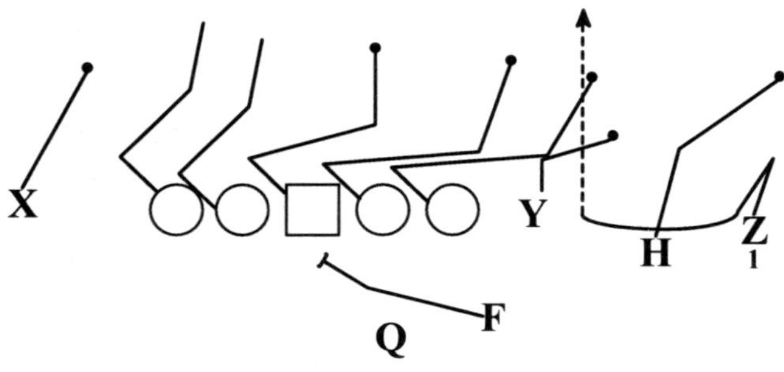

Diagram #9. Early 41 Solid

Our early 42 solid is very similar, except for now it is the #2 receiver getting the ball (Diagram #10). Our back drives up three steps, retraces his steps, catches the ball, and gets upfield at least five yards. We can run it from any formation. The only thing we do not do is run it to our back. We only run it to our receivers.

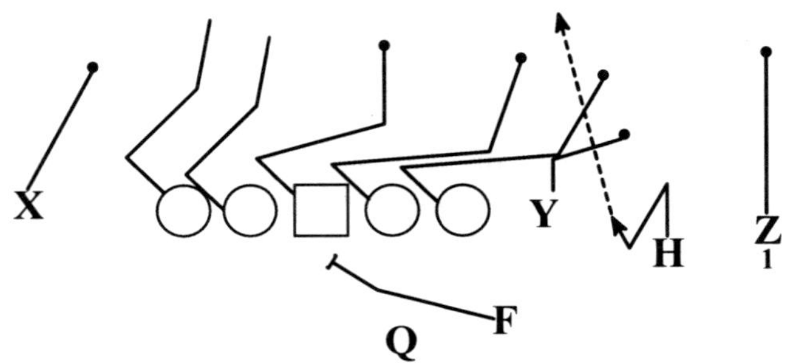

Diagram #10. Early 42 Solid

On 51 solid, we are faking the zone step to the right (Diagram #11). We are going to throw it back to the left. On the fast screen, we do not kick out. On the solid screen, his job is to kick out the first defender. We tell the running back that he is the one who sells the fake. The running back sells the fake more than the quarterback does. The running back will fake away on the solid screen. We can turn everything around and run everything to the left side. All we have to do is call 50.

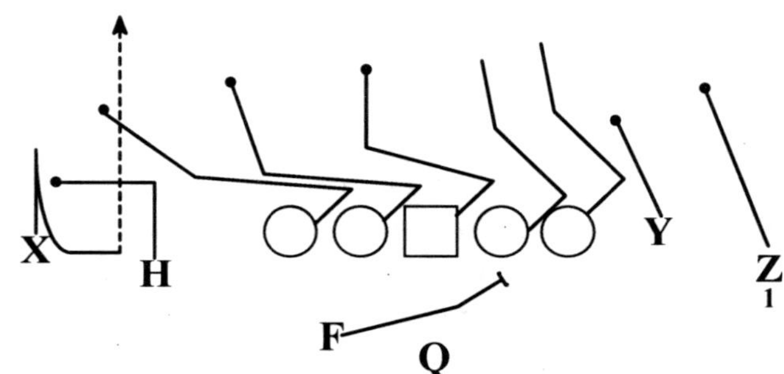

Diagram #11. Ace 51 Solid

The last thing we have is our jailbreak screen (Diagram #12). The jailbreak screen is just like a solid screen for our receivers. Our Z-back may have to come more inside to the line of scrimmage because of what our quarterback does. The F-back is lined up away from the play. As soon as the ball is snapped, he swings.

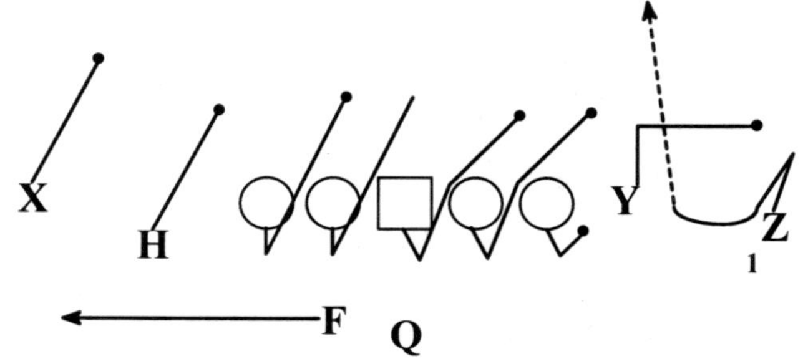

Diagram #12. Ace 41 Jailbreak

The biggest difference is that the tackle to the playside will try to push the defensive end up the field. We feel that we have to block him. He is the only one whom we feel can stop this play. The tackle really sells the pass to try to get the defensive end up the field. The rest of our linemen run our 90 pass set. That means they block just like our shotgun pass. They drop back, show their hands, and release toward the playside.

ACE 41 JAILBREAK RULES	
Position	**Rule**
Left tackle	90 set and show hands, flat release, work to the safety.
Left guard	90 set and show hands, flat release, block backside linebacker to the safety.
Center	90 set and show hands, flat release, block first linebacker in box (#3).
Right guard	90 set and show hands, flat release, block alley defender (#2).
Right tackle	90 set, and high wall defensive end.
X	Cut off backside most dangerous man.
Y	Two steps upfield, block #1 or most dangerous man.
Z	Jailbreak, drive upfield three hard steps, comeback at an angle toward quarterback, attack the ball, catch, and score.
H	Cut off backside most dangerous man.
F	Free swing numbers.
Quarterback reads	Pump fake opposite, retreat, get big, be athletic, throw to Z as he comes down line early.

For the quarterback, there is no fake. When he catches the ball, the first thing he is going to do is look the opposite way. He might even pump to the left. After he makes the pump, he backs up three steps and finds a way to get the receiver the ball. There will be guys coming after him. The quarterback does not have to look pretty; he may even lob it just over the defenders. I have found that our jailbreak screen works better against a good football team.

I did not realize how good the jailbreak screen was for us until I started putting together the cut-ups for my presentation. It was a great third-and-long play for us. We run this play to the outside receiver most of the time as well, because we want to get the ball to our fastest receiver. We can also run the jailbreak in the trips formation (Diagram #13).

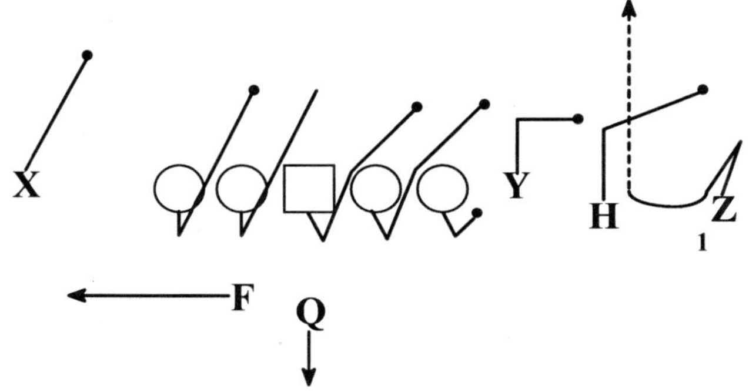

Diagram #13. Early 41 Jailbreak

Our screen package has been very good to us. Please feel free to give me a call anytime at Mayfield High School. I will be glad to go over this with you.

Good luck to you next season. Thank you very much.

Mike Newsome

DEVELOPING SIMPLE PASSING GAME CONCEPTS

Butler High School, North Carolina

I appreciate being here and to see the number of coaches here supporting this Nike Clinic. It is a pleasure to talk football with you today. I have slides and diagrams of the things I will cover with you. I want to share some passing game concepts with you.

We have been successful at Butler High School the last several years. There are three keys to that success. The first reason for our success is our coaching staff. I have a tremendous staff with 196 years of coaching experience within the total staff. Some of them have been head high school coaches, and I have one who was a head college coach. We have older coaches with experience and some good young coaches who have enthusiasm. Together, it makes for a good situation. We have several former players who have come back and wanted to coach with us. Wanting to come back and be a part of the success says a lot about our program.

The second thing you must have to be successful is good players. We have been fortunate to have great players. Coach Mark Richt of the University of Georgia just spoke, and they signed our quarterback from last year. I think he will be a great player for them. Great players always make you better coaches.

The third thing to having the success we have had is support. We have a great fan base, and the administration within the school is supportive. If you listen to my wife, she will tell you the key to our success was when I married her.

All my experience as a high school and college player is on the defensive side of the ball. Except for snapping the ball on extra-point situations, I have never been on the offensive side of the ball. When I became the head coach, I knew I needed to learn about the offense. I knew I had to understand the passing game because we had a couple of good quarterbacks in the program.

I went to clinics, and the coaches who lectured were speaking a foreign language as far as I was concerned. I did not have a clue what those coaches were talking about. However, I did learn that we had to make things simple. The first reason was so I could understand it, and secondly so the high school quarterbacks would understand it. I think that is what we have been able to do at Butler.

Six years ago, we came up with these concepts, and through style and patience we have developed them.

BULLDOG PASSING OFFENSE

- Six years (2005 to 2010)
- 7,700 yards QB (three years); 5,000 yards QB (two years); 2,900 yards QB (one year)
- 170 average passing rating (NCAA Top Ten = 161)
- 2,800+ yards rushing/year
- 550+ points/year (726 in 2009 and 734 in 2010)
- 6,500+ total yards offense / year (8,082 in 2010)
- Only 1 senior quarterback during this time

The player going to Georgia had a 259 passing rating in his junior year. He had 44 touchdowns and only two interceptions. We have had some great quarterbacks. Last year, when we finished the regular season, there was 10 yards difference in our passing and rushing yardage. We were very balanced in our offense, and that helped us to be successful.

PASSING CONCEPTS

- Curls and outs
- Fades and flats
- Curls and corners
- Double digs
- Crossing

- Four vertical
- 90 quick
- Spacing

These are the passing concepts we use. I started going to clinics and talking to other coaches and getting different kinds of advice about the passing game and the concepts in that part of the game. I wanted to make it as simple as I could. I am going to talk about the concepts we run. They are the same as many other people run. What we do differently is to make it easy to call formations and plays, and it and easy for our quarterbacks to understand.

I listened to a call Payton Manning made. It was a huddle call. and I could not believe it. He called, "Trips right, 255, X-block, slant, H-disco," and there was something else added on at the end. I could not understand it at all. I know some youth league coaches that call plays like that. I think coaches can get in the player's way and make things more complicated for them than necessary. I am a science teacher also. I do not think I am a great football coach. I do not think I understand the X's and O's as I should, but I think I do a good job of relating it to the players so they understand what we want.

When we call plays, we call "curls and outs." We do not call each individual receiver's route. The first thing I want to talk about is our pre-snap reads.

SNAP READS

- Pre-snap read
  - ✓ Find key read
  - ✓ Coverage to help with finding key read
  - ✓ Blitz, hot route
- Post-snap
  - ✓ Confirms pre-snap

I am going to talk about these two formations. I will talk about the quarterback a lot, but that is how we teach it. Until they understand one thing completely, we do not go to the next step. The first thing we teach is the key read. We do not worry about coverage until they understand their key read. We teach the coverage and finding the key read within the coverage. They have to see the blitz and know the hot routes that go with the blitzes. We also teach them a post-snap read to confirm what they saw at the beginning.

READ PROGRESSION

- Key read, first escape
- Key read, backside curl, escape
- Read coverage (finds key read)
- Backside routes escape

They must read the blitz from the first step. When I teach the young quarterbacks the concept, the first thing is the read key. If we run curls and outs, the key read is the outside linebacker. He reads the linebacker, and if he does not like what he sees, he escapes. We do not want him to hold the ball and take a sack. The second part of the progression is the key read, backside route, and escape.

This is something that the quarterbacks can pick up. When they are ready, we push them into the game. Christian LeMay, who is at Georgia, thought he was ready. His sophomore season was not very good. In his first game, he was 8 for 25 and had an interception for a touchdown. We quit throwing because he was not making it happen. We took him back to step one on the read key and worked him back through the process.

The quarterback has to read the blitz on his first step. However, the receiver has to read the blitz on the first step or the quarterback has no place to throw the ball.

The curls and outs is a double-sided pattern (Diagram #1). We run the same pattern on both sides. The outside receivers run the curl pattern, and the inside receivers run the out cuts. The quarterback's read is the curl/flat defender. In this diagram, he reads the outside linebacker. He looks for the best

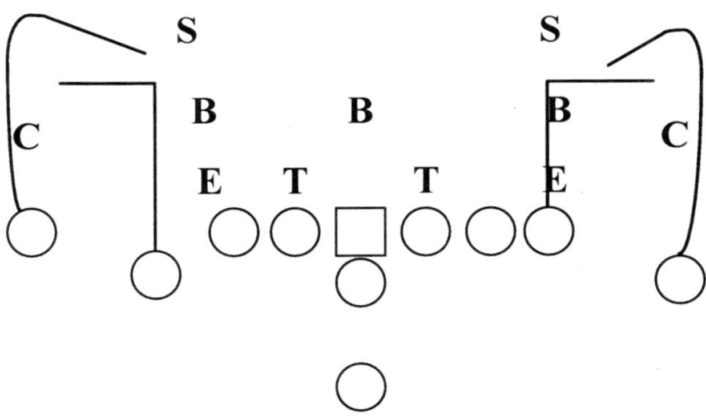

Diagram #1. Curls and Outs 2x2 Set

mismatch. If he has the best two receivers to the right, he takes that side. We teach him to read the backside to find a receiver. Finally, we teach him to read the coverage to find out where he should throw the ball.

At times, the tight end will not release on the pattern and stay in to block. The quarterback and receivers must know when he is not in the pattern. We can run the pass from multiple formations, but the combination of patterns does not change.

This pattern is an 80-protection pass, and the depth of the routes is 10 yards. We run the curl routes at 10 yards. The inside routes have the curl coming over the top. Anytime we have a route with another route run over the top, the inside route is cut to a shorter route. The curl is 10 yards, and the out route is a seven-yard pattern.

In a trips or any 3x1 set, we still run curls and outs (Diagram #2). The outside patterns are curls to both sides. However, there is only one receiver to the left in this formation. The inside receiver into the trips side runs the out cut from the opposite side. It is an in breaking route, which becomes an out cut to the other side of the formation.

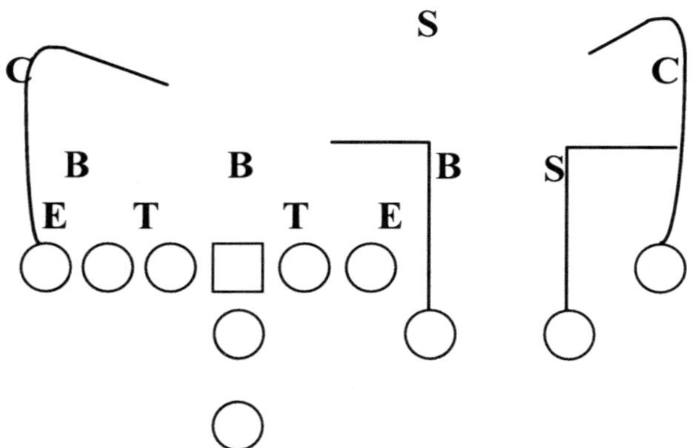

Diagram #2. Curls and Outs 3x1 Set

We have 16 different formations with a tight end. You can call any of those formations, and the receivers know what to do. They run curls and outs.

FADES AND FLATS

Read progression:

- Outside defender (corner)
- Best 1-on-1 mismatch
- Coverage to determine fade defender

On this concept, the outside receivers run fades and the inside receivers run flats (Diagram #3). However, if we are in a tight end set, the pattern is a one-sided pattern. The quarterback throws to the two-receiver side on this pattern. His read key on this concept is the outside defender. That defender is generally the corner.

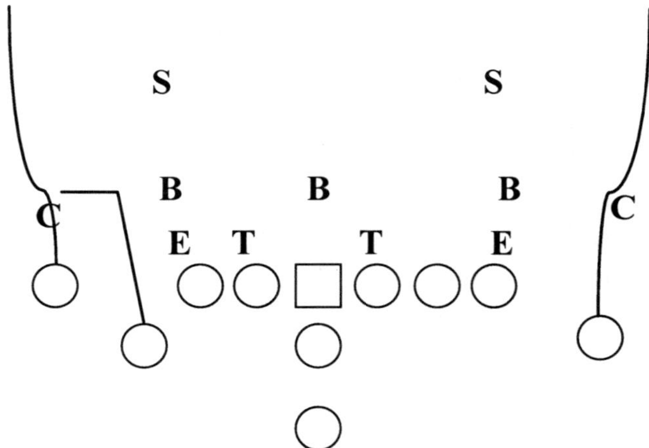

Diagram #3. Fades and Flats

In this formation, the tight end stays in and blocks. The quarterback reads the corner to the two-receiver side. If the corner bails out to cover the fade, the quarterback throws to the flat receiver. If the corner rolls in cover 2, he throws to the fade in the hole between the corner and the half-field safety.

Everybody runs this concept. The difference is we do not try to teach our quarterback to do too much. He reads one defender and throws the ball off what he does. The second rule in the progression is to take the best mismatch. In the 2x1 set, if the quarterback likes the mismatch with the backside single receiver, he throws the fade immediately.

We depend on defenders making mistakes. They coach the corner to roll up on the flat, but when the wide receiver runs at him on the deep route, he drops with the fade oftentimes. He is just as the linebacker is coached to sit on the curl. Instead of sitting on the curl, he chases the flat route. If the receiver runs the fade inside the corner, the corner sees the flat route coming to him. We want the receiver to run the fade to the outside of the corner, so the corner turns away from the flat and does not see it coming.

The release is the one thing I try to coach our receivers to do correctly. They are like water; they want to take the path of least resistance. If the corner gives them the inside release, do not take it. Fight through to the outside, and release upfield to the outside of the corner. Do not reroute to the inside. If the corner fights the wide receiver off the line of scrimmage, the flat pattern will be wide open.

If we align in a 2x1 set, we can get the tight end involved by tagging a call for him. If he is into the boundary, we tag the pattern "fades and flats, Y-bench." That gives us two patterns each way. We can run this concept out of any of our sets. The secret is to call it the same thing from every set.

With a 3x1 set, there is no backside flat pattern. We ran this route several times this year. We run the fade by the outside receiver and the flat by the inside receiver. The middle receiver runs a post and holds the half-field safety inside the hash. We call the pattern Florida, which is fades and flats, and tag it with "R-Post" (Diagram #4).

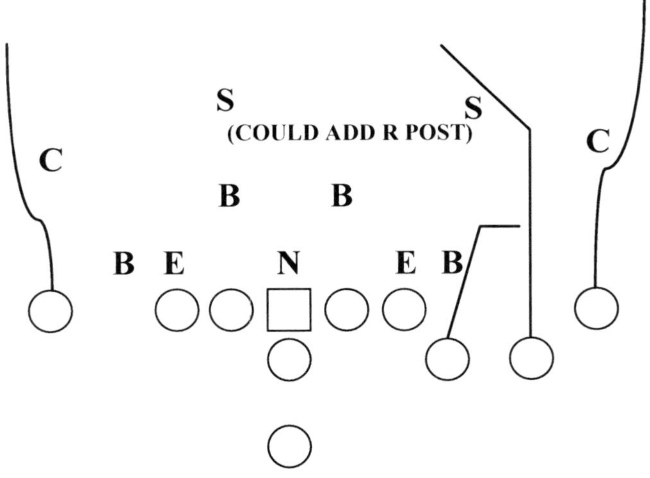

Diagram #4. Florida R-Post

If we call Florida without the tag, the inside receiver blocks and the middle receiver runs the flat route. It does not matter what formation or coverage the defense plays; the read for the quarterback is the same every time. On this play, he reads the outside defender. If we are in an empty set, he reads the same defender. He is not looking for safeties. The advanced quarterbacks know when they see man coverage and are way ahead of the novice quarterbacks. However, knowing the coverage usually leads to the same throw as reading the key.

There is the problem of tagging routes. If you use R-post, the quarterback thinks he has to throw the tag route instead of reading the key.

CURLS AND CORNERS

Read progression:

- Outside defender (corner)
- Outside defender to backside curl
- Coverage to determine outside defender

Curls and corners has turned out to be a great route for us (Diagram #5). The key read for the quarterback is the outside defender. This pattern is the same read as fades and flats. Since the curl has a route over the top of it, it becomes a shorter route. We tell the wide receiver to run the route at seven yards. He wants to push up on the corner up to eight yards, try to step on his toes, and break back to seven yards. We want the corner to break back with the outside receiver. We want to throw the corner route behind him. This is a good route against cover 2.

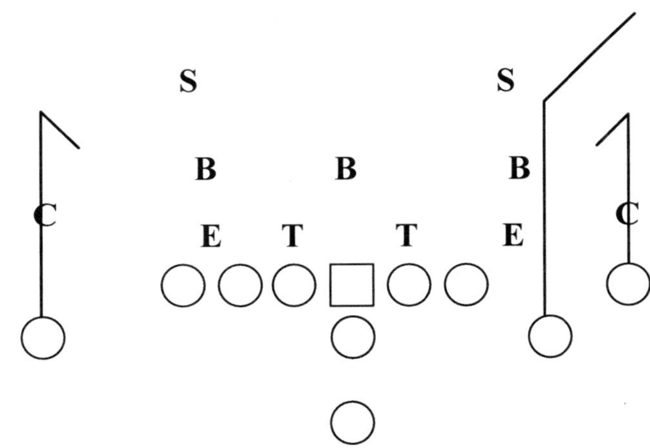

Diagram #5. Curls and Corners 2x2

The backside curl receiver runs a get-open route. He runs his curl at seven yards, but he finds a window in the coverage. He does not sit down behind a linebacker and stay there. He moves his pattern to get open. If the quarterback does not like what he sees on the two-receiver side, he comes back to the curl receiver to the backside. It is up to the receiver to get open. If we want two receivers to each side, we call Y-corner, and the tight end runs the corner route.

In the 3x1 formation, we send the inside receiver on a go route (Diagram #6). On this pattern, the inside receiver tries to hold the safety in the middle of the field. The outside receiver runs the curl, and the middle receiver runs the corner. The quarterback has the same read. He keys the corner and reads curl to corner. If he does not like either pattern, he comes off to the backside curl.

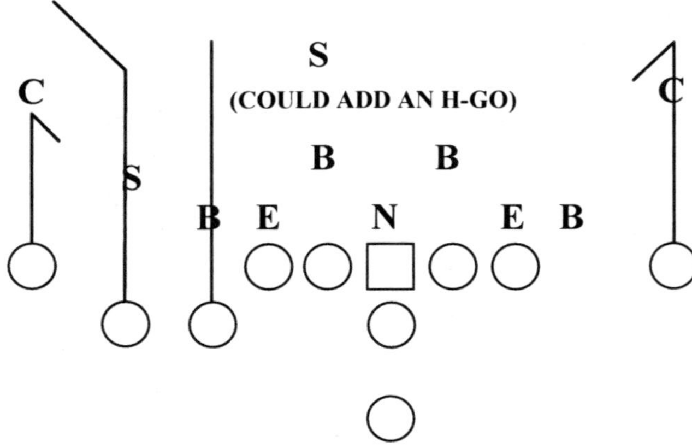

Diagram #6. Curls and Corners 3x1

When your receivers run their routes, they need to work the defenders with a stem move. That gets the defender going where the receiver wants him to go. If we want to run the corner route, we should stem the defender to the inside and break away from him. If the defender takes an inside leverage position, stem inside on the defender to move him further to the inside. The more space the quarterback has to throw the ball the less accurate he has to be. If he puts it in the vicinity, the receiver can go get it.

You can adjust the pattern with tags to take advantage of an over play by the defense. In the state playoff game, the opponent played the corner route on the curl and corner concept. We tagged the "curl and corner," ran a curl/post, and hit it for the touchdown. The corner rolled on the curl, and the safety played the corner route. The wide receiver ran the post behind the safety, playing over the top to the corner.

DOUBLE DIGS

Read progression:

- Curl/flat defender (outside backer)
- Curl/flat defender to backside curl
- Coverage to determine curl/flat defender

The double dig concept is a one-sided route (Diagram #7). We run it on the two-receiver side with a curl to the backside. However, we change up on the backside pattern and run a post route to hold the safety in the middle to keep him from breaking down on the dig route. On the double dig, we read the curl/flat defender. The thing I have trouble getting our players to understand is the depth of the outside dig. We run the route at 16 yards. That takes a long time to run that route. We need good protection on this pattern.

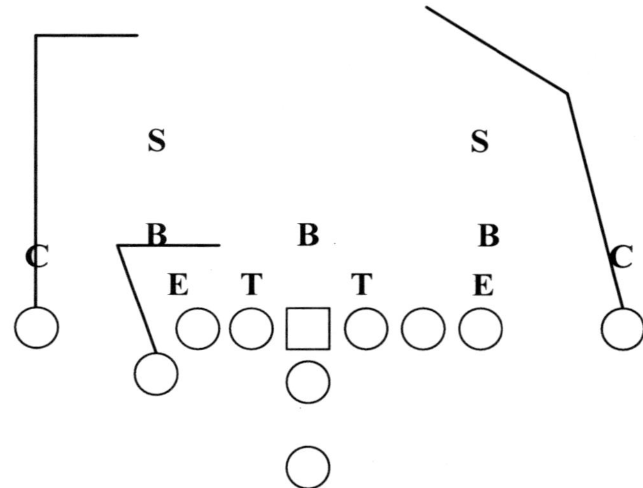

Diagram #7. Double Digs

The quarterback reads the outside linebacker. We want the receiver to run at the backer and try to step on his toes. We tell the receiver to smell the breath of the defender. He wants to get close on the defender and break inside at five yards. We want the defender to chase the receiver to the inside. If he chases inside, the quarterback throws a timing cut pattern to the deep dig receiver in the seam.

If the defender releases the inside dig pattern and sits in the zone, the receiver runs inside. He finds the window between the outside linebacker and the middle linebackers and sits down.

The quarterback reads the linebacker. If the linebacker chases, he delivers to the deep dig. If the linebacker sits in the zone, he finds the inside dig in the window. The corner rolls to the flat, and the safety stays on the hash mark, playing the post cut coming to the inside of the field by the backside receiver.

If we get into a wide alignment in the wideside of the field, the linebacker may not walk out on the slot receiver. If that happens, the slot receiver seeks out the defender and runs the same pattern. The receiver has to get the defender to recognize him so the defender has to react to what he does. He runs the same pattern.

In the 3x1 set, the linebacker stays over the tight end, and the safety walks down on the middle receiver (Diagram #8). The middle receiver runs the short dig, and the outside receiver runs the deep dig. The read is the same for the quarterback. If we feel the protection will hold up, we can run the tight end on an arrow route to the flat. We call "double-dig, Y-Arrow."

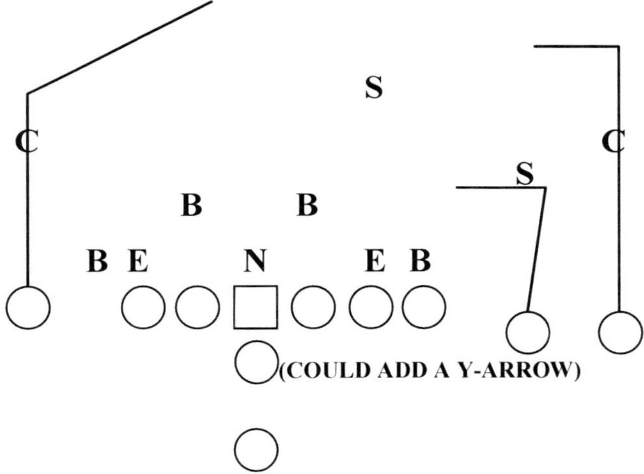

Diagram #8. 3x1 Double Dig

When the short dig runs his pattern off the linebacker, he wants to get as close as possible, but he does not want to get into a combative situation with the defender. He wants to get to the inside and bring him out of the passing lane. If the defender is fighting the receiver, he will chase him inside. If we run a trips set with a three-wide-receiver look, the H-back can run a go pattern to hold the safety. The go pattern threatens the safety and keeps him off the deep dig pattern.

FOUR VERTICALS

Read progression:

- Coverage read (MOF: open or closed)
- Receivers must also read coverage.

I did an entire clinic last year on four verticals (Diagram #9). I could talk an hour on this pattern. We run a four-vertical package. This package is like running five million patterns in one play. When we go to play in 7-on-7 camps, we run this play repeatedly. The thing that must happen is the quarterback has to read coverages. We do not run four verticals until our quarterback can read coverages. In addition to the quarterback, the receivers have to read the coverages.

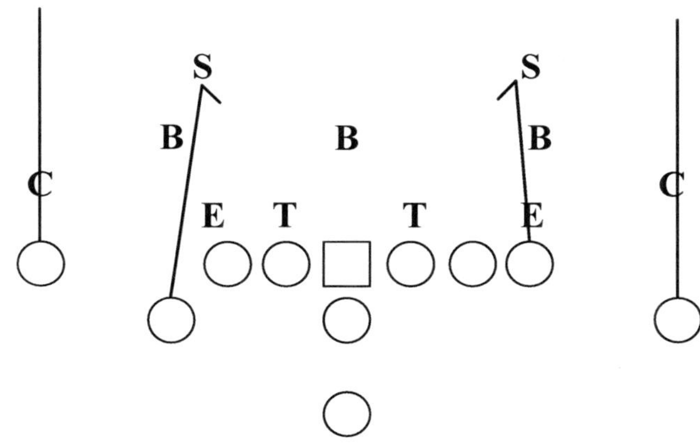

Diagram #9. Four Verticals

The first thing the quarterback has to know is whether the middle of the field is open or closed. In the four-vertical package, the receivers do not run deep all the time. The receivers read the coverage and curl up on occasions. When we run four verticals, the outside receivers run up the numbers, and the inside receivers run up the hash marks. Those are their landmarks.

When you run four verticals, it is critical to have everyone on the same page. We did not run this package this year as many times as we have in the past. The reason was we had trouble coaching our receiver on when to curl and when not to curl.

We want to run this against a cover-3 secondary. We try to put people in a cover-3 look when we can. We know they cover a certain set with cover 3. We get into that set and run the four-vertical package. The quarterback has to make good decisions in this package. In the cover-3 look, the inside receivers may be curling on the hash marks. You can do anything you want from this package if the receiver will get to the right places.

In the 3x1 set, the inside receivers have to get to their landmarks (Diagram #10). The middle receiver in the trips set takes the near hash mark, and the inside receiver must get across the field and up the other hash mark. On this type of pattern against the cover-3 secondary, the quarterback reads the middle of the field closed. He looks for the safety tilted one way or the other. If the corners try to squeeze the hash marks and stay as deep as the deepest, the outside receivers curl up on the numbers.

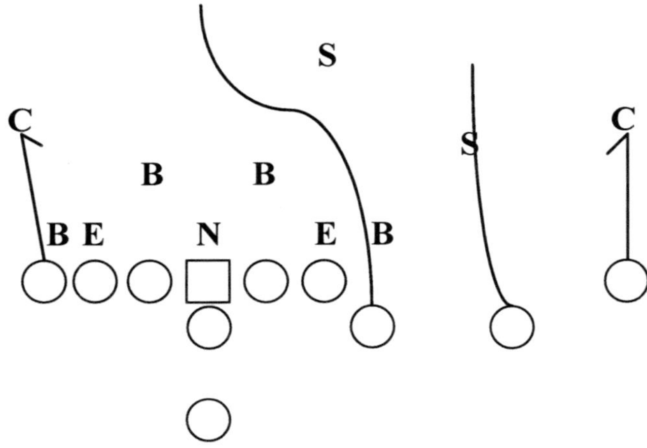

Diagram #10. Four Verticals 3x1

Knowing when to curl or come back is the tricky part. The outside receiver must see the corner squeezing to the inside and trying to help on the deep patterns before they can stop their patterns and hook up.

We can run switches out of the four-vertical game (Diagram #11). If we run a switch on the outside, it does not change what the receivers are going to do. The outside receiver comes inside and runs up the hash marks, and the inside receiver moves to the outside and runs the numbers. We can run a double switch, and both side switch their routes. It causes confusion, particularly if a defender is trying to carry a receiver to the safety.

The combinations are numerous with this package. You can run four receivers vertical. You can run two receivers up the hashes vertical and curl

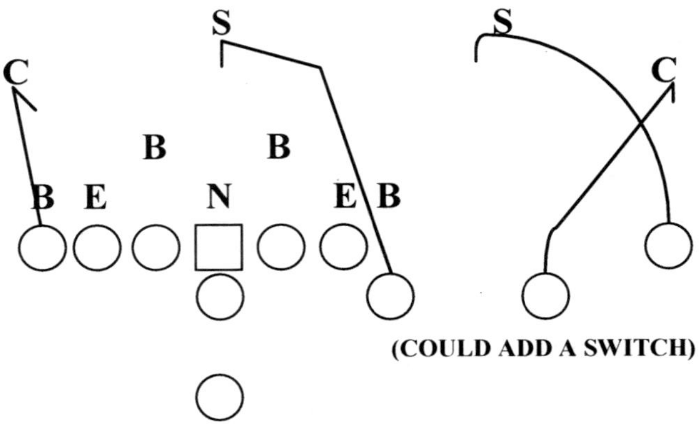

Diagram #11. Four Verticals Switch

the outside receivers. You can run two receivers up the numbers vertical and curl the inside receivers. You can run four receivers up the field and curl them all.

We played a 7-on-7 game and ran nothing but this pattern. We were no-huddle and ran the same play repeatedly. The opposing coach asked me after the game how we called the plays so quickly. I told him it was the same play. We ran different routes because of the coverage in the secondary. When he changed coverages, we adjusted our patterns.

90 QUICK GAME

Read progression:

- Best mismatch based on defensive back alignment

The 90 quick game is a quick pattern run to receivers. We call this "slant/sluggo spacing" (Diagram #12). We are thinking about changing the game this year to give the receiver an option to run whatever pattern he likes, according to the alignment and leverage of the defender. This is an

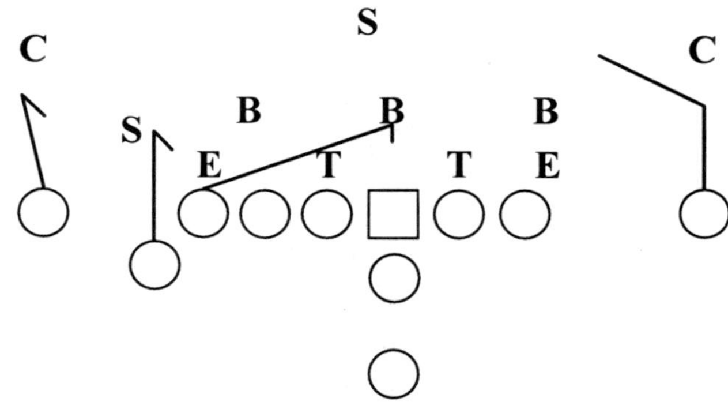

Diagram #12. Slant/Sluggo Spacing 3x1

NFL route. We like to run it out of the 3x1 formation. The single receiver runs the slant. It is a three-step slant at five yards. The tight end runs five yards over the center and hooks up in front of the middle linebacker. The middle receiver hooks up five yards just outside the tackle box. The wide receiver hooks up five yards in front of the corner.

If the quarterback has the slant pattern, he takes it immediately. If he cannot throw the slant, he comes over the ball to outside the tackle box.

The key thing I tried to do, because I was not too smart about offensive football, was to make this simple for me. When I made it simple for me, I made it simple for the quarterbacks. I think coaches do too much with the quarterback by trying to read coverages and defenses. We try to do too much with the quarterback.

I try to tell my quarterbacks that when they get to college, it will be tougher. The quarterbacks are expected in some places to call the coverages, read defenses, change blocking assignments, fronts, and everything else. It will get more and more complicated for them. However, as the quarterbacks I coach get better, we give them more to do.

The quarterback in this system always has the option to go back to the first step in the progression of reading keys. I teach the quarterback like that. If your quarterback gets confused, take him back to the beginning and go through it with him until he understands. Do not force progress down the quarterback's throat. We take our time with the quarterbacks. That is what we try to do, and our quarterbacks have been successful.

One thing I did not talk about but meant to was this: we are not an all shotgun team. We teach the quarterback to get under the center before we go to the shotgun sets. The reason we do that is so they can read coverages. Until they show you they can read coverages, they will be under the center. They want to get in the shotgun, but they have to read coverage first, and it happens faster under the center. If he is in the shotgun set, he has to take his eyes off the defense to catch the ball in the shotgun snap.

If he is under the center, he sees the defense the entire time. He can focus on what he is supposed to see. I would urge you to do that. If the quarterback has trouble reading coverage, he is taking his eyes off the defense.

I appreciate you coming, and I enjoyed being here. If I can help you, feel free to call. Thank you very much.

Josh Niblett

GAP SCHEMES AND PERIMETER RUNS

Hoover High School, Alabama

I tell everyone when I start that all the things I do are great. I love my job. I have a wife and three beautiful kids. However, those are not the most important things in my life. The most important thing is I serve an awesome God. On November 1, 1998, was the best decision I made in my life. I gave my life to Christ. On that day, something in my life changed. My entire outlook on life as a coach, father, and husband changed.

I am not going to tell you what to do or how to coach the game of football. Football is going to end one day, and judgment day is coming. How many games you have won, how many players you get signed to scholarships, or how many five star athletes you coached is not going to matter. What is going to matter is how you try to influence your player's lives in a spiritual way so that they become good fathers and husbands one day.

Every day, coaching is a ministry. Every day I wake up, I have a passion to go to my school. I do not start by blowing a whistle and start stretching. Every day when the players come in, we have a character education situation. We talk through it. I challenge them to do something good. Go home and tell your mom that you love her and kiss her cheek.

We all like coaching football and winning games because we are competitive. That is what we are supposed to do. We are supposed to compete to be the best we can possibly be. How you do it is more important to me than the outcome. This is about who you are and not what you have done.

I do not mean to get on the soapbox, but when I answer on judgment day, I want to answer for trying to do things the right way. I am not perfect, but I do know whom I serve and who gave me the breath of life.

I want to talk football and tell you what we do at Hoover High School. We are a zone and gap scheme team on offense. A few years ago, when I first came into coaching, we were a huge zone team. We run our zone play almost like running the veer. We are a vertical push, downhill zone team. We do not talk about bang, bend, and bounce. We hit the play going vertical. We hug the heels of the offensive linemen and jump cut. We do not jump cut to daylight. We look for butts. When we jump cut, we look for the butt of the next offensive lineman.

In the gap scheme, we tell our running backs to press the hole. If we have a running back who wants to cut three yards behind the line of scrimmage, we will find another position for him.

It does not take long to evaluate an offensive back. Hand it to him one time and see what he does with it. He will hit up inside or try to bounce. You have to develop the running backs to press the hole. When we run the gap or I-zone plays, we harp on that point. When the backs take their steps on the gap and zone, the steps almost look the same. We want it to look the same.

In our program, we do not claim that our way is the best way, but we do claim it to be our way.

The Hoover Program

It's not the hard way
It's not the easy way
It's not the only way
It's our way

"ONE PLUS TODAY" PHILOSOPHY—RELENTLESS EFFORT TO TAKE YOUR POTENTIAL TO ANOTHER LEVEL

Finish

- Know you are going to dominate.
- Quiet minded, focus—Compete to complete.

Compete

- You are either competing or not, no matter the circumstance.
- In a relentless pursuit of a competitive edge.
- Either win or lose—"It's all about us."

Commit

- Confidence and trust.
- Know what we do in preparation to be one plus today; it is how we do it.
- Practice is everything, how we practice defines who we are.
- Create a relentless tempo of high energy and great enthusiasm.

Believe

- Beliefs: It's all about the ball, do the little things right, and respect everyone.
- Three rules: Protect the family, the BUC rule, no excuses (no whining or complaining).
- Style of play: Fast, tough, finish.
- 2H Philosophy
- Learn from yesterday, prepare for tomorrow, and never be short today.
- Supported by our PHD (passion, hunger, drive).
- Be at your best because your best is required.

Vision

- We want to be one plus today, by competing to complete the task.

I want to talk about our gap and power running game. If you know how to block everybody on the gap scheme, talk to me when I finish today. The thing I like about the gap scheme is the fact we can build a wall away from where we pull. We want to build a wall so we can create a crease. We want to put as much pressure on the Mike linebacker as we can.

OUR RUNNING SCHEME WITH PERSONNEL GROUPS AND FORMATIONS

- I-Z: Zone with a read key (always); regular, base, seal, load, fold
  - ✓ Any personnel groupings: 10, 11, 12, 20, 21, empty (motion back)
  - ✓ Smoke and mirrors (jet action or mesh back)
  - ✓ 3x1 (I-Z bubble, I-Z look, I-Z quick); quick: one-receiver side
  - ✓ Bubble pre-snap off flat defender, QB can throw off pitch key to the bubble late
- Slice (Pistol): Zone while blocking read key (reg., backer); also be I-Z kick: no pistol
  - ✓ Any personnel groupings: 10, 11, 12, 21, 20
  - ✓ Smoke and mirrors (jet action or mesh back)
- Dash: Stretch read zone with read key (EMOL, 3 technique, shade)
- Jet sweep: Offensive line block inside zone away; read EMOL key playside; offensive line block long trap to the jet side
  - ✓ Any personnel groupings: 20, 21, 10, 11, 12, empty

We run the zone play with a read key. We can run the play and read the end man on the line of scrimmage (EMOL). We read an apex player verses a 4-1 alignment in the box. We can read the 3 technique and the 1 technique like the midline option. We can read everybody in the box.

If you do not read everybody in the box, the defense will tilt the defense on the backside. They run the defense down the line of scrimmage and "rock and roll" the Mike linebacker. That is the way people are stopping the zone these days. The Mike linebacker reads the I-zone coming to him. He steps into the gap as the center comes out to block him. Instead of filling the A gap, he rolls out and fills the cutback lane to the backside. The defensive line is running down the line and forcing the running back to cut the play back into the Mike linebacker. We must have a way to confuse the Mike linebacker.

On this play, we always have the bubble screen going with the zone play. We can throw the ball to the pitchback on the option as a one-man screen. From this scheme, we run the jet sweep, slice, and dash. We run the slice from the pistol look.

I want to talk about the gap scheme because it is a great complement to the zone play. The plays we run from the gap scheme are the power/blast, sweep, and gut play.

GAP SCHEME

- Power/Blast: Gap down with no read key (regular, Q, base, read)
  - ✓ Personnel groupings (10, 11, 12, 20, 21) (Cowboy)
- Sweep: Truck blocking
  - ✓ Personnel groupings (20, 21, 10, 11) (Cowboy)
- Gut: Influence sweep block, backside puller trap playside A- or B-gap defender
  - ✓ Same personnel groupings as sweep smoke and mirrors (jet action)

On the blast play, the guard pulls, kicks out, and the fullback is inside on the linebacker. If we run the power play, the fullback kicks out, and the guard turns up for the linebacker. The sweep we run in the gap scheme bases on the wing-T buck sweep. The blocking is not the same, but the play is similar. This is the companion play for the power and blast. When the C-gap defender squeezes to stop the power, we pin him inside and run the sweep with both guards pulling to the outside. The gut play is the companion for the buck sweep. The play is an influence trap, which looks like we are running the buck sweep.

When we run the power, the two-receiver side always runs the bubble screen. The defense will squeeze with their apex defender and try to get him in the box. When we see it, we want to throw the bubble screen.

That looks like a lot of complicated offense. However, if you break down what we do, it all fits together. It is not complicated, and what you will see is three or four of these plays grouped together as one play.

We do everything off signals. The offensive line coach signals to the offensive line, and the wide receiver coach signals to the skilled players. If the call is I-zone to the field, the offensive line gets a slice signal, which to them is a full zone blocking scheme.

When we run the jet sweep, we read the play a few different ways. We read the playside end. If he widens, we run the inside zone the other way with the quarterback. We can also run a long trap if the defensive end widens with the jet sweep motion coming to him. I am going to show you our blocking scheme, which may look like code. The initials are common nomenclature with coaches. Anytime you see the term box as part of the rules, it means a fullback or tight end is off the ball inside the box.

GAP BLOCKING SCHEME

- *Power:* Gap down PS/Box—Kick EMOL PS/BSG—Wrap for #1 LB (#2 bubble)
- *Gap Base:* PS T/TE Base EMOL—PSG/Gap down/Box—#2 LB; BSG—Wrap for #1 linebacker
- *Blast:* Gap down BSG—Kick EMOL PS/Box—Wrap for #1 LB (#2 bubble)
- *Stretch:* Gap down PS/Box—Load force/Q+T—Stretch/BSG—Wrap for #1 linebacker (#2 bubble)
- *Sweep:* Truck blocking/PST: Gap down/Box—EMOL/BSG/PSG—Pull/#2 WR—Crack
- *Gut:* Influence sweep block/BSG—Trap A-gap to B-gap defender

Using the power play example, gap down is the playside (PS) call for the offensive guard, tackle, center, and tight end. The fullback (box) to the playside kicks out on the end man on the line of scrimmage (EMOL). The backside guard (BSG) wraps around the double-team down blocks and up on the first linebacker in the box (#1 LB). The #2 receiver in the twin set to the outside runs a bubble screen.

We try not to call the player who aligns at fullback a fullback. We want him to be able to align as a tight end also. We want him to align in the backfield and be out in space. When we use the term "box," he knows that term refers to him.

The first play I want to show you is the power play (Diagram #1). This is a great complement to the zone play.

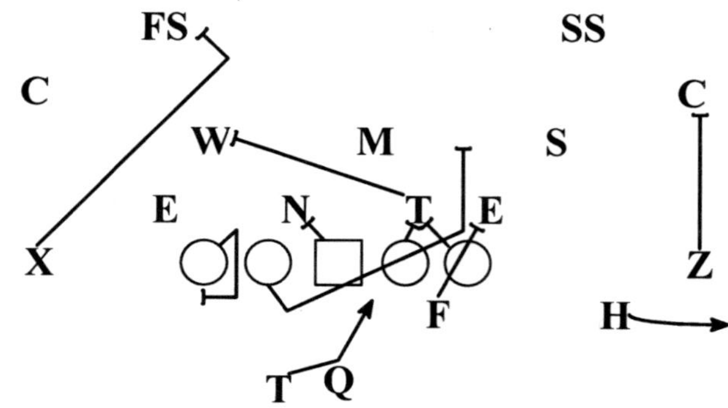

Diagram #1. Power vs. Over Defense

POWER ASSIGNMENT AND TECHNIQUE

- Quarterback: Step BS foot to 12 o'clock, reach ball back—two hands (pass drop fake)
- Running back: Align away from call, step over the bottle, attack playside A gap, press and hug
- Wide receivers: #1: Block MO (man); #2: bubble
- Box: No TE, pad out EMOL; with TE, vs. 5, 6, 7 technique pick up overhang, vs. 9 technique pad out
- Linemen: First level combo's first (vertical push), backer's second, build a wall
  - ✓ If PSTE vs. 7, 6, or 5 technique, man-block C-gap defender; No C gap, release to #2 linebacker
  - ✓ PST vs. 3, 2 technique, combo with PSG to #2 LB; If PSG has A-gap threat, then gap down man vs. 4, 4i technique; Flat inside read step, then vertical (no pressure: linebacker/pressure, take)
  - ✓ PSG vs. 3, 2 technique, combo with PST to #2 LB; If there is A-gap threat, then gap down man
  - ✓ Center vs. shade to 3 technique BS, block back; Vs. zero technique, combo with PSG unless a 3 technique backside
  - ✓ BSG Skip pull: Hug the combo or B-gap block; Wrap for #1 linebacker in the box
  - ✓ BST B-gap hinge
  - ✓ If BSTE butt block, C-gap threat

The quarterback's steps on the power play are the same as the zone read. The running back step is more at a 45-degree angle instead of downhill, but we do not want him flat. We want the quarterback's eyes to go to the backside defensive end. If the end sees the quarterback's eyes on him, he will sit and wait for the quarterback to pull the ball.

Getting the backside end to sit helps the center. If there is a 3 technique on the backside guard, the center has to block back for the pulling guard. The backside tackle can punch on the 3 technique until the center gets across to block him. When the center gets to the block, the tackle hinges to the backside. When the quarterback pulls his hand, he runs directly to the defensive end. We handle the defensive end with the quarterback. If the end does not squeeze, the quarterback can fake the dropback pass.

The running back aligns away from the call on the power play and to the call on the blast play. The receivers in the twin set run the bubble screen. The outside receiver blocks the man on him, and the slot runs the bubble.

If there is not a tight end, the fullback kicks out the EMOL. If we align with a tight end versus a 5-, 6-, or 7-technique defender, the fullback pick up the overhang defender. In the 43 over front, to the playside we have a 3 technique, 7 technique, and a Sam linebacker stacked on the 7-technique defender (Diagram #2). If we try to kick out the 7 technique with the fullback and let the tight end go to the linebacker, there is a problem. The tight end has to take an outside release to get to the Sam linebacker. If the Sam linebacker falls back inside, we cannot block him.

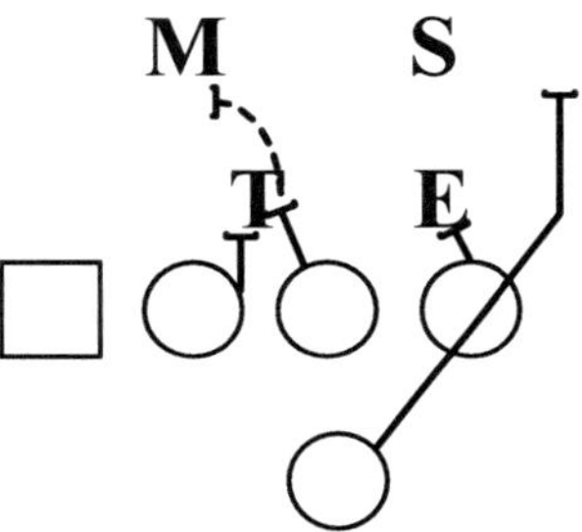

Diagram #2. Tight End/Fullback Block

The tight end blocks the 7-technique defender, using a man-blocking scheme. We want to block him down, but we want to block him any way we can. The fullback runs his scheme off the butt of the tight end. The 7 technique is a C-gap player, and the Sam linebacker plays the D gap. The fullback comes off the butt of the tight end and pads out on the linebacker.

The hardest block in this scheme is the combination block for the linebackers. We want to make sure we block the defender at the first level. You cannot worry about the linebackers until you get the first level secured. We do not want to drive the 3 technique down the line of scrimmage. We want to vertical push him off the line. We want to build a wall. The tight end blocks the C-gap defender. If there is no C-gap defender on the line, he releases to the second level.

The center IDs the linebacker in everything we do. When the center identifies the Mike linebacker, we know which backer the guard wraps around to block. The playside tackle has a gap scheme to the inside. If there is a 3- or 2-technique defender, he is in combination with the playside guard. If the guard has an inside defender, the tackle uses a man scheme to block the inside defender.

If the playside tackle has a 4 technique or 4i defender aligned head-up, he takes an inside read step (Diagram #3). This situation happens with 3-3 stack teams. The tackle takes a zone step inside. The zone step is a timing step, and the second step goes vertical up the field. If the 4-technique defender squeezes inside, the tackle blocks him. The fullback comes off the tackle's butt and wraps up on the linebacker or kicks out an outside blitzer.

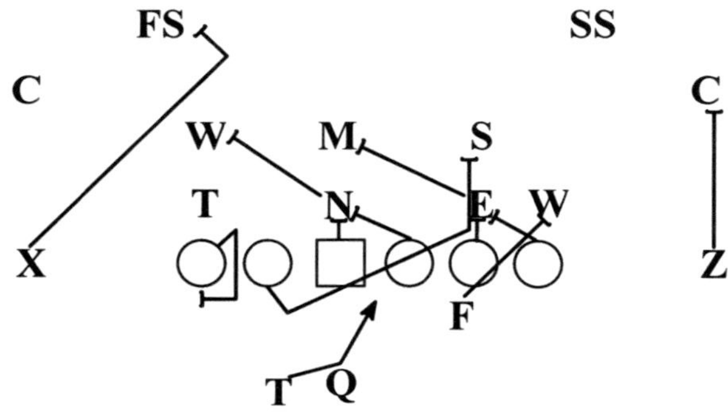

Diagram #3. 4-Technique Defender

The center's rule is simple: he blocks backside until he hits something. It does not matter if it is a shade, 2i-, 2-, or 3-technique defender. If he has a head-up defender, he combos with the playside guard unless he has a 3-technique defender to the backside. That would happen in a Bear front (double Eagle). In that case, the center, playside guard, and playside tackle all man-block to the backside.

The backside guard uses an open-skip pulling technique. He cannot turn his shoulders and run. The fullback will kick out, and he has to turn up inside. He has to have his eyes on the defender he is wrapping around to block.

If we have a tight end to the backside, he butt blocks the C-gap threat. The butt block is like a block-out technique in basketball. The tight end fires inside the 7-technique defender, turns his butt to him, and blocks him out of the inside. The reason we use this technique is most of our tight ends are basketball players. They do not like to stick their nose in there, but they will box him out.

Our offensive linemen align in a three-point stance. I do not believe you can come off the football and run-block from a two-point stance. However, I believe you can pass-block from a three-point stance.

We have changed our rule for our man-blocking scheme on the down block. We want the offensive linemen to block down on the defender and gnaw off the outside tip of the shoulder pad. If the blocker puts his head in front, the defender plays over the top of the blocker. If he puts his head behind the defender, the defender beats the blocker through the gap. We want them to aggressive attack the outside tip of the defender's shoulder and block him.

The running back has to find the pulling guard and hug the heels of the offensive blocker. We want the play to break in the A gap. If we can build the wall and the back hugs the heels in the wall, we have a good play. We did not design this play to get to the perimeter. It is a power play that runs up inside. The one thing you cannot have in a gap scheme is leakage through the wall.

BLAST

- Gap down/BSG—Kick EMOL PS; Box—Wrap for #1 LB (#2 bubble)

On the blast, the blocking rules for the offensive line are the same as the power (Diagram #4). The only difference is the block of the pulling guard and fullback. They exchange blocking assignments. The guard is the kick-out blocker, and the fullback is the

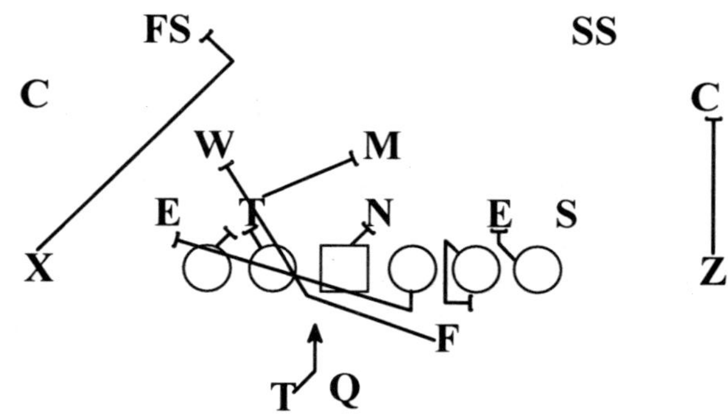

Diagram #4. Blast

wraparound blocker. On this play, the running back aligns to the side of the call. No rules change for anyone else.

The difference between the blast and the power is the alignment of the back. His position tells the defense it is a power play. However, they think the point of attack is opposite the alignment of the running back. We run a power play, blocking to the side of the back. The back still takes the play into the A gap, hugs the heels, and makes his jump cut off the butt of the offensive linemen. The most important thing the back can do is hug the wall. If he gets too wide, we do not have a play.

If we run the play from the pistol set, the running back goes away from the call and rocks back behind the fullback. He hits the play into the A gap and hugs the wall. We want the defense to read zone.

The sweep play is a perimeter run for us. We want to get the ball to the outside and stick it back inside. The offensive line scheme is "block down, backer."

SWEEP ASSIGNMENT AND TECHNIQUE

- Quarterback: Step flat playside—ride with two hands (pass drop fake)
- Running back: Align away from the call—crossover and flat stretch
- Wide receivers: #1—Block MO (man)/#2—Crack first linebacker in the box
- Box: Align to the call/Pen EMOL unless he disappears, then work up to the #2 LB in the box
- Linemen: Gap down truck
  - ✓ If PSTE vs. 7, 6, or 5 technique, man block C-gap defender; No C gap, release to #2 linebacker
  - ✓ PST vs. 3, 2 technique, gap down man; vs. 4, 4i technique, flat inside read step, then vertical (if no pressure, #2 linebacker/pressure, take)
  - ✓ PSG stretch pull, overhang defender
  - ✓ Center vs. no A-gap defender PS, block back; If A-gap threat, block A-gap defender
  - ✓ BSG stretch pull, backside linebacker (#2 or #3 backer in the box)
  - ✓ BST B-gap hinge
  - ✓ If BSTE butt block C-gap threat

The fullback on this play aligns to the side of the call (Diagram #5). He wants to pen or log the end man on the line of scrimmage. The #2 receiver, instead of running the bubble screen, cracks to the inside. He cracks the first linebacker in the box. The coaching point for the wide receiver as he comes to crack on the linebacker is to stay flat. If he does not come flat, the linebacker can get inside him and into the play. If the linebacker beats the crack block, it has to be over the top and not underneath.

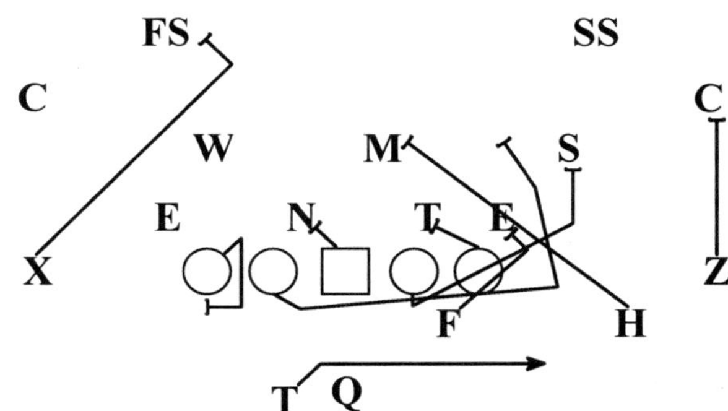

Diagram #5. Sweep

The playside guard uses a stretch pull and blocks the overhang or the first defender outside the box. If the center has a playside A-gap defender, he has to block it. It is a fast-flow play, and he has to get that defender. The backside guard uses a stretch pull and works for the #2 or #3 linebackers in the box.

When we run the sweep, the big linemen do not like to run wide. We want them to attack and take on the defender as soon as they can. When the playside tackle blocks down on a 3-technique defender, it is important for him to stop penetration. If the 3 technique penetrates, he picks off the backside pulling guard. The same thing is true of the fullback's block. He has to pen the defender and not let him get penetration up the field. We want to get outside his block quickly.

We do not run this play with the tight end, but we can. If the tight end is in the game and we run the sweep, his blocking assignment is what the fullback does. This is a good complement to what we do.

This is a good red zone play. However, in that area, we probably will get a crash coming from the edge. If we get that type of stunt or play, the guard kicks out, and the back sticks the ball back inside and gets to the end zone. If the defense stunts and we get the heat from the outside, we kick and stick the ball to the inside.

The backside guard has to run hard to get into the play. He wraps back inside for a box linebacker. The wide receiver to the playside has to block the man on him (MO). If we run this play with our fast wide receiver off the jet sweep action, he has to slow down. If he hits the play with too much speed, the blocks will not set up. We played a team in Alabama called Vestavia Hills High School. You look at them personnel-wise and think they are not much. They were the most fundamentally sound football team I have ever seen. They played an eight-man front and did not get out of it. We thought we could throw four verticals on them all day. They were always in the right place, and we had a heck of a time running or passing against them.

If the end man on the line of scrimmage blitzes inside the offensive tackle, the tackle blocks him, and the fullback moves up to the second-level block on the linebacker. The tackle and fullback exchange blocks.

The back has to stretch the play and make the defense run. Once he gets the defense running, he can cut the play up. We do not run out-of-bounds with this play. We have to get north and south when the defense runs.

We are probably 20 percent pistol in our offense. We run the zone from that set, and it has been good for us. Our Cowboy set is our version of the Wildcat. We can run the sweep from this set. The player we use in the Cowboy set is our slot receiver. He is also our punt returner. He is an unbelievable athlete and a good football player. We want a player in this set that is tough.

What we like to do with our formations is to fake the jet sweep going one way and run the buck sweep away from the motion. When the defense sees the jet motion, they start to move in the direction of the motion, and this sets us up to run against soft corners and support players.

When the guards pull, they want to look inside for their blocks. However, we try to make them aware of outside pressure. If there is no immediate threat to the inside, he wants to peek outside.

When we run the jet fake, the back has to finish the jet and make the defense respect what he does. They cannot stop running once the quarterback pulls the ball back from them.

GUT ASSIGNMENT AND TECHNIQUE

- Quarterback: Step flat playside—ride with two hands (pass drop fake)
- Running back: Align away from the call—crossover and flat get vertical inside trap block
- Wide receivers: #1—Block MO (man)/#2—Bubble
- Box: Align to the call—release to overhang defender
- Linemen: Gap down truck
  - ✓ If PSTE vs. 7, 6, or 5 technique, arc release to overhang defender
  - ✓ PST vs. veer release to #1 linebacker in the box. 4, 4i technique, flat inside read step, then vertical (if no pressure, #2 linebacker/pressure, take)
  - ✓ PSG 45-degree pull to trap EMOL
  - ✓ Center vs. no A-gap defender PS, block back; vs. zero, man block
  - ✓ BSG 45-degree pull to trap A- or B-gap defender
  - ✓ BST B-gap hinge
  - ✓ If BSTE butt block, C-gap threat

The last play in the gap scheme is the gut play (Diagram #6). It comes off the sweep play. It is an influence trap play. We pull the playside guard, and he traps the end man on the line of scrimmage. The backside guard pulls and traps the A- or B-gap defender. The fullback blocks the overhang defender on the playside, and the running back breaks on the block of the backside guard. We feel the 3-technique defender will run out when the playside guard pulls.

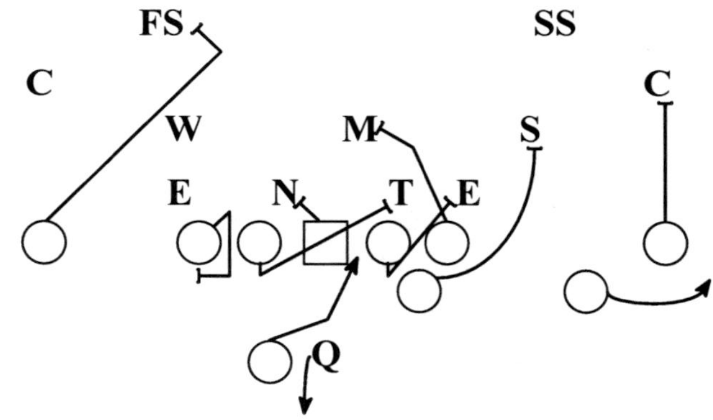

Diagram #6. Gut

Our play-action passing game has been good off the gap scheme series. This is a power play-action pass (Diagram #7). The twin receivers run the bubble screen as they do on the power play. The difference is the wide receiver does not block the defender that is on him. He runs past him and runs a post pattern. The fullback goes to the flat instead of the kick-out block on the Sam linebacker. The X-receiver on the backside runs a dig pattern.

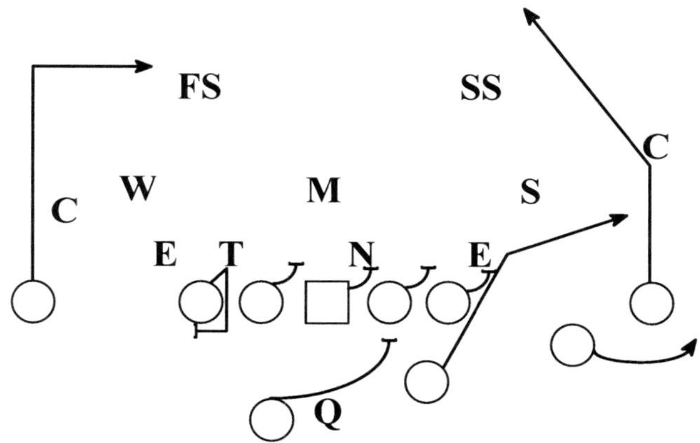

Diagram #7. Power Play-Action

The offensive line blocks the power play. They must keep their head down when they and not show pass action. The running back had to come off his fake early and look for the linebacker fill.

I will show you one more play. This play comes off our sweep action (Diagram #8). The formation ends up in a trips formation. The outside receiver runs a dig to the inside. The slot receiver runs a stem vertical route. It starts out looking like a crack block. The sweep back becomes the #3 receiver to that side and runs the flare route.

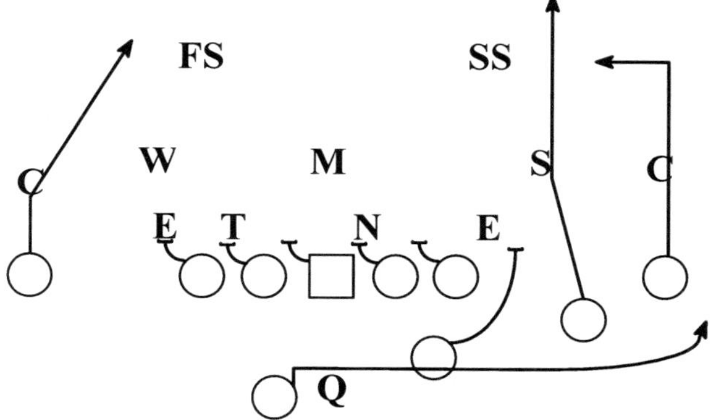

Diagram #8. Sweep Play-Action

The play-action passing game is a big part of any running game. The plays have to look exactly alike. We run them off jet sweep action and zone action. They are a big part of what we do. Everybody calls us a spread team, but we run the football. We balance our run to pass ratio.

I want to leave you with Paul's charge to Timothy.

Preach the word; be prepared in season and out of season; correct, rebuke and encourage—with great patience and careful instruction.

—2 Timothy 4:2

That is what we are called to do, and that is our ministry. We have to do that every day and have a passion for it. When it is all said and done, you have to go home to something. When I get home, I have my family. Win, lose, or draw, when I get home, there are five people in that house who care about each other. Do not every forget that, and all the rest of that stuff will take care of itself. If you are ever in Hoover, Alabama, come by and see us. Thank you very much.

Derek Pennington

THE 4-3 DEFENSE: PREPARATIONS AND DRILLS

Zeeland East High School, Michigan

I am going to talk about what we do defensively. I see there are a lot of coaches out there ready to listen to an offensive coach talk about defense. We did have a good defense this year. I wish I could take credit for it. I have a tremendous defensive coordinator who has been with me for a long, long time in Coach Troy Ayotte.

We play a tough schedule. We play against really good coaches as well, including Coach Elliot Uzelac at St. Joseph High School. Coach Uzelac was the offensive coordinator at The Ohio State University, the University of Colorado, and coached with the Cleveland Browns. We played against Coach John Shillito from Zeeland West High School, who is a tremendous coach of the T offense. Coach Wilson at Fruitport High School had a good T team as well. East Grand Rapids has a tremendous offense and averaged 48 points a game. Our defense held them to 17 points, even though on offense we were throwing interceptions, fumbling the ball, and causing him all kinds of problems.

I have been at Zeeland East High School for three years. In 2008, we were an odd stack team, but gave up a lot of yards on the ground. We were not very good on defense. After that year, we had to decide what we wanted to do differently. We went to clinics to hear about the 4-3 defense, because we were going to have some good defensive linemen. We decided to shift to the 4-3 defense. We were a 5-4 defense in 2009. If it had not been for our defense, we would have been worse. Our offense was bad. Our quarterback got hurt in our third game and was out the rest of the season. I had the worst offense I have ever coached out of the spread.

This year, we were fortunate, in that our quarterback stayed healthy. We played good offense and played real good defense. What we do defensively makes sense and is a good scheme. I have listed some defensive things that are important to me.

WHAT A HEAD COACH CARES ABOUT

- *Three-and-outs:* If you are not tracking this statistic, you are making a mistake. You can hold a team to 21 points, but if they had 20 first downs, you may have never had the ball. We want to get the other team off the field.
- *Takeaways:* We want to create turnovers with our defense. That creates good field position for our offense.
- *Do our athletes know what they are doing?* We as coaches may know what we are doing, but if we do not translate that to the players, it does not do us any good. We try to keep it simple for everyone. We line up one way: 4-3 cover 4.
- *Can we fix problems that arise?* If we are being hurt by something our opponent is doing, I want to know, from my defensive coordinator, what we are doing about it. You have to have answers to things that are hurting you.
- *Can we adjust to multiple formations?* I felt like we went against 10 different types of offenses this season. College guys do not see that. As a high school coach, you have to be ready for many different things.
- *How are we going to stop their best plays?* When I am in defensive meetings, I ask my staff, "How we are going to stop the opponent's best play?"

The 2009 conversion to the 4-3 defense was very difficult for me as a coach. When I first started coaching 15 years ago, I read a lecture in a Nike *Coach of the Year Clinics Football Manual* by Jackie Sherrill. Jackie Sherrill was a great defensive coach, and he said you play defense with two contain ends and a safety in the middle of the field. Everything else was horse manure.

I went 15 years thinking that is what you did. We had success with it over the previous 15 years. When we started going against four down offenses, we changed everything. Now, we spill everything. We are not a contain team. We no longer have a safety in the middle the field. We play split safeties. It was the total opposite of what I had known before, and out of my comfort zone.

Again, we are a spill and splatter team. We are doing everything we can to get the running back going east and west. Then, we are going to run his butt down. We are going to spill everything that you run, unless you are running right over center. The key point to this is if you are playing quarters, your safeties better come up and splatter the play. If you do not have good tackling safeties, you are not going to be good in this defense. We play linebackers at safety. Our best player on defense was a safety.

Everything starts with the defensive line. If you are going to play four defenders up front, you have to have good defensive linemen. We have been fortunate in that we had—and will have—some big kids up front. You have to have players who can hold the point of attack. We averaged 270 pounds on the defensive line. One of our opponent's coaches said, in an interview, we could show movies on the jerseys of two of our defensive linemen.

A couple of years ago, we went to hear Chuck Martin, who was at Grand Valley State University at the time, speak about pursuit angles and eliminating cutbacks on defense. We have all done the drill, where you pitch the ball out and have a running back run down the sideline. You tell your defense to pursue at an angle to where they think the ballcarrier is going to be. We do not teach it that way anymore. This was new and something that I was not accustomed to doing.

We talk a lot about how guys fit in on the run. In our old odd-stack defense, we were blitzing and playing games so much, I did not feel as if we had a good fit. We just had guys running around. If we blitzed and missed the ballcarrier, we did not have anyone with that responsibility.

Film work is important for us. We watched film every Monday or Tuesday with our players this year. We brought pizza in, and it cost me $1,500. If you tell moms and math teachers you are keeping kids until eight o'clock to watch film, you get a lot of complaining about it. If you tell them you are having a team dinner, all of a sudden you are a good guy. We had a team dinner every week where we watched film for two hours. We went through a lot of pizza this year.

We asked ourselves, "Can we make this film study more productive if we start using cut-ups?" What if we used cut-ups of the opponent's best plays? That way, you are not watching a whole film. We do cut-ups of the opponent's best five running and passing plays. You think kids are paying attention for two hours, but they are not. They are texting their girlfriends in the corner. If you give them pizza, you get them to pay attention for 20 or 30 minutes, especially if you have something good to say.

The strength and speed program we have has been very beneficial to us. If you talk to anyone who played us this year, they will tell you we were stronger and in better condition than they were. It is not because I am a genius or a great coach; it is because we had great athletes. We created some of them in the weight room and in the off-season program. You do not play defense for us and not train. We are going to take our toughest and best kids in the weight room, and put those 11 guys on the field and let them play defense. You have to have 11 guys on defense who are tough, physical, and can pursue the ball. Our players give us tremendous effort, and it starts in the weight room, not on Friday night.

At this point, I want to introduce my defensive coordinator, Coach Troy Ayotte, to tell you how we work our defense.

TROY AYOTTE, DEFENSIVE COORDINATOR

Thank you, Coach Pennington. Coach Pennington has the philosophy we are going to be a tough football team and going to be tough on defense. We talk about it quite a bit. As far as our staff goes, I have had the same staff with me since I have been at Zeeland East. It has been very instrumental to our success. All of our coaches really believe in the 4-3 defense, and enjoy the process of putting in and implementing this defense. I am the defensive coordinator, and I coach the defensive backs. Now, if the pass is over our defensive backs' heads, I can only yell at myself. I also coach the line on the offensive side of the ball.

As we said before, we spill everything. After we spill everything, we fill in by building what we call a picket fence. We tell our players we play defense one board at a time. We do not want players stacked on top of each other. We want to see boards, making offensive players go east and west.

Everything I have on the 4-3, I have stolen from somebody else. Shannon Wilson at Southlake Carroll High School in Texas runs this and does a great job. He has some good information out there on this defense. I have taken information from a lot of other coaches as well. The *2009 Coach of the Year Clinics Football Manual* has information about the 4-3 spill defense. In addition, Norm Parker at the University of Iowa is a very good resource.

On Sunday, I delegate responsibility to all of the defensive coaches. I identify any dropback passing routes and passing concepts. The first thing I do is draw up their top five passing routes. We are a quarters team, which is a zone match team. We line up in zone and then we match up man coverage as the play develops.

Our defensive line coach works to stop all the opponents' best interior runs. He develops the drills that are going to help us stop them. He looks at personnel and players we can go after, as a weak link. He looks at match-ups. He looks at their pass blocking schemes. This is important because we do not blitz. We practice with our down four to get pressure on the quarterback. If we can get pressure with four, that puts offenses in a tough situation.

Our linebacker coach works to stop play-action concepts, screens, draws, and goal-line sets. Play-action can give a defense that plays quarter coverage a dilemma. You have to decide, going into the week, what you are going to do. You have to study film to see what the other team wants to do and then make decisions as a staff on Sunday about how to stop it.

When we pull all of that together, we come up with their top five pass and top five run plays. This is what we are going to use to practice against at the beginning of the week. Following is our philosophy for the 4-3 defense:

- *Our aim is to be an aggressive attacking defense.* We do not blitz. We come after people. We line up the same, but we do not do the same thing every time. We read and react, and we are a stimulus-based defense. I explain to our players, I am coaching you and I trust you. Pull the trigger. I do not want players doubting themselves. You have to coach doubt out of them. This is why we keep things simple.
- *We believe in a "stop the run first" approach to defense.* This is nothing new for anybody.
- *We must have the ability to "affect" the quarterback.* No matter what offense we play against, if we rattle the quarterback, it is a less effective offense.
- *In order to be a successful defense, we must have 11 players who commit themselves to running to the ball.*
- *We will have simple and clear weekly goals.*
- *First and last, win the game.*

We never use a force player as a deep defender. Whoever forces or hammers the play back or gets the last spill in the splatter is never a deep defender. When I put things together, I keep this in mind. We protect the middle of the field. We always force the shortest and the widest.

We leverage the flats; we do not cover the flats. We never guard a zero or a one-yard route; we leverage it. When we go against a lot of passing, I coach our players: "No posts or pipes." I want our safeties to stay sticky with each other. If we are going to force the shortest and the widest, we have to keep those guys in the middle. You have to coach against posts in the middle if you are going to run this defense.

We have goals we try to achieve and give our kids something to aim for.

WEEKLY GOALS

- *Win!*
- *Allow less than 3.5 yards per carry.*
- *Allow less than 17 points per game.*
- *Recover three turnovers each game.* We stress this and do a lot of drill work during the week.
- *No big plays (15-yard run/25-yard completion).*

This is one reason we went to the 4-3 defense. We wanted to make them earn it.

- *50 percent or higher three-and-out.* Coach Pennington wants the ball back. He figures if we get enough plays on offense, we are going to win the ballgame.
- *Hold opponents to seven yards or less per catch.*
- *Hold opponents to 250 yards or less total offense.*

One of my favorite sayings is: we play defense, not defenses. We do not scheme a bunch; we are a stimulus defense. In the high school setting, I think addition by subtraction makes us better. What I mean by that is: by staying simple, it makes us better. Everybody knows what a white flag is. It signifies surrender. We named our defense the black flag. Our kids take the black flag with us everywhere we go. Right now, it is in our weight room. Our players make it, take care of it, and bring it out onto the field. They really like it and take pride in it.

WHY QUARTER COVERAGE?

When I first thought about running quarters defense, I thought college football and playing soft coverage. Now, I have embraced it.

- *Allows for nine players to play the run.* It allows us to play nine players in the box. We can play our safeties in double robbers. Our conference is a run conference. We are in a lot of nine-man fronts because of it.
- *Allows for a false quarterback read.* We run a matching zone. It is hard to tell if we are in zone or playing man. It messes with the quarterback.
- *Work one coverage, and master it.* We do not have a lot of time during the week; this makes it easier to coach.
- *Play one coverage that unfolds differently versus each route the offense runs.* Things change from week to week. We will man or zone based on what our opponent is doing for that week.
- *More interceptions because you have more eyes on the quarterback and subsequently on the football.*

Let me show you our base alignment (Diagram #1). We are a 4-3 defense. Here we are in cover 4.

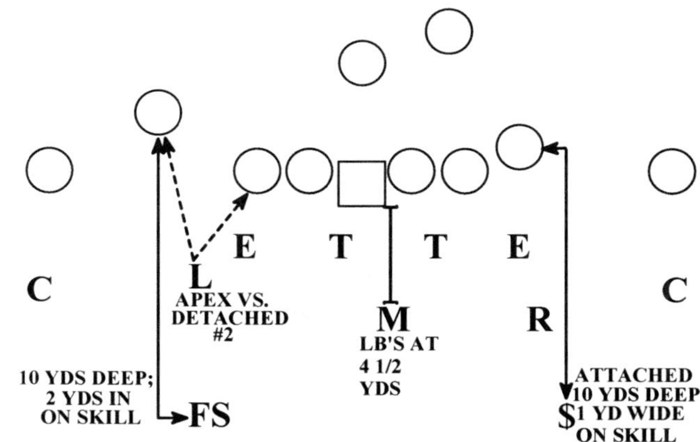

Diagram #1. Base Alignment, 4-3 Cover 4

We are in 1 and 3 techniques with our defensive tackles. On the tight end side, I believe in a 7 technique, partly because I am the defensive backs coach. This allows us to have a trigger for our safety in quarter coverage. If the tight end touches the defensive end, pull the trigger. It tells my safety he is coming right now. He is going to be the first board of the picket fence. If you line up your defensive end in an 8 or 9 technique, you cannot get a good read for your safety. The backside defensive end is in a 5 technique.

We apex or split the middle with our linebacker on a detached #2 receiver. This can change on a weekly basis and on down-and-distance. On run plays, the left and right linebacker spill plays, and the Mike linebacker plays over the top. Our down defensive lineman and our Lou and Rob linebackers run to the inside hip of the ballcarrier. The safeties are splattering. We do not flip-flop anybody. We have a Lou and a Rob linebacker. Lou and Rob cannot let the #2 receiver inside of them. We need to protect the middle of the field.

The corners have the #1 receiver, no matter what. We play two types of coverage with our corners. We play a clue technique, which is seven yards off and slightly inside, and we read the tackles. We run against a lot of spread option, and I know the tackle is a great read. If the tackle goes across the line of scrimmage, it is a run. We man-press out of quarters, too.

The safeties have the #2 receiver, once he passes the linebacker. That way, we do not have any confusion as to who has that responsibility. The safety knows to pick up #2, after he passes a linebacker in his drop zone area. We are in a match zone on #2, inside. We start our linebacker's four-and-a-half yards off the ball. The Mike linebacker opens up to the #3 receiver, in this case, the running back.

Our safeties line up based on the offensive formation. If the #2 receiver is attached to the offensive line, we line up 10 yards deep and one yard wide. If the #2 receiver is detached, we are two yards inside and 10 yards deep. We do not line up based on the field. We line up based on the offensive formation.

A WEEKLY SNAPSHOT: MAIN THEMES

Saturday

- Watch film at home. Our game film for corrections and any available scout film for the next week's game.

Sunday

- Staff meeting at 4:00 p.m.
- All film is ready to go by 4:00 p.m.
- Defensive line coach handles all film.
- Watch our game film once for corrections. I tell our kids that game film is like medicine; it is not supposed to taste good, but it is supposed to make you better. When we watch what we did on Friday night, we are just reporting the news.
- Watch all available film on our next opponent.
- Linebacker coach cards scout plays.
- We think in two terms on Sunday night.
  - ✓ Formations we will see.
  - ✓ Top five run and pass plays we have to stop.

Monday—Feel Good Monday

- Primary goals: Formation recognition and film.
  - ✓ Half of our time lining up to formations we might see.
  - ✓ Align and assign motion/shifts.
  - ✓ Opponent's game film and cut-ups of best five runs and five passes. Pizza and film.

Tuesday—Tough Tuesday (a.k.a. Teach 'em Up Tuesday Sub-Group and Team D)

- Primary goals: Implementation with contact
  - ✓ Individual drills
  - ✓ Sub-group
  - ✓ Run fit at thud tempo
  - ✓ Team with full contact
  - ✓ Pursuit

I stole the sub-group concept from our offense. It allows maximum repetition and technique time for a unit versus scheme, based on the needed skill set for the week. Do not confuse this with individual time that works more on individual techniques.

We can break out our defensive backs and linebackers and have them work on the corral drill and 7-on-7. At the same time, the defensive line can work on their trap breaker drill, pass rush techniques, and tackling progressions.

When I break down an opponent, I find out what percentage of runs versus pass they run. We run fit 70 percent of our time in sub-group. This is how the two sub-groups break down. We have run fit, and we have 7-on-7. When we do run fit, I have defensive lineman, linebackers, and the two safeties with me. We go against the five cards. We just practice fit repeatedly. We react to what we see, and we fit to it.

On Monday and Tuesday, and sometimes Wednesday, I will take the whiteboard into the defensive huddle, draw up each play, and show our players how they fit into the run. It takes a heck of a lot of time, but it gives our players a visual on where they are to fit in on the run. We went 11-1 this year, so we are going to do it again next year. Our players fit into the run a lot better because of it. Then, we run 7-on-7 the other 30 percent of the time. I have linebackers, safeties, and corners.

If we are working on run fit, the corners are working 1-on-1 against the #1 receiver. I have them with another coach. They are working their press-man, and they are working their off man with their reads. Then, we flip-flop it. When we run 7-on-7, the defensive line coach works on pass rush with the defensive lineman. This allows us to get in more work rather than running team periods.

One of the pass drills we use is the corral drill (Diagram #2). It is what we do when the ball is completed, and where we fit and what we do. You almost have to be a split safety team in order to do this. I do this at the beginning of 7-on-7 and figure out what spot the ball is likely going, based on our opponent's tendencies. We throw the ball there and figure out how we are going to converge on that spot. If you have a long pass, it is probably because of the cutback. This drill helps against cutbacks.

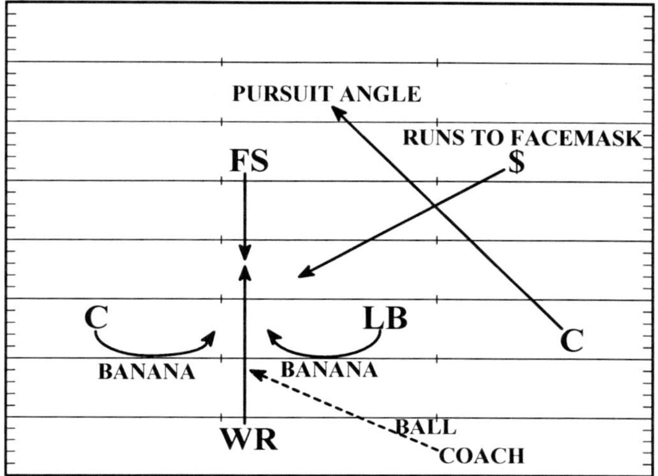

Diagram #2. Corral Drill

The free safety ladders down and has to make the ballcarrier stop. The corner and the linebacker banana back to the receiver on their back hip, to guard against the cutback. We are not great at it yet, but our yards after catch (YAC) have come down. We are going to keep working on it. This drill has helped us in that regard.

When we start our 7-on-7, we always start with the corral drill, and we get the ball to the position on the field where we think our opponent will be throwing. Our players will learn to go to spots for that opponent. The backside corner runs over the top, and the other safety runs to the face mask of the receiver.

After I saw this drill at a clinic, I went back and looked at some of my old tapes. Most of our long passes were cutbacks. The wide receiver would wiggle around, cut back across the grain, and make it a large gain. We work on this three to four times a week, maybe 150 times per week. It takes a lot of work. The safety assumes the ball is going to be pushed to him. The hard part is getting the linebacker not to go to the ball, but to force the ball into the safety.

Tuesday is our big hitting day. We get real physical on Tuesday.

Wednesday—Team D and Punt Defense

Because of the rugby punt, punts are a defensive play for us.

- Primary goals: Iron out the wrinkles.
  - ✓ Sub-group
  - ✓ 7-on-7 review with possible tricks
  - ✓ Defensive line varies by the opponent
  - ✓ Run fit at thud tempo
  - ✓ Limited team
  - ✓ Goal line

I do not put in our defense for trick plays right away. I wait until Wednesday to put those in. We have to make sure we have our five core plays defended. I will also put in any touchdown plays they have had that are not part of their five-core run or pass plays. We show the team these plays in our 7-on-7 drills on Wednesday.

Thursday—Thud Tempo and Prevent Defense, Go Through Game Scenarios

- Primary Goals: Have no doubt in our plan! We want to make sure our players are going to "pull the trigger" in the game.
  - ✓ Doubt is a heavy burden to bear!
  - ✓ Game plan review
  - ✓ Goal line review
  - ✓ Prevent

Friday—Game Night

Friday night is when the fur flies.

I want to thank everybody for your attention. It has been a pleasure to be with you today. If we can be of help, let us know.

Lance Pogue

THE EIGHT-MAN FRONT WITH ADJUSTMENTS

South Panola High School, Mississippi

It is a pleasure to be here. I have never been to this part of the country before. My assistant coach and I drove up here yesterday. We are 50 miles south of Memphis in Batesville, Mississippi. We drove from Memphis to Nashville and from Nashville to here. It was a beautiful drive and I am happy to be here.

The four years I have been at South Panola High School, we have had the good fortune to have good defensive linemen. If you play a four-man front, that is critical. We have been flexible in an eight-man front scheme. We will be 4-3 at times and other times some 50 front schemes. We play the over front. In the secondary, we play some cover 2 and cover 3. We also play the cover 3 alignment to get into some man free defenses.

My topic is defending the spread from the eight-man front. I want to give you some general thoughts before I get into what we do. We have some beliefs I want to share with you.

BELIEFS

- Being physical
- Creating turnovers
- Establishing field position

Everyone in this room knows the importance of being physical. To be a high caliber defensive football team, you have to be physical. If you are physical, you have the opportunity to create turnovers. From a defensive standpoint, establishing good field position is tremendously important. You want the offense to have to drive a long way to score. If you can get turnovers, that gives your offense the short field.

In our defensive scheme, we want to be *flexible*. If we play a two-back, power-running team, we need to have the flexibility to get into alignments that give us the best chance against that type of team. If we play a spread, four-wide offense, we need the flexibility to get into some coverage that will stop that type of offense.

On defense, you must keep it simple and let the players execute. In my opinion, we put too much emphasis in coaching. We put too much emphasis on something that looks good in the coaches meeting. It is not what the coach knows; it is what our players know.

Your defense, in addition to being flexible, must be *multiple in looks and pressures*. That is nothing original but I think it is critical.

I am going through different areas of our defense. After that, we will get into some schemes. We want three things from our front four.

FRONT FOUR

- Get off ball/attack
- Penetration
- Pass rush with four

The first two items are important, but the third thing is critical in defending a spread team. We have to be able to get pressure with our front four. We have the ability to rush three, four, five, six, or seven. I do not like to bring seven because that puts us in zero coverage and I do not like that. We have ways to get pressure. Stating the obvious, if you can get effective pressure with the front four, you are dealing the cards.

If you have to use extra blitzing to get the pressure, your coverage will suffer and the control goes back to the offense. Next year, we play Hoover High School in Alabama. Coach Josh Niblett is here and I am sure he is writing down everything I say. However, it is not what I say that is important. The players we put on the field make the difference. We cannot go to Hoover and blitz every down. If you do, they will have an answer for the blitz. You have to be multiple and you must be able to get pressure from your fount four if that is going to be your scheme.

LINEBACKERS

- Mike: Fit (A/B gaps), daylight
- Will: Adjuster

The Mike linebacker fits in the A and B gaps. Anything beyond that is gravy for us. That is all we ask from the Mike linebacker. The Will linebacker is the adjuster, and as we get further into the scheme, I will show you that. We do many things with the Will linebacker. On one play, he may align as a true linebacker, and on the next play, he is on the hash mark.

SECONDARY

- Strong safety/Rover: one has to be a man cover guy, other can use to blitz
- Cornerbacks: zone/man
- Free safety: hitter/cover guy

I am not trying to be funny when I say this is us in a nutshell. When we are looking for players, this is the position we try to identify. Our strong safety/Rover is the same thing. The strong safety travels to the strength of the defense and the Rover goes to the weakside. One of those players has to be a man cover player and the other has to be good on the blitz. If you have two players that can do that equally, that is great. However, for us to play effective defense, we have to find two players that can do those things.

The corners play zone and man coverage. We play cover 2, cover 3, and man free coverage. In a perfect world, at the free safety, we need a player that can cover and be a hitter. We have a sophomore right now that will be a junior and is probably one of the best players in the country at that position. He is 6'2" and 195 pounds. He played free safety and was a starter as a freshman. We moved him to strong safety last year to get him closer to the action. Next year, he will be the quarterback. We will move him back to free safety to take some of the physical play off him.

Do not let anyone tell you that you cannot use players both ways. We are in the 6-A class in Mississippi. Although we have a small population in the state, there is good football played there. Our top 10 or 12 football players every year will match up with anybody's.

Everyone knows that good football players make us all better coaches. I want to slide into our package and talk about it. We are very simple. We play with an eight-man front and a free safety. With the eight-man front, you will be a three-deep secondary or a man free team. The better you are at disguise, the better you can play.

The other part of the package is a two-safety scheme with a 4-3 front. In our 4-3 look, we are an over front. We have the capability of getting into an odd man front but the secondary will not change. If we go to the odd front, it is the 3-3 stack, which puts us back into a free safety look.

With our eight-man front, we load the box and get an extra defender. With eight men in the box, it gives us many ways we can pressure.

In the eight-man front, if we get formations with a tight end, we play a 7 technique or 6 technique with our C-gap defender (Diagram #1). We play a 3-technique tackle to the tight end side. We play the nose tackle in a shade to the backside. He plays in a 1 technique. Some people call it a 2i technique on the guard. If there is not a tight end to the backside, we play a 5-technique defender.

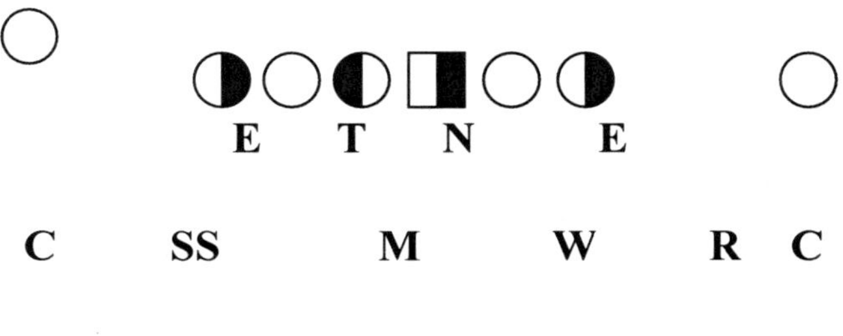

Diagram #1. Eight-Man Front

We play with a Mike linebacker and he plays the A or B gap. We do something that is unique with our Will linebacker. We play the Will linebacker as the B-gap defender to the weakside but we have the ability to stack him behind the Mike linebacker. He is an extra fitter and is hard to block. If we play a spread team where the quarterback can run the ball, he spies and mirrors the quarterback.

The 4-3 is an over front defense. We play a cover 2 shell behind the front (Diagram #2). It is important in this scheme to disguise what you do. We do many things from our cover 2 shell. I believe if you have the ability, in an even front defense, to play a cover 3 and cover 2 look, you can play at a high level in cover 3 and cover 2. Your front has to be good and hold up to what they have to do. When you go to the cover 2 look, you still have the ability to get to an eight-man front from the cover 2 shell.

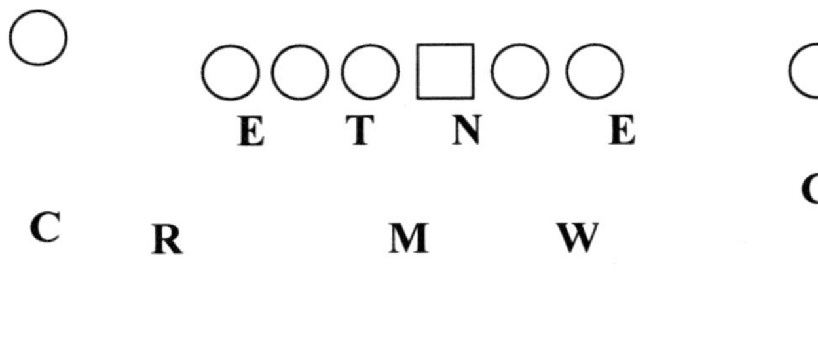

Diagram #2. 4-3 Cover 2

I think that is critical. If you play a 4-3 cover 2 defense, the offense will try to run the ball in the middle. If you can hold up, you can play the defense. If you cannot, you have to get into an eight-man front. The ability to be flexible is critical.

I talked about our free safety playing quarterback and players playing both ways. Playing players both ways means we get by with fewer reps with those players. I am a big fundamental coach and understand the importance of reps. To be the best football team we can be, we have to do it. That is especially true with our skill players.

We had a receiver this year that got involved in a big recruiting battle with The University of Alabama and The University of Mississippi. He signed with Ole Miss because it was close to his home. He was one of the best receivers in the country. We ran the Wildcat offense and got him the ball. However, we had to have him on defense. We played him as a cover player at corner or on the hash mark as a safety. He had tremendous ball skills. He did not require many reps because our scheme was so simple.

I know you can play athletes both ways and it makes you better. It is hot and humid in Mississippi but we get them in shape and utilize them. I know it is crazy to think about doing that with big, heavy linemen, but the skill personnel can do it.

OVER/4-3

- 2 shell
- Cover 4
- Make it look the same
- Very multiple in 2 shell

When we get in the 4-3 with the cover 2 look, we can drop down and play cover 4. The disguise has to be good. In a cover 2 look, you can get to an eight-man front on the snap of the ball. If you do a good job with the disguise, the offense will not know the difference from the look of the defense.

THREE-MAN LINE

- 3–3 stack (one safety)
- 3–4 look (two safeties)
- Change up/spread teams
- Coverage/calls stay the same

When we go to the 3-3 look, we take the least athletic defensive lineman out of the game (Diagram #3). We replace him with a linebacker/defensive back type and utilize the fact that we have more speed on the field.

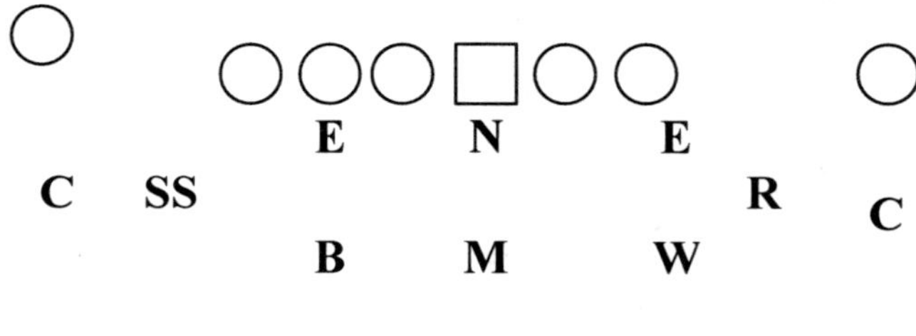

Diagram #3. 3-3 Stack

The defensive fronts are somewhat different, but from a coaching and teaching standpoint, it is the same. The terminology is consistent and simple.

DEFENSIVE LINE MOVEMENTS

- Cut 'er loose
- Heat up the offensive line
- Change techniques on snap

Playing this defense, you have to move the defensive linemen. We want to "cut 'er loose" in the defensive line. We want to put pressure on the offensive line. We want to change the defensive techniques after they snap the ball. We take the 3-technique defender across the face of the guard and into the A gap. Move the nose across the center's face into the A gap. We can put three different defenders into the strongside A gap. That will help the linebackers. Get the defensive linemen active. They like doing that.

That gets the defensive line's motor running, but it pressurizes a high school offensive line. Work hard on moving the defensive line from their normal alignment. I think it is a good deal and puts a lot of pressure on the offensive linemen.

PRESSURES

- Edge
- Gut
- Combo pressure with the defensive line

If you move the defensive line, you have to bring pressure from other places. We want to bring pressure off the edge and we can bring it up the middle. We can incorporate combination blitzes involving line movement with linebacker or secondary blitzes. When we get ready to play a spread team, we have to decide where we want to bring the pressure. That depends on what the offense can do and what they like to do.

DEFENDING SPREAD OFFENSES

- How much do they use the tight end
- True four wide
- Take away best running play
- Try to play cover 2 shell as much as possible—helps take away easy throws
- Set front to the running back; when the running back is in the gun, they have told you what they can and can't run

These things can be valuable to you. We found these things about the spread offense. The first thing I look for is how much they use the tight end. If they play with four wide receivers, are they all wide receivers? If the spread is an 11 personnel group, it makes a difference. With a tight end in the formation, there is an additional gap to control. When you begin to work your fits, you have to account for the extra gap. You need to know if the tight end is a pass receiver or just in there to block.

The third point is easier said than done. We want to take away their best running play. In my belief, you have to find a way to take away their best running play, whatever it may be.

We want to play the cover 2 shell as much as possible against a spread team. You have more pass defense in the cover 2 shell than the cover 3 scheme. We have played the same team three years in a row in the North Half championships in our state playoffs. Madison Central High School is a good team and they run the spread. They can throw the ball well. In addition to throwing the ball, they run every form of option known to mankind. We had more success defending them running a 4-3 scheme with a cover 2 shell. It takes away their easy throws and gets you in good shape to play the option.

When we play a spread team, we try to take away the cutback run from the zone play (Diagram #4). We do that by setting the 3-technique defender on the side that the running back aligns. If you set the 3 technique to that side, it takes away

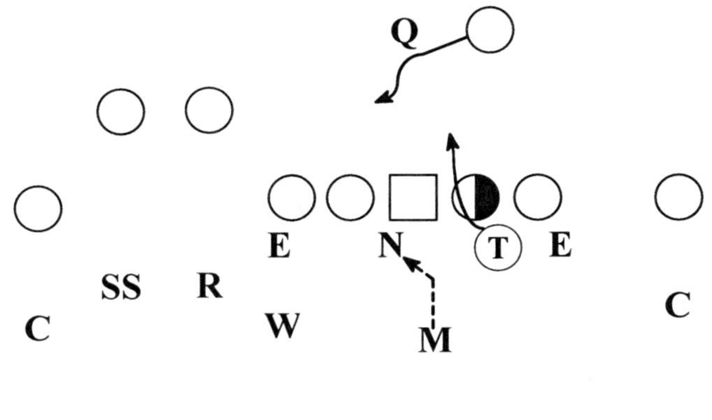

Diagram #4. 3 Technique to the Back

the cutback and forces the back to stay frontside with the ball. If you set him the other way, it gives the offense a cutback into the 1- and 5-technique defenders.

If they move the back after we align, we have no problem realigning the 1- and 3-technique defenders. All we have to do is stem down the line.

WHAT WE TRY TO IDENTIFY IN THE SPREAD

- Identify the quarterback (can he run or is he the primary runner?)
- What kind of running game with quarterback?
- Zone read/option
- How well does he throw the ball?

I think this is important. If the quarterback can run the ball and throw it too, you have some major problems. In high school, it is generally one or the other. It is rare to find a quarterback that can run and throw. Is the quarterback the primary runner, or does he run out of necessity? If we have a quarterback that is a running back, we want to load the box and force him to throw. If the quarterback cannot run but throws it well, you work in the other direction.

I know that sounds elementary, but that is how we prepare for every team we play. When we go into the Sunday meeting, these are the things we consider when we make the game plan.

DO THEY RUN OR THROW?

- Are they a check team versus a favorable box?
- What is their answer for pressure?
- What are their checks?

When we play a spread team, we want to know how they handle their automatics. If we can make the five-man box hold up against their run, you can make them one-dimensional. However, if they are good at checking their offense, you need to have an answer. We need to know what their answer is for pressure. A good football team will have an answer for your pressure if they cannot handle it. You need to know what they will do. Are they going to throw the screen or run the option? I think these things are critical when you put your plan for attack into action.

A favorable box tells the offense it is not loaded and there is a shortage of defenders in the box. They feel it is in their favor to run the ball into the box rather than to try to throw it on the perimeter. If they are a check team, your disguise has to be good. If the quarterback does not check to the right play, he has a bad play. That puts a lot of pressure on the quarterback. If he checks out of a run and into a pass in high school football, there is going to be an opportunity for us. We do not want to change our disguise until after the snap count. We look for these things when we play spread teams.

When we scout, we want to know where they align their best wideout. Most spread teams put their best receiver to the single receiver side. You need to know how to play him. Good teams will find ways to get their best receiver in a position so the defense cannot get their hands on him. They move him off the line of scrimmage or put him in motion to avoid all the hand checks and double-teaming. You have to plan for that.

If they have four good wide receivers, you are in trouble. Most of the time, high school teams do not have multiple wide receivers that can catch the ball. If one receiver is the go-to player, you need a plan.

OFFENSIVE LINE

- Can they block us consistently?
- How do they handle movements?
- Do they get to linebackers?
- Edge protectors?
- Look for heavy/light stances (high school kids)

If the offensive line cannot block us consistently, everything shifts to our advantage. If they can handle us consistently, you start thinking about pressure schemes and movement. We want to use movement to see if they can handle what we do on the defensive line. If they cannot block your linebacker, they have problems.

The edge protectors must have some talent to block the defenders we have coming off the edge. We are not big at the 5-technique end but he has speed. He comes off the edge well. Our 5 technique is 6'1", 215 pounds, and runs a 4.7. He is a pass rusher and we do not worry too much about his size.

In Mississippi, we do not play teams that line up in a two-back set and run at you. That is our style of play on offense. We want to line up and hit you in the mouth. We do not worry too much about size on defense. We want ability and speed on the field. If they take a bad step or their technique was not perfect, their speed overcomes that mistake. We try hard to coach techniques and fundamentals but these are high school kids.

The last point is a fact in high school football. When the linemen get tired, they tip everything they are going to do. You must coach it and be aware of it when you see it. You have to coach it and get your players to focus on it. That gives you an edge on the offensive blocker.

We are a downhill running team on offense and we want to stop the run on defense. We run the ball and are physical doing it. We are very multiple in formations but we only run four or five plays. In some years we are better at running the inside zone and not so good with the outside zone. When that happens, we put that one on the shelf and run the other one. We run the power and counter so we can gap scheme block it.

The point I am trying to stress is the defense takes the personality of what they work against in practice. If you want to be a physical defender and your offense is a finesse type offense, it is hard to become a physical defense. If you do not focus on what you want to be, you will become soft on defense. If the offense is a hard driving running team as we are, the defense takes on that personality and meets force with force.

The offense services the defense by being physical. If all you do in practice is pass rush and cover passes, you lose what you want to be. When you do play that team that wants to punch you in the mouth, it is hard to change gears. Every Monday, we have 10 plays of inside drills. We will be smart about it, but it could be the week of the state championships and we still will do it. We blow the whistle quick and hope we do not get anyone hurt but our players believe in it and we do it.

This is my fourth year at South Panola High School and we are 58-2. The reason we win like that is good players, not because of our coaching. We were fortunate this year. When we finished in December, we still had the same lineup we started with in August. We had no injuries and you know how big of an asset that was. I think if you can stop the run on defense and run the ball on offense, that makes you a physical football team.

This year, our strong safety was our leading tackler. The year before, it was the Will linebacker. He played in the box or on the hash. Two years ago, the Mike linebacker led the team in tackling. The point is that it is not one position that makes all the plays. Everyone has that chance because we penetrate and play aggressively.

In the state championship, we played Meridian High School, who was 14-0 and had a good football team (Diagram #5). They had a quarterback as the primary runner. We took the Will linebacker and stacked him behind the Mike linebacker and mirrored the quarterback, and he became the extra fitter on the defense.

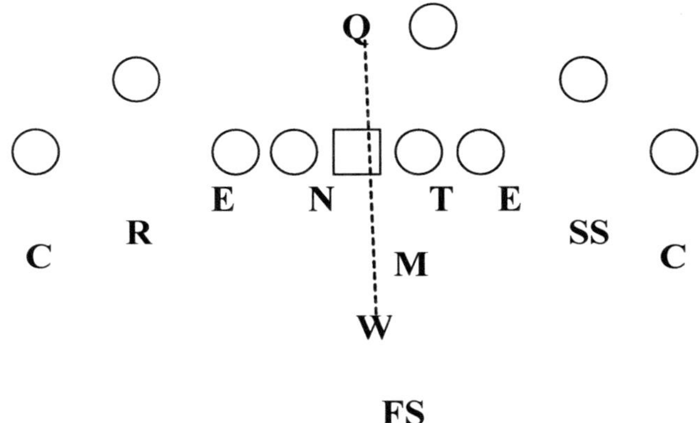

Diagram #5. Will Stack

In the secondary, the strong safety and Rover back align on the slot receiver and collision them if they try to release vertical up the field. We can play man free from this alignment or cover 3.

We use line movement along with linebacker blitzes to confuse the blocking of the offensive line (Diagram #6). One of our favorite movements is to bring the shade noseguard across the face of the center. He fills the strongside A gap and the Mike linebacker comes behind him into the weakside A gap. We call the stunt "Wildcat."

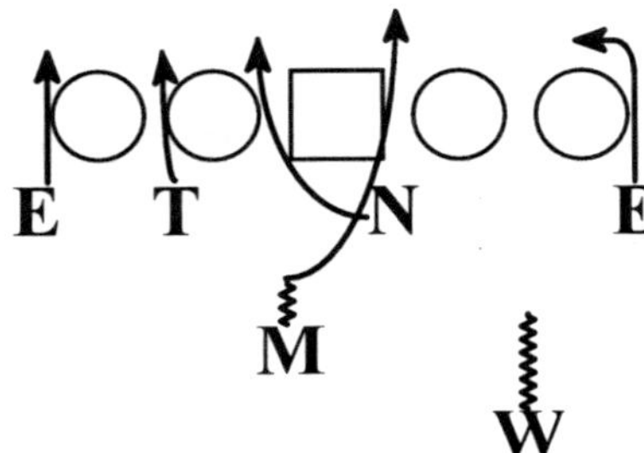

Diagram #6. Wildcat

Another stunt we use is the edge stunt by the strong safety (Diagram #7). The defensive end comes under the offensive tackle and becomes the B-gap player. The 3-technique tackle slants inside the guard and takes the A gap. The strong safety holds his disguise and comes off the edge at the last second. The free safety rolls down and replaces the strong safety. If they run the ball to that side, the free safety becomes the contain man. We protect the Mike linebacker and he can fast flow on the ball. We want the defensive line to penetrate.

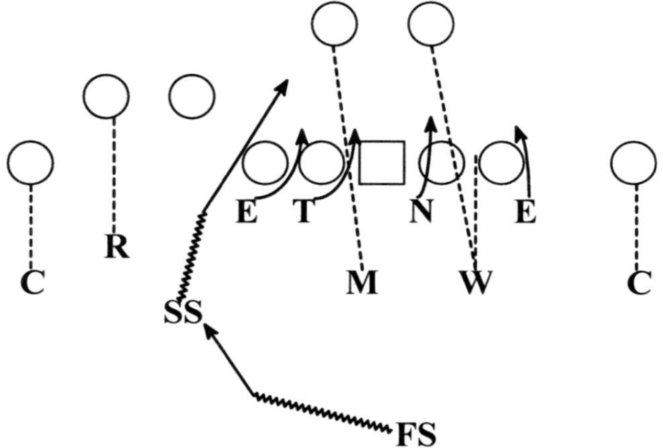

Diagram #7. Edge Smoke

When we run these little line movements, it cuts the defensive line loose and allows them to penetrate and make plays. The Mike linebacker and the shade nose exchange gap responsibilities and the Will linebacker plays soft and covers up in the middle. It is a simple but effective stunt. To make the stunt effective, the Mike fakes a blitz through his A gap. He gets the guard focused on his charge and at the last second pulls out and the shade player comes into that gap. The Mike blitzes the opposite A gap. Everyone has these types of stunts. It is a simple stunt but we turn the defensive line loose and let them make plays.

The last one I will show is the same stunt coming from the weakside of the formation (Diagram #8). We bring the Rover off the edge. The 5-technique defensive end goes inside into the B gap and the Will linebacker replaces the Rover coming off the edge.

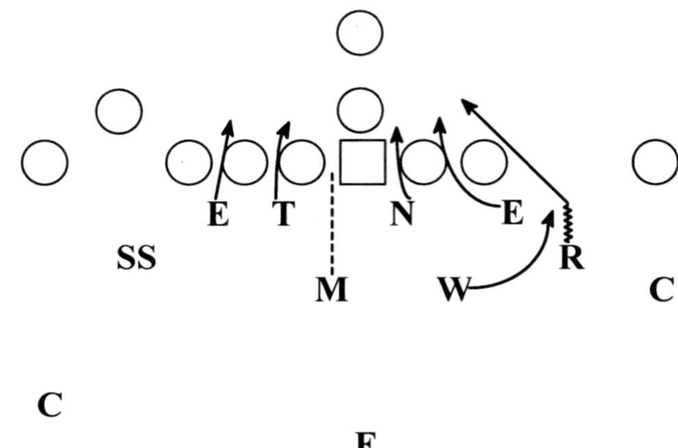

Diagram #8. Rover

The defense can be a multiple front team. It does not matter too much whether you are an odd or even front. The thing that does matter occurs in the secondary. That is the place where the confusion and breakdowns occur. You can be multiple up front but the secondary needs to have a consistent scheme. You need to scheme them up from a terminology standpoint where it is simple and not hard to understand. If we can pressure with the front and linebackers, it helps the secondary.

We have a lot of our defense coming back. We have all the front and linebackers, but we have a lot of work to do on offense. I appreciate what you coaches stand for. When football practice and the Friday night events are over, we are in the business of helping the players that play for us. The winning is good but that is not why we are in the game. There are a lot of things the kids can get into and there is not too much love out there for them. At times, we are the last guy they can lean on. Continue to fight hard to have a positive difference in their lives. The key is to keep fighting hard to help these kids make it in life. I appreciate your time and I enjoyed it.

Scott Reed

GUN RUN FROM THE PISTOL AND EMPTY SETS

El Dorado High School, Arkansas

Thank you. I am going to talk about our gun and run game, which is our pistol offense.

We have won back-to-back 6A state titles in Arkansas. John Painter, our defensive coordinator, and I went to El Dorado High School four years ago. The reason we went there was because El Dorado, Arkansas is the home of Murphy Oil Company. Murphy Oil had just endowed $50 million to our school to pay for our high school kids' college education. I have two sons. It made sense to me. My two sons will get between 65 percent and 75 percent of the highest annual in-state college tuition for up to five years, provided they pass 24 hours and keep a 2.0 or higher grade point average. This is awesome for us. It has helped our football program at El Dorado High School.

In 2009, we won the state title for the first time in 51 years. We went to our community and raised $600,000 to put in professional turf and a new scoreboard with a video screen for replays. It is first class. We have a positive atmosphere in El Dorado and it is a great place to be a football coach.

A year ago, and for the previous seven years, I had an offset backfield. The quarterback had his heels at five yards and we sat the tailback in the tackle's tracks with his toes at five yards. Then, like a lot of you, we started finding out more about the pistol offense. Last winter, I heard Chris Klenakis, the offensive line coach for the University of Arkansas, who they hired from the University of Nevada, Reno. We all know Nevada does a great job on the pistol, as Coach Chris Ault is the person that started the pistol offense. A lot of things he said made sense to me. There were things about our running game I did not like and had trouble with in the past. I went to watch Arkansas practice and saw things in the pistol that I liked.

It is hard to change things when you have been successful. Why try to fix something that is not broken? That, and the fact that we did not know about the pistol, made it difficult to make the change.

The way he explained it, and after watching his film, it just made sense to me. I knew our game had to evolve, so we jumped in with both feet. The debate we had was, if we were going to change, what were the advantages?

OFFSET ADVANTAGES

- Had been successful with offset and used it for eight years
- Kids in program had been raised up with it
- Back could get out on "free release" routes faster-closer to edge
- Back set closer to line and protections
- Tackle-pull series

As I said, we had been successful with the offset formation for eight years. Our players were used to lining up and used to the fundamentals and mechanics of it. It was faster for the back to get out on a free release. Another thing that I liked to do out of the offset was, what you probably call "dart," we call "T read," where you are pulling the tackle and reading the end from where he is pulling. We are still running T read from the pistol, but now we are doing it out of an empty set and having the quarterback carry the ball.

PISTOL ADVANTAGES

- Running back gets ball deeper, allows him to set blocks, increases vision
- Hides the running back
- Defense cannot set front based on alignment of back
- Hides protection keys

- Back aligns at same depth in "gun" or "under"—carryover in timing on run game (cut/read, power, counter)

We are a multiple personnel offense. We could be in the gun, or we could be under center. We can have no one in the backfield or run from a full backfield. We run the inside zone from under center. We run a zone read out of the gun. We block them very similarly and want to have some carryover. We run the following series out of our pistol offense:

- Zone read
- Stretch
- T read (dart)
- Power
- Nose
- Counter
- Flash (tie in with any series)

We can run the stretch play out of the gun. We have not been good at running the stretch. I found if we run a naked out of the gun, off the stretch, it gives people problems. The backer wants to come fast and we get a real good stretch on the backside backer in a hurry. If you take the quarterback, whose heels are at four yards, and you run the stretch, naked with pistol, it is difficult for the defense.

We run flash out of empty. We also will run our dart series where we pull the tackle. Also, we run a new play that we got from the University of Oregon out of our nose play.

The more we got into using the pistol, the more I liked running it. If you are debating or have not gone to it, I can tell you I am sold on it. Any time you change something, you probably are not going to like everything about it anyway. In the past, we had a problem of being consistent at our mesh point. When we went to the pistol, we only had one exchange problem.

We eliminated turnovers by going to the pistol. Defenses cannot base their front on keying an offset back. We come up to the line of scrimmage, and the defense does not know where we are going. We can run the option very easily and we do not have to move anybody. We can change the direction of the play without moving anybody. The defense does not know which direction we are going. That is a major advantage.

It hides our protection scheme. It messes up the way the defense keys our backs. It is a major pain in the butt for the defense, which is good for me. I will trade two steps for the defense not knowing which direction we are going for pass protection.

Following is the information I got from Coach Klenakis for the inside zone series out of the pistol:

- One-man game (running back gets ball, predetermined)
- Two-man game (quarterback and running back)
- Two-man with lead (cover 1)
- Two-man with double lead (cover 2)
- Three-man (triple option) (quarterback, running back, pitchback)
- Four-man (triple option with lead or load)

We have used the three two-man games and the three-man games at El Dorado High School. Our best success has been with the two-man combinations (Diagram #1).

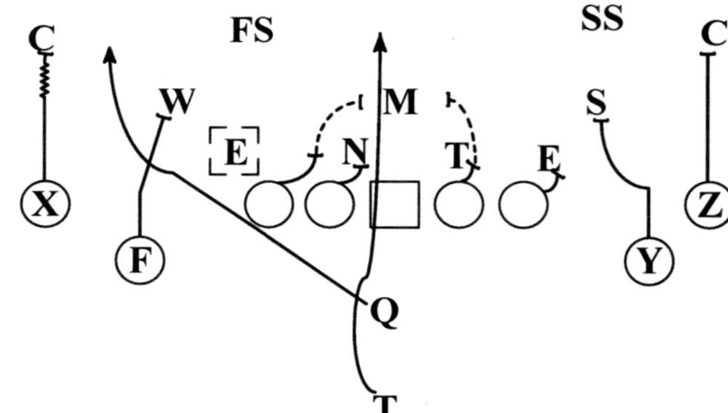

Diagram #1. Two-Man Game, Two High Safeties

We run the same play against the three-deep alignment. We are reading the end. If we want to give the tailback the ball, we call 42 read (Diagram #2). It is still the two-man game.

Against the two-deep look, if we need to account for the free safety, we can bring the Y-receiver in motion and pick up the free safety (Diagram #3). We can still run the play, we just have one fewer blocker outside if the quarterback keeps the ball.

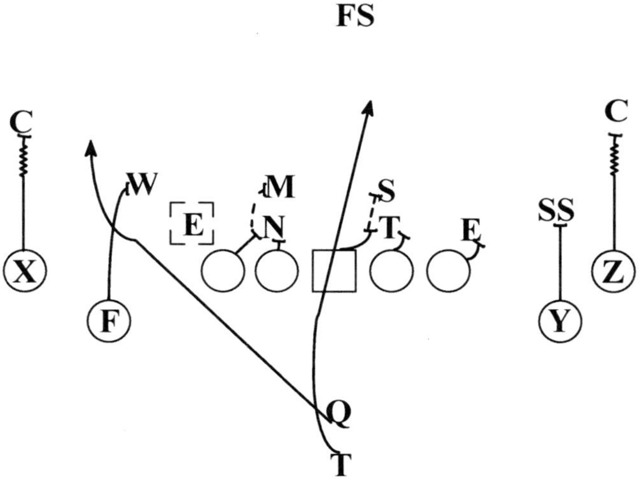

Diagram #2. Two-Man Game, One High Safety

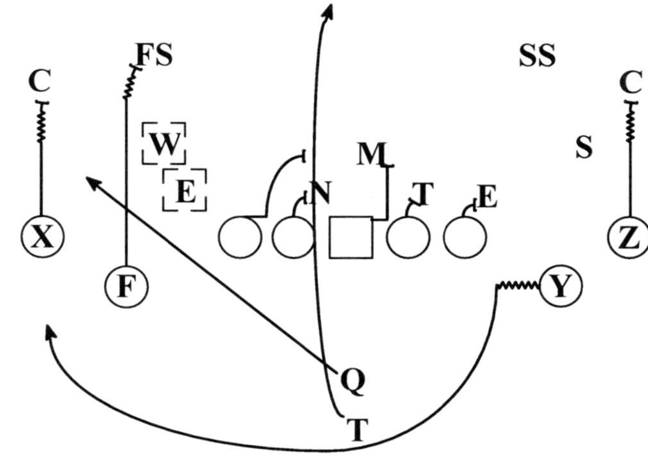

Diagram #4. Three-Man Game, Y Motion

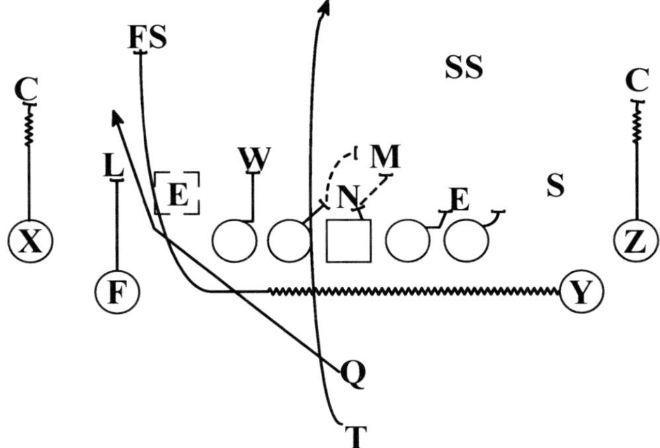

Diagram #3. Two-Man Game, Motion Y

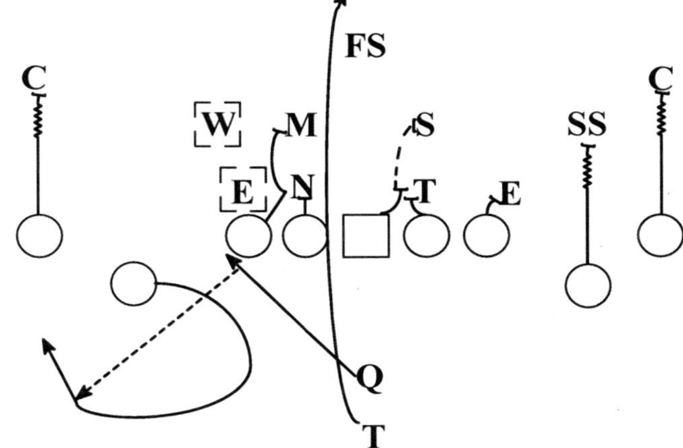

Diagram #5. Three-Man Game, F-Back Read

On the three-man game, we can run the play several ways. We can have the Y-receiver go in rocket motion and he becomes the pitchman (Diagram #4). We run the same play with one additional man in the option.

We can run the same play without having the Y-receiver going in motion. We can have the F-back counter away from the playside and curl back outside looking for the pitch from the quarterback (Diagram #5). We are reading the end man on the line of scrimmage. Now, we want to attack the outside shoulder of the pitch support.

We do not run the one-man game where it is predetermined. Coach Klenakis said he starts out running the option. We did not run much option this year because we did not feel we had the need to. We thought we were good enough offensively that we did not need to. We preach to the players to eliminate turnovers and fumbles.

If we had not been good this year and if we had to pitch the football all over the pasture, we would have. I know we would have had more turnovers, but if we had to, we would live with it. His thought is if you start out running the option, you should find a way to give yourself an advantage. A lot of what they called on offense, they based it on coverage. We had enough depth at running back this year that we could rest our running backs. This year, we ran the two-man game most of the time.

This is the most important part of teaching the pistol. This is taken verbatim from Coach Klenakis.

RUNNING BACK PRINCIPLES/RULES

- Has right to vertical push; only "opposite color" takes him off his track
- Take half of quarterback (nose through shoulder tip); must lateral step if running back is fast
- Work back to quarterback; running back must stay into quarterback and away from the defensive end.
- Always run as if you have the ball.
- Find the wall, space is not your friend, stay tight to the wall.
- Quarterback will read defensive end.

In the past, when we were in the offset and running the inside zone read, we taught our tailback to read from the 3 technique to the backside guy once we handed him the ball. Guys, it does not happen. We made it tough on him by asking him to read two defensive linemen after he had the ball. He was running to daylight. The other thing is, I do not want him to stop and look around. This is one of the best parts about going to the pistol. It teaches him to get on a track, and the only way he gets off track is if he sees the opposite color. It makes him more decisive.

We teach the tailback to run his nose right through the shoulder tip of the quarterback. It is almost like running power. The tailback does not have an aiming point on the line of scrimmage. He is running through the quarterback's shoulder and away from the defensive end. The quarterback has his heels at four yards. That one yard makes a big difference on the quality of the gun snaps you have.

We did not have any gun snap problems. The tailback is sitting with his toes at seven yards. That is the same place we put him when we are under center and in the I formation. He is in the same spot and his timing is the same. Now, he is running downhill rather than sliding and reading.

The quarterback will pivot and replace with his shoulder open so the back can go frontside if he wants to. That is what we mean by "he has the right to a vertical push." We do not want the quarterback forcing him to the backside A gap. We want the tailback to have the right to vertical push.

Our tailback is quick, so he has to take a vertical step. He is working back through the quarterback and away from the defensive end. We are going to make the defensive end commit in order to catch him. We do not pull the ball much, maybe 10 percent of the time. The end has to come flying to make the quarterback pull the ball. The ball is gone before that can happen.

Both the running back and the quarterback have to run as if they do not have the ball. They must carry out their fakes, depending on who has the ball.

We want to be right on the wall because it will hide the running back. We do not want him running to space, we want him as close to the wall as possible. We want it as hard as possible for the linebacker to find him.

QUARTERBACK PRINCIPLES/RULES LATERAL STEP TO SIDE (HOP TO OPEN), AND REPLACE

- Eyes to defensive end (read path and eyes of defensive end)
- Running back has the right-of-way to vertical push
- Extend ball early, bend knees
- Decision must be made by the time he gets to the front hip
- Run as if you have the ball

We tell the quarterback, when in doubt, give the ball to the tailback. We want the back to carry the ball. It is important the quarterback carry out the fake. We had a problem with it in the first game, but after we had a meeting, we got better.

OFFENSIVE LINE PRINCIPLES/RULES

Inside Zone Blocking Rules

- 6x2 inch step; stay square
- Covered: Stretch-base
- Uncovered: Stretch-double

Push the Front

- Create double-teams "clamps"
- No penetration (do not climb unless gap is threatened)

Backside Guard and Tackle

- Know who the quarterback "player" is
- Backside tackle is "married" to backside linebacker and must engage him square-up

In the past, when we were running the zone read, it seemed as if we were always catching the defensive linemen. Now, we come off the ball with a six-inch width step and a two-inch vertical step. We are now coming off the ball better. We make a big deal out of pushing the front. Our zone rules have not changed. If we are covered, we are to stretch base block. If we are uncovered, we are to stretch double-team block.

One reason why we have gotten better at blocking is because we are not leaving the double-team block unless we have a threat. This has been important for us. In the past, we were too quick to come off the double-team block to the linebacker. We work the double-team block as long as we can. We call them "clamps." We want to get as many double-teams as we can. When the linebacker comes to us, that is when we are going to come off. I am sold on the pistol offense because it has allowed us to have more push and, therefore, more space to run.

The backside tackle is married to the backside linebacker. It is important that the backside guard and tackle know who is responsible for the quarterback. We want to make sure our shoulders stay square.

WIDE RECEIVER PRINCIPLES/RULES

- Outside—Stalk/base the corner nose to the midline.
- Inside—Same technique as outside receiver; you have #2 outside the box. If no #2 outside the box, block the near safety.
- #3 receiver—Same technique and rule as inside, but you have #3.

We teach our outside receivers to stock the corner and put their nose in the middle of the defender. If it is press coverage, we run the defender off and then we block him. Our inside receiver is blocking #2 at less than 10 yards and outside of the box. If there is no #2, he is going to the near safety. The hard thing is, if you are running it against a 4-3 team and the linebacker is sitting outside the box, our #2 receiver has to go block him. The backside guard and tackle are not going to go get that guy.

This makes game planning important. We will make our play call based on where the defense plays their guys in the box. Sometimes we will run it to our 3x1 formation, and sometimes we will run it away from our 3x1 formation. It depends on where they put their guys in the box.

Sometimes we use a tight end and let him release to the linebacker. Again, it depending on how they line up in the box. We decide this during our film study for the upcoming week. We do not just run it from the same formation and personnel group every week. We have to find an advantage.

We tell our receivers to go and engage. If it is a run and they do not go engage a defender, we grade them at a minus. If their grade is not good enough, they have a problem. Our offensive linemen are engaged on every play. We expect our receivers to do the same. If they want to play for us, they have to be complete athletes and be able to block as well as catch.

The next thing I want to talk about is the T read. The good thing about running the T read out of the pistol is there is carryover for the quarterback and the tailback concerning their footwork.

T READ "DART" PRINCIPLES/RULES

Quarterback

- Same footwork as zone read.
- Same read as zone read.
- On Q-T, you read the defensive end and use running back rules for keepers.

When we run Q-T, it means the quarterback is the running back and our tackle is pulling on the play.

Running Back

- Same footwork as zone read.
- Same rules/points as zone read.
- Set in hip of pulling tackle and get vertical in same gap.

Wide Receivers

- Outside—Stalk/base the corner; nose to midline
- Inside—Same technique as outside receiver. You have #2 outside the box. If no #2 is outside the box, block near safety.
- #3 receiver—Same technique and rule as inside, but you have #3

Offensive Linemen

- Playside tackle—Covered: Stretch drive; Uncovered: Stretch double
- PSG—Covered: Stretch drive; Uncovered: Zone to backside linebacker
- Center—Zone backside A gap to backside linebacker
- Backside guard—Zone B gap area
- Backside tackle—Pull for playside linebacker; take first available gap
- Tight end—Playside D gap
- Backside—Zone D gap
- Do not touch read

On the T read, or dart, we are not getting the double-teams from the offensive linemen. We are back to blocking where we are catching. We do not run this play with a predetermined read. We always read everything in the past so we kept it that way. The rules for the offensive line carryover for odd fronts or even fronts.

The last thing I want to talk about is the nose man. We got this from Oregon last year. This is when we are running the stretch and reading the backside defensive tackle.

NOSE PRINCIPLES/RULES

Quarterback

- Signal back to initiate motion
- Get ball snapped with back outside backside tackle
- Read true nose versus odd front or backside tackle versus even front

Running Back

- Motion at 7/8 speed, slightly away from the line of scrimmage.
- Circle field; do not get vertical until opposite color takes you off your path.
- Flash rules apply. (Instead of reading the end, we are reading the defensive tackle.)

Receivers

- Block stretch, no crack
- Nose to outside number
- All flash rules apply
- 2H Offensive Linemen
- Playside tackle—Covered: Rip and reach (hat to outside armpit); Uncovered: Rip and reach to first removed down lineman; take first threat (hat to outside armpit)
- Playside guard—Same as above
- Center—Same as above
- Backside guard—Zone to backside linebacker
- Backside tackle—Turn out defensive end; hips work to inside

The playside tackle, guard, and center are running the stretch play. They are blocking an outside zone play. If we call 46 nose, we are running outside zone to the right. The backside guard and tackle are man blocking, leaving the backside defensive tackle alone so we can read him. I like to run this offense against a team that is very athletic.

My time is up. If you have any questions, I will be around. Thank you very much.

Jamie Riggs

BOOTLEG PACKAGE OFF THE COUNTER TREY

T.R. Miller High School, Alabama

I can see you are the real football coaches. You can handle getting up at this time of the morning, so you must be football coaches. I am very happy to be here. This is the first time I have been to the Northwest. They told me if I talked slowly, you could understand me. I am from Alabama and represent the Alabama Football Coaches Association. We have many good football coaches in Alabama, and we take pride in training our coaches. They do a good job for us. I represent over a 1,000 coaches. The association is doing some good things in trying to promote football in our state.

Our school is in Brewton, Alabama, which is eight miles from the Florida line. It is extreme south Alabama. We are a small school with approximately 360 students. I am originally from there, as I came back as the head coach, and have been there for 22 years. I do not stay there because I am from there. I stay there because of the situation. Our sport and fans are the best. Our players have good spirit. They work hard and love to play the game. The biggest thing in our community on Friday night is the high school football game. The community comes out, and it has been a great deal.

We have a rival in our area. The name of my school is T.R. Miller, and right next to us is East Brewton, Alabama. Their high school is W.S. Neal High School. I would not say we hate each other, but we do respect each other. We tolerate each other, play against one another in everything, and it means something to win the game when we play them. It does not get any better in high school football.

We have a shotgun intermarried situation with our community. Some of the parents of my players went to Neal High School, that other school. A creek separates the two communities. There is a bridge over the creek. The fitting name for the creek is Murder Creek. Every year, the last game of the season is the "Battle of Murder Creek." It does not get any better than that.

Five years ago, I had double bypass surgery. For years, I did not eat right or take care of myself, and I almost had a heart attack. Now, I go every year for a physical. I see a dermatologist every year. We have lost some fine football coaches to cancer and heart attacks. I talked to the doctor after the procedure. Everything he told me I should not do was like a picture of my life up to that point. If you want to stay in coaching and coach for a long time, take care of yourself. I want to encourage you to go every year for a physical and watch the skin in relationship to the sun. We have a tendency to take care of everyone else and not ourselves. I have been coaching for 33 years, and I have a bit of coaching left in me.

In coaching, we strive to do something better than anyone else does it. If you cannot do it, better do something different. I have run the counter trey play since the 1980s. I wanted to do it better than anyone else did it in our state. I am an I formation and a one-back kind of coach. I run the bootleg off this play, and I am one of two coaches in our state who run the play. It is different. The thing that makes it different: we use the guard and tackle to pull on the counter, and we do the same thing on the bootleg.

I got this idea back in the early 1990s. Dennis Erickson was the coach at Miami and went out to play Brigham Young University. He was in the one-back set and running the counter trey from that set. He ran a play, faked the counter trey, and let the quarterback run the ball away from the fake. He cracked on the defender assigned to the quarterback. The thing that impressed me was the fact that he pulled the guard and tackles, and ran away from them.

I thought if you could make the running play and the bootleg look the same, the defense could not tell the difference. I coached defense early in my career. When we started playing wing-T teams, I became fascinated with the offense. I found the concept was good, and when we played a wing-T team, the defense slowed down. All the misdirection drove us crazy. If you did not read your keys right, you were in trouble.

For years, I looked for a play you could run and did not have to block. I do not know whether it happens in Oregon, but it does in Alabama. After the game, the offensive line coach comes in, sits down in a chair, looks at you, and says, "We didn't block nobody tonight." One of my offensive line coaches came in and told me that one night. I told him, "I do not know about not blocking nobody, but our line sure did not block #78 because he kicked our tail all night long."

In Alabama, we have some good defensive linemen, and you had better have ways to deal with them because you cannot always block them. I found out it is easier to deal with those linemen when they run the wrong way. It was funny watching how many people were sucking into the counter play when we ran the bootleg.

We run the counter trey as a power off-tackle play (Diagram #1). We can run the play to the tight end or split end sides. To the callside of the play, we use a gap-blocking scheme. Everyone to that side blocks down. We pull the backside guard, and he kicks out the C-gap defender to the playside. The

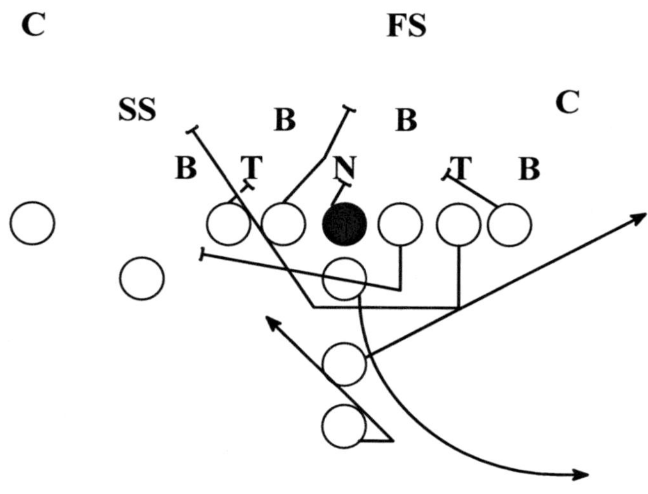

Diagram #1. 25 Counter Trey

backside tackle pulls, turns into the hole, and wraps up for the inside linebacker.

To the tight end side, the tailback takes a counter step and aims for the outside leg of the tackle. If he runs to the split end, his aiming point is the guard-tackle gap. He picks up the pulling tackle, gets on his inside hip, and follows him inside the kick-out block.

The quarterback extends the ball and sprints out. He does not come straight, but at a slight angle to the tailback. He extends the ball and hands it to the tailback. Most people want the fullback to go opposite the running back and block off the edge. I want the fullback to go to the flat area. That is where he goes when we run the bootleg.

We want to split the defense. The players to the run side are thinking about how to deal with the counter play. The defenders to the backside have to think about defending the bootleg. If we have an odd-numbered play, it goes to the split end side. The even numbers go to the tight end side. A 25 counter goes to the split end side. We flip-flop the offensive line. We can run a 25 counter to the left or right, depending on the location of the tight end.

We can run the counter trey from the I formation, offset fullback, or a one-back set. If the defense is in a 43 under alignment, the playside guard blocks down on the noseguard. We run a combination blocking scheme on the 5-technique defensive end to the backside linebacker. The center blocks back on the 3-technique defensive tackle. The backside guard pulls and kicks out the outside linebacker. The tackle pulls and turns up inside the guard's block and tries to wrap up on the inside linebacker.

If we run the play to the tight end side, we call it "26 counter" (Diagram #2). It is the same blocking, except the aiming point for the running back changes to the outside leg of the tackle. We get gap blocking inside, and most of the time we get some kind of combination block to the backside linebacker.

If we run 25 counter boot, we want the play to look like the counter trey (Diagram #3). We pull the guard and tackle into the split end side. We do not always pull the tackle. He may have to seal the edge with a reach block on the last defender. The playside linemen block the 25 counter trey. It is a

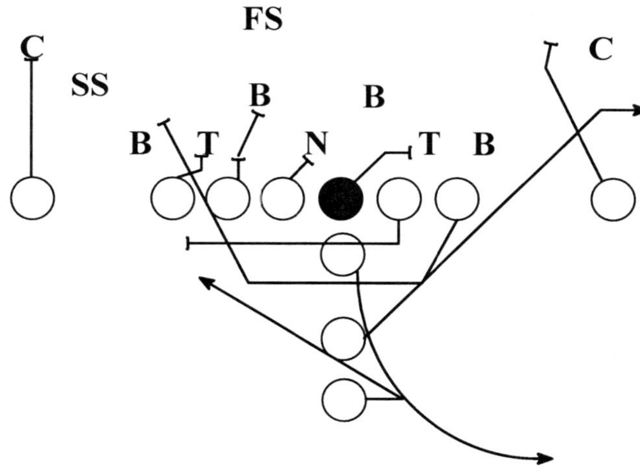

Diagram #2. 26 Counter

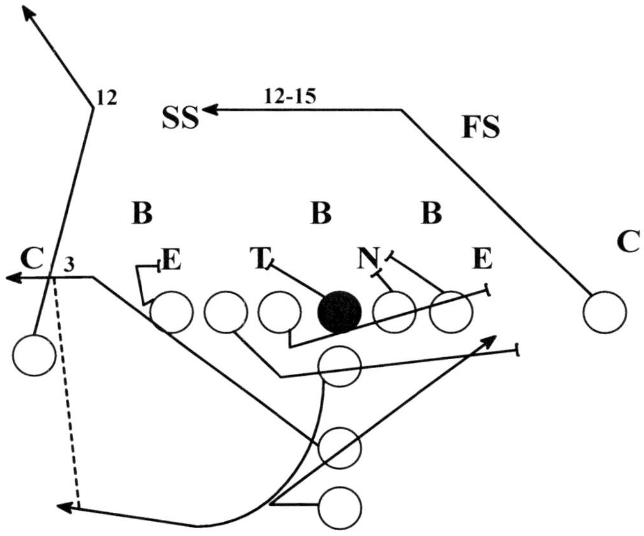

Diagram #3. 25 Counter Boot

running play for them. If their assignment takes them to a linebacker, they block down on the next man on the line of scrimmage. The pad levels of the offensive linemen have to stay down as they would in a run block. The center blocks back as he did on the counter trey, although the ball is coming that way. He blocks back so the defender will fight over him going away from the play.

The quarterback does exactly the same thing he did on the counter trey play, except he keeps the ball. The tailback does the same thing, and runs as if he has the ball. He rocks the baby and fakes the run. The fullback goes off the edge and into the flat area. He turns around at about three yards and looks for the ball.

The patterns for the other receivers are the standard patterns for a bootleg. The split end runs a drag pattern, coming across the middle. The wide receiver to the side of the bootleg runs a deep clearing pattern or a deep comeback.

The key to the play is to get the quarterback on the edge. If you can get the quarterback on the edge, good things are going to happen. You have to make one block to get the quarterback outside the backside contain defender. In this set, we reach the defender with the tight end.

If the tackle has no tight end, he may have to reach the 5-technique defensive end. The offensive tackle, instead of pulling, reaches the 5-technique defender. In Alabama, teams like to put the openside 5 technique in a wide-angle charge to the inside. The most effective technique we have found is to cut him down.

The best way to seal the edge is to do it with the wide receiver (Diagram #4). If we align in a twins set, we motion the slot receiver back to the inside and seal the edge. We bring him in motion, step him inside on the defensive end, and seal the contain defender.

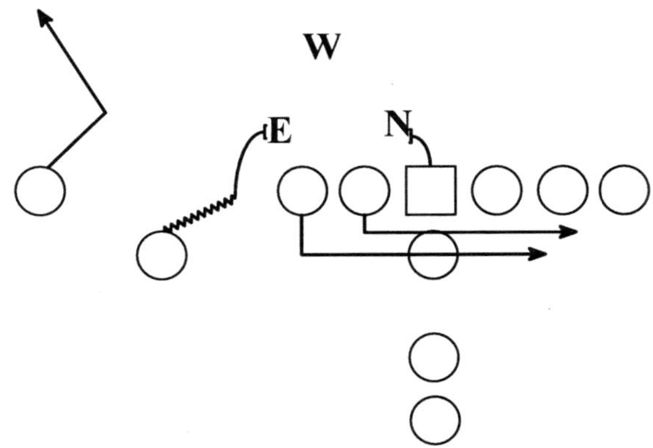

Diagram #4. Receiver Motion Seal

Those are the two ways to seal the edge on this play. If you seal the edge with the motion back, you can make the play look exactly like the counter trey.

I want to give you a couple of things to think about. You must insist the two plays look the same. I stay on the quarterback and running back to make the mesh and fakes looks the same. I think of it as one play. It does not bother me that I run the counter trey for only two yards. I know that the bigger chunk of yardage comes off the bootleg pass.

One thing I learned early on about running this play. If you run the bootleg and the linebackers cover the drag pattern, you need to run the counter. They are not attacking the line of scrimmage if they can cover the drag pattern. The general rule is to run two counters for every bootleg pass you run. We played 12 games, and we ran about 100 counters and 50 bootleg passes. That amounts to about 25 percent of our offense. Next year, I want it to be about 30 percent of the offense.

In my play calling, I have a simple rule: when in doubt, run the counter. If it is third-and-four and you are not sure what to run, run the counter. If it is first-and-10 and you are not sure what to run, run the counter. Every time you run the counter, it will pay dividends when you run the bootleg.

The bootleg is a great first-and-10 play. It is a great red zone play. People try to play man coverage in the red zone. I promise you, they have difficulty covering the fullback out of the backfield. We use this play as a two-point play. It is the single-best play to run on the first play of the game. The better the defensive team is, the better it is to run the bootleg on the first play of the game.

We do not run the bootleg on the first play of the game every week. I did it three or four times. If the defense loves to stunt and load the line of scrimmage, run the bootleg at them. The offensive linemen on the bootleg pass love to be actors. The thing they cannot do is get downfield. The guard has a block on the line of scrimmage with his kick-out block. When the tackle pulls, he cannot turn up. He has to continue to run down the line of scrimmage.

When we run the bootleg, the offensive linemen want to cut their splits to no more than two-foot splits. We want to bring the edges of the defense closer to the inside.

The quarterback extends the ball to the running back on the fake. The running back comes over the ball but does not clamp down on it. The quarterback pulls the ball and hides it on his inside hip. The next thing he must do is get his head and eyes around to see what is happening on his backside. The fullback runs hard to the flat area. The quarterback and running back are responsible for drawing the defenders. I want the fake to draw the linebacker and the secondary.

If we run a great fake, we draw eight people to the back faking the counter. On the first play in the "Battle of Murder Creek" this year, we drew 10 defenders. If you draw 10 defenders toward the counter when you are running the bootleg, it is a great fake. You have 10 defenders running the wrong way. That is what we want to be able to do.

If we do not think the 5-technique defender can be a threat to our quarterback, we run the bootleg naked. If our quarterback is faster and a better athlete than the defender playing that position is, we run it naked. If we do that, the quarterback has to be a good ball mechanic. He has to handle the fake and get the ball into throwing position on the run.

If you play a 3-4 slanting defense, on occasion the defensive tackle slants to the outside. If we pull the tackle and the defender slants to the outside, he can pressure the quarterback. The quarterback needs to learn to read the hot pattern. Before the quarterback snaps the ball, he has to see the edge to the side of the bootleg. If the defender to that side has walked down, he should suspect a blitz. If he thinks the blitz is coming, he needs to work for depth and width and dump the ball to the fullback immediately.

When we run the play, there are four possible parts to the play. We have the fullback in the flat and the wideout on the comeback. The tight end runs the drag coming across the field. The last thing is the quarterback outside the containment with the ball. He can always run the ball.

I want to mention the coverage before I go on with the next part. I love to run this against a cover-3 secondary. Many times, the defender responsible for the flat ends up chasing the bootleg. The drag is open many times on this play. The deep route and comeback route are good against that coverage. If you play a cover-2 team, the drag is open almost every time.

The coverage we are starting to see is quarters, or cover 4, and man coverage. When we play one of those teams, the first thing I do is cheat the receiver in slightly. I want to know one thing in a quarter coverage. I want to know who is covering the fullback. Many times, the defense does not know who has that coverage. You will see us throw to the fullback many times. I promise you, the teams that are playing quarter coverage do not cover the fullback.

We run this play from all different formations. We run it from one split end, twins, pro, slot, to the tight end side, and away from the tight end side. If the defense uses man coverage, it is advantageous to run the bootleg away from the motion.

When the fullback runs his pattern, he has to avoid all the trash and clutter at the line of scrimmage. As soon as he gets to the line of scrimmage, he has to get his head around and look for the ball. If he gets his head around quickly, there is no need for communication between him and the quarterback. He should see the blitz coming and know the quarterback is dumping the ball immediately.

We run the play from multiple formations. I like to use motion with the scheme. We can use the motion to seal the edge or confuse and distract the secondary. If you find a secondary who is moving with your motion, you need to run the bootleg away from the motion.

When the quarterback comes away from the center, I want him to show the ball. If the quarterback extends the ball and the tailback makes a good fake everyone in the stadium, including the defense, will think he has the ball. With the pulling linemen and all the action, the defense loses sight of the ball.

The quarterback throws the ball to the fullback if he is open. We do not look to the deep ball as the first option. The fullback, drag route, and deep route, are the progressions we look to throw. The good thing about throwing to the fullback is he is a running back. He will not fall down and can make people miss in the open field.

The fullback will be open early and the drag route late. If we fool the defense, the drag route will be open. People always scramble to cover the deep route and can see the flat route, but the drag route is in the traffic and hard to see.

The thing about this play is any offense can run it. If you have a counter play, you can run the bootleg off that play. The thing the fullback must do is catch the ball. If he cannot catch, you cannot use him. This is an easy throw for the quarterback, and the fullback has to catch the ball. We try to drill this play with a two-ball drill. The quarterback hands the ball off, and we give him another ball to throw to the fullback as he continues the play.

I did not like the timing of the drill. When we run the counter trey, the quarterback throws an imaginary ball to the fullback, and he catches it. That gets us used to the timing of the play. We do not block the fullback on the counter. We run him to the flat as we do on the bootleg. The reason I run him to the flat was he would not block anyone. I run him to the flat, and instead of chewing him out, I am bragging on him.

We like to run the bootleg away from motion (Diagram #5). We ran a pro set with the flanker tighter than normal. We bring him in motion to the openside of the formation. The motion back will be the drag runner coming from the backside. The tight end runs the corner pattern. We run the counter fake to the split end side. Against the 3-4 look, we keep the tackle in and reach the 5-technique defensive end. The outside linebacker has the flat coverage on the fullback.

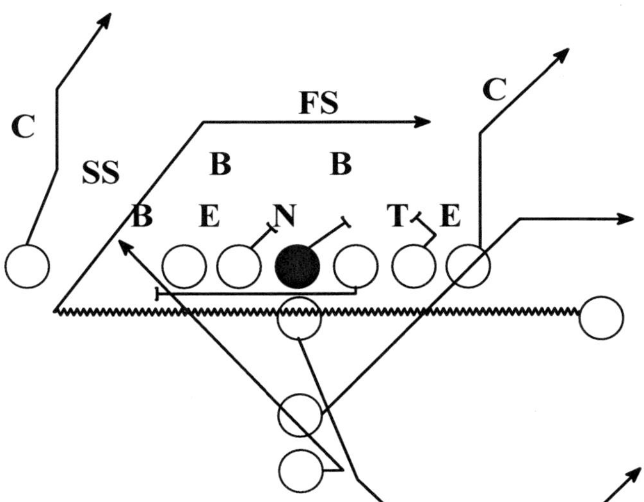

Diagram #5. Bootleg Away From Motion

The quarterback has the same read on the play. He wants to find the outside linebacker right away. If he is coming, he dumps the ball. If he reads the fullback and plays him, the drag to the flanker will be open.

In the first game of the season, my quarterback, who happens to be my son, got hurt. He had surgery and missed the next game. During the week of practice, my second quarterback broke his hand. I played the second game of the season with the third quarterback. He can run this play and run it well. It is not that hard to do if you work on it. The third quarterback had 140 yards passing all on this play.

We throw hot off any unblocked defender coming off the bootleg side. I think we could run this play naked and get away with it. However, we like to secure the C-gap defender with a reach block.

The reality of this play is we are not blocking anyone on the bootleg side of the ball and getting away with it. The only block we attempt is the reach block by the tackle or tight end. It does not need to be a good block. It needs to be an occupying block. The quarterback throws the ball quickly, or he runs the ball.

The most success we had this year was bringing the back in motion and sealing the edge (Diagram #6). We run this play to the twin-receiver side. We motion the slot receiver back, and he seals the edge of the defense. The guard and tackle pull, and we fake the counter to the tight end side. The wide receiver runs a corner route. However, we like to bring him back on a comeback. The tight end runs the drag route at 10 to 15 yards coming across the middle.

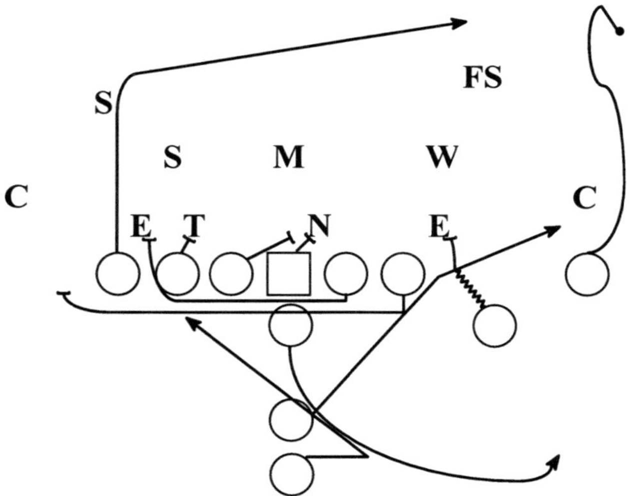

Diagram #6. Bootleg to the Motion

We teach the motion back to block the edge. He has a simple rule: he is to seal the last man on the line of scrimmage. It does not matter if he is standing up or down in a stance. It could be a linebacker, defensive end, or a defensive tackle. If they run stunts, he seals whatever comes to the C gap.

When we get the quarterback outside the edge defender, good things happen. It puts defenders in no-man's land. If they cover, the quarterback runs the ball. If the defender comes up, the quarterback throws the ball. Most good defenders will force the throw. They know if they force the throw, there is a chance the receiver will drop the ball.

This play works well against teams that play quarters or cover 2. If linebackers are assigned pass coverage on running backs, it is extremely difficult for them. If the linebacker reads the #3 receiver in the backfield and has to pass him to someone else, you win. He is a run player. When he sees the counter trey with pulling linemen, he is playing run. We see it repeatedly. The fullback comes to the flat, and no one is in sight.

When we call the comeback pass to the outside receiver, he is in great position to come back and block for the fullback. The deep receiver knows the only way he will get the ball is if they cover the fullback. He becomes a great blocker on this play and comes back to spring the fullback for bigger chunks of yardage.

When we play man coverage teams, we found the tight end is open many times on the drag pattern. The reason he is open is the counter fake draws the man covering him. We run the drag route behind the linebackers. When he gets to the position at which we snapped the ball, we want him to be 10 yards deep. He continues to climb to a depth of 12 to 15 yards behind the linebackers. He runs across the field, headed for the sidelines. We expect to throw the ball when he gets to the opposite hash marks.

We ran a play this year that was successful for us. It is a good play in a third-and-five-yards for the first down. We call the play "counter shoot" (Diagram #7). It is a bubble screen to the fullback. We set up in the twins set and ran the counter trey fake to the tight end side. The quarterback runs the counter fake, pulls the ball, and runs the bootleg naked. The fullback, instead of going three yards downfield, ran along the line of scrimmage or

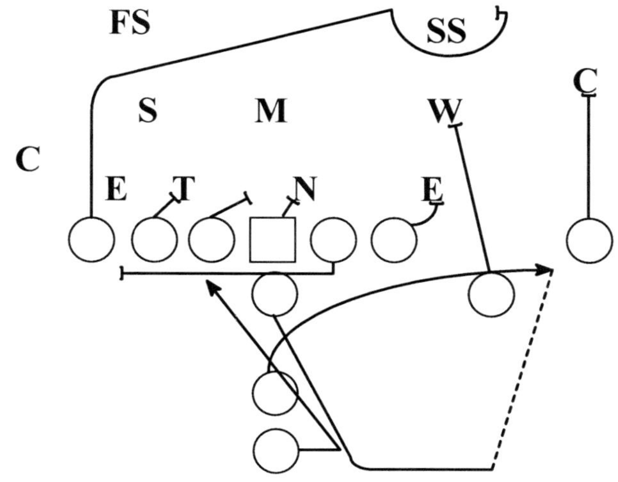

Diagram #7. Counter Shoot

slightly behind it. The twin receivers release and drive the defenders off the line of scrimmage. Once the defenders recognize the screen, the receivers are in position to block them.

We throw the ball behind the line of scrimmage, so it is legal to block downfield. One thing I did learn about this play is running it naked. You do not need to run this play naked. What happens is the defensive end penetrates and forces the fullback too deep. The quarterback dumps the ball, and the fullback is too deep off the line of scrimmage. I think the better way to do it is to motion the slot, seal the edge, and block the corner with the wideout.

When we ran the play, the outside linebacker tightened down as the motion came inside. We drove off the corner with the outside receiver, threw the ball to the fullback, and had a good one-man bubble screen down the sidelines.

It is a good concept. Make sure, if you decide to do something similar, that the fullback is a player who can do something after he catches the ball.

I have enjoyed this very much. Thank you for your attention.

Rob Robertson

THE 3-4 DEFENSE ALIGNMENT AND DESIGNS

Lawrence Central High School, Indiana

Eight years ago, we chose to switch from a 4-4 defense to the 3-4 defensive scheme. We wanted to build a team with the wing-T and 3-4 defense. We wanted to have something simple as our template with X's and O's. We believed the way you win games is through hard work in the weight room, with discipline, and good athletic football principles.

We found we did not have enough answers in regard to how to switch up our defense versus the different types of offenses we faced. With the 3-4 defense, we found a defense where we could create our own simple rules and language to accommodate any offensive look we may see. We can reduce our 3-4 concept to about anything we see on offense.

I did some research on the high schools in Indiana. From 1994 through 2010, the losers averaged scoring less than 14 points per game. This tells me if you want to win football games, you want to hold teams to two touchdowns or less. I took this information from John Harrell's Indiana High School Football website.

If you look at the 5A state champions from 2001 through 2010, they allowed an average of 13.8 points per game. Fishers High School, who beat us in the state championship this year, averaged allowing 16 points per game.

We changed to the 3-4 defense because we wanted a different language. I did not really care about X's and O's, and I did not care about any particular defense. We wanted a language that the players could plug into and we could use in any situation. The 3-4 defense is very adaptable. We have a language that is simple and that makes it easy to diagnose problems and to come up with a fix. If you keep things simple, you always have an answer.

WINNING AND LOSING BY THE NUMBERS
YEARLY AVERAGE SCORING

Year	Winner Points	Loser Points
1994	31.0	10.8
1995	30.1	10.2
1996	32.6	11.0
1997	33.4	11.2
1998	32.7	11.4
1999	33.6	11.4
2000	34.3	11.3
2001	31.6	10.4
2002	33.0	10.8
2003	32.9	10.9
2004	34.2	11.9
2005	34.5	12.4
2006	33.8	11.6
2007	33.7	12.1
2008	35.0	12.5
2009	34.0	11.0
2010	37.1	13.3

Year	School	Points Allowed
2010	Fishers	16
2009	Warren Central	20
2008	Center Grove	14
2007	Carmel	13
2006	Warren Central	8
2005	Warren Central	14
2004	Warren Central	21
2003	Warren Central	11
2002	Ben Davis	11
2001	Ben Davis	10

When we look at offenses today, they have athletes in all positions and practice 12 months a year. They know how to spread you out and get you into 1-on-1 situations. If the offense is going to have multiple formations, we want to use simple concepts to make it easier for us to defend in any situation. Teams have a bread-and-butter play when they "got to have it." They may do a lot of different things during the game, but they always come back to just one or two things when the game is on the line.

We align our techniques as shown in Diagram #1. We use A-, B-, C-, and D-gap responsibilities.

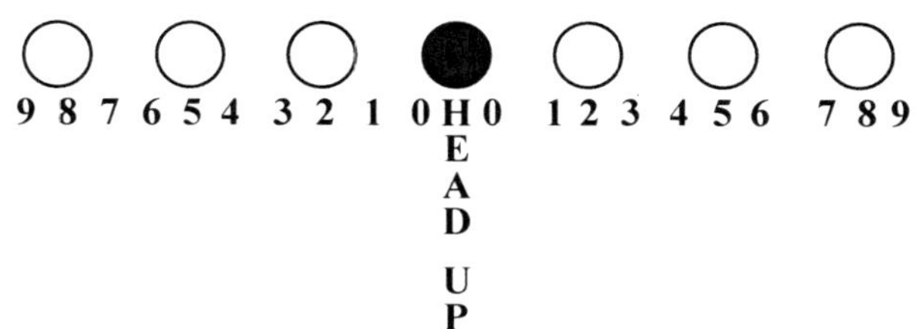

Diagram #1. Alignment Techniques

This is our base defense (Diagram #2). We have called strength to our left, even though the offense has two tight ends. The triangle shows our strongside and the circle shows the weakside. We can flip-flop it any time. The best thing we did last year was to line up correctly on formations. Our kids spend a lot of time in the summer going against formations. They practice it repeatedly. It is an automatic way to line up. We may have a plan B against a formation, but our plan A is already in our players' heads.

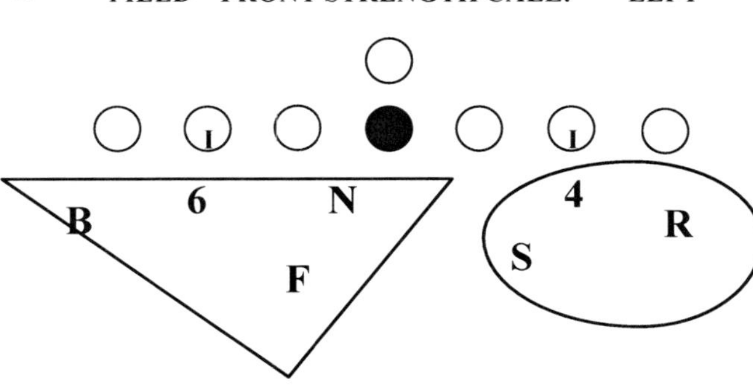

Diagram #2. Base

We have three down linemen. We have a 6 tackle, a nose man, and a 4 tackle. I changed a little this year in that I like having the tackles line up head-up to the offensive tackles. We do not want the offense to know, based on our alignment, which side our strength call is to. We still call them 6 tackle and 4 tackle. The 6 tackle has C-gap responsibility, and the 4 tackle has the B-gap responsibility. The 6 tackle goes to the strength, and the 4 tackle goes to the weakside. The nose is in a 0 technique.

The strongside of our defense consists of a 6 tackle, a nose, a strongside inside linebacker that we call Fox, and a strongside outside linebacker that we call Bandit. The Bandit is in a 9 technique and in a two-point stance. His stance is heel to toe with his inside foot up. The important thing about Bandit is where his eyes are. His key every single time is the end man on the line of scrimmage to the back.

The key for the inside linebackers is the fullback down to the guard if it is an I formation. If we face a wing-T, a team that pulls guards and down blocks guards, we read the guard to the back. Every move he makes is based on the guard's movement.

The weakside of our defense consists of a 4 tackle, an inside linebacker we call Stud, and an outside linebacker we call Ram. Our Ram is our C-gap outside linebacker. Our linebackers line up in a slightly outside shade 3 technique on the guard. They line up at about four to five yards deep.

If I call a shade strong, my three defensive linemen are going to shade to the strength (Diagram #3). Their gap responsibility is the same. The 6 tackle has C gap, the nose has A gap, and the 4 tackle has B gap. The strongside Fox has the B gap, the Stud linebacker has A gap, the Bandit has the D gap, and Ram has the C gap.

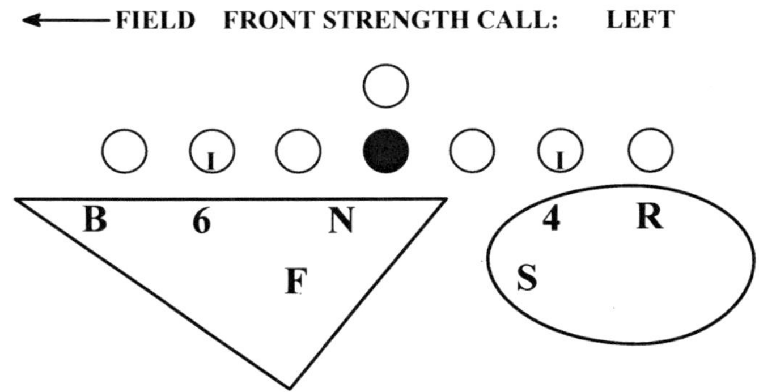

Diagram #3. Shade Strong

Both outside linebackers need to be disciplined enough to stare at the man in front of them. Most high school players want to look into the backfield immediately to try to find the football. The outside linebackers have to stare at the last man on the line of scrimmage because every move the offensive man on the end makes will dictate what we will do.

It does not matter if it is a tight end, a tackle, or a wingback; we treat a wingback just like a tight end when he is in front of us. We know if the offense puts their wingback in motion, they have just narrowed their world down. If they motion him away, then a bootleg or a counter is coming back at us. If the opposite wing is motioning to us, we know it is time to play ball because the wing-T is coming back at the end.

Here is why I love this defense. We can mosey our linebackers down into a four-man front. I make a Mojo call to our defense (Diagram #4). The kids know when we call Mojo, the nose bumps over to head-up over the guard, and our 4-tackle bumps over to head-up over the other guard. Our Ram lines up in a two- or three-point stance depending on his preference. This gives us a four-man front. We can run a 4-4 cover 3 out of this alignment. In this case, I have rolled the strong safety down on the weakside. The strong safety has flat coverage to the weakside and the Bandit has flat coverage to the strongside.

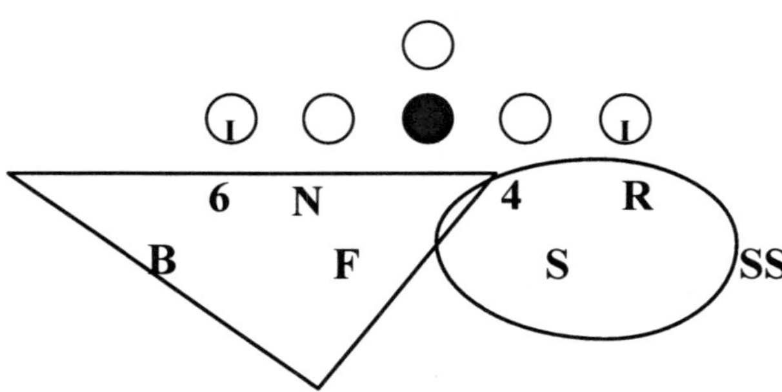

Diagram #4. Mojo

We have gap responsibility the same as if they were head-up in a three-man front. Our nose still goes to the A gap. He can exchange gap responsibility with the Fox and take the B gap and the Fox will take the A gap. We can call 31 to let the nose and tackle know which way to shade. We like to run 11 in short-yardage situations to put two down linemen into the A gaps.

If we call heavy down, we are making a quick adjustment to the weakside (Diagram #5). We are now shaded to the strength. The 4 tackle bumps down the A gap to the guard. The Ram bumps down to the tackle. They still have B- and C-gap responsibility; they are just a little bit tighter.

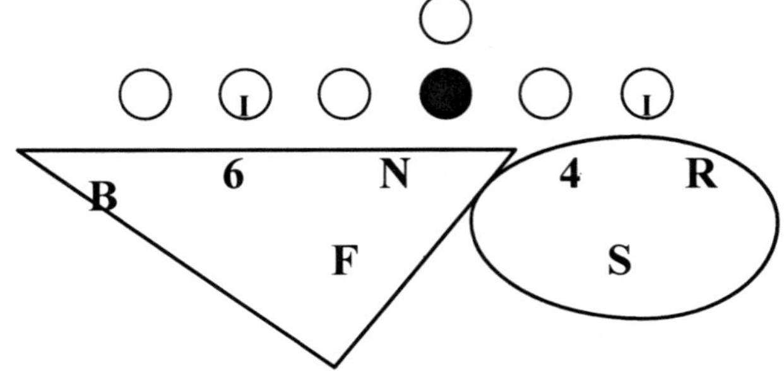

Diagram #5. Heavy Down

Everyone in here knows that if you do not stop the C gap, the offense is not going to do anything but run to the C gap. It is a high percentage play for the offense. We are ready to exhaust all resources in order to stop anything going to the C gap.

Miami is nothing but a 4-3 concept (Diagram #6). We are still running it from a 3-4 thought process. The Fox is still going to read the guard. He is not backing off and he is not trying to spill the play; he still has his same rules. We are just moving people around.

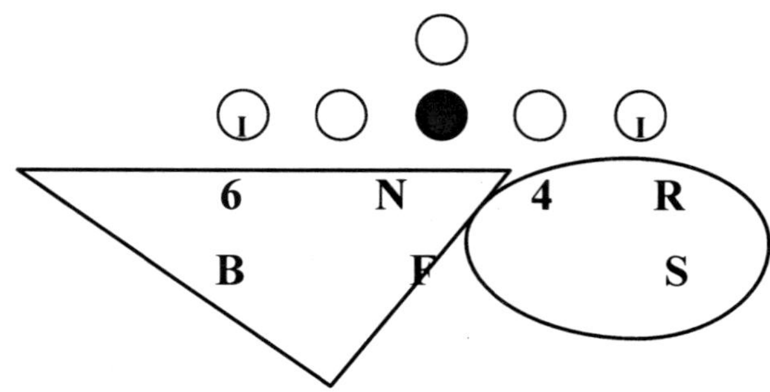

Diagram #6. Miami

A lot of times, we have our strongside predetermined. Other times, we can change it up.

For instance, if we are on the hash, we can call "field." That means we are putting the strength of our defense to the field. Our Bandit, 6 tackle, nose, and Fox will go to the fieldside. If I call boundary, we are going to put our strength to the shortside of the field. We still have our 4 tackle, the Stud, and the Ram to the wideside.

Look at our alignment versus some other formations. The first one is our base defense versus a pro set (Diagram #7). When we break our huddle and see the quarterback under center with a tailback and a fullback in the backfield, our kids know our world has been narrowed. They do not think zone option because of the fullback, and the fact that the quarterback is under center.

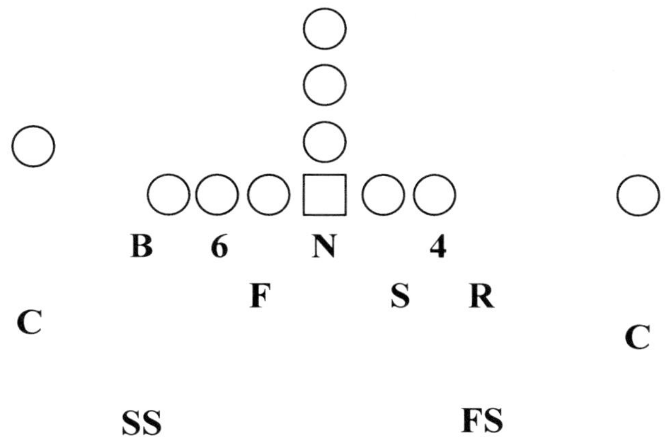

Diagram #7. Base vs. Pro

We have the 6 tackle, 4 tackle, and nose man head-up. The Bandit is in a 9 technique. We show a strong and a free safety on the diagram, but we did not use it much this year. We did not differentiate between the two. We had a left safety and a right safety. You can have a strong corner and a weak corner or a boundary corner and a field corner depending on your personnel. It worked out well for us this year because we had one corner that needed our help, so we kept him near our sideline for the entire game. He needed to be about five feet from a coach all the time, just to check in with him.

We can call base away and change the strength to the opposite side of the formation (Diagram #8). This comes in handy if we want to reduce our 3-4 down to a 4-4 look.

We have the Bandit on the weakside. We do not want to have two players in the same gap. It

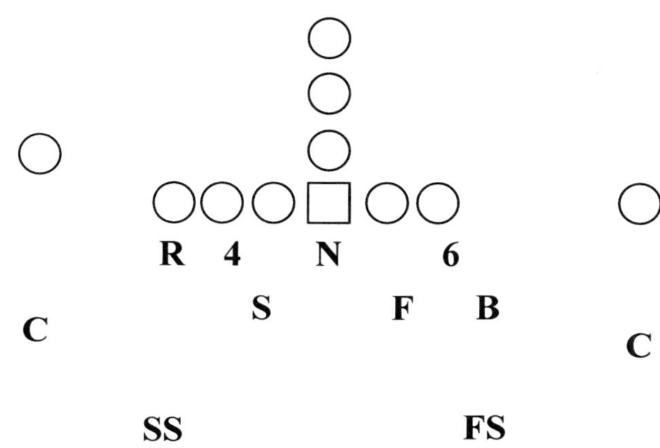

Diagram #8. Base Away vs. Pro

looks like we have the 6 tackle and the Ram taking the C gap. What we will do up front is move to the weakside. This means even though we have the strength to the right, the 6 tackle, nose, and 4 tackle are going to go to their weakside gaps. The Ram is going to bang the tight end straight back in his stance.

We have a drill where we have a blocker and a running back about five yards back, and the Ram works to hit, engage, and drive the blocker back. He wants to get his eyes to the inside. The number one thing to teach outside linebackers is to keep their eyes to the inside and not to look over the blocker's shoulder. He has to dominate the blocker and drive him back and not look over him.

Base versus a spread look is a good diagram to look at. People ask me about this formation. They want to know what the rules are for the Ram and for Bandit (Diagram #9). We have a seven-yard rule on the slot. If the slot is within seven yards, the Bandit can go out on him. He lines up three to four

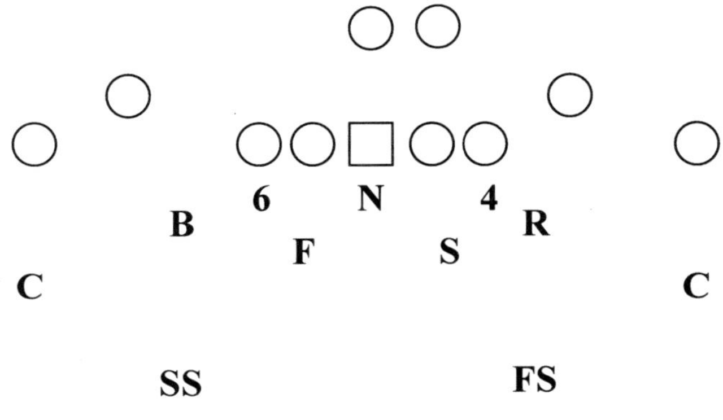

Diagram #9. Base vs. Spread

yards off the receiver. We play games with the Bandit. He can line up on an inside shade, head-up, or on an outside shade. If the receiver is past seven yards, we have to split the difference.

We love balanced sets. We are a two-deep concept team with outside linebackers. Each week our safeties get a visual key for the run. We tell the safeties if it is an A-gap run, they come downhill in first gear. If it is a B-gap run, we want them running in second gear. If it is a C-gap run, they are in third gear. If the run is going to the D gap, the safeties are in a full blast attack on the D gap.

For option responsibilities, the 6 tackle, nose, and 4 tackle have the dive. They ask me, "Coach, what about the...," and I tell them, "The dive! You have got the dive!" The Bandit and the Ram have the quarterback. In cover 4, the safeties have the pitch. In cover 2, the corners have the pitch.

If we see jet action, whatever coverage we had called is now off. We are automatically going to a cover 2. We knife on the jet back. We are going to have extreme violence at the point of attack.

If we use a base alignment versus a one-back shotgun, nothing has changed. It is still a balanced set (Diagram #10).

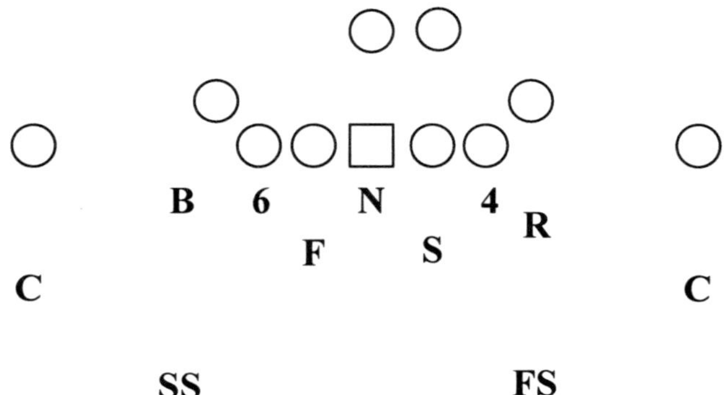

Diagram #10. Base vs. Shoot/Ace

If we go to cover 4, it is obviously quarters coverage. If we read the high hat pass, the safety is reading the #2 receiver. If the #2 receiver runs an out, he immediately eyeballs #1.

The corner is obviously staying over the top of #1. He is going to line up about a yard to a yard and a half with an inside shade and backpedal. The Bandit has the sideline flats. Fox and Stud have hook/curl responsibility. We say hook/curl, but they locked onto the back almost man-to-man. Ram is, almost all the time, automatically rushing. He will be the fourth guy blitzing nearly all of the time. If he is not, we are going to designate it.

I got this idea from another coach last year and I love it. We call our blitzes by color. This may be the best nugget I give you today. You have to know your color wheel. The primary colors are red, blue, yellow, and, for our purposes, black. I give a single color call for all blitzes. If I want to send our Fox, I call red. If I want to switch the Fox with the nose, I call red 30. That means they are crossing or switching gaps. Blue is for the Stud. If I want to send the Fox and the Stud, what do I do? If you mix red and blue, you get the color purple. I just call purple. Bandit is black, and Ram is yellow. If I want to send Bandit and Ram, I call gold.

The kids bought it. Ram and Stud are green (yellow and blue). Bandit and Fox are maroon (black and red). My players picked this up in 15 minutes. I felt like a genius for a day.

Let me get to our base defense versus trips (Diagram #11). Trips gives us more problems than anything else does. We have a plan A and a plan B for trips.

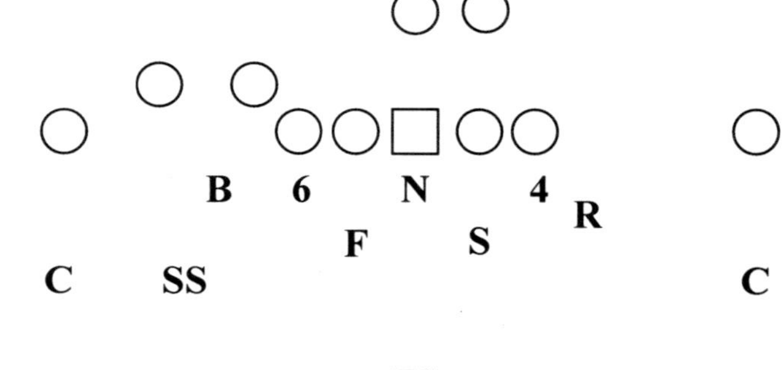

Diagram #11. Base vs. Trips

When we go against trips, our corner is in deep coverage. The strong safety has to make contact with the #2 receiver, and the Bandit has to make contact with the #3 receiver. The free safety stays on top. We have modified man coverage on the backside. If you want to pick on our lone corner, go ahead. He is going to be our best coverage defender. We always have our best defender on the backside of a trips set.

The secondary call against this is our stack. We stack our backers. We put the Fox behind the 6 tackle and the Stud behind the nose. The Bandit slowly moves out just a little so he can get contact on the #3 receiver. If we see a tight end trips set, it is the same thing. Our players signal special. The Bandit has to hit the tight end. We drum that into our Bandit and Ram repeatedly. The tight end is concerned with the defender in front of him.

We spend a lot of time with our safeties in their drill work, reading the pass run and reading and playing the downhill game. If you run outside to the weakside, our free safety comes hard and our strong safety rolls over and replaces the free safety.

This is what we look like against the two-back shotgun (Diagram #12). From the two-back shotgun, you know they are going to ride one of the backs and then run the option back the other way. How do we play against the zone option?

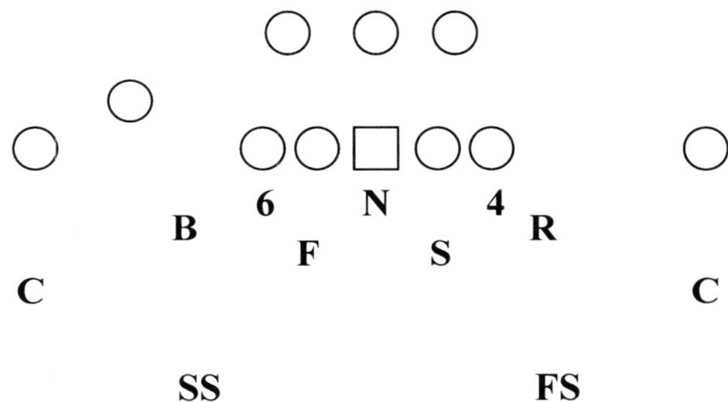

Diagram #12. Base vs. Deuce Slot

Our three down linemen and the Stud and Fox linebackers have the dive. The Bandit and Ram have the quarterback. They need to play disciplined on the fake and stay home. If the Bandit sees the quarterback ride the running back on his side away, he will shuffle, shuffle, shuffle, and stay at home. If the option comes his way, he is going to tattoo the quarterback.

We treat our base set versus a bunch formation just as we do trips. It is still our special coverage (Diagram #13). We start out with our two high safeties. The strong safety rolls downhill. We do this as a timing thing. As the ball is snapped, the strong safety should be on the #2 receiver and the free safety replaces him.

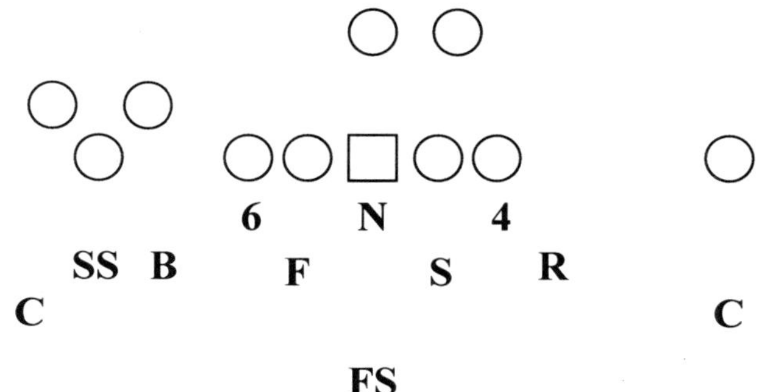

Diagram #13. Base vs. Bunch

The strong safety has to make contact with the #2 receiver. He cannot let the #2 receiver cross in front of him and get the inside seam and go across the field. The Bandit uses the seven-yard rule. He splits the difference or he moves out on him. He makes contact with the #3 receiver. He walls him off. We call it "wall #2" and "wall #3."

If we see an unbalanced look, the Ram and a corner make a call when they see they are all alone with the guard and a tackle (Diagram #14). The call is UBI. The strong safety automatically rolls down. The free safety is rolling over. The outside linebacker has the sideline flat. The corner has a deep one-half, and the free safety has a deep one-half. The only change we have to make is by the strong safety. Our best tackler on the team is going to roll down to the D gap and lay some wood on somebody. We still are in a 2-deep coverage.

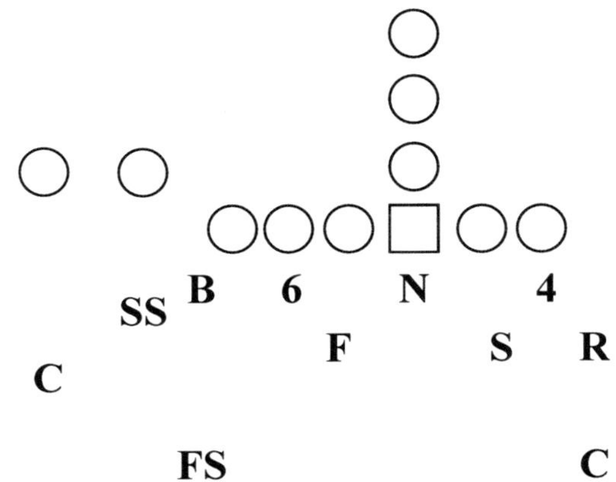

Diagram # 14. Base vs. Unbalanced

In the 3-4 defense, the Ram and Bandit are the elephants in the room. They have to be able to play the C gap, and they have to be able to play man coverage. They are the first players you have to go out and find.

When we look at a double tight end formation, it is a balanced set (Diagram #15). On a double tight end set the Bandit is in a 9 technique. The Ram is head-up to an inside shade.

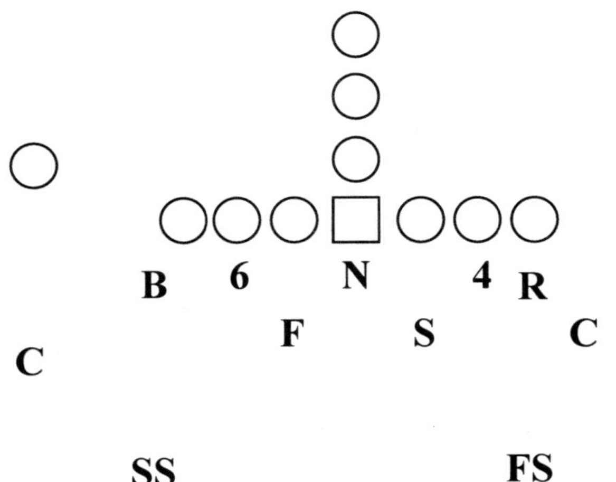

Diagram #15. Base vs. Double Tight

Our linebackers coach is Rick Carrico. He has been coaching for quite a while. He has pounded a few things into me in the last few years. Two years ago, we were slanting, twisting, and we had all kinds of things going on. Coach Carrico looked at me and said, "You are just doing way too much." He said, "I don't understand it and that means the kids don't understand it. You need to break this thing down and you need to make it simple."

The most profound thing he said was, "You are just trying to beat 16-year-olds." We have 16-year-old players that we are trying to beat 16-year-old players with. You have to keep a simple mind-set and you will be a lot better off.

If you need anything from us, please feel free to contact us. We will be glad to help you any way we can. Thank you.

John Shannon

THE ONE-BACK SET PLAY-ACTION PASS

Biloxi High School, Mississippi

I am pleased to be here today. I hope I can give you something that will be useful within your program. I am going to jump right into my talk and make the most of the time I have available.

It does not matter what type of offense you run; the thing you have to do is make sure you have a play-action pass to go with those plays. If you run the power, zone read, or the counter, make sure you have a play-action pass off each play.

I want to show you how we put a play together. One of the biggest things we are doing now is evaluating the plays we want to use in our offense. When we look at the play, we want to know its strengths and weaknesses. We want to evaluate the attitude and techniques of the play.

I want to show you how we would look at a play we are considering for our offense. If we were looking at a naked play and the protection of that play, here is the thing we would consider.

PHILOSOPHY

> We want to establish a "run look" appearance to the entire defense. We accomplish this by selling the run with contact. We expect our linemen to be overly aggressive, have a low pad level, and accelerate their feet through their gaps. We must have a great fake between the quarterback and running back. Protect what your quarterback can do.

The contact refers to the offensive linemen and tight ends. You have to protect what you want the quarterback to do. If you run the naked, play-action, sprint-out, or bootleg, you must protect the quarterback. From one season to the other, you have to change from one quarterback to the one who follows him. Your modes of protection depend on what you do with him.

KEYS TO THE PLAY

- The mesh of the running back and the quarterback must resemble the run look perfectly.
- Offensive line must come off the ball as if it is an actual run. The emphasis is low pad level. We must sell the run.
- The quarterback must push the perimeter.
- The quarterback must be a threat to run the ball.

The quarterback and running back must mirror the running play that you are using for play-action. It has to look exactly alike. It does not matter what level you play, as soon as you tell the offensive line it is a play-action pass, they do not play with the same intensity as if it were a run. That is the biggest problem you must overcome in the play-action game. When you study your game tape during a play-action pass, stop the film after the linemen take three steps. You have to answer an important question: Does the play look like a run or a pass? The pad level of the offensive linemen is the biggest problem we have. The last key that says the quarterback must be a threat to run the ball is not necessary, but it helps if he can.

- Favorable defenses or looks
  - ✓ Backside defensive ends who bend hard on zone and do not have to contain
- Unfavorable defenses or looks
  - ✓ Upfield defensive ends or slow-playing defensive ends who respect naked and boot
  - ✓ Any outside pressure

When you run this play, make sure you know what looks are favorable to the play. In the naked play, if we have a backside defensive end bending hard on a zone read and he does not have contain, that is a favorable look for this play. If you have a quarterback who runs just okay, it makes more sense for him to throw the ball on the naked play instead of running it on the zone read. The unfavorable looks for the naked play are a defensive end who slow plays or plays up the field, or any kind of pressure coming off the edge. The player who must understand that situation is the quarterback.

You coach the quarterback to recognize the favorable looks and the unfavorable looks. If the defensive end is charging up the field or playing slow off the backside, continue to run the football. If the quarterback sees any kind of pressure coming off the edge, he does not run this play. When you get into a naked scheme, you must be prepared to do two things.

If the quarterback is in the shotgun and sees the pressure, he can automatic and get out of the play. If he is under the center and is not sure, he shifts into the shotgun so he can see. If he stays under the center and attempts to run the play with edge pressure coming, he is hit in the back. The coach can handle the play from the sideline if the quarterback cannot read what is happening. We have a system where I can take the quarterback out of a bad play.

Whenever you put together a concept of a play, make sure to list your philosophy, the keys to the play, the favorable looks, and unfavorable looks.

FORMATTING THE PLAY

- Formations
- Motions
- Shifts
- Trades
- Unbalanced

When we format a play, we like to use as many personnel groupings, formations, shifts, trades, or unbalanced sets as we can. We feel it gives us an advantage. If you have four good wide receivers, a great tight end, and you can line up in a 2x2 set every play and win, you need to do it. However, I know the more looks I can show a defense, the less they can do with their blitzes, pressures, and movements. We want to do as much as we can in relationship to those things. The determining factor is to do things that do not affect your execution.

COMPLEMENTARY PLAYS

- Zone
- Outside zone
- Tight zone
- Read zone

If the defensive coordinator knows that I run the zone play from this particular formation, I must have complementary plays from that formation. That linebacker has to worry more about more than one play when he sees that particular formation. The complementary play could be any of the plays I have listed, or it could be a gadget play such as a reverse. Make sure going into the game that you have complementary plays from each formation or shift you use. Make sure you know what you are showing in your previous game. You have to self-scout so you can avoid tendencies. The defensive coordinator is looking at more than the previous game to scout you.

RULES

- Wing rules
- Stack rules
- Bunch rules

The last thing as you develop your plan is to have special rules that handle everything you do. Make sure, when you formulate your plan, build it and put it together so that it handles everything you want to do. Your rules have to handle all your formations, shifts, motions, trades, or any unbalanced situation. Once you have built the play and established the rules, you do not have to worry about changing rules to handle something you will do in game six or seven later in the year.

When we teach the naked play, we teach out of the 2x2, 3x1, or 3x2 concepts and formations. Those are the only possibilities we have. When you build your pass and naked concepts, build them that way.

2X2 CONCEPTS

- 2x2 Double slot
- 2x2 Tight end frontside
- 2x2 Tight end backside
- 2x2 Double tight end

These combinations of formations are the only ways you can align in a 2x2 formation. You can have two-man combinations to the front and backsides of the formations.

TWO-MAN COMBINATIONS

- Two-man combo frontside (flag, corner, curl)
- Two-man combo and tight wing backside
- Two-man combo tight wing frontside
- Three-man combo from 2x2 tight wing backside
- 2x2 from a two-back set

These are the possibilities from a 2x2 formation. The three-man combination is a possibility if you use the back from the backfield or a receiver from the other side.

From the 3x1 concept, we have more possibilities for combination patterns. We are taking the naked concept and building it from one back, two backs, or any combination of formations you can align.

3XL CONCEPTS

- Single receiver/double slot
- Single receiver/double slot (special)
- Single receiver/tight end backside
- Single receiver/tight end backside (special)
- Single receiver/tight wing backside
- Single receiver/individual cut (corner/comeback/post)
- Tight end (deep concept)
- Tight end (bunch concept)
- Three-man combo frontside (curl)
- Three-man combo frontside (stay concept)

The single receiver/double slot special means the #2 and #3 receivers switch responsibilities. If we call "choice special" from the 3x1 concept, the #2 and #3 receivers switch their routes. If we call "flag special," the same thing occurs.

If you have an exceptional receiver, you can use him as the single receiver and run individual cuts to him. Once you go back to the tight end, it changes the rules. That puts us into a B concept, and I will talk to you about that as we go though the lecture. We can use the tight end in the bunch concept. If you want more protection for your quarterback, we go to a two-man combination to the three-receiver side and use a stay call to keep the tight end in to block.

When you teach a concept, the first things you teach are the alignments. After you teach the alignments, teach the depths of the patterns. It does not matter if you are under the center, zone read, pistol, or a two-back formation.

If we run the naked to the left side of the formation, the outside receiver to the left has a clear route. If their pattern is a clear route, they are not in the progression of the pattern. They are to take the top off the coverage and clear out the deep area. If we use the word "takeoff" instead of "clear," the receiver is in the progression read of the quarterback. We run a fade streak, fade, and corner with our vertical routes. That language tells the quarterback and receiver the vertical route is in the read progression.

I want to show you the naked play from a 2x2 double-slot formation (Diagram #1). The combination patterns are clear, late, over, and diagonal routes.

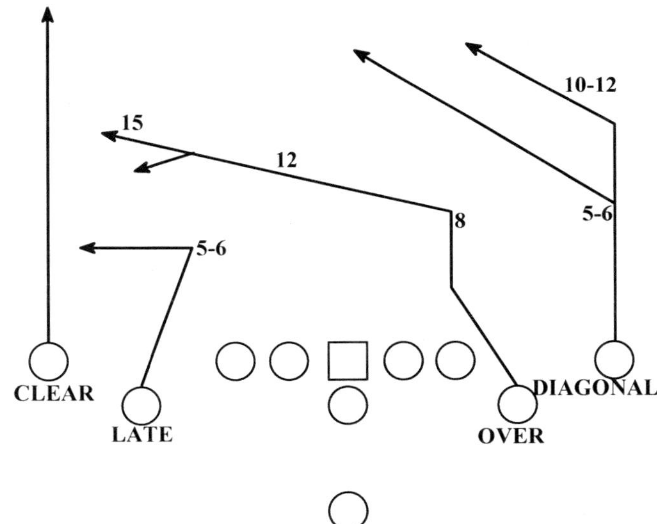

Diagram #1. Naked 2x2 Concept

The #1 receiver runs the clear route and takes the top off the coverage. The #2 receiver is the late receiver and comes out of his route as the quarterback comes out of his fake to the running back. The slot receiver on the zone running play is responsibility for the nickel or Will linebacker in his blocking assignment. We want him to get into a running lane to that defender so he can block the inside shoulder. When he runs the late route, it is the same concept, but he wants to aim at the backside shoulder of the defender. He does not want to get any closer than arm's length from the defender. We do not want the defender to be able to grab the #2 receiver.

We run the late route at five to six yards. We want to give the quarterback a place to throw the ball immediately. We want him to see the jersey color as he comes out of his fake of the running back.

The #3 receivers runs the over route. The slot receiver on the backside runs the over route. The slot wants to stem inside and climb to a vertical spot between five to eight yards deep. He cannot let the frontside linebacker grab him. The linebacker coach will teach the linebacker to look for the receiver coming into the middle and grab him. He wants to run over the top of the linebackers and not in front of them.

After he gets over the top of the frontside linebacker, he climbs to a depth of 12 yards. At that point, he can settle in a hole if the coverage is zone coverage, or he can continue to run getting no deeper than 15 yards. The over receiver has to feel the area as he comes into that part of the field. If it is open, he settles, or he stays on the move working outside.

The #4 receiver is the outside receiver to the backside. He runs the diagonal route. His job is to occupy the safety. His pattern will depend on whether there are one or two safeties in the middle of the field. If there is a single safety in the middle, his break point is five to six yards, and he runs through the safety. His main objective is to keep the safety off the over route. If it is a two-safety look to the middle, his break point is 10 to 12 yards, breaking through the safety.

If the formation has a tight end as the #2 receiver to the frontside of the naked, the pattern changes slightly (Diagram #2). We do not run a late route as the slot receiver ran. The tight end runs a late shoot. The tight end will have a 7 technique, 6 technique, or 9 technique aligned on him. If he has a 9 technique or outside shoulder defender aligned on him, he wants to leave that defender alone. The 9-technique defender will bend to the inside and chase the running back on the fake. The tight end steps to the inside, delays for a count of three seconds, and releases on a shoot pattern to the flat.

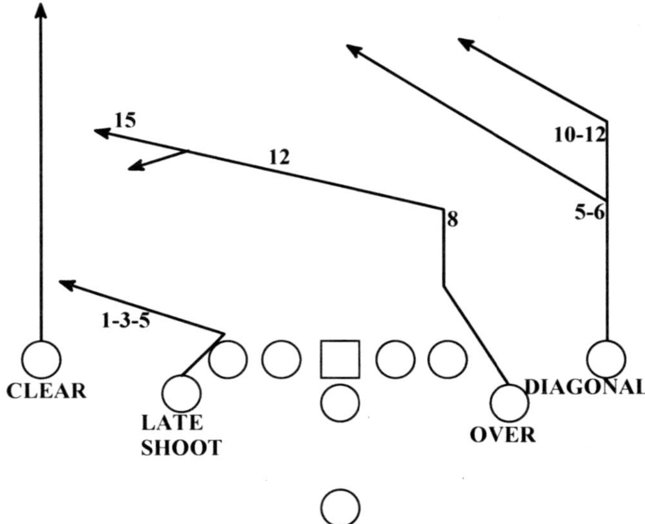

Diagram #2. Naked Late Shoot

The tight end wants to come out on the pattern as the quarterback comes out of his fake to the running back. The tight end does not want to be in front of the quarterback or behind him. He wants to be at the same place as the quarterback. If the defender is a 7 technique on his inside shoulder, the tight end locks the outside arm of the defender and drives for two steps before he releases on his late shoot route. If the defender aligns in a head-up or 6 technique, the tight end pauses slightly. If the defender jumps outside, the tight end closes inside and releases on his time schedule. If the defender moves inside, the tight end locks the outside arm and drives inside for two steps before releasing.

If the defender is head-up or inside, the tight end blocks him. If he is outside, he belongs to the quarterback. If you run the true naked, the 9 technique belongs to the quarterback. If you pull the guard on a naked bootleg, the 9 technique belongs to the pulling guard.

The shoot pattern starts at one yard and climbs to a depth of five yards. The tight end usually catches the ball at one to three yards. We want him to build his depth as he approaches the boundary. The other patterns in the combination do not change. The outside receiver clears the top of the coverage, the slot receiver to the backside runs the over, and the backside receiver runs the diagonal.

If the tight end is to the backside of the naked play, he runs the over route (Diagram #3). He

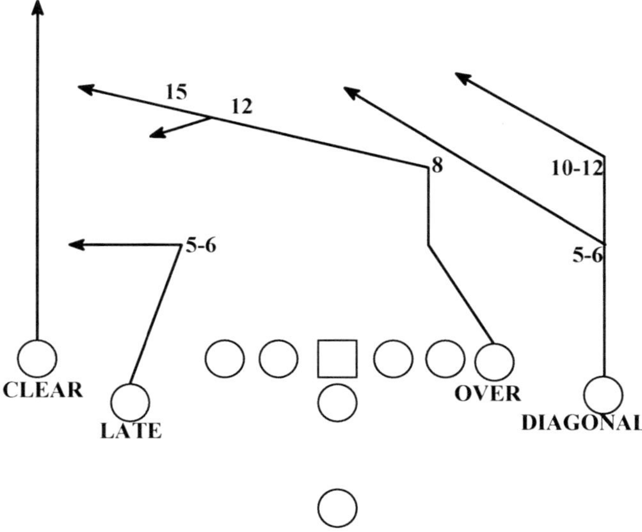

Diagram #3. Naked Tight End Over

cannot allow the inside linebacker to cover him. He must get up the field and over the top of the inside linebacker. If he tries to run the over without getting up the field, he will never get to the other side of the formation.

With a double tight end formation with two wideouts, the defenders will be a 7 technique to the boundary and 9 technique to the field (Diagram #4). If they play you with two 9 techniques, you should be running the ball inside. We like to run the naked to the 7-technique defender. Generally, the 7-technique defender plays to the boundary side of the formation. If the defense plays a 7-technique

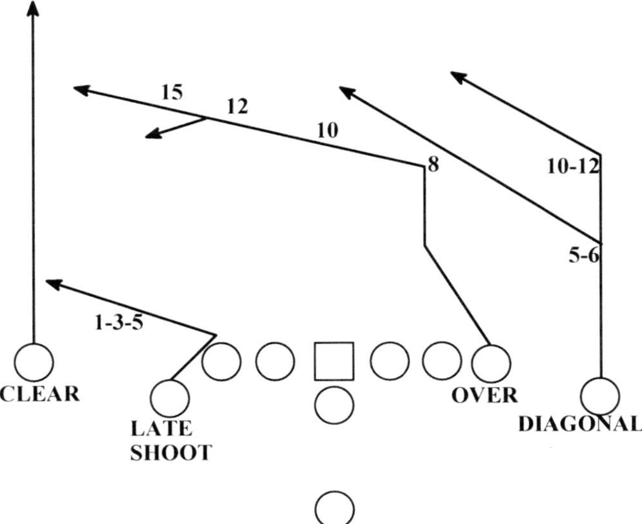

Diagram #4. Naked Double Tight Ends

defender to the field, the safety will roll up for support to the outside. If they do that, the diagonal pattern could be the pattern to throw.

We want to run the naked toward the 7-technique defender because he cannot win in any situation. On a double tight end formation, the frontside tight end runs the late shoot, and the backside tight end runs the over pattern. The outside patterns are the same. The front side clears, and the backside runs the diagonal.

That is the base concept of the play. Once you get out of the base concepts, you can go to two-man combinations. To build these combinations, you need to know what you run best. You need to decide what you do best and plug it into the concept. The first combination we run is flag (Diagram #5). We change up on this play sometimes. We run the regular smash route with the flag. On the regular flag route, our break point is 10 to 12 yards on a dropback pass. On the naked, we want to get deeper with the exit point for the flag at 26 yards.

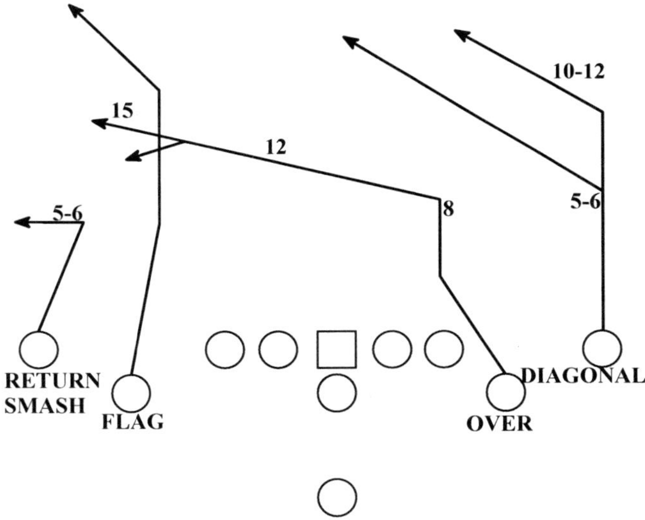

Diagram #5. Naked Flag

In a double slot formation, the slot runs the flag route. He stems his pattern much as he did on the late route. He goes vertical and aims for a point on the sidelines 26 yards deep. The outside receiver does the smash route. However, we do not want to sit down at five to six yards and stay there. We run a smash return route and work to the outside. The backside patterns do not change. The #3 receiver does the over, and the #4 receiver runs the diagonal.

The quarterback reads the play from the top down unless he has immediate pressure in his face. If he has pressure, he does the opposite. He reads from low to high. With no pressure, the quarterback looks to the flag first, the over second, and the smash third. If the quarterback comes out and has a defensive end in his face, he looks for the smash route.

Base your two-man combos on what your quarterback throws best. If he cannot throw a deep ball or sideline cut, do not use those patterns. In my case, I match my combinations as to what type of secondary I expect to see. Always have a reason for what you do. We can change up the patterns by using a call. That means the outside receiver runs the seam corner, and the inside receiver runs the rail smash. The smash rail looks like a wheel coming behind the seam corner at a depth of five to six yards. The backside remains the same because those are the rules. Because the flag and corner routes are outside breaking routes, the over receiver can stay on the move across the field.

We run a two-man curl combination (Diagram #6). The outside receiver runs the curl at 14 yards, coming back to 12 yards. The inside receiver runs an arrow route at five to six yards. The curl route is an inside breaking route, which means the over pattern has to sit down at the hash mark. He cannot stay on the move without running into the curl route. A coaching point is the depth of the routes. On a dropback pass, the curl is 12 yards, coming back to 10 yards. To keep the timing the same for the receiver and the quarterback, the receiver has to go to 14 yards and back to 12 yards.

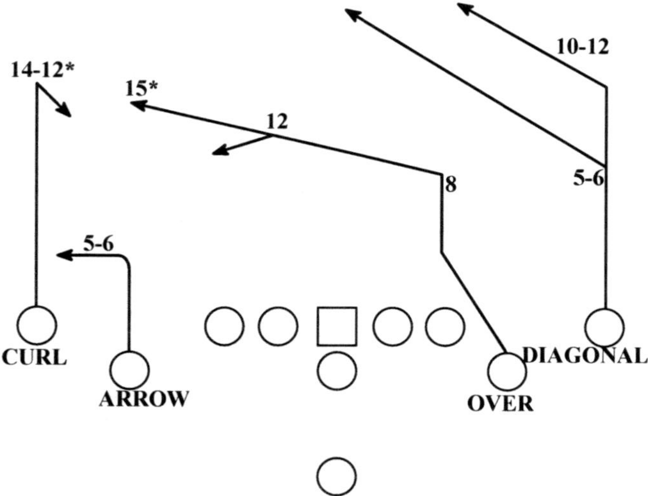

Diagram #6. Naked Curl

Because of the play-action, the timing of the throw is later. If the curl receiver runs his pattern at 12 yards, he has to wait on the quarterback. The defense has time to see the pattern and cover it. In addition, when the over route stops at the hash mark, the quarterback has a triangle read with the curl, arrow, and over patterns. You may have to tag the play so that you remind the curl to go two yards deeper and the over not to go past the hash mark.

If you have a tight wing set, frontside or backside, it can work well for you (Diagram #7). When we get into a tight wing set, we switch responsibilities of the two receivers to the backside of the formation. With the tight wing to the backside, the tight end runs the diagonal pattern, and the wing runs the over route. The tight end becomes responsible for the safety on the backside. With a single safety in the middle, the tight end runs 10 to 12 yards and right at the free safety. If the defense is a two-high-safety look, the tight end runs at the safety to his side and runs a skinny post inside of him. The wing could be a slot receiver, running back, or a second tight end.

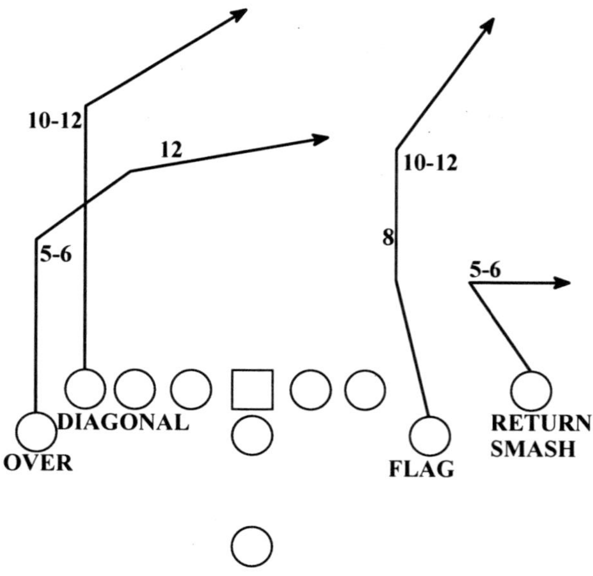

Diagram #7. Naked Tight Wing Back

The wing receiver runs the over route. He starts his pattern and mirrors the vertical push of the #2 receiver, which is the tight end. When he gets to eight yards, he starts his over route. He hides behind the tight end, and the route opens up nicely. If we run the play with normal rules, the pattern is not as good. We automatically switch the routes when we get into a wing, bunch, cluster, or a stack formation.

If the wing is to the frontside, the normal rules apply to the route (Diagram #8). If there is a tight wing to the frontside, the wing runs the flag, and the tight end runs the late shoot. The backside patterns are the same for the slot and wide receivers. The tight wing runs the flag instead of a clear because by running the flag, he can affect the corner and the safety. He can get both defensive backs involved in coverage on him. The vertical route causes problems for the deep secondary.

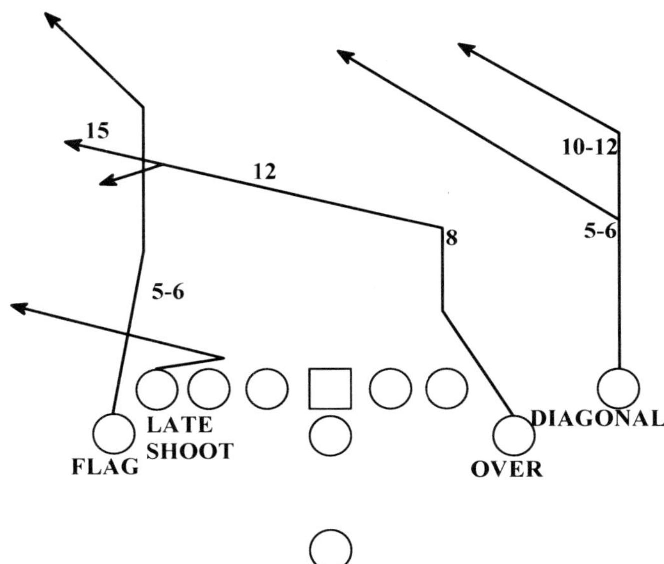

Diagram #8. Naked Tight Wing Front

If the corner squats, the wing is wide open on the flag. If the corner runs with the flag, the tight end is open on the shoot.

From the 2x2 formation, I want to have a three-man combination to the frontside of the play (Diagram #9). We do this off split zone action. On a split zone, the wing runs backside and blocks the defensive end. We tag the play to give it a split zone play-action and run the three-man combination to the frontside. The outside receiver clears. Against the two-deep secondary, he runs vertical. Against the single safety, he runs a deep post to occupy the corner and safety. The slot receiver runs a 10- to 15-yard bench pattern. The wing comes under the

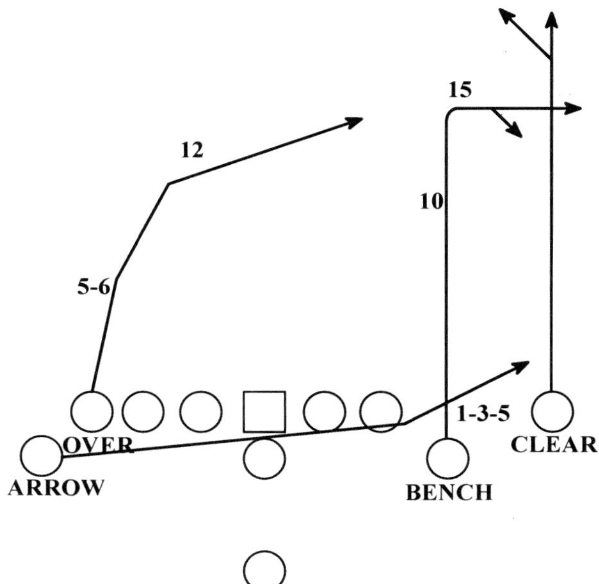

Diagram #9. Three-Man Combo

line of scrimmage and runs a one- to five-yard arrow route. The backside tight end runs the over route.

The quarterback reads from the top down if there is no one in his face. The bench route is an out breaking route, working back toward the sidelines.

The only other thing we have with this concept is with two backs in the backfield. If the #2 receiver comes from the backfield, the pattern is an arrow pattern rather than a late route. The rules for the #2 receiver are simple. If he splits, he runs the late route. If he is tight, he runs the late shoot pattern. If he is in the backfield, he runs the arrow route.

I want to show you the 2x2 concept from a two-back set with motion to the backside (Diagram #10). The naked play will be away from the motion. The motion brings the #1 receiver down in to a cluster or stack position with the #2 receiver. Going back to the rules for a tight wing or stack to the backside, the patterns switch. Since the #2 receiver to the frontside comes from the backfield, his pattern is an arrow. The backside #2 receiver runs the diagonal. The motioned #1 receiver runs the over. The frontside #1 receiver clears, and the running back runs the frontside arrow pattern. Using motions and shifts can free up good players.

These are the base rules for a 3x1 concept (Diagram #11). If we run toward the single receiver, his rule is to clear. The late shoot has to come from

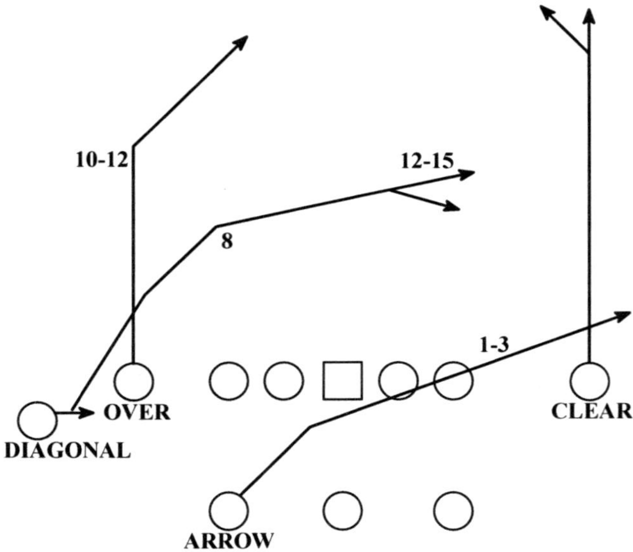

Diagram #10. Two Backs Stack Motion

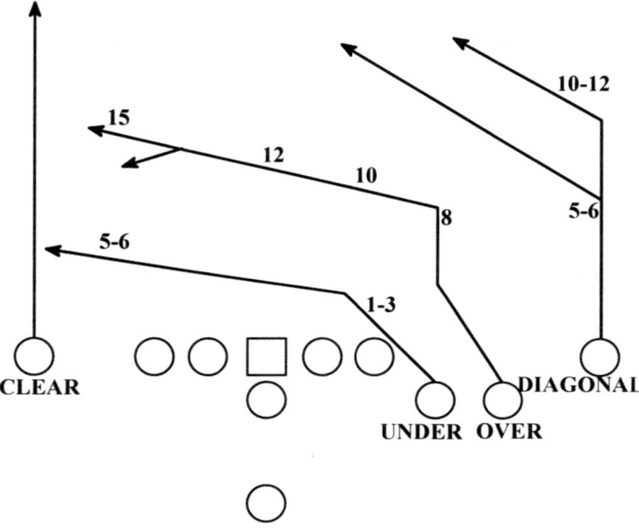

Diagram #11. 3x1 Concept

the three-man side. That is the #2 receiver or inside slot to the three-man side. His pattern is an under route. That means he is coming under the drops of the linebackers. He may have to stay tight to the line of scrimmage until he reaches the other side of the formation. His depth on the other side is from one to five yards deep. It all depends on the drops and play of the inside linebackers. The #3 slot receiver runs the over, which is the same pattern as before and the #4 receiver runs the diagonal.

If we want to adjust the patterns, we use the term "special." The special call means the #2 and #3 receivers switch their patterns. The #2 receiver runs the over and the #3 receiver runs the under. They apply the rules for the depths and routes of the patterns. We like to run special against man coverages.

The progression read for the quarterback does not change. However, if he sees two safeties in the middle, he has to think about the clear pattern. That is an alert for him and the single receiver. Otherwise, the read is the same. If there is one safety in the middle, the clear is not in the thought process. If he has no pressure, he looks over to under. If he gets pressure, he goes under to throwaway.

If you run this play with a tight end to the three-receiver side, you must run this play as special. By the rules of the concept, the tight end has to run the under route. He will not get across against the linebackers. He has to run the over, and the inside slot runs the under. The linebacker plays the tight going up the field, and the slotback has clear sailing under the linebackers.

If we align with a tight wing on the three-man side, we can tag it with a split zone call (Diagram #12). That call brings the wing under the offensive line into an arrow route. The tight end runs the over and the wide receiver runs the diagonal. The single receiver runs his clear. The patterns are the same, and nothing changes for the quarterback read.

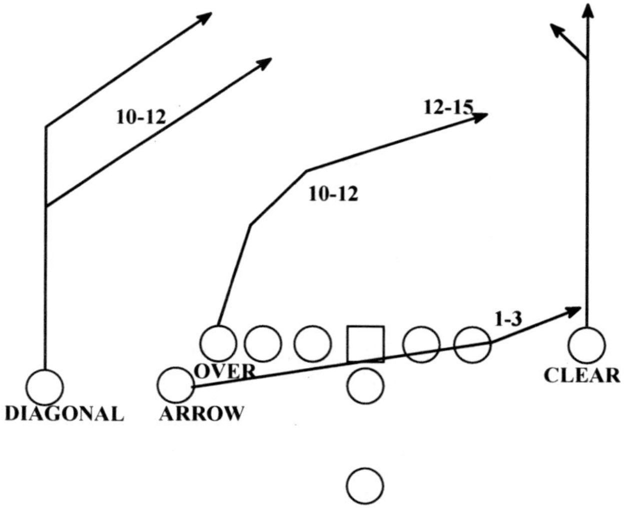

Diagram #12. 3x1 Tight Wing

The advantage of doing these things is it makes the defense think. If a great defensive end is thinking, he is not playing fast.

If you have a great receiver, you want to play him at the single receiver position. This concept gives you the option of working that way at any time. To get him involved, all you need is a tag. The three-receiver side runs the concept pattern, and the single receiver runs the pattern you call.

The only time a pattern can change is if the single receiver runs an inside breaking route. You have to stop the over route at the hash mark. You can call comeback, seam corner, hitch, post, or whatever you can complete. If you have that great receiver, the defense will do special things to stop him. They have to commit more defenders, which opens other areas for the other receivers. Play-action passing is the best way to get your star receiver the ball. If the single receiver runs a post cut, the diagonal route on the backside becomes a dig or square in route. We still want to influence the safety to play up on that route.

When we roll our quarterback on the naked, we pull him up to throw the ball. If the safety stays deep on the post cut from the single receiver, the deep in could be the pattern that comes open over the linebackers. The linebackers will chase the over and under patterns.

In the 3x1 formation, if the single receiver is the tight end, we go to a deep concept (Diagram #13). The depths of the routes in the pattern change. The under becomes a deep under at 8 to 10 yards. The over is a deep over at 18 to 20 yards deep. The diagonal takes the top off the coverage at 25 to 30 yards deep. The tight end follows his rules for the late shoot and runs his pattern.

When we teach for run or pass, we start everything off the left hash mark. That goes for our alignment rules, split rules, or our thought process. Once the ball gets four yards off the hash mark, you can consider that the middle of the field. If you run this play from the left hash mark, it gives you a vertical and horizontal stretch in the back third. You have three receivers, and they have two defenders. This play is good in the red zone.

I try to hold this play for the red zone because if I can hit the deep hole in the middle, it is a touchdown. In cover 2, the flat-defender has the late shoot, the safety takes the deep over, and there is no one on the deep under.

We can run the deep concept out of a three-man bunch. However, the inside receiver in the bunch runs the deep over instead of the deep under. That is our rules for bunched sets. The middle receiver in the bunch runs the deep under and the outside receiver runs the deep diagonal. Everything else is the same.

We can run a three-man combo to the three-receiver side (Diagram #14). The inside receiver runs the late route. The outside receivers run the two-man combo I talked about earlier. You run the patterns you want to run. If we run the curl, the #3 receiver runs the seam flag, and the outside

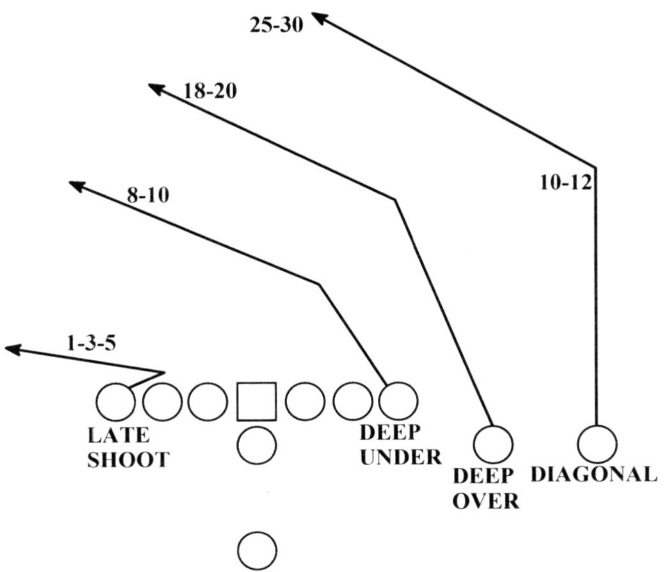

Diagram #13. 3x1 Deep Concept

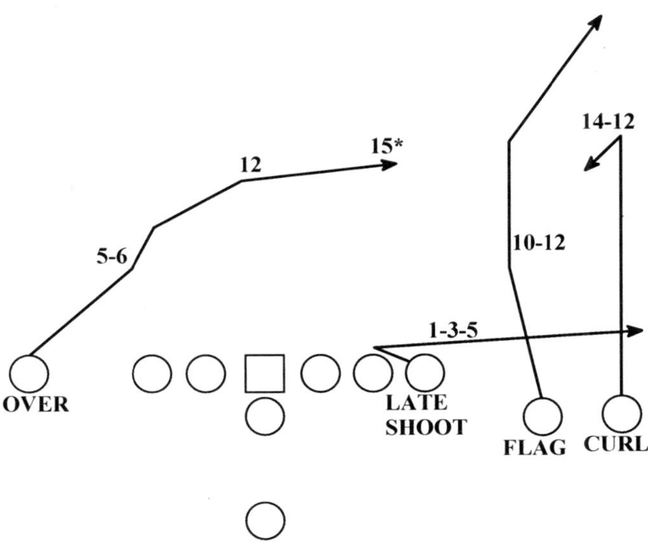

Diagram #14. Three-Man Combo Front

receiver runs the 12-yard curl. The adjustment has to be on the single-receiver side. He has to run the over route. That is a long way for him to come. He has to tighten his split to get there. However, if he is into the boundary side of the field, it is almost unnoticeable. His split cannot be wider than eight yards for him to help you with that route.

There are reasons to put three receivers into the boundary. The defense will cover or they will not. If they do not, you have a running as well as passing advantage. If they do cover into the boundary, they leave the Stud single receiver into the open field. Playing a 2x2 formation into the boundary gets complicated. You have to keep the outside linebacker out of the box. He wants to creep back into the box. You need to figure what the defense is doing and take advantage of your formations into the boundary.

We use the stay concept many times (Diagram #15). You get into a 3x1 tight end set. The tight end stays in and blocks the defensive end. That is the best of both worlds. You are protecting the quarterback and giving him a two-man concept to the three-man side. The pocket is moving, and the quarterback is outside the containment with no one

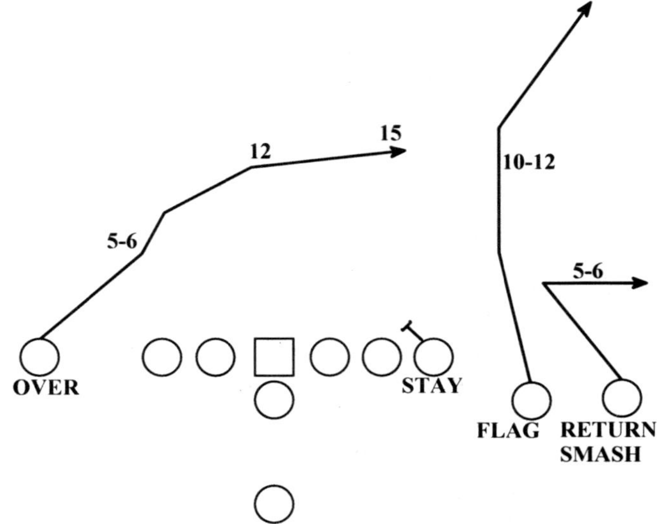

Diagram #15. Stay Flag

in his face. You can run stay flag, stay curl, or stay tube, which are two vertical routes. If the tight end has a 9 technique, we tell him to jump him and get to his outside. If the 9 technique is wide, the only thing we can do is cover him up and ride him.

I want to thank you for your attention. I hope I gave you something you can use.

Benji Sonnichsen

RECEIVER BASICS, DRILLS, AND ROUTES

Prosser High School, Washington

It is an honor to be here. I believe coaching is the best profession to be in. The impact that we have on kids is tremendous. The life lessons we can teach and we learn ourselves is really great. Being men, I think we all gravitate toward the violence of the game. I want to thank you all as coaches for inspiring me to be a better coach and a better teacher of men. My goal for this presentation is that you are able to take at least one thing back with you and it is relevant to you as a football coach.

I want to tell you a little story. There was a guy who was stranded on an island. Every day, though, it was getting a little bit easier for him to survive. He built a shelter, learned how to hunt, and was able to build fire. Every day, it got easier and easier as he learned about his environment. One day, he was on the other side of the island, and over the mountain he saw smoke billowing up. He felt pretty nervous about that. He hustled back to his camp and saw everything he worked for was on fire. There was no way for him to stop or put out the fire, because it had become too aggressive. He was in despair and thought that life was coming to an end. Everything was not working out as he had hoped. He drank his last bottle of tequila and laid out on the beach and thought about how bad things were. He passed out and slept through the night. The next day, he woke up and saw a cruise ship in the bay, and the ship's captain yelled over to him, "Hey, I saw your signal." That is how I see my coaching journey and how it relates to me.

I had a pretty good career playing at Prosser High School and went on to play in college. When I got out of college, I went back to Prosser as an assistant coach, and we had a lot of success there. I took the first head coaching job offered to me at Mount Vernon High School. Our first year, we were 0-9. We got the snot beat out of us by all of the tough 4A football teams. I felt like the guy on the island. I felt like I was stranded and had lost everything. I questioned the profession I had chosen. I went back to Prosser as a head coach, and we were 9-0 in our league. I felt I had come full circle. What I am saying to you is to stick with it; things are going to work out.

My college coach used to talk about the journey and the destination. Everyone is caught up in getting to the destination. We want to get to the finish line, and we want to hold up the trophy. It is refreshing and rewarding to remind ourselves of the process. It is about the journey, not the destination. Enjoy it; life is too quick.

Coach Kelly from the University of Oregon made a comment earlier about going into the national championship game with Auburn. He talked about faceless opponents. They were playing themselves; they were not playing Auburn. They were playing against everything that they had worked for and against their preparation. It is not against their opponent; it is against themselves. That is a great reminder for us to focus on our excellence and the things we can control.

Okay, let's talk about wide receivers. First of all, we talk about wide receiver effort. They need to get somewhere. When I talk about wide receiver effort, I am looking for three things. First, we want to see finish line effort. Where are they going to get to? What type of desire do they have to cross the goal line or to get a first down? The second thing is hands on. How active are they going to be? This could be hands-on blocking, getting dirty and doing what it takes to become a better blocker. It could be hands-on learning in practice. It is a roll-up-your-sleeves mentality of getting after stuff and learning. The third thing is stay inbounds. It is about toughness and scrapping to get the extra yard.

I want to discuss wide receiver fundamentals. I will cover ball drills, route breaks, blocking, and routes with the quarterback.

The practice script is the first thing we need to talk about. We make sure we ink what we think. Everything we are going to do is scripted. We can set a great life lesson as a coach by being prepared. Everything we do as a position coach, and in our area of responsibility, is scripted. Our kids will see that and carry it into their life after football.

This is a cut-up of the front of our practice script. What I am showing here is the right half. The left half will be our practice schedule with all of the periods listed and the activities during those periods. The right side here would be the wide receivers coaches' script. Each position coach would have a script based on his area of responsibility. We have found that this is something that works for us.

Ball Drills		Individual		Red Zone
Settle				
Above eyes		#1 WR		10-Yard Line
Front	1	Stop	1	Fade
Sideline	2	Comeback	2	Slant
Drag foot	3	Slant		5-Yard Line
Side	4	Hook	1	Back shoulder
Behind	5	LOS dig	2	Post up
Low				
In		#2 WR		Installs
High	1	Post		99
Right Breaks	2	Wheel		99 Mustang
Snap	3	Sit		978 levels
Curl wrap	4	Vertical		
Leverage snap	5	Deep out		
Four turns				
Low drive		#3 WR		
Blocking	1	Bubble		
Shadow	2	Quick out		
Departure				
Steer				
Chute				
2-on-2				

Do not let your players stand around and play catch before practice. In the game of football, they do not just stand there and catch the ball; they move around. Have them catch the ball from the quarterback, and have them move, even if it is just a few shuffle steps. We call it the settle drill.

The above eyes drill requires them to have an arm pump motion, where they get their hands from a running motion, up into a catching motion. Let me mention here that our drills do not cover a long distance.

I was with Coach Adams from Eastern Washington University a couple of years ago at a football camp. I was coaching defensive backs at the time. I asked him what type of drills I should take our safeties through. He said, "Coach, I cannot tell you that because I do not know what type of coverage you run and what kind of defense you are going to run." I said that we were a cover-4 team. He said, "Coach, look at everything your kids are going to be required to do in a game, in order to be successful. Take that concept, and put it into practice. Shorten your drills down, so they do not have to run a lot. Work on the top end of the drill in whatever you do."

We have shortened all of our drills to get more repetitions in a shorter period of time. We want to get the receivers different looks, in different spots, where they have to do different things with their feet. Where they are on the field, what the down-and-distance is, and what type of catch it is will determine what they need to do with their hands and their feet. We have to have FBI: football intelligence. We want to get reps on all of those things. Shortening the drills helps us accomplish that. We can get all of this done before practice.

The front drill is where we catch the ball in front of us. The next drill is the sideline drill, where we catch the ball and have to turn up the sideline. We have to know where we are on the field. We cannot just catch it on the sideline. We have to work on dragging our foot out-of-bounds. The side drill is catching the ball on the side of our body. We have to turn differently, and we have to set our hands differently. We have to catch the ball, and then tuck it. We have to get reps on all of these different things.

In the behind drill, we just throw the ball behind them. We are going to experience this situation in a game where we have to turn back around and catch a ball. We do not want to do this for the first time in a game; we want them to get reps and practice it. The low drill is where we have to scoop the ball from down below our knees. Palms have to be up. The in drill is where we have an in cut or some type of curl/hook concept, whatever it is you might do. Now, we have to come differently toward the football. The high drill is where they have to elevate to get the ball, and then tuck it and run. We have a lot of different things that we need to do with our kids to help them improve on catching the football.

Now, back to the script. The next thing we will work on is route breaks. We list everything we are going to do. The first thing is snap. We are working on stances and starts here. We want to make sure we are in a good starting position, where our feet are not too close and are not too far apart. Our hands are not too high, and they are not too low. We will snap around some bags. We want to work on sticking a foot in the ground and cutting around bags, getting into a window, and separating from a defender. The ball is coming. You look for their hips sinking, and their foot sticking in the ground.

In the curl wrap drill, we push, we curl/slant, and then we come back toward the ball and get into the window. We can relate this drill to the hook concept and see it on our game film. We have to find the window, and then wrap around the bag.

In the leverage snap drill, we are getting leverage on the defender, as in press coverage. Then, we are bursting or snapping away from the defender.

The four turns drill is an individual drill. This is a drill where we work on the different types of cuts we have.

I want to talk about three types of releases. The first release is a low drive release or speed release. We are looking for a great takeoff, and then being able to drive underneath a defender. We want to rip our shoulders through as soon as we experience pressure.

The stick release is where we have a cover-2 corner. We press him, and then we stick inside of him. We push the corner out. We do not want to let him collapse on us. We want to press him outside, and then stick inside of him.

The jump to balance release is where we square a guy up. We start in a receiver stance, we run and get to a square position, we give him a shoulder fake, and then we can go either way. Jump to balance is great on the goal line when we are facing press coverage.

Stalk blocking drills are next. Again, it is scripted. The shadow drill is a great drill. As I have studied stalk blocking and talked to a lot of coaches about it, they talk about patience. Have patience when you stalk block as a wide receiver. We will start out on our normal track, then we settle down with a good base and with our shoulders square while buzzing our feet. We will shadow, and then we will engage.

The steer drill is at the top end of the stalk block. He has already engaged the guy; now, he is working on steering him. If he understands where the ball is going, he will know which direction to steer the defender. The goal is always to take drills and shorten them down. We will show them the big picture, but we will work on the individual parts. This will give them more reps, but will save their energy so they can have great team reps.

In the chute drill, we put them in the chute, and we practice getting physical and aggressive. We challenge these guys. We make a big deal out of it. We know, as coaches, that we get what we emphasize. If you emphasize stalk blocking, you will get good stalk blocking. We match them up, best player on best player.

In the 2-on-2 drill, we work on a zone-blocking track. All of the receivers should be working to track based on where the ball is going. If it is an inside zone run, the receivers track should be to the inside. We have to understand which direction we are going to steer the defender, based on the play call.

Goal setting is a very important part of what we do. We watch Friday night's game film with our players on Saturday, and then we let them go. On Monday, we meet with the varsity players after school. The freshman and JV teams have games, so it is just the varsity players. The first thing we do is spend 10 to 15 minutes doing a character lesson. After that, we hand out goal setting cards. These goal setting cards have four categories: offense, defense, team, and family. We ask them what they are going to do and when they are going to do it. We want them to pick something specific that they can get better at in each category. It could be a certain route, it could be blocking—we want something specific. We have five or six guys stand up and share one of their goals with the rest of their team. I did this while playing at the college level. They took it a step further and wrote comments on our goal cards. They would give us good feedback.

I want to share an experience with you about goal setting and how we can make an impact with the players on our team. Every year, we go to the Boise State football camp. Last year, we were there with practically a whole new offensive line. One of our players by the name of Hayden, who was going to be a senior, did not get many reps at the camp. If he did, it was after everything was pretty much over and done with. Hayden was not someone we counted on.

During the summer, he would show up in the weight room and did a good job. When we got together in the preseason, we started goal setting. He started taking goal setting seriously. We saw him getting better every single day.

By week three, we realized as a coaching staff, that we needed to make a change on the offensive line. Hayden took that spot in week three against a very good opponent and a very important game for our league title. Hayden did not let go of that spot for the rest of the year. At the end of the year, all of Hayden's goal setting cards were plastered all over his locker. This is an example of a kid making the most out of his opportunity and using goal setting to help him stay focused and have a purpose.

The next part of our script is individual routes with our quarterback. We want to get on the same page as the quarterback here. The #1 receiver is the closest to the sideline, #2 is the second from the sideline, and #3 is third. We will list all of the routes they are going to have for the week. Any new installs or special routes and concepts for the week we will list here. This part of practices is the individual offense time allotted on our practice schedule. A lot of coaching goes on during this time.

The script that we are working from for this lecture is from later in the season and during a playoff week. The first route we are working on is the stop route (Diagram #1). We are working on taking five hard steps, turning inside, catching the football, and then turning back outside. We can run the fade route if we face bump coverage.

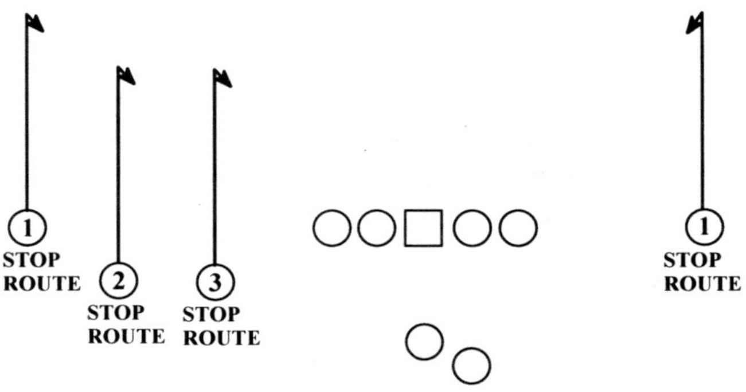

Diagram #1. Stop Route

Stop Route

- Five hard steps
- Turn inside
- Catch ball, turn outside
- Fade option if bump coverage

This is where all of the coaching happens. We are talking about stance, route running, catching the ball, and all of their different breaks during this time. It is real important to have coaches available. Our coaches play the different defensive positions as it relates to our opponent. The stop route is the foundational route that we start with. We throw this route six to eight times per game. It is important for our players to run this route hard. This will set up everything else that we will run.

The next route is the comeback route (Diagram #2). As a coach, we are thinking about how our opponent will be playing their defense. The coach will line up in different defensive positions and switch it up based on our opponent, so our quarterback and receivers get a game-type look. We do all of our teaching and correcting at this time.

The comeback route should be your unstoppable route. This should get you your first down when you need a first down. We really push this route and put emphasis on teaching and coaching it. We want

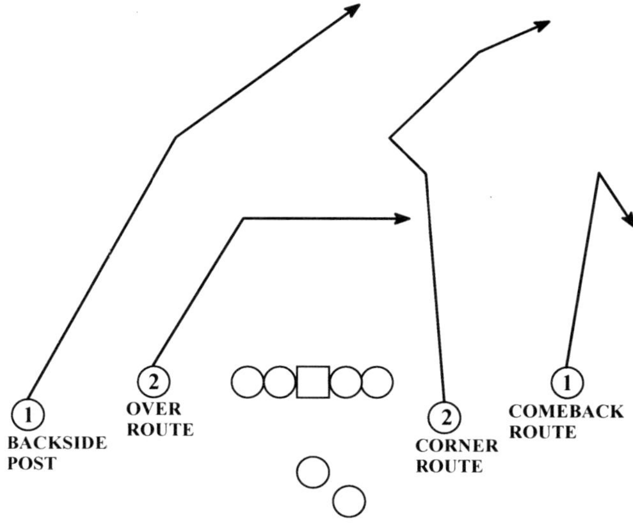

Diagram #2. Comeback Combo Route

to make sure we sell the fade, push to 12 yards, and come back to 10. A point of emphasis is to know the down-and-distance. If it is third down and 15, we are not going to push to 12. We are going to make sure we get the first down.

Comeback Route

- Sell the fade.
- Push to 12 yards.
- Come back to 10 yards.
- Know the down-and-distance.

On the corner route, we are looking for the receiver to stem the defensive back. You can see this in the comeback combo diagram. Any time we can get the defender's hips turned, it is game over. We want to really push the defender and bank him inside. We make our cut at 10 to 12 yards, take the route high, and then adjust to grass. If we take our route high, the pass can be outside and we can adjust to it. The pass is to grass.

Corner Route

- Stem the defensive back.
- Cut at 10 to 12 yards.
- Take the high route.
- Adjust to grass.

Over Route

- Freeze the linebackers.
- Run at them.
- Dip under-over; burst over-under.
- Stay away from the comeback route.

Backside Post

- Run hard to the backside.
- Take the high route.
- Take the top off the coverage.

Let's talk about the hook concept (Diagram #3). We want to push to 10, slant to 15, and then slide into the window. Some people will teach it differently, but this is what I believe in. In practice, sometimes I have to play safety and have him push at me as if I am defending a post pattern. Sometimes, I will play the corner. Sometimes, I play the linebacker and have them find the window behind me. It is all going to depend on what I want my quarterback and receivers to see and how our opponent plays pass defense. The important part is for him to find the window.

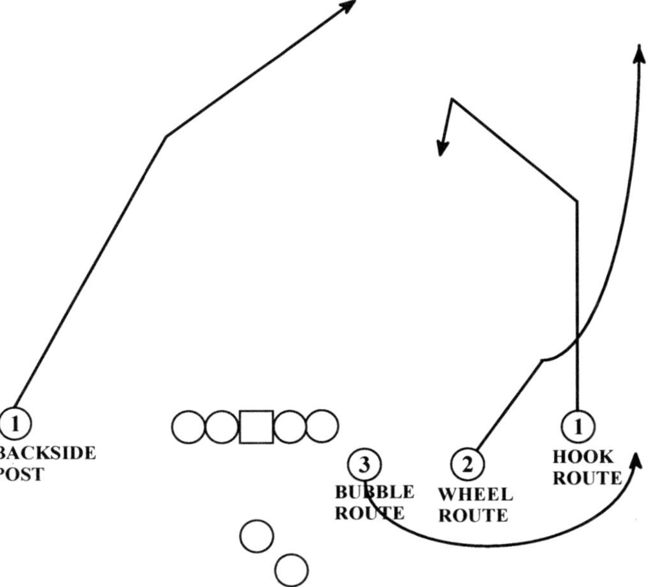

Diagram #3. Hook Combo Route

Hook Route

- Sell the out route.
- Turn up the sideline.
- Stay on the sidewalk.

The wheel route, in this instance, is a speed wheel concept. We are just trying to clear the top off of the route. We are looking to take the corner out of the play. We are looking to sell the out route, then we are going to turn up the sideline, and we are going to stay on the sidewalk. The sidewalk area is the area between the numbers and the sideline. It is a buzzword for the kids so they know what we are talking about on the plays. We do not want them drifting inside.

Wheel Route

- Push to 10 yards.
- Slant to 15 yards.
- Slide into the window.

On the bubble route, we want to take a back step and go. We want to beat the defender to the sideline and put tremendous pressure on the defense to have to cover us. Anytime we get even numbers here, we are taking this. The bubble is built into our running game, and the quarterback just knows to throw it. The bubble route has to be a quick route.

Bubble Route

- Back step and go.
- Beat defender to the sideline.

Backside Post

- Run hard to the backside.
- Take the high route.
- Take the top off the coverage.

On the dig route, we are looking for three hard steps, and then we are coming down the line of scrimmage. We are coaching all the time during these drills. On the dig route, I am coaching them to push me three hard steps.

Dig Route

- Three hard steps
- Come down the line of scrimmage.

Our sit route concept is our deep stop route. We complement our four verticals with a 10 to 12 yards deep sit route. This is a nice complement. We go 10 to 12 yards, sit down, and find a window inside. Use your body as a shield. The ball is coming to the outside hip. As you can see, it is incorporated into the levels combo route (Diagram #4). We can also run it as four verticals, and then they will all sit.

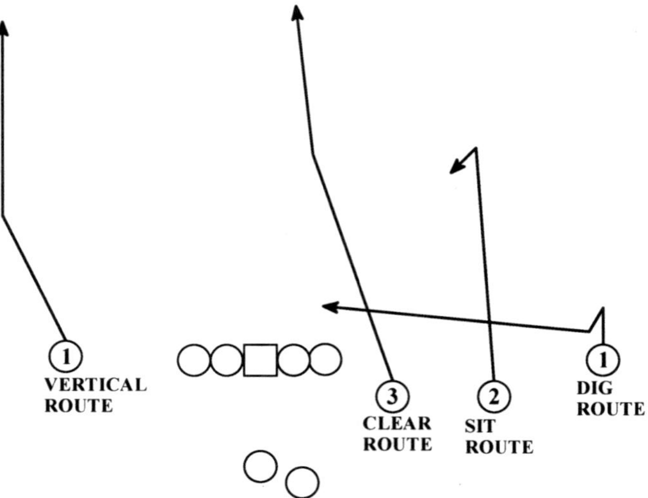

Diagram #4. Levels Combo Route

Sit Route

- 10 to 12 yards
- Sit down.
- Find the window.
- Turn inside.

Clear Route

- Clear the linebackers.
- Take a peek.
- Take the top off the defense.

Vertical Route

- Outside release.
- Stay on the sidewalk.

It is important to give the quarterback different looks as well. Make him have to throw it underneath arms, over-the-top, off-balance, with pressure in his face, and just a normal throw. We want to make sure he gets a lot of different looks as well.

A smash route is where we really work on stemming the defender. For the post route, we want the defenders hips to turn to the outside and then we want to come inside to the post (Diagram #5). The coaching point is to get the defenders hips to move. We want to make the defender think that we are going a different way.

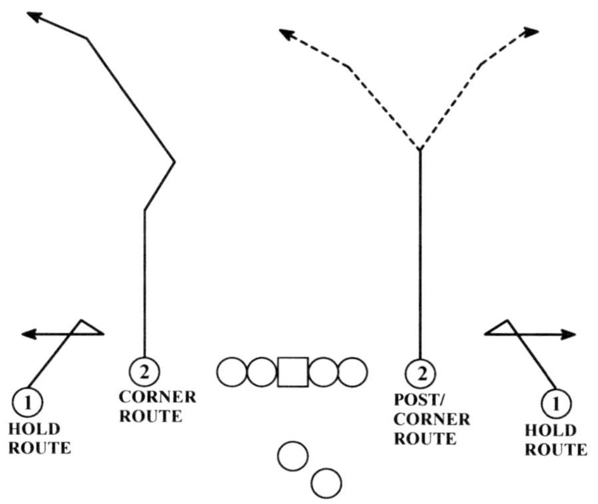

Diagram #5. Smash Route

Smash Route

- Pivot back outside.
- Widen to the sideline.
- Occupy the cornerback.

We coach our receivers to keep their speed. At times, you see a receiver sprint down the field and make a move and he loses all of his speed. You become a better receiver when you keep your speed. When we go to the corner, we take the route high, and then adjust to grass. It is not as important on the post route because it is a much easier read for the quarterback.

Post/Corner Route

- Stem the defensive back.
- Cut at 10 to 12 yards.
- Take the high route.
- Adjust to grass.

Corner Route

- Stem the defensive back.
- Cut at 10 to 12 yards.
- Take the high route.
- Adjust to grass.

Hold Route

- Slant inside.
- Pivot back outside.
- Widen to the sideline.
- Occupy the cornerback.

We run routes for our red zone in every single practice. We are going to run the fade, slant, post up, back shoulder, and the pivot route. We will throw from the five-yard line, the 10-yard line, the right side, the middle, and the left side. It takes us about seven minutes to get through both sides of doing that.

One thing I have learned over my years of coaching is we do not go on a cadence in practice in the red zone. It will save your quarterback's voice, and it will make sure the receivers are ready to go. The quarterback gets ready, and they go. It is just a little thing.

For the first seven minutes of red zone practice, we are working on our fundamentals. For the next eight minutes, we work on our installs. This is at the end of our goal line passing and our two-minute drill practice periods.

As far as throwing the ball in the red zone, we are always going to look for a mismatch. If we have a bigger guy on a smaller defender or if we have a quicker guy on a slower defender, we are going to look to throw the fade first. If we have first down and we see a mismatch, we are going to take a shot. We practice these things every single day so we will be comfortable with it when it comes to game time. It is all about getting reps in practice.

What do we consider the red zone? We consider the red zone to be when the defense changes. There are different kinds of red zones. When the defense changes, that is when the red zone begins. There is red zone at the 20- or 30-yard line. We call that red zone shot. We look at what we can run to take a shot at the end zone from that position. There is also goal-line red zone. If we have a mismatch, we will take a shot.

I would like to thank you for having me here today. If you need anything, I am available.

Bob Sphire

SPREAD OFFENSE ATTACK PASSING GAME

North Gwinnett High School, Georgia

I want to go over some passing concepts out of our spread offense. These concepts have been successful for us the last couple of years. The first one I am going to talk about is the "Y cross." This is one of the staples in the spread passing game.

Our offensive motto on the field is "Do not be afraid to throw. Pass, pass, pass." From year to year, our philosophy about throwing comes back to our ability to run the football. This year, we were probably more two-back than ever before. We had a tremendous amount of ability to run the football. This year, we had four players, counting our quarterback, that all rushed the ball for over 600 yards.

OFFENSIVE PHILOSOPHY

- Stay loose
- Go reckless
- Score now

When we first arrived at North Gwinnett, we had to install the system. Those early years we aired the ball out probably more than we should have. We tweak the system every year, but philosophically we have not changed must over the years. Even though we ran the ball more, we increased the tempo and tried to get more snaps in the games. We tried to make it more difficult for defenses to align to our formations. We changed personnel and got into multiple formations that stressed the defenses.

The cross pattern can be a 2x1 route with two backs. We like to run it from a 2x2 formation. We can run it out of a 3x1 and we do some good things. We can run it with two tight ends or we can run the cross from the empty set.

We label our personnel with letters. Our one-back is the F-back (Diagram #1). Some people call him the ace, but we like the F-back. Our slotback this year played in the backfield and as a receiver. In some years, you have to substitute to fit the situation you need. This year, that was one player. That is the ideal situation because it makes it tougher on the defense. If they can substitute a defensive back when you put your pass receiver in the game, it makes less of an adjustment for them. If you have to put a running back into the game, they put in a linebacker. If the player can do both, the defense does not know how to adjust.

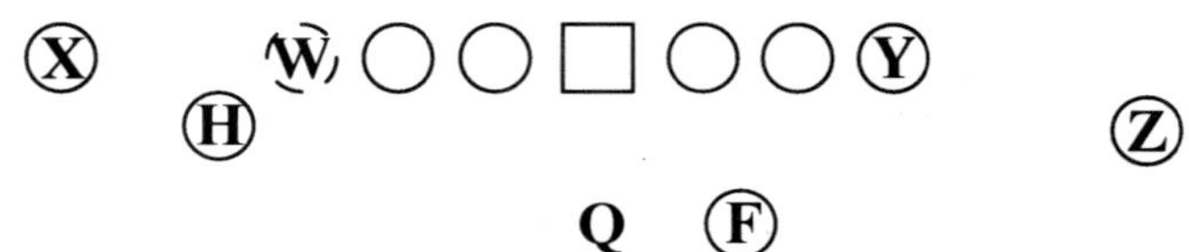

Diagram #1. Personnel

We play with a split receiver called the X-receiver. He is always on the line of scrimmage. The Z-receiver is a wide receiver and is always off the line of scrimmage. Our X-receiver this year was a 6'3", 215-pound wide receiver. He was physical and could get off jams at the line of scrimmage. The Z-receiver was 5'8" and weighed 155 pounds. He was a great route runner and a tough player. He returned punts for us. We could put him in motion to help him get off jams when the defense tried to hold him up.

The H-back is a slotback and played in and out of the backfield. The Y-end is the tight end and aligned on the line of scrimmage most of the time. We played the entire year with the Y-end in an open position. We like a player that plays in an open formation as well as a closed.

This year, we played our tight end in an open position instead of tight to the tackle. He aligned three to five yards outside the tackle. When I refer to a 2x1 alignment, it resembles a 2x2 because the tight end is detached from the tackle. In our terminology, we use the letter "W" to represent the second tight end in the game. Following is a chart of general rules for our crossing scheme.

We have some general rules about route running (Diagram #2). If we are in a red 2x1 formation, the Y-end and Z-receiver are to the right side of the formation. The X-receiver and the H-back are to the left side of the formation. In the cross concept, the Z-receiver's automatic pattern is a post route. The #2 receiver to the right is the Y-end. He runs the crossing route. Against zone coverage, we want him to run under the Sam linebacker and over the Mike linebacker.

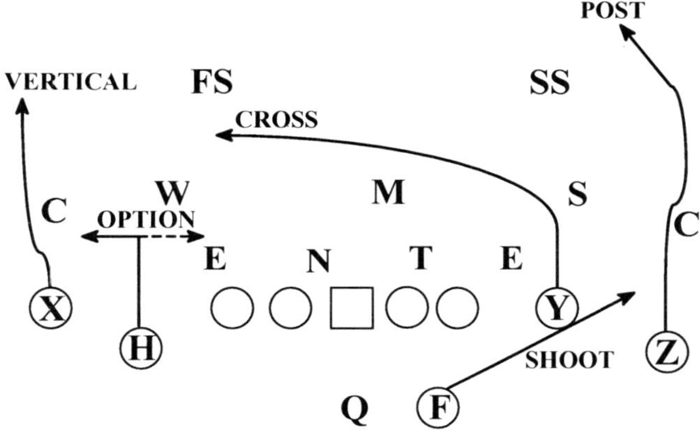

Diagram #2. 80 Y Cross

80-81 CROSS		
Pos.	**General Rules**	**Adjustments**
X Y Z	PS #1 post PS #2 run crossing aiming for 17 yards BS outside vertical	If W is for H, run option route
H	Backfield run option route Slot option hot	Drive call: six to nine yards under Mike LB Follow call: 12 yards dig/curl over OLB unless he expands wide
F	Check release to shoot	Trips drive and follow concept: requires overtake position on the opposite side for pass protection
QB	Read progression: 1)Outside vertical 2)Option route unless from the backfield 3)Cross route 4)Post 5) Shoot	Drive progression: OSV, cross, drive, post, shoot Follow progression: OSV, cross, curl/dig, post, shoot

We coach the Y-end to climb over the Mike linebacker even if he plays a Tampa-2 technique. That could put his depth at 17 yards. We do not want to come under him unless it is the last resort. Man coverage is a little different and we will talk about stairstepping later.

The slot receiver or H-back to the left side of the formation runs an option route. It is hard to teach high school players option routes. When we teach them, we start with no option. He runs an "up and out" pattern at five yards. He wants to stem the defender inside and break outside at five yards. After he understands the package, we teach him how to sit in a window in the coverage and work back inside. If he aligns in the backfield, he has the same pattern with a read-out blocking assignment.

The X-receiver takes an outside vertical release. The release is nonnegotiable. He must take an outside release to make sure the corner turns his back to the crossing and the option routes. The F-back is in a one-back alignment to the right of the quarterback in the backfield. He sets, checks, and releases on a shoot route in the right flat. If he runs out of bounds, he is four yards deep. The quarterback is in the shotgun. We can align him under the center. When we do it, we make it part of the huddle call. We call "under" before we call the play.

When we install the Y-cross in the spring, we start from a two-back set. In our pass protection, the offensive line is responsible for the four down defenders and the Mike linebacker (Diagram #3). We try to identify the Mike linebacker in a way so that the H-back can be a single read blitz protector. If his blocking assignment does not blitz, he can release into a pattern. The F-back ends up with the

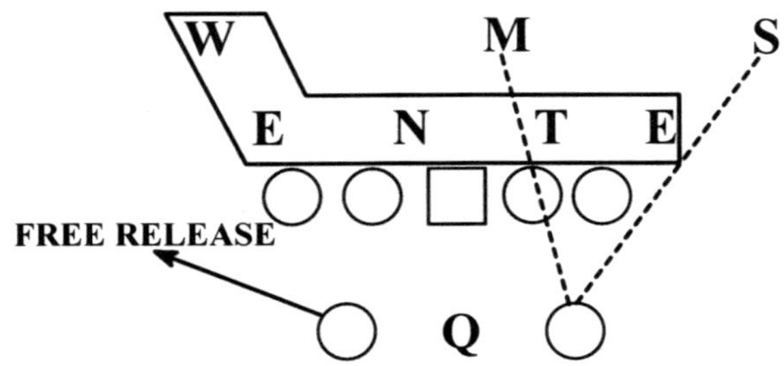

Diagram #3. Pass Protection Rules

dual read in our pass protection. He has to check two defenders before he can become a receiver. If he does not get out in the pattern, it is okay.

To make these rules work, the center identifies the Will linebacker as the Mike linebacker. The offensive line is responsible for him and the H-back has a free release. The F-back reads from the Mike to the Sam linebacker in his dual read.

The way we call the direction of the play is a little different than most spread people. Our 80s patterns are five-step drop patterns. The quarterback aligns in the shotgun. He can also align under the center. If we call 80 protection, that sets the protection to the right. The shoot pattern by the F-back is to the right. If we call 81 protection, the protection is to the left and the shoot pattern is to the left. The red and blue calls set our receivers. If we call red, the tight end and Z-receiver are to the right. If we call blue, they are to the left. That gives us a playside and a backside.

In Diagram #2 we show 80 Y cross. This is 80 cross. The X-receiver runs the outside vertical release. The H-back runs his option route. In the beginning, it is an out cut. As he understands the package, we allow him to option cut to the inside and look for the windows in the coverage. The Y-end runs the cross and the Z-receiver runs the post route. The F-back runs his shoot route to the flat to the right. Some spread coaches run a swing route with the F-back instead of the shoot. I like the shoot, but that pattern is a matter of choice.

From a protection standpoint, we have to identify the Mike linebacker. The identified Mike may not be the middle linebacker. He is the defender we say he is. If we want to give the H-back a free release, we identify the Will linebacker as the Mike and the center tilts the protection to him.

The F-back has a dual read from the middle linebacker to the Sam linebacker. That is a logical progression. He protects to the inside first and fans to the outside. If neither the middle nor the Sam linebackers come on a blitz, he has a shoot route in the direction of the protection. In this case, he goes right.

We game plan our protection schemes so that we know which linebacker in the scheme is most likely to blitz. We try to designate that linebacker in our offensive line protection and read the linebackers that are less likely to blitz.

When we designate the Will linebacker as the Mike, the center works with the guard and tackle to that side (Diagram #4). The guard and tackle to the right block big on big on the defensive end and tackle. To the left, the center, left guard, and left tackle are responsible for the nose, defensive end, and Will linebacker. The F-back reads the Mike linebacker to the Sam linebacker for his protection assignment.

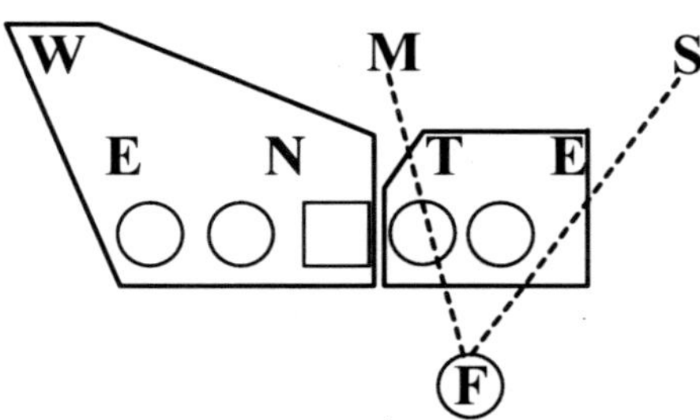

Diagram #4. Protection Scheme

Those are the base rules for protection. The scheme changes with the designations and game planning. That is why we practice each week. We adapt the plan to the opponent and their tendencies.

If we call 81 Y cross, it is the same pattern except the formation flips to the left and the protection becomes a left protection scheme. It is a 2x1 formation with the tight end to the left and the X-receiver to the right. The callside is left and the backside is right. The receivers apply their callside and backside rules.

We ran the entire year with the tight end in an open position. His alignment was three yards outside the tackle in a two-point stance. On occasion, we brought a second tight end into the game. We called him the "W-end." When we made that move, we substituted for the H-back. When the second tight end was in the game, he ran the assignments of the H-back. On the 80 cross pattern, he ran the backside option route. We aligned him in an open position off the line of scrimmage. It was a three-yard tight slot alignment.

I want to talk about the 2x1 routes and talk about the teaching points. There will be a number of designated calls in this part of the lecture. They are call changes that go with the general rules. A red formation, for us, is a right formation. The first play I want to talk about is an open right formation. The set has the Y-end to the right in an open position and the Z-receiver outside of him. The backside is the twins formation of the H-back and X-receiver.

The pattern I want to talk about first is the F shoot (Diagram #5). If the F-back does not get pressure, he can check and release on the shoot route. We always teach the quarterback when he is in trouble to find a running back. The route is a simple throw for the quarterback and can lead to big gains. We put the ball in the hands of a running back in space. In a spread offense, the more you can get the running backs involved with the game, the better off you are.

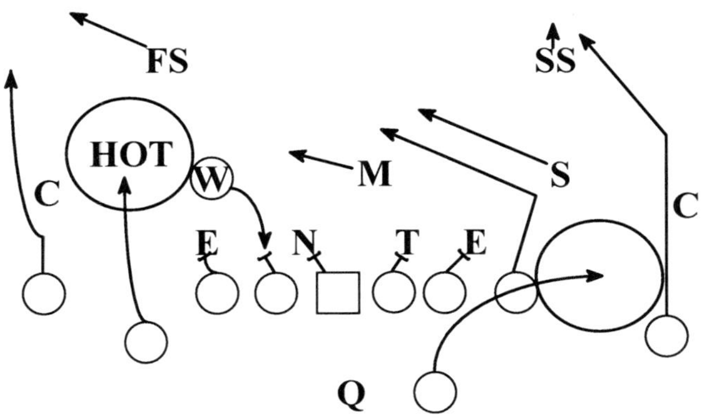

Diagram #5. F Shoot

The Y-end runs the cross route on this play. He comes under the Sam linebacker and over the Mike linebacker. In zone coverage, if the quarterback throws the ball to the Y-end, he throws the ball before the Y-end gets into the open window. If he waits for the tight end to run into the window, the ball will come out too late.

In the defensive alignment against this set, the quarterback, in his pre-snap read, eliminates the X-receiver from his read. The safety is back playing over the top of the pressed corner. His *hot* read is the H-receiver running the option route. If the Will linebacker blitzes, the H-back works to the inside instead of to the outside. He has the option to do what he wants within his limits.

We teach the quarterback to attack the point at which the defense attacks. If they blitz the Will linebacker, we want to attack the area he should cover. When we run our blitz pickup drills in practice, I constantly tell the quarterback to attack the defense from where the pressure is coming.

The option pattern can come from the two-back set in the backfield. When the H-back runs this play from the backfield, he has to check his way into the pattern. He may have a blocking assignment and cannot release until he sees the assignment drop into coverage. The problem we most often encounter is the receiver not getting far enough downfield. They get impatient trying to get to the sideline. They need to work vertical up the field before they break to the sideline.

In the past two years, we ran the cross pattern 55 times. In those 55 plays, the Z-receiver made several big plays. We had an unusual situation right before the half against a good football team two years ago. We used a play-action pass because their safeties were aggressive. You can window-dress this concept a number of different ways. The quarterback looked for the post pattern matched against their safeties. The post pattern is the fourth pattern in the progress unless we feel it is the right pattern to throw in a situation. That play ended up as a touchdown to the post receiver.

Each year about this time, we start evaluating our playbook for next year. We go back through the playbook and look at what we have and try to figure what we want to emphasize for the next year. That emphasis depends on the personnel we have returning.

The 2x2 formation is the set we like to use in this offense (Diagram #6). This formation spreads the defense more in their underneath coverage. On this defensive set, the Mike linebacker and strong safety blitzed from the wideside of the field. The quarterback missed the hot read and threw to the option route. There was man coverage on the

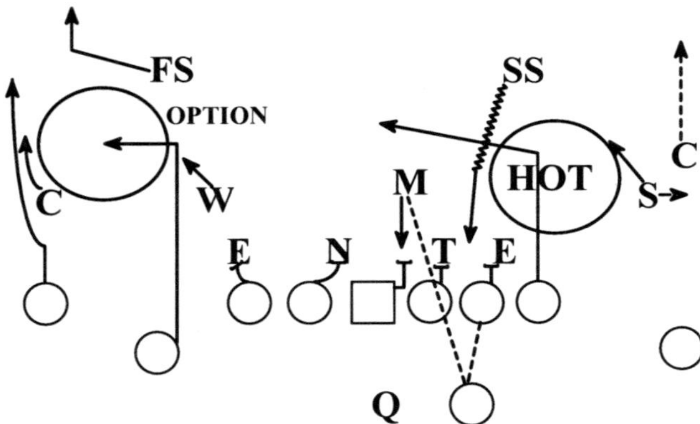

Diagram #6. 2x2 H Option

H-back and he beat the coverage into the sideline. The easy throw was to the tight end on the crossing route uncovered by the blitz of the strong safety. The tight end reads the blitz and looks immediately for the hot throw.

The quarterback has two choices against the pressure. He throws to the Y cross or the H option. The coaching point is to throw where the defense is pressuring.

You can use motion with any of these formations without changing any of the pattern concepts. We use motion to get from one alignment to another and to move defenders into areas we want them to be.

When the Y-end runs the crossing route, he has to know what to do when he gets over the Mike linebacker. We tell him to go under the Sam linebacker and over the Mike linebacker; however, once the tight end gets over the Mike linebacker, he has to flatten his pattern. If he continues to get depth, he brings the safety into the coverage. Once he gets behind the Mike linebacker, he wants to flatten his route and run toward the sideline.

One thing that can help the Y-end is to tag the backside vertical pattern with a corner route. Running the corner pulls the safety to the outside and deeper. This helps the crossing route thrown late.

In the pre-snap read, the quarterback always looks to the outside vertical route as his first option. The receiver is big and fast. When the quarterback sees a pressed corner or a walked-down corner with no safety support over the top, he throws the vertical takeoff by the X-receiver.

In 2006, when we first arrived at North Gwinnett, we had one athlete. We had zero offensive weapons. We were good defensively but we put all our best athletes on the defensive side of the ball. We had to squeeze our offense as much as we could to this receiver without overdoing it. We did not want the defenses to load up on him and take him away. The thing you can do with the route concept is not always run the cross with the Y-end.

There are two ways to look at that situation. You can rep what you have or involve more people in the concept. We decided to involve other receivers so we could choose when we had multiple good receivers. Running cross concepts with any of the three receivers (X, Y, or Z) can help get the match-up or personnel working the concept that may force the best defensive look to work against, or the best man-to-man beater available.

What we did was align the Z-receiver outside the X-receiver (Diagram #7). In a 2x1 set, the Y-end was on the line of scrimmage on the backside of the set. The H-receiver in this set aligned in the backfield. To the playside of the formation, we aligned in a twin-receiver set with the X-receiver on the line of scrimmage. We let the Z run the post and the X-receiver ran the X cross pattern. To the backside, the Y-end ran the outside vertical and the H-back ran the option route.

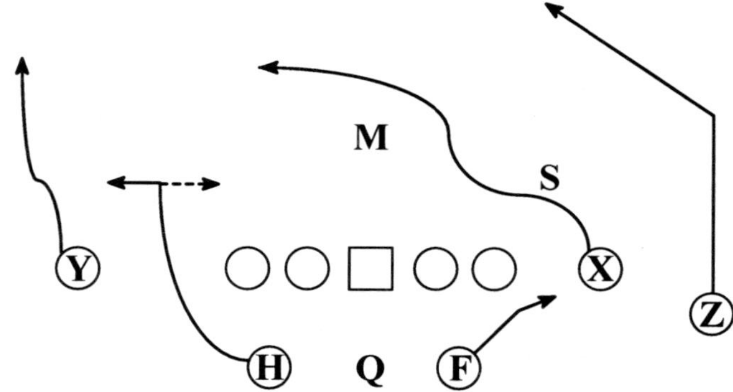

Diagram #7. 80 X Cross

This gives us a different look but it is the same concept for everyone in the pattern. There are different ways to package the routes you want with the personnel you want running them.

I want to get into the trips formation. When you get into the trips set and run crossing patterns, you have to make sure the F-back goes opposite for the protection schemes. When we set the F-back to the single receiver side, we hope to get him out to hold the outside linebacker to that side. However, we base that on whether the defense brings pressure.

In our trips formation, the H-back comes to the trips side of the formation and is the middle receiver between the Y-end and Z-receiver. The X-receiver is to the single side with the F-back set in that direction.

We do four things when we bring the H-back to the Y- and Z-receiver side:

- H option
- H follow
- H drive
- H under

In the first concept, the H-back runs his option route from the three-receiver side (Diagram #8). In this combination, the Z-receiver runs the post and the Y-end runs the cross. The H-back runs his five-yard out or comes underneath looking for a window to the inside. The X-receiver runs the outside vertical and the F-back reads his way out to the shoot.

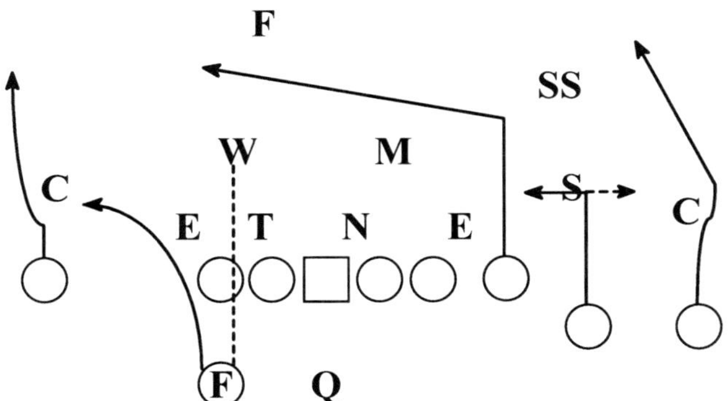

Diagram #8. Trips H Option

We can run a route combination called "H follow" (Diagram #9). We teach the follow route as a 10-yard dig route. The H-back follows the cross route across the field. That is the adjustment we like from the trips set. We have the post over the top to hold the safety and the H-back following the cross route. If the Mike runs with the tight end, the window behind him is open.

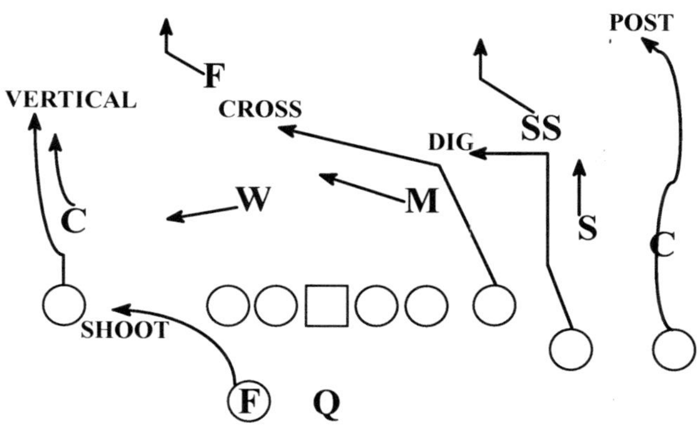

Diagram #9. Trips H Follow

We also can run the H-back on a six-yard cross route, which we call "drive." The object of this route is to draw the Mike linebacker to the route. We want him to attach to this route and the cross is open in front of him. The secret to all these routes is spacing.

The last thing you can do with the H-back is run an "under," which brings him under the linebackers on a shallow cross through the heels of the defensive linemen area.

SCRAMBLE DRILL

- Deep work back
- Away work toward
- Shallow work deep

If you run the spread offense, you must work scramble drills in practice. It is part of the spread game. If the quarterback cannot scramble with the ball and the receivers do not know where to go when the quarterback scrambles, you will not be successful throwing the ball. If the receivers are deep, they have to work back to the quarterback. If they are away from him, they have to work toward him. If the receiver is shallow, he has to work deep. You must do those three things in the scramble drill.

We run a bunch set with the trips formation. In the set, the Y-end runs the cross, the Z-receiver runs the post, and the H-back runs the wheel route (Diagram #10). The Y-end is on the line with the H-back two yards behind him. The Z-receiver is outside the Y and H-back, in the gap separating the Y and H-back. On the snap, they break downfield. The Z-receiver stems his route to the outside before heading for the post.

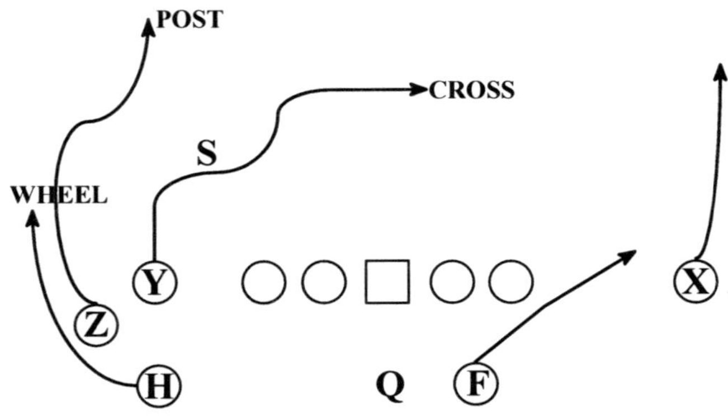

Diagram #10. Trips Bunch Y Cross

The H-back is the hot receiver and must see the blitz and know the ball is coming on the stem part of the pattern. The H-back starts behind the Z-receiver and breaks out on the wheel. The Y-end runs the cross pattern. It has been a good combination for us. The critical element to this pattern is the spacing between the receivers. The Z-receiver has to do a good job of stemming to the outside to give him a chance to run down the seam.

EMPTY CROSS CONCEPT

- Two tight ends with no F-back
- F-back in cannon, near or mid on shoot
- F-back in an angle route from the backfield with a "free release"

We can align the F-back at a wide receiver's position and call it a cannon position. We can align him in between two receivers in a mid position, or we can put him in a wing outside the tackle in a near position. We can create an empty set by aligning the F-back in the backfield and free releasing him. We can also run him on the cross pattern with a tag.

MAN COVERAGE

- Kill shot to outside receiver
- Hot throws
- Stairstep technique

When we play man coverage, the first thing the quarterback wants to know is, "Does he have the kill shot?" He has to assess whether the X-receiver has favorable coverage to go for the house. The hot routes are the option routes, shoot, and cross routes.

The stairstep technique is for a player running a crossing route. If the receiver feels man coverage, he has to climb vertically in his pattern. He has to make the defender get north and south movement to get to him. Once he climbs, he snaps off his pattern and continues across the field. He cannot let the defender simply trail him and chase him across the field. He has to climb and make the defender do the same thing. That will help him get separation when he breaks back across the middle.

I want to talk about the shallow route before I run out of time.

80/81 SHALLOW		
Pos.	**General Rule**	**Adjustment**
X, Y	Called route run shallow through defensive line (must continue on route); playside no-call outside vertical	Backside: outside vertical
Y, H	Base rule: PS-vertical BS Dig	If called on shallow, run shallow through defensive line (must continue on route) Dig-route runner-stem is hot Trips rule: #3 is #2 backside except if #3 is called on shallow and #2 becomes #2 backside
H	Called route—run shallow through defensive line (must continue on route); playside no-call) outside vertical	Backside: outside receiver has outside vertical. Inside receiver has 10-yard dig (hot) looking for window vs. zone and continue across vs. man
F	Check shoot	
QB	Pre-snap read: either vertical or read progression 1) Shallow 2) Dig (stem to hot route 3) Shoot	

The pattern in the shallow concept is a vertical by the playside #1 receiver (Diagram #11). The #2 receiver runs the shallow cross through the defensive line. The backside patterns are an outside vertical by the #1 receiver and an inside dig by the #2 receiver. We can run all the receivers on the shallow route.

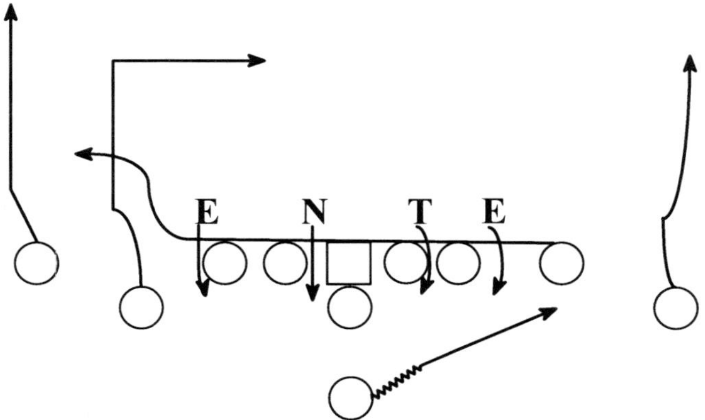

Diagram #11. Red 80 Y Shallow

The next set is a red 2x1 formation. We run 81 H shallow (Diagram #12). Red sets the formation to the right and 81 sets the callside to the left. The backside patterns are an outside vertical by the Z-receiver and a dig route by the Y-end. The playside pattern is the shallow cross by the H-back and the vertical by the X-receiver.

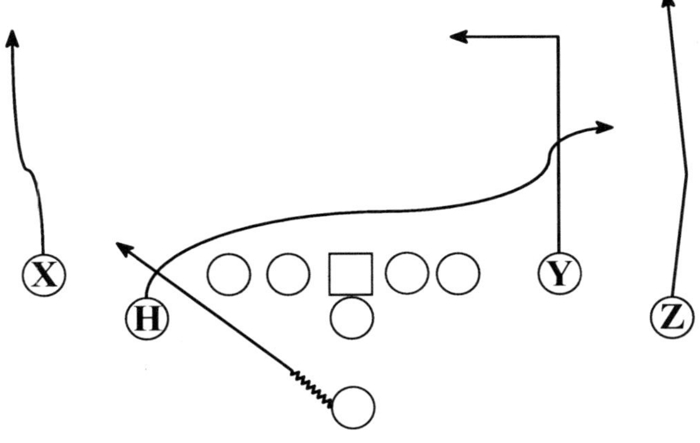

Diagram #12. Red 81 H Shallow

We flip the formation from a red to a blue formation and run 81 Z shallow (Diagram #13). The playside is the left and the backside is the right. The playside runs the vertical and shallow and the

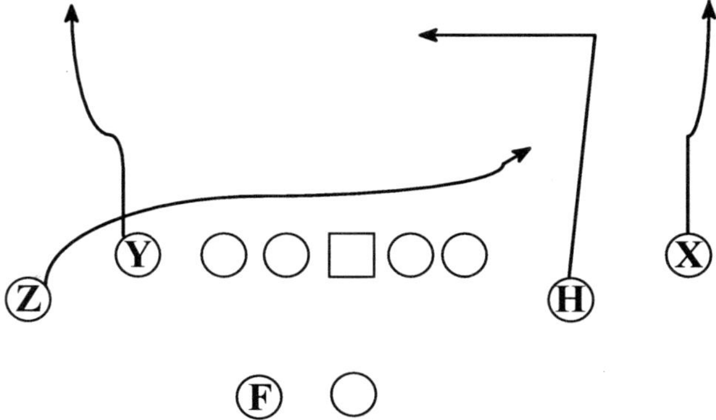

Diagram #13. Blue 81 Z Shallow

backside runs the vertical and dig. It is the same concept with a different receiver running the cross.

The last play is a red formation. We call 81, which puts the playside to the left. The backside is to the right. The call is 81 X shallow. It is the same pattern as the Z shallow except the X-receiver runs the shallow. We coach our receivers to catch the shallow, get to the numbers, and turn it north and south.

The quarterback on the shallow looks at his pre-snap read for the kill shot by the wide receivers. If that is a favorable option, the quarterback wants to keep that in his head. However, on the shallow route, his eyes are on the stem of the dig route runner. If the Will linebacker blitzes, he throws hot to the dig route runner right now. If the Will drops into coverage, his eyes go to the window that the dig route comes into. That window is the same window that the shallow route is coming.

The shallow receiver runs through the defensive line. That means he runs through the heels of the defensive line. The defensive line is rushing the quarterback and is no longer there. The drops of the linebackers cause them to lose him as he runs under them. When he gets through the line, he starts to climb in his pattern. He works toward the number gaining depth as he goes.

The trips set, for shallows, can sometimes help rotate coverage to help this route package or allow for man coverage rub off to occur. We can add tags to the patterns that give us the type of match-up we look for in the defense.

Thank you, again.

Art Walker

ELEMENTS OF THE DRAW PACKAGE

North Allegheny High School, Pennsylvania

Thank you. I appreciate you having me here today. I would like to spend some time talking about some of the things I think you have to do to be successful. Some things have changed based on our personnel, but other things are fundamental to success.

Our school is located in the tradition rich western Pennsylvania area, about 15 miles north of Pittsburgh. We compete in the largest classification in Pennsylvania, which is AAAA. We typically have about 85 to 100 players on our squad in grades 10 through 12.

We played in the state championship game on December 18. For those teams who run the spread offense all of the time, I can tell you when it is 18 degrees and snowing in Pennsylvania, it is hard to run your spread offense in those conditions. In this type of weather, you have to be able to run the football. So we have come up with what we think allows us to do that.

We are an I-based football team. We are also a no-huddle team. We have not been a no-huddle team exclusively during my time at North Allegheny High School, but for the last three years, we have. Contrary to what you might think when you hear the no-huddle offense, we do not spread our offense as most no-huddle teams do.

We may be in a double tight end set, but we are still calling plays at the line. Tempo can vary based on your personnel. This year, we hung our hat on running the ball and playing defense. We are a balanced offense between the run and the pass. In most years, we are somewhere near 50/50 with the run and the pass. The running game is what we try to establish. We do use the play-action pass, and it is very important to our offense.

Probably one of our most successful plays has been our draw play. We have a number of different ways we run the draw play. We can be in multiple formations, and we can run the play-action passing game off this scheme. I am going to talk about the different elements to our draw package and then show you some footage of it all later. I have kept it basic for you here today so you can adapt it to fit into your system if you see something you like.

We have to start with our numbering system (Diagram #1). We try to keep it simple for the kids. I know some people use an even and odd numbering scheme, but we like to use a basic 1 through 9 numbering system, going from right to left We have our wide plays on the right side as #1 and the wide plays on the left as #9. We also number our backs. The quarterback is #1, the halfback is #2, the fullback is #3, and the wingback, or power back, is #4.

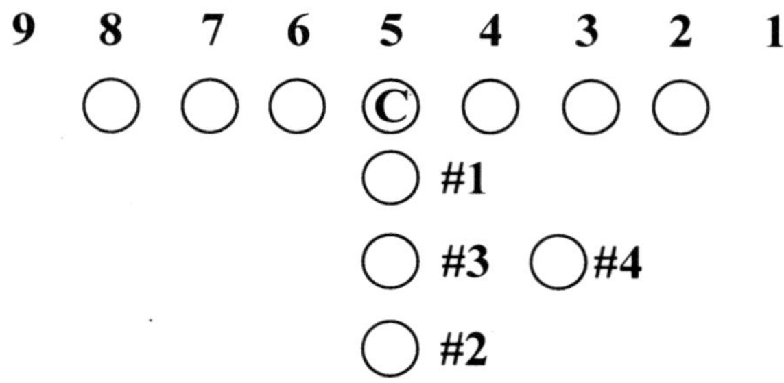

Diagram #1. Numbering System

You can see how simple our system is. You have to take what system you use and fit any offensive play to your system. It is easy for us to adapt and install offensive concepts into our system.

We are not a wing-T offense. We do run the waggle play, and we do run some other wing-T type plays. Our power play is our 22 power. The opposite of that play is 28 power.

We are a shoulder blocking football team. We are not a zone team, and we do not reach block, and we do not come off the line with our hands out in front of our face. We want to take a step off the line and get our shoulders on the defender, and move the defenders off the line of scrimmage. We want to get as many double-team blocks on the plays as possible. We are a shoulder blocking team. We want to ride the defender off the line and get to the next level.

We purchased a big chute where we could work as many as five players under the chute. Our linemen are under the chute three days a week.

My offensive line coach was an old wing-T coach. He is a great coach and is very meticulous. He works with the line from the start of practice to the end of practice and shows a great deal of patience. He is a good teacher. Our kids know the blocking rules, and these rules do not change regardless of the defensive front we face.

Let me tell you why we use the draw series. It allows us to utilize our personnel. This means we focus on our tailback, quarterback, wide receiver, and tight ends. We can utilize our play-action passing game with our simple five-step protection. Screens to the fullback are used. We think this confuses the defense because we have so many different formations and various personnel that it makes us harder to prepare for and to defend.

I want to cover our draw blocking rules. Following are our rules for our pro 24 draw:

- C: Backside A/backer
- LG: Backside B/backer
- LT: Backside C/backer
- RG: On/inside
- RT: On/outside
- TE: Arc release/block force
- SE: Run off/block force
- FL: Run off/block force
- FB: Power step/check backer blitz/replace tight end/force
- TB: Lateral step/gather/read hole/accelerate through handoff/stay low/score
- QB: Simulate three-step drop/eyes upfield/ handoff/pass set

I am not sure what front you see the most, but we see both the odd and the even defense. This is what it looks like versus an odd front (Diagram #2).

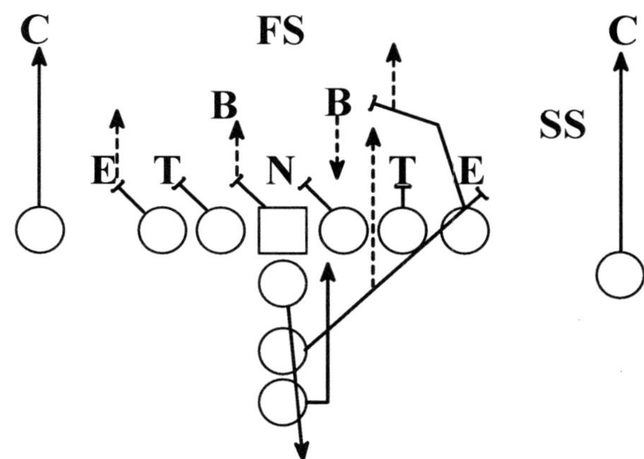

Diagram #2. 24 Draw vs. Odd Front

We see teams that like to mix their defensive front during the game, so we have to be prepared to run the play against the even defense as well (Diagram #3).

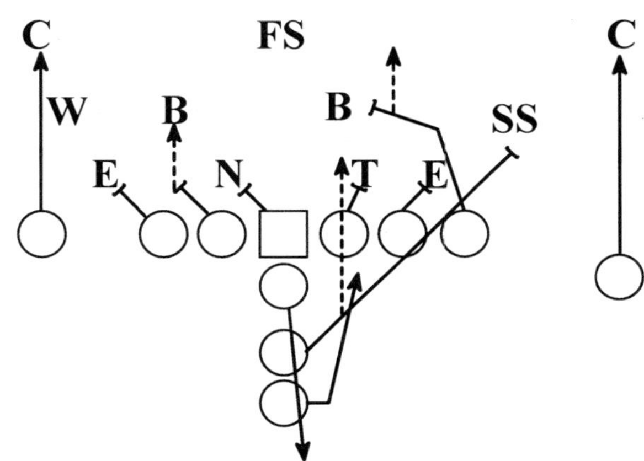

Diagram #3. 24 Draw vs. Even Front

Following are our rules for our lead draw. We call this "pro 24 lead draw":

- C: Backside A/backer
- LG: Backside B/backer
- LT: Backside C/backer
- RG: On/inside
- RT: On/outside
- TE: Arc release/block force
- SE: Run off/block force
- FL: Run off/block force
- FB: Lateral step/attack inside linebacker
- TB: Lateral step/gather/read hole/accelerate through handoff/stay low/score

- QB: Simulate three-step drop/eyes upfield/handoff/pass set

I want to show you the play against the odd and the even fronts. First is against the odd front (Diagram #4). We want the tight end to arc release to occupy the defensive end.

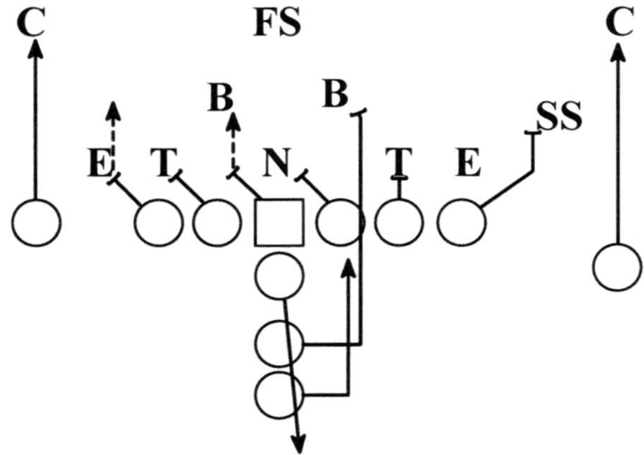

Diagram #4. Lead Draw vs. Odd Front

The lead draw against the even front is similar to the isolation play inside (Diagram #5).

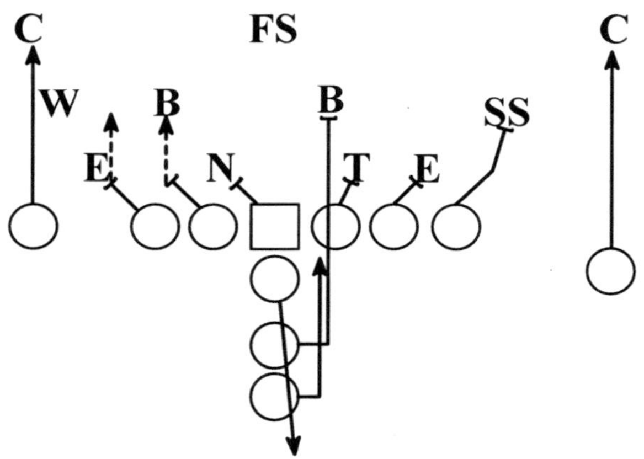

Diagram #5. Lead Draw vs. Even Front

We can run the lead draw to the split side as well (Diagram #6). We run a slot look to the right side and run the lead draw to that side.

We can run this same lead draw scheme out of a shotgun formation (Diagram #7). This is what that would look like from the shotgun look. The quarterback is the ballcarrier.

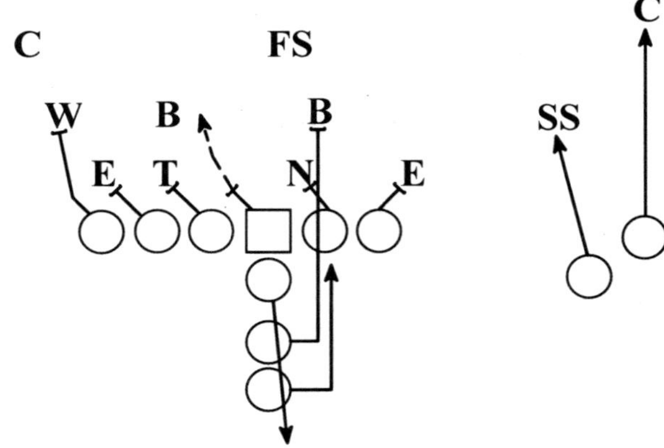

Diagram #6. Lead Draw to the Split Side

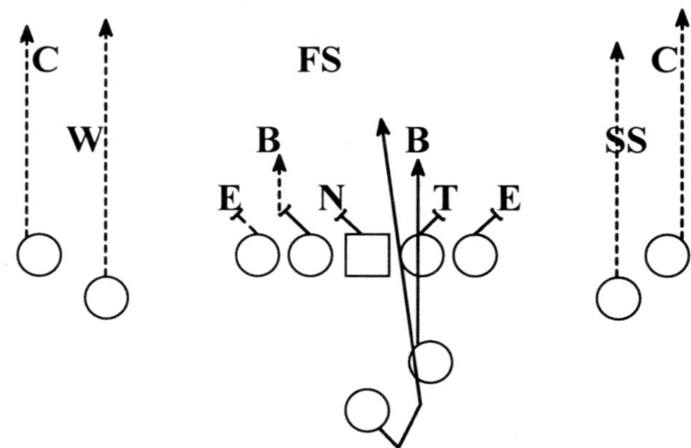

Diagram #7. Lead Draw from Shotgun

I want to go over our play-action draw pass blocking rules. We call this "pro 24 draw pass" (Diagram #8). This is against the even front. The quarterback sets up on the pass, and reads the defense to find the hole.

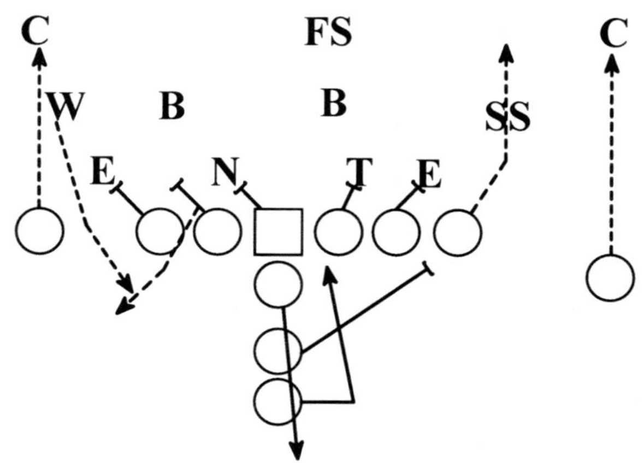

Diagram #8. Pro 24 Draw Pass Blocking vs. Even Front

Play-Action Draw Pass Blocking Rules

- C: Backside A/bug out
- LG: Backside B/bug out
- LT: Backside C/bug out
- RG: On/inside
- RT: On/outside
- TE: Pattern
- SE: Pattern
- FL: Pattern
- FB: Block playside outside/read playside edge blitz/clean up
- TB: Lateral step/gather/fake handoff/read backer blitz/clean up/release
- QB: Simulate three-step drop/eyes upfield/fake handoff/pass set/read progressions

Against the Bear front, the center gives the fullback the Bear alert (Diagram #9). The fullback and center are responsible for the nose and middle linebacker.

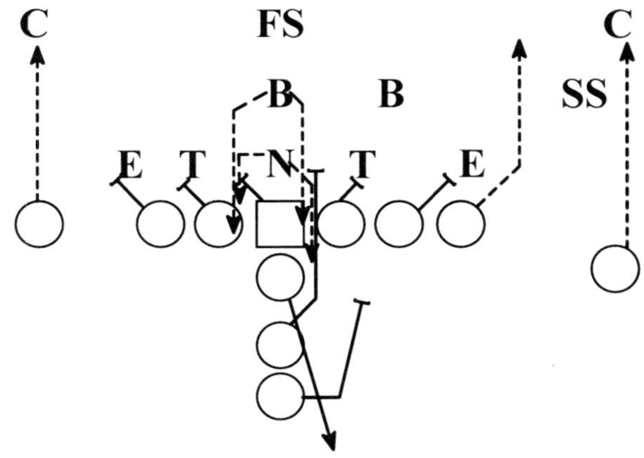

Diagram #9. Pro 24 Draw Pass vs. Bear Front

We like to run combination routes with our receivers. We like the curl route with our wide receiver and a wheel route from our tight end. The backside receiver is going to run the dig route. Our quarterback reads the playside corner. We have found versus cover-3 defenses, the playside linebacker bites on the run fake and will not get underneath our curl route (Diagram #10).

We can also try and key on the free safety. We do this by running a deep post with our playside wide receiver (Diagram #11). Our backside split end

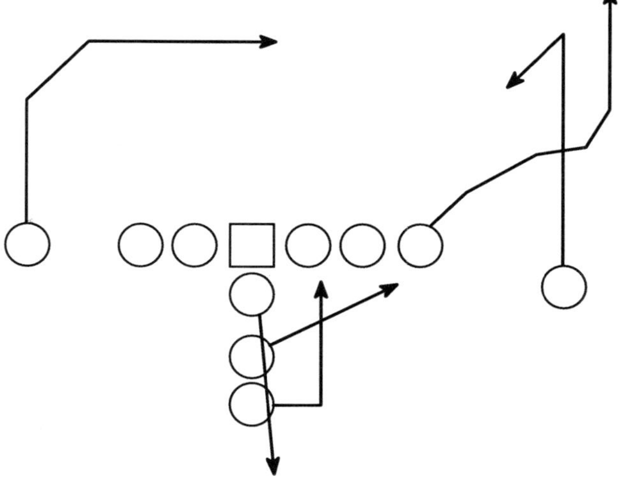

Diagram #10. Curl Route

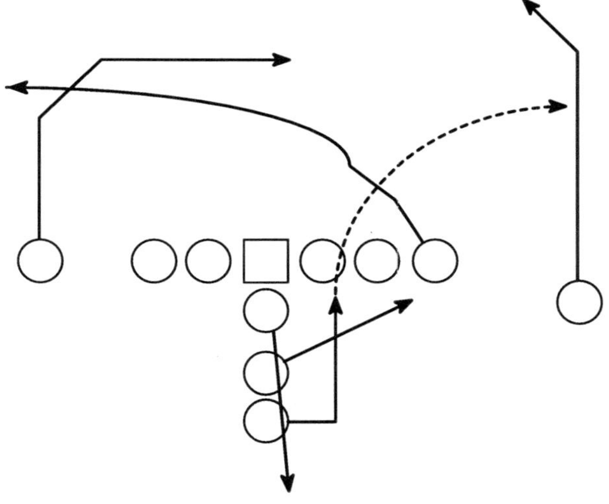

Diagram #11. Post Route

runs a dig route. The tight end runs a drag behind the linebacker. Our quarterback reads the free safety and delivers the ball based on his read.

This scheme allows us to run the draw out of a variety of shotgun and spread formations. We like to run the draw to a trips set with the sprint-out passing game (Diagram #12).

One wrinkle you can run out of shotgun set is our gut draw play (Diagram #13). It is very simple. Our frontside linemen follow their on blocking rules. Our backside linemen follow their backside draw rules progressions. Our backside tackle pulls and guts to the playside inside linebacker. This play works great from a one-back set from the shotgun.

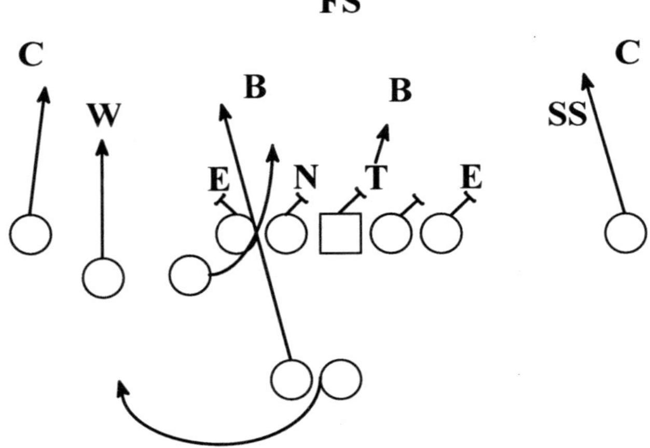

Diagram #12. Draw to Trips

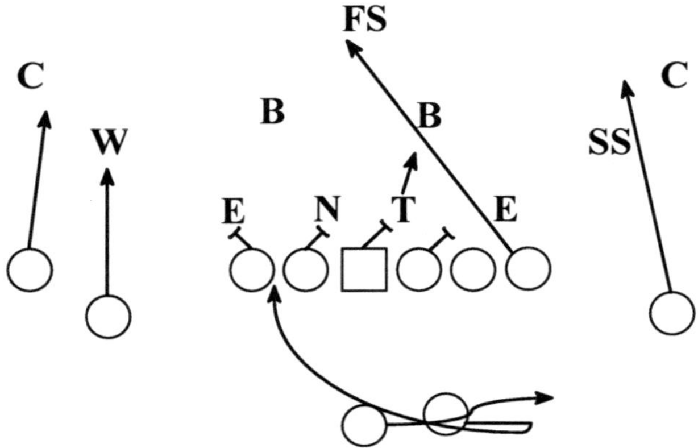

Diagram #13. Gut Draw

It is a misdirection shotgun/spread type running play. Play-action passing is very simple to add to this play.

Following are the rules for our blocking on the gut draw:

- Frontside: On blocking rules.
- Backside blocking: Follow backside draw rules progression.
- Backside tackle: Pulls and guts to the playside inside linebacker.
- Great from a one-back set and shotgun action.
- Misdirection shotgun/spread run play.
- Play-action very simple to add to this play.

We do a lot of walk through prior to practice. After playing 16 weeks, our guys knew how to practice. We did not want to beat them up day in and day out. We get a lot accomplished mentally on whom to block in those walk-throughs. I will be glad to meet with you and talk about the screen game if you want.

I know I have gone over a lot of information. I am going to show you some video that will make it come together for you. I appreciate your time today. Thanks.

Steve Warren

DEFENSIVE PRACTICE SCHEDULE AND DRILLS

Abilene High School, Texas

I appreciate you being here this morning. I want this to be as informal as you want it to be. Stop me and ask questions at any time. I am going to be the first one to tell you, I do not have all the answers. In 2009, we were fortunate to go 16-0 and win the state 5A championship in Texas. That is a huge accomplishment in Texas. It takes you 16 weeks to get it done. If you are fortunate to do that, they invite you to places like this to talk football. I am excited to be here and I want to talk about defense. I want to show you our defensive practice schedules and later on some drills we use.

I am at a high school with 2,200 students. That is small by Class 5A classifications. We played schools with a student enrollment of up to 6,000 students. I know our size is bigger than some of you have in your state. We have a good mix of students at our school. We are unlike any other school in our classification. We do not have an abundance of Division I players. What we do fits what we do well on the football field.

I will do anything I can do to help you. I think coaching is a great fraternity. I am proud to be a part of it and proud to represent our staff and our state. I have been the head coach at Abilene High School for 15 years. If you are talking about X's and O's, everyone in our state has a tremendous amount of knowledge. We are a 3-4 defense.

I am going to start out today's lecture by telling you that I think you are missing the boat if you spend all of your time teaching your players X's and O's. When we went to Abilene High School 15 years ago, the 10 years prior to our coming, they had won eight games. It was a bad job and probably was the reason I got it. I came from a little Class A high school with an enrollment of about 150 students. Abilene was the worst 5A job in Texas.

When I got there, I found a group of people who had no expectations whatsoever of the football program. The principal, athletic director, teachers, custodians, cafeteria workers, and students had no expectations for the program. All they did was lose and that was all they expected. In the 12 years before we got there, they had eight different football coaches. All of them did the same thing. They stayed for a year or two and left. We tried to do something different, and it has worked well for us in the past 15 years.

The reason I am talking about it is that I think it was so important for our development and our program. All of you are in programs that are in different stages of development. Some of you have just gone to a new job and some of you have been at the same place for a period. When we went into Abilene, we told anyone and everyone who would listen to us that we were going to win. You can imagine the reaction we got from people. They thought since no one else had won, we would not either. They fired everyone before us or the coaches left on their own and we wanted to try something different.

The first year, we went 5-4. We did not set the world on fire and I did not get an invitation to speak at a clinic that year. The second year, we went 6-3 and showed some progress. The third year, we went 4-6 but we were still talking about winning. We kicked our expectations up a notch. We told them we were not just going to win, but we were going to be a playoff team. The same people told us they were glad we were winning a few games but the playoffs were out of the question.

They had not been to the playoffs since 1958. In 1999, we made the playoffs at Abilene High School for the first time in 41 years. The thing that got us to the playoffs was our expectation level. We talked to our players and convinced them we could win. After we made the playoffs, our next step was to start talking about winning district championships. The playoffs were not good enough for this program. We wanted to go further. Five or six years ago, we started talking about winning the state championship.

I firmly believe we would not have won the 2009 state championship if we had not started talking about it five years ago. The players on those teams helped lay the foundation for our state championship team. They bought into the idea that we could win a state championship. They fought their butts off trying to win one. We did not win until 2009, but the teams that went before them were a part of that championship. Those teams before helped the mind-set. We feel we are one of the 20 to 30 schools in 5A football in Texas that has a chance to win the state championship every year. We believe that at our school, and that has been a huge part of our success.

It does not matter the size of your school or what state you play in. If you do not have an expectation level with your players, you will not get there. If you are sitting around telling everyone that you are a playoff team but have never had the players to win it all, you will not win it all. If you do not think you can win it all and do not talk about it with your players, you never will. They have to talk about it.

I heard this statement somewhere and it is the truth: "You will never exceed your own expectations." I get on my coaches all the time for talking about what a player cannot do. If all you expect out of him is cannot, then that is all he will do. If you start taking a different approach that he can, then you have a chance.

I think that is critical. We can talk about defensive practice plan, offense, defense, or special teams; none of that makes a difference unless you have a level of expectation that you are going to succeed. Is it risky at first? Of course it is, and people will laugh at you, especially if you have been bad. They look at you as if you were crazy and think you will be gone in a couple of years. When you take little successes and turn them into big things, you have a chance.

The first year we went to Abilene, we had to find things outside the program that our players were doing well and build them up. We had a player, who I felt had a chance to be a good player, who liked farming. He came to school with his pants tucked into his boots and he loved farming. He had just won a stock show with a pig. I went down and watched him show the hog. He won the show and we turned that into a Super Bowl at our place. It did not have anything to do with football. It had to do with success. We blew it up into a big deal and the lights came on for that player. His attitude about himself improved to thinking he was good. It caught on to everyone on the team.

In 2009, when we won it all, it was not because we had a bunch of Division I football players. We had one player who tried to play college football. He went to Rice. I am not saying Rice is not a good football school, but the experts do not mention Rice in the sentence when they talk about football powers. He went to Rice because he was a good student who played offensive line.

In 2009, the MVP on defense for the championship game was our outside linebacker. He stood 5'8" and weighed 165 pounds. Every coach in here has one of those types of players on your team. He was one of those players that believed in what was going on in our program. He is a farmer now and a great one. The level of expectations you have with your players makes a huge difference in what goes on in your program.

We went into the last season fully believing we were going to win another state championship. It did not happen. We ended up 10-3 and got beat in the third round of the playoffs. I promise you, every step we took, our players believed it. The players in our off-season program right now believe they can win the state championship and they will fight like hell to do it.

We are a 3-4 team and I want to talk about how we prepare and teach that. If you want to talk about schemes afterward, I have no problem with that. I do not have any secrets. My father is an old, retired football coach. He coached for about 30 years. We call the defense a 3-4, which wears him out. He tells me it is nothing but an old 50 defense. He is exactly right. That is all it is. You younger coaches might be wondering what I am talking about, but back in the day, that is what it was called.

In our discussion from a defensive standpoint, we never talk about the size of the players. We have never said a player was too small to play. The player who started as our noseguard last year was 180 pounds. He was tough and could run but was not very big. Next year, when we take the field, we will start one player on defense who weighs over 200 pounds. However, they can all run. That is where we put our fast players. We are fortunate at Abilene High School to play platoon football. At the beginning of their sophomore season, we make a decision as to what side of the ball they will play.

We play the players both ways as freshmen and some of them play two ways as sophomores. On occasion, we have a player good enough to play both ways but that is seldom. The players that cannot catch play defensive back for us. Linemen that are not very big but can run play defense. They must be mean. We stock our defense first. I am an old defensive coordinator and that is how I have coached.

For years, in practice, we worked off a segment timing schedule. We had a manager keeping time and he blew a horn at the end of each period. I found myself watching the clock wondering when that next period was going to start. I was wasting time doing that. We have evolved to a practice schedule where most of the time is scripted. We get our work done in a certain amount of time and get off the field.

That throws the accountability of how well you practice onto the players. I am a firm believer that if you are on the practice field for more than two hours, you are spinning your wheels. Players are different these days. They want to get out of practice and play Xbox or do something with their friends. They have so much they want to do rather than practice football. If you keep them in practice forever, you have a hard time keeping their attention. You may be able to practice for three hours and get something out of it, but we do not believe it.

During our school day, we have fourth period athletics at our place. That means I get my players from 11:20 to 12:20 during the day. I will show you the practice schedule we use after school and follow that up with what we do during the class period.

Question: If you were at a school that did not have an athletic period in school, would you still restrict the practice time to two hours?

Yes! If we did not have an athletic period, we would spend more time on the grass.

I take exactly what we do fourth period in the athletic period and transfer it to the practice field after school. As I progress through this, you will see what we do in that athletic period. However, if you do not have an athletic period, it means you will have to practice longer to get everything done.

Our idea about practice deals with the tempo of practice. We want to practice extremely fast. I do not want "standing around coaching" going on during practice. I do not want a player pulled out of a drill and talked to for two or three minutes. That leaves 9 or 10 other players standing around doing nothing. If a player makes a mistake, we coach him on the way back to the huddle. I want as many repetitions as we can possibly get.

Having said that, let me go back and correct myself. The only mistake you can make at Abilene High School is lack of effort. That does not have anything to do with scheme. That has everything to do with effort. We talk about this all the time and our players take it to heart. All you have to do when you come to practice at Abilene High School is play hard. That is all we ever talk about to our players.

If the player made a technical mistake, that is our fault. We did not coach him up enough. If the player is playing his butt off, then he is good. He may miss a tackle because he went with the wrong leg, but as long as he went a thousand miles an hour, that is the effort we look at. We will get him to the place where he will make that tackle at some point.

We sell them on the fact that we do not want them thinking a lot. We want them to play the game. Playing is fun. That is especially true on defense. We played a game when I was little. We called it "kill the guy with the ball." Whoever had the ball, everyone went after him. We played in a vacant lot. You did not need a team and whoever had the ball the others tried to tackle him. When someone tackled the ballcarrier, the ball went to someone else. We played that for hours. That is all defensive football is. I think we understand there is more to defensive football than that, but that is the primary object.

The only mistake you can make at our place is lack of effort. We stress that in practice, in the weight room, and in the off-season. We teach it more than anything else we teach. We do not want our players to worry about the rest of the game.

At the top of our practice schedule is Abilene High Defensive Workout with a blank line with the opponent written in. We have a place to write the date. The next things are consistent. We have special teams, bags, pursuit, and blitz drills.

Abilene High Defensive Workout

Opponent: ____________________

Date: ________________________

Special teams
Bags
Pursuit
Blitz drill

If you have a better way to stretch, please let me know. Stretching wears me out. We do not do a lot of stretching. We warm up by running around and moving. We run with high knees, walking lunges, backward runs, carioca, and things like that. We line up in 11 lines offensively and defensively. We line up according to position and work across the field to the hash mark and back. That is what we do before we go into our practice.

After we warm up, we go to a special teams drill with our offense and defense. The defense goes to punt protection and the offense goes to extra point and field goal. We feel those are the two most important teams there are. A blocked punt or a great punt can change the momentum of a game in a heartbeat. A blocked extra point or a field goal to win a game is tremendously important. All the special teams play is important, but we feel these are the most critical parts of the game.

We are not on a clock. This is untimed. We are not on the clock so no one has to watch the clock. We work. We may protect three punts or 19 punts. If a player is on the punt team, it is up to him to determine the number of reps we do. I am in control of the punt team and we have a scout team rushing the punter. We do the drill until I am satisfied we have done the work to get the job done. It may take five minutes to do that or it could take 15 minutes.

The offense works on extra points and field goals. They know when Coach Warren is done with punt protection, they are finished with extra points and field goals. At that point, I blow the whistle and we go to the next period.

Defensively, the next thing we do is bag drills. However, the offense controls that block of time. We script what we want to do offensively. The offense works on a net drill, screen drill, and blitz drill. That takes about 15 minutes. All three of those drills are untimed drills. When the offense finishes, the practice moves on to the next exercises. The defense, during that time, works on bags, pursuit, and blitz. We work those drills in an untimed block of time.

After we finish that drill, we go to an individual instruction period. We call it our "indo" period. The players go to their position coaches for the next block of time. The individual time is six periods on the clock. That is the only time of the day we spend on the clock.

Period	DL	ILB	OLB	SAFE	COR	Period
1	tac	tac	tac	tac	tac	1
2						2
3						3
4						4
5						5
6						6

This is an example of how the sheet looks. The first period for everyone is a tackling period. An example of the second period would be hog pen, four-cone drill, and the ladder drill for the defensive line. The inside linebackers work on footwork. The outside linebackers work on a float and post drill. The safeties and corners work on pedal progression.

I need to tell you how we break down our squad. The junior varsity players and varsity players are practicing together. If a player plays inside linebacker, they work with the inside linebackers coach. Our JV players work with the varsity linebackers coach in these individual drills with the varsity players. During the second half of practice, the JV players become the scout team players. They get individual work along with the varsity players.

I do not want our coaches working with two players and six standing. I want to work with all eight players at the same time. I tell my coaches to make sure their drills do not have anyone standing around watching someone else do the drill. The only way to get better is through repetition. If the player goes every time instead of every sixth time, he gets more reps and gets better.

During those six individual periods, the inside and outside linebackers may come together during one of those periods. The safeties and corners do the same thing. The same thing holds true for the receivers and running backs, but this is an individual period. The skills for each position overlap to a certain extent.

After the individual time, we go to a part of our kicking game. We work kickoff on Monday and kickoff return on Tuesday. This is an untimed part of practice. The players on those teams determine how much time we spend during that period. If we cover three kicks well, then that is all we cover. The players learn that I am hotheaded. We have covered as many as 13 kicks in one session. That is a lot of kickoffs. That made me tired. As the season progresses, we take less and less time in the untimed periods because of the experience of the players.

The second half of practice is different. I want to talk about the JV team before I get into what we do. After the special teams drill, our JV players become scout players for the remainder of the practice. The offensive JV players go with the defensive groups and the defensive players go with the offense. We tell our JV players that football techniques are the same for the opponent as they are for the home team. They need to work on their offensive techniques against the varsity defense. If the opponent runs the zone play, the JV guard practices his technique that we use on the zone play.

Everyone has issues with the scout team. How do you get a good picture with your scout team? We tell our scout team if they do the things they are supposed to do with great enthusiasm, they do not have to condition at the end of practice. When practice is over, they leave the field and go home. We run the JV teams two to three times during the season for conditioning. We never tell them it is punishment conditioning. It is conditioning. They did not get their conditioning done because they did not practice hard enough.

If you tell them it is punishment, it becomes a negative deal. They get mad at you and you get mad at them because they do not run hard. It gets to be a headbutting contest. That only happens about twice during the season. The rest of the time, they are good to go. It all plays into practicing fast. We do have down time, but it is not during the course of practice.

We have a film tower at our practice facility. When we do our inside drill, we film it. We film the drill from both sides. We do it for two reasons. On occasion, we have players that play both sides of the ball. More importantly, I can stand there and watch both drills. The coaches are in close proximity and can hear any comments made about his young players. He may be watching his position, but he can also see and hear what is going on in the other drill.

When we run the inside drill, we work off the offensive script. We have 15 plays scripted for this drill on Monday and Tuesday. When we get the 15 plays run, the drill is over and we go on to something else. If they can get the work done in 15 plays, that will take about 10 minutes. On occasion, we have to run 25 plays to get the 15 plays we want. The accountability of drills is on the players and not on the clock. We do not stop in the middle of the script because we are out of time. We will run the 15 plays at our pace.

This is a full-contact drill with the exception of taking the ballcarrier to the ground. We never take a running back to the ground or hit a quarterback during the season.

While the inside drill is going on with the interior players, on an adjacent field the defensive backs and receivers are going 1-on-1. We put the best on the best in this drill. The offense runs routes and the defense covers them. They continue with that drill until we finish with the inside drill. We flip our quarterbacks between the two drills. The first quarterback may start in the inside drill and flip to the passing drill halfway through.

Halfway through the drill, or eight plays, the first offensive line gets a break. They take a water break along with the JV defensive players. The second line players work for two or three plays. The first line comes back and finishes the drill. We substitute that way unless we have to go longer for some reason. Fifteen plays is a long time for an offensive line to work, especially if it is early in the season. The position coach can substitute an individual on his own schedule if he thinks the player needs more repetitions at a certain position. However, we do not have a scripted time that the second-line players go into the drill during the season. In spring football, we do script when the second-line players go into the drill.

After we do the inside drill, we go to our 7-on-7 drill. We work the offensive receivers and running backs against a defensive secondary and linebackers. The defensive drill works off the offensive script. We run 15 scripted plays in this drill.

While the offensive and defensive skeleton drills are going on, the offensive and defensive lines work against one another. They work ones against ones, working on pass blocking versus pass rush or run blocking against run defense. The same thing is true about the 15 plays. Until we get the 15 plays run the way we want them, we continue to work. The linemen are finished with their drill when the skeleton drills are finished. This is an untimed drill.

When we do our inside drill and pass skeleton drill, the scout teams work off play cards. One of the things our defensive coaches do to help practice go fast is to color-code the play cards. This lends itself to doing a better job scout-team-wise. We color-code the receivers. Instead of calling them X, Y, Z, or A, we use colors. We use blue, red, green, and black for the receivers and match up their scrimmage vests with that color. The blue receiver wears the blue scrimmage vest.

Our defensive coordinator is horrible with player names. He may call a player "blue dot" until the player is a senior. If he needs that player to do something, he may refer to him as green dot or blue dot because that is how he knows you from the scout team. Our scout team players know what color they are on the scout team card. They keep the same color all week. As many formations as there are in today's football, this helps us to get it done faster.

After we finish the secondary shell drill, we go to the team drill. It is a 15-play scripted drill. When the offense gets through 15 plays, we are finished with practice. The team period is an untimed period. We take as long as it takes to run the 15 scripted plays.

If we have a veteran team and practice well, we will not be on the field but an hour and 45 minutes. If we do not practice well, we could be on the field for two and a half hours. The length of time we are on the field depends on the practice ethics of the players. You have all been part of practices that the longer practice goes, the worse it gets. We have found out, if practice starts out fast, it will end fast. If they want to get it done and get off the field, they will. We base Monday and Tuesday practices on the scripted plays.

Wednesday is a lighter day for us. We cut back to about half the periods. Instead of six individual periods, there are three periods. The scripts, instead of being 15 plays, will be 10 plays. On Wednesday, we are in shorts and shoulder pads. There is less physical contact. It is a slower pace day in regard to butting heads. The practice is still fast-paced but scaled back on hitting.

We stress the idea that we are less intense because we take off the pants. We still have high expectations of our players. Our entire idea is about fast, fast and do not stand around.

I want to tell you what our players do Monday through Thursday during the course of a week. On Monday morning before school, the players come in and meet with me for about 15 minutes. This is a scouting report meeting. The assistants are not there. There is no one in the room but me. I talk about the opponent. I talk about their record, outstanding players, what the game means to us, and things of that nature. That is the time we spend talking about our opponent. We spend very little time the remainder of the week talking about the opponent.

I cannot control what they are doing in Midland or Odessa. I cannot control it, so I do not worry about it. I worry about my team and get them as good as I can. If you spend a lot of time talking about teams that you play, you are wasting time. We worry about the things we can control at Abilene.

Fourth period, during the season, our players understand that is the teaching time. We do not pad up and we wear only shorts and helmets. Monday during the athletic period, we have the scouting report on the grass. We line up, stand in position, and we teach the scouting report. From a defensive standpoint, we base our defense on formations. We align as sound as we can to every formation the opponent has. We do not talk in specifics about what they do. We make our adjustments to the formations they run. We call this "Jojo" time. Anytime we can steal some time during the day, we refer to that as Jojo time.

On Tuesday, we bring the team in at 7:30 before school to watch the practice tape from the day before. That is when we correct the mistakes from the practice time on the grass. We spend time slowing down and watching what we need to do. Make sure your coaches know that when they talk to one player, they are talking to everyone in that group. The players need to listen to what the coach is telling the other players. During the athletic period, we are in the weight room the entire time. We lift two times a week during the season. We lift on Tuesday and Saturday.

Wednesday morning, we do the same thing. We come in and watch practice tape from the preceding day's practice. We make corrections and sometimes we walk through the corrections. We do that particularly in the offensive line. We could split the time watching tape and walking through the practice. However, I do not want them to spend more than 25 minutes in that meeting.

Wednesday, during the athletic period, we are on the grass working on our special teams. We hit all the special teams and the rest of the time is Jojo time. We spend about 40 minutes doing special teams work and 20 minutes in Jojo, which is a repetition time for us. The defensive coordinator works on the opponent's formations. We do not have an offensive line. We use trashcans with the receivers and backs. He calls the formation, comes to the line, and the defense aligns to that formation. He goes back to the huddle, calls the next formation, and goes to the line. The defense adjusts to the formations repeatedly. We align between 50 to 75 plays during this time. If you align correctly on defense, you have a chance to be successful. All we ask is that the defense align correctly.

Thursday is different. We do not come in early on Thursday. We start to play the game on Thursday. Thursday, we base everything we do off the script I have. We create game-type simulations. The position coaches do not know what I am going to call. We want it to be just like the game. We work situational offense and defense off the sideline as if it were a game. We use the kicking game in those situations also. I call all kinds of situations and the players and coaches have to react to what I call. I may call for the onside kick team or the punt team. I give the offense situations and they run three or four plays within that situation. I do the same thing with the defense. We work every scenario you could see in that game.

We do these things during the athletic period. We cover taking a safety, pooch punts, one-minute offense, prevent defense, and everything that could happen in that game. We run the last play of the game for the offense and defense. We simulate injuries, no time-outs, and clock plays. The pace is relaxed unless I tell them it is an urgent situation.

We do not practice on the grass on Thursday after school. The JV and freshman teams are playing games and the coaches are with them. I bring the varsity back and we have a special teams meeting. We watch cut-ups for about 15 minutes. The last thing we do is try to take the edge off the week and have some fun. I want them to leave feeling good. The coaches put together a highlight tape from the game the week before. We fill it up with the music they like to listen to and let them have a good time. They whoop, holler, and have a big time. They have a blast doing it and I want them to have a blast.

People ask me if our players watch film during different times of the day. Our seniors do not have full schedules. There is always time in the day and places for them to watch film. We make it available for them and encourage them to do it. We can make them DVDs so they can take them home. I do not have the capability to do that, but the young coaches on our staff know all about the technology. We have the hardware and equipment to make those things happen.

That is what we do during the course of a week. The classroom is a fast-paced mental process but the physical aspect is slow. We do the teaching and coaching during these times. It is slow down and learn. The learning and teaching phases of the tempo occurs during Jojo time. Before we had the classroom time, we did it before practice with no shoulder pads. However, it would be only 30 minutes as opposed to an hour in the classroom period.

On Friday, if we are in town, we do our Jojo period. I usually bring someone from the community to talk to the team. It could be a former player or a minister from the community. The purpose of the meeting is a devotional/motivational type of setting. If we have to travel, we miss that activity. We may have to travel three hours to get to the game site.

Question: What do you do in the spring?

We go fast and it is all good-on-good competition. Leading up to spring practice, we have a month where we are on the grass every other day teaching. That gets us ready for the fast-paced reps of the spring.

Every clinic where I speak, I like to finish the same way. I think it is important. I love the fact we have many coaches in here that like to coach. I think it is important for you to understand the responsibility you have as a coach. Too many players out there need something we can give them. They do not get it anywhere else. You have a player that comes to school because of you. You will know that fact 10 years from now when he comes back and tells you that. Do not take that responsibility lightly. Do not be an X's and O's football coach. There are young men out there trying to get somewhere but without coaching, they do not stand a chance. Without good coaches and role models, where are they going to get help? It is something special you can provide at your school that no one else can.

I appreciate your attention and this has been awesome. If I can help you, please call on me. I am thrilled to be here and I hope your remaining clinic is productive.

2011
CLINIC NOTES
Lectures by Premier High School Coaches

Edited by Earl Browning.

$34.00 (S & H included)
265 pages • 978-1-60679-172-1

Also available:

2010

978-1-60679-109-7
260 pp. • $30.00

2009

978-1-60679-065-6
272 pp. • $25.00

2008

978-1-58518-740-9
256 pp. • $20.00

2007

978-1-58518-074-5
268 pp. • $20.00

2006

1-58518-982-0
256 pp. • $20.00

Title	Item #	Price	Qty	Total
Kentucky residents must include tax form 51A-126 or pay 6% sales tax. Shipping & Handling: Included in cost for orders within the USA; $8.00 for each Clinic Notes to Canada; $10.00 for each Clinic Notes for international orders.	PLUS	KY Tax 6%		
	PLUS	Shipping		
		TOTAL		

Name ______________________ Organization/School ______________________

Address ______________________

City ______________________ State __________ ZIP __________ Phone (   ) ______________________

Method of Payment: ☐ VISA ☐ MasterCard ☐ American Express ☐ Discover ☐ Check #__________ ☐ P.O. #__________

Account # ☐☐☐☐ ☐☐☐☐ ☐☐☐☐ ☐☐☐☐ Expiration: ___/___ CVC #: __ __ __

Signature: ______________________ Email Address: ______________________

Mail check or credit card info to:
Earl Browning, Telecoach, Inc.
3512 Foxglove Lane, Louisville, KY 40241

Make checks payable to: Telecoach, Inc.
Website: www.nikecoyfootball.net
Email: 4earl@nikecoyfootball.com